Lecture Notes in Computer Science   16096

Founding Editors

Gerhard Goos
Juris Hartmanis

Editorial Board Members

Elisa Bertino, *Purdue University, West Lafayette, IN, USA*
Wen Gao, *Peking University, Beijing, China*
Bernhard Steffen , *TU Dortmund University, Dortmund, Germany*
Moti Yung , *Columbia University, New York, NY, USA*

The series Lecture Notes in Computer Science (LNCS), including its subseries Lecture Notes in Artificial Intelligence (LNAI) and Lecture Notes in Bioinformatics (LNBI), has established itself as a medium for the publication of new developments in computer science and information technology research, teaching, and education.

LNCS enjoys close cooperation with the computer science R & D community, the series counts many renowned academics among its volume editors and paper authors, and collaborates with prestigious societies. Its mission is to serve this international community by providing an invaluable service, mainly focused on the publication of conference and workshop proceedings and postproceedings. LNCS commenced publication in 1973.

Ivo Martinac · Bo Nørregaard Jørgensen ·
Zheng Grace Ma · Rúnar Unnþórsson ·
Chiara Bordin
Editors

Energy Informatics

First Nordic Energy Informatics Academy
Conference, EIA Nordic 2025
Stockholm, Sweden, August 20–22, 2025
Proceedings, Part II

Editors
Ivo Martinac
KTH Royal Institute of Technology
Stockholm, Sweden

Bo Nørregaard Jørgensen
University of Southern Denmark
Odense, Denmark

Zheng Grace Ma
University of Southern Denmark
Odense, Denmark

Rúnar Unnþórsson
University of Iceland
Reykjavík, Iceland

Chiara Bordin
Arctic University of Norway
Tromsø, Norway

ISSN 0302-9743   ISSN 1611-3349 (electronic)
Lecture Notes in Computer Science
ISBN 978-3-032-03097-9   ISBN 978-3-032-03098-6 (eBook)
https://doi.org/10.1007/978-3-032-03098-6

© The Editor(s) (if applicable) and The Author(s), under exclusive license
to Springer Nature Switzerland AG 2026
Chapters "Proper Definitions of Micro Grid Metrics are Needed! – A Generalizable Framework" and "Towards a Taxonomy for Application of Machine Learning and Artificial Intelligence in Building and District Energy Management Systems" are licensed under the terms of the Creative Commons Attribution 4.0 International License (http://creativecommons.org/licenses/by/4.0/). For further details see license information in the chapters.

This work is subject to copyright. All rights are solely and exclusively licensed by the Publisher, whether the whole or part of the material is concerned, specifically the rights of translation, reprinting, reuse of illustrations, recitation, broadcasting, reproduction on microfilms or in any other physical way, and transmission or information storage and retrieval, electronic adaptation, computer software, or by similar or dissimilar methodology now known or hereafter developed.
The use of general descriptive names, registered names, trademarks, service marks, etc. in this publication does not imply, even in the absence of a specific statement, that such names are exempt from the relevant protective laws and regulations and therefore free for general use.
The publisher, the authors and the editors are safe to assume that the advice and information in this book are believed to be true and accurate at the date of publication. Neither the publisher nor the authors or the editors give a warranty, expressed or implied, with respect to the material contained herein or for any errors or omissions that may have been made. The publisher remains neutral with regard to jurisdictional claims in published maps and institutional affiliations.

This Springer imprint is published by the registered company Springer Nature Switzerland AG
The registered company address is: Gewerbestrasse 11, 6330 Cham, Switzerland

If disposing of this product, please recycle the paper.

Preface

The Nordic Energy Informatics Academy Conference 2025 (EIA Nordic 2025) brought together researchers, innovators, and professionals across Europe and beyond to explore how digitalization and informatics can accelerate the sustainable transformation of the energy sector. Held over three days, the conference served as a vibrant forum for knowledge exchange, collaboration, and innovation at the intersection of energy systems and digital technologies.

Thanks to the dedicated efforts of the organizing and technical program committees, a total of sixty-five (65) submissions were received for EIA Nordic 2025. Each submission was evaluated through a rigorous single-blind peer-review process, with three expert reviewers assigned to each paper. Reviews were based on relevance, scientific quality, originality, and clarity. According to the review policy, a manuscript was accepted only if it received at least two positive recommendations.

As a result, fifty-one (51) high-quality research papers were accepted and presented across eleven thematic sections, including 43 full papers and 8 short papers. The strong alignment of submissions with the conference's specific scope, as well as the high standard of contributions from experienced research groups and ongoing collaborations within the Nordic energy informatics community, contributed to this acceptance outcome. All accepted papers are published in the Springer Lecture Notes in Computer Science (LNCS) series, ensuring global visibility and scientific impact.

The conference opened with keynote speeches that set the tone for deep discussion on emerging energy informatics challenges and opportunities. The technical program included insightful presentations organized around the following focused themes:

- Energy Forecasting and Intelligent Control Systems
- District Heating, Thermal Systems, and Retrofit Strategies
- Building Simulation, Urban Energy, and Environmental Sensing
- Industrial Process Efficiency and Biomass Utilization
- Energy Informatics for Electric Vehicles and Mobility Systems
- Multi-Agent Systems and Local Market Coordination
- Policy, Metrics, and Infrastructure Performance
- Smart Building Systems and Semantic Data Integration
- Prosumer Optimization and Energy Storage in Local Energy Communities
- Grid-Oriented AI, Simulation, and Resilience
- Non-Intrusive Load Monitoring and Data Competitions

Each session provided a platform to present cutting-edge methods, innovative applications, and empirical case studies that address real-world energy challenges—from grid flexibility and urban energy sensing to semantic data modeling, battery storage, and AI-based resilience strategies.

In addition to the paper sessions, the conference featured a technical site visit to the KTH Live-in Lab, offering participants further opportunities to network and experience real-world energy innovation in action.

EIA Nordic 2025 once again demonstrated the value of interdisciplinary research and the power of digital tools to drive impactful solutions in energy systems. The conference fostered new ideas, strengthened collaborations, and inspired the community toward the continued advancement of energy informatics.

July 2025

Ivo Martinac
Bo Nørregaard Jørgensen
Zheng Grace Ma
Rúnar Unnþórsson
Chiara Bordin
Zheng Grace Ma
Signe Rude Madsen

Organization

General Chairs

Ivo Martinac KTH Royal Institute of Technology, Sweden
Bo Nørregaard Jørgensen University of Southern Denmark, Denmark

Program Chairs

Zheng Grace Ma University of Southern Denmark, Denmark
Rúnar Unnþórsson University of Iceland, Iceland
Chiara Bordin Arctic University of Norway, Norway

Publication Chair

Zheng Grace Ma University of Southern Denmark, Denmark

Operations Officer

Signe Rude Madsen University of Southern Denmark, Denmark

Program Committee

Abbas Fotouhi Cranfield University, UK
Abdulsalam Yassine Lakehead University, Canada
Agus Hasan Norwegian University of Science and Technology, Norway
Ahmed Yousif Mohamed Idries Norwegian University of Science and Technology, Norway
Aikaterini Chatzivasileiadi Cardiff University, UK
Alexander Kies Aarhus University, Denmark
Alireza Afshari Aalborg University, Denmark
Amjad Anvari-Moghaddam Aalborg University, Denmark
Aoife M. Foley University of Manchester, UK
Arianna Fonsati KTH Royal Institute of Technology, Sweden

Bjørn Austbø	Norwegian University of Science and Technology, Norway
Carlos Fernandez	Robert Gordon University, UK
Cathryn Peoples	Ulster University, UK
Daniel Donaldson	University of Birmingham, UK
Di Wu	Norwegian University of Science and Technology, Norway
Eduard Petlenkov	Tallinn University of Technology, Estonia
Etienne Saloux	Natural Resources Canada, Canada
Hamid Reza Shaker	University of Southern Denmark, Denmark
Hans-Peter Schwefel	Aalborg University, Denmark
Hassam ur Rehman	VTT Technical Research Centre of Finland, Finland
Hicham Johra	SINTEF, Norway
Himanshu Nagpal	EURAC Research, Italy
Hossam Gaber	Ontario Tech University, Canada
Hung Cao	University of New Brunswick, Canada
Igor Sartori	SINTEF, Norway
Ivan Korolija	University College London, UK
Jarek Kurnitski	Tallinn University of Technology, Estonia
Jianguo Ding	Blekinge Institute of Technology, Sweden
Joy Dalmacio Billanes	University of Southern Denmark, Denmark
Joyjit Chatterjee	University of Hull, UK
Juri Belikov	Tallinn University of Technology, Estonia
Kai Heussen	Technical University of Denmark, Denmark
Katja Sirviö	VTT Technical Research Centre of Finland, Finland
Kristoffer Christensen	University of Southern Denmark, Denmark
Kun Zhang	Université du Québec, Canada
Laurent Georges	Norwegian University of Science and Technology, Norway
Linas Martišauskas	Lithuanian Energy Institute, Lithuania
Louis Gosselin	Université Laval, Canada
Magnus Værbak	University of Southern Denmark, Denmark
Mahshid Javidsharifi	Aalborg University, Denmark
Majid Ali	Aalborg University, Denmark
Manuel Llorca	Copenhagen Business School, Denmark
Mohamed Emad Farrag	Glasgow Caledonian University, UK
Najmeh Bazmohammadi	Aalborg University, Denmark
Niklas Lavesson	Blekinge Institute of Technology, Sweden
Ólafur Pétur Pálsson	University of Iceland, Iceland
Paula Carroll	University College Dublin, Ireland

Pei Huang	Dalarna University, Sweden
Qian Wang	KTH Royal Institute of Technology, Sweden
Ravi Pandit	Cranfield University, UK
Risto Kosonen	Aalto University, Finland
Saleh Abdel-Afou Alaliyat	Norwegian University of Science and Technology, Norway
Sebastian Büttrich	IT University of Copenhagen, Denmark
Seyed Shahabaldin Tohidi	Technical University of Denmark, Denmark
Stefán Thor Smith	University of Reading, UK
Touraj Ashrafian	Northumbria University, UK
Umit Cali	University of York, UK
Vahid Nik	Lund University, Sweden
Weiqi Hua	University of Birmingham, UK
Yasunori Akashi	University of Tokyo, Japan
Yushuai Li	Aalborg University, Denmark
Zeeshan Afzal	Linköping University, Sweden

Contents – Part II

Policy, Metrics, and Infrastructure Performance

Proper Definitions of Micro Grid Metrics are Needed! – A Generalizable Framework 3
   Jonathan Fellerer, Jana Helbrecht, and Reinhard German

Solar-Geothermal Power "HGS-ORC" System for Energy Co-generation: Energy, Economic and Environmental Analysis: Algerian Case 24
   Mohamed El-Amine Slimani and Maria Sigríður Guðjónsdóttir

Towards the Integration of Data Space Technology in Hydrogen Research Workflows 36
   Ryan Ford, Rita Beigaitė, and Lius Daniel

Comparison of Outages Trends and Statistics in Nordic Countries Across Distribution Networks and Their Impacts 51
   Seema, Andreas Theocharis, and Reza Sirjani

Managing Risk in Distribution Systems with Solar Generation: A Case Study Using the MATPOWER Optimal Scheduling Tool 67
   Johanna Bolaños-Zuñiga and Alberto J. Lamadrid L.

Smart Energy Management System with Individual Load Monitoring 78
   A. Alex, Jayarama Pradeep, T. S. Aiswarya, N. Harini, and Nikith Jude Serrao

Smart Building Systems and Semantic Data Integration

Towards a Taxonomy for Application of Machine Learning and Artificial Intelligence in Building and District Energy Management Systems 95
   Klaus Lichtenegger, Florian Ahammer, Fabian Schopper, Daniel Muschick, and Markus Gölles

A Dynamic Semantic Data Modeling Approach: Application to Flexible HVAC Zones 114
   Shoya Marumoto, Shohei Miyata, Keiichiro Taniguchi, and Yasunori Akashi

Leveraging Generative AI and Semantic Data for Improved Operation
of a Real-Life Building 130
    John Clauß, Luis Caetano, Knut Nordanger, Thomas Elvrum Lassen,
    and Reidar Kind

Development of an LSTM-Based Model for High-Resolution
Downsampling and Reconstruction of HVAC Chiller Flow Data 144
    Yue He, Shanrui Shi, Shohei Miyata, and Yasunori Akashi

Data-Driven Optimal Air-Balancing Control for Multizone Ventilation
Systems with Design-to-Operation Adaptation 154
    Shanrui Shi, Shohei Miyata, and Yasunori Akashi

Prosumer Optimization and Energy Storage in Local Energy Communities

Evaluating the Potential for Developing Local Energy Communities
in Sweden: Case Studies at Jättesten and Chalmers Campus 173
    Mohammadreza Mazidi, Araavind Sridhar, David Steen,
    Elena Malakhatka, Sara Abouebeid, Felix Niklasson, Le Anh Tuan,
    and Holger Wallbaum

Data-Driven Correlated Uncertainty Sets for PV Generation and Electricity
Demand 187
    Debajyoti Biswas, Cristian Aguayo, Anna Mutule, and Paula Carroll

Scheduling Heat Pumps for Balancing Thermal Storage and Grid Export 204
    Aditya Somawanshi and Anupama Kowli

Battery Energy Storage Integration with BIPV Systems: A Multi-scenario
Economic Analysis and Optimization 221
    Hashem Amini Toosi

Grid-Oriented AI, Simulation, and Resilience

A Data-Driven Analysis of Unscheduled Flows in the European Power
System 237
    Maurizio Titz and Dirk Witthaut

Green Hydrogen Under Uncertainty: Evaluating Power-to-X Strategies
Using Agent-Based Simulation and Multi-criteria Decision Framework 254
    Frederik Wagner Madsen, Joy Dalmacio Billanes,
    Bo Nørregaard Jørgensen, and Zheng Ma

Synthesizing Fault Localization Datasets 271
    Zhonghe Chen, Adi Botea, Paula Carroll, and Deepak Ajwani

Machine Learning-Based Cyberattack Detection in Power Data 285
    Robert A. Becker, Nikolai Kamenev, Celina Koelsch, Aashay Kulkarni,
    and Thomas Bleistein

Optimization of Second-Life Battery Energy Storage System in Buildings
with Photovoltaic Panels: A Norwegian Case Study 300
    Italo Aldo Campodonico-Avendano, Amin Moazami, Aileen Yang,
    and Hicham Johra

Non-Intrusive Load Monitoring and Data Competitions

ADRENALIN: Energy Data Preparation and Validation for HVAC Load
Disaggregation in Commercial Buildings 321
    Balázs András Tolnai, Zheng Grace Ma, Igor Sartori,
    Surya Venkatesh Pandiyan, Matt Amos, Gustaf Bengtsson,
    Synne Krekling Lien, Harald Taxt Walnum, Akram Hameed,
    Jayaprakash Rajasekharan, Rafeal Gomez Garcia,
    and Bo Nørregaard Jørgensen

Advancing Non-intrusive Load Monitoring: Insights from the Winning
Algorithms in the ADRENALIN 2024 Load Disaggregation Competition 338
    Balázs András Tolnai, Rafael Sudbrack Zimmermann, Yangxinyu Xie,
    Ngoc Tran, Cihat Emre Çeliker, Zheng Grace Ma, Igor Sartori,
    Matt Amos, Gustaf Bengtsson, Synne Krekling Lien, Clayton Miller,
    Akram Hameed, and Bo Nørregaard Jørgensen

Comparison of Three Algorithms for Low-Frequency
Temperature-Dependent Load Disaggregation in Buildings
Without Submetering 355
    Balázs András Tolnai, Zheng Ma, and Bo Nørregaard Jørgensen

Lessons Learned from the ADRENALIN Load Disaggregation Challenge 371
    Balázs András Tolnai, Zheng Ma, Igor Sartori, Clayton Miller,
    Stephen White, Matt Amos, Gustaf Bengtsson, Akram Hameed,
    and Bo Nørregaard Jørgensen

Business Model Innovation in Data Competitions: Insights from the 2024
ADRENALIN Load Disaggregation Challenge 388
    Zheng Grace Ma, Balázs András Tolnai, and Bo Nørregaard Jørgensen

Author Index 407

Contents – Part I

Energy Forecasting and Intelligent Control Systems

A Multi-stage Deep Learning Framework for Short-Term Electricity Load Forecasting 3
    Ege Kandemir, Agus Hasan, and Saleh Abdel-Afou Alaliyat

Solaris AI: Enhancing Solar Energy Forecasting with Generative AI and Deep Learning 15
    Mohammed Farhan Faisal, Nimisha Nixon, and Pamba Raja Varma

A Tool for Synthesizing and Implementing Medium Voltage Load Profiles 32
    Hendrik Plompen, Ranier Alexsander Arruda Moura, Khawaja Khalid Mehmood, Anne van der Molen, Peter van der Wielen, and Phuong Hong Nguyen

Decentralized Reinforcement Learning for Adaptive Power Sharing in Hybrid DC Microgrids 60
    Abd Alelah Derbas, Chiara Bordin, Sambeet Mishra, and Frede Blaabjerg

District Heating, Thermal Systems, and Retrofit Strategies

Digitalization in District Heating: Comparative Insights from Denmark and Sweden on Adoption, Barriers, and Value Creation 79
    Zheng Ma, Joy Dalmacio Billanes, and Kristina Lygnerud

Evaluating Retrofit Strategies and Decentralized Systems for the Transition to Low-Temperature District Heating: A Simulation-Based Case Study in Borlänge, Sweden 95
    Vignesh Pechiappan Ayyathurai and Abdelmomen Najmadin

Parametric Study Model for Observing Exergy Balance Through the Series of Subsystems in District Heating 110
    Genku Kayo

Demand-Side Frequency Response Based on District Heating System Integrated with Heat Pump 119
    Hui Yan and Sara Walker

A Parametric Optimization Approach for Enviro-Economic Evaluation
of Energy Renovation Strategies – A Case Study on a Congregation House
in Southern Sweden 131
   *Md Parvaz, Einar Örn Þorvaldsson, Jesper Engström,
   Dennis Johansson, and Henrik Davidsson*

Building Simulation, Urban Energy, and Environmental Sensing

Development of an Automated 3D Building Modeling Method
and Urban-Scale Analysis of Heating and Cooling Loads 149
   Hisato Osawa, Taro Mori, and Konatsu Suzuki

Research on 3D Modeling for Thermal Environment Simulation Using
Publicly Available Map Data 164
   Kazuma Otani, Taro Mori, Hisato Osawa, and Konatsu Suzuki

Rooftop Irregularity Segmentation in Aerial Imagery Using Deep Learning 173
   Konatsu Suzuki, Taro Mori, Hisato Osawa, and Kazuma Otani

Autonomous Air Quality Monitoring System with Photovoltaic Energy
Harvesting: A Sustainable Approach for Public Policies 185
   Emerson Santana and Eduardo Liberado

How Clean is the Air You Breathe During Urban Walk? A Case Study
of Central London 198
   Nikhil Ravindra, Amin Al-Habaibeh, and Benachir Medjdoub

Industrial Process Efficiency and Biomass Utilization

Examining the Role of Digital Technologies and Artificial Intelligence
in Climate Resilience and Energy Adaptation Within Energy-Intensive
Industries 215
   Joy Dalmacio Billanes, Bo Nørregaard Jørgensen, and Zheng Grace Ma

Energy Efficiency Optimization in Plastic Pyrolysis: A Data-Driven
Modeling Study 230
   Aysan Safavi, Christiaan Richter, and Runar Unnthorsson

Globally Optimal Scheduling for Industrial Energy Cost Reduction Under
Dynamic Electricity Pricing 237
   Lu Cong, Bo Nørregaard Jørgensen, and Zheng Grace Ma

Energy Informatics for Electric Vehicles and Mobility Systems

The Irish Highway Network: A Novel Test Instance for the Charging
Station Location Problem 255
  Jingyu Xiang, Paula Carroll, and Annunziata Esposito Amideo

Enhancing EVRP Benchmark Instances with Energy Estimates 267
  Clíodhna Ní Shé and Paula Carroll

Economic and Environmental Benefits of Centralized MILP Optimization
of EV Fleet Charging 283
  Lucija Hajsok and Tea Žakula

Electric Vehicle Based Virtual Electricity Network (EVEN) Solution
for Performance Enhancement in Distribution Networks 299
  Pei Huang and Rehman Zafar

Variational Quantum Eigensolver-Based CaaS Business Model for V2G 309
  Desh Deepak Sharma, Ramesh C. Bansal, and Jeremy Lin

Multi-Agent Systems and Local Market Coordination

Towards ICT-Enabled Multi-agent Based Operations in Local Energy
Communities: A Proof of Concept 323
  *Haoyu Huang, Natascha Fernengel, André Xhonneux,
  Alexander Holtwerth, Michael Hehemann, Eugen Hoppe,
  Simon Waczowicz, Kevin Förderer, Veit Hagenmeyer, and Dirk Müller*

Peer-to-Peer Energy Management Model for Residential Homes 341
  Najmeh Khajoei, Runar Unnthorsson, and Steinn Gudmundsson

Agent-Based Flexibility Aggregation for a Distributed Redispatch 354
  Malin Radtke, Sanja Stark, and Stefanie Holly

A Visualization Framework for Exploring Multi-agent-Based Simulations:
Case Study of an Electric Vehicle Home Charging Ecosystem 371
  Kristoffer Christensen, Bo Nørregaard Jørgensen, and Zheng Grace Ma

Author Index 387

Policy, Metrics, and Infrastructure Performance

Proper Definitions of Micro Grid Metrics are Needed! – A Generalizable Framework

Jonathan Fellerer[✉][iD], Jana Helbrecht[iD], and Reinhard German[iD]

Friedrich-Alexander-Universität Erlangen-Nürnberg, Martensstr. 3, 91058 Erlangen, Germany
{jonathan.fellerer,jana.helbrecht,reinhard.german}@fau.de

Abstract. The rapid adoption of renewable energy and energy storage technologies has accelerated the deployment of micro grids (MGs), highlighting the need for clear, standardized metrics to evaluate performance. Current definitions of several metrics for MGs vary widely, often ignoring key aspects such as internal losses, storage dynamics, and grid interactions, limiting comparability and practical applicability. This paper presents a comprehensive set of twelve well-defined metrics ranging from 0 to 1, which are inherently aligned with energy conservation principles and explicitly capture system losses. These generalized metrics serve as a framework for deriving use-case-specific metrics and framework-compliant equations. Synthetic yet realistic use case scenarios are used to demonstrate their flexibility and suitability for different technological and regulatory contexts. The results emphasize clarity, consistency, and practical relevance, laying the groundwork for broader empirical validation, standardization, and regulatory integration. Future work should focus on approximation methods to deal with real-world measurement limitations.

Keywords: metrics · key performance indicators · micro grid · energy storage system

Nomenclature

Other

ΔQ	The difference of stored energy at the start and end of the approximation period
η_{sdch}	The approximated efficiency due to self-discharge
C	The nominal capacity of the ESS

Demand related

ψ_{SS}	The self-sufficiency metric
ψ_{IR}	The import reliance metric
ψ_{CD}	The curtailed demand metric
E_{d}	The maximum possible or the effective demanded energy amount
E_{cd}	The curtailed demanded energy amount
E_{sd}	The energy amount from storage to demand
η_{sd}	The efficiency from storage to demand

Export related

ψ_{SE}	The self-export metric
ψ_{IE}	The imported export metric
ψ_{CE}	The curtailed export metric
E_{e}	The maximum possible or the effective exported energy amount
E_{ce}	The curtailed exported energy amount
E_{se}	The energy amount from storage to export
η_{se}	The efficiency from storage to export

Generation related

ψ_{SC}	The self-consumption metric
ψ_{EG}	The exported generation metric
ψ_{CG}	The curtailed generation metric
E_{g}	The maximum possible or the effective generated energy amount
E_{cg}	The curtailed generated energy amount
E_{gd}	The energy amount from generation directly to demand
E_{ge}	The energy amount from generation directly to export
η_{gd}	The efficiency from generation directly to demand
η_{ge}	The efficiency from generation directly to export
E_{gs}	The energy amount from generation to storage
η_{gs}	The efficiency from generation to storage
E_{gsd}	The energy amount from generation via storage to demand
E_{gse}	The energy amount from generation via storage to export
ψ_{SCL}	The internal losses due to self-consumption.
ψ_{SEL}	The internal losses due to self-export.

Import related

ψ_{SI}	The self-import metric
ψ_{EI}	The exported import metric
ψ_{CI}	The curtailed import metric
E_{i}	The maximum possible or the effective imported energy amount
E_{ci}	The curtailed imported energy amount

E_{id}	The energy amount from import directly to consumption
E_{ie}	The energy amount from import directly to export
η_{id}	The efficiency from import directly to consumption
η_{ie}	The efficiency from import directly to export
E_{is}	The energy amount from import to storage
η_{is}	The efficiency from import to storage
E_{isd}	The energy amount from import via storage to demand
E_{ise}	The energy amount from import via storage to export
ψ_{SIL}	The internal losses due to self-import.
ψ_{IEL}	The internal losses due to import-export.

1 Introduction

The growing penetration of worldwide energy systems by Renewable Energy Sources (RESs), particularly Photovoltaic Systems (PVs) and Wind Turbines (WTs), combined with advances in energy storage technologies, has significantly accelerated the adoption of micro grid (MG) solutions globally. MGs, which integrate localized energy generation, storage, and consumption, are increasingly recognized for their ability to enhance energy autonomy, grid resilience, and sustainability. This benefit of Energy Storage Systems (ESSs) within MGs has been studied worldwide in several publications in the past decade [1,3,8,13,16,19,23]. However, the performance evaluation of these MGs critically dependent on clear, consistent, and standardized metrics. In particular, "self-consumption (SC)" and "self-sufficiency (SS)" have emerged as central indicators reflecting the effectiveness and sustainability of MG operation.

Despite their importance, the existing literature reveals substantial variability and ambiguity in the definitions and applications of these metrics. Recent studies, notably by Helbrecht [7] and Zepter et al. [25], have highlighted significant limitations and inconsistencies in the way SS is quantified in the literature, particularly in systems involving energy storage with active energy market (EM) interactions. The introduction of flexible or local EMs will lead to more interaction of ESSs and different markets in the coming years. Traditional definitions often neglect important system parameters like storage and inverter losses, or have implicit assumptions that can lead to wrong interpretations and impractical performance assessments.

This paper addresses these critical gaps by proposing a comprehensive set of 12 well-defined metrics specifically tailored for MGs with ESS. The basis for eight of those metrics has been developed and thoroughly discussed by Helbrecht [7], and two have been elaborated by Zepter et al. [25]. Our work extends their ideas and forms a generalized metric framework. The 12 metrics can also be applied to MGs without energy storage or even systems without energy generation and only ESS. The introduced metrics range from 0 to 1 and are categorized into groups of three, inherently ensuring compliance with fundamental principles of energy conservation and explicitly incorporating system losses. Four additional selected metrics are introduced to describe internal losses which result in a total of 16 metrics in this paper. More metrics can be easily constructed using the proposed energy balance network and it's metrics as a framework. Complemented by a suitable visualization, this study aims to contribute significantly to the standardization and comparability of MG performance evaluations in different technological and regulatory contexts.

We want to elaborate on some of the related literature and the identified discrepancies and implicit assumptions in Sect. 1.1. Within Sect. 2 we will introduce the generalizable metric framework, the 12 core metrics, and the four additionally selected metrics. Since visualization is a fundamental instrument for communicating information about complex systems, we will propose an aggregated view within Sect. 2.1. In Sect. 3 we apply it to a set of MGs with increasing complexity and different objectives to showcase the adaptability and versatility of the proposed metric framework. Section 4 concludes the work and opens up relevant future research directions.

1.1 Relevance, yet Ambiguity in the Research Community

A classification of different metrics into "load matching" and "grid interaction" has been presented in [17]. They classify both SS and SC in the first category and indicate the rather simple nature of these metrics, as their calculation only requires load and generation profiles. They use the term load matching index for the SS and base their calculations on the definition of [24]. This common definition relates "on site generation" to the "load" and cuts at a load matching index of 1 whenever the generation exceeds demand. This is one of the big shortcomings of many definitions, since this simplifies the overall system model significantly to a degree that does not match modern energy systems. Although the definitions used might have been applicable for the state of technology in 2010, the increased usage of ESS and the potential direct participation of MG at the EM, would lead to misleading results without an updated set of metrics.

In [18], arguments for and against increased prosumage (producers, consumers and storage) are summarized and discussed within a global context with a focus on the European Union (EU). Some of those are directly linked to decisions made by possible prosumers based on data that could be obtained by looking at metrics like SS and SC. They also highlight the potential benefit of MGs by utilizing spare ESS capacity to participating at the EM, whether by providing ancillary services or by offering their buffer capacity to some degree. According to empirical data from Germany published in [6,14], there is a preference for self-generation and independence from the grid that can be expressed by a wish for a rather high SS and SC, as then the percentage of energy given or taken from the grid is lower. Taken a step further, reliable numerical metrics for those and similar metrics could incentivize and guide prosumers to manage their consumption based on the generation profile if possible.

The metrics SS and SC are not only relevant for prosumers but also for algorithms, models, and simulations to analyze system sizing and operation. The Effective Energy Shift (EfES) algorithm is introduced by Fellerer et al. [5] that computes the total energy that can be discharged from an ESS over some period of time, as well as the metrics SS and SC depending on the capacity of the ESS. This can therefore be used to calculate the energy that remains to be imported from or to be exported to the grid. An analytical solution based on the algorithm for the cost-optimal capacity of an ESS has been introduced by Fellerer et al. [4]. The definition used for the two metrics assumes that the ESS does not interact with the EM, either by being charged from imported energy or discharged to sell energy. These assumptions are explicitly stated, and their definition therefore inline with the one we introduced in our article.

A simulation study by [9] determined the economic viability of PV and ESS in the residential context. They highlighted the interdependence of these two system components and the large effect on overall system performance. To calculate the actual net present value (NPV) a model calculating the metric SC is used. Again, the assumption is made that there is no interaction between the market and the ESS. They concluded that ESS will remain an important and economically viable technology.

A system sizing methodology that solves a single-objective Mixed Integer Linear Programming (MILP) and a multi-objective Non-Linear Program (NLP) has been presented in [20]. The single-objective utilizes the net energy exchanged with the grid, while the multi-objective depends on the SS, the SC, as well as the NPV, which highlights the importance of reliable and preferable bounded and normalized numerical values for those metrics. Especially since their definitions will not produce accurate and potentially wrong results for MGs with ESS and EM interaction.

Among other metrics, SS and SC play a significant indicator in [11] to determine the optimal tilt angles and orientation of PVs in different regions of China. Even though they correctly state, that those metrics should be computed based on the directly used energy amounts, they do not elaborate on the effect or size of ESSs on those metrics. Based on their literal description, we assume that the ESS are not participating in the market and only serve to increase the autarky level of a system, which is equivalent to maximize SS.

The set of definitions described in [12] is based on a rather simple model without an ESS. They define the SC as a fraction of the self-consumed energy and the sum of the surplus PV generation and the self-consumed energy. The SS is the fraction of self-consumed energy and the sum of the surplus demand and self-consumed energy. It should be noted that their statement that efficiency losses of ESSs should not be counted as SC is not reasonable. Even though this simplifies relating SS and SC, it also removes those losses from minimization targets and therefore potential real-life decisions, when those are based on minimization results. This might have been the reasoning behind that statement, but better alternatives exist. One alternative is to optimize for the effectively used energy from own generation (hence minimizing the total losses described by the later proposed curtailment metrics, representing external and operational losses, and internal, mostly technical, losses Equation (5)). Optimizing for SC alone is a questionable objective, since it will be biased toward inefficient technologies.

There are definitions that use ambiguous language. An exemplary pair of these is shown in [2,10]. The SC is the simple fraction of the self-consumed energy ("Eigenverbrauch" in German) divided by the total production. This is not a very exact definition, since it does not differentiate the energy meant for consumption from the energy actually used to cover the demand. In the context of the metric SS [2] uses again the self-consumed energy ("Eigenverbrauch" in German) in the nominator. No matter the interpretation of self-consumed energy, the subtle difference between energy meant for consumption and the energy actually being consumed is lost.

A typical set of definitions uses imported and exported energy to define the self-generated energy used for consumption. For SC, [10,15,22] use the difference between generated energy and the energy exported to the grid to define the self-generated energy intended for consumption. Similarly the definition for SS in [15] uses the difference between consumption and import to determine how much of the consumed energy was actually self-generated. As [7] discusses, this combination of definitions can significantly impact the possibility of modeling trading via an ESS or the grid in general, since the metrics become unbounded and can even assume negative values.

Another possible way to calculate the metric SS is shown in [22]. It uses the difference between generation and export to calculate the amount of consumed energy that was self-generated. This seems even more problematic than the previous definitions, as the values of generation and export are farther away from the demand, and with that prone to more efficiency losses, than the import.

Instead of the nominator, the denominator can also be expressed differently. In [21], for example, all of the generated energy is defined by the sum of the self-consumed energy and the exported energy. This aligns well with our proposed definition.

1.2 Closing the Gap

As seen in the previously named examples, the definitions of the MG metrics found in literature differ a lot. The identified gap is not only the differences in definition but also the difficult expansion to a system using an ESS for trading.

The work of Zepter et al. [25] takes a look at the SS and discusses the disadvantages and problems of commonly used equations as soon as a ESS with the option of active EM trading is added to a MG. They state three main points of criticism and possible improvements. First, there is the oversimplification of the capabilities of the ESS by not giving it the option for active grid exchange.

Secondly, current definitions are not able to represent the initial and change of the energy storage level. The third criticism is the ambiguous handling of efficiency losses and not assigning them to the actual components of the system.

In particular, the first and third points of criticism were addressed by Helbrecht [7]. Some of the definitions that come up in the literature are compared with those based on a more general and detailed model. The MG was modeled rather generally and by splitting the ESS virtually, the energy flows created by the energy exchange between storage and the external grid could be explicitly addressed. The basis for proposed definitions includes the "intention" of energy usage, e.g.:

$$SS = \frac{\text{effectively covered demand by own generation}}{\text{energy demand}} \text{ and}$$

$$SC = \frac{\text{effectively consumed own generation intended for own demand}}{\text{self-generated energy}}.$$

Together with the model of a generalized MG, concrete definitions for SS, SC, and some additional metrics were presented. To prove the equality between definitions derived from the generic model and those originating from the literature, some of the energy flows and efficiency losses used in the definitions had to be set to 0. This consequently identified the limitations and implicit assumptions of each literature definition as well as the differences between them, e.g., that some definitions only hold, as long as there is no interaction between ESS and an EM.

Our work in this article presents a MG model that is based on the most comprehensive model proposed by Helbrecht [7] which is based on the model introduced by Fellerer et al. [5]. This model can serve as a generalized framework for clearly defined and bounded metrics for any MG composition.

2 The Generalizable Micro Grid Metric Framework

Based on the identified discrepancies and insufficiencies within the existing definitions, we introduce generalizable definitions for several important metrics. The same framework can be used to assess other definitions and prove the equivalency, differences, or assumptions made. Several examples and comparisons have been made in [7] and eight metrics proposed in our paper have been inspired by it. This includes large parts of the energy balance network shown in Fig. 1. A summary of the 12 core metrics that will be introduced is added in Appendix A.1.

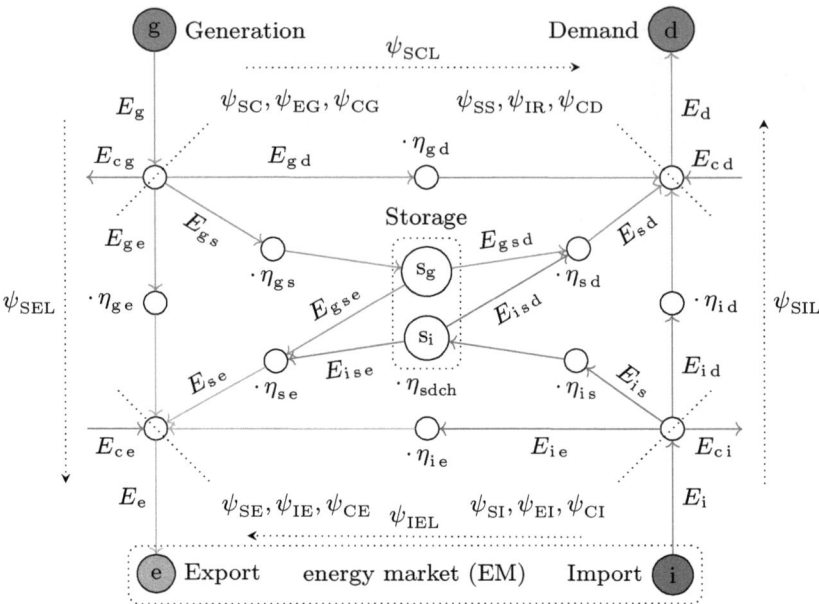

Fig. 1. Generalized energy balance network for MGs (Color figure online)

It describes two potential sources of energy, namely the internal generation and the external import, as well as two energy sinks, the internal demand and the external export. All other nodes in the directed network follow the basic rule of energy conservation. Two categories of losses are assumed within the model; technological losses and operational losses. To distinguish those two, technical losses use a label with a multiplication by some factor η_x, which replaces an outgoing flow for $\eta_x < 1$ or an incoming flow for $\eta_x > 1$. Operational losses are indicated by arrows in red (E_{cg}, E_{cd}, E_{ci}, and E_{ce}). The self-discharge η_{sdch} belongs to both categories, since it depends on the technological implementation of the ESS as well as on the operational decision on how long energy should be stored.

One of the concepts described in [7] is the virtual split of any ESS that is necessary, once the same ESS is used for internal consumption and market interaction. The virtual split separates the ESS with an effective storage capacity C into two storage parts s_g and s_i. While s_g can only be charged by the own generation, s_i can only be charged by importing energy from the market. This ensures that any energy that is charged from import and later used internally to cover demand does not increase self-sufficiency. Although this virtual split is easy to perform on a conceptual level, it is not as easy when applied to real systems. Approximations could be achieved by performing bookkeeping of energy that gets charged and discharged and assigning individual energy packets to either virtual part of the ESS. Any self-discharge during storage of energy has to affect the ESS as a whole.

Within the introduced energy balance network it is now possible to derive several different metrics. We will get triplets for each of the outer nodes demand, generation, import, and export, as well as metrics for internal losses between the outer nodes. This results in a total of 12 core metrics and four selected loss metrics. All efficiencies are positive and not zero; hence $0 < \eta_x \in \mathbb{R}^+$. When mapped to a real system or any use case, each η_x can correspond to multiple and even the same physical device. An AC-coupled PV will most likely only have a single inverter with efficiency η_{PV} that connects it to the AC-grid. Hence $\eta_{gd} = \eta_{ge} = \eta_{PV}$, since they correspond to the efficiency of the same inverter. Once we add an AC-coupled ESS, there is at least one other inverter with efficiency η_{ESS} between the PV and the ESS, which will lead to $\eta_{gs} = \eta_{PV} \cdot \eta_{ESS}$. The same concept applies to all other efficiencies, and some more real-world use cases and mappings have been explored in [7]. Since the presented system does not specify the actual energy carrier, it can be easily extended by interpreting all variables as vectors. The number of elements in the vector is the number of different energy carriers. The adaptation of the presented equations is straightforward. Especially when we consider a system with electricity generation that has electricity demand on one hand and heat demand on the other, we can use a heat pump to cover the own heat demand by electricity generation. We will get three metrics for electricity generation, three metrics for electricity demand, and another three metrics for heat demand. This example also makes it obvious that efficiencies should only be non-zero but are not limited, since heat pumps typically have a coefficient of power larger than 1.

To ensure meaningful metrics, all energy values have to be positive $E_x \geq 0$ along their respective arrows in Fig. 1. This leads to the interpretation of the four energy values E_g, E_d, E_i, and E_e to be either effective energy values (hence without additional losses or curtailment) or the maximum possible energy values (hence with additional losses or curtailment). An overview of the 12 metrics and whether they are adapted versions or newly introduced is available in Table 1.

Metrics relative to E_d are the **self-sufficiency (SS)** $\psi_{SS} \in [0, 1]$, the **import reliance (IR)** $\psi_{IR} \in [0, 1]$, and the **curtailed demand (CD)** $\psi_{CD} \in [0, 1]$. The first describes how much demand has been covered by the own generation, the second describes how much demand has been covered by importing energy, and the last serves as a slack variable describing deficits or external curtailment. The def-

Table 1. Overview of the 12 core metrics.

Demand E_d	Generation E_g	Export E_e	Import E_i
ψ_{SS} [a]	ψ_{SC} [a]	ψ_{SE} [b]	ψ_{SI} [b]
ψ_{IR} [b]	ψ_{EG} [b]	ψ_{IE} [c]	ψ_{EI} [b]
ψ_{CD} [c]	ψ_{CG} [c]	ψ_{CE} [c]	ψ_{CI} [c]

[a] adapted from common definitions; [b] adapted from Helbrecht [7]; [c] newly introduced

initions are as follows:

$$\psi_{SS} = \frac{\eta_{gd} \cdot E_{gd} + \eta_{sd} \cdot E_{gsd}}{E_d} \quad \text{if } E_d \neq 0, \text{ else } 1 \quad (1a)$$

$$\psi_{IR} = \frac{\eta_{id} \cdot E_{id} + \eta_{sd} \cdot E_{isd}}{E_d} \quad \text{if } E_d \neq 0, \text{ else } 0 \quad (1b)$$

$$\psi_{CD} + \psi_{SS} + \psi_{IR} = 1. \quad (1c)$$

Alternatively, we can use $\psi_{CD} = E_{cd}/E_d$ which might only be relevant, when load curtailment happens or if no import is possible.

Metrics relative to E_g are the **self-consumption (SC)** $\psi_{SC} \in [0,1]$, the **exported generation (EG)** $\psi_{EG} \in [0,1]$, and the **curtailed generation (CG)** $\psi_{CG} \in [0,1]$. The first describes how much generation has been consumed by the own demand and the resulting internal losses. The second is how much generation has been consumed by exporting it and the corresponding internal losses. Any excess generation that has not been consumed or external curtailment will be reflected in the last metric. Similar to before they are defined as follows:

$$\psi_{SC} = \frac{E_{gd} + \frac{E_{gsd}}{\eta_{sdch} \cdot \eta_{gs}}}{E_g} \quad \text{if } E_g \neq 0, \text{ else } 1 \quad (2a)$$

$$\psi_{EG} = \frac{E_{ge} + \frac{E_{gse}}{\eta_{sdch} \cdot \eta_{gs}}}{E_g} \quad \text{if } E_g \neq 0, \text{ else } 0 \quad (2b)$$

$$\psi_{CG} + \psi_{SC} + \psi_{EG} = 1. \quad (2c)$$

Alternatively, we can use $\psi_{CG} = E_{cg}/E_g$ and external curtailment or excess generation will lead to $\psi_{CG} > 0$.

On the import side and relative to E_i we define the metrics the **self-import (SI)** $\psi_{SI} \in [0,1]$, the **exported import (EI)** $\psi_{EI} \in [0,1]$, and the **curtailed import (CI)** $\psi_{CI} \in [0,1]$. The first defines how much energy has been imported and later consumed by the own demand or lost in-between. The second describes how much energy has been imported and later exported again, including the corresponding internal losses. The last indicates how much import has not been possible, even though it was intended. Those are defined as:

$$\psi_{\text{SI}} = \frac{E_{\text{id}} + \frac{E_{\text{isd}}}{\eta_{\text{sdch}} \cdot \eta_{\text{is}}}}{E_{\text{i}}} \quad \text{if } E_{\text{i}} \neq 0, \text{ else } 1 \tag{3a}$$

$$\psi_{\text{EI}} = \frac{E_{\text{ie}} + \frac{E_{\text{ise}}}{\eta_{\text{sdch}} \cdot \eta_{\text{is}}}}{E_{\text{i}}} \quad \text{if } E_{\text{i}} \neq 0, \text{ else } 0 \tag{3b}$$

$$\psi_{\text{CI}} + \psi_{\text{SI}} + \psi_{\text{EI}} = 1. \tag{3c}$$

Alternatively, we can use $\psi_{\text{CI}} = E_{\text{ci}} / E_{\text{i}}$. Any external or operational limit on the imported power will lead to $\psi_{\text{CI}} > 0$.

Finally, we can define the metrics relative to E_{e}: **self-export (SE)** $\psi_{\text{SE}} \in [0, 1]$, **imported export (IE)** $\psi_{\text{IE}} \in [0, 1]$, and **curtailed export (CE)** $\psi_{\text{CE}} \in [0, 1]$. The first describes how much export has been generated internally, the second how much imported energy has actually been exported, i.e., after losses, and the last describes any remaining losses or deficits. Hence we get:

$$\psi_{\text{SE}} = \frac{\eta_{\text{ge}} \cdot E_{\text{ge}} + \eta_{\text{se}} \cdot E_{\text{gse}}}{E_{\text{e}}} \quad \text{if } E_{\text{e}} \neq 0, \text{ else } 1 \tag{4a}$$

$$\psi_{\text{IE}} = \frac{\eta_{\text{ie}} \cdot E_{\text{ie}} + \eta_{\text{se}} \cdot E_{\text{ise}}}{E_{\text{e}}} \quad \text{if } E_{\text{e}} \neq 0, \text{ else } 0 \tag{4b}$$

$$\psi_{\text{CE}} + \psi_{\text{SE}} + \psi_{\text{IE}} = 1. \tag{4c}$$

Alternatively, we can use $\psi_{\text{CE}} = E_{\text{ce}} / E_{\text{e}}$ which is only relevant, if an export target should be achieved and is 0 otherwise. In most setups E_{ie} is 0, but, e.g., a MG that imports energy as electricity and exports as hydrogen could have a direct import-export flow that does not require intermediate storage.

In addition, we can easily define four metrics that describe internal losses. Those are the **self-consumption losses** ψ_{SCL}, **self-export losses** ψ_{SEL}, **self-import losses** ψ_{SIL}, and **import-export losses** ψ_{IEL}:

$$\psi_{\text{SCL}} = 1 - \frac{\psi_{\text{SS}} \cdot E_{\text{d}}}{\psi_{\text{SC}} \cdot E_{\text{g}}} \quad \text{if } E_{\text{g}} \neq 0, \text{ else } 0, \tag{5a}$$

$$\psi_{\text{SEL}} = 1 - \frac{\psi_{\text{SE}} \cdot E_{\text{e}}}{\psi_{\text{EG}} \cdot E_{\text{g}}} \quad \text{if } E_{\text{g}} \neq 0, \text{ else } 0, \tag{5b}$$

$$\psi_{\text{SIL}} = 1 - \frac{\psi_{\text{IR}} \cdot E_{\text{d}}}{\psi_{\text{SI}} \cdot E_{\text{i}}} \quad \text{if } E_{\text{i}} \neq 0, \text{ else } 0, \text{ and} \tag{5c}$$

$$\psi_{\text{IEL}} = 1 - \frac{\psi_{\text{IE}} \cdot E_{\text{e}}}{\psi_{\text{EI}} \cdot E_{\text{i}}} \quad \text{if } E_{\text{i}} \neq 0, \text{ else } 0. \tag{5d}$$

The self-discharge and the corresponding η_{sdch} can be approximated with an estimate of the difference of the stored energy amount ΔQ between the start and the end of an analysis period:

$$\eta_{\text{sdch}} = \frac{E_{\text{gsd}} + E_{\text{gse}} + E_{\text{isd}} + E_{\text{ise}}}{\eta_{\text{gs}} \cdot E_{\text{gs}} + \eta_{\text{is}} \cdot E_{\text{is}} - \Delta Q}. \tag{6}$$

For long analysis periods the unbounded energy values E_x and the bound $-C \leq \Delta Q \leq C$ will result in $\Delta Q \ll E_x$ and might therefore be ignored for sufficiently long approximation periods. If either the nominator or the denominator is 0 we can safely use $\eta_{\text{sdch}} = 1$.

2.1 Visualization

In addition to the mathematical definitions presented, we propose a way to visualize all relevant metrics in a compact way. It follows the same four dimensions of generation, demand, import, and export and utilizes the normalization that is already at the core of all metrics presented. The color coding within the visualization follows a traffic light schema that describes metrics related to "oneself", the "outer world" and "losses". These are also used when referring to variables inside the text in the remaining document. The proposed visualization is a stacked radar or spider web chart with additional annotations and can be seen in Fig. 2.

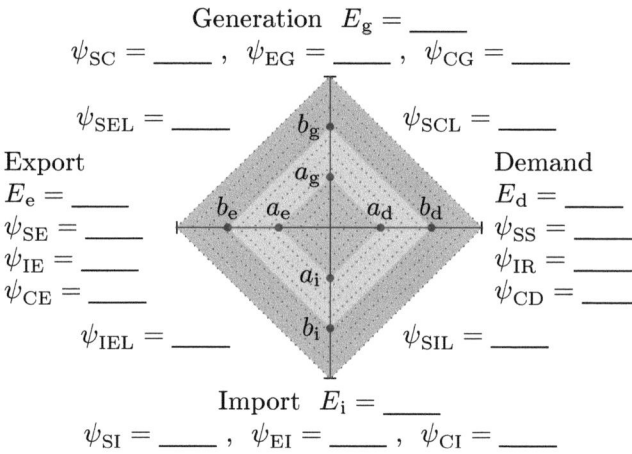

Fig. 2. Proposed visualization suitable for the generalized metric framework.

The numerical values of the 12 metrics of Eqs. (1) to (4) are located on the corresponding axis. The total energy amounts per dimension should be annotated, to convey the size context of a specific MG. Between the four dimensions, the arrows indicate the main energy flows and allow a suitable location to display the four different internal losses from Eq. (5). Within the radar chart, we define eight different points for the 12 different metrics. The length of each axis is exactly 1, since this represents the balancing equations. The inner points are $[a_d, a_g, a_e, a_i] = [\psi_{\text{SS}}, \psi_{\text{SC}}, \psi_{\text{SE}}, \psi_{\text{SI}}]$. The outer points are $[b_d, b_g, b_e, b_i] = [\psi_{\text{SS}} + \psi_{\text{IR}}, \psi_{\text{SC}} + \psi_{\text{EG}}, \psi_{\text{SE}} + \psi_{\text{IE}}, \psi_{\text{SI}} + \psi_{\text{EI}}]$. Any dimension without any energy flow, i.e., $E_d = 0$, $E_g = 0$, $E_e = 0$, or $E_i = 0$ should be left blank.

3 Explanation and Visualization of Proposed Metrics Through Use Cases

Using a series of synthetic, yet realistic scenarios, we illustrate the effectiveness of the proposed metrics along with their corresponding visualizations. Each scenario progressively incorporates complexity, starting from a basic reference case to a fully integrated MG combining RES, ESS, and EM interactions.

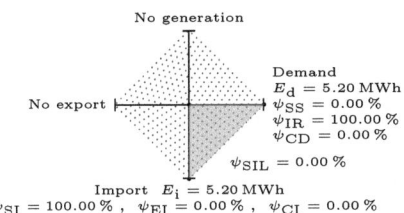
(a) Standard single-family house without own generation or storage.

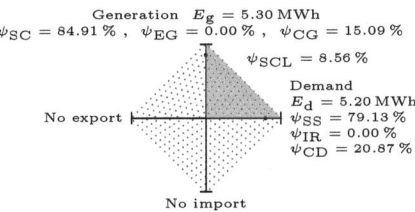
(b) Standalone MG system, hence no import or export.

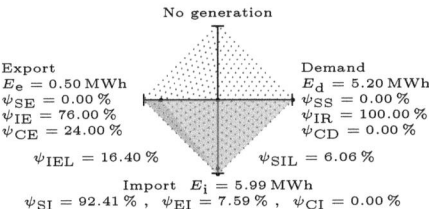
(c) MG without RES, but ESS that is used for trading.

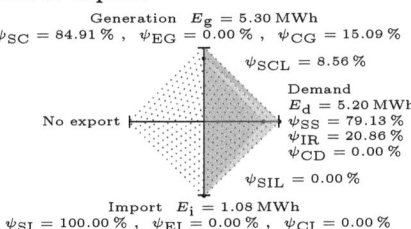
(d) MG with own RES, no export, but additional import.

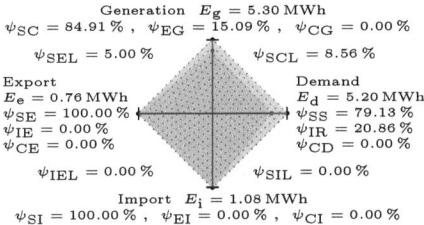
(e) MG with own RES, only direct export, and additional import.

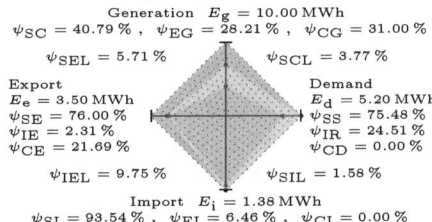
(f) MG with own RES, ESS with curtailment and trading.

Fig. 3. Exemplary use cases of different complexity.

Use Case 1: Standard Single-Family House (Reference) (see Fig. 3a)
The initial use case involves a standard single-family home without local generation or storage. Although typically not classified as a MG, this scenario serves as a fundamental reference point. As the household does not generate energy locally, it must import 100 % of its energy demand from the grid. Consequently, dimensions related to generation and energy export in the visualization are intentionally left blank, as they provide no meaningful data in this context.

Use Case 2: Islanded MG with RES (see Fig. 3b) In the second use case, the same household operates as an islanded MG exclusively relying on its own RES. Due to the absence of a grid connection, neither energy import nor export occurs. Consequently, the metrics for export and import remain blank. Instead, curtailment occurs in both generation and demand, as renewable production and load consumption do not always align temporally. Those losses are reflected in the curtailment metrics ψ_{CG} and ψ_{CD}, and any optimization for load shifting could utilize those as part of the objective function. Internal losses due to inverter inefficiencies and battery storage operations - including charging, self-discharge, and discharging—are captured by the metric ψ_{SCL}, which can support decision-making regarding investment in specific technologies or equipment.

Use Case 3: Grid-Connected MG with ESS for EM Trading, but no RES (see Fig. 3c) This scenario explores a grid-connected household equipped exclusively with an ESS, engaging in active energy market trading. Here, internal losses arise as a result of battery operations, namely charging cycles, self-discharge, and discharge processes. Since a local RES is absent, the visual representation excludes generation, instead focusing on interactions and efficiency losses related to energy storage operations and market participation. Similarly to before, we can use the internal losses ψ_{SIL} and ψ_{IEL} to support investment decision-making. By approximating the maximum possible export, here 0.5 MWh, we can minimize for ψ_{CE} to address export targets that have not been met (or simply maximize for $E_e - E_{ce}$).

Use Case 4: Grid-Connected MG with RES and ESS, But No Export Possible (see Fig. 3d) The fourth scenario depicts a grid-connected household with RES and ESS but without the possibility of energy export to the grid. This limitation significantly influences system behavior, as surplus generation can lead to curtailed demand or generation curtailment when the ESS capacity is exceeded or operational limits are encountered. Import reliance remains relevant during periods of insufficient local generation or storage depletion. Internal losses can now be attributed to two major subsystems, i.e., the PV and the ESS. Individual metrics can be easily derived from the presented metric framework and can then be used as key performance indicators within a combined investment decision process.

Use Case 5: Grid-Connected MG with RES, But Only Direct Energy Export and Import (see Fig. 3e) The fifth scenario introduces direct grid export capabilities alongside RES and continues to feature energy imports. The hypothetical ESS is never charged from the grid or discharged to the grid. With direct export permitted, surplus RES generation is fed into the grid, reducing curtailment and maximizing the utility of the installed renewable capacity. As before, we have several metrics to support a multitude of optimization problems.

Use case 6: Comprehensive MG Scenario (Mixed Operation with RES, ESS, and EM Trading) (see Fig. 3f) The final and most complex scenario demonstrates a fully integrated MG, combining larger RES capacity, a large ESS, and operational strategies that involve both internal energy management and active participation in external EMs. Given the wide range of dedicated metrics, intricate interactions between generation, demand, storage, import, and export, as well as efficiency losses across all four dimensions can be analyzed at one glance.

4 Discussion and Conclusion

This study has introduced a clearly defined set of metrics to evaluate the performance of microgrid systems with RESs and ESSs. These metrics provide a robust and unified framework that is applicable in diverse scenarios, from standalone microgrids to complex grid-connected hybrid systems.

The practical implications of adopting standardized metrics are substantial. They provide clarity and comparability, enabling researchers, system designers, policymakers, and stakeholders to evaluate system performance and make informed decisions uniformly. Unlike previous definitions, which suffered from ambiguity and inconsistency, as already highlighted in [7,25], the metrics proposed in this article are explicitly defined, range consistently from 0 to 1, and inherently account for energy losses, thus preserving the principle of energy conservation.

These metrics have demonstrated compatibility across different technological setups and regulatory contexts. For standalone microgrids, the self-sufficiency (SS) and self-consumption (SC) metrics directly assess the proportion of locally generated energy that meets local demand, while the curtailed generation (CG) and curtailed demand (CD) metrics indicate the degree of operational mismatch within the system. For grid-connected systems, the import reliance (IR) and self-import (SI) indicate the dependence on external resources. Market interactions such as energy trading and energy export can be furthermore described by the metrics exported generation (EG), imported export (IE), and exported import (EI). External curtailment or unmet import and export targets reflect in the metrics curtailed export (CE) and curtailed import (CI).

The illustrative scenarios presented, ranging from simple single-family homes without generation or storage to complex grid-connected hybrid systems, underscore the metrics' adaptability. Through synthetic yet realistic data, these cases highlight the practical utility of these metrics in diverse operating conditions, making them suitable for both theoretical analyses and real-world applications.

To further strengthen the proposed metrics, several future research directions should be pursued. Empirical validation through real-world microgrid data is essential to ensure practical applicability and robustness. Extending the metric framework for energy systems with multiple types of energy carriers, e.g., electricity and heat, should prove beneficial. Promoting standardization within the broader research community and industry will facilitate widespread adoption, enabling consistent benchmarking and regulatory integration. Finally, collaboration with regulatory bodies will be necessary to integrate these standardized metrics into existing energy policies and market structures.

In conclusion, clearly defined and standardized metrics for MG performance evaluation, as introduced here, provide essential tools for advancing the integration of renewable energy and storage technologies. However, effective application in real systems requires additional exploration into practical approximation methods with low accuracy or incomplete measurements.

We hope that our proposed generalized metric framework with its variability and applicability to a multitude of different MG structures and objectives will lead to a better definition of the multi-faceted characteristics of MG, a higher transparency regarding implicit assumptions and internal operation, and finally a potentially easier comparison of one of the most relevant technological concepts for the future of global energy grids.

A Appendix

A.1 Summary Table for Quick Reference

	Energy Sinks	Energy Sources
	Demand E_d	Generation E_g
oneself	$\psi_\mathrm{SS} = E_\mathrm{d}^{-1} \cdot (\eta_\mathrm{gd} \cdot E_\mathrm{gd} + \eta_\mathrm{sd} \cdot E_\mathrm{gsd})$ if $E_\mathrm{d} \neq 0$, else 1	$\psi_\mathrm{SC} = E_\mathrm{g}^{-1} \cdot \left(E_\mathrm{gd} + \frac{E_\mathrm{gsd}}{\eta_\mathrm{sdch} \cdot \eta_\mathrm{gs}}\right)$ if $E_\mathrm{g} \neq 0$, else 1
outer world	$\psi_\mathrm{IR} = E_\mathrm{d}^{-1} \cdot (\eta_\mathrm{id} \cdot E_\mathrm{id} + \eta_\mathrm{sd} \cdot E_\mathrm{isd})$ if $E_\mathrm{d} \neq 0$, else 0	$\psi_\mathrm{EG} = E_\mathrm{g}^{-1} \cdot \left(E_\mathrm{ge} + \frac{E_\mathrm{gse}}{\eta_\mathrm{sdch} \cdot \eta_\mathrm{gs}}\right)$ if $E_\mathrm{g} \neq 0$, else 0
curtailment losses	$\psi_\mathrm{CD} = 1 - \psi_\mathrm{SS} - \psi_\mathrm{IR}$	$\psi_\mathrm{CG} = 1 - \psi_\mathrm{SC} - \psi_\mathrm{EG}$
	Export E_e	Import E_i
oneself	$\psi_\mathrm{SE} = E_\mathrm{e}^{-1} \cdot (\eta_\mathrm{ge} \cdot E_\mathrm{ge} + \eta_\mathrm{se} \cdot E_\mathrm{gse})$ if $E_\mathrm{e} \neq 0$, else 1	$\psi_\mathrm{SI} = E_\mathrm{i}^{-1} \cdot \left(E_\mathrm{id} + \frac{E_\mathrm{isd}}{\eta_\mathrm{sdch} \cdot \eta_\mathrm{is}}\right)$ if $E_\mathrm{i} \neq 0$, else 1
outer world	$\psi_\mathrm{IE} = E_\mathrm{e}^{-1} \cdot (\eta_\mathrm{ie} \cdot E_\mathrm{ie} + \eta_\mathrm{se} \cdot E_\mathrm{ise})$ if $E_\mathrm{e} \neq 0$, else 0	$\psi_\mathrm{EI} = E_\mathrm{i}^{-1} \cdot \left(E_\mathrm{ie} + \frac{E_\mathrm{ise}}{\eta_\mathrm{sdch} \cdot \eta_\mathrm{is}}\right)$ if $E_\mathrm{i} \neq 0$, else 0
curtailment losses	$\psi_\mathrm{CE} = 1 - \psi_\mathrm{SE} - \psi_\mathrm{IE}$	$\psi_\mathrm{CI} = 1 - \psi_\mathrm{SI} - \psi_\mathrm{EI}$

A.2 How to Apply to Time-Series Data?

Since the proposed metrics are based on accumulated energy, deriving those from power time series is only a question of algebraic integration and is therefore most of the time straight forward time-weighted addition of all values ($E = \int P dt \approx \sum_i P_i \cdot \Delta t_i$).

This also indicates that the metrics are mostly meaningless for extremely short periods of time. To align with typical analysis methods found in the literature, we suggest to have at least a week of data that is not influenced by the initial transient period anymore.

Since the correct energy values required by the different metrics highly depend on the intersection/overlap of multiple power time series, almost none of them can be calculated without power time series accurately. Exceptions from this rule are the realized flows $E_d - E_{cd}$, $E_g - E_{cg}$, $E_e - E_{ce}$ and $E_i - E_{ci}$ since those are accumulations of different power time series.

A.3 Potential Integration with Simulation Tools or Building Automation Platforms

Integrating the introduced metric calculations into simulation tools or real-life MGs require the measurement or at least approximation of the relevant energy flows. This is obviously easier within simulation tools, typically operating on power time series, but still requires the ability to somehow integrate the required energy flows. It does not matter whether it is only integrated on RAM during run-time to compute the final values or if time series are logged for a post-processing step that calculates the metrics of interest.

In real-life systems this ability to measure is much lower, since typically only a small number of measurement devices is present within the system. The most common one for grid connected systems is at the grid connection point where we can measure E_i and E_e, yet only if the energy meter can count both energy flow directions independently. Most PV inverters nowadays have an integrated measurement that can provide us with $E_g - E_{cg}$, since it will not be able to measure energy that does not flow. However, E_{cg} can easily approximated by small PV simulation models parametrized to the PV system in question. Almost any ESS that has a relevant size will also measure the power that it is charged or discharged with, providing us with $E_{gs} + E_{is}$ and $E_{sd} + E_{se}$ or $\eta_{gs} \cdot E_{gs} + \eta_{is} \cdot E_{is}$ and $E_{gsd} + E_{gse} + E_{isd} + E_{ise}$, depending on, wheather internal losses of the charging controller and its components are accounted for or not. Additionally, most ESS will provide and approximation of the state of charge and hence Q. We assume that this attribution and potential splitting of measured energy flows to specific sources and targets is the most challenging open topic that will be addressed in future publications. The actual demand is not measured on most systems, but the technical components like smart plugs or current clamps for different phases or power lines exist off-the-shelf.

Additional care must be taken when assigning the correct values to the different efficiencies η_x since they correspond to different physical components depending on the coupling method within your MG (DC- or AC-coupled). To get the correct η_x, all physical components efficiency on the path, e.g., from generation to ESS have to be included and multiplied which has been shortly discussed in Sect. 4.7 in [7].

References

1. Anaza, S.O., Haruna, Y.S., Amoo, A., Sadiq, A.A., Yisah, Y.A.: Micro-grids system: a review of control techniques and strategy, distributed energy sources and energy storage system. In: 2023 2nd International Conference on Multidisciplinary Engineering and Applied Science (ICMEAS), vol. 1, pp. 1–6 (2023). https://doi.org/10.1109/ICMEAS58693.2023.10429898
2. Brusermann, M.: Autarkiegrad: Unterschied Eigenverbrauch & Autarkie – Klarsolar (2022). https://klarsolar.de/unterschied-eigenverbrauch-autarkie/
3. Cunha, P.H., Saavedra, O.R., Oliveira, D.Q.: Critical review of multi-microgrids. In: 2023 15th IEEE International Conference on Industry Applications (INDUSCON), pp. 443–450 (2023). https://doi.org/10.1109/INDUSCON58041.2023.10374924
4. Fellerer, J., German, R.: Analytical solution for the cost optimal Electric Energy Storage size based on the Effective Energy Shift (EfES) algorithm. In: Jørgensen, B.N., Ma, Z.G., Wijaya, F.D., Irnawan, R., Sarjiya, S. (eds.) Energy Informatics, pp. 224–246. Springer, Cham (2025). https://doi.org/10.1007/978-3-031-74741-0_15
5. Fellerer, J., Scharrer, D., German, R.: Analytic closed-form expressions for energetic measures as a function of the capacity of Electric Energy Storage - Effective Energy Shift algorithm. In: SSRN. SSRN (2024). https://doi.org/10.2139/ssrn.4804780. https://ssrn.com/abstract=4804780, submitted version (currently in review)
6. Gährs, S., Mehler, K., Bost, M., Hirschl, B.: Acceptance of ancillary services and willingness to invest in PV-storage-systems. Energy Procedia **73**, 29–36 (2015). https://doi.org/10.1016/j.egypro.2015.07.554. https://www.sciencedirect.com/science/article/pii/S1876610215013223
7. Helbrecht, J.: Analysis of Calculation Methods for Energetic Measures in Systems with Electric Energy Storage. Master's thesis, Friedrich-Alexander-Universität Erlangen-Nürnberg, Computer Science 7, 91058 Erlangen, Germany (2024). https://doi.org/10.25593/open-fau-1858. https://open.fau.de/handle/openfau/36088
8. Hirsch, A., Parag, Y., Guerrero, J.: Microgrids: a review of technologies, key drivers, and outstanding issues. Renew. Sustain. Energy Rev. **90**, 402–411 (2018). https://doi.org/10.1016/j.rser.2018.03.040. https://www.sciencedirect.com/science/article/pii/S136403211830128X
9. Hoppmann, J., Volland, J., Schmidt, T.S., Hoffmann, V.H.: The economic viability of battery storage for residential solar photovoltaic systems – a review and a simulation model. Renew. Sustain. Energy Rev. **39**, 1101–1118 (2014). https://doi.org/10.1016/j.rser.2014.07.068. https://www.sciencedirect.com/science/article/pii/S1364032114005206
10. Klein, M., Ziade, A., de Vries, L.: Aligning prosumers with the electricity wholesale market – the impact of time-varying price signals and fixed network charges on solar self-consumption. Energy Policy **134**, 110901 (2019). https://doi.org/10.1016/j.enpol.2019.110901. https://www.sciencedirect.com/science/article/pii/S0301421519304793
11. Liu, C., Xu, W., Li, A., Sun, D., Huo, H.: Analysis and optimization of load matching in photovoltaic systems for zero energy buildings in different climate zones of China. J. Clean. Prod. **238**, 117914 (2019). https://doi.org/10.1016/j.jclepro.2019.117914. https://www.sciencedirect.com/science/article/pii/S0959652619327842

12. Luthander, R., Widén, J., Nilsson, D., Palm, J.: A Photovoltaic self-consumption in buildings: a review. Appl. Energy **142**, 80–94 (2015). https://doi.org/10.1016/j.apenergy.2014.12.028. https://www.sciencedirect.com/science/article/pii/S0306261914012859
13. Monchusi, B.B.: A comprehensive review of microgrid technologies and applications. In: 2023 International Conference on Electrical, Computer and Energy Technologies (ICECET), pp. 1–7 (2023). https://doi.org/10.1109/ICECET58911.2023.10389254
14. Oberst, C.A., Madlener, R.: Prosumer preferences regarding the adoption of microgeneration technologies: empirical evidence for German homeowners. In: Working Papers 2015.07, International Network for Economic Research - INFER (2015). https://ideas.repec.org/p/inf/wpaper/2015.07.html
15. Rücker, F., et al.: Self-sufficiency and charger constraints of prosumer households with vehicle-to-home strategies. Appl. Energy **317**, 119060 (2022). https://doi.org/10.1016/j.apenergy.2022.119060. https://www.sciencedirect.com/science/article/pii/S0306261922004561
16. Saeed, M.H., Fangzong, W., Kalwar, B.A., Iqbal, S.: A review on microgrids' challenges & perspectives. IEEE Access **9**, 166502–166517 (2021). https://doi.org/10.1109/ACCESS.2021.3135083
17. Salom, J., Widen, J., Candanedo, J.A.: Understanding net zero energy buildings: evaluation of load matching and grid interaction indicators. In: Proceedings of Building Simulation 2011: 12th Conference of IBPSA. Building Simulation, vol. 12, pp. 2514–2521. IBPSA, Sydney (2011). https://doi.org/10.26868/25222708.2011.1787. https://publications.ibpsa.org/conference/paper/?id=bs2011_1787
18. Schill, W.P., Zerrahn, A., Kunz, F.: Prosumage of solar electricity: pros, cons, and the system perspective. Econ. Energy Environ. Policy **6**(1), 7–32 (2017). https://doi.org/10.5547/2160-5890.6.1.wsch. https://www.jstor.org/stable/26189569
19. Shahgholian, G.: A brief review on microgrids: operation, applications, modeling, and control. Int. Trans. Electr. Energy Syst. **31**(6), e12885 (2021). https://doi.org/10.1002/2050-7038.12885. https://onlinelibrary.wiley.com/doi/abs/10.1002/2050-7038.12885
20. Simoiu, M.S., Fagarasan, I., Ploix, S., Calofir, V.: Optimising the self-consumption and self-sufficiency: a novel approach for adequately sizing a photovoltaic plant with application to a metropolitan station. J. Clean. Prod. **327**, 129399 (2021). https://doi.org/10.1016/j.jclepro.2021.129399. https://www.sciencedirect.com/science/article/pii/S0959652621035824
21. Stippe, B.: Eigenverbrauchsquote: Wieviel Solarstrom kann ich selbst nutzen? (2023). https://solarwissen.selfmade-energy.com/eigenverbrauchsquote-was-ist-das/
22. Team, X.: Eigenverbrauch und Autarkie - Was ist der Unterschied? (2021). https://x2energy.de/ratgeber/fachwissen/photovoltaik-solaranlage/eigenverbrauch-und-autarkie-was-ist-der-unterschied

23. Uddin, M., Mo, H., Dong, D., Elsawah, S., Zhu, J., Guerrero, J.M.: Microgrids: a review, outstanding issues and future trends. Energy Strategy Rev. **49**, 101127 (2023). https://doi.org/10.1016/j.esr.2023.101127. https://www.sciencedirect.com/science/article/pii/S2211467X23000779
24. Voss, K., et al.: Load matching and grid interaction of net zero energy buildings (2010). https://doi.org/10.18086/eurosun.2010.06.24
25. Zepter, J.M., Engelhardt, J., Gabderakhmanova, T., Marinelli, M.: Re-thinking the definition of self-sufficiency in systems with energy storage. In: 2022 International Conference on Smart Energy Systems and Technologies (SEST), pp. 1–6 (2022). https://doi.org/10.1109/SEST53650.2022.9898436

Open Access This chapter is licensed under the terms of the Creative Commons Attribution 4.0 International License (http://creativecommons.org/licenses/by/4.0/), which permits use, sharing, adaptation, distribution and reproduction in any medium or format, as long as you give appropriate credit to the original author(s) and the source, provide a link to the Creative Commons license and indicate if changes were made.

The images or other third party material in this chapter are included in the chapter's Creative Commons license, unless indicated otherwise in a credit line to the material. If material is not included in the chapter's Creative Commons license and your intended use is not permitted by statutory regulation or exceeds the permitted use, you will need to obtain permission directly from the copyright holder.

Solar-Geothermal Power "HGS-ORC" System for Energy Co-generation: Energy, Economic and Environmental Analysis: Algerian Case

Mohamed El-Amine Slimani[1](✉) ⓘ and Maria Sigríður Guðjónsdóttir[2]

[1] Department of Fuels and Renewable Energies, University of Adrar, Adrar, Algeria
mslimani@univ-adrar.edu.dz, mosl@grogtp.is
[2] School of Engineering, Reykjavik University, Reykjavik, Iceland

Abstract. This study focuses on modeling a power and heat generation system utilizing an Organic Rankine Cycle (ORC) power plant, with the geothermal source of Hammam Debagh in northeastern Algeria serving as a case study. The ORC geothermal power plant is integrated with a solar Fresnel Lens Reflector and a parabolic Trough collector system, creating a hybrid geothermal solar ORC system (HGS-ORC), which is linked to a heating application system for district heating and drying purposes. An analysis of thermodynamics, energy, and exergy was conducted for four potential system configurations. The analyzed configurations include the basic HGS-ORC, two HGS-ORC setups without a recuperator—one with a mass flow control system for the working fluid (WF) and one without—and two additional HGS-ORC setups with a recuperator, also with and without a mass flow control system. A study was conducted to analyze the economic and environmental aspects of various system configurations, utilizing design data as well as local and global economic and environmental factors. The results show that the HGS-ORC configuration equipped with recuperator and control system has the best energy, economic and environmental performances. The estimated annual production of this configuration is about 10 GWh of electricity and more than 76 GWh of heat available for heating and drying. Based on a conventional power plant working with coal fired as heat source, the avoided CO_2 emission by this configuration is about 12.84 t CO_2/h.

Keywords: ORC power plant · Fresnel Lens Reflector · Parabolic Trough Collector · hybrid geothermal solar ORC

1 Introduction

The exhaustion of fossil fuel reserves and their environmental consequences, such as climate change, have motivated numerous scientists to explore alternative energy sources that are both renewable and eco-friendly. Geothermal energy, one of the renewable energy sources, refers to the thermal energy stored within the Earth. This energy is found in the rocks and fluids beneath the Earth's crust and can be harnessed through steam and hot water to heat buildings or produce electricity. With more than 280 hot springs, Algeria has a high potential for geothermal energy resources of low-enthalpy type. This section will concentrate mainly on Algeria's geothermal resources, their geographic location, and their utilization.

Algeria has important thermal water reserves, which appear on the surface by the numerous thermal springs in the North and by the artesian wells that capture the Albian aquifer in the South.

Geothermal research has primarily been conducted in northern Algeria, with notable contributions including the work of Kedaid et al. [1] and Rezig [2], among others. According to these studies, Northern Algeria is home to numerous geothermal sources, with approximately 280 identified, featuring temperatures ranging from 22 to 98 °C [3]. The majority are found in Mesozoic rocks, sometimes at their contact with other formations, and are scattered across northern Algeria.

Out of the 280 hot springs cataloged by Algeria's National Agency of Hydraulic Resources (ANRH), certain geothermal spas and resorts are designated for public sector use. Many small spas are also appreciated for their therapeutic benefits. The leading spas and resorts, renowned for offering a variety of services like physical rehabilitation, massages, and other health treatments provided by professional medical teams, are situated in Meskhoutine, Guergour, Bouhanifia, Bouhadjer, Boughrara, Righa, Chiguer, Elssalhine, and Zalfana [3–5].

The organic Rankine cycle (ORC) is an efficient technology for producing electrical power for capacities up to 10 MW, and source temperatures of up to 400 °C [6]. Due to the good compatibility between the working temperatures of solar thermal collector technologies and the power cycle temperature requirements, using solar irradiation to drive an ORC is a viable renewable energy-based technique. Flat plate collectors, vacuum tube collectors, compound parabolic collectors, parabolic dish collectors, linear Fresnel reflectors, parabolic concentrators, and solar towers are among the solar thermal technologies studied in the literature that can drive ORC. Different thermal storage techniques can be used to assist hybrid solar-geothermal systems for energy delivery [6].

The purpose of this study is to give a model of a configuration of hybrid solar geothermal power plant with enhanced parameters for maximum power and heat generation adaptable for regions with significant solar potential.

2 Theoretical Relations for Modeling the System

2.1 Thermodynamic Model

For a basic ORC configuration, a heat recovery system (HRS containing preheater, evaporator, and superheater), a turbine, a condenser, and a pump are all part of the cycle. To increase the enthalpy of the working fluid and evaporate it, the HRS is fed with heat from an energy source. In Fig. 4, at the HRS input (State 1), the working fluid is a subcooled liquid, and at the HRS outlet, it is a superheated vapor (State 4). The HRS can be divided into three sections: preheater, evaporator, and superheater. In the preheater, the subcooled liquid changes into a saturated liquid (State 2). The evaporator is responsible for the latent heat exchange so that a saturated vapor can be produced (State 3), while the superheater produces a superheated vapor (State 4). In the ORC system, the superheating component is generally small, and, in some cases, no superheating is performed. For dry refrigerants, superheating is not beneficial or only beneficial in small amounts (5–10 °C) because of its T-S curve [7]. The superheated vapor enters the turbine, where it is expanded to low pressure (State 5). The condenser is responsible for heat rejection to the atmosphere to produce a saturated liquid with low pressure (at State 7). To complete the cycle, the saturated liquid enters the liquid pump, where the pressure is increased with a small amount of work consumption (but not insignificant). In Fig. 1b, the entire thermodynamic process is depicted.

The heat transfer rate in the HRS (Qin) can be calculated from an energy balance on the working fluid control volume, where $\dot{m}$ refers to the mass flow rate, and the state numbers refer to the points of Fig. 1.

$$\dot{Q}_{in-ORC} = \dot{m}_{wf}(h_4 - h_1) = \dot{m}_{geo}(h_{s2} - h_{s4}) \tag{1}$$

And

$$\dot{Q}_{in-ORC} = Q_{Pre} + Q_{eva} + Q_{Sup} \tag{2}$$

The power generation in the turbine (W_T) is calculated as:

$$\dot{W}_T = \dot{m}_{wf}(h_4 - h_5) \tag{3}$$

The electricity production by the shaft (P_{el}) is calculated as:

$$P_{el} = \eta_{mg} \dot{W}_T \tag{4}$$

Where η_{mg} is the generator efficiency.

Usually, the turbine process is modelled using an isentropic efficiency ($\eta_{is,T}$) as shown below:

$$\eta_{is,T} = \frac{h_4 - h_5}{h_4 - h_{5,is}} \tag{5}$$

The heat rejection rate from the condenser to the ambient (Q_{out}) is calculated as:

$$\dot{Q}_{out} = \dot{m}(h_5 - h_7) \tag{6}$$

The power consumption and the efficiency (η_p) of the pump (Wp) are calculated as:

$$\dot{W}_p = \dot{m}_{wf}(h_1 - h_7) \tag{7}$$

$$\eta_p = v_7 \frac{P_1 - P_7}{h_1 - h_7} \tag{8}$$

The net electricity produced by the ORC (Pel,net) is calculated as:

$$P_{el-net} = P_{el} - \dot{W}_p \tag{9}$$

Exergy is a measure of the departure of a state of a system from that of the surroundings. It is defined as the maximum theoretical work that can be produced from a system as

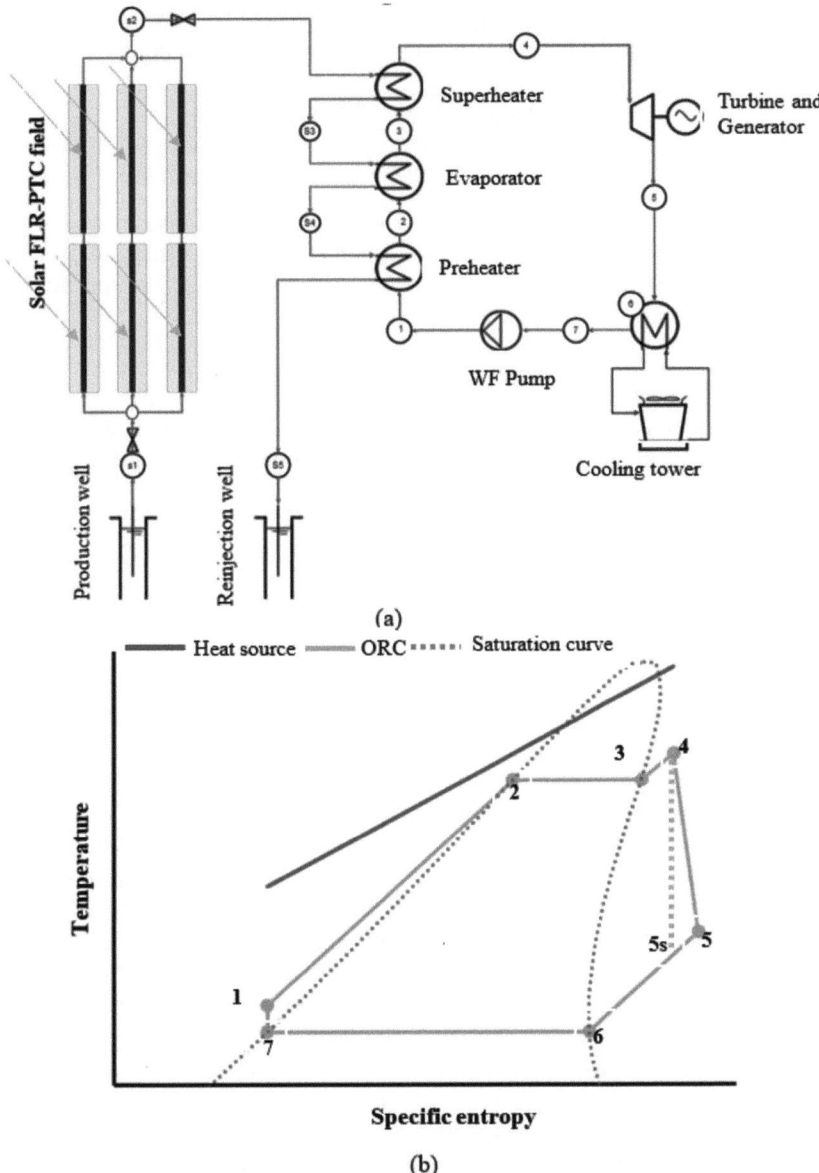

Fig. 1. (a) Basic hybrid Geoth-Solar ORC system (reference case) layout with key components; (b) Temperature-specific entropy (T-S) diagram of ORC system.

it interacts with the equilibrium state (surroundings). For the steady-state condition, the exergy balance equation of the system and its components can be expressed as follows:

$$\sum_i \dot{m}_i ex_i + \dot{E}x_Q = \sum_i \dot{m}_e ex_e + \dot{E}x_W + \dot{E}x_D \tag{10}$$

Where $\dot{Ex}$ is the exergy rate, subscripts Q and W represent heat and work, respectively, ex is the specific exergy of the process. $\dot{Ex}_D$ is the exergy distruction.

$$\dot{Ex}_Q = \left(1 - \frac{T_{am}}{T_i}\right)\dot{Q}_i \qquad (11)$$

$$\dot{Ex}_W = \dot{W} \qquad (12)$$

Exergy generally consists of four parts which are physical exergy (ex_{ph}), chemical exergy (ex_{ch}), kinetic exergy (ex_{ke}), and potential exergy (ex_{pe}). The specific exergy is given as follows;

$$ex = ex_{ph} + ex_{ch} + ex_{ke} + ex_{pe} \qquad (13)$$

The chemical, kinetic, and potential exergy are neglected because there is no chemical reaction, speeds are negligible, and the process's elevation difference is low. The physical exergy rate of any flow is written as follows;

$$ex_{ph} = (h_i - h_o) - T_o(s_i - s_o) \qquad (14)$$

The exergy rate of the component flow can be calculated as follows;

$$\dot{Ex}_i = \dot{m}_i ex_i \qquad (15)$$

2.2 Economic Model

The economic feasibility and financial profitability are the most important factors that investors assess when deciding whether to engage in resource development. The situation is more complicated for Geothermal energy because geothermal power facilities typically have longer payback times (about 5–7 years) than other renewable-energy power plants due to higher capital investments (basically in drilling and equipment). The main economic decision factors encouraging an investment are Lowest Initial Cost; Lowest Life-Cycle Cost; Average Annual Rate of Return; Payback Period; Social and Environmental Context; and Net Present Value (NPV).

The economic performance of the hybrid geothermal, solar system should also be addressed when evaluating it. The cost of CTP solar collectors has steadily decreased in recent years, and current research assumes a price of 150 \$ US/m^2 (Zhou et al., 2013). Drilling costs for the geothermal subsystem are projected to be calculated based on a unit price per meter of drilling for a known field.

As indicated in Table 1, the costs of the hybrid geothermal, solar ORC system are estimated using cost correlations.

2.3 Environmental Impacts: Greenhouse Gases Emissions

The emission of greenhouse gases (GHGs) represents the factor number one contributing to world climate change. There are numerous options for reducing greenhouse gas emissions from power generation, transmission, and distribution by:

Table 1. Economic cost estimation equations [8, 9].

Item		Cost (USD)
Solar field		$C_{sol-field} = 150 \times A_{field}$
Exploration cost	Surveys	$C_{surv} = 119.8 \times W_{net}$
Confirmation and drilling cost	Administration	$C_{admin} = 0.075 \times W_{net}$
	Drilling	$C_{well} = 240000 + 690 \times L_w + 0.205257 \times L_w^2$
	Well test/well	$C_{w-test/w} = 70000 \times F_w$
	Well test/field	$C_{w-test/f} = 100000 \times F_w$
	Other costs/project	$C_{other} = 20000 \times F_p$
	Compliance reports	$0.1 \times (C_{surv} + C_{well} + C_{w-test/w} + C_{w-test/f} + C_{other})$
Power plant	Gathering systems	$C_{se} = 280 \times W_{net}$
	ORC turbine	$C_{ORC} = 820 \times W_{net}^{0.8} - 19000$
	Generator	$C_{Gen} = 2447 \times W_{net}^{0.49}$
	Heat exchanger and condenser/Unit	$C_{HEX} = 120 \times W_{net}$
	Cooling system	$C_{cs} = 90 \times W_{net}$
	Buildings and auxiliary systems	$C_{pu} = 360 \times W_{net}$
Operational and maintenance cost		$C_{OpM} = 0.06 \times T_k$

$A_{field} \equiv m^2$; $W_{net} \equiv kW$; $L_w \equiv m$;
F_w: well test correction factor; F_p: project correction factor

- Increasing the efficiency of Fossil-fired power plants and fuel Switching;
- Using renewable energy resources;
- Increased end-use energy efficiency;
- Using carbon capture and sequestration.

Dissolved gases are commonly found in deep pressured hot water sources (CO_2, H_2S, NH_3 and CH_4) for geothermal sources. During depressurization and cooling, these are released, resulting in oxidation products such as SO_2 and NOx. Mercury, boron, arsenic, and other metal salts in solution may either precipitate in geothermal brine ponds, generating pipe scale that must be disposed of, or be discharged to the environment as fine-grained particulate matter from cooling towers. Dry-steam and flash-steam geothermal power plants account for most gas emissions. Because dry-steam plants do not produce mineral-laden brine, they have a smaller environmental impact than flash-steam plants. Binary plants (EGS) work in a closed-loop mode, with fluids directly returning to depth, hence not emitting liquids or gases [10].

Compared to fossil fuel power plants, which may generate GHGs, geothermal power plants have a minor environmental impact. GE impacts have been greatly decreased by advancements in technology and the realization of the necessity for environmental protection.

Table 2 below shows the approximate gaseous emissions per unit of power generated in MWh for different fossil fuels.

Table 2. Approximate greenhouse gases (carbon dioxide, nitrogen oxides, and sulfur dioxide) for different fossil fuels [11].

Emission	CO_2 [kg/MWh]	SO_2 [kg/MWh]	NO_x [kg/MWh]	Particulates Matter [kg/MWh]
Lignite	940–1250			
Coal fired	994	4.71	1.955	1.012
Oil fired	758	5.44	1.814	
Gas fired	550	0.0998	1.343	0.0635

The avoided GHGs emission from the hybrid power plant can be calculated by the following formula:

$$Emissions = Fuel \times HHV \times EF2$$

Where:

Emissions = mass of gas emitted.

Fuel = mass or volume of fuel combusted.

HHV = Fuel heat content (higher heating value), in units of energy per mass or volume of fuel.

EF2 = gas emission factor per energy unit.

In this formula, the heat input for power generation via a power plant must be equivalent to Fuel × HHV.

3 Proposed System Configurations

The binary power plants are considered the less efficient power plant compared to the other types of power plants, which means that the amount of heat rejected by binary PP is very high compared to the electricity generated. To increase the overall efficiency of the binary cycle, the use of the rejected heat by the cooling system is recommended by using a recuperator. The heat economized by the recuperator can be used for some heating applications (like district heating and drying).

For that reason, the following configurations (cases) with different modes are chosen for this study.

Case 1: Hybrid Geothermal-Solar ORC without recuperator: with mass flow control of WF (case 1- mode 'a') and without (case 1- mode 'b').

Case 2: hybrid Geothermal-Solar using recuperator: with mass flow control of WF (case 2-a) and without (case 2-b).

The recuperator is an element that can be important in a thermal power plant if we want to both save source heat and use the heat rejected by the HGS-ORC in applications requiring heat (district heating).

The integration of a recuperator reduces the heat required by the preheater and rejects the heat saved by the latter element outside the ORC.

The Table 3 resume the operating conditions used for the simulation.

Table 3. Operating conditions

Geothermal source temperatures	98 °C
ORC working fluid	R227ea
DNI	750 W/m^2
Masse flow rate	110–135 kg/s

4 Results and Discussion

4.1 Estimation of Annual Production

In this section, the annual energy production is estimated based on the power and heat obtained for each configuration (case and mode). The yearly output is calculated by estimating that the solar irradiation manifests by an annual average of 8 h per day (with Direct Normal Irradiation, DNI = 750 W/m^2), and consequently 16 h of no sunshine per day (with DNI = 0 W/m^2). An estimated operating time of the HGS-ORC system is 8160 h per year (the remaining 600 h are considered for maintenance and other operations).

The results show that the mode "b" (control system) presents the maximum production of electric power with an annual power of more than 10.29 GWh (Fig. 2), while the second configuration (with recuperator) shows the highest annual production of the heat (Fig. 3) with more than 76 GWh (for case 2, mode b). The intersection of the conclusions shows the 2 -mode b configuration that produces the most electrical and thermal energy.

4.2 Economic Analysis

The main economic factors used for the Algerian case study are listed in Table 4.

The economic parameters, net present value (NPV), and payback period of the different configurations are given in Figs. 4 and 5.

As the NPV is the difference between the present value of cash inflows and the present value of cash outflows over 30 years of a lifetime for each configuration, this parameter is considered a key economic factor for the investment in any project. This parameter is evaluated for each system configuration in two scenarios and two economic

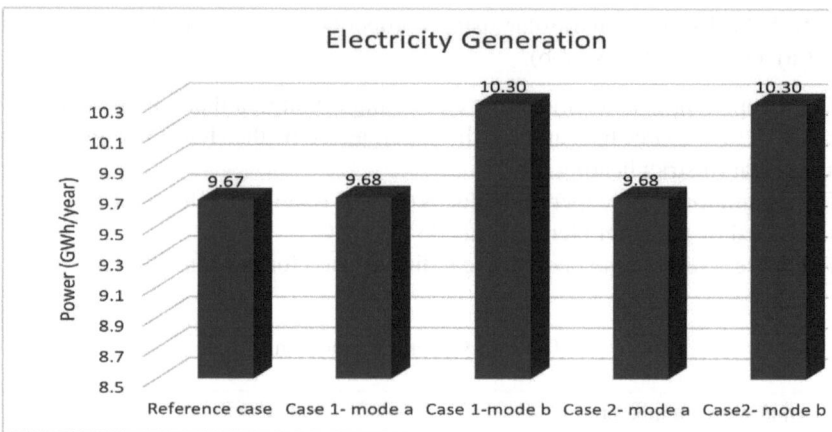

Fig. 2. Annual power generation by each system configuration of HGS-ORC

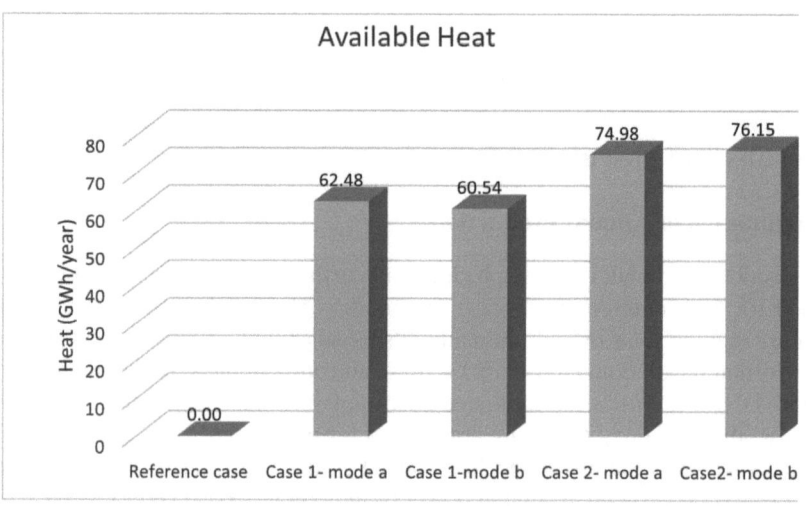

Fig. 3. Annual available heat by each system configuration of HGS-ORC

data. The first scenario is that no exploration and drilling activities are needed for the HGS-ORC system. In our case study, we used the natural hot spring of 'Hammam debagh' as a source of geothermal energy. The second scenario is by supposing the need of exploration and drilling activities in that area for 3 shallow wells (of 100 depth m each) to provide the same temperature and mass flow rate of the natural hot spring. The economic calculations are based on the use of two economic data, Algerian economic data, and world average economic data, to have estimated information of the feasibility of the HGS-ORC system both in Algeria and worldwide (for similar external operating conditions).

Table 4. Parameters assumption for economic calculation

Item	Symbol	Unit	Design value
Tax rate	tax	–	17%
Electricity price	c_{el}	$/kWh	0.039
Gaz price	c_{gz}	$/kWh	0.003
Lifetime	$LT(N)$	year	30
Interest rate	i	–	5%

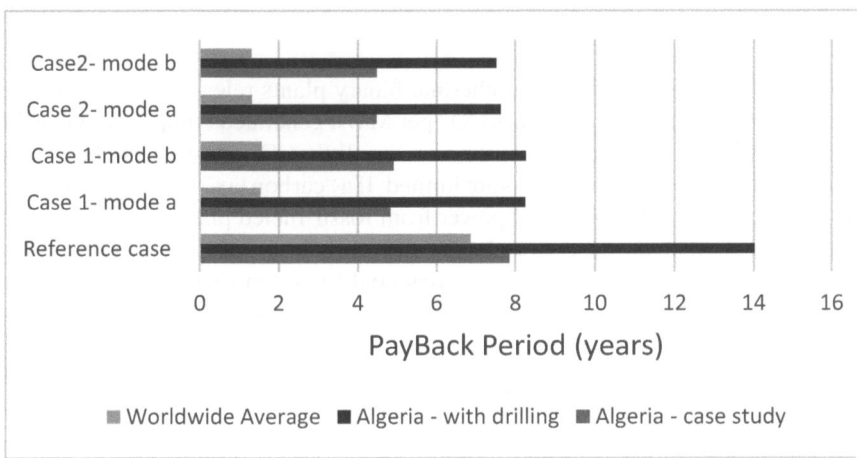

Fig. 4. Payback period given by each system configuration of HGS-ORC

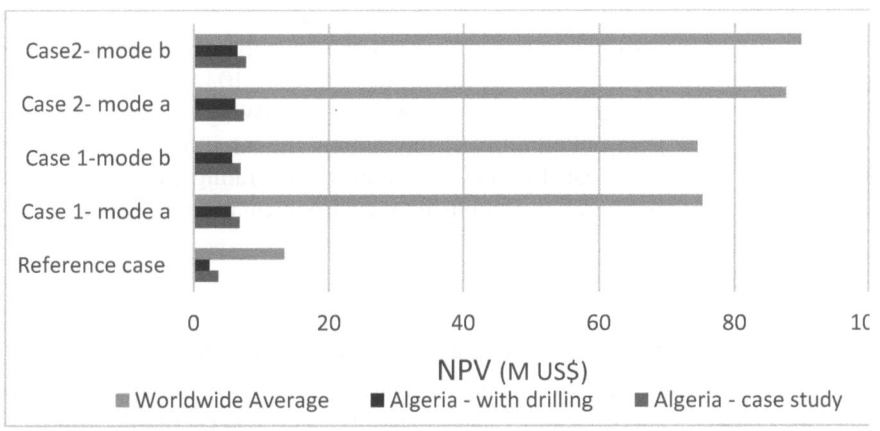

Fig. 5. Net Present Value given by each system configuration of HGS-ORC

The results show that case 2 – mode b presents the highest NPV and the lowest payback period in all the scenarios and economic data. The NPV and payback period for this configuration is about 7.7 MUSD and 4.5 years for the case study; The NPV and payback period becomes lower (6.4 MUSD) and higher (7.5 years), respectively, if exploration and drilling are needed. The NPV reaches 90 MUSD if that configuration of the HGS-ORC system is implemented worldwide with the same external operating conditions with a payback period of 1.3 years.

The reference configuration with 2.3 MUSD of NPV and 14 years of payback period shows the low economic performance (low NPV and hight payback period) among the other configurations because of its single output (just electricity).

4.3 Environmental Aspect

Compared to fossil-fueled plants, geothermal binary plants release no CO_2, but steam and flash plants emit substantially less CO_2 per MWh generated compared to fossil fuel plants. Because geothermal plants emit no or very little CO_2, they should be in a good position if and when carbon emissions are limited. If a "carbon tax" was implemented, the cost of producing a kilowatt-hour of power from fossil-fueled plants would be affected significantly more than the cost of producing electricity from less polluting technologies like geothermal. Geothermal power facilities could gain an extra revenue stream by selling carbon credits on a trading market under a program known as "carbon emission credits".

Here the avoided greenhouses gas emissions are calculated based on the required quantity of fossil fuel for operating a conventional power plant (with 36% of efficiency) to generate the same amount of power given by the different configurations.

The values of the avoided CO_2, SO_2, and NO_x emissions for each configuration of the HGS-ORC system are calculated based on the fossil fuels emissions commonly used as a heat source in thermal power plants to produce electricity.

Compared to other configurations, the 'b' mode configurations show significant values of the avoided emissions of CO_2, SO_2, and NOx due to its high electrical power output. Coal-fired would be the most polluting fuel with over 104.8 kt CO_2/year, 573.8 t SO_2/year, and 191.3 t NOx/year if used to generate 10.3 GWh/year.

Natural gas is the least polluting fossil fuel among the three fuels, with values of 58 kt CO_2/year, 10.5 t SO_2/year, 141.6 kt NOx/year for generating the same amount of power. The reference configuration exhibits poor environmental performance.

5 Conclusion

Given that Algeria possesses over 280 geothermal sources primarily located in the northern region, utilizing this renewable energy resource emerges as a promising option to enhance the country's energy security and expand its renewable energy portfolio.

This study examines the geothermal source at Hammam Debagh in northeastern Algeria, recognized as one of the world's hottest springs with a surface temperature of 98 °C and a notable flow rate, as a case study for designing a power production system utilizing an ORC. The geothermal ORC system is combined with a combined Fresnel

Lens Reflector – Parabolic Trough Collector (FLR-PTC) solar concentrator to constitute a hybrid geothermal solar system called HGS-ORC. A thermodynamic, energy, energy, economic, and environmental (4E) analysis was carried out for five configurations of the HGS-ORC system: basic configuration (reference case), two configurations without recuperator (case 1) with the existence and not of mass flow control system (case 1 - mode a and case 1 - mode b, respectively), and two other configurations equipped with a recuperator (case 2) with and without a mass flow control system.

The results show that the configuration of case 2 (with and without a control system) presents the best energy and exergy performance compared to case 1 and the reference configuration. The maximum annual energy production is ensured by HGS-ORC configuration using a recuperator and control system with about 10.3 GWh/year of power and more than 76 GWh/year of available heat for district heating and drying.

The environmental analysis of the avoided greenhouse gases emissions (mainly, carbon dioxide 'CO_2, nitrogen oxides NOx, and sulfur dioxide SO_2) for each configuration was done by taking into consideration three possible fossil fuels (coal-fired, oil-fired, and gas-fired) as a potential heat source for the systems. The results show that the configuration of the HGS-ORC-heating system equipped with a recuperator and mass flow control system gives the best environmental performance.

References

1. Kedaid, F.Z., Rezig, M., Abouriche, M., Fekraoui, A.: Carte geothermique preliminaire du nord de l'Algerie au 1/1000.000. Internal report. Centre de Developpement des Energies Renouvelables, Algeria, 35 pp. (1988)
2. Rezig, M.: Etude Géothermique du Nord-Est de l'Algérie. Université des Sciences et des Techniques du Languedoc, Montpellier, France, DEA (1991)
3. Lebbihiat, N., Atia, A.M.A., Meneceur, N.: Geothermal energy use in Algeria: a review on the current status compared to the worldwide, utilization opportunities and countermeasures. J. Clean. Prod. **302**, 126950 (2021)
4. Fekraoui, A., Kedaid, A.: Geothermal resources and uses in algeria: a country update report. In: Proceedings of the World Geothermal Congress 2005, pp. 24–29. Antalya, Turkey (2005)
5. Saibi, H.: Geothermal resources in algeria. Renew. Sustain. Energy Rev. **13**(2544–2552), 19–25 (2009)
6. Loni, R., Mahian, O., Markides, C.N., et al.: A review of solar-driven organic Rankine cycles: recent challenges and future outlook. Renew. Sustain. Energy Rev. **150**, 111410 (2021)
7. Tchanche, B.F., Lambrinos, G., Frangoudakis, A., Papadakis, G.: Low-grade heat conversion into power using organic Rankine cycles – a review of various applications. Renew. Sustain. Energy Rev. **15**, 3963–3979 (2011)
8. Jónsson, M.Þ.: Feasibility study. DGPP - Mechanical Design of Geothermal Power Plant and District Heating System. Presented at "Specialized courses" Organized by GRO-GTP, pp. 17–39. Reykjavik, Iceland (2021)
9. Van-Erdeweghe, S., Van-Bael, J., Laenen, B., D'haeseleer, W., 2019: design and off-design optimization procedure for low-temperature geothermal organic Rankine cycles. Appl Energy **242**, 716–731 (2021)
10. Sayed, E.T., et al.: A critical review on environmental impacts of renewable energy systems and mitigation strategies: wind, hydro, biomass and geothermal. Sci. Total Environ. **766**, 144505, 15 (2021)
11. Soltani, M., et al.: Environmental, economic, and social impacts of geothermal energy systems. Renew. Sustain. Energy Rev. **140**, 110750 (2021)

Towards the Integration of Data Space Technology in Hydrogen Research Workflows

Ryan Ford, Rita Beigaitė[✉], and Lius Daniel

VTT Technical Research Centre of Finland, Espoo, Finland
{Ryan.Ford,Rita.Beigaite,Lius.Daniel}@vtt.fi

Abstract. The increasing importance of hydrogen in the clean energy transition highlights the critical need for secure, interoperable, and efficient data management within research environments. Many hydrogen laboratories still rely on fragmented, manual, and non-standardised data exchange practices that hinder interoperability, traceability, and collaboration. This paper presents a tailored framework that integrates key components of Data Space technology, specifically the International Data Spaces Association (IDSA) connector, into hydrogen research workflows. A Minimum Viable Data Space (MVDS) architecture is designed and deployed using a real-world use case from a hydrogen research lab. The approach includes mapping laboratory operations to data space principles, implementing containerised connectors, and validating the setup through an experimental data exchange scenario. The results demonstrate a practical and scalable pathway for modernising laboratory data infrastructure, enhancing collaborative research, and advancing Europe's digital and sustainable energy goals.

Keywords: Data Spaces · Data Exchange · Data Management · Hydrogen · Research Infrastructure · Energy Data Space

1 Introduction

Hydrogen technologies are emerging as key enablers of a sustainable energy transition, offering potential solutions to decarbonize hard-to-electrify sectors, balance electricity grids, and transport renewable energy across regions [1,6,19]. Among these technologies, water electrolysis and hydrogen fuel cells are central to hydrogen production and application. They continue to evolve through advancements in electrochemical materials and system integration [11,22].

Such technological developments are supported by experimental validation in hydrogen research laboratories, generating high-frequency, high-volume datasets [13,18]. These include performance metrics, catalyst efficiency data, sensor outputs, material characterisations, and operational parameters, all collected from rigorous experimentation and continuous testing. However, data exchange within and between laboratories and stakeholders remains challenging due to fragmented practices. Data is typically compiled, filtered, transformed, and then shared via email, manual file transfers, or cloud platforms, often lacking standard procedures and documentation. This leads to data inconsistency, reduced interoperability, and inefficiencies, ultimately hindering collaborative research.

As hydrogen research scales, the limitations of traditional data-sharing approaches particularly in terms of security, traceability, and compliance with regulations such as the General Data Protection Regulation (GDPR)[1] become increasingly apparent. A robust, federated data-sharing model is needed to ensure laboratories and stakeholders can manage and exchange sensitive research data securely and efficiently. The Data Space concept [4], as advocated by the European Union, offers a structured, decentralised, and policy-driven framework that supports secure data flows, preserves data sovereignty, and facilitates scalable interoperability across research networks.

In this paper, we propose and experimentally validate a practical framework that leverages Data Space components specifically those provided by the International Data Spaces Association (IDSA) [3] to enable secure and efficient data exchange tailored to the data management workflows of a hydrogen technology research laboratory. We design a Minimum Viable Data Space (MVDS) and validate its operational feasibility in a controlled experimental setup using VTT's Hydrogen Lab as a real-world use case. Our contributions are threefold:

- a structured analysis of current data-sharing practices and their limitations within the context of a hydrogen laboratory;
- the design and implementation of a tailored Data Space framework based on IDSA principles and technologies;
- an experimental validation demonstrating the operational feasibility and benefits of Data Space-based data exchange compared to legacy methods.

The remainder of this paper is structured as follows: Sect. 2 provides an overview of Data Spaces and their relevance to the energy sector. Section 3 outlines our methodological approach. Section 4 describes the current practices and challenges in hydrogen data exchange. Section 5 introduces our proposed framework and its architecture. Section 6 presents the experimental validation. Section 7 discusses key findings and future research directions. Section 8 concludes the paper.

2 Background

A data space is a decentralized infrastructure paradigm that facilitates secure and governed data sharing among participants based on clearly defined agreements [2]. At its core, the concept prioritizes interoperability, data sovereignty, and trust [21], enabling autonomous organizations to exchange information without relying on centralized storage solutions [17]. In contrast to conventional centralized models such as data warehouses and data lakes [14], data spaces empower

---

[1] https://eur-lex.europa.eu/legal-content/EN/TXT/?uri=CELEX:32016R0679.

each stakeholder to maintain full control over their data assets, thereby enhancing resilience, security, and regulatory compliance [4].

In recent years, the European Union (EU) has strongly advocated for data spaces, recognizing them as strategic components essential for the digital economy and critical infrastructures [15]. The EU's vision involves creating a federated ecosystem of Common European Data spaces[2], aiming to enable secure and interoperable data sharing across critical sectors, including health, mobility, manufacturing, finance, and notably energy. The development of these sector-specific data spaces is intended to facilitate secure and efficient data flows, underpinning data-driven innovation, new business models, and enhanced competitiveness at both national and EU-wide scales. Several EU-funded initiatives and projects have explored the development and practical application of data spaces, contributing significantly to the creation of blueprints [5], standards [15], and reference architectures [9,16,20] that guide their implementation.

In the energy sector, the EU-funded IntNET project has recently published the Common European Energy Data Space (CEEDS) Blueprint [7]. This document outlines the creation of the CEEDS to enhance energy data infrastructure by integrating legacy systems with federated data spaces. It specifically focuses on developing viable business use cases, such as collective self-consumption and optimised energy sharing for communities or residential home energy management integrating distributed energy resources flexibility aggregation, alongside designing a supporting data space architecture. Several EU projects are currently contributing to the development of the CEEDS. The main ones include Data Cellar[3], Enershare[4], Omega-X[5], EDDIE[6], and SYNERGIES[7].

All of the above-mentioned projects are ongoing and propose different architectures for energy data spaces. Still, their architectural components show significant overlap, indicating a convergence toward emerging trends in energy data management systems [12]. These architectures are primarily built using components from Gaia-X[8], a European initiative that provides a reference architecture for federated and sovereign data infrastructure; FIWARE[9], an open-source framework offering standardised software building blocks for smart applications; and IDSA[10], which provides a reference architecture and trust framework for secure, controlled data exchange. For example, the Omega-X project adopts a layered architecture based on Gaia-X principles, combining secure federated data exchange with FIWARE enablers and IDSA connectors to support data sovereignty. Similarly, Data Cellar builds its platform around FIWARE com-

---

[2] https://digital-strategy.ec.europa.eu/en/policies/data-spaces.
[3] https://datacellarproject.eu/.
[4] https://enershare.eu/.
[5] https://omega-x.eu/.
[6] https://eddie.energy/.
[7] https://synergies-project.eu/.
[8] https://gaia-x.eu/.
[9] https://www.fiware.org/.
[10] https://internationaldataspaces.org/.

ponents and applies IDSA standards to manage data sharing between energy communities in a trusted way.

However, despite significant progress, current implementations of data space solutions still face considerable challenges related to standardization, operational maturity, and clarity in practical deployment guidelines [15]. While the earlier-mentioned initiatives have produced valuable frameworks and tools, the gap between high-level concepts and their application in real-world energy contexts remains substantial. This hinders adoption and creates uncertainty for both technology developers and end users. Closing this gap is essential to unlocking the full potential of data spaces, particularly in fast-evolving domains like hydrogen research, where secure and efficient data exchange is crucial for innovation and achieving sustainability goals.

In this paper, we advance the field by presenting a hydrogen-lab-specific Data Space framework. Through empirical validation, we move towards bridging the gap between theoretical data space concepts and their practical implementation.

3 Methodology

Our approach is structured around three primary steps: defining a representative use case, designing a practical data space framework, and conducting experimental validation to assess its feasibility and effectiveness.

First, we defined a real-world use case based on the operational data management workflows at the Hydrogen Lab of the Technical Research Centre of Finland (VTT). The practices of the laboratory were characterized by manual data transfers, email-based communication, fragmented documentation, and minimal policy enforcement. This setting provided a realistic and relevant foundation for identifying practical requirements, pain points, and constraints common in hydrogen research environments.

Next, we mapped core data space principles and components to the identified workflows. Guided by the reference architecture of the International Data Spaces Association (IDSA), we proposed a tailored framework that replaces traditional manual data-sharing methods with an automated, secure, and policy-driven Data Space model. The framework defines how key components such as data connectors, identity and access management (IAM), and policy enforcement mechanisms interact to enable governed and auditable data exchange aligned with European data sovereignty goals.

In the third and final step, we designed and deployed a Minimum Viable Data Space (MVDS) for experimental validation. This proof-of-concept was implemented in a controlled testbed environment replicating provider and consumer roles using containerized IDSA connectors. Supporting services, including Keycloak for identity management and Django REST APIs for metadata handling, were integrated into the testbed. We used MicroK8s for lightweight orchestration and ArgoCD for automated GitOps-based deployment.

Through this setup, we conducted a detailed simulation of secure data exchange workflows. We focused on validating the correct functioning of data publication, contract negotiation, access control, and audit logging. The use of Postman test suites enabled systematic testing and reproducibility of all API interactions. This hands-on implementation allowed us to observe practical outcomes, evaluate system behavior under realistic constraints, and confirm the operational feasibility of our proposed approach.

4 Data Exchange in Hydrogen Research Lab

Hydrogen laboratories are inherently data-rich environments, requiring effective and secure data exchange mechanisms to advance research and foster collaboration. The VTT Hydrogen Lab in Helsinki exemplifies this scenario, conducting extensive experimental studies on hydrogen production technologies. While current practices have been effective historically, evolving data management standards necessitate revisiting and potentially modernizing these methodologies.

4.1 Current Practices

At the VTT Hydrogen Lab, experimental workflows typically begin with the setup and calibration of electrolysis systems, followed by continuous data collection through integrated sensors and Supervisory Control and Data Acquisition (SCADA) systems. Key parameters such as voltage, current, gas purity, temperature, pressure, and humidity are recorded at high frequency, typically at least once per second, to enable real-time monitoring and accurate analysis of system responses to operational changes. Electrolysers often consist of one or more stacks, each comprising numerous individual cells that require separate voltage measurements. This high-resolution monitoring across multiple components results in the generation of extensive datasets. The combination of a large number of variables and frequent logging produces significant data volumes, which, if manual filtering is required, can lead to time-consuming and labor-intensive data handling.

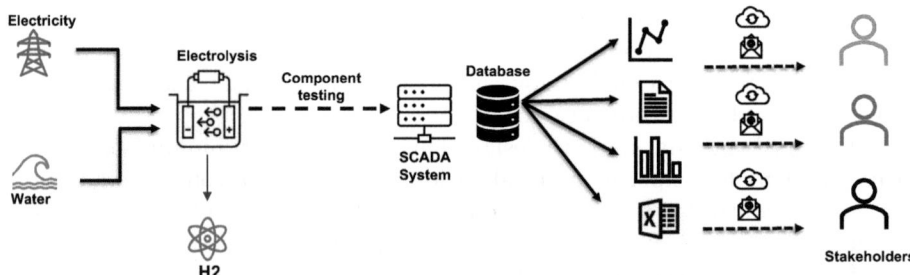

Fig. 1. Data flow within a typical hydrogen research laboratory illustrating the integration of electrolysis experiments, sensor data collection, SCADA systems, and client interactions.

Figure 1 illustrates the current workflow within the laboratory, capturing the stages from initial sensor measurements to the final dissemination of data. Upon completion of experiments, researchers manually extract raw data, conduct validation procedures, and prepare comprehensive reports. Data is formatted into spreadsheets or PDF documents and shared via email or cloud storage links directly with stakeholders, typically including industrial partners and academic institutions (Fig. 2).

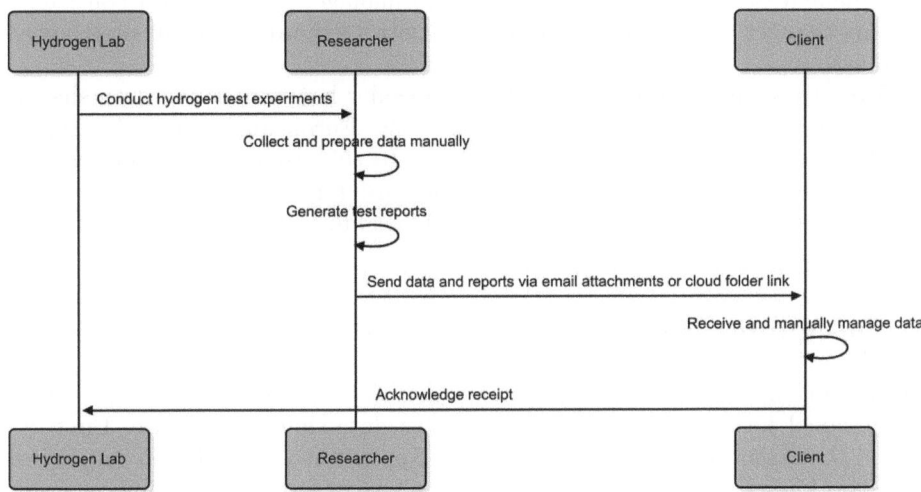

Fig. 2. Traditional data exchange workflow in a hydrogen lab.

This workflow is common across hydrogen laboratories. It effectively supports current collaborative research efforts and demonstrates reliability at a small scale with well-established routines.

4.2 Limitations

Although familiar and still widely used, existing workflows in hydrogen research labs face limitations as data volumes and complexity increase. These workflows rely heavily on manual tasks. Data cleaning, formatting, and sharing are often done by email or shared links. Though common, these methods require a lot of human effort and are not suited to frequent or large-scale data exchange. This can slow down work and cause errors, especially when the same data is sent to different recipients or reused in new contexts.

Security and governance are also important concerns in these workflows. Common tools such as email and general cloud platforms do not always ensure encrypted transfers or proper access controls. This increases the risk of unauthorised access or accidental sharing of sensitive data. Once data is shared, there are often no tools to track how it is used or to apply any limits. Laboratories have little control over whether data is used as agreed, deleted when no longer needed, or kept up to date. This reduces transparency and accountability, and can create problems with data protection rules such as the General Data Protection Regulation (GDPR).

Interoperability and scalability add more challenges. Data is often shared in fixed formats like spreadsheets or PDFs, which need manual changes before they can be used in other systems. This slows collaboration and makes it harder to reuse data across different projects. As research grows in size and complexity, these manual tasks become more difficult to manage. Keeping data consistent, tracking changes, and maintaining version control is harder without more structured systems.

Given these limitations, it is useful to consider how structured data-sharing frameworks, such as those promoted under the European Union's data space initiatives, could improve current workflows. In this work, we explore whether such frameworks can address existing issues around security, governance, and interoperability, and evaluate their practical feasibility through the lens of a real hydrogen research use case.

5 Designing a Framework for a Hydrogen Lab Data Space

This section introduces a tailored and practical data space framework explicitly designed for the hydrogen research lab's data-sharing use case. First, we outline the essential components of a data space, then map these components to the workflows identified in Sect. 4. Recognizing that even a Minimum Viable Data Space (MVDS) based strictly on industry standards may pose adoption challenges, we propose a simplified, practical deployment. This simplified model incorporates key data space components to ensure interoperability and ease the transition towards a fully standardized data space.

5.1 Minimum Viable Data Space (MVDS) Based on Industry Standards

A Minimum Viable Data Space (MVDS) incorporates essential components and principles recommended by industry standards and current best practices in data spaces. The following core components provide a robust foundation for secure, interoperable, and policy-driven data exchange:

- **Connector:** a software enabling secure, policy-controlled data exchanges between data providers and consumers, aligned with data sovereignty principles [10,16].
- **Identity and Access Management (IAM):** mechanisms that ensure authenticated identity verification and enforce access rights through policy-defined authorizations in federated environments [4,8].
- **Broker Service:** catalog systems managing metadata of available data assets, enabling participants to publish, search, and discover data offerings [5].

- **Governance Layer:** a structured set of organizational, legal, and technical agreements defining rules and conditions for data exchange, ensuring compliance, certification, and policy enforcement [5,9].
- **Standardized Data Models and APIs:** common semantic representations and standardized software interfaces facilitating interoperability and effective communication across different systems and sectors [15].

These components, inspired by industry-leading initiatives such as IDSA and Gaia-X, constitute the backbone of the MVDS architecture, balancing robustness and flexibility to enable rapid, practical adoption in hydrogen research environments.

Utilizing these MVDS concepts, we mapped specific operational requirements and workflows of a hydrogen research laboratory into a tailored data space framework, as depicted in Fig. 3.

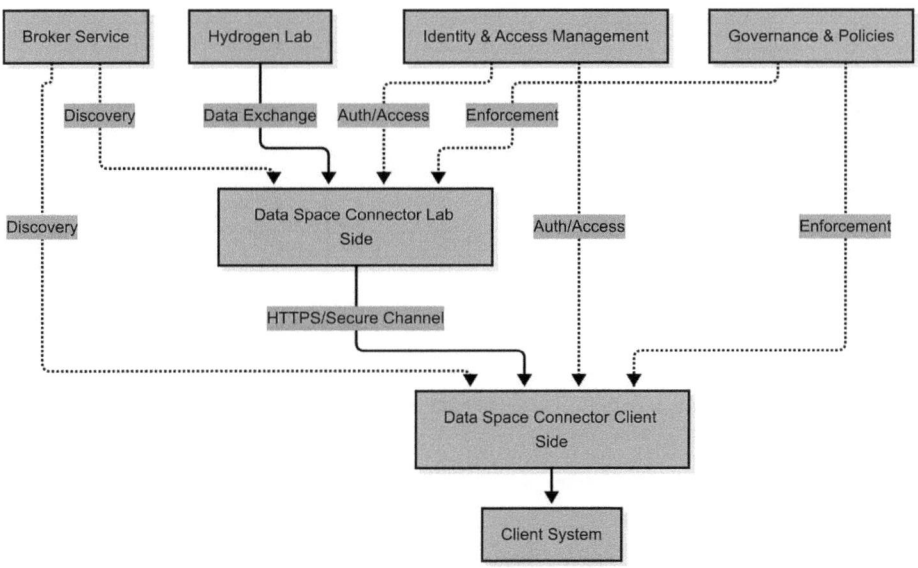

Fig. 3. Minimum viable data space for hydrogen lab: data space architecture interaction diagram.

This architecture integrates primary connectors for the data provider (Hydrogen Lab) and the data consumer (e.g., stakeholders). Secure HTTPS channels handle data exchange, while IAM supports authentication and policy-based authorization. The Broker Service ensures data discoverability, and the Governance Layer enforces compliance with usage policies.

Figure 4 illustrates the detailed sequence for secure data sharing within the data space. The process starts when the Hydrogen Lab prepares its data and shares it through its local connector. This connector first confirms its identity by logging in with the Identity and Access Management (IAM) system. After authentication, the connector checks and applies the relevant data usage policies using the Governance and Auditing service. It then registers a description of the dataset, or metadata, with the Broker Service. A client system that wants to find data sends a search request to the Broker. The Broker replies with a list of available metadata that matches the query. Once the client chooses a dataset, it sends a request to its own local connector. This connector also verifies its identity with the IAM system and checks the data usage rules with the Governance service. If access is approved, the client-side connector sends a secure, encrypted request to the lab's connector to retrieve the data. The Hydrogen Lab's connector then sends the data back through the secure channel. Throughout this process, both connectors keep records of the data exchange. These logs are sent to the Governance system, making it possible to audit who accessed the data and under what conditions, helping ensure accountability and compliance.

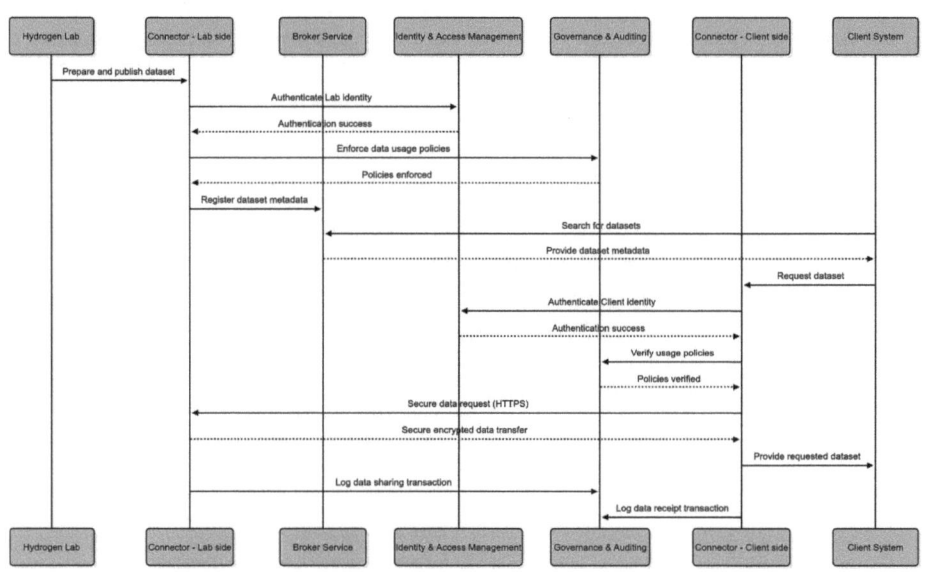

Fig. 4. Secure data-sharing sequence using data space connectors, highlighting publication, discovery, negotiation, and governed access phases.

5.2 Proposed Simplified Architectural Model for the Hydrogen Lab

Recognizing that the MVDS model based on industry standards, although minimal, may still present complexity barriers, we propose a simplified architecture for practical deployment. This alternative is not a full-fledged data space according to comprehensive blueprints or reference architectures but retains essential data space components to ensure interoperability and support a smooth future transition.

Figure 5 illustrates the simplified minimum viable data space. It includes only essential elements: data connectors, simplified governance mechanisms, and secure data transfer channels. Unlike the full, industry-standard MVDS, this simplified model does not include advanced broker services or complex governance rules at the start. This makes it much easier and faster to set up, while still respecting important rules about data ownership and control.

In this simplified setup, data connectors still manage secure data exchange based on policies. However, instead of using a full Broker Service, a basic method for cataloguing metadata is used. Also, the Identity and Access Management (IAM) system is made simpler, to make deployment easier. This model keeps data systems able to work together (interoperability) and offers a clear way to move towards the full MVDS setup over time.

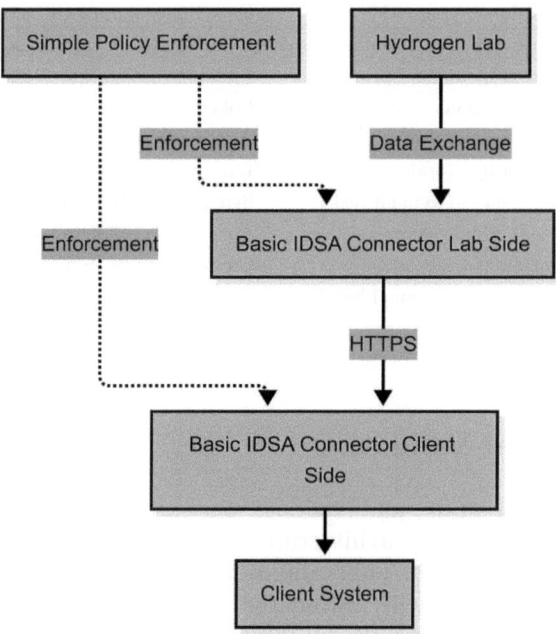

Fig. 5. Simplified Minimum Viable Data Space (MVDS) architecture for hydrogen laboratory.

5.3 Comparative Analysis of Traditional and MVDS Approaches

We conducted a comparative analysis using selected criteria (Table 1) to evaluate the possible advantages of adopting a data space model compared to traditional email-based data sharing. The table compares both approaches across criteria such as security, scalability, governance, compliance, interoperability, efficiency, collaboration, traceability, and risk of data loss.

The traditional approach, typically based on email exchanges, has the following limitations: weak access control, manual processes, limited oversight, and a higher risk of errors or data loss. The data space model addresses these issues by enabling encrypted and governed access, automating compliance checks, supporting policy-based governance, and using standard formats and APIs for interoperability.

The comparison shows that the data space model (if correctly implemented) offers better support for secure, efficient, and well-managed data exchange. The simplified MVDS further reduces complexity, making onboarding easier and encouraging broader adoption.

Table 1. Comparative Analysis of Data Sharing Approaches

Criteria	Traditional Approach	Data Space Approach
Security	Higher risk of unauthorised access	Enforced access control and encryption
Scalability	Limited by manual processes	Scalable through automation and standards
Governance	Often informal	Policy-based, structured governance
Compliance	Manual, error-prone	Automated compliance checks
Interoperability	Limited by proprietary systems	Improved with standardised formats and APIs
Efficiency	Slower due to manual tasks	Streamlined through automation
Collaboration	Siloed, ad hoc sharing	Structured, collaborative sharing
Traceability	Poor audit trail	Comprehensive audit and logging
Risk of Data Loss	Higher due to manual handling	Lower with managed transfers

6 Experimental Validation

To practically demonstrate and validate our proposed simplified Minimum Viable Data Space (MVDS) architecture, we implemented and tested a real-world data exchange scenario. This validation aimed to replace traditional manual or email-based methods with automated, secure, and compliant data-sharing practices. We specifically tested the simplified architecture depicted in Fig. 5, utilizing industry-standard components to ensure the experiment's reproducibility.

6.1 Experiment Design and Execution

We deployed dockerized instances of data space components onto bare-metal servers to simulate realistic operational conditions. We chose open-source IDSA connectors for their proven capability in secure data governance and alignment with European data governance standards. We selected Keycloak for identity and access management due to its robust OAuth2 support and compatibility with federated authentication scenarios. We developed the backend API for metadata management and policy enforcement using the Django REST Framework to leverage rapid prototyping capabilities. Finally, we orchestrated deployments using MicroK8s, with automated deployment and management via ArgoCD, ensuring a scalable and reproducible infrastructure.

The following enumerated steps outline the detailed experimental workflow for clarity and reproducibility:

1. **Server Preparation:** Provisioning and securing bare-metal servers to simulate provider and consumer environments.
2. **Dockerisation:** Containerising the IDSA connector instances and supporting components to standardise deployments.
3. **Component Deployment:** Deploying the Docker containers onto prepared bare-metal servers using MicroK8s and automated GitOps principles with ArgoCD.
4. **Identity and Access Management:** Integrating Keycloak to manage authentication and authorisation processes.
5. **Resource Creation and Cataloguing:** Creating data resources, metadata catalogues, and associated representations through API calls.
6. **Policy Enforcement Definition:** Implementing usage policies, such as read-only access, explicitly linked to resources and artefacts.
7. **Contract Agreement:** Simulating consumer-provider contract negotiations and automating agreements.
8. **Data Exchange Execution:** Validating secure data exchange, policy enforcement, and logging through extensive Postman API testing.

To provide a detailed and structured overview, Table 2 summarises the data exchange workflow that was tested using Postman collections. The table outlines each step involved in the process, from the creation of the initial catalog to the final stage of data retrieval, ensuring that all stages were properly validated. Table 3 provides a description of the technology stack selected for the implementation. It details the specific components and justification for each choice, emphasising their relevance and suitability within the context of a research lab environment. Table 4 presents a summary of the test coverage and validation status of the system. It demonstrates that all critical functions, including policy enforcement, token authentication, and data retrieval, were tested and successfully validated.

Our experimental validation showed that automated and secure data exchanges could be achieved using the simplified MVDS architecture. The results indicated improvements in governance, compliance, interoperability, and operational efficiency compared to traditional manual data exchange methods. These findings suggest progress towards more practical data sovereignty solutions in hydrogen research laboratory contexts.

7 Discussion

A key strength of our data space deployment is its incremental and modular architecture. By starting with a minimal setup based on essential IDSA components such as connectors, identity management, and basic governance, the model

Table 2. Summary of Data Exchange Workflow Validated via Postman

No.	Step	Description
1	Create Catalog	Provider registers a new catalog entry
2	Create Resource	Define data resource and metadata
3	Add Representation	Associate resource format (e.g., JSON)
4	Create Artifact	Provide access endpoint for the data
5	Create Rule	Define usage policy (e.g., read-only)
6	Contract Agreement	Consumer negotiates and signs contract
7	Data Retrieval	Consumer securely accesses dataset

Table 3. Data Space Component Choices and Justifications

Component	Technology Used	Reason for Selection
Connector	IDSA Java	Standard-compliant and extensible
Identity Management	Keycloak	OAuth2 support, open-source, SSO capabilities
Backend API	Django REST Framework	Rapid prototyping and flexibility
Deployment	MicroK8s + ArgoCD	Lightweight Kubernetes with GitOps automation

Table 4. Experimental Test Coverage and Validation Status

Component	Test Type	Validation Status
Policy Enforcement	Postman Contract	✓ Passed
Token Authentication	Postman Login Flow	✓ Passed
Data Retrieval API	Postman Artifact Download	✓ Passed
Catalog Publishing	Manual API Check	✓ Passed
Audit Logging	Log Trace Review	✓ Passed

supported rapid prototyping and lowered the barrier to adoption. This practical approach allows researchers to engage with data governance principles without the overhead of full-scale implementations.

The pilot setup also reveals some limitations. One concern is the absence of a user-facing interface, which may limit accessibility for non-technical users and slow early adoption. Configuring connectors, managing tokens, and understanding policy rules can require technical setup and training. The lack of standard deployment tools across institutional IT environments may further complicate implementation. Performance under load has not yet been fully tested, so further evaluation is needed to confirm the system's scalability and reliability with large datasets or frequent access. These factors point to a need for better usability, improved robustness, and closer alignment with existing systems.

The proposed framework is transferable to other research laboratories with similar data governance needs. Its modular design and use of interoperable standards make it suitable across scientific domains where secure and compliant data sharing is essential. However, despite efforts to simplify the setup, user training remains crucial. Clear documentation and structured onboarding are needed to support adoption and reduce setup time.

To realise the full potential of the framework, future iterations should address current usability challenges. Introducing user interfaces, such as interactive dashboards and guided workflows, would make Data Space services more accessible to all laboratory users, regardless of technical background. This will be key to moving from technical validation to sustained daily use.

In addition, improving interoperability with current European data infrastructure initiatives can strengthen the framework. Integrating Gaia-X principles would support trust and federated identity management. Adopting tools like Eclipse Dataspace Connector (EDC) [10] may offer more flexible orchestration, while lightweight frameworks such as Simpl[11] could enable faster experimentation.

8 Conclusions

This paper aimed to bridge the gap between theoretical data space concepts and their practical implementation, focusing on the energy sector. We proposed a hydrogen-lab-specific data space framework as a practical use case for energy data spaces. Through empirical validation using a real-world hydrogen lab workflow, we assessed how the framework enhances key aspects of data management, including security, compliance, scalability, and traceability.

Our findings show that starting with a simplified set of core data space components lowers adoption barriers and facilitates smooth integration into existing research workflows. This highlights the framework's practicality and relevance for hydrogen research. As energy data spaces evolve, our approach offers a clear path for early adoption, enabling hydrogen labs to connect more easily with broader energy data spaces once they are fully operational.

The next steps involve developing user interfaces for the proposed architecture and testing it beyond the simulation environment, with the active involvement of relevant stakeholders. These future iterations aim to address usability challenges and support broader adoption across the research community.

Acknowledgements. This research was funded by the European Union NextGenerationEU. The project is part of the strategic research opening 'industrial energy efficiency and low-carbonisation' of VTT, launched with the support of the additional chapter of the RePowerEU investment and reform programme for sustainable growth in Finland.

References

1. Bampaou, M., Panopoulos, K.: An overview of hydrogen valleys: current status, challenges and their role in increased renewable energy penetration. Renew. Sustain. Energy Rev. **207**, 114923 (2025)

---

[11] https://digital-strategy.ec.europa.eu/en/policies/simpl.

2. Big Data Value Association (BDVA) and Centre of Excellence for Data Sharing and Cloud (CoE-DSC): Leveraging the benefits of combining data spaces and privacy enhancing technologies (2024)
3. Braud, A., Fromentoux, G., Radier, B., Grand, O.: The road to European digital sovereignty with gaia-x and idsa. IEEE Network **35**(2), 4–5 (2021)
4. Curry, E., Scerri, S., Tuikka, T.: Data spaces: design, deployment and future directions. Springer Nature (2022)
5. Data Spaces Support Centre (DSSC): Data spaces blueprint v2.0 (2025). https://dssc.eu/space/BVE2/1071251457/Data+Spaces+Blueprint+v2.0
6. Dincer, I., Acar, C.: A review on clean energy solutions for better sustainability. Int. J. Energy Res. **39**(5), 585–606 (2015)
7. Dognini, A., et al.: Blueprint of the common European energy data space (2024)
8. Fotiou, N., Siris, V.A., Polyzos, G.C.: Access control for data spaces. In: 2025 28th Conference on Innovation in Clouds, Internet and Networks (ICIN), pp. 54–58. IEEE (2025)
9. Gaia-X European Association for Data and Cloud: Gaia-x architecture document (2024). https://docs.gaia-x.eu/technical-committee/architecture-document/24.04/
10. Gieß, A., Hupperz, M., Schoormann, T., Möller, F.: What does it take to connect? unveiling characteristics of data space connectors. In: Proceedings of the 57th Hawaii International Conference on System Sciences (2024)
11. Hauch, A., et al.: Recent advances in solid oxide cell technology for electrolysis. Science **370**(6513), eaba6118 (2020)
12. Karagiannis, V., Nagy, B., Jodkowski, A., Kranner, M., Ignjatović, D.: A review of emerging trends in energy data management systems. In: 2024 11th International Conference on Internet of Things: Systems, Management and Security (IOTSMS), pp. 74–81. IEEE (2024)
13. Li, Z., Outbib, R., Hissel, D., Giurgea, S.: Data-driven diagnosis of pem fuel cell: a comparative study. Control. Eng. Pract. **28**, 1–12 (2014)
14. Nambiar, A., Mundra, D.: An overview of data warehouse and data lake in modern enterprise data management. Big Data Cognitive Comput. **6**(4), 132 (2022)
15. Noardo, F., Atkinson, R., Bastin, L., Maso, J., Simonis, I., Villar, A., Voidrot, M.F., Zaborowski, P.: Standards for data space building blocks. Remote Sensing **16**(20), 3824 (2024)
16. Otto, B., Hompel, M.t., Wrobel, S.: International data spaces: Reference architecture for the digitization of industries. Digital transformation, pp. 109–128 (2019)
17. Otto, B., Ten Hompel, M., Wrobel, S.: Designing data spaces: The ecosystem approach to competitive advantage. Springer Nature (2022)
18. Paredes-Baños, A.B., Molina-Garcia, A., Mateo-Aroca, A., López-Cascales, J.J.: Scalable and multi-channel real-time low cost monitoring system for pem electrolyzers based on iot applications. Electronics **13**(2), 296 (2024)
19. Sazali, N.: Emerging technologies by hydrogen: a review. Int. J. Hydrogen Energy **45**(38), 18753–18771 (2020)
20. Seidel, A., et al.: Towards a seamless data cycle for space components: considerations from the growing European future digital ecosystem gaia-x. CEAS Space J. **16**(3), 351–365 (2024)
21. Soininen, J.P., Laatikainen, G.: What is a data space–logical architecture model. Data in Brief, p. 111575 (2025)
22. Ursua, A., Gandia, L.M., Sanchis, P.: Hydrogen production from water electrolysis: current status and future trends. Proc. IEEE **100**(2), 410–426 (2011)

Comparison of Outages Trends and Statistics in Nordic Countries Across Distribution Networks and Their Impacts

Seema(✉), Andreas Theocharis, and Reza Sirjani

Karlstad University, 65188 Karlstad, SE, Sweden
{seema.seema,andreas.theocharis,reza.sirjani}@kau.se

Abstract. This research compares the frequency and duration of outages within distribution networks for main Nordic land countries (Sweden, Denmark, Finland, and Norway). In addition, this paper focuses on planned and unplanned outages for low- and medium-voltage networks; the consequences of outages for distribution networks and companies; and the level of discomfort experienced by consumers during both planned and unplanned outages. This study highlights the countries with the highest incidence of outages by collecting data from their official reports, compares the frequency and duration of unplanned outages, focuses on SAIFI (System Average Interruption Frequency Index), SAIDI (System Average Interruption Duration Index), and CAIDI (Customer Average Interruption Duration Index)-based outage indices, and examines their outage trends.

Keywords: Unplanned and planned outages · Distribution network · Outages trends

1 Introduction

In the field of power systems, maintaining the safety and reliability of the grid operation is the primary objective of the grid operators and distribution companies [1]. The reliability of the power system is closely related to outages and is a measure of the ability of the power grid to deliver electricity consistently and without interruptions [2]. A reliable power system has minimum frequency of occurrence and short duration of planned and unplanned outages caused by extreme weather condition, component failure, and operational issues [3]. In addition, a reliable power system ensures continuous demand supply during planned outages [4]. Almost all Nordic countries have used the same customer-related continuity indices or system reliability indices, such as SAIFI, SAIDI, and CAIDI [5,6]. In this article, we compare outage trends in Nordic countries using the same reliability indicators. Research on outage trends is driven by the goal of measuring grid dependability, determining whether outages are occurring frequently enough to pose a threat to the electricity system, and utilizing modern technology to find solutions for unexpected outages. Furthermore, the primary drivers for reviewing outage trends and statistics include improving grid resilience [7], ensuring readiness for future disasters [8], optimizing investments in energy infrastructure [9], minimizing economic losses [10], and fostering customer satisfaction and trust. In addition to analyzing outage patterns in Sweden, Denmark, Finland, and Norway, this research explores the effects of these outages on utility companies and consumers. In [11], the authors explored the research question regarding the financial impact on Swedish distribution grid operators due to both short- and long-term grid interruptions. Their conclusion indicates that in Sweden, distribution companies experience a significant loss in value during power outages. The findings reveal that the average revenue loss associated with sold electricity for all businesses operating the grid annually amounts to roughly 13.6 million SEK, while companies incur approximately 131.5 million SEK each year in penalty fees due to these outages. In [12], the authors investigate the economic effects of power outages in Finland. According to the Electricity Market Act of 2013, a total of 7,361,479 euros were paid out to customers as compensation in 2016. Their analysis indicates that the majority of these compensations were due to interruption events lasting between 12–24 and 24–72 hours. Power outages affect not just distribution companies and businesses, but also the overall economic development of the nation. In [13], researchers investigate the influence of SAIDI on economic growth across both developing and developed nations. Furthermore, the authors declare that a 1% decrease in the system average interruption duration time correlates with an average increase of 2.16% in the national economic growth rate [13]. Consequently, distribution companies have dedicated significant resources to minimizing outages, as seen in Sweden and Finland, where they have substituted overhead transmission lines with underground cables. However, households and various consumers are still looking for a reliable energy supply, show willingness to invest more to prevent power outages [14,15]. In this paper, the authors analyse the existing records of the outages occurring in Nordic countries aiming to emphasize the main points of correlation between electricity grid outages with the energy transition and future social development. Therefore, the authors have compiled outage data for Sweden, Denmark, Finland, and Norway to demonstrate the duration and frequency of planned and unplanned outages in this study.

2 Dataset

We have compiled data on outages from four Nordic countries to produce a comparison study and highlight the frequency and duration of outages: Sweden, Denmark, Finland, and Norway. Sweden gathers its outage statistics from DARWin annual statistics reports [16], and we utilised their reports to compile the SAIFI, SAIDI, and CAIDI dataset from 2013–2020. Additionally, Energiföretagen Sverige has assembled its own event-oriented statistics. Since the early 2000s, Sweden has initiated the collection of outage data to assess reliability [17]. Since 2010, electricity companies have been submitting their outage reports annually to the Electricity Markets Inspectorate. The outage data for Denmark have been compiled using the ELNET website [18]. This report covers the SAIFI, SAIDI, and CAIDI datasets spanning from 2013 to 2022 for only 1–24 kV voltage levels. Energiateollisuus published a report on Finland's outage statistics, covering the years 2010 to 2019 [20]. We utilised this report to collect data on SAIDI, SAIFI, and CAIDI for Finland. The annual interruption statistics from 2006 to 2023 for Norway are available on the Energy Regulatory Authority (RME) webpage [21]. In Norway's national statistics, the SAIDI, SAIFI, and CAIDI are computed somewhat differently than in other countries; they incorporate both planned and unplanned outages in their calculations of these metrics. For Sweden, Denmark, and Finland, they distinguished between planned and unplanned reliability and outage indices as shown in Table 1.

Table 1. Outages Metrics for Outages Trend Analysis.

Country	Outage Indices	Voltage Level
Sweden	Unplanned and planned SAIDI, SAIFI, CAIDI	LV (0.4 kV), MV (<10 kV, 12 kV, 24 kV)
Denmark	Unplanned and planned SAIDI, SAIFI, CAIDI	MV (1–24 kV)
Finland	Unplanned and planned SAIDI, SAIFI, CAIDI	MV (1–45 kV)
Norway	SAIDI, SAIFI, and CAIDI [1]	from <1 kV to 420 kV

[1] SAIFI, SAIDI and CAIDI are available for planned, unplanned, and mixed (unplanned+planned) outages.

3 Methodology

This section describes the strategy utilised to examine the occurrence and duration of planned and unplanned outages in Nordic nations, including Sweden, Denmark, Finland, and Norway. The approach includes collecting and classifying data, including planned and unplanned outages, various voltage levels within the distribution network, and a comparative time series analysis to identify trends and significant differences between the chosen countries. Time series data from national grid operators were collected for the years [2013–2019], and plotted to perform a multi-country comparison of electricity reliability metrics. The analysis focuses on temporal changes and patterns in SAIDI, SAIFI, and CAIDI. This section has covered outages key performance indicators (KPIs), and their importance in outage studies and voltage levels of the distribution network for a specific country. Each of the four countries presents a unique set of years for outage data. Consequently, we have selected the period 2013 to 2019 for our data analysis. A dataset file has been prepared for Sweden, Denmark, and Finland, while the data for Norway is plotted separately for outages comparison. This is due to the fact that Norway's reports integrate both unplanned and planned outage indices, such as SAIDI, SAIFI, and CAIDI, from 2019 and from all years, such as from 2013; their outage indices are collected for all medium, high, and extra high voltage levels. Nevertheless, Sweden, Denmark, and Finland each provide their yearly data on SAIDI, SAIFI, and CAIDI for planned and unplanned outages separately and for separate voltage levels. This study investigates outages through the analysis of key performance indicatorsÂăsuch as SAIDI, which measures the average outage duration per customer in minutes, SAIFI, representing the average frequency of outages per customer, and CAIDI, indicating the average duration of outages per customer per interruption.

3.1 Planned and Unplanned Outages

The definition of planned outages is uniform across all Nordic countries. According to the Denmark grid operator [18], scheduled or planned outages are the types of interruptions for which energy consumers have been given adequate notice, such as 48 h before the interruption [19]. However, unplanned outages are defined differently in different countries. According to Denmark's power grid companies, unplanned outages occur when a sudden error causes the power supply to be cut off without prior notification to the customer [18]. According to the Danish grid, they have seven categories of outages, planned, unplanned, interruption due to third parties, interruption due to force majeure, interruption due to error/work outside their own statistical area, interruption as a result of agreements on the delivery of flexibility service and last interruption as a result of research, development and demonstration of projects [19]. Unplanned outages lack a clear definition in [20]; however, if they do not fit any of the other six categories mentioned above, they are classified as unplanned outages. The Sweden report [16] classifies the outage data into two distinct types: planned and unplanned. In [23], unplanned outages are classified based on the reasons for failure, including unknown factors, technical errors, weather conditions, excavation activities, accidents, overload situations, sabotage (excluding cyber-attacks) and testing procedures. These interruptions happen suddenly without prior warning. The report on outages in Sweden [16] indicates that unplanned interruptions primarily originate from weather conditions, technical failures, and unknown causes.

3.2 Voltage Levels in the Distribution Network for Nordic Countries

The 7th CEER-ECRB benchmarking report on the quality of electricity and gas supply, 2022 [5], reveals that all European countries operate with four different voltage networks: low-voltage, medium-voltage, high-voltage and extra-high-voltage networks. Table 2 below details the voltage networks for each Nordic country, specifying the minimum and maximum kV values across four distinct networks. Furthermore, considering the minimum and maximum kV range of Nordic countries, the network is classified into two distinct system types: the distribution system and the transmission system, as shown in Table 3 below. This research focuses on analyzing trends and information on interruptions in the distribution network. Consequently, our data on outages is limited to the distribution system voltage level. Furthermore, the seventh CEER-ECRB benchmark report on the quality of electricity and gas supply, 2022 [5], details the classification of the Swedish distribution system into regional and local DSOs.

Table 2. Nordic countries Line to Line voltage level network.

Country	LV Networks	MV Network	HV Network	EHV Network
Sweden	1 kV (Max)	>1 kV (Min)–36 kV(Max)	36 kV(Min)–150 kV(Max)	220 kV(Min)–380 kV(Max)
Denmark	0.4 kV(Min)–0.4 kV (Max)	0.4 kV [1](Min)–10 kV [2](Max)	10 kV [3](Min)–50 kV [4](Max)	50 kV(Min)–132 kV(Max)
Norway	0.23 kV (Min)–1 kV (Max)	1 kV (Min)–22 kV(Max)	36 kV(Min)–132 kV(Max)	220 kV(Min)–420 kV(Max)
Finland	0.4 kV (Min)–1 kV (Max)	1 kV (Min)–70 kV(Max)	70 kV(Min)–110 kV(Max)	220 kV(Min)–400 kV(Max)

[1] For SAIDI/SAIFI, the lower limit of MV is taken 1 kV, [2] For SAIDI/SAIFI, the upper limit of MV is taken 24 kV, [3] For SAIDI/SAIFI, the lower limit of HV is taken 25 kV, [4] For SAIDI/SAIFI, the upper limit of HV is taken 99 kV.

Table 3. Nordic countries distribution and transmission system.

Country	Distribution System	Transmission System
Sweden	0.4 kV (Min)–<220 kV (Max)	220 kV (Min)–400 kV(Max)
Denmark	0.4 kV(Min)–100 kV (Max)	100 kV (Min)–400 kV(Max)
Norway	0.23 kV (Min)–132 kV (Max)	132 kV (Min)–420 kV(Max)
Finland	0.4 kV (Min)–110 kV (Max)	110 kV (Min)–400 kV(Max)

3.3 Role of Outages KPIs

The roles of SAIFI, SAIDI and CAIDI in the electricity system include measuring the reliability of the power system, the performance of the utility benchmark, planning and investment of the grid infrastructure, regulatory compliance and penalties, and last but not least, customer satisfaction and economic effect. High SAIFI means that customers frequently experience outages, and SAIFI is defined as the average number of outages per customer per year as formulated below [22].

$$SAIFI = \frac{\text{Total number of customer interruptions}}{\text{Total number of customers served}} \quad (1)$$

High SAIDI means customers experience long total outages time, and SAIDI is defined as the average total outages duration per customer over a given period (mostly a year) as formulated below [22].

$$SAIDI = \frac{\text{Sum of customer interruption durations}}{\text{Total number of customers served}} \quad (2)$$

High CAIDI means customer experience each outage takes a long time, and CAIDI is defined as the average duration of a single outage event per customer per year as formulated below [22].

$$CAIDI = \frac{\text{Sum of customer interruption durations}}{\text{Total number of customer interruptions}} \quad (3)$$

Or

$$CAIDI = \frac{\text{SAIDI}}{\text{SAIFI}} \quad (4)$$

To evaluate the effectiveness of utility performance, various objectives for outage rates are established for urban and rural energy systems, as detailed in [6]. The annual operating target of SAIFI for the urban energy system is established at 1.0, while for the rural energy system it is set at 1.5 per year. The urban energy system has a target of 60 min per year for SAIDI, while the rural system has a goal of 90 min per year for the same measure. The CAIDI target in both rural and urban systems is established at 60 min or 1.0 h per outage. The established goals for SAIDI, SAIFI, and CAIDI serve as valuable benchmarks for assessing improvements in energy supply over time, guiding actions to upgrade the grid infrastructure and develop improvement strategies. A high SAIFI number indicates that outages occur often, suggesting that the utility needs to improve weak feeder areas through redundancy or grid strengthening. A high value of SAIDI and CAIDI indicates that the utility system required a long time for restoration, prompting the utility to focus on improving automation maintenance or their contingency strategies and encouraging them to adopt smart grid technologies [24]. Moreover, high values of SAIFI, SAIDI, and CAIDI indicate significant customer dissatisfaction, which adversely impacts industries and hospitals. Furthermore, it adversely affected utilities due to penalties, highlighting the economic consequences for utilities caused by higher values of SAIFI, SAIDI, and CAIDI [11].

4 Results and Discussion

This section presents our comparative time series analysis of the unplanned and planned outages metrics for SAIDI, SAIFI, and CAIDI in Denmark, Sweden, Norway, and Finland. We utilised the Python libraries pandas and matplotlib to illustrate the results. Figure 1 presents the recorded planned SAIDI for Denmark, Sweden, and Finland covering the period from 2013 to 2019. In Denmark, we demonstrate data exclusively pertaining to medium-voltage levels ranging from 1 to 24 kV. The Figure (see Fig. 1) clearly indicates that for Denmark the value is quite minimal. Between 2013 and 2019, Denmark's planned SAIDI was set to be below 2.5 min (see Fig. 1). Nonetheless, the planned SAIDI pattern for Finland is notably elevated—approximately 10–20 min across all years for the 1–45 kV voltage level. The outage data in Sweden are collected from various voltage levels, illustrated in the graphs: 0.4 kV, <10 kV, 12 kV, and 24 kV. When we compare the planned outages within Sweden for different medium voltage levels, we found that 24 kV voltage levels experience a long duration of planned outages compared to other low and medium voltage levels; however, the duration of interruptions for Sweden remains minimal from Finland while being significantly higher from Denmark.

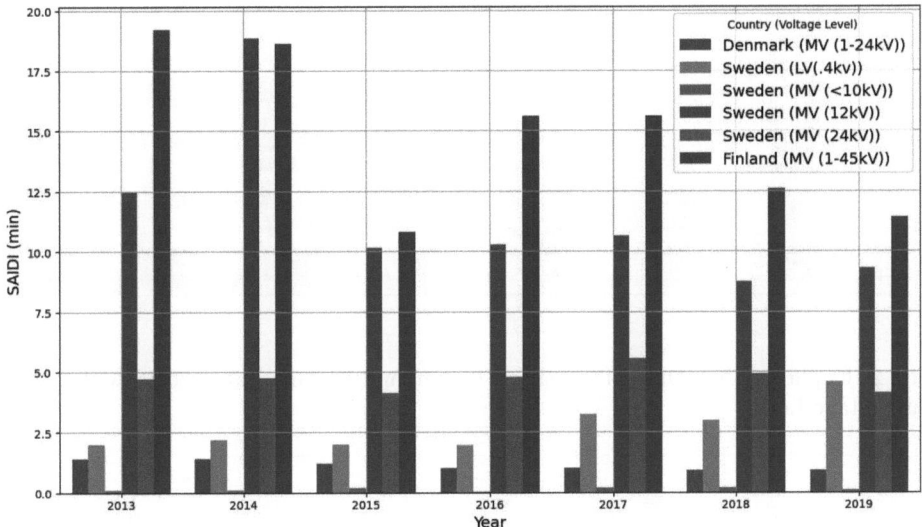

Fig. 1. Planned SAIDI for Denmark, Sweden, and Finland (2013–2019) with different Voltage Level.

Figure 2 illustrates the unplanned SAIDI metrics for Denmark, Sweden, and Finland. The unplanned SAIDI for Denmark remains the lowest compared to other countries, with a duration of under 15 min, which is quite commendable. Nonetheless, Finland is experiencing a minimum duration of 70.8 min and a maximum of 234.6 min, which is quite significant and suggests a concerning level of reliability in the power grid. On the other hand, Sweden's low and medium voltage distribution network exhibits an impressively low SAIDI, generally under 20 min. Nonetheless, the 24 kV medium voltage line experiences a prolonged interruption, usually exceeding 50 min.

Figure 3 presents the planned SAIFI for three Nordic countries, SAIFI referring to the yearly occurrence of outages. The aim of the outage rate is that it should be less than 1.0 for urban systems and 1.5 for rural systems according to [6]. In this context, the planned SAIFI is below the target across all Nordic countries, indicating a positive outlook for power grid reliability. Nevertheless, Finland is again facing higher SAIFI levels in comparison to other countries, however, it is still within the limits and low (see Fig. 3). Finland's unplanned SAIFI is significantly high, as seen in Fig. 4, primarily as a result of weather-related problems.

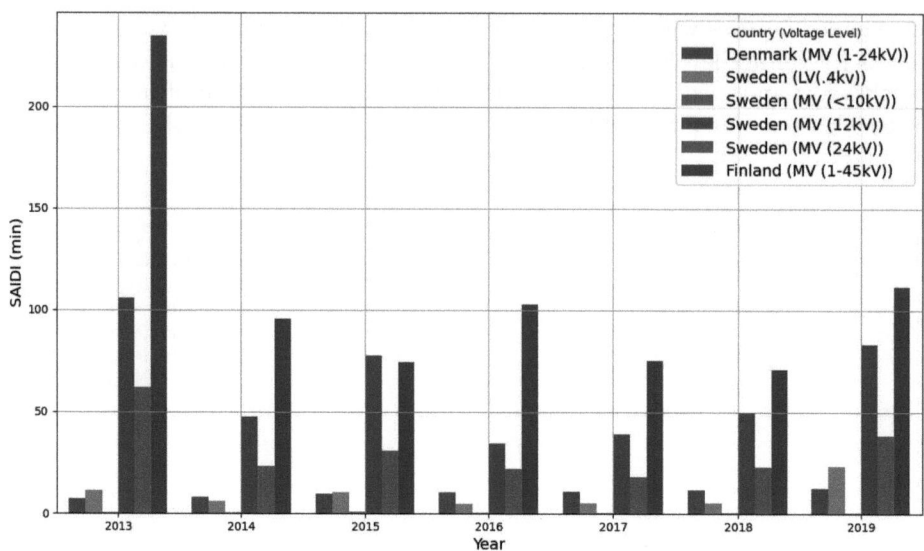

Fig. 2. Unplanned SAIDI for Denmark, Sweden, and Finland (2013–2019) with different Voltage Level.

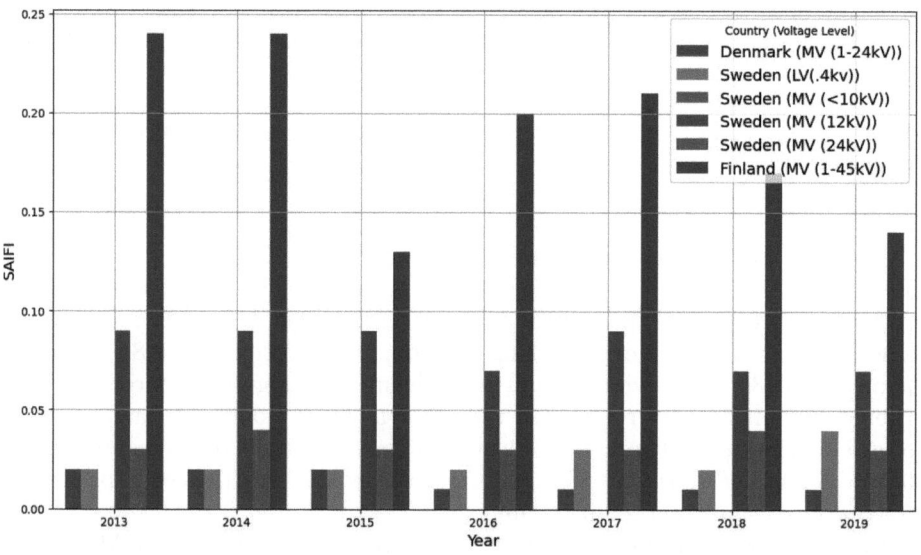

Fig. 3. Planned SAIFI for Denmark, Sweden, and Finland (2013–2019) with different Voltage Level.

Figures 5 and 6 illustrate both the planned and unplanned CAIDI. The CAIDI indicates the typical duration of power interruptions faced by customers. It represents the average time required to restore service to a customer after an

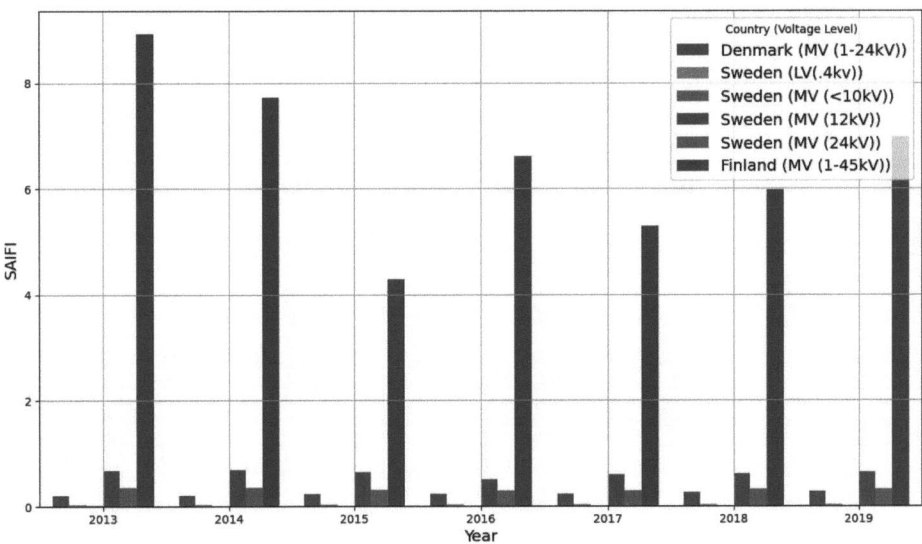

Fig. 4. Unplanned SAIFI for Denmark, Sweden, and Finland (2013–2019) with different Voltage Level.

unplanned and planned outage. The main difference between SAIDI and CAIDI is in their priority: SAIDI quantifies the overall duration of the outage experienced by each customer annually, which includes all served customers, while CAIDI measured the time required to restore power after an outage, taking into account only those customers impacted by the outages. According to Fig. 5, Sweden's planned CAIDI is higher than that of other countries; for the <10 kV voltage network, the lowest CAIDI is around 148 min, and the highest is 275 min. Furthermore, Sweden exhibits a significant value for unplanned CAIDI, particularly within the 0.4 kV voltage network (see Fig. 6).

Figure 7 illustrates the SAIDI, SAIFI and CAIDI metrics for Norway over the years from 2013 to 2019. Outages metrics include both planned and unplanned events combined, covering medium, high, and extra-high voltage-level networks, as detailed in Table 2. Consequently, the authors have omitted comparisons with outage metrics of Denmark, Sweden, and Finland in relation to Norway. Figure 7 illustrates that the minimum and maximum minutes for SAIDI are 181.2 and 110.9, respectively. Nonetheless, the durations of individual outages are relatively short, as indicated by CAIDI, which records a maximum of 81.9 min and a minimum of 63.0 min. However, the SAIFI values for all years exceed 1. Furthermore, as shown in Figs. 8 and 9, we have separate information for planned and unplanned outages, although these are available only up to 2018. On the website, separate metrics for planned, unplanned, and combined (planned and unplanned) outages were available until 2018; starting in 2019, only combined outage metrics are provided. Consequently, Figs. 8 and 9 illustrate the planned and unplanned SAIDI, SAIFI, and CAIDI only up until 2018, whereas Fig. 7

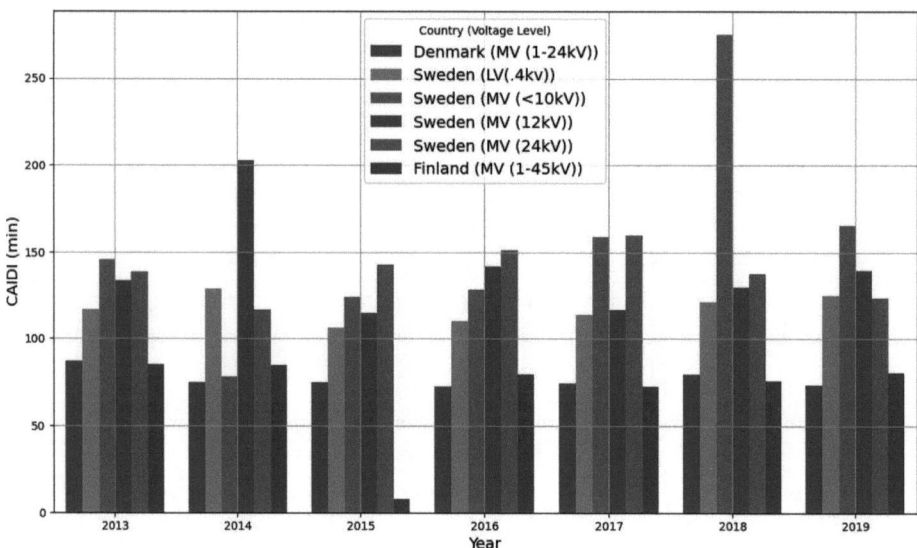

Fig. 5. Planned CAIDI for Denmark, Sweden, and Finland (2013–2019) with different Voltage Level.

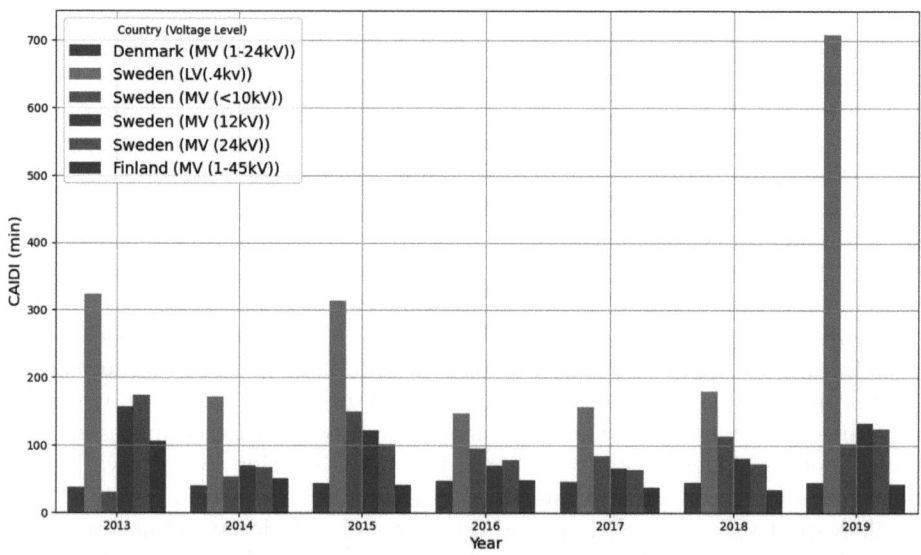

Fig. 6. Unplanned CAIDI for Denmark, Sweden, and Finland (2013–2019) with different Voltage Level.

presents the unplanned and planned SAIFI, SAIDI, and CAIDI up until 2019. Moreover, all these metrics in Figs. 7, 8, and 9 are associated with medium, high, and extra-high voltage level networks.

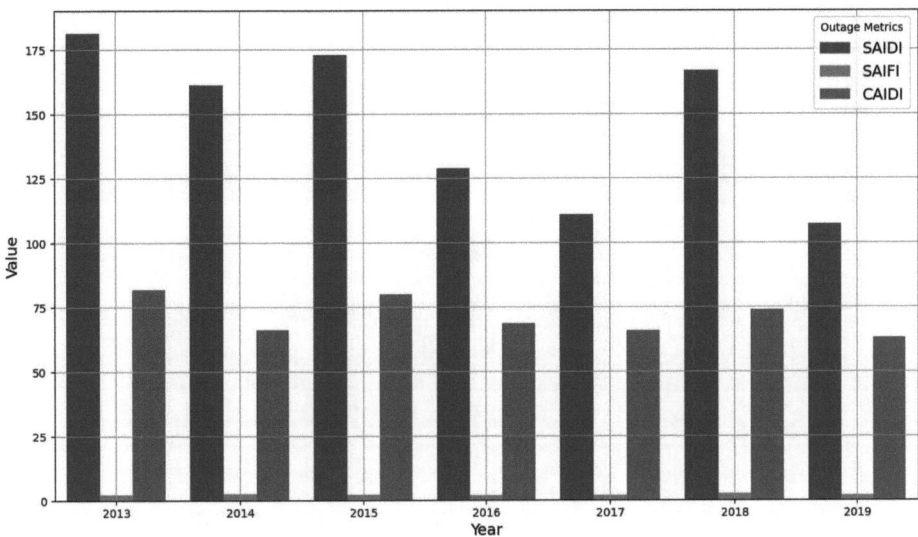

Fig. 7. Total planned and unplanned SAIDI, SAIFI and CAIDI for Norway (2013–2019) for medium, high and extra high Voltage Levels (<1 kV, 1–22 kV, 33–110 kV, 132 kV, 220–300 kV,420 kV).

This study highlights the frequency of occurrence and duration of outages in Nordic main-lands countries as summarized in Table 4.

Table 4. Summary of outages KPIs for mainland Nordic countries.

Outages KPIs	Sweden	Norway	Finland	Denmark
Unplanned SAIDI	for 24 kV and 12 kV oscillated, for <10 kV stable and 0.4 kV increasing	oscillated	improvement but not so much	stable
Unplanned SAIFI	stable for 0.4 kV, <10 kV, 12 kV and 24 kV	increasing	worsening	very stable
Unplanned CAIDI	for 0.4 kV worsening but for <10 kV, 12 kV and 24 kV oscillating	oscillating	stable	stable
Planned SAIFI	12 kV and 0.4 kV increasing and <10 kV stable	oscillating	improving	stable
Planned SAIDI	0.4 kV increasing, 12 kV improving, <10 kV stable and 24 kV improving	improving	very oscillating	stable
Planned CAIDI	0.4 kV stable, 12 kV improving, <10 kV increasing and 24 kV stable	worsening	stable	stable

This study reveals that Finland experiences the longest unplanned SAIDI duration, ranging from approximately 111 to 70 min, recorded only once in 2013 at 234.6 min, more than Denmark and Sweden. However, the longest unplanned SAIDI duration in 100 min. In Norway, the data includes all medium, high, and extra voltage levels, while in Finland, it is limited to the medium voltage level (1–45 kV). Therefore, it is difficult to compare the duration of the unplanned SAIDI in Norway and Finland. However, Norway and Finland have notably higher unplanned SAIDI value compared to Sweden and Denmark, and this suggests that Finnish and Norwegian customers experience more frequent and longer-lasting outages. Such disparities underscore the need to address specific resilience challenges within the grid. The SAIDI planned across the Nordic

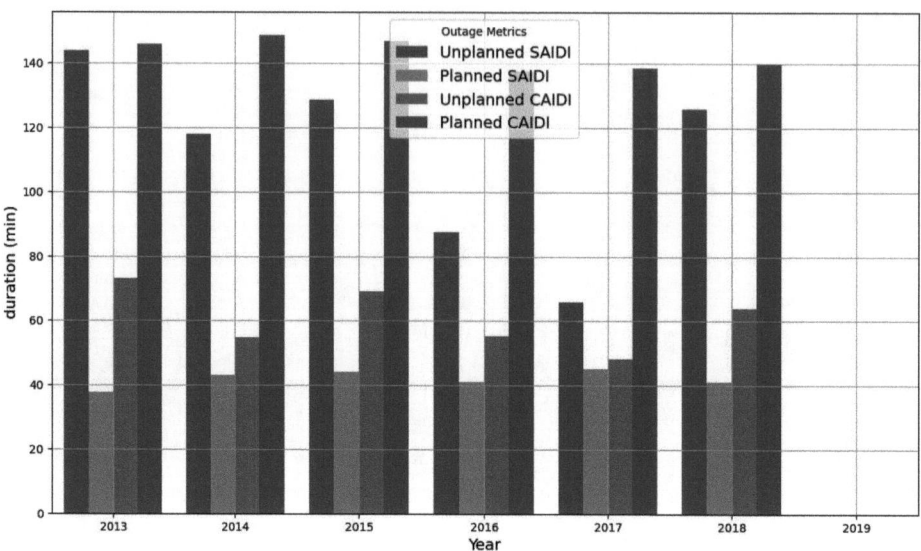

Fig. 8. Planned and unplanned SAIDI and CAIDI for Norway (2013–2019) for medium, high and extra high Voltage Levels (<1 kV, 1–22 kV, 33–110 kV, 132 kV, 220–300 kV, 420 kV).

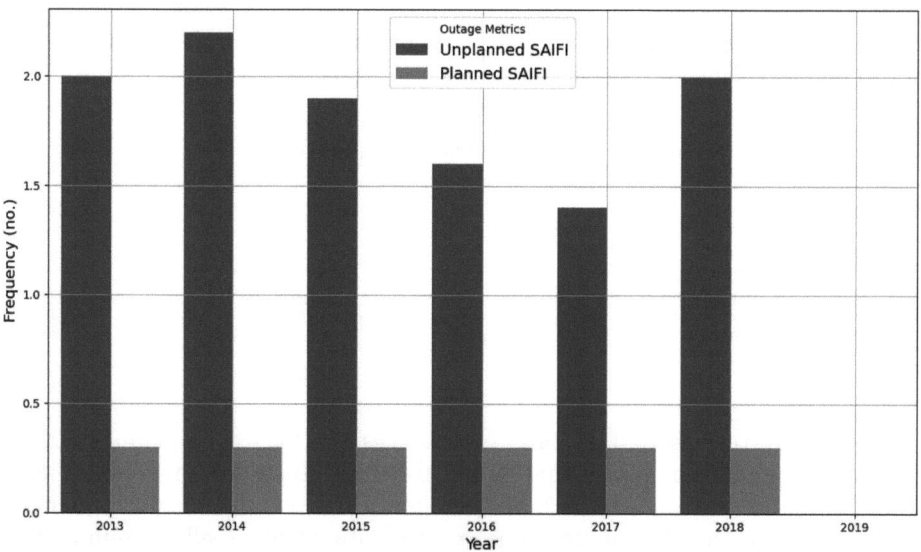

Fig. 9. Planned and unplanned SAIFI for Norway (2013–2019) for medium, high and extra high Voltage Levels (<1 kV, 1–22 kV, 33–110 kV, 132 kV, 220–300 kV, 420 kV).

nations shows that Finland is once again experiencing the longest duration, yet remains within the 10- to 19-minute framed. However, when it comes to unplanned CAIDI, Sweden shows the longest duration compared to all other countries, particularly at low and medium voltage levels. Additionally, Sweden's low-voltage networks have longer unplanned CAIDI durations than medium-voltage networks. Furthermore, it should be noted that Finland is experiencing a significant number of unplanned outages compared to its Nordic country peers. Although the analysis uses an adequate dataset, variations in data collection methods between countries could lead to certain uncertainties in the analyzes as described in Sects. 3.1 and 3.2.

5 Concluding Remarks

In this paper, the authors aim to examine the frequency and duration of outages in Nordic countries. Modern grids are characterized by intelligent mechanisms to minimize power disruptions during outages by grid reconfiguration using switching control and load shedding. However, such corrective measures do not consistently result in effective outage mitigation due to their sluggish response and computational inefficiency. [25]. Power outages have a significant impact on production, transportation, communication, and health supply services. They may lead to considerable financial setbacks. [26]. Consequently, examining system outages is crucial for maintaining the stability and resilience of modern life. [27]. The examination of the recordings in Nordic countries revealed that there is no specific indication of changes in the duration and the frequency of the outage events. However, the changes in the energy sector that are undergoing, in which the electricity grid is a reforming sector, may raise some questions about outages implications on the Nordic energy transition. At this point, it is imperative to highlight that national recordings should be as accurate as possible, aiming for a better understanding and management of system outages [23]. In particular, we would like to emphasize the following three main points of correlation between outages with the energy transition and future development.

1. May electricity grid outages have a negative impact on the energy sector's coupling? For example, the transport sector, which is continuously electrified, is highly dependent on the electricity sector [28]. In recent incidents of wide outage (blackout) in Spain, transport sector problems have raised the question of social security and acceptance in modern smart cities. The electrification of industry is also a big question about how it is going to be affected by outages as regards loss of revenue, risk of operation, and business activity.
2. How energy communities could help against outages [29]. When an outage occurs, there are parts of the downstream grid that are still healthy. However, they might not be operational because of the power electronics of renewable energy resources, which are usually capable of grid-connected operation only. The distributed energy resources could provide power to the connected loads, provided that the power electronics can operate in islanded conditions. At this point, one can mention that there are thoughts to develop energy communities by developing a parallel DC distribution grid that connects the resources

of the energy community. This DC network has the potential to facilitate power distribution among the connected entities during an AC grid outage, assuming that the power electronics, like grid-forming inverters, are equipped to support such operations. Grid forming inverters ensure the continuity of grid operations during main grid failures and facilitate real power balancing to maintain grid stability.
3. How are the energy markets affected? The local energy markets play an important role in the reliability and the social acceptance of the energy communities. The establishment of energy communities, via the development of local energy markets, system flexibility in combination with the sectors' coupling, and related social acceptance, is a key challenge in Sweden nowadays.

More dedicated research needs to be done in this direction. Digital twins of the systems with energy management alternatives under outage conditions are of paramount importance. Real-time indicators that capture the risk of an outage might be useful to improve the system's operation [30]. As such, data-based models could forecast unforeseen outages and provide timely insights to distribution companies, customers, and aggregators, allowing them to efficiently handle the frequency and duration of power interruptions [31–33].

Acknowledgements. The authors acknowledge the financial support from KKS funding (2023–2027) (Project code: 20210059) and Interreg SV-NO GränsEnergi project code: 20369648 (2025–2027).

References

1. Carvallo, J.P., Frick, N.M., Schwartz, L.: A review of examples and opportunities to quantify the grid reliability and resilience impacts of energy efficiency. Energy Policy **169**, 113–185 (2022)
2. Zhang, D., Li, G., Bie, Z., Fan, K.: An analytical method for reliability evaluation of power distribution system with time-varying failure rates. Reliab. Eng. Syst. Saf. **250**, 110–290 (2024)
3. Yao, Y., Liu, W., Jain, R.: Power system resilience evaluation framework and metric review. In: 2022 IEEE Power & Energy Society Innovative Smart Grid Technologies Conference (ISGT), pp. 1–5, New Orleans (2022)
4. Yao, Y., Liu, W., Jain, R.: Optimal energy interruption planning and generation re-dispatch for improving reliability during contingencies. In: 2020 IEEE Power & Energy Society Innovative Smart Grid Technologies Conference (ISGT), pp. 1–5, Washington (2020)
5. Council of European Energy Regulators (CEER). https://www.ceer.eu/publication/7th-ceer-ecrb-benchmarking-report-on-the-quality-of-electricity-and-gas-supply/. Accessed 18 Feb 2025
6. Hussen, S., Ayalew, F., Ibrahim, K.: Analysis of distribution system reliability and outage rates. Reclosers Technical data, pp. 1–7. Copper power series (2017)
7. Eskandarpour, R., Khodaei, A., Arab, A.: Improving power grid resilience through predictive outage estimation. In: 2017 North American Power Symposium (NAPS), pp. 1–5, Morgantown (2017)

8. Paul, S., Poudyal, A., Poudel, S., Dubey, A., Wang, Z.: Resilience assessment and planning in power distribution systems: past and future considerations. Renew. Sustain. Energy Rev. **189**, 113991 (2024)
9. Alsenani, T., Zhang, K., Qiu, J.: Studying power outage trends and impact of investments in the smart grid technologies. IET J. (2015)
10. Chen, H., Jin, L., Wang, M., Guo, L., Wu, J.: How will power outages affect the national economic growth: evidence from 152 countries. Energy Econ. **126**, 107055 (2023)
11. Economic repercussions of power outages for Swedish electrical distribution companies. https://www.diva-portal.org/smash/get/diva2:1771989/FULLTEXT01.pdf. Accessed 18 Feb 2025
12. Kufeoglu, S., Gündüz, N., Winzer, C., Lehtonen, M.: Regional differences in economic impacts of power outages in Finland (2018)
13. Chen, H., Jin, L., Wang, M., Guo, L., Wu, J.: How will power outages affect the national economic growth: evidence from 152 countries. Energy Econ. **126**, 107055 (2023). ISSN 0140-9883
14. Carlsson, F., Martinsson, P., Akay, A.: The effect of power outages and cheap talk on willingness to pay to reduce outages. Energy Econ. **33**(5), 790–798 (2011). ISSN 0140-9883
15. Carlsson, F., Kataria, M., Lampi, E., Martinsson, P.: Past and present outage costs – a follow-up study of households' willingness to pay to avoid power outages. Resour. Energy Econ. **64**, 101216 (2021). ISSN 0928-7655,
16. DARWin Annual Statistics Reports. https://www.energiforetagen.se/statistik/elstatistik/tidigare-statistik-darwin/darwin-arsstatistik-rapporter/. Accessed 18 Feb 2025
17. Security of supply - electricity networks. https://ei.se/om-oss/statistik-och-oppna-data/leveranssakerhet---elnat. Accessed 18 Feb 2025
18. Interruption statistics 2013-2022 (RA645). https://elnet.dk/materialesamling/afbrudsstatistik-2013-2022-ra645. Accessed 18 Feb 2025
19. Forsyningstilsynet, Vejledning til indberetning af afbrudsstatistik for netvirksomhe-dens leveringskvalitet i 2022 (2022)
20. Sähkön keskeytystilastot 2010-2019. https://energia.fi/tilastot/sahkon-keskeytystilastot-2010-2019/. Accessed 18 Feb 2025
21. Avbruddsstatistikk. https://www.nve.no/reguleringsmyndigheten/publikasjoner-og-data/statistikk/avbruddsstatistikk/. Accessed 18 Feb 2025
22. IEEE 1366- Reliability Indices. https://site.ieee.org/boston-pes/files/2019/03/IEEE-1366-Reliability-Indices-2-2019.pdf. Accessed 18 Feb 2025
23. Outage Statistics and Trends in Sweden – What does data tell us?. https://kth.diva-portal.org/smash/get/diva2:1831794/FULLTEXT01.pdf. Accessed 18 Feb 2025
24. Yeliz, Y., Ahmet, O., Irfan, A., Robert, B.: Distribution automation effects on reliability during major contingencies, pp. 1–5 (2018). https://doi.org/10.1109/ICHQP.2018.8378919
25. Jacob, R.A., Paul, S., Chowdhury, S., et al.: Real-time outage management in active distribution networks using reinforcement learning over graphs. Nat. Commun. **15**, 4766 (2024)
26. Sullivan, M.J., Schellenberg, J., Nexant, M.B.: Updated value of service reliability estimates for electric utility customers in the United States (2015). https://eta-publications.lbl.gov/sites/default/files/lbnl-6941e.pdf

27. Salman, H.M., Pasupuleti, J., Sabry, A.H.: Review on causes of power outages and their occurrence: mitigation strategies. Sustainability. **15**(20), 15001 (2023). https://doi.org/10.3390/su152015001
28. Qiu, Y., Deng, N., Wang, B., et al.: Power supply disruptions deter electric vehicle adoption in cities in China. Nat Commun **15**, 6041 (2024). https://doi.org/10.1038/s41467-024-50447-1
29. Younesi, A., Wang, Z., Siano, P.: Enhancing the resilience of zero-carbon energy communities: leveraging network reconfiguration and effective load carrying capability quantification. J. Cleaner Prod. **434**, 139794 (2024). ISSN 0959-6526, https://doi.org/10.1016/j.jclepro.2023.139794
30. https://www.anl.gov/esia/outage-prediction-and-grid-vulnerability-identification-using-machine-learning-on-utility-outage
31. Ghasemkhani, B., et al.: Machine learning model development to predict power outage duration (POD): a case study for electric utilities. Sensors **24**, 4313 (2024). https://doi.org/10.3390/s24134313
32. Dehbozorgi, M.R., Rastegar, M., Sami, A.: Data mining-based cause identification of momentary outages in power distribution systems. Sustain. Cities Soc. **77**, 103587 (2022). https://doi.org/10.1016/j.scs.2021.103587. ISSN 2210-6707
33. Taylor, W.O., Cerrai, D., Wanik, D., Koukoula, M., Anagnostou, E.N.: Community power outage prediction modeling for the Eastern United States. Energy Rep. **10**, 4148–4169 (2023). https://doi.org/10.1016/j.egyr.2023.10.073. ISSN 2352-4847

Managing Risk in Distribution Systems with Solar Generation: A Case Study Using the **MATPOWER** Optimal Scheduling Tool

Johanna Bolaños-Zuñiga[1] and Alberto J. Lamadrid L.[1,2](✉)

[1] Institute for Cyber Physical Infrastructure and Energy (I-CPIE), Lehigh University, Bethlehem, PA 18015, USA
job323@lehigh.edu
[2] Laboratory for Information and Decision Systems (LIDS), Massachusetts Institute of Technology (MIT), Cambridge, MA 02139, USA
ajlamadrid@mit.edu
https://www.lehigh.edu/~all512/

Abstract. The increasing integration of renewable energy sources, particularly solar power, introduces variability that poses significant challenges to power system reliability. This research addresses the management of solar generation uncertainty in a distribution system using real data from the E.W. Brown Universal Solar Facility and electricity demand (load) data in Kentucky, U.S.A. The objective is to determine the amount of reserves to mitigate operational risks and maintain system stability under different uncertainty scenarios. We simulate the expected dispatch over 24 h by solving a multi-period, stochastic, security-constrained DC optimal power flow (SCOPF) using the MATPOWER Optimal Scheduling Tool (MOST). Unlike traditional unit commitment models, we assume all generators remain continuously active throughout the dispatch horizon. To highlight the role of reserves, we compare four different operational cases. The results underscore the importance of reserves as a fundamental tool for managing renewable energy variability and ensuring dispatch reliability, denoting that optimal dispatch must balance supplying demand, maintaining sufficient reserves to handle uncertainties, and minimizing operational and financial risks.

Keywords: Stochastic dispatch · optimal power flow · renewable energy sources · uncertainty · reserves

1 Introduction

The transition to variable renewable energy sources (VRES) is a key component of the global strategy to manage the risks derived from climate change, as high-

---

This work was supported by the Advanced Research Projects Agency-Energy (ARPA-E), U.S. Department of Energy, under Grant DE-AR0001277 and the Pennsylvania Infrastructure Technology Alliance (PITA) Grant PIT-24-22.

© The Author(s), under exclusive license to Springer Nature Switzerland AG 2026
I. Martinac et al. (Eds.): EIA Nordic 2025, LNCS 16096, pp. 67–77, 2026.
https://doi.org/10.1007/978-3-032-03098-6_5

lighted in [12]. The growing adoption of VRES is also a component essential to meeting climate targets while diversifying the generation portfolio and reducing dependency on any particular fuel. However, integrating intermittent resources like solar energy into the grid introduces significant challenges to power system reliability due to its inherent variability and dependency on weather conditions. This variability makes maintaining a stable balance between supply and demand challenging, requiring innovative strategies to ensure reliable system operations and cost efficiency [10].

Several studies emphasize the importance of managing the uncertainty introduced by renewable generation. In [10], the authors argue that stochastic optimization frameworks are essential for balancing the dual objectives of minimizing operational risks and controlling costs. Unlike deterministic models, assuming perfect foresight, stochastic approaches consider the probabilistic characteristics of the renewable generation and the unpredictability of real-world conditions, providing more robust and realistic dispatch solutions across multiple time horizons [11] and security constraints, especially considering contingencies like outage probabilities [13]. Likewise, this method is applicable to solar energy adoption, where forecast errors and sudden drops in generation can lead to shortages or over generation, resulting in higher costs and reliability risks [3].

To address these risks, system operators use operating reserves to maintain power system stability. Reserves serve as a buffer, allowing the system to respond to fluctuations in generation and demand. Studies highlight the importance of spinning reserves for renewable-rich systems [14], emphasizing that reserve strategies must evolve to support growing renewable penetration without increasing costs [17]. Dynamic reserve management is crucial under multi-uncertainty scenarios, such as solar variability and transmission contingencies, ensuring operational reliability through real-time adjustments [16]. Furthermore, stochastic security-constrained operational planning ensures that reserves are economically allocated and positioned to handle forecast errors and unforeseen events.

Using real data offers a more accurate reflection of the complexities in renewable generation. Real datasets capture actual forecast errors, system constraints, and weather-induced variability, which simulations may overlook. For example, sudden drops in solar output due to weather changes are better represented with real data, leading to more effective dispatch strategies and reserve management [6].

We focus this research on linking the two strands above, first addressing the uncertainty of renewable energy, particularly solar; and second using high resolution data from a solar farm already in production. The variability in solar generation risks causing shortages, over generation, and increased costs, making effective reserve management necessary for reliable power system operations. We use the open-source MATPOWER Optimal Scheduling Tool (MOST) [21] to evaluate reserve strategies under different solar scenarios by solving a multi-period stochastic security-constrained DC optimal power flow or stochastic security-constrained economic dispatch (S-SCED). Since we incorporate real data from Kentucky, our approach more accurately captures the operational complexities of forecast errors and variability [6]. Moreover, by treating load as dispatchable, we introduce flexibility, allowing demand to adjust to solar availability [7]. Our findings provide practical insights for system operators and planners, helping optimize reserve management to ensure reliability and cost efficiency as renewable penetration increases.

The following sections in this article present the formulation of the problem, Sect. 2, information about the considerations and assumptions of simulation, Sect. 3, results and discussion 4, and conclusions and future work, Sect. 5.

2 Formulation

We simulate the scheduling of the power system following the architecture used in restructured electricity systems in the U.S. Here, a system operator optimizes an objective function (e.g., maximize social welfare, minimize cost), subject to both physical (e.g., Kirchoff's laws) and regulatory (e.g. reliability requirements) constraints.

Table 1. Nomenclature for the problem

Variable	Description
$\mathcal{X}$	Set of discrete variables
$\mathcal{Y}$	Set of continuous variables
$\mathcal{T}$	Set of all time periods, n^t elements
$\mathcal{B}$	Set of all nodes (buses), n^b elements
$\mathcal{I}$	Set of generating units, n^i elements
Θ, V	Vector of n^b bus voltage angles and magnitudes $\in x$
U	Vector of binary variables from assets $\in \mathcal{I}$, e.g., associated to unit commitment costs
P	Vector of n^i active power injections from assets $\in \mathcal{I}$
R	Vector of n^i reserves from assets $\in \mathcal{I}$
$f_P^{it}(\cdot), f_r^{it}(\cdot)$	Cost for injection i in period t for active injections and reserve capacity
$f_{uc}^{it}(\cdot)$	Cost for discrete events for unit i in period t e.g., associated to unit commitment costs

$$\min_{x,y} \& \{V(x,y) = F(x) + G(y)\} \tag{1a}$$

$$\text{subject to } h_x(x) + h_y(y) \leq b$$
$$x \in \mathcal{X}, y \in \mathcal{Y},\} \tag{1b}$$

where $F(x) = \sum_{it} f_{uc}^{it}(u^{it})$, and $G(y) = \sum_{it} f_P^{it}(p^{it}) + f_r^{it}(r^{it})$. The constraints are the required constraints for unit commitment and optimal power flow, please refer to [2,5] for the classical formulations and to [4,20] for recent surveys. The constraints include, among others, operating limits,

$$u^{ti} P_{\min}^{ti} \leq p^{ti} \leq u^{ti} P_{\max}^{ti}, \tag{1c}$$

balance between supply and demand,

$$p^{ti} - \sum_{l \in n_B} |V^{ti}||V^{tl}|\left[G^{ti,tl}\cos(\theta^{ti} - \theta^{tl}) + B^{ti,tl}\sin(\theta^{ti} - \theta^{tl})\right] = 0, \quad (1d)$$
$$\forall t \in \mathcal{T}, \forall i \in \mathcal{I}^t,$$

and ramping constraints,

$$p^{ti} - p^{(t-1)i} \leq \delta_+^{(t-1)i} - \delta_-^{(t-1)i}, \quad \forall t \in \mathcal{T}, \forall i \in \mathcal{I}^t. \quad (1e)$$

3 Simulation

The variability of renewable energy presents significant challenges for power system reliability. To address these challenges, we perform a simulation to analyze the expected dispatch, considering the uncertainty of real solar generation data per hour by solving a S-SCED, where the main objective is to minimize the expected cost over a set of scenarios and consider constraints such as power and generation levels, reserves requirements, demand, storage capacities, ramp rate limits, and contingencies. Fig 1 shows the diagram of the process developed in this work.

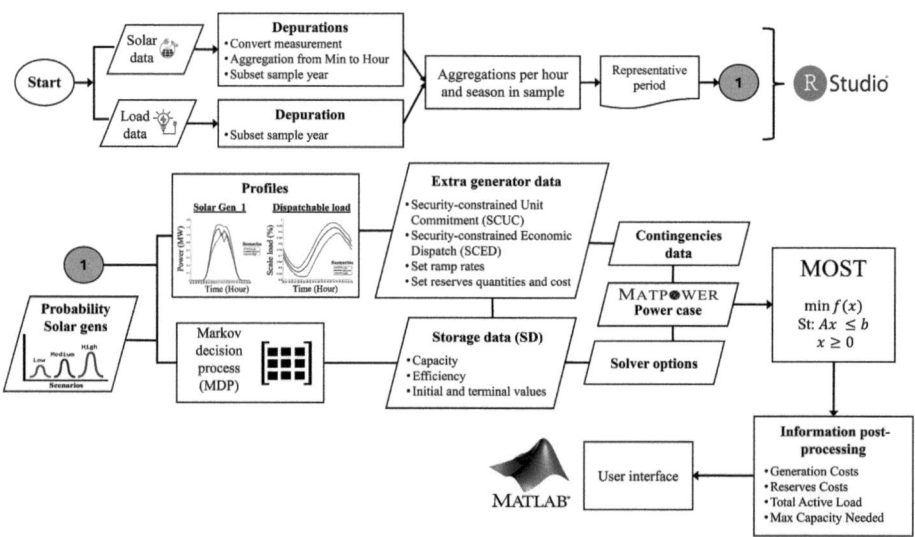

Fig. 1. Workflow for multiperiod S-SCED simulation.

We represent the current distribution system using a modified 3-bus system and modified an existing MATPOWER case file (case3sc.m). In Bus 1, we host 11 generators: 10 solar gens (units) and one backup generator, natural gas (Ng).

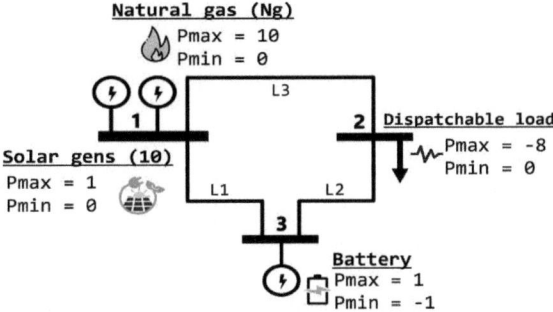

Fig. 2. Scheme of the modified 3-buses MATPOWER case.

Bus 2 has the load of the system, and Bus 3 has the electrochemical battery. Figure 2 shows the simplified configuration of this case.

We model the uncertainty of solar generation as a Markov Decision Process (MDP) and define different scenarios to capture this variability [8]. We treat each level of solar generation as a state and represent transitions between states over time using a transition probability matrix based on data from a representative period.

We process load profile values as scaled or percentage-based rather than absolute values and calculate a series of scaled values between 0 and 1, where 1 represents the maximum load value, and the remaining values correspond to proportions of that maximum.

We define representative periods as convex combinations of aggregate data at chosen time intervals (e.g., minutes or hours) and a number of observations based on electric market behavior, as energy consumption patterns differ daily (e.g., Monday vs. Sunday). This methodology allows for analyzing how solar and load values fluctuate over a defined planning horizon.

3.1 Dataset

We source real-time solar generation and demand data at the E.W. Brown solar farm in Kentucky from September 1st, 2016, to October 31st, 2023, with minute-level granularity[1] The solar generation measurement is in kilowatts (kW), while the demand is in Megawatt-hours (MWh). However, since the load information from September 1st, 2016, until October 31st, 2023, has gaps, we use public information about Kentucky demand data from the U.S. Energy Information Administration (EIA) [1]. The granularity of the EIA data is per hour, and the measurement is in MWh.

The E.W. Brown Plant is a 10-megawatt universal Solar Facility divided into 10 units, each rated at 1MW, covering 50 acres of the plant property of LG&E

---

[1] The database used in this work is confidential. However, readers can find publicly available portions of the solar data on the website of E.W. Brown Solar Facility [9].

and KU. The plant began commercial operations in the spring of 2016. On the other hand, the U.S. Energy Information Administration is an independent agency that gathers, analyzes, and publishes energy-related data.

3.2 Assumptions

The assumptions, parameters, and variables based on the characteristics of the Kentucky case are described below:

- We use 2022 as the sample year because it is one of the years with complete EIA load data and the least missing solar generation data.
- We consider three scenarios for solar generation uncertainty: low, medium, and high.
- We determine the seasons as follows: Winter includes the months of January, February, and December of the same year; Spring includes March through May; Summer covers June through August; and Fall envelops September through November.
- We aggregate the data per hour because we used the load data from the EIA dataset.
- We compute the average of the 60 min within each hour to aggregate the solar generation values per hour. Additionally, the measurement is converted from kW to MW.
- We establish the representative period as one day (24 h) per season, with seven observations representing each weekday (Monday to Sunday). Thus, we set the planning horizon at 24 h per season, using one representative day for each season.
- We calculate the solar/load values for each hour of the representative day by season by taking the average for each hour corresponding to the same weekday across all weeks within the season (average-hour). For example, for hour 0 on Mondays during the summer, we compute the average solar/load values from all Mondays in that season and repeat this process for the remaining hours. Therefore, there are 672 average-hours for load (24 h × 7 weekdays × 4 seasons) and 6,720 average-hours for solar (24 h × 7 weekdays × 4 seasons × 10 sections).
- We compute the maximum load value from the 672 average-hours to calculate the scale load. Then, we divide each average-hour by this maximum value.
- We designate the battery values based on the BESS specifications from the E.W. Brown Universal Solar Facility (Power: 1 MW, Energy: 2 MWh).
- We set the Pmax (maximum real power output) for each solar generator at 1 MW (maximum daily generation) and the Ng at 10 MW. Meanwhile, we assign the Pmin (minimum real power output) at 0 for both, the Pmax for the battery at 1 MW, and the Pmin at -1 MW.
- We set the peak load value (real power demand) at 8 MW based on historical maximum data and scale it hourly according to the behavior observed during the sampling season. Additionally, we set the Pmin value for the dispatchable load at -8 MW.

- We define linear costs [19], setting the cost of solar generation and battery operation at zero. Meanwhile, we set the cost of the Ng generator at 20 USD/MWh, and the cost of dispatchable load at the default value of 5,000 USD/MWh.
- We regard prices for positive reserves as lower than those for negative reserves based on the assumption that supply must exceed demand. This pricing structure provides a more flexible modeling approach, facilitating problem optimization for the differing reserve requirements.
- We decide ramp rates and reserve quantities for each generator according to its Pmax value.
- All generators are active throughout the planning horizon. Therefore, we did not consider Unit Commitment (UC), as the generators for commitment, combined cycle gas turbines, can respond quickly and be dispatched in the time scales considered [15]. Consequently, we do not include startup times as decision variables.
- We set the energy capacity of the battery to a maximum of 2 MWh. Additionally, we initialize the storage level at 0 and assume that the charge level at the beginning would match the level at the end of the planning horizon.
- We use the default branch values from the MATPOWER case file, including resistance, reactance, susceptance, and ratings.

4 Results and Discussion

We develop our simulation in Matlab R2024a to analyze the expected dispatch for each day (24 h) per season. We use MOST from MATPOWER 7.1 to perform all simulations, with Gurobi version 11.0.0 as the solver.

The simulations are carried out on a computer with a 2.3 GHz 11th Gen Intel(R) Core(TM) i7-11800H processor, 32 GB RAM, and 1 TB hard disk.

Figure 3 depicts the expected dispatch by generators per season in 2022. Notice that the white spaces represent periods when the battery is discharging while the battery is charging during overgeneration. In the same way, Table 2 summarizes the expected generation costs, reserve requirements, and maximum dispatch for each generator.

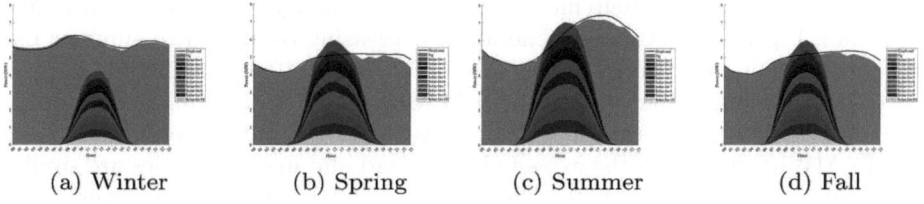

(a) Winter   (b) Spring   (c) Summer   (d) Fall

Fig. 3. Hourly expected dispatch by generators per season in 2022.

Table 2. Summary of the key optimization results per season in 2022

Metrics	Fall	Spring	Summer	Winter
e[Generation Costs, ($)]	1,619.40	1,509.40	1,835.96	2,372.43
e[Reserves Costs (Positive), ($)]	4.49	3.13	5.13	12.8
e[Total Active Load (MWh)]	120.07	118.43	150.46	141.45
Max Capacity Needed (MW)	11.64	11.33	14.3	11.31
a) Max Solar (MW)	6.34	6.13	7.4	5.23
b) Max Ng (MW)	5.29	5.2	6.9	6.08
c) Max ESS (MW)	0.67	0.52	0.6	0.66

In Fig. 3a and Table 2, we can observe that in Winter, max solar generation is minimal ($\sim$ 46%), requiring a heavy reliance on using max Ng ($\sim$ 51%) to supply most of the demand throughout the day. Therefore, the generation cost is highest in this season (2,372.43). Moreover, the reserve costs are the highest (12.8), reflecting the uncertainty and increased need for reserves during this period of low renewable generation and higher demand.

In spring, solar generation increases significantly, reducing the need for Ng during daylight hours, particularly between 11:00 and 14:00, when solar output peaks (see Fig. 3b). Solar generation reached a maximum capacity of 6.79 MW ($\sim$ 52%), reducing generation costs to 1,509.4, the lowest among all seasons, possibly due to increased dependence on solar energy and lower demand. Besides, reserve costs also decrease (3.13), which could indicate more stable generation patterns. Despite the increased solar generation, reserves remain important to manage variability, particularly during low solar hours.

In Fig. 3c, we see the highest levels of solar generation in summer, with a significant reduction in natural gas use during peak hours (between 09:00 and 15:00) and battery charging during those hours. Table 2 shows that solar generation reaches its highest value of 7.4 MW ($\sim$ 50%), and max Ng output increases to 6.9 MW ($\sim$ 46%) to supply the load, which is the highest among the seasons (150.46 MWh). The generation costs are higher in summer than in spring, at 1,835.96, primarily due to the increased total load, though the notable solar contribution helps offset the cost. The reserve cost also rises to 5.13, possibly due to the variability in solar generation during the day. Finally, the battery discharges to help meet the load, particularly during low solar hours.

In fall, Fig. 3d depicts solar generation decreasing compared to summer but still providing enough energy during midday (between 10:00 and 13:00). According to Table 2, max solar capacity is 6.34 MW ($\sim$ 52%), and max Ng supplies 5.29 MW ($\sim$ 43%). Generation costs decrease to 1,619.4 due to reduced demand (120.07 MWh). Although the expected total load and max capacities are similar to spring, reserve costs at 4.49 indicate lower uncertainty than in summer but higher than in spring.

In conclusion, solar energy reduces the use of conventional energy, especially in spring and summer. However, reserves remain essential year-round, ensuring system reliability by providing backup during periods of low solar generation or increased demand. Their importance is most evident in winter and fall when solar output is lower and demand for conventional generation is higher.

Importance of Reserves. We consider four cases for operational cost analysis to illustrate the importance of reserves:

- Case A: Solar production is perfectly known. We mean, there is a deterministic solar generation.
- Case B: Solar generation is uncertain in keeping with the three scenarios.
- Case C: Security-constrained. Solar production is uncertain as in case B, and there is a probability (6%) contingency on a transmission line (L3).
- Case D: Solar generation is removed. Therefore, the load is supplied by natural gas.

We focus only on the results for the four cases during the summer since the explanation remains consistent across seasons. Figure 4 compares the generation costs and reserve requirements of the four cases analyzed. We observe that in Case A, where solar production is deterministic (perfectly known), no reserves are needed, as indicated by the 0 value. With uncertain solar generation, Case B shows increased reserve costs (5.13), highlighting the need for reserves to manage variability. In Case C, the added transmission line contingency (6% probability) reduces reserves to 3.48 due to additional risk management mechanisms. Finally, in Case D, solar generation is removed, requiring full reliance on Ng. Again, no reserves are needed as the system is fully predictable. However, the operational cost is the highest among the cases.

Therefore, increased uncertainty in solar generation directly raises the operational risk for the power system, which is reflected in the need for reserves to

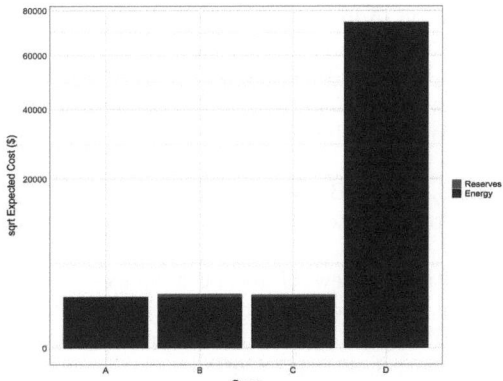

Fig. 4. Illustration of the expected cost breakdown for the four cases analyzed in the summer of 2022.

mitigate solar variability [16]. When solar generation is uncertain or contingencies arise, reserves are essential for ensuring energy supply reliability. In contrast, scenarios with deterministic solar generation or total dependence on natural gas do not require reserves due to their predictability, resulting in lower operational risk.

5 Conclusions

Reserves represent a risk factor in load dispatch because, although load dispatch is based on predictions and models, the actual behavior of the system is uncertain and can vary. Reserves are the safety net that allows the electrical system to adapt to unforeseen changes and avoid failures. Hence, if these reserves are inadequate or poorly managed, the risk of interruptions and cost overruns could increase significantly [18].

Optimal dispatch must balance the need to generate enough energy to meet demand and have enough reserves to mitigate unexpected events, minimizing operational and financial risks. In future work, we will explore sampling methods to extend the analysis beyond a single year because stratified, random, or seasonal sampling, as suggested by [6], could better reflect variability while balancing accuracy and efficiency, improving reserve management in multi-year scenarios.

Acknowledgements. This work was supported by the Advanced Research Projects Agency-Energy (ARPA-E), U.S. Department of Energy, under Grant DE-AR0001277. We sincerely thank PITA XXVI for Award PIT-24-22 and team PPL.

References

1. U.S. Energy Information Administration. Open data - API dashboard (2024). https://www.eia.gov/opendata/
2. Baldwin, C.J., Dale, K.M., Dittrich, R.F.: A study of the economic shutdown of generating units in daily dispatch. Power Apparatus and Systems, Part III. Transactions of the American Institute of Electrical Engineers **78**(4), 1272 –1282 (1959)
3. Bessa, R., Moreira, C., Silva, B., Matos: Handling Renewable Energy Variability and Uncertainty in Power System Operation, chapter 1, pp. 1–26. John Wiley & Sons, Ltd. (2019)
4. Capitanescu, F.: Critical review of recent advances and further developments needed in AC optimal power flow. Electric Power Syst. Res. **136**, 57–68 (2016)
5. Carpentier, J.: Contribution a l'etude du dispatching economico. Bull. Societe Francaise des Electriciens **3**, 431–447 (1962)
6. Chen, Y., Xu, J.: Solar and wind power data from the Chinese state grid renewable energy generation forecasting competition. Sci. Data **9**, 1–12 (2022)
7. Hungerford, Z., Bruce, A., MacGill, I.: The value of flexible load in power systems with high renewable energy penetration. Energy **188**, 115960 (2019)

8. Lamadrid, A.J., et al.: Using the matpower optimal scheduling tool to test power system operation methodologies under uncertainty. IEEE Trans. Sustain. Energy **10**(3), 1280–1289 (2019)
9. LG&E and KU. E.W.: Brown Solar Facility historical data (2024). https://lge-ku.com/live-solar-generation/historical-data
10. Integrating Renewables in Electricity Markets. ISORMS, vol. 205. Springer, Boston, MA (2014). https://doi.org/10.1007/978-1-4614-9411-9
11. Mégel, O., Mathieu, J.L., Andersson, G.: Hybrid stochastic-deterministic multi-period dc optimal power flow. IEEE Trans. Power Syst. **32**(5), 3934–3945 (2017)
12. Newell, R., Raimi, D, Villanueva, S.: Prest B. Global energy outlook 2021: Pathways from paris (2021)
13. Nycander, E., Söder, L.: Comparison of stochastic and deterministic security constrained optimal power flow under varying outage probabilities. In: 2019 IEEE Milan PowerTech, pp. 1–6 (2019)
14. Ortega-Vazquez, M.A., Kirschen, D.S.: Estimating the spinning reserve requirements in systems with significant wind power generation penetration. IEEE Trans. Power Syst. **24**(1), 114–124 (2009)
15. Sharf, M., Romm, I., Palman, M., Zelazo, D., Cukurel, B.: Economic dispatch of a single micro gas turbine under chp operation with uncertain demands. Appl. Energy **309**, 1–13 (2022)
16. Sun, B., et al.: An effective spinning reserve allocation method considering operational reliability with multi-uncertainties. IEEE Trans. Power Syst. **39**(1), 1568–1581 (2023)
17. Tsai, C-H.: Operating reserves in the three most windy U.S. power markets: a technical review. Renew. Sustain. Energy Rev., **135**, 1–20 (2021)
18. van Stiphout, A., De Vos, K., Deconinck, G.: The impact of operating reserves on investment planning of renewable power systems. IEEE Trans. Power Syst. **32**(1), 378–388 (2017)
19. J Wood, A., F Wollenberg, B., B Sheblé, G.: Power generation, operation, and control. John Wiley & Sons (2013)
20. Zheng, Q.P., Wang, J., Liu, A.L.: Stochastic optimization for unit commitment; a review. IEEE Trans. Power Syst. **30**(4), 1913–1924 (2015)
21. Zimmerman, R.D., E Murillo-Sánchez, C.: Matpower optimal scheduling tool most 1.3. user's manual (2024). https://matpower.org/docs/MOST-manual.pdf

Smart Energy Management System with Individual Load Monitoring

A. Alex, Jayarama Pradeep, T. S. Aiswarya, N. Harini, and Nikith Jude Serrao[✉]

Department of Electrical and Electronics Engineering, St. Joseph's College of Engineering, Chennai, India
`hodeeestaffaffairs@stjosephs.ac.in` , `nikithserrao03@gmail.com`

Abstract. As household energy costs rise, consumers need intelligent solutions to monitor and optimize electricity usage. This paper presents a smart IoT-based energy management system aimed at enabling real-time tracking of individual appliances through an intuitive mobile app, web dashboard, Short Message Service (SMS), and offline interface. The system allows users to view detailed usage trends, perform datalogging, set custom power thresholds for devices, and establish cost limits to prevent budget overruns. It provides remote control capabilities via app, web, or SMS—even without internet—helping households identify wasteful consumption, receive automatic alerts during excess usage, and manage devices proactively. By combining granular energy insights with flexible control options, the system supports reduction of electricity bills, prevention of appliance overload, and encouragement of sustainable energy habits. Considering India's 294 million households, even a modest conservation of 1 unit per home could result in a nationwide saving of 294 million units daily, highlighting the system's potential contribution to India's sustainable development goals and energy conservation efforts.

Keywords: IoT · Energy Monitoring System · Energy Conservation · Wireless Control · Multi-platform Alerts

1 Introduction

India's rising energy demands reveal a major issue: inefficient electricity use, especially in the residential sector. Households consume 24% of the nation's electricity (Fig. 1), yet most users are unaware of their energy waste. Inefficient habits—like leaving lights on, running appliances during peak hours, or keeping electronics in standby—stem from limited awareness and lack of real-time usage visibility. This disconnect between energy supply and informed consumption leads to unchecked wastage, straining infrastructure and increasing costs for both users and providers.

Our research addresses this knowledge gap through an intelligent monitoring system that:

- Educates users by making energy wastage visible in real-time
- Identifies inefficient usage patterns during non-productive hours
- Promotes behavioural change through actionable insights
- Prevents unnecessary consumption via smart threshold alerts

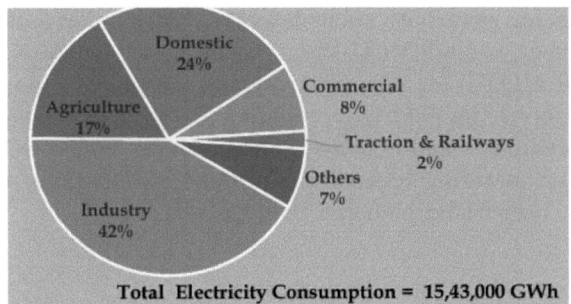

Fig. 1. Consumption of Electricity by Sectors in India during 2023-24

The solution empowers consumers with information instead of enforcing restrictions. By revealing when and where wastage occurs—such as appliances left on standby—it promotes awareness and voluntary conservation. This people-centric approach is a vital step toward sustainable energy management. When users understand their consumption patterns and receive timely feedback, they become active participants in conservation rather than passive bill payers. Such informed usage helps optimize existing energy resources and meet growing demands through awareness and education, not just infrastructure. This work presents an open-source smart building automation setup with affordable hardware, making it accessible and scalable for residential use.

2 Literature Survey

The paper proposed by India Ratings and Research (Ind-Ra) [1] in 2024 projects a 5.5% surge in electricity consumption in FY 2025, primarily driven by rising incomes, rapid urbanization, and extreme weather conditions. This highlights the urgent need for effective energy management strategies to meet demand while minimizing environmental impact. According to the India Energy Outlook 2021 by the International Energy Agency (IEA) [2], India is expected to become the world's third-largest energy consumer by 2030, overtaking the European Union. In response to this challenge, recent advancements in IoT-based energy monitoring systems have shown considerable promise. Chella Santhosh and S.V. Aswin Kumer [3] introduced a GSM-enabled smart meter for real-time alerts and energy data transmission. Shishir Muralidhara and Niharika Hegde [4] proposed a low-cost Arduino-based Wi-Fi solution for appliance-level monitoring. M. Prathik and K. Anitha [5] integrated GSM for alerts on excessive power usage and outages, while Bibek Kanti Barman and Shiv Nath Yadav [6] developed a cloud-based ESP8266 system for monitoring and theft detection. B. Sahani [7] added SMS alerts and monthly usage reports to an Arduino meter, and G. Harsh and V. Preethi [8] used Zigbee and GSM for prepaid/postpaid billing with remote access. R. Tiwari and S. Joshi [9] implemented an ESP32-Firebase solution for web-based smart metering, and Kedi Zheng et al. [10] applied clustering techniques for electricity theft detection. A. Kumar and P. Sharma [11] created a cost-effective NodeMCU-Blynk based meter, while N. Srivastava and K. Das [12] used MQTT for secure data transmission. M. Jain and A. Mishra [13] further advanced the field by combining AI with IoT meters for anomaly detection and predictive maintenance. These studies collectively highlight the evolution of smart metering technologies toward automation, real-time analytics, and efficient, user-friendly energy management.

2.1 Limitations of the Existing System

Despite advancements, a key gap remains: most existing systems lack integrated individual appliance-level monitoring with both online and offline control in a single solution. This fragmentation limits real-time energy management, especially where internet access is unreliable. A unified approach combining monitoring, control, and alerts across platforms can greatly enhance the effectiveness of smart energy systems in meeting India's rising energy demands.

Few other issues with the existing systems are:

- They only measure and calculate the total power consumed and not the individual power consumed by each load.
- Does not support per-appliance cost tracking or budget controls
- The system does not give any multi-platform alerts when the load is misbehaving.
- They do not log data for extended period. Thus, depriving users of viewing their long-term usage.

3 Proposed System

The proposed system section deals with the model and block diagram of the proposed system.

3.1 Model of the Proposed System

The proposed system (Fig. 2) offers an intuitive home energy management solution that monitors and controls individual loads like Load 1 and Load 2 (Fig. 3) through a user-friendly interface. It continuously tracks each appliance's power consumption and analyzes usage trends to identify inefficiencies. Key parameters—voltage, current, and power—are visualized in real-time on accessible dashboards. When thresholds are exceeded or irregularities occur, users are alerted via multiple channels. This proactive monitoring helps prevent equipment damage, optimize energy use, and reduce electricity bills.

Users enjoy flexible control options including; Web portal access, Mobile application interface, SMS-based commands and Manual override capability

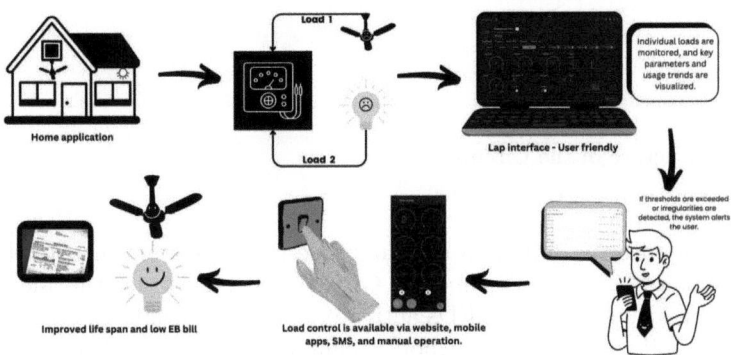

Fig. 2. Block Diagram of the Circuit

The system's dual-interface design (combining digital and physical access points) (Fig. 4) ensures reliable operation for all users regardless of technical proficiency. By making energy consumption visible and controllable through these multiple touchpoints, the solution effectively bridges the gap between awareness and action in household energy management.

3.2 Workflow

The system implements an energy monitoring and control process (Fig. 5) through a structured workflow. It begins with device control, allowing users to toggle appliances ON/OFF via both online (web/mobile app) and offline (SMS/manual) interfaces, ensuring uninterrupted operation. Monitoring starts with continuous voltage measurement, displayed on a real-time gauge with threshold markers. If limits are exceeded, the gauge turns red, and email alerts notify users of voltage instability.

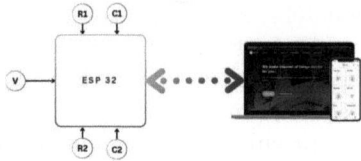

Fig. 4. Overview of Interface

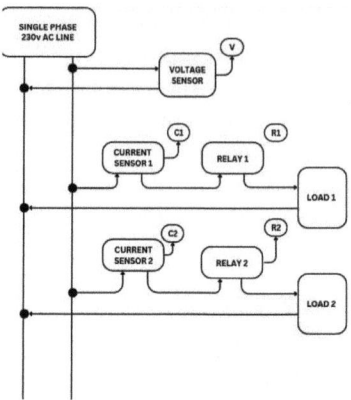

Fig. 3. Structure of the Circuit

Current monitoring follows a similar process. The system measures and displays current with visual thresholds. On detecting a surge, the alert system triggers: the gauge turns red, LEDs activate, and notifications are sent via SMS, email, and mobile app. If auto-turnoff is enabled, the system disconnects power to the affected device to avoid hazards.

Power consumption is continuously calculated and displayed through dynamic gauges, giving users real-time insights into energy usage. The system tracks each device's contribution to the electricity bill, enabling accurate cost attribution. It also presents unit consumption per appliance to help identify energy-intensive devices and optimize usage. All data is logged to Google Sheets for detailed tracking. This workflow integrates real-time monitoring, intelligent alerts, and user-configurable controls to support efficient energy management and equipment protection.

3.3 Hardware Setup

The system (Fig. 6) uses an ESP32 microcontroller for real-time monitoring and wireless communication, chosen for its built-in Wi-Fi/Bluetooth and dual-core processing. Current is measured using the ACS712 (20A) Hall-effect sensor, offering safe and accurate isolated sensing. Voltage is monitored via the ZMPT101B module, which provides precise AC mains measurement with isolation. The setup also includes JQC-3FC relays for safe switching, a 16 × 2 LCD for local display, and a SIM800C GSM module for SMS alerts without internet. These components together form a robust and cost-effective smart energy monitoring solution.

The ESP32 was selected over alternatives like Arduino due to its superior processing power and built-in wireless capabilities. The ACS712 (20A) offers better safety and isolation than shunt resistors, while the ZMPT101B provides more accurate AC voltage measurement than basic voltage dividers. This

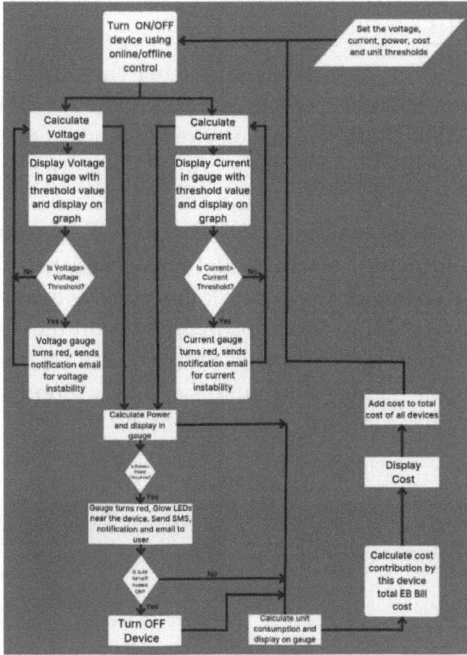

Fig. 5. Flow Chart of the Proposed System

combination delivers reliable performance for household energy monitoring while keeping costs reasonable. The GSM module adds crucial offline functionality, making the system practical for areas with unstable internet.

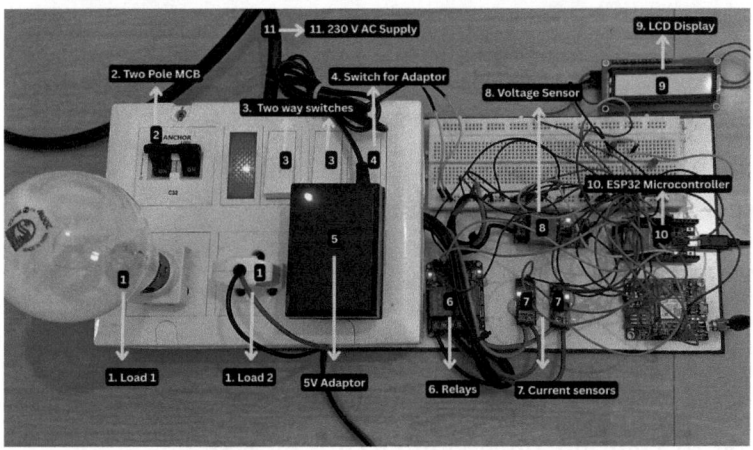

Fig. 6. Hardware Setup of the System

3.4 Software Setup

The system's software (Fig. 7) is developed using the Arduino IDE for programming the ESP32 microcontroller. The firmware handles real-time data acquisition from ACS712 and ZMPT101B sensors, performs power calculations, and implements control logic for device switching. A key feature includes per-appliance cost calculation, helping users understand each device's contribution to their electricity bill. For user interaction, the Blynk IoT platform is integrated to provide real-time monitoring, alerts, and remote control via a mobile app. A comprehensive web dashboard visualizes long-term usage trends through interactive graphs and charts. Gmail integration enables online alerts, while the GSM module ensures SMS-based alerts during internet outages. Google Sheets logging provides extended usage history and analysis. The system thus offers real-time energy insights and multi-platform control access.

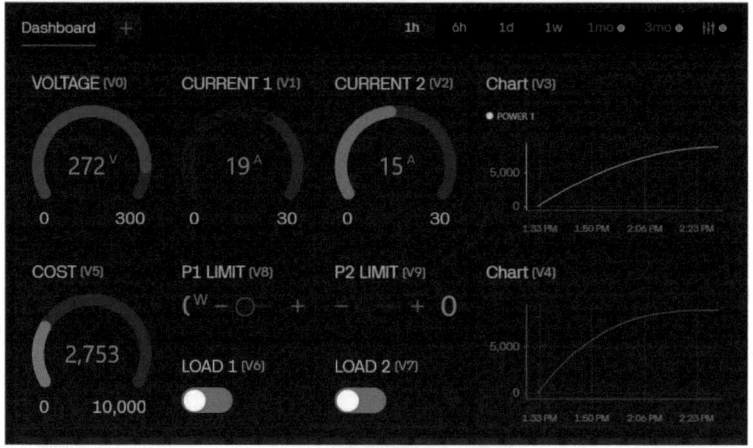

Fig. 7. Blynk Interface

4 Working of the Proposed Model

1. Raw Data Acquisition:
The ACS712 sensors measure instantaneous current drawn by each connected device (tested with two 200W bulbs) on the 230V AC line, outputting an analog voltage proportional to the current. The ZMPT101B sensors similarly measure AC voltage and provide a scaled-down analog signal.

2. Analog to Digital Conversion (ADC) by ESP32:
Analog voltage signals from the current and voltage sensors are fed into the ESP32's 12-bit SAR ADC pins, each capable of 4096 digital levels. With multiple

ADC channels, the ESP32 supports simultaneous or multiplexed readings. It averages five readings per second per sensor to minimize noise and fluctuations.

3. Digital Value to Voltage and Current Calculation

- The ESP32 converts the averaged digital readings from the ADCs back into voltage values. The relationship depends on the ADC's reference voltage (typically 3.3V on the ESP32):
  Sensor Voltage (V) = (Averaged Digital Reading/4095) × Reference Voltage (V)
- **Current Calculation:** The current drawn by a device is calculated from the ACS712 sensor's output voltage using its sensitivity (provided in mV/A in the sensor's datasheet) and the zero-current offset voltage (typically half of the sensor's supply voltage):
  Current (A) = (Sensor Voltage (V) − Zero Current Voltage (V))/Sensitivity (V/A)
- **Voltage Calculation:** The AC line voltage is derived from the ZMPT101B sensor's output using a calibration factor based on specifications and experimental tuning, followed by RMS calculation from the sampled data.

4. Data Processing and Power Calculation:

- The ESP32 processes the calculated RMS voltage and current values for each connected device.
- The instantaneous power consumed by each device is calculated as:
  Power (W) = RMS Voltage (V)×RMS Current (A)×Power Factor
- The power factor for each device is also calculated using zero crossing method to provide a more accurate estimate of real power consumption.

5. Displaying Data on the 16×2 **LCD:** The ESP32 sends real-time voltage, current, and power values to the 16×2 LCD for immediate local monitoring. It uses appropriate libraries based on the LCD interface, such as LiquidCrystal for parallel or I^2C libraries for serial communication.

6. Data Transmission to Blynk Cloud: The ESP32 connects to the internet via Wi-Fi and uses the Blynk library to establish a secure connection with the Blynk cloud. It transmits calculated RMS voltage, current, power, and cost values for each device, mapped to virtual pins in the Blynk app. These values are visualized in real-time on the mobile and web interfaces using gauges and interactive charts.

7. Threshold Monitoring and Notifications: The Blynk software continuously checks real-time voltage and current values against user-defined thresholds (overcurrent, overvoltage, undervoltage). When a threshold is breached, the corresponding gauge in the app turns red, and the ESP32 sends notifications via email, SMS (through the GSM module), and the Blynk app. LED indicators near the devices also provide local visual alerts.

8. Remote Control via Blynk App/Website: Users can control auto cutoff and turn-on functionalities through the Blynk app or website. When a command is sent, the Blynk cloud relays it to the ESP32, which activates a relay via its GPIO pins to switch the corresponding device ON or OFF. Threshold limits can also be configured directly within the Blynk interface.

9. Offline Control via SMS (using GSM Module): The GSM module connected to the ESP32 enables device control without internet access. Users can send specific SMS commands to the system's SIM card, which the ESP32 parses to operate the relays and turn devices ON or OFF.

10. Data Logging: Periodically or upon specific events, the ESP32 sends processed voltage, current, power, energy, and cost data to a Google Sheet using HTTP requests directed to a Google Apps Script web app. This enables the creation of a historical energy consumption database.

11. Adaptability for Different Electricity Tariffs: Depending on where the system is integrated, that location specific tariffs are used for cost calculations for each device. Thus, it makes the system adaptable for consumers across various geographical locations ensuring proper calculations are performed. Currently Tamil Nadu tariff has been implemented in the device.

Category	Slab	Subsidy/Unit
Domestic (IA)	**Upto 500 units** 0 – 100 units (bimonthly)	Rs.4.80/unit.
	101 – 200 units (bimonthly)	Rs.2.45/unit.
	201-300 units	Rs.0.10/unit
	301-400 units	Rs. 0.10/unit
	401-500 units	Rs. 0.15/unit
	Above 500 units 0-100 units (bimonthly)	Rs.4.80/unit.
	101-200	Rs.0.10/unit
	201-300	Rs.0.10/unit
	301-400	Rs.0.10/unit
	401-500	Rs. 0.15/unit
	501-600	Rs. 0.15/unit
	601-800	Rs. 0.20/unit
	801-1000	Rs. 0.20/unit
	Above 1000	Rs. 0.25/unit

Fig. 8. Tamilnadu Tarrif

5 Results and Discussions

The system successfully performed real-time monitoring, control, alerts, and data logging using low-cost components, and incorporated nudging methods such as visual alerts and per-appliance cost feedback to encourage energy-conscious behaviour.

5.1 Hardware Implementation

The physical prototype (Fig. 6) shows the complete hardware setup comprising:

- ESP32 microcontroller with sensor connections
- Properly installed ACS712 and ZMPT101B sensors
- Relay modules for load control
- LCD display for local monitoring
- GSM module for offline communication
- All components remained stable during continuous 72-hour operation without overheating or performance degradation.

5.2 Real-Time Monitoring Interface

The Blynk interface provided consistent real-time monitoring:

- Live device status (ON/OFF)
- Instantaneous parameter updates (voltage, current, power)
- Color-changing gauges that turned red during threshold violations (Fig. 9)
- Smooth graphical trends of usage patterns

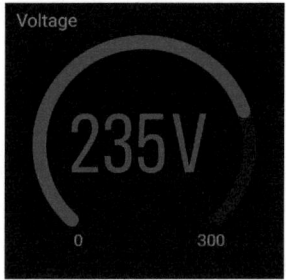

Fig. 9. Gauge turns red when threshold is crossed (Color figure online)

5.3 Alert System Performance

The multi-channel notification system performed reliably:

- Immediate Gmail alerts received for all threshold crossings (Fig. 10)
- Visual indicators (gauge color change, LCD alerts) activated consistently
- No missed alerts during the testing period

Fig. 10. Gmail Alerts

5.4 Data Logging and Analysis

The system maintained accurate historical records:

- Google Sheets automatically updated with timestamped entries (Fig. 11)
- Usage trends clearly visible in weekly/monthly views (Fig. 8)
- No data loss observed during network transitions
- Real-time logging of all parameters

Energy Management							
Date	Time	Volt	Cur1*	Cur2	Pow1	Pow2	
5/1/2025	11:57:54 PM	223.54	0.8	0	178.832	0	
5/1/2025	11:58:25 PM	222.99	0.79	0	176.1621	0	
5/1/2025	11:58:47 PM	225.26	0.81	0	182.4606	0	
5/1/2025	23:59:09	221.56	0.78	0	172.8168	0	
5/1/2025	23:59:31	221.54	0.77	0	170.5858	0	
5/1/2025	23:59:51	217.26	0.79	0	171.6354	0	
5/2/2025	0:00:10	221.38	0.8	0	177.104	0	
5/2/2025	0:00:30	221.76	0.78	0	172.9728	0	

Fig. 11. Data-logging in Google Sheets

5.5 Control System Operation

Load control functionality worked as intended (Fig. 12, 13):

- Successful ON/OFF switching via both app and SMS
- Immediate response to commands (<2 s for app, <5 s for SMS)

Fig. 12. SMS alerts

Fig. 13. Relay Control

5.6 User Experience

The system delivered intuitive monitoring through (Fig. 14):

- Clear mobile interface showing all critical parameters
- Comprehensive web dashboard with historical data
- Instant visual feedback via LCD display (Fig. 15)
- Multiple control options (app, web, SMS)

The collected evidence demonstrates that the system meets all design objectives, providing:

- Accurate real-time monitoring
- Reliable alert mechanisms
- Flexible control options
- Comprehensive data logging
- Seamless dual-mode operation

This successful validation paves the way for real-world deployment in residential and small-scale industrial settings (Figs. 15, 16, 17 and 18).

Fig. 14. Offline LCD Display

Fig. 15. Web Interface when Off

Fig. 16. Web Interface when On

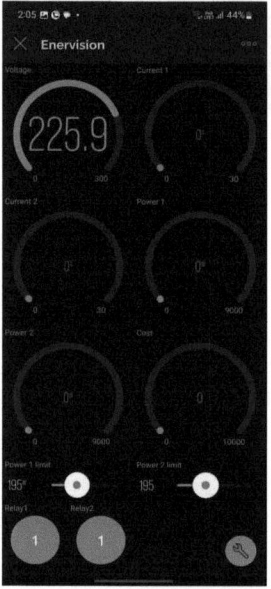

Fig. 17. Mobile Interface when Off

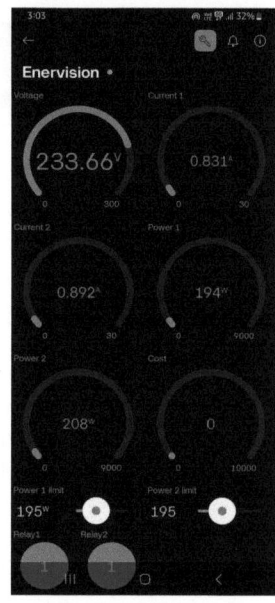

Fig. 18. Mobile Interface when On

5.7 Total Cost Estimation

While products like TP-Link Tapo P110, Wemo Insight, and Sonoff POW Elite offer smart control features, they are limited to single-device monitoring and typically cost up to Rs.5,000, making them less suitable for multi-load, low-cost residential applications compared to the proposed system which has a cost of approximately Rs.1800 (Fig. 19)

Component	Model	Quantity	Approx. Cost (INR)
ESP32 microcontroller	ESP32 DevKit	1	₹300
Current Sensor	ACS712 (20A)	2	₹200
Voltage Sensor	ZMPT101B	1	₹150
GSM Module	SIM800C	1	₹450
Relay Module	JQC-3FC	2	₹150
LCD Display (16x2)	I2C Compatible	1	₹120
Miscellaneous (PCB, casing, wiring)	-	-	₹200
Total Estimated Cost			₹1,570 – ₹1,800

Fig. 19. Cost Estimation

6 Conclusion

The developed energy monitoring system—with both hardware and software components fully operational—provides a comprehensive solution for efficient electricity management. By enabling real-time, appliance-level tracking with intelligent alerts and controls, this system empowers users to significantly reduce energy wastage. Given India's massive residential sector, widespread adoption of this technology could lead to substantial conservation of non-renewable resources while lowering household electricity costs. The system's proven effectiveness makes it an essential tool for sustainable energy management that should be implemented across all consumer levels to optimize India's power utilization. It thus offers a complete solution to individual and global energy issues by reducing energy costs and promoting sustainable energy usage.

Disclosure of Interests. The authors declare that they have no conflict of interest.

References

1. India Ratings and Research (Ind-Ra). Electricity Consumption Report (2024)
2. International Energy Agency (IEA), India Energy Outlook 2021
3. Santhosh, C., Aswin Kumer, S.V.: IoT-Based Smart Energy Meter Using GSM. J. Energy Syst. (2023)
4. Muralidhara, S., Hegde, N.: Appliance-Level Energy Monitoring with IoT. IEEE Internet Things J. (2022)
5. Prathik, M., Anitha, K.: Arduino-GSM smart meter for energy optimization. Energy Eng. (2023)
6. Barman, B.K., Yadav, S.N.: Cloud-Based Real-Time Energy Monitoring. Sustainable Energy Technologies (2024)
7. Sahani, B.: Arduino-Based Smart Meter with SMS
8. Alerts, Journal of Power Electronics (2023). Harsh, G., Preethi, V.: Zigbee-Enabled Smart Energy Meter. Renewable Energy Focus (2024)

9. Tiwari, R., Joshi, S.: Web-Based Smart Meter Using Firebase. In: Proc. Smart Grid Conf. (2023)
10. Zheng, K., Chen, Q., Wang, Y., Kang, C., Xia, Q.: Data-driven electricity theft detection, arXiv preprint, arXiv:2411.06649, November 2024
11. Kumar, A., Sharma, P.: Cost-Effective Smart Meter with NodeMCU. Int. J. Eng. Res. Technol. (IJERT) (2023)
12. Srivastava, N., Das, K.: MQTT-based energy metering system. IEEE Trans. Internet Things (2023)
13. Jain, M., Mishra, A.: AI for anomaly detection in smart meters. Procedia Comput. Sci. (2023)
14. Zheng, K., Chen, Q., Wang, Y., Kang, C., Xia, Q.: A combined data-driven approach for electricity theft detection using maximum information coefficient and clustering techniques. arXiv preprint, arXiv:2411.06649, November 2024
15. M. Aashik S., Abishlal, A.N.S., Abinayaa, A.S.T., Benedict, J., Pradeep, J.: IoT-Based Energy Monitoring and Controlling System Using ESP32 Microcontroller. In: E3S Web Conf., vol. 405, p. 02013 (2023)

Smart Building Systems and Semantic Data Integration

Towards a Taxonomy for Application of Machine Learning and Artificial Intelligence in Building and District Energy Management Systems

Klaus Lichtenegger[1,2](✉) [iD], Florian Ahammer[1,2] [iD], Fabian Schopper[2,3] [iD], Daniel Muschick[1] [iD], and Markus Gölles[1] [iD]

[1] BEST – Bioenergy and Sustainable Technologies GmbH, Inffeldgasse 21b, Graz 8010, Austria
{klaus.lichtenegger,markus.goelles}@best-research.eu

[2] FH JOANNEUM – University of Applied Sciences, Institute Business Informatics und Data Science, Eckertstraße 30i, Graz 8020, Austria
klaus.lichtenegger@fh-joanneum.at

[3] Graz University of Technology, Institute of Software Engineering and Artificial Intelligence, Inffeldgasse 16b, Graz 8010, Austria

Abstract. Building and district energy management increasingly requires advanced control strategies. For several tasks that arise, Machine Learning (ML) and Artificial Intelligence (AI) have found widespread application, but often the interaction with existing elements and the integration into the productive system are done in a rather unsystematic way. Thus, one faces problems concerning interface design, data requirements and reliability/trustworthiness. In order to improve this situation, we outline the general control structure of such systems, review key concepts from ML/AI and discuss approaches for conventional high-level control. This is followed by a literature review on ML/AI applications for energy management. Based on the systematics and the literature findings, we establish a taxonomy for the integration of ML/AI methods for energy management, which leads as a main result to a comprehensive guide for such applications, taking into account both characteristics of the method and the affected elements of the system. This is supplemented by a quick guideline for choice of an appropriate method and for subsequent evaluation. The target readership are control engineers who would like to get a systematic overview of ways to integrate ML/AI methods in their work, and data scientists who want to get a better understanding for main tasks and challenges for applying their tools for control tasks.

Keywords: Taxonomy · Control · Energy Management · Buildings · Districts · Optimization · Machine Learning · Artificial Intelligence

1 Introduction

1.1 Buildings and Districts in the Energy System

Buildings are responsible for 33 % of our final energy consumption, [38], but also have increasing potential to contribute to the decentral generation of energy. Currently, limited grid transfer capacities and lack of sufficient long-term storage in our energy system severely restrict the possibilities for decentralized energy generation.

Fortunately, parts of the current lack of proper hardware can be compensated by software solutions like intelligent energy management. Thus, the *smart operation* of buildings and interconnected buildings, like residential estates, city quarters and districts, has received increasing attention. For the *high-level control* tasks that arise, approaches from traditional control engineering are increasingly supplemented or replaced by systematic optimization-based approaches or by methods from Machine Learning (ML) and Artificial Intelligence (AI).

1.2 Missing Systematics for ML/AL in Energy Systems

While many companies claim to offer AI-based solutions, few give details on the models they use. Even in research, there is often some confusion about reasonable ways to apply ML and AI, about the requirements concerning data and domain expertise and about evaluation of performance. This situation has been made worse by AI becoming quite "fashionable", a development fueled first by the Deep Learning revolution (which started around 2012 with AlexNet for image recognition, [25], and Word2Vec for Natural Language Processing, NLP, [27]) and later by the advent of Large Language Models (LLMs), which became particularly popular by the release of Chat-GPT in 2022.

This development has led to project proposals that include AI methods in order to increase the chance for funding, regardless of whether these methods actually make sense for the task at hand and with often little *systematic* evaluation of the method. Thus, while ML and AI techniques are increasingly common, different approaches are hard to compare, and potential synergies are yet under-explored. The main objective of this article is to improve this situation by establishing a taxonomy for the integration of ML/AI methods for energy management and a resulting guideline/checklist.

1.3 Structure of This Article

In Sect. 2 we examine the general structure of control and information flow in building/district energy systems and review some key terms from ML and AI. In Sect. 3, we review three current popular approaches to high-level control, and in Sect. 4, we present an overview of current applications of ML/AI in building and district energy management. As the original contribution, in Sect. 5, in response to the issues described in Sect. 1.2, we propose a systematic approach for integration of ML/AI in high-level control. This leads to a taxonomy and, in Sect. 6, to a set of criteria for choosing and evaluating methods.

2 Control Structure and Clarification of Key Terms

In Sect. 2.1 we discuss the main levels of control and the corresponding information flow, in Sect. 2.2 we briefly review key terms of Machine Learning (ML) and Artificial Intelligence (AI). The discussion can of course only give a rough overview; details on basic control engineering can be found e.g. in [34], on ML and AI e.g. in [8,9,20,29,30].

2.1 Levels of Control and Information Flow

For control tasks, it usually makes sense to distinguish between two levels:

- *Low-level control* (also termed *component-level control* or *subordinate control*) is the control of a single technological device or transmission system. The typical objective is to keep some target quantities at or at least close to prescribed values, the *set points*. A typical and important example is the control of temperature in a room.
  This type of control is often realized with simple rules (like a two-point controller that lead to a hysteresis) or linear methods (like PID controllers with corrections proportional to the error itself, to its integral and to its derivative), although various superior methods exist, [2]. Also, when serious problems during operation occur, emergency measures to prevent further damage are typically initiated and handled by the low-level control.
- *High-level control* (also termed *system-level control*, *supervisory control* or *superordinate control*, often also referred to as *energy management system*, EMS, though this term can have a broader meaning, see ISO 50001) operates on top of the low-level control. Its task is to create a schedule of set points that optimizes the operation of the whole system, usually also taking into account the expected near future. Classical rule-based and more sophisticated optimization-based approaches for this task are discussed in Sect. 3.

The simplified structure of a typical building/district energy system with both levels control is illustrated in Fig. 1. The main strands of information flow are also summarized in Table 1.

Table 1. Main strands of information flow in a system with high- and low-level control

information type	from	to	sampling rate
measurements	physical system	pre-processing	high (almost continuous)
forecasts	forecasting system	high-level control	usually discrete
processed data	pre-processing	{ subordinate control	(quasi-)continuous
		high-level control	needed only at discrete t_k
set points	high-level control	subordinate control	discrete, e.g. $\Delta t = 15$ min
actuator values	subordinate control	physical system	(quasi-)continuous

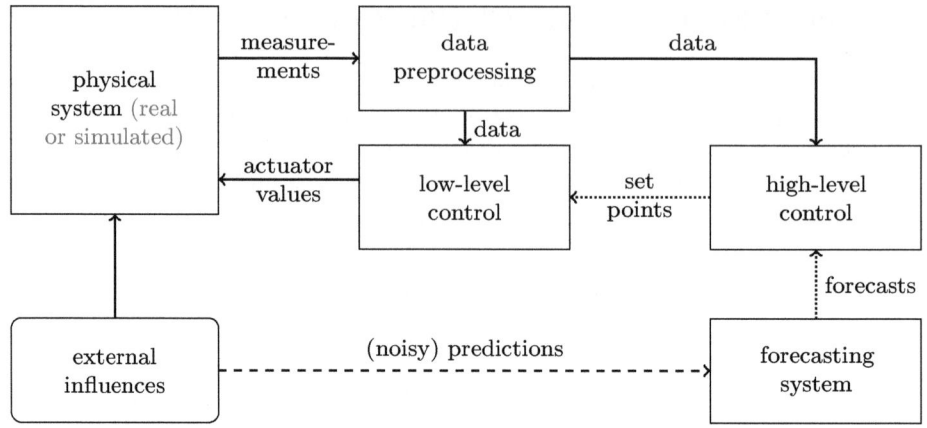

Fig. 1. Modular structure of a building or district energy system

2.2 Machine Learning and Artificial Intelligence Some Key Terms

Machine Learning (ML). In its broadest sense, ML makes use of computers to extract relevant information from data and to allow for predictions or decisions based on it. Since such a broad definition would even include simple statistical analysis methods, like linear or logistic regression, it is often narrowed down to the use of somehow advanced models or on methods that repeatedly update with new data. Still, the border of ML to traditional statistics and to system- and information-theoretic approaches like sensor fusion and Kalman filtering is quite blurred, [13,36].

Essentially, one distinguishes three basic types of ML, [40]:

- *Supervised Learning*: The model learns to predict values for output variables (continuous ones for regression tasks, discrete ones for classification tasks) depending on input *features*, i.e. descriptive variables or combinations thereof. The training is usually based on historic data, often expanded by data augmentation techniques. Due to its similarity traditional statistical tasks, supervised learning is sometimes mocked as "glorified curve fitting".
- *Unsupervised Learning*: For this type of learning, no target variable is given. Instead, one aims at finding patterns in data, e.g. by identifying clusters or by discovering particularly useful combinations of variables that lead to dimensionally reduced representations.
- *Reinforcement Learning*: Instead of historic data, this branch of machine uses an *environment* (usually some simulation model) to learn a *policy*, i.e. a strategy for choosing actions, given the state of the environment. In the training process, the agent learns to maximize some suitably defined *reward function*, [41].

In addition to and beyond those three basic types, there exist intermediate and mixed approaches, most notably:

– *Semi-supervised Learning*: While the task is the same as for supervised learning (regression or classification), only part of the training data has labels for the target variable that is to be predicted. The unlabeled data points can still be used to improve the model, [29, Sec. 19.3].
 – *Self-supervised Learning*: For some tasks, it makes sense to artificially convert unsupervised learning problems to supervised ones by *masking* certain variables that have to be predicted. Such approaches have been particularly successful in the Natural Language Processing, e.g. by training a model to predict masked words.
 – *Data Imputation*: In many cases, the imputation of missing data can be posed as a supervised learning problem with varying target variables. One can even regard many problems in supervised learning as a special case of the general data imputation task.
 – *Imitation Learning*: Often, reinforcement learning can be significantly accelerated and improved, if some examples for high-quality policies are provided. Including such supervised elements in reinforcement learning leads to the field of *imitation learning* (also *apprenticeship learning*). If one specifically tries to learn a reward function from examples, this is called *inverse reinforcement learning*.

Artificial Intelligence (AI). In a broad sense, AI is the ability of computers to perform tasks that require some *intelligence* – which is for itself a rather fuzzy concept. The comprehension of which tasks require intelligence has evolved over time, and thus AI itself seems to be a moving target. Performing mathematical calculations, playing chess or translating texts are tasks that at some times have been regarded as requiring intelligence. By now, all these tasks can be handled quite well by computers, but one would not attribute true intelligence to them for being able to do so.

A main distinction is between *narrow* (or *weak*) AI, which is designed to solve a single problem (like playing chess or recognizing cats in images) and *broad* (or *strong*) AI, which can perform various different tasks that require intelligence. Another important distinction can be made between *generative* AI, which is designed to create new content, and *discriminative* AI, which is designed for evaluation and decision-making. Much of the current confusion concerning potential and limits of AI methods arises from missing distinction between these forms of AI, in particular by using generative AI for discriminative tasks.

While there are forms of AI that work without ML, e.g. swarm intelligence methods, based on rule-based agents, most AI methods heavily rely on ML, and often AI is just used as a more fashionable synonym for ML. But, while one can find such very broad uses of the term AI, one often also encounters a rather narrow point of view, where AI is limited just to the most recent, most popular methods (which would currently be generative LLMs).

Deep Learning. A subset of ML are techniques built on *deep* neural networks, i.e. those with many layers (at least 3, but typically > 10). Such approaches are particularly versatile, and their use often requires only little domain knowledge, since elaborate *feature engineering* can usually be circumvented. There are numerous architectures in use, including Convolutional Neural Networks (CNN), Recurrent Neural Networks (RNN, also with various extensions like LSTM), stacked Restricted Boltzmann Machines, Transformers and Sequential State Space Models (SSSM), [3,9].

Such models can easily have millions of parameters (network weights), and strategies against *overfitting* have to be used. The training usually requires large amounts of data, though often *data augmentation*, i.e. the creation of additional training data by simple transformations (rotations, flips, cropping, ...) from the original data, set can be used. Often, also *Transfer Learning* is employed, i.e. the pre-training of a model on large, but rather general data set, with subsequent training on the specific task. A specific challenge in Deep Learning is *few-shot*, *one-shot* or even *zero-shot* learning, i.e. the ability to correctly deal with classes, for which only a few, only one or even no samples are contained in the training data, [17,46].

Deep Learning can be contrasted with *Statistical Learning*, i.e. methods that are directly derived from statistical approaches (like Decision Tree Learning, Support Vector Machines and Mixture Models), and with *Shallow Learning*, i.e. neural networks with only few layers (or without explicit layer structure, but only a small number of neurons). Many statistical models can also be expressed as shallow neural networks, [3, Ch. 2].

Theory-Guided ML. While some statistical learning methods allow to some extent the integration of domain knowledge and fundamental laws (by model design and feature engineering), this is no longer possible in straightforward deep learning. There are, however, methods to also integrate information like physical laws in ML models. A promising approach are physics-informed neural networks (PINN), [37], for which the conventional loss (deviation between model prediction and ground truth) is extended with a second term that describes the violation of physical laws. Training with such an extended loss yields models that also tend to respect physical laws and thus should be able to generalize better to situations significantly different from all those observed in the training data. The performance of such models can be further improved by integration of state-based elements and corresponding leaning of event functions, [14].

3 Approaches to High-Level Control

Since the integration of ML/AI methods in high-level control is both promising and challenging, as a foundation for the subsequent discussion, we first review three main approaches to this task, namely rule-based, central optimization-based and decentral optimization-based.

3.1 Rule-Based Methods

The most basic (and most transparent) approach for superordinate control is based on expert rules. Such rules are often rather simple, based only on the current state of the system. The incorporation of forecasts, however, is possible also with rule-based approaches and will in general improve the performance, [43,48]. For increasingly complex and interacting systems, however, it is becomes hard to define rules that lead to (near-)optimal operation.

3.2 Central Optimization-Based Methods

A systematic approach to supervisory control is offered by optimization, minimizing a cost function by optimal choice of set point values of the underlying low-level controllers, such as demanded energy flows or temperature levels. The cost function typically contains operational expenses (OPEX), like electricity and fuel costs, but may also include terms for emissions and extra costs for unwanted behavior like repeatedly turning on and off boilers or heat pumps.

Optimization-based strategies require some type of model for the system and thus sound domain knowledge. Such models can be closely entwined with the solution strategy, e.g. by using piecewise affine-linear models for a mixed-integer linear programming (MILP), [22,23,28]. This approach offers high performance, at the price of limited flexibility in the modeling process.

Alternatively, one can use generic optimizers with black-box models, effectively running simulations with different sequences of actor values. This approach allows for greater flexibility concerning the models and the optimization methods, but it is less systematic and usually cannot compete in terms of performance with the integrated approach.

3.3 Distributed Optimization-Based Methods

Due to the unfavorable scaling properties of typical optimization methods, centralized optimization is often not applicable to complex systems. If a single entity is in the authority of all producers, this is an algorithmic problem, which can be addressed with methods from distributed optimization, e.g. [10].

Usually, however, in increasingly complex energy systems, one tends to encounter several (semi-)independent actors. For such energy system, local market-based interactions can be combined with individual optimization to reduce the total cost, [26]. Such an approach can be interpreted as an optimization method based on swarm intelligence, which takes advantage of the emergent behavior produced by interacting agents.

Swarm intelligence for orchestrating production and consumption can be elevated to very large systems and, by establishing energy markets, leads to time-variant tariffs that indicate when there is increased demand or a surplus of energy. A sufficiently pronounced time dependence of energy tariffs (together with a favorable design of grid transmission fees) helps to optimally use flexibility options and can even make the operation of intermediate storages as a service to the grid economically viable.

4 ML and AI for Building and District Energy Systems

ML and AI are in use in several parts of the energy sector, for various forms of renewable energy, [21], for assistance in the design of energy systems, [35] and their operation, [6]. A comprehensive bibliographic overview of essential terms is presented in [16]. We briefly review some key applications and aspects.

4.1 Anomaly Detection

Methods from unsupervised learning are suitable for detection of anomalies, which may be indications of errors and failures. One can use, for example, approaches borrowed from multivariate statistics, in particular Principal Component Analysis (PCA) and its extension to probabilistic PCA, [8, Sec. 12.2], tree-based methods like isolation forests or autoencoders as special types of neural networks.

Supervised methods can be applied to anomaly detection as well, by comparing the model output with the measured value and flagging instance with large deviations as potential anomalies. Such an approach, based on Random Forests, for solar thermal plants, has been developed in [18].

4.2 Forecasting

Accurate forecasting is crucial for efficient energy system operation and planning. It provides the basis for informed decision making in grid management, enabling optimal scheduling of generation assets, maintenance planning, and balancing of supply and demand. In modern smart grids and buildings, load forecasts help operators perform unit commitment, demand response, and peak shaving strategies to maintain reliability and cost effectiveness, [49]. Better predictions lead to more efficient resource planning, cost savings, and grid stability, [7].

Methods from traditional time series analysis (like ARMA, ARIMA and ARIMAX, [19]) are increasingly replaced by neural networks, in particular recurrent neural networks (RNN), their extensions like Long Short-Term Memory (LSTM) and, more recently, transformer models, [45]. Still, already conceptually simple adaptive methods, like a linear-regression model for each hour of the day (with possible distinction between working days and holidays), with parameters that are updated day-to-day based on measurement, are quite powerful, while at the same time computationally lean enough for implementation on almost any programmable logic controller (PLC), [33, 44].

For medium/long-term predictions, in [5], the authors demonstrate effectiveness of ML models on a city-wide scale. The results suggest that among ML models, the simpler, more interpretable ones have greater generalization capacity in long-term energy prediction.

Challenges in Energy Forecasting. Despite advances, several key challenges must be addressed to achieve consistently accurate forecasts in building and district energy systems:

1. *Overfitting Complex Models*: Advanced machine learning models, e.g. deep neural networks or ensemble boosters, are at risk of overfitting to historical data patterns, which degrades their performance on new situations. Overfitting is widely recognized as a common challenge in energy load forecasting; accordingly, solutions like cross-validation, regularization, and data augmentation are employed to improve generalization.
2. *Dependence on High-Quality, Long-Term Data*: Accurate forecasting, especially for long horizons, requires large amounts of high-quality historical data. Poor or limited data can lead to model inaccuracies. Data quality issues such as missing values, sensor errors, or changes in consumption behavior can significantly skew forecasts if not properly handled. Thus, robust preprocessing (cleaning, outlier removal, imputation) and careful data validation are necessary to maintain forecast fidelity over time, [4].
3. *Feature Relevance and Domain Knowledge*: In energy applications, there may be many candidate input features (weather variables, occupancy, calendar info, etc.), but not all features are relevant. Including extraneous or redundant inputs can confuse models and inflate computational complexity. Domain-specific knowledge is helpful in selecting meaningful features and exclude irrelevant ones.

Key Insights and Best Practices in Energy Forecasting.

1. *Neural Networks Excel at Nonlinear and Time-dependent Patterns*: Especially deep and recurrent architectures are highly effective for capturing nonlinear relationships and temporal dependencies in energy data. They often outperform classical linear models in complex scenarios, [15].
2. *Multivariate Models Outperform Univariate Models*: Incorporating relevant inputs generally improves forecast accuracy compared to using only the target variable's history. Multivariate approaches can explain variability that a univariate model would treat as random. The improved performance comes at the cost of higher complexity, so feature selection remains important, but overall, the consensus is that well-chosen external inputs boost predictive power, [24].
3. *Hybrid and Ensemble Models Show Great Promise*: No single model type is universally best for all situations or all forecast horizons. Combining models either in hybrid models (integrating different modeling techniques) or in ensemble methods (aggregating multiple models' outputs) is a powerful strategy to improve accuracy and robustness. Practitioners should consider ensemble techniques, e.g. stacking an ARIMA with a neural network, or blending multiple neural networks, especially when aiming to generalize well across different conditions, [31].
4. *Real-Time Adaptability with Advanced Architectures* Energy systems are dynamic, and the ability to adapt forecasts in real time as new data arrives is necessary. ML methods with this adaptability leads to more resilient operations, as the EMS is always using the most current expected conditions to make decisions, [7].

4.3 Surrogates and World Models

A task beyond just forecasting external influences is the modelling of system responses. While this is the traditionally the domain of white- or gray-box physical modelling, typically using differential equations, ML/AI models may, as discussed in Sect. 5.4, find some use as *surrogates*, in particular for system which are computationally expensive to simulate. Recently, for ML/AI models that can predict the state of a system or an environment, given some actions of an agent, the term *world model* has been coined, [39]. For such objectives, physics-guided ML approaches are particularly promising.

Surrogates can be useful both for general optimization-based control (Sect. 3.2), where black-box models are evaluated by the optimizer, and for training reinforcement learning agents (Sect. 4.4).

4.4 Operation of Systems via Reinforcement Learning

Agents that have been trained with reinforcement learning (RL) can perform high-level control, which makes them an alternative to the approaches outlined in Sect. 3. Also conventional swarm intelligence approaches can be extended to Multi-Agent Reinforcement Learning (MARL) strategies, by now supported by open-source packages like Gymnasium, [42].

The reward function is usually similar to the cost-function for optimiziation-based approaches and typically contains energy prices and costs for violation of comfort levels or unwanted behavior (like frequent on-off cycles). Apart from the different sign convention, a main difference is that RL typically does not used a fixed prediction horizon, but instead uses *discounting* to reduce the impact of events that are expected to occur at later times and are thus more uncertain.

An overview of RL approaches to EMS is presented in [47]. In addition, in [12] a fully observable, discrete Markov decision process has been used for training the agent. The reward function reflected the negative energy costs and comfort losses, weighted by multi-objective constants. The study showed that multi-objective RL can outperform linear model predictive control in multi-energy systems given sufficient training, but its success depends on costly, potentially unsafe training and careful hyper-parameter tuning. In [1], the goal of the agent was to learn how to manage the battery energy storage operations. The results show that a suitable discretization can improve the performance of the Q-learning agent, especially by increasing the discrete states for the electricity price. A more complex system, a microgrid that also contains a wind turbine generator and thermostatically controlled loads, has been studied in [32]. Various methods for RL training show quite different performance; some approaches achieve near-optimal policies.

Main issues that up to now preclude the use of RL in productive systems are the computational effort required for training, the potential influence of modelling errors on the policies and missing explainability, since state-of-the-art RL methods like deep Q-learning or Proximal Policy Optimization (PPO) produce extremely opaque results.

5 Characterization of ML and AI for Control Tasks

In this section, we summarize main aspects that should best be known before application of ML/AI models for tasks in building or district energy management, but at least be cleanly documented once the method has been developed. A graphical summary, suitable as a checklist, is given in Fig. 3 on p. 14.

5.1 Type of ML/AI Approach

A key information is of course the method used, together with a detailed characterization. This includes a characterization according to the terms discussed in Sect. 2.2, but should also give more detailed information in the type of model actually used and, if applicable, further details. In particular, it is not sufficient to just state that one has used "a neural network", but one should give detailed information on the architecture, the number of weights, the activation function and the strategies used against overfitting.

5.2 Foundation of Training

It should clearly be noted, which type and amount of data has been used for training, if the data is open or private, possibly GDPR-relevant, ...

If data augmentation techniques are used, this should be documented as well. For reinforcement learning (and imitation learning), the training environment should be characterized (general modelling approach, known model errors, ...)

5.3 Objective of the ML/AI Application

An ML/AI method may completely replace a conventional element (providing a *surrogate*), improve its performance, be used for an explainability analysis, e.g. by training a decision tree on an existing black-box solution, or fulfill some other task. It should be clear, *why* an ML/AI solution is sought for the task at hand (faster inference, better performance, ...). This objective together with the resulting information flow to and from the ML/AI model should be clearly defined.

5.4 System Element(s) Affected by ML/AI Application

Based on the modular system structure depicted in Fig. 1, we can derive a systematic way for characterizing the application of ML/AI methods due to the system element where they are used. The six basic elements are:

(S) the physical *system* to be controlled
(E) *external* influences ("the world")
(F) *forecasts* for future evolution of external quantities
(P) data *pre-processing*
(H) *high-level* control ("energy management system")
(L) *low-level* control

From this list, five basic applications for ML/AI methods can be derived:[1]

- **(S)** For an AI surrogate, the model learns the properties of the physical system. This application makes sense for use cases in which systems are not transparent or the fundamental principles are unknown. Since this rarely the case for energy management tasks, a physical gray-box model is usually the better choice, since it is easier to fit, has better generalization properties and provides much higher interpretability.
- **(F)** Forecasting of relevant time series (like expected solar gains, expected consumption or time-variant tariffs) is a major application of ML methods, and most forecasting methods make use of some sort of ML.
- **(P)** In data pre-processing, ML methods are heavily used, in particular unsupervised learning and data imputation techniques, e.g. for de-noising, dimensional reduction or dealing with missing data.
- **(H)** An ML/AI system for high-level control learns to predict the set points that a high-level controller would obtain or, using Reinforcement Learning, finds policies that maximize the cumulative reward. Once trained (which requires significant computational effort), such an AI system can be useful as a computationally cheap black-box replacement for the original controller.
- **(L)** While AI-based methods are usually too slow and too computationally expensive to fully replace low-level control, they can be useful for anomaly detection. For certain applications like sun tracking, computer-vision-based low level control works fine, [11].

It is also possible to replace or augment a combination of two or three elements of the system. Among the many possible combinations, some are particularly promising:

- **(SL)** AI surrogate for the physical system, including low-level control: The AI learns the dynamical properties of the physical system, including low-level

---

[1] Only at rare occasions, one will use AI methods to exclusively learn the external influences **(E)**. Usually, if these are included, they will be combined either with the system **(SE)** or with the forecasting **(EF)**.

control, i.e. the response of the controlled system to prescribed set points. This constitutes an interesting application, since one often wants to set up a high-level control for a system with some legacy low-level control, which cannot be altered, but still has to be integrated in the final control solution.

(HL) AI solution for the complete control system: The AI learns to predict the (quasi-)continuous actuator values that the full control system high-level and low-level control) would yield, based on measurements and forecasts. This might be useful in some situations where an integrated control system is to be installed instead of the more flexible, more modular approach of separate high- and low-level control. It might also be interesting for applications where a clear separation of these layers is not possible or where even the low-level control has to include predictive elements, e.g. due to long delay times.

Some important applications for ML/AI solutions replacing/augmenting one or more system elements are shown in Fig. 2.

6 Criteria for Choice and Evaluation

Several criteria are relevant for choosing an appropriate ML/AL method for a task at hand Together with standard performance measures, these criteria can also be used for subsequent evaluation.

Data Requirements. The amount of data available often limits the model that can be successfully used. For situations with scarce data, deep learning is usually not viable, unless pretraining and transfer learning can be used. For evaluation, it is usually instructive to study the performance of models depending on the amount and diversity of data used for training.

Computational Effort and Hardware Requirements. While simple ML models can already run on a Programmable Logic Controller (PLC), many deep learning models require large computational resources, including Graphical Processing Units (GPUs). For many methods, training the models requires far more computational effort than evaluating them.

Explainability. While simple models, e.g. linear regression, decision trees, typically do not achieve the performance of more complex ones, they are transparent and thus can be considered as far more trustworthy than black-box models with a large number of parameters – an important aspect, particularly in view of the EU Artificial Intelligence Act, https://artificialintelligenceact.eu/.

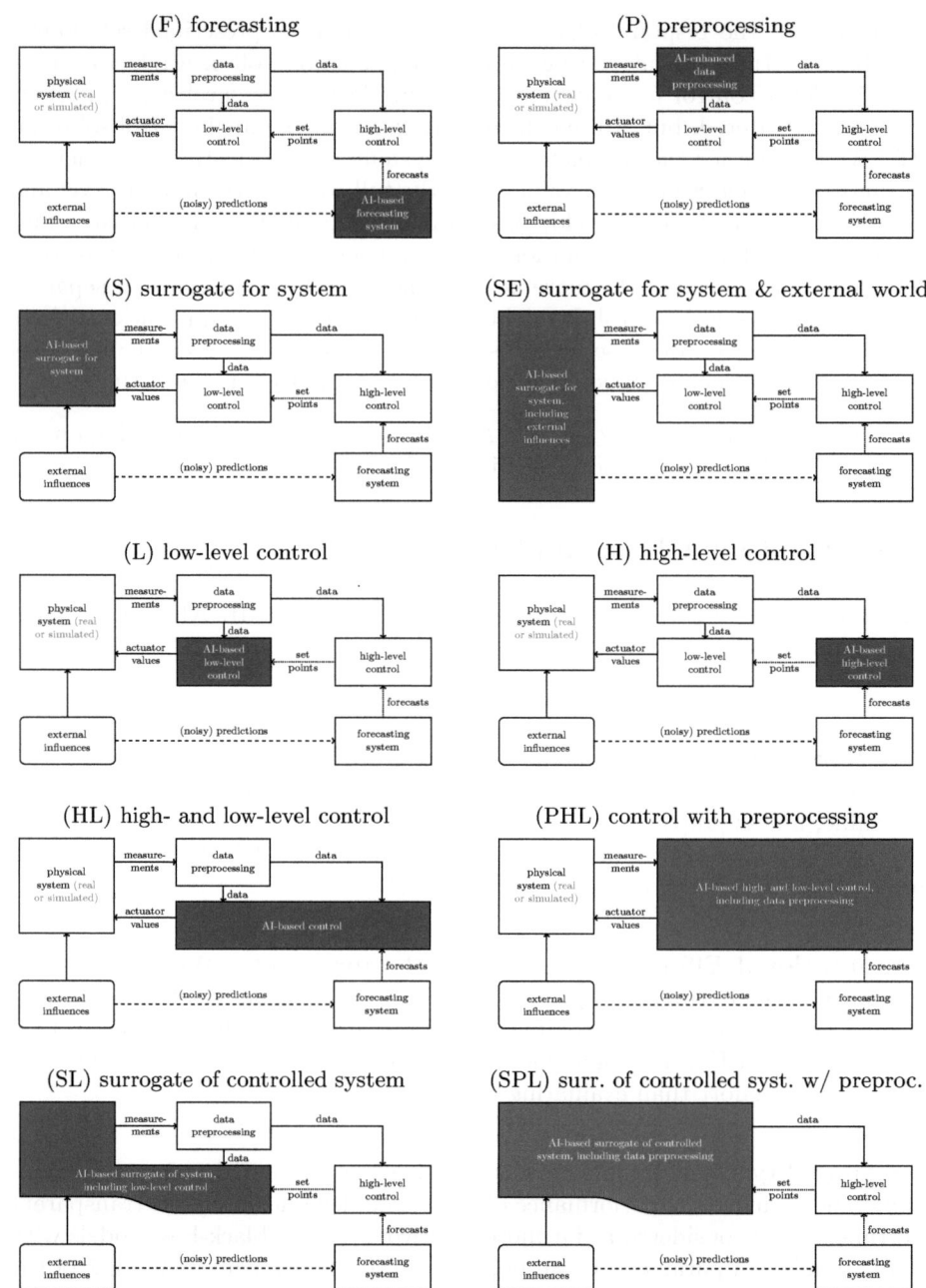

Fig. 2. Some applications of ML/AI-based methods in the control of energy systems

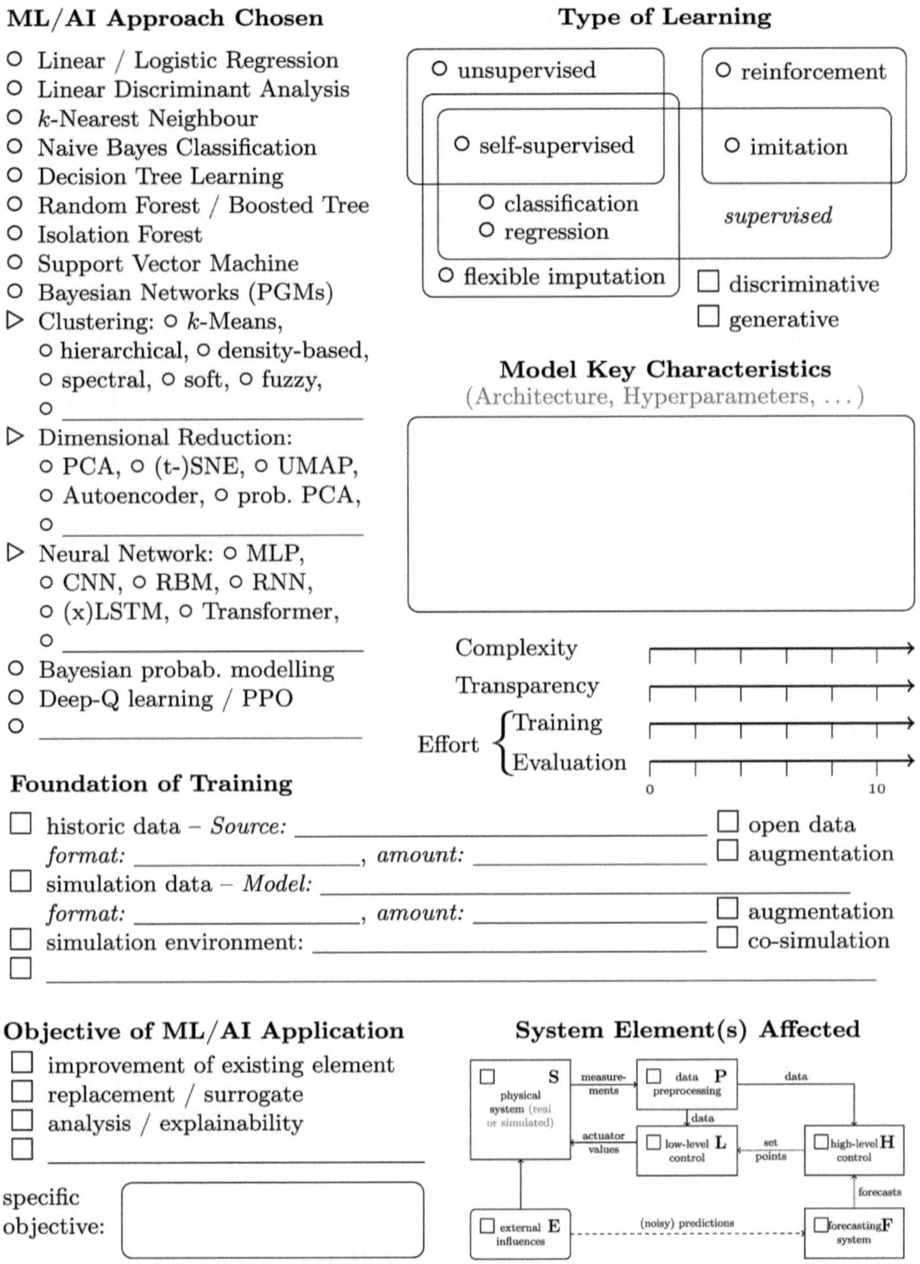

ML/AI Approach Chosen

- ○ Linear / Logistic Regression
- ○ Linear Discriminant Analysis
- ○ k-Nearest Neighbour
- ○ Naive Bayes Classification
- ○ Decision Tree Learning
- ○ Random Forest / Boosted Tree
- ○ Isolation Forest
- ○ Support Vector Machine
- ○ Bayesian Networks (PGMs)
- ▷ Clustering: ○ k-Means,
  ○ hierarchical, ○ density-based,
  ○ spectral, ○ soft, ○ fuzzy,
  ○ _____
- ▷ Dimensional Reduction:
  ○ PCA, ○ (t-)SNE, ○ UMAP,
  ○ Autoencoder, ○ prob. PCA,
  ○ _____
- ▷ Neural Network: ○ MLP,
  ○ CNN, ○ RBM, ○ RNN,
  ○ (x)LSTM, ○ Transformer,
  ○ _____
- ○ Bayesian probab. modelling
- ○ Deep-Q learning / PPO
- ○ _____

Type of Learning

- ○ unsupervised
- ○ reinforcement
- ○ self-supervised
- ○ imitation
- ○ classification
- ○ regression
- _supervised_
- ○ flexible imputation
- ☐ discriminative
- ☐ generative

Model Key Characteristics
(Architecture, Hyperparameters, ...)

Complexity
Transparency
Effort { Training
         Evaluation
0   10

Foundation of Training

- ☐ historic data – _Source:_ _____   ☐ open data
  format: _____, _amount:_ _____   ☐ augmentation
- ☐ simulation data – _Model:_ _____
  format: _____, _amount:_ _____   ☐ augmentation
- ☐ simulation environment: _____   ☐ co-simulation
- ☐ _____

Objective of ML/AI Application

- ☐ improvement of existing element
- ☐ replacement / surrogate
- ☐ analysis / explainability
- ☐ _____

specific objective: [   ]

System Element(s) Affected

☐ S physical system (real or simulated) — measurements → ☐ P data preprocessing — data →
actuator values → ☐ L low-level control — set points → ☐ H high-level control
☐ E external influences — (noisy) predictions → ☐ F forecasting system — forecasts →

Fig. 3. Graphical representation of a basic checklist for characterization of ML/AI application for building and district energy management

7 Conclusions and Outlook

We have presented a systematic overview and a guideline for the integration of ML/AI methods in the control of building and district energy systems. The checklist developed in this article is expected to be useful for concretizing the use of ML and AI for the control of energy systems. It should, however, not be regarded as final, but rather as one step towards a fully comprehensive systematic for application and evaluation. It is planned to apply it to ongoing and future research projects in order to provide empirical case studies.

Acknowledgements. The concepts presented in this article have been used in research that is performed in the project DISTEL, funded by Zukunftsfonds Land Steiermark (PN: 1515). They have profited from discussions in RISE (project FO999902661), funded by the Austrian Ministry of Climate Action and Energy.

Furthermore, parts of the research leading to these results has received funding from BMK, BMAW and the Federal States Vienna, Lower Austria and Styria within the scope of the Austrian COMET – Competence Centers for Excellent Technologies Programme under the Grant Agreement no 892426. The COMET Programme is managed by the Austrian Research Promotion Agency (FFG).

The authors are grateful to Thomas Hirsch, Gerald Schweiger and Catherine Laflamme for valuable discussions and insights.

References

1. Abedi, S., Yoon, S.W., Kwon, S.: Battery energy storage control using a reinforcement learning approach with cyclic time-dependent markov process. Int. J. Electric. Power Energy Syst. **134**, 107368 (2022)
2. Adamy, J.: Nonlinear Systems and Controls. Springer, 2 edn. (2024). https://doi.org/10.1007/978-3-662-68690-4
3. Aggarwal, C.C.: Neural networks and deep learning: a textbook. Springer, 2 edn. (2023). https://link.springer.com/book/10.1007/978-3-031-29642-0
4. Ahmad, T., Chen, H.: Short and medium-term forecasting of cooling and heating load demand in building environment with data-mining based approaches. Energy and Buildings **166** (2018). https://doi.org/10.1016/j.enbuild.2018.01.066
5. Ahmad, T., Chen, H.: Nonlinear autoregressive and random forest approaches to forecasting electricity load for utility energy management systems. Sustain. Cities Soc. **45**, 460–473 (2019). https://doi.org/10.1016/j.scs.2018.12.013
6. Ahmad, T., Madonski, R., Zhang, D., Huang, C., Mujeeb, A.: Data-driven probabilistic machine learning in sustainable smart energy/smart energy systems: Key developments, challenges, and future research opportunities in the context of smart grid paradigm. Renew. Sustain. Energy Rev. **160**, 112128 (2022). https://doi.org/10.1016/j.rser.2022.112128
7. Benti, N.E., Chaka, M.D., Semie, A.G.: Forecasting renewable energy generation with machine learning and deep learning: current advances and future prospects. Sustainability **15**(9) (2023). https://doi.org/10.3390/su15097087, https://www.mdpi.com/2071-1050/15/9/7087
8. Pattern Recognition and Machine Learning. ISS, Springer, New York (2006). https://doi.org/10.1007/978-0-387-45528-0_9

9. Bishop, C.M., Bishop, H.: Deep Learning. Springer Cham (2023). https://doi.org/10.1007/978-3-031-45468-4
10. Boyd, S., Parikh, N., Chu, E., Peleato, B., Eckstein, J.: Distributed optimization and statistical learning via the alternating direction method of multipliers. Found. Trends Mach. Learn. **3**(1), 1–122 (2010). https://doi.org/10.1561/2200000016
11. Carballo, J.A., Bonilla, J., Berenguel, M., Fernández-Reche, J., García, G.: New approach for solar tracking systems based on computer vision, low cost hardware and deep learning. Renew. Energy **133**, 1158–1166 (2019). https://doi.org/10.1016/j.renene.2018.08.101
12. Ceusters, G., et al.: Model-predictive control and reinforcement learning in multi-energy system case studies. Appl. Energy **303**, 117634 (2021)
13. Chen, B., Dang, L., Zheng, N., Principe, J.C.: Kalman Filtering Under Information Theoretic Criteria. Springer (2024)
14. Chen, R.T.Q., Amos, B., Nickel, M.: Learning neural event functions for ordinary differential equations (2021). https://arxiv.org/abs/2011.03902
15. Di Piazza, A., Di Piazza, M.C., Vitale, G.: Solar and wind forecasting by narx neural networks. Renew. Energy Environ. Sustain. **1**, 39 (2016). https://doi.org/10.1051/rees/2016047
16. Entezari, A., Aslani, A., Zahedi, R., Noorollahi, Y.: Artificial intelligence and machine learning in energy systems: a bibliographic perspective. Energ. Strat. Rev. **45**, 101017 (2023). https://doi.org/10.1016/j.esr.2022.101017
17. Fei-Fei, L., Fergus, R., Perona, P.: One-shot learning of object categories. IEEE Trans. Pattern Anal. Mach. Intell. **28**(4), 594–611 (2006). https://doi.org/10.1109/TPAMI.2006.79
18. Feierl, L., Unterberger, V., Rossi, C., Gerardts, B., Gaetani, M.: Fault detective: automatic fault-detection for solar thermal systems based on artificial intelligence. Solar Energy Adv. **3**, 100033 (2023). https://doi.org/10.1016/j.seja.2023.100033
19. Hamilton, J.D.: Time Series Analysis. Princeton University Press (1994). https://press.princeton.edu/books/hardcover/9780691042893/time-series-analysis
20. Hastie, T., Tibshirani, R., Friedman, J.: The Elements of Statistical Learning: Data Mining, Inference, and Prediction. Springer, 2nd edn. (2017)
21. Jha, S.K., Bilalovic, J., Jha, A., Patel, N., Zhang, H.: Renewable energy: present research and future scope of artificial intelligence. Renew. Sustain. Energy Rev. **77**, 297–317 (2017). https://doi.org/10.1016/j.rser.2017.04.018
22. Kaisermayer, V., et al.: Smart control of interconnected district heating networks on the example of "100% renewable district heating leibnitz". Smart Energy **6** (2022). https://doi.org/10.1016/j.segy.2022.100069
23. Kaisermayer, V., et al.: Predictive building energy management with user feedback in the loop. Smart Energy **16**, 100164 (2024). https://doi.org/10.1016/j.segy.2024.100164
24. Koukaras, P., Mustapha, A., Mystakidis, A., Tjortjis, C.: Optimizing building short-term load forecasting: a comparative analysis of machine learning models. Energies **17**(6) (2024). https://doi.org/10.3390/en17061450
25. Krizhevsky, A., Sutskever, I., Hinton, G.E.: Imagenet classification with deep convolutional neural networks. Commun. ACM **60** (2017). https://doi.org/10.1145/3065386
26. Lichtenegger, K., et al.: Decentralized heating grid operation: a comparison of centralized and agent-based optimization. Sustain. Energy Grids Netw. **21**, 100300 (2020). https://doi.org/10.1016/j.segan.2020.100300
27. Mikolov, T., Chen, K., Corrado, G., Dean, J.: Efficient estimation of word representations in vector space (2013). https://arxiv.org/abs/1301.3781

28. Moser, A., et al.: A MILP-based modular energy management system for urban multi-energy systems: Performance and sensitivity analysis. Appl. Energy **261**, 114342 (2020). https://doi.org/10.1016/j.apenergy.2019.114342
29. Murphy, K.P.: Probabilistic Machine Learning: An introduction. MIT Press (2022). http://probml.github.io/book1
30. Murphy, K.P.: Probabilistic Machine Learning: Advanced Topics. MIT Press (2023). http://probml.github.io/book2
31. Mystakidis, A., Koukaras, P., Tsalikidis, N., Ioannidis, D., Tjortjis, C.: Energy forecasting: a comprehensive review of techniques and technologies. Energies **17**(7) (2024). https://doi.org/10.3390/en17071662, https://www.mdpi.com/1996-1073/17/7/1662
32. Nakabi, T.A., Toivanen, P.: Deep reinforcement learning for energy management in a microgrid with flexible demand. Sustain. Energy Grids Netw. **25**, 100413 (2021). https://doi.org/10.1016/j.segan.2020.100413
33. Nigitz, T., Gölles, M.: A generally applicable, simple and adaptive forecasting method for the short-term heat load of consumers. Appl. Energy **241**, 73–81 (2019). https://doi.org/10.1016/j.apenergy.2019.03.012
34. Nise, N.S.: Control Systems Engineering. Wiley, 8 edn. (2022)
35. Perera, A., Kamalaruban, P.: Applications of reinforcement learning in energy systems. Renew. Sustain. Energy Rev. **137**, 110618 (2021)
36. Information Theoretic Learning. ISS, Springer, New York (2010). https://doi.org/10.1007/978-1-4419-1570-2
37. Raissi, M., Perdikaris, P., Karniadakis, G.E.: Physics informed deep learning (part i): data-driven solutions of nonlinear partial differential equations (2017). https://arxiv.org/abs/1711.10561
38. REN21: Renewables 2024 Global Status Report Collection (2024). https://www.ren21.net/gsr-2024/
39. Ser, J.D., Lobo, J.L., Müller, H., Holzinger, A.: World models in artificial intelligence: sensing, learning, and reasoning like a child (2025). https://arxiv.org/abs/2503.15168
40. The Data Science Design Manual. TCS, Springer, Cham (2017). https://doi.org/10.1007/978-3-319-55444-0_9
41. Sutton, R.S., Barto, A.G.: Reinforcement learning: an introduction. Adaptive computation and machine learning series, The MIT Press, Cambridge, Massachusetts, second edition edn (2018)
42. Towers, M., et al.: Gymnasium: a standard interface for reinforcement learning environments (2024). https://arxiv.org/abs/2407.17032
43. Unterberger, V., Lichtenegger, K., Gölles, M.: Predictive rule-based control strategy for optimizing the operation of solar district heating plants. In: Proceedings of EuroSun 24 (2024). https://doi.org/10.18086/eurosun.2024.03.03
44. Unterberger, V., Lichtenegger, K., Kaisermayer, V., Gölles, M., Horn, M.: An adaptive short-term forecasting method for the energy yield of flat-plate solar collector systems. Appl. Energy **293**, 116891 (2021). https://doi.org/10.1016/j.apenergy.2021.116891
45. Vaswani, A., et al.: Attention is all you need. In: Guyon, I., et al., (eds.) Advances in Neural Information Processing Systems. vol. 30. Curran Associates, Inc. (2017), https://proceedings.neurips.cc/paper/2017/file/3f5ee243547dee91fbd053c1c4a845aa-Paper.pdf
46. Xian, Y., Schiele, B., Akata, Z.: Zero-shot learning – the good, the bad and the ugly (2020). https://arxiv.org/abs/1703.04394

47. Yang, T., Zhao, L., Li, W., Zomaya, A.Y.: Reinforcement learning in sustainable energy and electric systems: a survey. Annu. Rev. Control. **49**, 145–163 (2020)
48. Zemann, C., Deutsch, M., Zlabinger, S., Hofmeister, G., Gölles, M., Horn, M.: Optimal operation of residential heating systems with logwood boiler, buffer storage and solar thermal collector. Biomass Bioenerg. **140**, 105622 (2020). https://doi.org/10.1016/j.biombioe.2020.105622
49. Zhao, D., Piao, X., Chen, Z., Li, Z., Taniguchi, I.: A unified energy management framework for multi-timescale forecasting in smart grids (2024). https://arxiv.org/abs/2411.15254

Open Access This chapter is licensed under the terms of the Creative Commons Attribution 4.0 International License (http://creativecommons.org/licenses/by/4.0/), which permits use, sharing, adaptation, distribution and reproduction in any medium or format, as long as you give appropriate credit to the original author(s) and the source, provide a link to the Creative Commons license and indicate if changes were made.

The images or other third party material in this chapter are included in the chapter's Creative Commons license, unless indicated otherwise in a credit line to the material. If material is not included in the chapter's Creative Commons license and your intended use is not permitted by statutory regulation or exceeds the permitted use, you will need to obtain permission directly from the copyright holder.

A Dynamic Semantic Data Modeling Approach: Application to Flexible HVAC Zones

Shoya Marumoto(✉) ⓘ, Shohei Miyata ⓘ, Keiichiro Taniguchi ⓘ,
and Yasunori Akashi ⓘ

The University of Tokyo, 7-3-1 Hongo, Bunkyo-ku, Tokyo 113-8654, Japan
`s-maru42317@g.ecc.u-tokyo.ac.jp`

Abstract. The semantic data model (SDM), which is considered a foundation for uniting data that are currently dispersed individually, was not envisioned to change intrinsically during daily use. Thus, the SDM needs to adapt to spatial flexibility for more advanced data-driven control using dynamically changing spatial information. Based on this issue, this study proposes a dynamic description approach of the SDM with examples. Specifically, a method for describing an SDM that reflects the changes in the HVAC zones of each air conditioner owing to the movement of partitions and the operation status of the air conditioners is proposed. The changes in the SDM are classified into two types: addition of telemetry data and changes in the graph structure. As an example of application which associates with the dynamic SDM, a method for estimating each changing HVAC zone was proposed and the results were analyzed. Although the changes were observed in the HVAC zones, some cases were difficult to consider in practically. However, the results show the possibilities for more sophisticated estimation methods and its applicability to the dynamic SDM. As a case study in constructing an information system incorporating a dynamic SDM, a prototype was developed using a physical model. The system encompasses the sensing of partitions and occupants within the model, data integration to the SDM, and display of application outputs. The system was analyzed in comparison with previously proposed system architectures to demonstrate the potential use of dynamic SDM in smart building operations.

Keywords: Semantic Data Model · Flexible HVAC Zones · Data-Driven

1 Introduction

Building operations account for 30% of global final energy consumption [1], and improving energy efficiency in buildings is expected to contribute significantly to the reduction of GHG emissions. Advanced applications, such as demand response [2] and fault detection and diagnosis [3], are currently being developed to support this goal.

Simultaneously, comfort in buildings is becoming more important to improve productivity. The latest applications that utilize motion sensors and the Internet of Things technologies, such as personalized air conditioning [4], open space management [5], and autonomous robot-driven deliveries [6], are aimed at improving comfort.

With the adoption of smart applications, smart building systems generate a large amount of input and output data. However, at present, these data are individually dispersed, and there is a growing need for a platform that integrates and links the data [7].

Advanced applications often require a variety of input data. When sensing and control data are properly managed, it becomes possible to utilize these heterogeneous data sources in combination. Moreover, in conventional systems, introducing a new application typically requires considerable effort for data acquisition and preprocessing. By managing data in an integrated manner, the workload involved in implementing new applications which needs existing data can be significantly reduced.

The SDM, which is a conceptual data model and enables machines to understand the semantic structure of data, is expected to be a resolution for these issues. It has a general-purpose data format that describes the relationships between elements using a network structure, which also makes it easier for humans to understand. System architectures that use SDMs as the core of the building OS have been discussed, and BIM-based building OS [8] and WoT-based building OS [9] have been proposed. Also, several applications utilizing SDM have been reported. Kato et al. developed a prototype defect investigation system using the SDM [10]. In addition, description of the SDM and data integration with surrounding systems were verified for a CO_2 concentration monitoring system [11]. Kogure et al. have developed a graph auto-generation application and a measurement data completion application using an SDM for multiple heat source systems [12]. In addition, development of applications such as fault detection in VAV units using metadata [13] and temperature sensor error detection [14] have been reported.

Although linkages with spatial information are essential for data-driven operations, most existing research has primarily focused on the facility systems, especially HVAC equipment. In contrast, the spatial components, such as fixtures, occupants, and zones, have received comparatively little attention.

Based on this issue, this study focuses on describing spatial components using an SDM. In facility systems, equipment connections like piping or ductwork tend to remain static, so previously developed SDMs have generally assumed a fixed structure. However, spatial configurations are often more variable, depending on the location and state of fixtures, human occupancy, and other factors. By responding to these flexible changes on the spatial side, applications such as facility management and robotic control can become more advanced and responsive.

For instance, the optimal HVAC control strategy may vary depending on the position of movable partitions, requiring real-time information on partition location to adjust control algorithms accordingly. Similarly, if occupant location data is available, autonomous robots can plan paths that avoid densely occupied areas, improving both safety and efficiency.

To enable higher-level applications that adapt to such spatial flexibility, SDMs must be capable of dynamically representing spatial conditions. This study therefore proposes the creation and use of a dynamic SDM tailored for such spatial dynamics. Specifically, this study pursues the following three objectives. The overarching objective is to explore the feasibility of using the proposed dynamic SDM through prototyping applications and information systems that operate based on dynamic spatial semantics.

1. To describe dynamically changing spatial elements including air-conditioning control zones in the SDM. The zones change depending on the movement of partitions and the operating status of air conditioners, in a room with multiple individual air conditioners.
2. To propose a method for HVAC zoning as an example of applications which utilize dynamic SDMs and discussing the results.
3. To develop an information system incorporating a dynamic SDM using a simplified physical model and a laptop.

2 Creating the Semantic Data Model

2.1 Overview of SDM

An SDM is a conceptual data model that utilizes metadata to structure data based on its meaning. The term "metadata" is defined as data that represents the attributes and features of data, thereby giving meaning to the data. For instance, when there are time-series data of the temperature obtained from sensor A, the information "obtained from sensor A," "time-series," and "temperature" are given as metadata.

Building Information Modeling (BIM) is a data model, which is a combination of a 3D model and a metadata model, where each object is given metadata. In contradistinction to BIM, the SDM can describe relationships between the elements instead of incorporating 3D information. In a facility system, the connection between the equipment is important, making the SDM more compatible and useful.

The SDM is described using a method called the Resource Description Framework (RDF) triple [15] (Fig. 1). The RDF data can be represented by a directed graph structure, with the subject and object as nodes and the predicate as edges. The right side of Fig. 1 shows the graph structure of the latter half of the example RDF description.

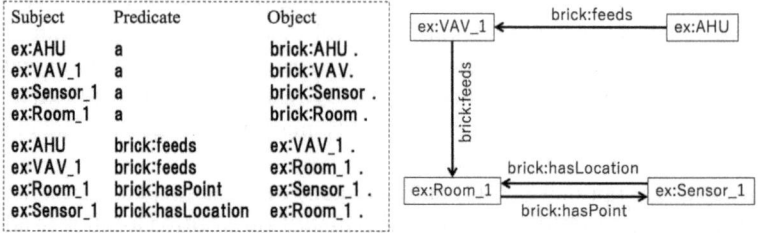

Fig. 1. Example of the RDF description and SDM graph structure

In the example, Uniform Resource Identifiers (URIs) beginning with "brick:" are URIs obtained from Brick Schema [16]. Similarly, the RDF Schema provides a URI "rdf:type," which is shortened to "a" in the example description. This has the same meaning as the be-verb. Thus, various frameworks offer a shared vocabulary in the SDM, and the dictionary of the vocabulary provided by each framework is called an ontology. Table 1 shows the ontologies used in the modeling. However, the elements not provided in existing ontologies are defined independently.

Table 1. Ontologies used in the modeling

Ontology	Abbreviation	Main description target
Brick	brick:	Building facility system
Building Topology Ontology [17]	bot:	Building spatial topology
Quantities, Units, Dimensions and Data Type Ontology [18]	qudt: unit:	Units and quantities of measurement data
OWL-Time [19]	time:	Time

2.2 Subject Room

The subject room was a graduate students' room at the University of Tokyo Engineering Building I (Fig. 2). There are four individual air conditioners and three ventilation units in this room. Thirty-five sensor boxes were installed on the walls and desks to measure the air temperature and humidity. In addition, five movable partitions were placed on the rails (Fig. 3), and it was assumed that the HVAC zone of each air conditioner changes as the partitions move. However, this study focuses only on air-conditioning system, and the HVAC zone shall represent the area where each air conditioner has priority control.

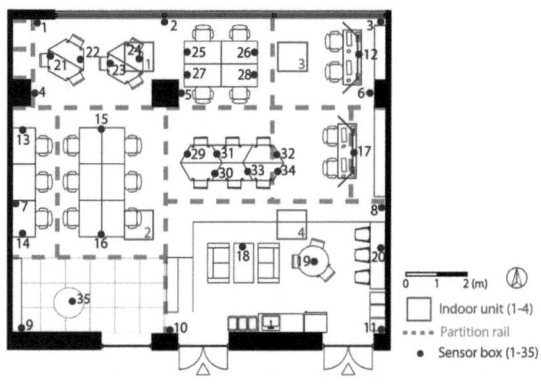

Fig. 2. Floor plan

Fig. 3. Movable partitions on the rail

2.3 Modeling and Changes in the SDM

Figure 4 shows a simplified diagram of a portion of the created SDM. The SDM includes telemetry data such as the location data of partitions utilized for HVAC zoning and temperature/humidity data, in addition to equipment and space elements and their property data. These telemetry data are connected to the equipment entities where the data is obtained, so that they can be accessed by following the graph structure. In addition, telemetry data are connected to the time and the unit nodes. As time nodes are common, any telemetry data at the same time can be retrieved with the correspondence using the time nodes. This is expected to increase the versatility of the SDM in applications that use more types of data. The sensor box and the zone in which it is located are connected by "brick:hasLocation." Moreover, virtual boundary surface entities are established between HVAC zones or the external space, and they are connected by the relationship "bot:interfaceOf." If partitions or windows are part of the virtual boundary, they are connected by "brick:isPartOf."

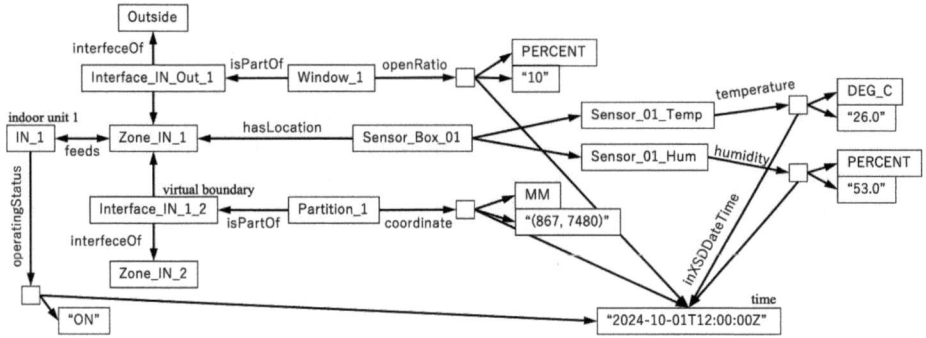

Fig. 4. Simplified diagram of the SDM

The following two types of changes occur in an SDM created in this manner. An example of changes in the zones and the SDM is shown in Fig. 5. The data flow for these changes is shown in Fig. 6.

- The telemetry data are added over time (light-blue boxes in Fig. 5).
- The relationships between elements such as the sensors and zones that are connected by "brick:hasLocation" and "brick:isPartOf" changes through the application of HVAC zoning, using telemetry data (red arrows in Fig. 5).

SPARQL queries are used to extract the data required for HVAC zoning and other applications from the SDM. This is a partial extraction of a specific graph structure from the RDF data graph structure. For instance, when obtaining information on the HVAC zone in which each sensor box is and the temperature at the sensor box, the extraction of the graph structure shown in Fig. 7 yields the output shown in Table 2.

3 HVAC Zoning

As an example of applications that works in conjunction with the dynamic SDM, an HVAC zoning is proposed in this section. In this application, the control area of each air conditioner is estimated based on the position of movable partitions and the operational status of the air conditioners. The results of the HVAC zoning are then analyzed to explore the future potential and challenges of the application.

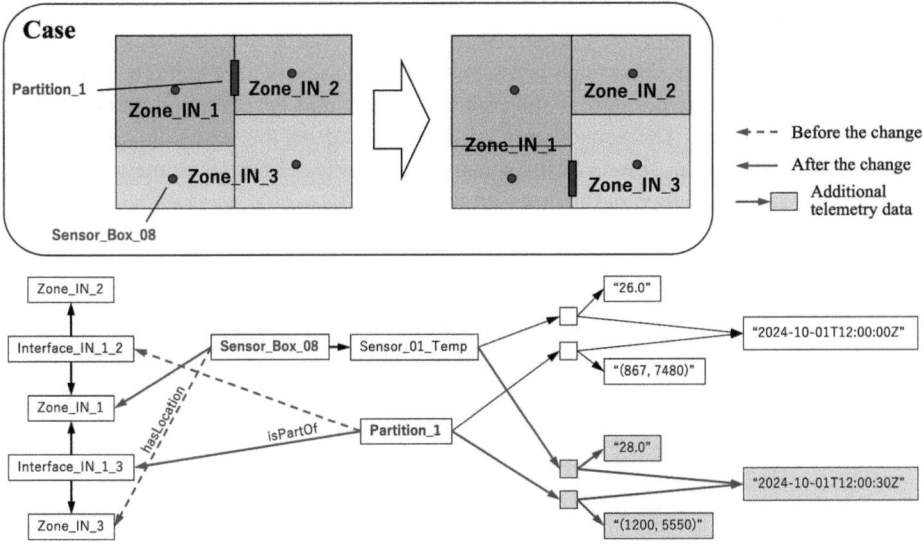

Fig. 5. Example of changes in the SDM

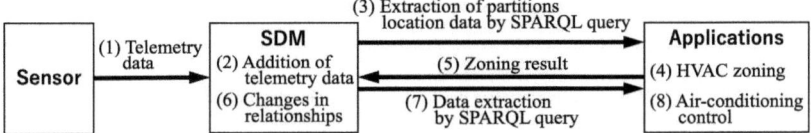

Fig. 6. Data flow for the changes in the SDM

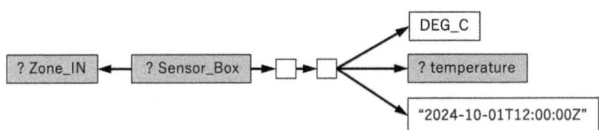

Fig. 7. Example of the graph structure of a SPARQL query

Table 2. Example of the output of the SPARQL query

?Zone_IN	?Sensor_Box	?temperature
Zone_IN_1	Sensor_Box_1	"26.0"
Zone_IN_4	Sensor_Box_2	"24.3"
Zone_IN_2	Sensor_Box_35	"25.8"

3.1 Methodology

As shown in Fig. 8, each sensor box is assigned a unique sensor area that it is responsible for. This sensor area is defined as the minimum unit, and an HVAC zone consists of multiple sensor areas. The sensor area is set up based on the partition rails and the Voronoi diagram with positions of the sensors as the sites. However, some adjustments were made for convenience in the creation of the SDM.

Fig. 8. Sensor area allocated to each sensor box

The HVAC zone which each sensor area is in is determined by the distance between the sensor box and the indoor unit. To determine the distance, the shortest path wherein partitions, pillars, and walls as obstacles were avoided was used. The indoor unit with the shortest path from each sensor box was taken as the predominant indoor unit in that sensor area. Figure 9 shows a simplified diagram of the shortest path. In the figure, although indoor unit 1 is closer to sensor box 1 in terms of the linear distance, indoor unit 2 is closer to sensor box 1 in terms of the shortest path because the partition is an obstacle. Therefore, sensor area 1 is in HVAC zone 2.

If the shortest path is greater than a certain distance, the sensor area is considered to be outside of the control range of the indoor unit and be in the non-air-conditioned zone (Zone_IN_0). In this study, the threshold value was set to 5500 mm based on a study in which one air conditioner was in operation.

When the partitions are lined up with a small gap between them, they are assumed to function as a single large partition. If the coordinates of the partitions are used as they are, the shortest path through the gaps is formed, and the calculation does not function as a large partition (Fig. 10a). To eliminate this gap in the calculation, the shortest path was formed with a partition width equal to 1.5 times the partition width (Fig. 10b).

3.2 Results and Analysis

This section analyzes the results of the proposed HVAC zoning. The overall results and those for each of the three special cases are analyzed separately.

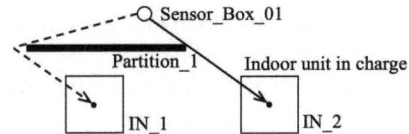

Fig. 9. Simplified diagram of the shortest path

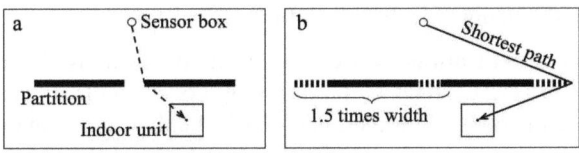

Fig. 10. Gap between partitions

Overall Analysis. Figure 11 shows the overall results for six cases. Cases (a−1)(a−3) represent those with stowed partitions. Cases (a−1), (a−2), and (a−3) represent the zones when all the air conditioners are in operation, when air conditioners 1 and 2 are in operation, and when air conditioners 2 and 3 are in operation, respectively. Cases (b−1) and (b−2) represent the cases in which the partitions are placed together while all air conditioners are in operation, and case (c) represent a case in which the partitions are dispersed. In case (a−1), the shapes of zones 2 and 4 are uneven. Particularly, the sensor areas in the center of the room, such as 29–31 and 33, have a strong tendency to show this behavior. This is similar for sensor areas 32 and 34 in case (a−2) and sensor area 23 in case (a−3). For these cases, where all partitions are stowed and there are no obstacles other than the pillar, it is difficult to assume that the zones will have such an uneven shape in practice. This may be owing to the density of the sensor boxes and the elongated shape of their sensor areas.

In case (a−1), sensor box 30 is located 3014 mm away from the indoor unit 2 and 3083 mm away from the indoor unit 4. Although these distances can be considered almost the same, the sensor area 30 is in zone 2 owing the slight difference. However, depending on the other factors, such as the size of the respective HVAC zone, the heat load in the zone, and the direction of the outlet, its location could easily be in zone 4. The method used in this study to estimate HVAC zones has the disadvantage that the sensor area, which is susceptible to the influence of multiple air conditioners, is clearly defined to be in one of the zones. By establishing an intermediate area that is susceptible to multiple air conditioners, the zone estimation would be closer to the actual situation.

As shown in cases (a−2) and (a−3), zone 2 is larger than the other zones in many cases because the placement of indoor units is closer to the upper-right corner and indoor unit 2 is closer to the center of the room. This causes many sensor boxes to be close to indoor unit 2. For the proposed method, zone estimation was performed based on only the distance between the indoor units and sensors; however, the estimation is expected to be closer to the actual situation if the zone area is also used as a parameter.

A comparison of cases (a−1), (b−1), and (b−2) shows that HVAC zones change with the movement of the partitions. For example, the location of sensor area 10, which is in zone 2 in case (a−1), changes to zone 4 in case (b−2) because of the partitions between indoor unit 2 and sensor box 10, which increases the length of the shortest path connecting them. A comparison of cases (a−1), (a−2), (b−1), and (b−2) shows that the central part of the room is prone to changes in the location of the HVAC zones. This is owing to the fact that the center of the room is closer to all air conditioners (less than 5500 mm) and the sensor boxes are densely located.

In many cases where the partitions are distributed as shown in case (c), the HVAC zones do not change. This indicates that the longer distance to avoid a single partition does not significantly change the distance of the shortest path.

Cases of Zoning by Partitioning. Cases (d−1) and (d−2) in Fig. 12 show examples of the differentiation in HVAC zones by partitioning. For example, in case (a−2), sensor areas 13 and 15 are in zone 1; however, in case (d−1), their location changes to zone 2 owing to the partition between them and indoor unit 1. Similarly, the location of sensor areas 29–31 and 33 changes from zone 2 in case (a−3) to zone 3 in case (d−2). When the temperature preferences of a person seated in the sensor area 21–24 and that of a person seated in the sensor area 13 and 15 are different, it is conventionally difficult to differentiate the temperatures in case (a−2). However, the predominant indoor unit can be changed, by installing a partition between them, thereby enabling more advanced personalized air-conditioning control. At that time, the SDM can be used as a data infrastructure to change the reference sensor box.

Cases Representing Zones Divided into Disconnected Areas. Cases (e−1) and (e−2) in Fig. 13 represent cases wherein an HVAC zone is divided by another zone. In case (e−1), the sensor area 32, which is in the non-air-conditioned zone (zone 0), is surrounded by zone 3. In case (e−2), sensor areas 5 and 27, which are in zone 3, are surrounded by zone 4 and zone 0, and are separated from zone 3 that consists of sensor areas 3, 6, and 12. Case (e−1) shows the result that the non-air-conditioned zone is isolated, and this can be a real case depending on the capacity of the air conditioner and arrangement of the partitions.

On the other hand, case (e−2) represents a case wherein zone 3 is divided, and the air-conditioned zone is not originally divided by other air-conditioned or non-air-conditioned zones. In fact, it is considered that the upper part of sensor areas 31–33 is in zone 3 and there is a path connecting the zone 3, which is divided. However, because HVAC zoning is discreet in this method, the path is not shown. In case of such a division, an intermediate area that is affected by multiple air conditioners as described above can be used. At that time, sensor areas 6, 17, 29–34, which are in the control area for both indoor units 3 and 4, were used as the intermediate areas. However, because the ratio of influence of each indoor unit differs for each sensor box, data of the ratio of influence, which is obtained from the information such as the shortest path length, can be associated with the sensor box.

Cases Where Zones Were Not Separated by Partitions. Cases (f−1) and (f−2) in Fig. 14 represent cases of failure to differentiate HVAC zones by partitioning. In case (f−1), sensor area 10 is assumed to be in zone 4 owing to its partition arrangement. However, using the proposed method, the sensor area is in zone 2. In case (f−2), sensor area 6, which is assumed to be in zone 0, is in zone 4.

This is because the shortest path is formed in the small gap between the partition (expanded by 1.5 times) and the wall/pillar, and the sensor box is not located at the

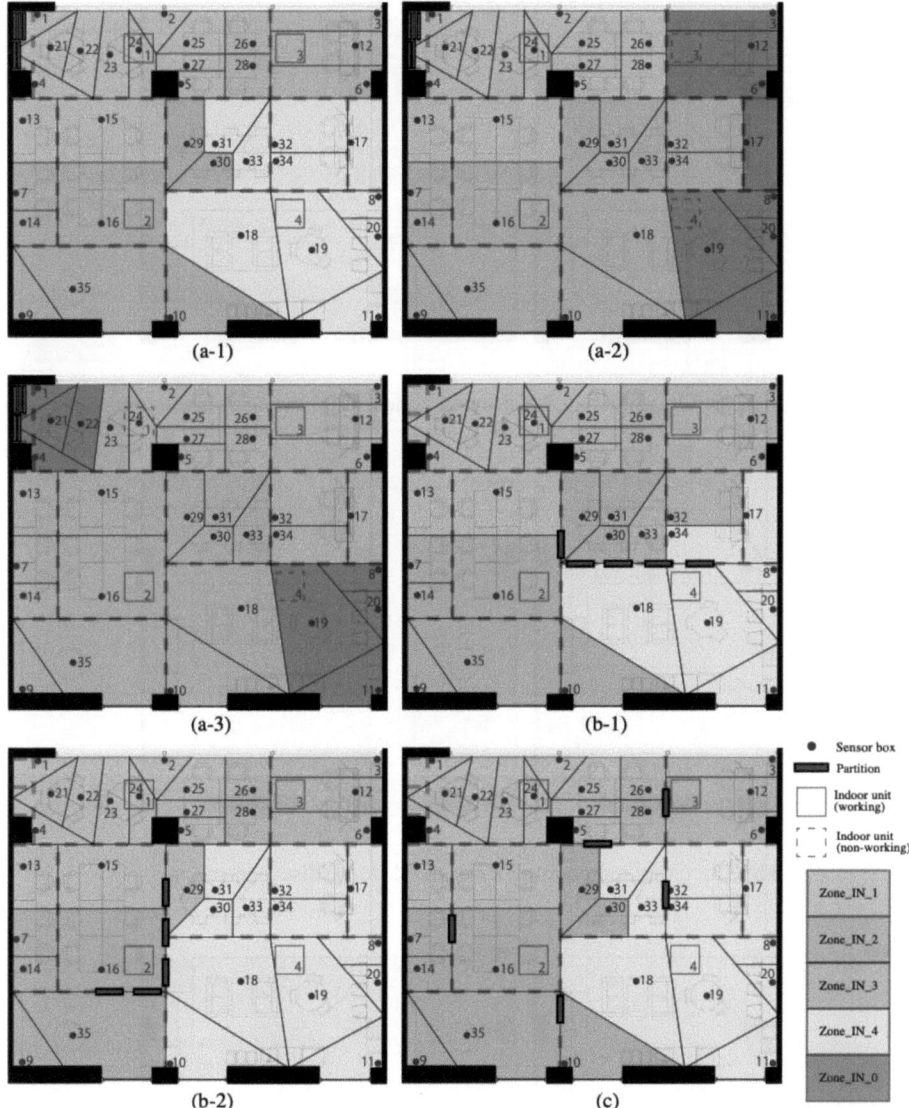

Fig. 11. The changes of HVAC zones in some cases

center of the sensor area. When a sensor is installed on a wall, the sensor is located near the boundary of the sensor area. Cases (f−1) and (f−2) show the shortcomings of the proposed method, wherein the sensor area is judged based on the sensor box as a point.

3.3 Challenges and Future Prospect of HVAC Zoning

Although changes in the HVAC zoning were demonstrated, some cases lacked accuracy, resulting in issues such as irregularly shaped, oversized, or fragmented zones. To

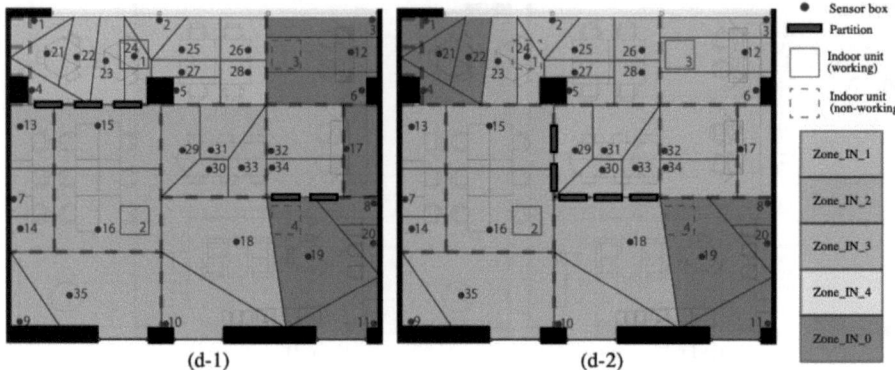

Fig. 12. Differentiation in the air-conditioned zones owing to partitioning

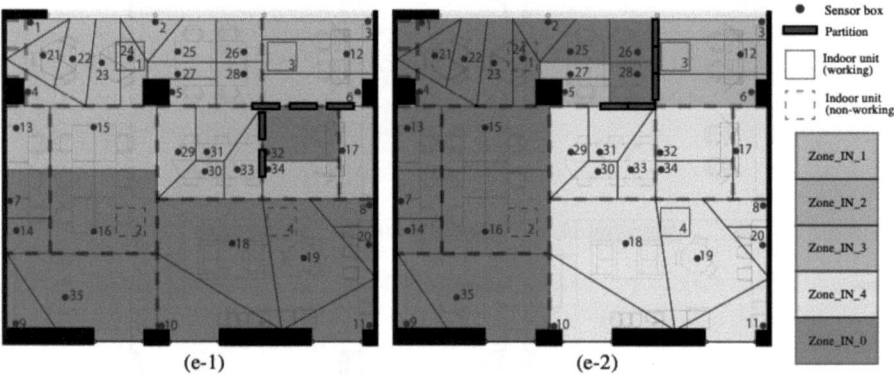

Fig. 13. Cases representing zones divided into disconnected areas

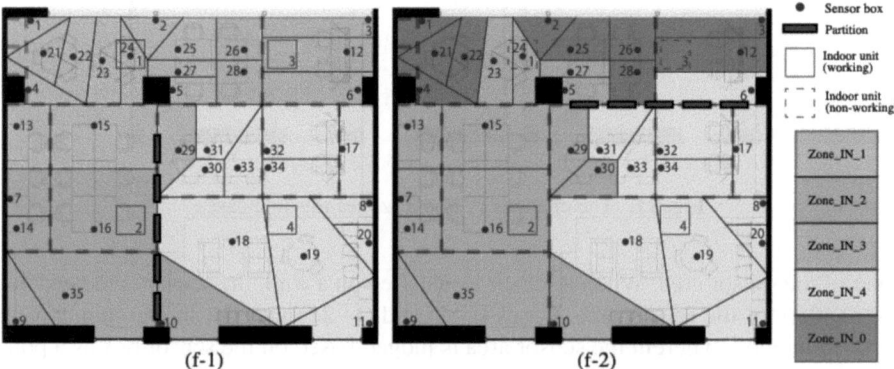

Fig. 14. Cases where zones were not separated by partitions

address these issues, potential solutions include incorporating zone area as parameter and introducing intermediate area that is influenced by multiple air-conditioning units.

In this study, zoning was performed based on the position of movable partitions and the operational status of air-conditioning units. However, other parameters—such as internal heat loads (e.g., human occupancy) and external heat loads (e.g., solar radiation through windows)—can also be considered in future applications. For example, reducing the size of an HVAC zone that includes a densely occupied area may enable more energy-efficient climate control. In addition, the distance threshold for the non-air-conditioned zone (5500 mm) was set arbitrarily, however, its validation needs to be demonstrated in the future research.

Despite these challenges, the prospects for utilizing the dynamic SDM have broadened. Traditionally, sensors used for HVAC control were fixed; however, by utilizing a dynamically changing SDM, it becomes possible to flexibly reassign or reconfigure the sensors in response to changes in HVAC zoning.

4 Prototype Development of the Information System

A prototype information system that utilizes the proposed dynamic SDM was developed (Fig. 15). The prototype consists of three main components: sensing of spatial changes, integration of data into the SDM, and utilization of these data in applications. The system is implemented using a simplified physical model and a laptop.

This chapter introduces the developed system (Fig. 16) and compares it with the smart building system architecture proposed by the Digital Architecture Design Center of the Information-technology Promotion Agency (IPA DADC) [7] (Fig. 17). The objective is to demonstrate the feasibility and the challenges in constructing and operating such a system in practice.

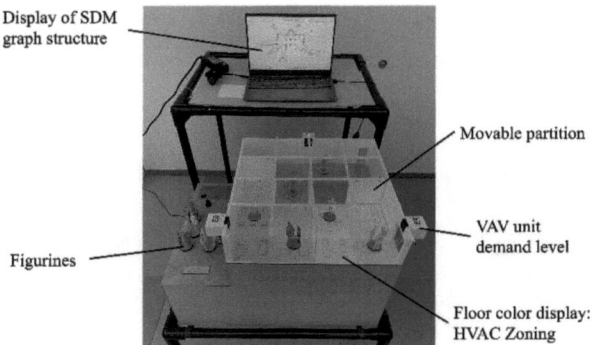

Fig. 15. Constructed prototype model

4.1 Room Setting

The subject room of the prototype is a virtual co-working office. In this room, partitions can be moved along a grid layout. The HVAC system is based on a VAV configuration using three units. Each occupant is represented by a figurine that is assigned a set of attributes, as shown in Fig. 18.

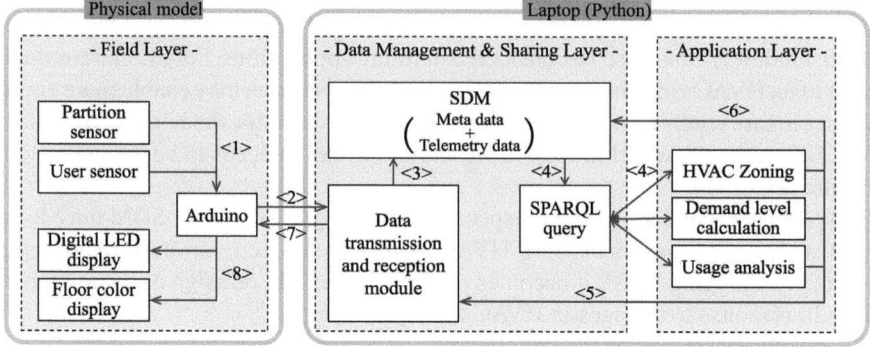

Fig. 16. System architecture used in the prototype

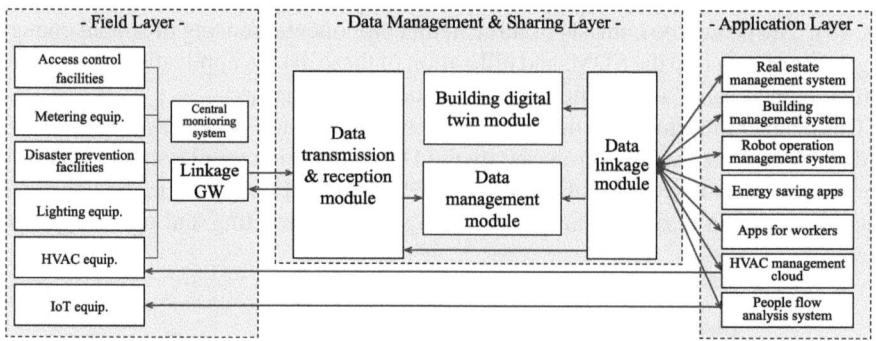

Fig. 17. System architecture proposed by IPA DADC

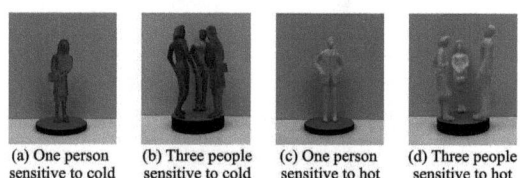

(a) One person sensitive to cold (b) Three people sensitive to cold (c) One person sensitive to hot (d) Three people sensitive to hot

Fig. 18. Occupant attributes

4.2 System Architecture

Sensing. Magnets are attached to both the partitions and the figurines. Magnetic sensors are installed beneath the floor surface of the room model. The sensors used for detecting the partitions operate on a binary principle, outputting either 0 V or 5 V depending on the presence or absence of the magnetic field. The sensors used for detecting the figurines measure both the strength and direction of the magnetic field and output different voltage values accordingly (<1> in Fig. 16).

Unlike the actual room introduced in the previous chapter—where partitions could be moved continuously—in this prototype, sensing is only possible at designated locations due to technical limitations. Similarly, only one figurine can be placed per grid cell. In a real-world implementation, technologies such as UWB (Ultra-Wide Band) positioning are expected to allow continuous tracking of partition movement. As for acquiring occupants' location and thermal preference data, personal devices such as smartphones or smartwatches can be used to automatically transmit this information.

Telemetry Data Transmission and Integration into SDM. The data sensed by the magnetic sensors is first transmitted to a microcontroller (Arduino) <1>. The Arduino processes this data and sends it via serial communication to a connected laptop <2>.

In a smart building, various types of data collected at the field layer are typically aggregated by a gateway before being transmitted to the data management and sharing layer. In the prototype system, the Arduino functions as such a gateway. Furthermore, it standardizes the format of the sensing data from both partitions and figurines, mirroring the gateway's role in unifying communication protocols among heterogeneous devices. The sensing data, which a data transmission and reception module receive, is used to update the SDM in real time <3>.

Applications. Each application retrieves input parameter values from the SDM via SPARQL queries <4>, serving as the data linkage module in the smart building.

The output from each application is transmitted to the data transmission and reception module <5> and simultaneously sent back to the SDM to update it <6>. The data transmission and reception module send control commands via serial communication to the Arduino <7>, which in turn converts the command into the appropriate data format for the display device designated to present the application output <8>. In this process as well, the Arduino serves the function of a gateway.

The applications implemented in the prototype include:

- Proposed HVAC zoning (Fig. 19)
- A simplified calculation of demand level of VAV units based on parameters such as the zoning result, the number of occupants, and their thermal preferences (Fig. 19)
- Spatial usage analysis based on occupants' attribute data accumulated in the SDM.

4.3 Lesson Learnt from Prototyping

While the system architecture proposed by IPA DADC separates the data model and sensing data management into different modules, the prototype developed in this study integrates the data model with the sensing data. This integration enables applications to retrieve multiple types of sensing data while preserving their semantic context. For example, in the prototype's VAV demand level calculation application, both the number of occupants and their thermal preferences can be retrieved together in a semantically structured form, making the data easier to use.

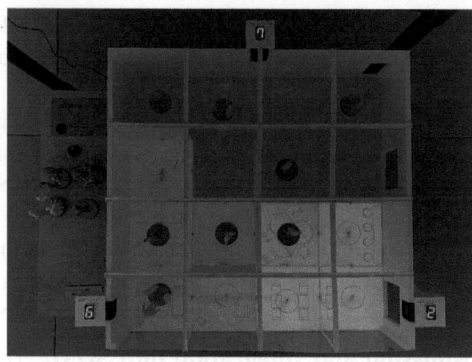

Fig. 19. Floor colors represent HVAC zoning result. Each demand level is displayed digitally.

In the IPA DADC architecture, data acquisition typically requires two steps: first, querying the data model to identify the location of the required data; second, accessing the values from a separate data management module. In contrast, the proposed system allows applications to directly access the data values from the integrated semantic data model, eliminating the need for separate data lookup and access procedures.

However, this integrated approach also has drawbacks. Specifically, the data model grows significantly in size. When the prototype was operated continuously for about two weeks, the increasing size of the data model led to longer loading times. While expanding the system to multiple rooms or an entire building would make application development and adaptation easier, it also highlights the need for more efficient data management strategies to handle increased data volume.

5 Conclusion

In this study, dynamic description approach of the SDM was proposed, and its applicability was demonstrated through its implementation in HVAC zoning. While conventional HVAC control is based on zoning configurations determined during the design phase, this study showed the potential for more efficient or personalized HVAC control by performing zoning in a data-driven manner according to spatial changes.

Although the HVAC zoning method used in this study was simplified, the results suggest that more advanced applications can be realized by incorporating additional parameters. As the number of the input and output data increases, the usefulness of the dynamic SDM as a data infrastructure also increases.

Future work includes exploring the use of SDMs in data-driven applications beyond HVAC zoning. Additionally, while all data transmission in the prototype was conducted via wired connections, wireless communication will be essential when expanding the system to real-world buildings. Considering this and other differences, future research should address the expansion and deployment of the proposed system in actual building environments.

Disclosure of Interests. The author has no competing interests to declare that are relevant to the content of this article.

References

1. https://www.iea.org/energy-system/buildings. Accessed 6 July 2025
2. Vardakas, J.S., Zorba, N., Verikoukis, C.V.: A survey on demand response programs in smart grids: pricing methods and optimization algorithms. IEEE Commun. Surv. Tutor. **17**(1), 152–178 (2015)
3. Gao, Z., Cecati, C., Ding, S.X.: A survey of fault diagnosis and fault-tolerant techniques—part i: fault diagnosis with model-based and signal-based approaches. IEEE Trans. Indust. Electron. **62**(6), 3757–3767 (2015)
4. Jeoung, J., Jung, S., Hong, T., Choi, J.: Blockchain-based IoT system for personalized indoor temperature control. Autom. Construct. **140** (2022)
5. Monrós, G., Delgado, C., Badenes, J.A., Monrós-Andreu, G., Llusar, M.: Metallised sol-gel coatings on ceramic glazes with photocatalytic activity. Acad. Mater. Sci. **1**(4) (2024)
6. Srinivas, S., Ramachandiran, S., Rajendran, S.: Autonomous robot-driven deliveries: a review of recent developments and future directions. Transport. Res. Part E: Logist. Transport. Rev. **165** (2022)
7. IPA DADC.: Smart Building System Architecture Guidelines (2023)
8. Eneyew, D.D., Capretz, M.A.M., Bitsuamlak, G.T.: Toward smart-building digital twins: BIM and IoT data integration. IEEE Access **10** (2022)
9. Owaki, K., et al.: Proposal of a scalable building operating system architecture and data model toward software-defined building. In: 2024 IEEE 48th Annual Computers, Software, and Applications Conference (COMPSAC), pp. 1586–1591 (2024)
10. Kato, S., Yashiro, T., Murai, H.: Prototype of a Functional relationship model using semantic data model - case study of ceiling radiant heating and cooling system. Techn. Report Archit. Inst. Japan **29**(73), 1636–1641 (2023)
11. Kato, S., Yashiro, T., Murai, H.: A study on the semantic structure of building elements for the development of autonomous distributed systems - using "semantic data model. J. Inst. Indust. Sci. The University of Tokyo **74**(1), 135–138 (2022)
12. Kogure, Y., Miyata, S., Akashi, Y., Taniguchi, K.: Metadata model of multiple heat source systems using brick schema and its deployable applications (in Japanese). J. Soc. Heat. Air-Condition. Sanit. Eng. Japan 319, 11–18 (2023)
13. Duarte Roa, C., Raftery, P., Rupam, S., Pritoni, M., Peffer, T: Detecting passing valves at scale across different buildings and systems: a brick enabled and mortar tested application. Berkeley National Laboratory (2022)
14. Zhang, L., Guo, J., Fu, X., Tiong, R.L.K., Zhang, P.: Digital twin enabled real-time advanced control of TBM operation using deep learning methods. Autom. Construct. (2023)
15. Kaneiwa, K.: The semantic web and linked data. 1st edn. Corona, Japan (2017)
16. https://brickschema.org. Accessed 2 May 2025
17. https://w3c-lbd-cg.github.io/bot/. Accessed 2 May 2025
18. https://www.qudt.org. Accessed 2 May 2025
19. https://www.w3.org/TR/owl-time/. Accessed 2 May 2025

Leveraging Generative AI and Semantic Data for Improved Operation of a Real-Life Building

John Clauß(✉), Luis Caetano, Knut Nordanger, Thomas Elvrum Lassen, and Reidar Kind

SINTEF Community, 7034 Trondheim, Norway
{john.clauss,luis.caetano}@sintef.no

Abstract. The operation of modern buildings generates large volumes of sensor data that, if effectively utilized, can significantly improve energy efficiency and fault detection. However, conventional fault detection and diagnosis (FDD) systems often rely on rule-based methods that lack context-awareness, generate excessive false alarms, and demand expert interpretation. This paper presents a novel framework that combines Large Language Models (LLMs), time series data, and semantic knowledge graphs to enhance building operation and diagnostics. The approach is implemented and evaluated in the ZEB Laboratory, a full-scale zero-emission building and research infrastructure in Trondheim, Norway.

The proposed system integrates structured sensor metadata from a Neo4j-based knowledge graph with real-time measurement data from an InfluxDB time-series database. An LLM (GPT-4o) processes this data to detect anomalies and generate contextual explanations and recommended actions in natural language. One exemplary room serves as the primary testbed, showcasing how knowledge-driven reasoning enables accurate, actionable alerts with reduced false positives. Test scenarios demonstrate the framework's ability to identify faults and guide operational decisions. Structured outputs support seamless dashboard integration and potential for automated control. This work shows how generative AI combined with semantic metadata and real-time data streams can transform building management into a more intelligent, interpretable, and proactive process.

Keywords: generative AI · semantic data · building operation · anomaly detection

1 Introduction

The building sector is a major contributor to global greenhouse gas (GHG) emissions and energy consumption. Within the European Union (EU), buildings account for approximately 36% of total GHG emissions and about 40% of total energy use [1]. Despite efforts toward energy-efficient technologies, the sector remains a prime candidate for operational improvements, especially within existing buildings, where 75% of the stock is deemed energy inefficient [1]. Improving operational efficiency is a core strategy for achieving climate targets, such as the EU's commitment to reducing emissions by 55% by 2030 compared to 1990 levels [1]. Key to this transformation is the use of data-driven building management systems, advanced control strategies, and Fault Detection and Diagnostics (FDD) methods to minimize avoidable energy waste and increase system reliability.

Studies show that 15%–30% of energy use in buildings is wasted due to faults in heating, ventilation, and air conditioning (HVAC) systems, along with suboptimal control and maintenance practices [2, 3]. These issues not only lead to higher energy bills and GHG emissions but also reduce occupant comfort and accelerate equipment wear. FDD systems, especially automated fault detection and diagnostics (AFDD), are designed to detect such issues, ideally before they cause major inefficiencies. However, in practice, many tools rely on static rule-based logic, where faults are defined by threshold violations. This method often leads to alarm fatigue, where facility managers are inundated with non-critical alerts and have limited tools for prioritizing real issues [4]. More advanced FDD methods leverage time series data and machine learning to identify anomalies that evolve over time, offering improved precision. However, despite significant academic progress in this domain, real-world deployment remains limited, due to issues such as poor interoperability, lack of labeled fault data, and integration complexity [2, 5].

Even when faults are detected, following up requires substantial time and human expertise. Facility managers often must review raw time series data or consult static fault reports without contextual insight. Moreover, documentation of building conditions over time is often lacking, despite its value for audits, performance tracking, and tenant communication. Dashboards and digital twins have been proposed to address these limitations, but few existing systems allow facility managers to interact naturally with the underlying data or to generate contextual explanations and summaries of building performance. This gap between detection and action continues to hinder scalable improvements in operational efficiency [4].

The emergence of Generative AI, especially Large Language Models (LLMs), opens new possibilities for augmenting FDD and building management tools. By combining semantic models, e.g., ontologies like Brick and Project Haystack, with LLMs trained on diverse datasets, it becomes possible to build systems that not only detect faults but also explain them, reason across systems, and provide actionable summaries in natural language. Early semantic frameworks such as Brick Schema [6] and Project Haystack [7] enable structured representation of building metadata and relationships. These can be combined with time series anomaly detection models and LLM-based interfaces to translate data into actionable insights, even for non-expert users. However, integration between LLMs, time series data, and building ontologies remains largely unexplored. The potential for these technologies to improve explainability, reduce false positives, and streamline communication with human operators represents an important research frontier.

This paper presents a novel approach that couples generative AI (LLMs) with time series data and semantic metadata models to enhance near real-time understanding and management of building performance. The contribution of this work is threefold:

1. Proposal of a *conceptual and technical framework* integrating LLMs, semantics, and a time series database for building operation.

2. Demonstration of the application of this framework on data from *a real-life building*, showing how it enhances interpretability, fault explanation, and user friendliness.
3. Showcasing the framework to *support facility managers* in day-to-day operations and long-term documentation, reducing follow-up burden and improving decision support.

The paper is divided into five sections. Section 2 introduces the real-life pilot building, Sect. 3 the methodology, and Sect. 4 presents the results of various exemplary faults to be detected and communicated to the facility manager. Section 5 concludes the work and outlines further work.

2 ZEB Laboratory

2.1 General Information

The Zero Emission Building (ZEB) Laboratory, located at the Gløshaugen campus of the Norwegian University of Science and Technology (NTNU) in Trondheim, Norway, is a state-of-the-art research infrastructure jointly operated by NTNU and SINTEF. It serves as a real-world testbed for advanced studies in sustainable building technologies, including energy efficiency, indoor environmental quality, and data-driven building operation. The building is designed to meet the ZEB-COM performance target, aiming for net-zero CO_2 emissions over its 60-year life cycle, including embodied, operational, and end-of-life emissions [8]. In addition to being a demonstrator for climate-resilient and energy-efficient construction, the ZEB Laboratory functions as a living lab where new control strategies, digital tools, and smart services can be tested under realistic conditions. Among its notable research assets are two "Twin Rooms" equipped with dedicated HVAC systems and sensor networks, allowing controlled experimentation and side-by-side comparison of interventions such as data-driven control or fault detection strategies.

2.2 Data Infrastructure and Data Flow

A cornerstone of the ZEB Laboratory's functionality is its advanced data infrastructure, designed to support real-time monitoring, control, and experimentation. More than 1500 sensors are deployed across the building, capturing high-resolution data on parameters such as temperature, humidity, air quality, energy flows, occupancy, and equipment status. These sensors are integrated through a Building Management System (BMS), Siemens DesigoCC, which communicates via the building network BACnet. To support data-driven applications, a dedicated data pipeline has been established. Operational data is continuously streamed from BACnet devices to an InfluxDB time-series database via a gateway server (Fig. 1) and a custom-developed middleware, *BACnet2Influx*. This setup enables high-frequency data ingestion and robust query handling for analytics and machine learning applications.

A parallel control interface, BACforsk (Fig. 2), allows researchers to temporarily override standard BMS logic and deploy custom control scripts. This is critical for testing novel supervisory control strategies, or services leveraging LLMs or semantic reasoning

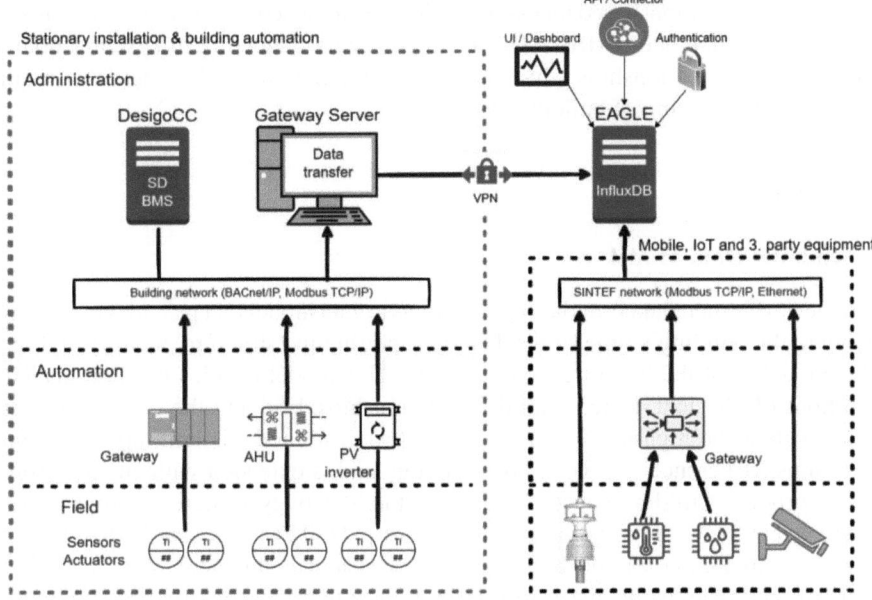

Fig. 1. Instrumentation and data flow in the ZEB Laboratory in Trondheim, Norway [8].

engines. The platform is compatible with MQTT, enabling lightweight, distributed access to live data and control endpoints, facilitating integration with external (cloud) services. More detailed information on the technical infrastructure is provided in [9].

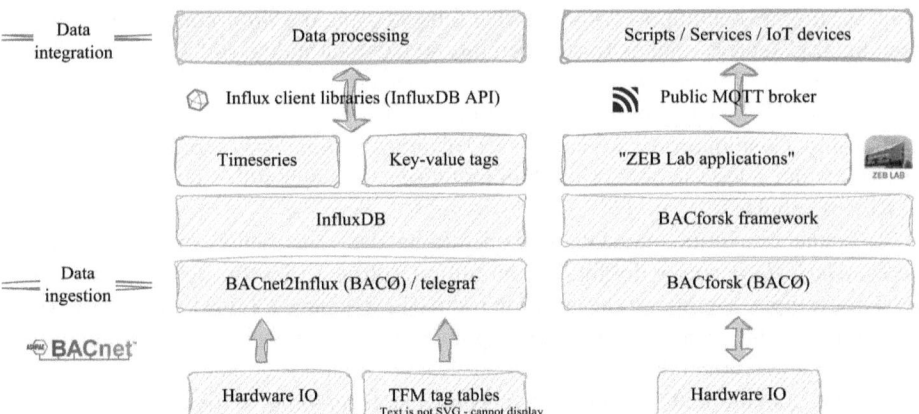

Fig. 2. High-level schematic illustration of the established framework [9].

Additionally, a graph-based metadata model is established using Neo4j and semantic ontologies like Brick and SAREF. This enables semantic labeling of systems, components, and spatial relationships which is crucial for generative AI models that require contextual understanding of building systems.

3 Methodology

3.1 Semantic Data Model

The framework's metadata foundation is a semantic data model that provides context and meaning to the building's time series data by capturing the structure, identity and sensing functionality of the building's components. This model enables machine-readable descriptions of physical devices and their relationships, bridging the gap between raw time series data and high-level operational context. The model is built upon the Smart Applications REFerence (SAREF) [10] ontology and is extended with custom properties to incorporate building-specific needs and the Statsbygg's interdisciplinary classification system TFM (Tverrfaglig merkesystem) [11]. TFM is a standardized system used across Norwegian public buildings for consistent component identification. At the core of the model is the class *saref:Device*, used to represent physical components such as room units, sensors, and actuators. Standard SAREF properties are employed to store metadata such as manufacturer and model number. Each device is uniquely identified using TFM codes. The TFM classification system is represented through a custom *skos:ConceptScheme* [12] and with properties such as *hasTFMSystemCode* (e.g. 569 signal systems), *hasTFMComponentType* (e.g. RT for temperature sensors) and *hasTFMComponentIdentifier* (e.g. RT601).

A typical example is a multifunctional room unit (e.g., RT601), modelled as a *saref:Device* and decomposed into internal sensors using the *saref:consistsOf* property. Each internal sensor, such as for temperature, relative humidity, or CO_2 concentration, is modeled as a distinct *saref:Sensor* instance. Sensor types are further specified using *saref:FeatureKind*, with the measured property being defined via the *saref:observes* relationship. Custom properties such as $CO_2Concentration$, *DewPointTemperature*, and *Brightness* are added to reflect the building's sensing capabilities beyond the default SAREF vocabulary.

To connect semantic metadata with operational data, each sensor instance includes a *hasTimeSeriesId* property linking it to an InfluxDB time series through a unique identifier. For example, a temperature sensor in room 312 will have a 1:1 relationship to a time series through this identifier, thus enabling the retrieval and contextual interpretation of real-time and historical data.

Spatial containment is represented using the *saref4bldg:isContainedIn* property, linking each device to its corresponding room or spatial zone (e.g., room 312). This spatial anchoring is essential for contextual reasoning, such as associating environmental conditions with occupancy or supporting localized control strategies.

Figure 3 shows the knowledge graph representing the interconnected network of sensors and devices associated with room 312 in the ZEB Laboratory. At the core of the graph lies room 312 itself, depicted centrally, which interfaces with numerous surrounding entities. These entities include various sensors (such as temperature, relative humidity, dew point, and CO_2 concentration), brightness sensors for lighting optimization, and presence detection sensors to facilitate occupancy-driven controls. Additionally, the graph includes equipment like supply air and variable air volume (VAV) sensors for airflow management, and window status sensors. Connected actuators, control devices with sensors are represented by nodes with TFM label, include heating valves, radiator valve positions, and blinds/shutter actuators, allowing for precise environmental adjustments within the space. Overall, this knowledge graph provides a comprehensive overview of the smart infrastructure in room 312 in the ZEB Laboratory, highlighting the integration of environmental monitoring, occupancy comfort management, and energy-efficient controls.

3.2 Developed Framework

Figure 4 illustrates the workflow designed to detect and respond to anomalies in room conditions using a Large Language Model (LLM). The integration of LLMs significantly improves/simplifies anomaly detection and diagnosis by incorporating contextual insights from knowledge graphs that connect various sensor metadata. This approach helps the system effectively distinguish genuine changes in room conditions from equipment-related issues such as sensor drift or hardware malfunctions. As a result, the system can achieve greater accuracy, significantly reducing false positives and ensuring alerts are both meaningful and actionable.

The workflow process begins with the integration of sensor data sourced from both a graph database (Neo4j) and a time-series database (InfluxDB), complemented by user-defined reasoning prompts. This comprehensive dataset is then processed via API calls to an LLM, currently GPT-4o, which was selected for its advanced reasoning capabilities. The LLM analyzes the current status of room conditions, identifies anomalies, and assesses their potential underlying causes. Structured responses generated by the LLM are returned in a predefined JSON format, facilitating smooth integration and clear visualization in the front-end user interface. While the approach currently depends on a proprietary API, the system is designed to be modular, allowing for future substitution with open-source or locally hosted LLMs to enhance replicability and long-term scalability. The initiation of this anomaly detection workflow can occur through continuous real-time monitoring of time-series data or through periodic snapshots of sensor conditions. As represented in Fig. 4, the detailed workflow proceeds as follows: Initially, structured snapshots of room conditions, including information from room ontology and sensor time-series data, are combined with user-defined prompts and analysed by the LLM. These prompts guide the model to perform anomaly detection and failure identification based on sensor readings, using domain-specific knowledge such as the expected comfort levels for office buildings in Norway. The LLM then produces actionable insights and recommendations in a structured JSON format.

If the LLM successfully identifies the cause of an anomaly, it logs the relevant information into the alerting system, accompanied by clear fault messages and recommended actions. If the cause cannot be determined, the anomaly will be escalated for manual intervention and further investigation to ensure a timely and effective resolution.

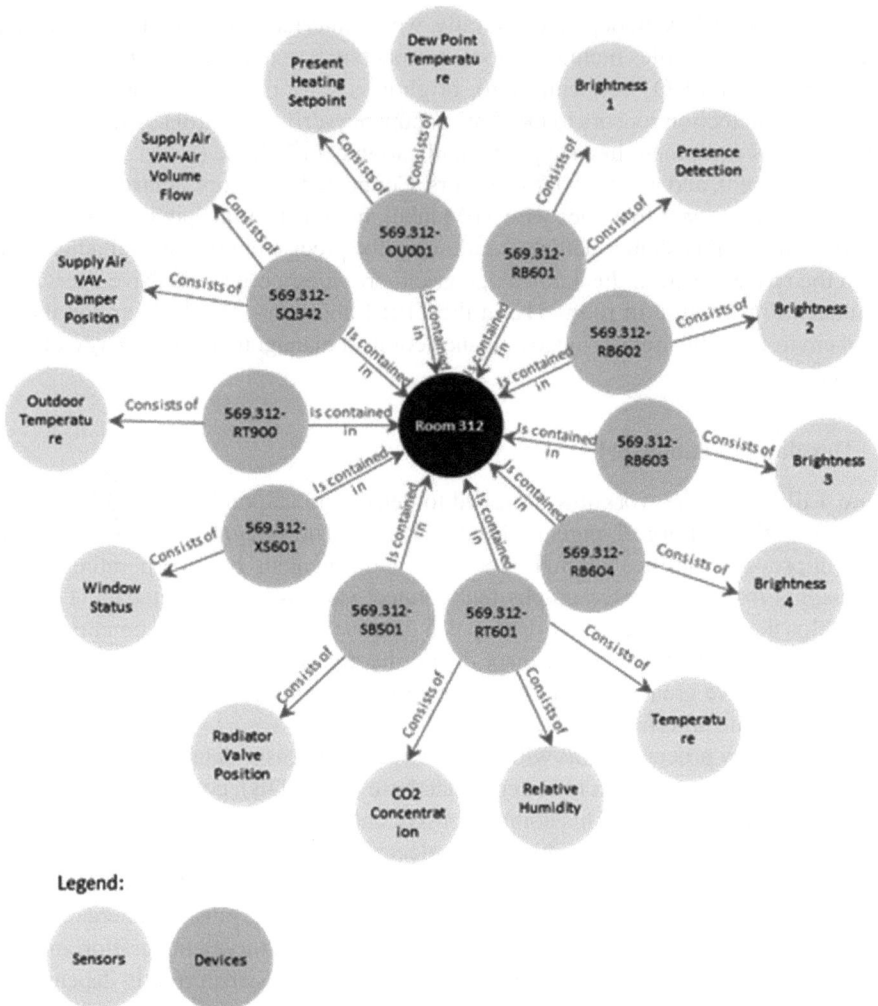

Fig. 3. Knowledge graph representing relationships between devices and sensors in the room.

3.3 Dashboard

To support better decision-making in building operations, we developed a dashboard to make data on room conditions more accessible and actionable. The dashboard, demonstrated in Fig. 5, provides an overview of indoor environmental conditions across building spaces, helping users quickly identify and address potential comfort and operational issues. Sensor data is summarized to highlight the status of key parameters such as temperature, humidity, brightness, and occupancy.

When anomalies or deviations from ideal conditions occur, the system alerts the user by clearly describing the problem and recommending immediate corrective actions. This ensures prompt resolution of issues to maintain optimal indoor comfort and energy efficiency. Additionally, the dashboard presents detailed sensor readings and explanations,

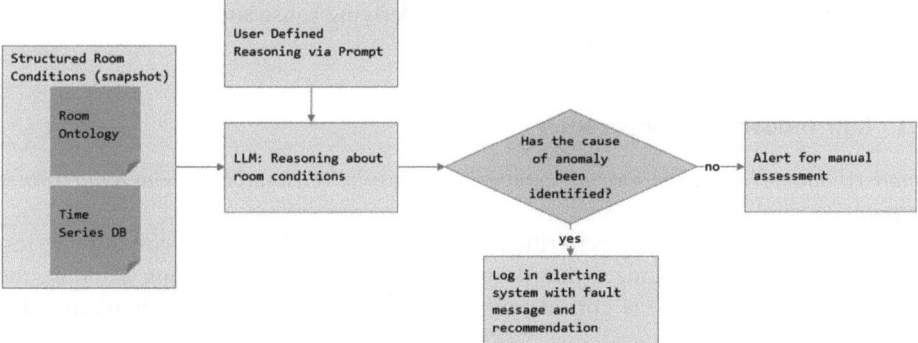

Fig. 4. Development of a Server-Client relation.

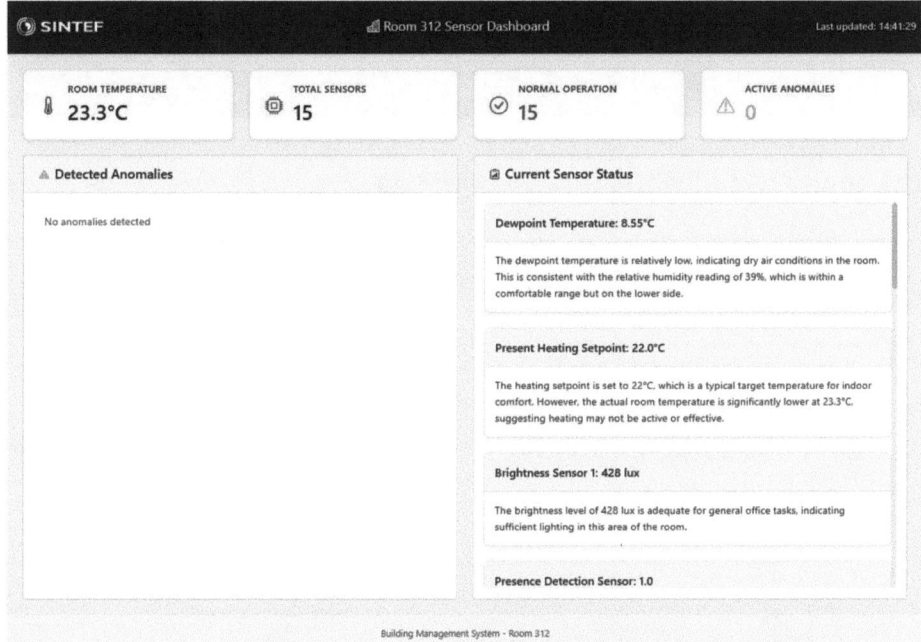

Fig. 5. Dashboard for room conditions.

helping users understand the context behind each measurement and effectively make informed decisions for building management.

4 Evaluating Anomaly Detection and LLM-Based Reasoning

This section presents a series of test scenarios designed to evaluate the framework's ability to detect various environmental anomalies using sensor data and LLM-based reasoning. Each scenario introduces a specific fault or irregular condition and examines whether the system can correctly identify the underlying cause and provide appropriate recommendations based on contextual cues.

4.1 Low Indoor Air Temperature

Imposed anomaly: Low indoor air temperature despite reasonable "room temperature setpoint"

In this scenario we have overwritten specific readings of the room condition to test whether the system recognizes that despite having an adequate heating setpoint, the actual indoor temperature is considerably lower. The values used for simulating this situation are:

- An indoor temperature significantly lower than the setpoint (e.g. 10 °C).
- A normal heating setpoint (e.g., 22 °C) indicating that heating should be active.

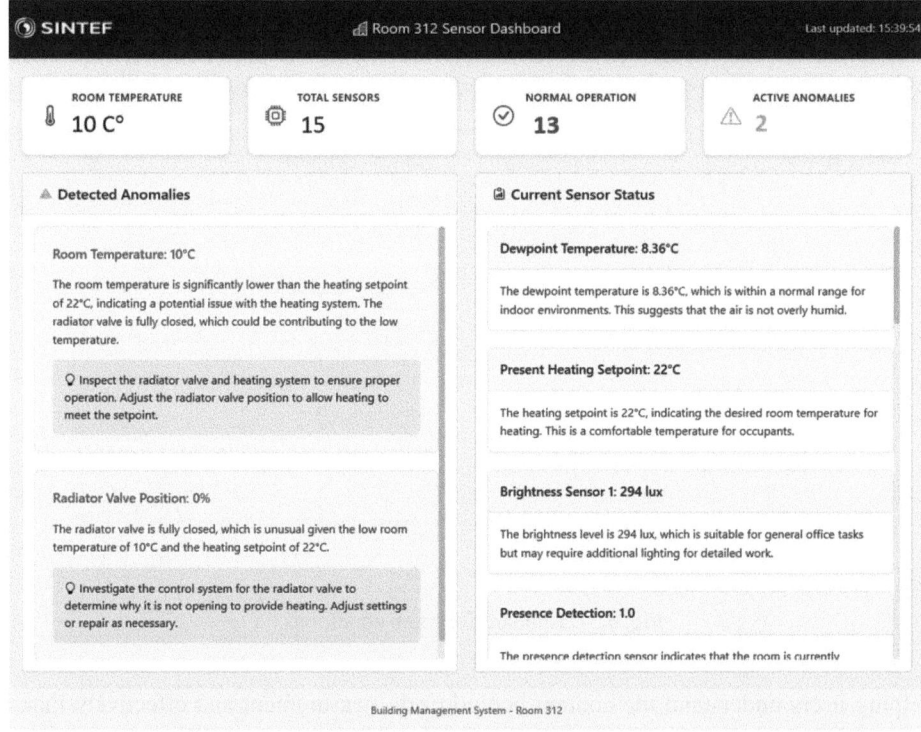

Fig. 6. Dashboard results when testing low indoor temperature and normal heating setpoint.

Figure 6 showcases the system's ability to detect a malfunction in the heating system despite an adequate heating setpoint. The system concludes there may be a fault in the heating system, particularly the radiator valve actuator or control mechanism, and suggests checking the valve actuator and related controls.

Imposed anomaly: Low indoor air temperatures with "window open"

In this scenario, the system tests if it can detect that the indoor temperature is unusually low because a window has been left open. The indicators used to represent this are:

- A low indoor temperature reading, here imposed 10 °C.
- An active status from the window sensor indicating the window is open.

The dashboard in Fig. 7 demonstrates how the system detects an unusually low indoor temperature due to an open window. The system correctly flags this as an active anomaly and recommends closing the window to reduce heat loss and help the heating system maintain the desired temperature.

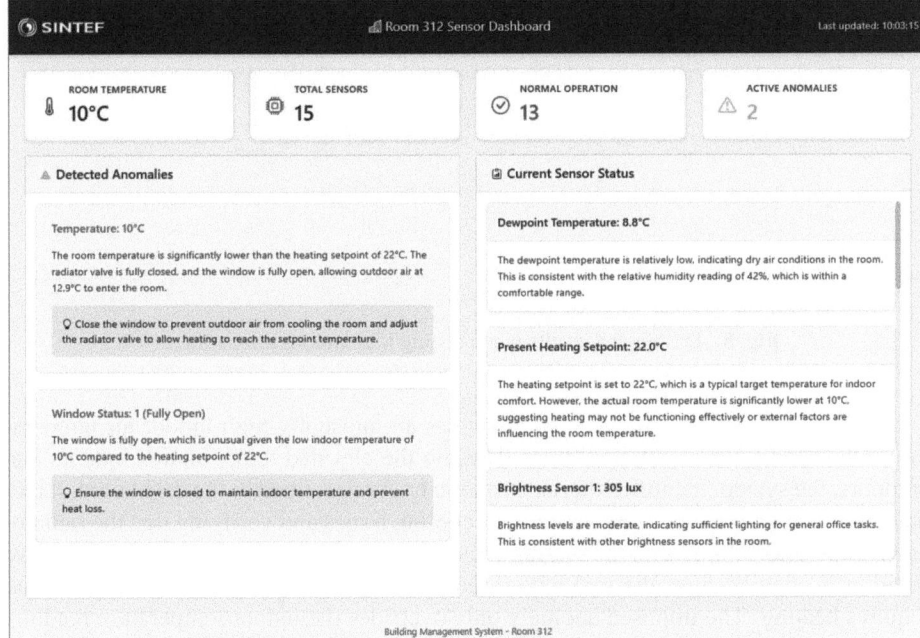

Fig. 7. Dashboard results when testing low indoor temperature and window open.

4.2 High Indoor Temperature

Imposed anomaly: High indoor air temperature

In this scenario, the system is tested to test if it can recognize that high indoor air temperature are influenced by similarly high outdoor air temperatures. The indicators used to represent this are:

- Elevated indoor temperature, here imposed 30 °C.
- Similarly elevated outdoor temperature, here imposed 30 °C.

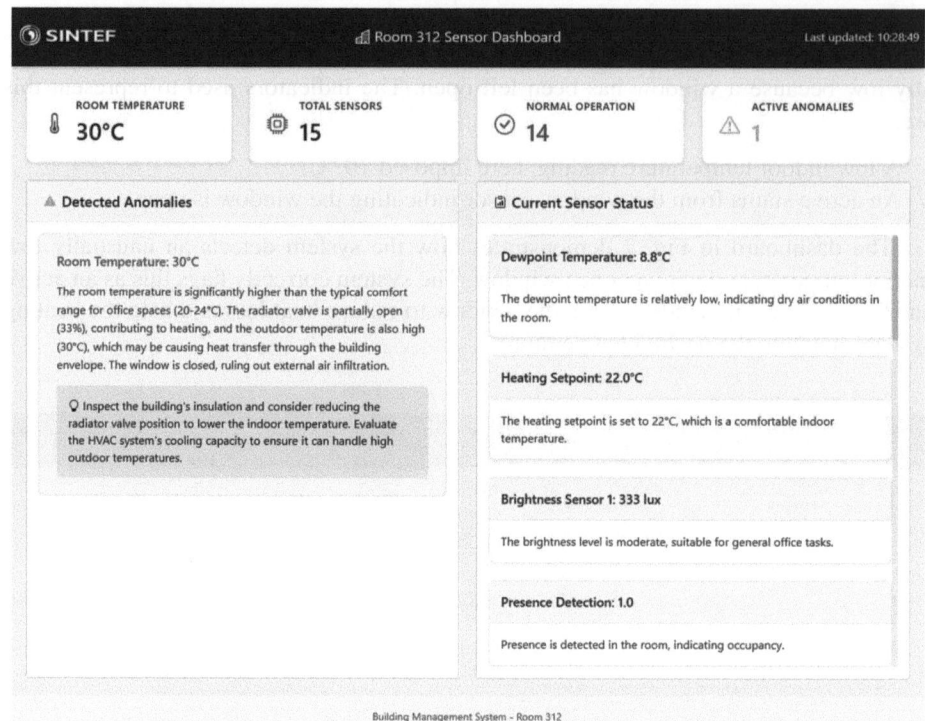

Fig. 8. Dashboard results when testing high indoor temperature.

Figure 8 illustrates how the system detects an unusually high indoor air temperature influenced by external conditions. Despite the elevated temperatures indoors and outdoors, the system identifies this as an anomaly. As described in the dashboard, it recommends inspecting the HVAC system for cooling issues and verifying that the radiator valve's operation aligns with the heating setpoint. Note that in this case, the radiator valve position is open because the real indoor temperature is in fact under the setpoint and requires heating. The imposed anomaly only overrides the indoor temperature reading, not other parameters such as the valve position. As a result, the system detects a mismatch between the open valve (indicating a need for heating) and the high indoor temperature (imposed 30 °C, exceeding the setpoint), and correctly flags it as an anomaly.

4.3 High CO_2 Concentration

Imposed anomaly: High CO_2 concentration and ventilation "off"

In this scenario, we imposed a situation with poor indoor air quality caused by insufficient ventilation. The indicators used to represent this are:

- Elevated CO_2 concentration, here imposed 1000 ppm.
- A ventilation airflow sensor indicating that ventilation is currently off or providing no airflow.

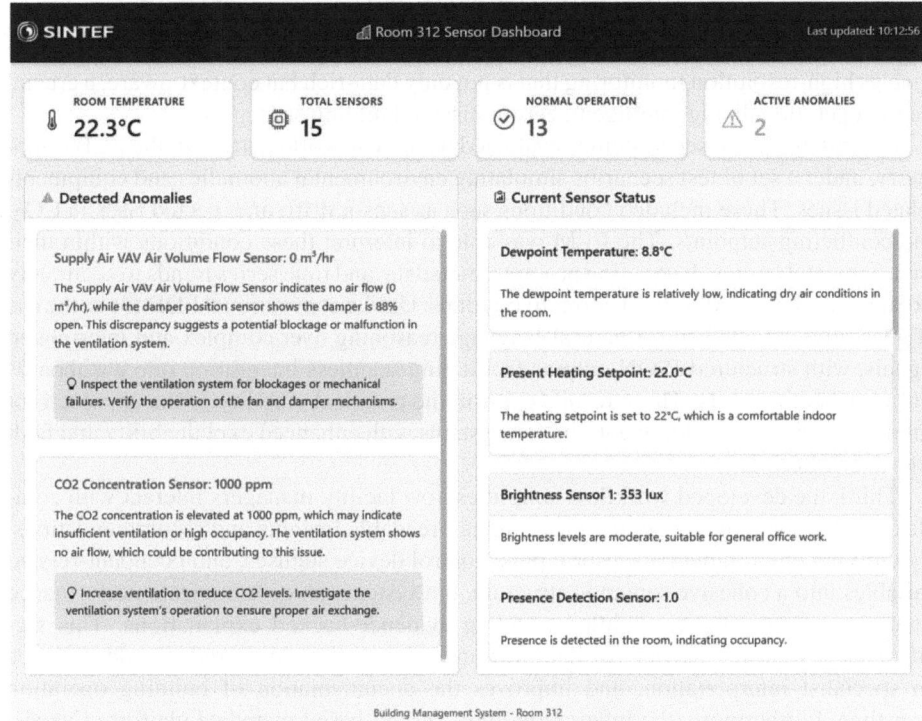

Fig. 9. Dashboard results when testing high CO_2 and ventilation "off".

Figure 9 demonstrates the system's ability to detect poor indoor air quality due to insufficient ventilation, confirming that the system can effectively correlate high CO_2 levels with inactive ventilation, helping to maintain healthy indoor air quality.

5 Conclusions

This work presents an integrated framework for enhancing building operation through the combination of Large Language Models (LLMs), time series data, and semantic knowledge representations, applied and tested in the ZEB Laboratory, a state-of-the-art zero-emission building and research infrastructure. The contributions of this work address critical needs in building management: contextual fault detection, improved decision support, and accessible documentation of building performance. We conclude by reflecting on the three key contributions:

First, we introduced a framework that connects the rich, structured semantics of a building's metadata, represented as knowledge graphs, with real-time sensor data stored in a time series database. Through this integration, LLMs such as GPT-4o can interpret dynamic room conditions, identify anomalies, and provide reasoning-informed diagnoses that go beyond threshold-based alerts. For instance, in Room 312 of the ZEB Laboratory, a knowledge graph was used to semantically map the interplay between sensors (e.g., temperature, humidity, CO_2, light) and actuators (e.g., heating valves, blinds), forming the foundation for intelligent LLM-driven analysis. This architecture enables high-resolution monitoring that is not only data-rich but context-aware, a crucial step in operationalizing intelligent, zero-emission building strategies.

Second, the proposed system is evaluated using real-world data from the ZEB Laboratory, under a set of test scenarios simulating environmental anomalies and equipment-related issues. These included conditions such as sensor drift, unexpected rises in CO_2, and conflicting setpoints. The LLM was able to interpret these conditions within their environmental context leveraging prompts, metadata, and time series trends to accurately isolate root causes and suggest corrective actions. Unlike conventional FDD tools, the use of generative AI allowed for natural-language reasoning over complex and interrelated signals, with structured JSON outputs facilitating seamless integration into dashboards and visualization tools. These results confirm the practical viability of the approach for augmenting current building automation systems with enhanced explainability and fault relevance filtering.

Third, the developed workflow simplifies how facility managers interact with complex building data by generating clear, human-readable insights and recommendations. By unifying environmental sensor inputs, control device statuses, and occupant-related variables into a cohesive semantic structure, the system can communicate performance status in natural language while providing evidence-backed explanations. This significantly lowers the barrier for data-informed decision-making, reduces dependence on specialist interpretation, and improves the documentation of building operation over time. Furthermore, the integration with a graph-based metadata platform (Neo4j) and lightweight front-end via structured API responses demonstrates the potential for scalable deployment in operational settings.

Building on the promising results from room-level integration, future work will focus on scaling the framework to cover the entire ZEB Laboratory (rooms and technical systems), enabling system-wide diagnostics, control, and optimization. One key direction is the differentiation between anomalies and physical failures, where anomalies can be addressed through system adjustments, while failures require physical intervention. This distinction will allow the system to trigger alerts for failures and perform self-correcting actions for anomalies, improving operational efficiency. For example, the detection of anomalies in the HVAC system operation that may cause energy waste without affecting the indoor environment, will be incorporated into the framework. Additionally, detected failures will be annotated in the dataset to enrich future training data for predictive models to be used for control of the HVAC system.

Acknowledgements. This authors gratefully acknowledge the financial supported by the Research Council of Norway and the ZEB Laboratory project under grant number 245663.

References

1. European Commission. Communication from the commission to the european parliament, the council, the european economic and social committee and the committee of the regions (2020). https://eur-lex.europa.eu/legal-content/EN/TXT/PDF/?uri=CELEX:52020DC0562

2. Chen, Z., et al.: A review of data-driven fault detection and diagnostics for building HVAC systems. Appl. Energy **339** (2023). https://doi.org/10.1016/j.apenergy.2023.121030
3. Katipamula, S., Brambley, M.R.: Review article: methods for fault detection, diagnostics, and prognostics for building systems—a review, part I. HVAC R Res. **11**(1), 3–25 (2005). https://doi.org/10.1080/10789669.2005.10391123
4. Heimar Andersen, K., Pommerencke Melgaard, S., Johra, H., Marszal-Pomianowska, A., Lund Jensen, R., Kvols Heiselberg, P.: Barriers and drivers for implementation of automatic fault detection and diagnosis in buildings and HVAC systems: an outlook from industry experts. Energy Build. **303**, 113801 (2024). https://doi.org/10.1016/j.enbuild.2023.113801
5. Chen, Y., Crowe, E., Lin, G., Granderson, J.: What ' s in a Name ? developing a standardized taxonomy for HVAC System faults (2020). https://escholarship.org/uc/item/351568bv
6. BrickSchema, BrickSchema (2022). https://brickschema.org/blog
7. Project Haystack, "Project Haystack." https://project-haystack.org/
8. Goia, F., Nordanger, K., Clauß, J.: ZEB laboratory (2024). https://static1.squarespace.com/static/5a156c44ccc5c5ef7b893553/t/67b89479d7118313afa5ba47/1740149899912/ZebLab_Rapport_2024_v12.pdf
9. Clauß, J., Lassen, T.E., Caetano, L., Skeie, K.S.: Towards automated energy flexibility deployment in buildings: a solution at the ZEB laboratory. In: 9th International Conference on Smart and Sustainable Technologies, SpliTech 2024 (2024). https://doi.org/10.23919/SpliTech61897.2024.10612479
10. Garcia-Castro, R., Lefrancois, M., Poveda-Villalon, M., Daniele, L.: The ETSI SAREF ontology for smart applications: a long path of development and evolution. In: Moreno-Munoz, A., Giacomini, N. (eds.) Energy Smart Appliances: Applications, Methodologies, and Challenges, pp. 183–215 (2023). https://doi.org/10.1002/9781119899457.ch7
11. Statsbygg. Tverrfaglig merkesystem. https://www.statsbygg.no/tfm
12. Miles, A., Bechhofer, S.: SKOS simple knowledge organization system reference. W3C Recommendation (2009). https://www.w3.org/TR/skos-reference/

Development of an LSTM-Based Model for High-Resolution Downsampling and Reconstruction of HVAC Chiller Flow Data

Yue He[✉], Shanrui Shi, Shohei Miyata, and Yasunori Akashi

The University of Tokyo, 7-3-1 Hongo, Bunkyo-ku, Tokyo 113-8656, Japan
heyue-1122@g.ecc.u-tokyo.ac.jp

Abstract. High-frequency time-series data from HVAC systems offer detailed insights into dynamic performance but incur significant storage and processing burdens. This paper presents an intelligent, deep-learning-based downsampling framework that simultaneously compresses data and preserves critical temporal features. Raw one-second measurements of chiller supply temperature and instantaneous flow rate are aggregated into multi-resolution feature sets (1 min, 30 s, 20 s, and 10 s) using statistical descriptors, and a long short-term memory (LSTM) network is trained to reconstruct the original one-second flow profile from these low-dimensional summaries. Comprehensive evaluation, including storage efficiency and mean squared error (MSE) against ground truth, demonstrates that the 20-s aggregation achieves the best trade-off, reducing average reconstruction error (MAE = 19.8 L/min, MAPE = 2.40%) and peak deviation (146.4 L/min) while cutting storage requirements by an order of magnitude. The model also reduces the MSE during rapid ramp-up peaks by approximately 12% relative to one-minute baselines and maintains high fidelity in steady-state regimes. These results confirm that LSTM-based downsampling can dramatically lower data volumes with minimal loss of high-frequency information, enabling more efficient monitoring and fault detection in HVAC applications.

Keywords: Heating ventilation and air conditioning (HVAC) · Long short-term memory (LSTM) · High-resolution data

1 Introduction

With the advancement of indoor environmental monitoring technologies, acquiring high-resolution data at one-second intervals has become possible. Such data are essential for heating, ventilation, and air conditioning (HVAC) system optimization, energy consumption analysis, and fault detection and diagnosis (FDD) [1, 2]. However, the use of high-resolution time-series data introduces several key challenges:

1) High storage demand: Continuous monitoring generates massive datasets. For example, storing 1-s interval data from 40 sensors over two months requires 2.53 GB, whereas 1- and 5-min downsampling reduces the size to 41.16 MB (−98.4%) and 10.29 MB (−99.6%), respectively (Fig. 1 and Table 1).

2) Data redundancy: Many recorded data points exhibit minimal variation and provide limited new information, causing storage inefficiencies. Naive downsampling can reduce file size but may discard valuable transient behaviors.
3) Potential information loss: Fixed-interval downsampling (e.g., 5 or 10 min) may overlook short-term fluctuations that are critical for timely and accurate FDD.

To address these challenges, this paper proposes an intelligent data storage optimization approach based on deep learning. Specifically, we aim to reduce data storage requirements while preserving important time-series characteristics; explore the potential of long short-term memory (LSTM) networks to enhance storage efficiency while preserving critical temporal information necessary for fault detection and system-level analysis in HVAC systems [3]. In summary, this study developed an LSTM-based dimensionality reduction method to improve storage efficiency without compromising the critical temporal information required for fault detection and system-level analysis.

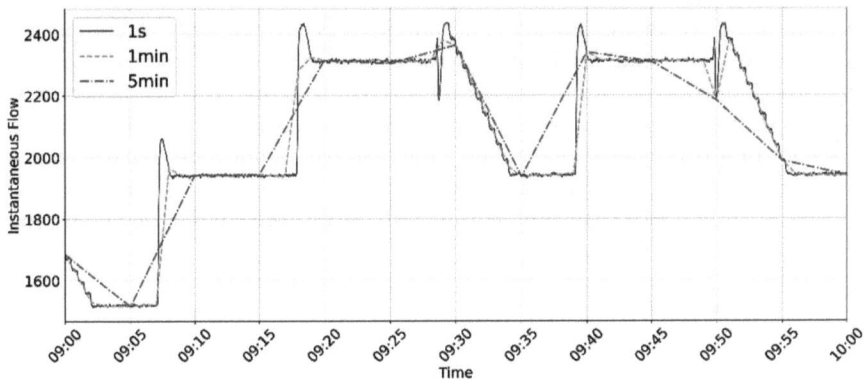

Fig. 1. Comparison of data at different sampling intervals

Table 1. Storage capacity of the sensor system by sampling interval

60-day data (40 sensors)		
Dataset	Data Points	File Size (KB)
1-s Interval	207 360 000	2 590 720 KB ($\approx$ 2.53 GB)
1-min Interval	3 456 000	41 160 KB ($\approx$ 41.16 MB)
5-min Interval	691 200	10 540 KB ($\approx$ 10.29 MB)

2 Background

The key challenge in managing high-resolution data for HVAC systems lies in determining a balance between reducing storage requirements and preserving critical time-series information. Traditional downsampling methods are often employed to reduce data volume, but each has limitations. Fixed-interval downsampling (e.g., 1, 5, and 10 min) is simple and computationally efficient but tends to ignore transient events and anomalies, thereby reducing the accuracy of FDD [4]. Statistical downsampling (e.g., mean, median, max) is advantageous for long-term trend analysis and minimizing data fluctuations but often conceals subtle variations that are critical for detecting faults. In summary, conventional methods struggle to optimize storage efficiency while retaining essential information, potentially compromising FDD performance.

To overcome these limitations, recent research has explored deep learning–based dimensionality reduction, most notably LSTM networks, which compress data while retaining underlying temporal dynamics. For example, Zhu et al. [5] introduced an LSTM-SVDD framework that dynamically adjusts fault residual thresholds based on the discrepancy between predicted and observed values, achieving real-time HVAC fault detection across varying severity levels. Similarly, Jin et al. [6] developed an LSTM-based autoencoder as a virtual temperature sensor for chilled water supply, reporting F1-scores from 0.935 to 1.000 under diverse fault conditions and demonstrating strong robustness and generalization.

Despite these advances, research on applying LSTM networks to compress and reconstruct truly high-frequency HVAC measurements is rare. Most studies have focused on lower resolution aggregates or leveraging LSTM for sensor anomaly detection without evaluating its ability to recover fine-grained, one-second temporal dynamics. This study focused on two central challenges: How can we significantly reduce data storage without losing critical temporal information? How can we ensure that time-series patterns necessary for FDD can still be accurately reconstructed after downsampling?

3 Research Method

3.1 LSTM Method

In this study, we adopted an LSTM network as a unified approach to data compression and information preservation [7]. LSTM, a specialized variant of recurrent neural network (RNN), is explicitly designed to capture long-term dependencies in time-series data. Conventional RNNs often suffer from information loss and the "vanishing gradient" problem as the sequence length increases; LSTM overcomes these limitations through internal memory cells regulated by input, output, and forget gates (Fig. 2) [8, 9].

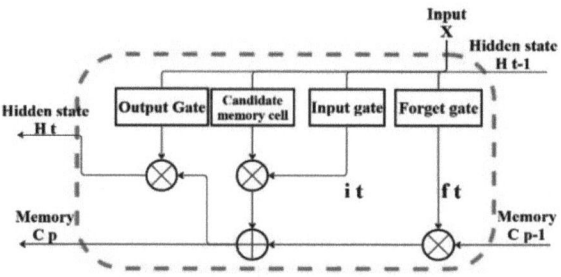

Fig. 2. LSTM conceptual diagram

The network is trained by minimizing the mean squared error (MSE) between predicted and ground-truth flow values:

$$MSE = \frac{1}{T}\sum_{t=1}^{T}(y_t - \hat{y}_t)^2 \tag{1}$$

where y_t is the actual value, $\hat{y}_t$ is the model prediction, and T is the length of the time series data. LSTM offers several key advantages for this task: it effectively models long-range temporal correlations, captures nonlinear dynamic behaviors more accurately than traditional statistical approaches, and readily handles irregular, high-frequency data, thereby enabling intelligent downsampling without significant loss of fine-scale information [10].

3.2 Data and Framework

The original dataset comprised time-series measurements sampled at one-second intervals [11, 12]. We evaluated three downsampling and prediction strategies: first, a full-resolution approach that retains the raw one-second data as ground truth; second, a fixed-interval baseline that uniformly subsamples at 1 min, 30 s, 20 s, and 10 s; third, an LSTM-based downsampling method. Evaluation metrics included storage efficiency and MSE between the reconstructed and original signals [13].

As shown in Fig. 3, our forecasting framework consists of three sequential stages. In the data ingestion stage, raw time-series measurements sampled at one-second intervals undergo formatting, cleaning, and scaling before being split into a high-resolution training set (one-second data) and a compressed validation set (1 min/30 s/20 s/10 s aggregated data). One-second supply temperature (°C) and flow rates at various aggregation intervals serve as input features, whereas the one-second instantaneous flow rate is defined as the target variable.

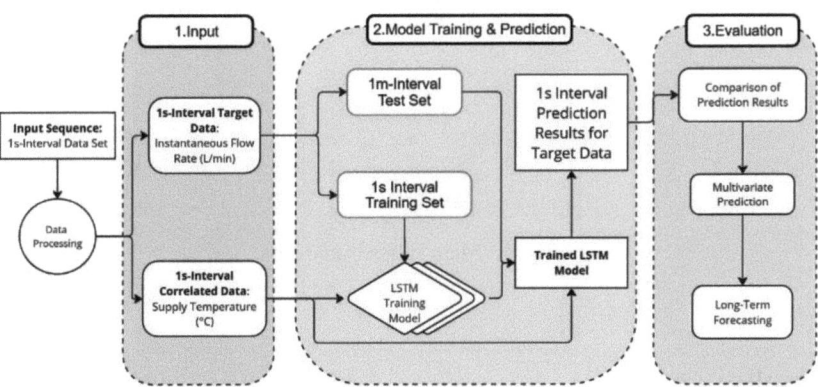

Fig. 3. Flowchart

In the model development and prediction stage, this study employed an LSTM network to map each compressed input vector to its corresponding sequence of sixty flow values every second. By training exclusively on low-dimension summaries paired with high-resolution targets, the model learns to reconstruct fine-grained dynamics from aggregated data.

Finally, in the performance evaluation stage, prediction accuracy is quantified by comparing the LSTM's reconstructed one-second outputs against the actual measurements using the MSE, thereby rigorously assessing the framework's ability to recover high-frequency signal characteristics.

3.3 Target Measurement Points to Be Downsampled and Reconstructed

The building targeted in this study is a human resource development center located in Japan. This facility is equipped with Internet-of-Things (IoT) sensors that comprehensively cover HVAC, water supply and drainage, and electrical systems. Among them, 40 sensors can collect high-frequency data at one-second intervals, which is a notable feature. Such high-resolution and diverse sensor data include subtle fluctuations essential for accurately capturing the dynamic behavior of HVAC systems and detecting anomalies, making them suitable as empirical data for verifying the effectiveness of storage optimization and high-precision estimation.

In particular, physical quantities with significant temporal variation, such as supply temperature and instantaneous flow rate, were used as benchmarks to evaluate prediction accuracy and time-series pattern retention performance. This study focused on reproducing the characteristic data of flow rate changes associated with chiller control adjustments. As shown in Fig. 4, the target data was limited to two weeks of weekdays during the winter of 2024 (from November 18 to 29), and the model evaluation was conducted to reflect the chiller load and operating characteristics under cold weather conditions.

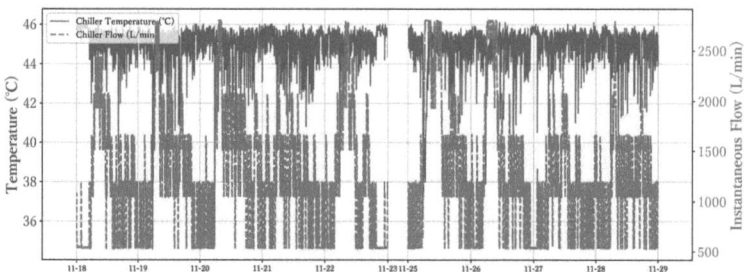

Fig. 4. Main subjects and data

4 Results

Figure 5a shows the actual data of the chiller flow over a two-hour test window. Here, the signals subsampled at 1 min, 30 s, 20 s, and 10 s overlapped nearly perfectly with the one-second ground truth, indicating that during relatively stable operating periods, fixed-interval downsampling—even at one-minute intervals—introduced negligible distortion.

In contrast, Fig. 5b magnifies the rapid ramp-up segment around 09:35–09:55. In this transient event, both the 1 min and 30 s series failed to reach the true peak flow recorded at one-second resolution, underestimating the maximum by a noticeable margin. The 20-s and 10-s intervals captured the peak more faithfully, although slight smoothing remained.

The predicted results at various aggregation intervals against measured data were compared both at the macro level and over specific time segments. As shown in Fig. 6, during the one hour from 09:00 to 10:00 on November 28, the LSTM model fed with one-minute aggregates consistently tracked the measured flow. In particular, during the rapid ramp-up phases between 09:35–09:40 (600 → 1200 L/min) and 09:45–09:50 (1200 → 1600 L/min), the model's predictions more faithfully reproduced the true peak values than the one-minute baseline. During the subsequent steady-state interval (09:40–09:45), the predicted and measured time series exhibited nearly identical fluctuation patterns. Conversely, in the low-flow region (≈600 L/min), the model exhibited slight deviations from the actual data, resulting in higher relative errors than during peak periods. These findings demonstrated that, although the proposed method excels at reconstructing dynamics during transient ramp-up phases, improving accuracy in low-flow regimes remains an avenue for future research.

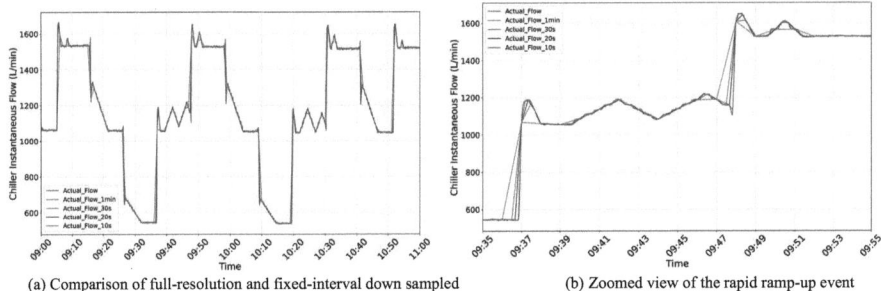

(a) Comparison of full-resolution and fixed-interval down sampled   (b) Zoomed view of the rapid ramp-up event

Fig. 5. Comparison of downsampling intervals

As shown in Fig. 7, these predicted results evaluated the LSTM model's ability to reconstruct the ramp-up peak between 09:35:00 and 09:55:00 using these four aggregation intervals. The original flow signal increased sharply from approximately 600 to 1200 L/min and stabilized at 1,150–1200 L/min by 09:37:00. All four schemes captured the overall rise and return to steady-state but with varying fidelity. Under 1-min aggregation, the model reproduced the peak with a maximum absolute error of ±38.53 L/min (≈3.2%) but displayed a noticeable temporal lag and an overly smooth, linear transition. Reducing the interval to 30 s decreased the peak error to ±23.79 L/min (≈2.0%), although the peak timing remained offset. A 20-s aggregation further improved accuracy, yielding a peak error of ±13.92 L/min (≈1.17%). The 10-s input series achieved near-synchronous peak detection (within 1 s) and limited the maximum error to ±2.5 L/min (≈0.21%).

During the subsequent steady-state interval (09:38–09:46), all predictions exhibited some drift relative to the ground truth; however, the 10-s and 20-s models more effectively

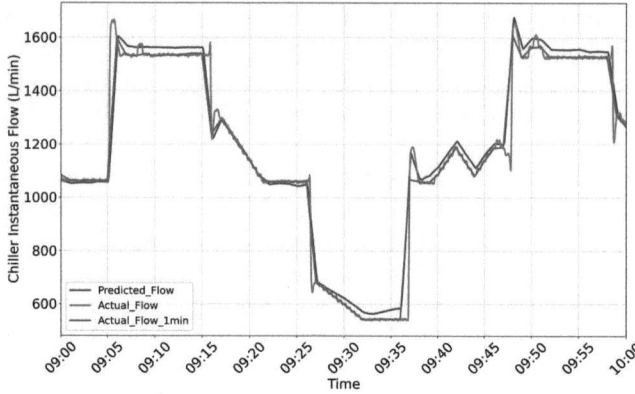

Fig. 6. Comparison of measured and LSTM-predicted flow time series using 1-min internal

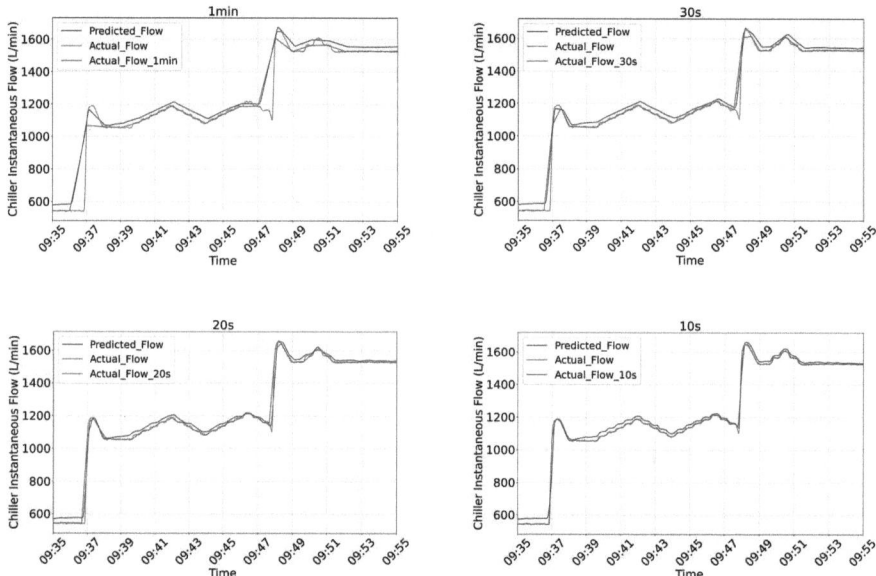

Fig. 7. Comparison of performance for the ramp-up peak under different downsampling intervals (1 min, 30 s, 20 s, 10 s).

captured the chiller's stepwise operating characteristics. These results demonstrated that predictive accuracy under stable conditions remains an area for further improvement.

As shown in Fig. 8, the absolute prediction error between the LSTM's one-second predictions and actual measurements data remained low during relatively steady-state periods (09:30–09:35 and 09:38–09:45), at 10–20 L/min for the 20-s and 10-s schemes versus 20–40 L/min for the 1-min and 30-s baselines. In contrast, the rapid ramp-up

Development of an LSTM-Based Model for High-Resolution Downsampling

events around 09:36 and 09:48 produced pronounced error spikes—approximately 300 L/min for the 30-s interval and 150 L/min for the 20-s interval.

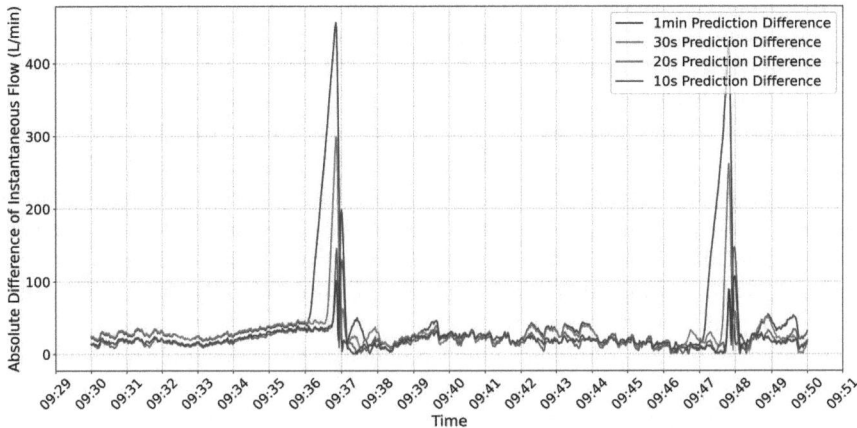

Fig. 8. Absolute prediction error of instantaneous flow

A quantitative evaluation over the entire 09:30–09:50 window (Table 2) showed that the 20-s aggregation achieved the lowest overall error (mean absolute error (MAE) = 19.8 L/min, mean absolute percentage error (MAPE) = 2.40%) and a maximum deviation of 146.4 L/min, demonstrating the best trade-off between storage reduction and prediction fidelity. Coarser sampling degraded the performance: the 30-s baseline yielded MAE = 29.7 L/min (MAPE = 3.80%), and the 1-min interval incurred the highest errors (MAE = 43.5 L/min, MAPE = 5.55%). These findings confirmed that finer downsampling intervals (20 or 30 s) markedly improve average and worst-case predictive performance for high-frequency transient flows in chiller systems.

In summary, our multi-scale evaluation, spanning both the hour-long series and the focused ramp-up peaks, demonstrates that the 20-s aggregation interval consistently delivers the best compromise between data compression and reconstruction fidelity.

Table 2. Prediction error metrics for different downsampling intervals

Downsampling Interval	MAE (L/min)	MAPE (%)	Max. Absolute Deviation (L/min)
1 min	43.49	5.55	456.06
30 s	29.70	3.80	298.29
20 s	19.81	2.40	146.39
10 s	21.17	2.58	197.83

5 Conclusion and Discussion

This study demonstrated that an LSTM-based intelligent downsampling framework can effectively tackle the storage burden of high-resolution HVAC time-series data while preserving essential dynamic features. By aggregating one-second chiller flow measurements into multi-resolution summaries (1 min, 30 s, 20 s, and 10 s) and training an LSTM network to reconstruct the original one-second signal, our approach achieves up to 90% data reduction with only marginal increases in reconstruction error. During the critical ramp-up peak ($\approx$600 $\rightarrow$ 1200 L/min), one-second predictions reduced the MSE by 12% relative to one-minute aggregates. Among the tested intervals, the 20-s aggregation had the optimal balance, yielding the lowest overall MAE (19.8 L/min) and peak deviation (146.4 L/min) while maintaining excellent fidelity in steady-state periods. Although the method excels at capturing rapid transient peaks, it exhibits slightly higher relative errors in low-flow regimes (~600 L/min), highlighting room for future refinement.

The proposed method, although validated here using chiller supply temperature and instantaneous flow rate, shows potential for extension to other HVAC measurements such as pressure and power consumption. These variables often exhibit similar transient behaviors but may require adjustments to aggregation strategies or model parameters to accommodate their unique temporal characteristics. Further validation on a wider variety of HVAC data would help confirm the method's general applicability.

Despite its advantages, the framework introduces computational overhead during the LSTM training phase. Although this cost is manageable for offline processing, it may pose scalability challenges when deployed across multiple systems. Strategies to improve training efficiency, such as model simplification or transfer learning, should be explored in future research.

Planned extensions include exploring intermediate aggregation scales with additional input features, integrating Transformer-based architectures for improved nonlinear modeling, and developing multi-scale, automated data management workflows. These efforts aim to enhance the framework's applicability for HVAC control optimization and fault detection, ultimately contributing to more efficient building energy management.

Overall, the proposed approach offers a practical solution to balance data reduction and information retention in high-resolution HVAC monitoring, creating the foundation for more efficient and intelligent building management systems.

Acknowledgment. This research was conducted with the support of the Smart Building System Research Initiative, Graduate School of Engineering, The University of Tokyo.

References

1. Cash, M., et al.: On false data injection attack against building automation systems. In: 2023 International Conference on Computing. Networking and Communications (ICNC), pp. 35–41. IEEE, Honolulu (2023)
2. Hosamo, H., Mazzetto, S.: Data-driven ventilation and energy optimization in smart office buildings: insights from a high-resolution occupancy and indoor climate dataset. Sustainability **17**(1), 58 (2025)

3. Fadel, M.A.: Data-driven fault detection and diagnostics for HVAC systems in buildings. Doctoral dissertation, Politecnico di Milano (2024)
4. Sharma, A., Sharma, V., Sharma, S., et al.: Fault detection and diagnosis in Air-Handling Unit (AHU) using deep learning models. Systems **13**(5), 330 (2023)
5. Zhu, H., Yang, W., Li, S., Pang, A.: An effective fault detection method for HVAC systems using the LSTM-SVDD algorithm. Buildings **12**(2), 246 (2022)
6. Jin, X., Fang, X., Zhou, W., Qian, K.: A virtual sensor of LSTM-autoencoder for detecting faults in chilled water supply temperature sensors. Appl. Sci. **14**(3), 1113 (2024)
7. Marino, D.L., Amarasinghe, K., Manic, M.: Building energy load forecasting using deep neural networks. In: IECON 2016 – 42nd Annual Conference of the IEEE Industrial Electronics Society, pp. 7046–7051. IEEE, Florence (2016)
8. Wang, Y., Zhan, C., Li, G., Zhang, D., Han, X.: Physics-guided LSTM model for heat load prediction of buildings. Energy Build. **294**, 113169 (2023)
9. Kim, D., Lee, Y., Chin, K., Mago, P.J., Cho, H., Zhang, J.: Implementation of a Long Short-Term Memory Transfer Learning (LSTM-TL)-based data-driven model for building energy demand forecasting. Sustainability **15**, 2340 (2023)
10. Yang, X., Gao, W., Qian, F., Li, Y.: Potential analysis of the attention-based LSTM model in ultra-short-term forecasting of building HVAC energy consumption. Front. Energy Res. **9**, 202 (2021)
11. Yang, K., Liu, Y., Yao, Y., Fan, S., Mosleh, A.: Operational time-series data modeling via LSTM network integrating principal component analysis based on human experience. J. Manuf. Syst. **61**, 746–756 (2021)
12. Zhang, Y., Li, Y., Wang, Y., et al.: LSTM-autoencoder based anomaly detection using vibration data. Sensors **23**(2), 246 (2023)
13. Liguori, A., Markovic, R., Dam, T.T.H., Frisch, J., van Treeck, C., Causone, F.: Indoor environment data time-series reconstruction using autoencoder neural networks. Build. Environ. **191**, 107623 (2021)

Data-Driven Optimal Air-Balancing Control for Multizone Ventilation Systems with Design-to-Operation Adaptation

Shanrui Shi[✉], Shohei Miyata, and Yasunori Akashi

Department of Architecture, Graduate School of Engineering,
The University of Tokyo, Tokyo, Japan
shishanrui1910@gmail.com

Abstract. Accurate air-balancing control is important for maintaining indoor air quality and reducing fan energy consumption in multizone ventilation systems. While data-driven approaches can outperform conventional control methods, their performance depends on their access to large volumes of high-quality operational data. To address this limitation, this study proposes an ANN-based optimal air-balancing strategy that bridges the design and operational phases. A physics-based duct network model was developed using Modelica to generate synthetic operational data. An artificial neural network (ANN) surrogate was then trained to capture the nonlinear actuator–airflow relationship. A hybrid optimization algorithm combining improved particle swarm optimization and Adam was developed to compute the optimal combinations of fan frequency and damper positions while satisfying the operational and energy-saving constraints. Simulation results benchmarked against the ASHRAE Guideline 36 trim-and-respond sequence show that the proposed strategy delivers more accurate air balancing with improved energy efficiency. To assess the robustness to parameter drift across project phases, both uniform and random perturbations are applied to the physical model. Fine-tuning the ANN with as little as 3% of new operational data restored, and often exceeded, the accuracy of the model retrained from scratch. These results demonstrate that the proposed strategy enables high-precision, phase-resilient air-balancing control with minimal real-world measurement effort.

Keywords: Air balancing · Multizone ventilation system · ANN model · Transfer learning

1 Introduction

People generally spend more than 90% of their lives indoors, making the indoor air quality (IAQ) critical for their physical and mental well-being as well as overall work efficiency [20]. Ventilation systems are essential for delivering fresh outdoor air (OA) to maintain the IAQ, but they are also among the most energy-intensive components in buildings [4]. Therefore, developing energy-efficient ventilation control strategies that maintain the IAQ is of great importance.

Demand-controlled ventilation dynamically modulates airflow based on real-time indoor conditions [19]. In systems equipped with gas sensors, the controller maintains indoor CO_2 concentrations below a prescribed threshold. In systems without gas sensors, airflow is scheduled according to measured or forecasted occupancy patterns [17]. The latter approach often referred to as air balancing, aims to match the delivered outdoor airflow to a zone's instantaneous demand with minimal error [17]. However, achieving precise air balancing in multi-zone buildings, remains challenging due to intricate duct interactions that cause significant deviations between intended and actual airflow at terminal units [14]. Such deviations can result in underventilation, compromising IAQ, or overventilation, leading to unnecessary fan energy consumption.

Early air-balancing solutions relied on manual, trial-and-error tuning of damper positions. Recent efforts have sought to automate the process using advanced control and estimation techniques. For instance, Jing et al. [11] formulated steady-state pressure balance as a multivariate regression problem, identifying model parameters through supervised learning to enable direct computation of damper settings without iterations. Subsequent studies enhanced robustness using support-vector regression [10] and incorporated Bayesian linear regression to simultaneously improve airflow accuracy and reduce fan energy consumption [13]. Despite these advances, physics-based methods often require detailed duct geometry and fitting parameters, which are seldom available in practice and costly to calibrate [6].

Data-driven approaches offer an alternative by learning system dynamics directly from operational data. Cui et al. [6] introduced a branch-and-black-box (B^2) model that predicts terminal pressures with a radial basis function (RBF) kernel and computes damper settings accordingly. Jing et al. [12] trained a feed-forward neural network to map airflow to pressure drop and then relied on a look-up table to infer damper openings. However, such indirect mappings can be inaccurate when construction deviates from design specifications and fails to enforce the desirable constraint that at least one damper remain nearly fully open to minimize system resistance [5]. Cheng et al. [5] therefore proposed an end-to-end neural network method that embeds energy-saving constraints, and Li et al. [18] further enhanced the approach by integrating multiple constraints into an improved perceptron formulation.

Although these data-driven approaches offer improved accuracy and energy savings, several limitations remain.

First, the kernel-based models in [5,18] exhibit limited model capacity in complex, high-dimensional, or highly nonlinear duct networks. Their constraints are implemented as penalty terms, expanding the optimization landscape and necessitating careful hyperparameter tuning (e.g., kernel bandwidths, regularization weights), which increases computational cost. Second, purely data-driven schemes require large amounts of high-quality operational data, meaning they can be deployed only after sufficient data have been collected [22]. In contrast, model-based development enables the creation of physical models during the design phase; yet, how to leverage such models for operational optimal control remains underexplored. Third, system parameters—such as fan performance curves—often differ between the design and operational phases [21]. Although prototype models developed during the design phase can be fine-tuned using operational data, the effectiveness of this adaptation and its impact on closed-loop control performance have yet to be systematically evaluated.

Therefore, this study proposes a data-driven, model-based optimal air-balancing control framework that delivers both accurate airflow distribution and energy-efficient operation. Leveraging information available during the design stage, we build an initial predictive model and formulate a constrained optimal control problem. After installation, the controller is fine-tuned using limited operational data, thereby significantly reducing the data requirements typical of black-box approaches. We further investigate how this design-to-operation adaptation influences control accuracy, energy consumption, and robustness, offering new insights into the fusion of model-based development and data-driven optimal control for ventilation systems.

2 Methodology

2.1 Overview of the Research Methodology

The proposed workflow, illustrated in Fig. 1, consists of two chronological stages—design and operation—followed by control design and performance evaluation.

Design Phase. Using readily available design information (e.g., room area, expected occupancy, duct geometry, and fan or damper performance curves), a physics-based ventilation model is first constructed. Synthetic operational data are generated by running this model under a wide range of representative boundary conditions. These data form a large, labeled dataset used to pre-train a feed-forward, data-driven surrogate model (artificial neural network, ANN) that captures the nonlinear behavior of the duct network.

Operation Phase. After installation and commissioning, discrepancies inevitably arise between the as-built system and its design specifications. These parameter variations are simulated by perturbing the original physics-based model. The modified model then generates a smaller but more realistic dataset, which is used to fine-tune the pre-trained ANN through transfer learning. This process adapts the surrogate to the real system using only a limited amount of new data.

Control and Evaluation. The original or fine-tuned ANN now serves as the predictive core of an online, optimal air-balancing controller. A hybrid optimization algorithm is employed to minimize airflow tracking error and fan energy consumption while satisfying operational constraints. Control performance is subsequently evaluated to assess the effectiveness of the model transfer and the minimum operational data required for reliable adaptation.

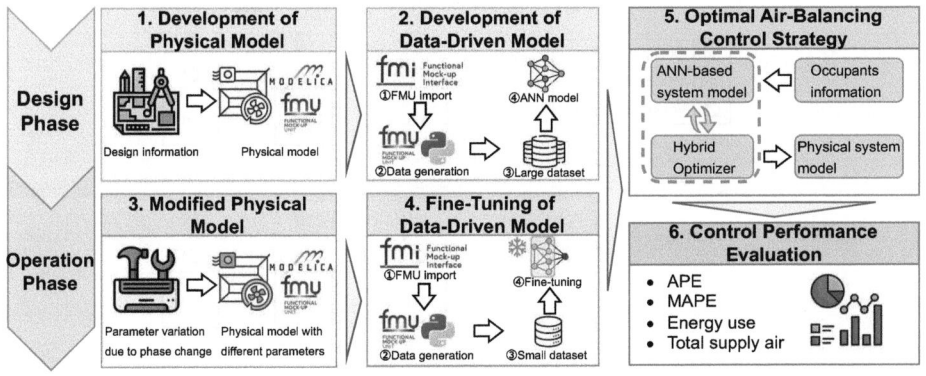

Fig. 1. Research methodology.

2.2 Modelica-Based Physical Model of the Multizone Ventilation System

The target plant is a hypothetical six-zone ventilation system derived from the experimental setup described in [24]. As illustrated in Fig. 2, the system consists of six independent rooms, each equipped with a variable-air-volume (VAV) terminal unit. The OA is supplied by a single variable-speed supply-air (SA) fan. Since thermal loads are assumed to be handled by auxiliary air-conditioning units (e.g., fan-coil systems), the focus of this study is solely on the ventilation loop.

A physics-based model was built using the Modelica Buildings Library [25] and simulated with OPENMODELICA. The model architecture is shown in Fig. 3. Control inputs comprise the fan frequency and the six damper positions, while the measured outputs are (i) the realized actuator signals of fan and dampers, (ii) six zone airflow rates, (iii) total airflow rate, (iv) static pressure downstream of the fan, and (v) fan electricity usage. The model was exported as a Functional Mock-up Unit (FMU) and co-simulated from Python via FMPy [1].

2.3 ANN Surrogate Model

An ANN surrogate was trained to approximate the nonlinear mapping:

$$\mathbf{y} = F(\mathbf{x}), \tag{1}$$

where the input vector $\mathbf{x}$ consists of seven control variables, and the output vector $\mathbf{y}$ consists of the six zone airflow rates. A five-layer multilayer perceptron (MLP) [9] with three hidden layers was adopted, as illustrated in Fig. 4.

Using the FMU, a total of $4^7 = 16,384$ input-output samples were generated through random sampling within the feasible input domain: $0.2 \leq inv_{\mathrm{SA}}, d_i \leq 1.0$. Data points falling outside the designed ventilation range (0–10 persons per zone) were discarded. Prior to training, inputs and outputs were normalized to

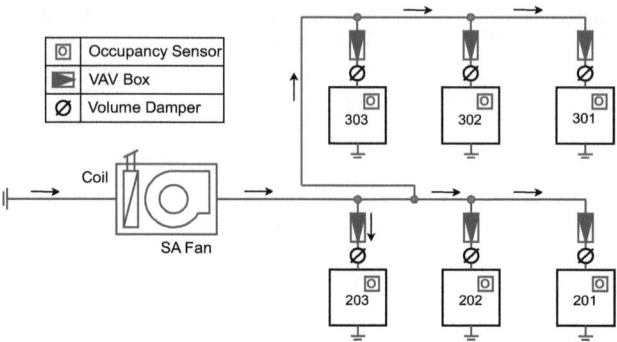

Fig. 2. Schematic of the hypothesis ventilation system.

the range [0, 1]. The ANN was trained using the Adam optimizer [16], incorporating a learning rate scheduler and early stopping as described in [23].

2.4 Simulated Parameter Deviations and Transfer Learning

To emulate post-installation discrepancies, the following parameters in the physical model were varied by up to ±20%: fan *P-Q* curve coefficients, damper characteristic coefficients, and duct resistances. Three deviation scenarios were considered: (i) uniform upscaling, (ii) uniform down-scaling, and (iii) parameter-wise random scaling within [0.8, 1.2]. For each scenario, the full 16,384 sample dataset was regenerated.

To adapt the surrogate model using a limited quantity of new data, parameter-based transfer learning was employed: early ANN layers were frozen to retain general features, whereas the deeper layers were fine-tuned using subsets of the updated dataset. This approach enabled assessment of the minimum data volume needed to restore predictive performance comparable to a model fully retrained from scratch.

2.5 Optimal Air-Balancing Control Formulation

Given the trained surrogate model, the optimal control problem at each time step is formulated as:

$$\min_{\mathbf{x}} J(\mathbf{x}) = \sum_{i=1}^{6} (Q_i(\mathbf{x}) - Q_i^{\text{set}})^2 + \lambda + w \cdot inv_{\text{SA}}, \tag{2}$$

subject to $0.2 \leq inv_{\text{SA}}, d_i \leq 1.0$.

Here, the first term penalizes deviations between the predicted airflow $Q_i(\mathbf{x})$ and the setpoint Q_i^{set}, which is derived from real-time occupancy. λ is a constraint penalty to ensure that at least one damper opening exceeds 0.85, thus reducing

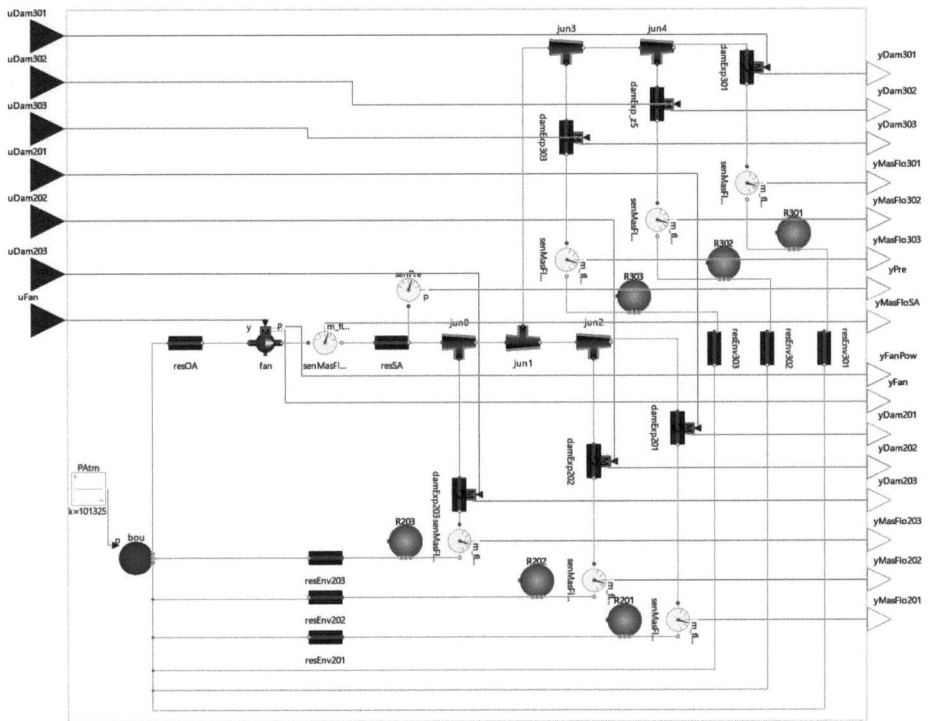

Fig. 3. Modelica model of the ventilation system.

system resistance. The third term penalizes fan power usage, scaled by a tuning weight w.

To solve the non-convex and highly nonlinear optimization problem $J(\mathbf{x})$, a hybrid IPSO–Adam algorithm is used. Improved particle swarm optimization (IPSO) with a double linearly decreasing inertia weight [7,15] performs global search to identify a feasible initial solution. This is followed by local refinement using the Adam algorithm, which leverages the surrogate's analytic gradients for fast convergence.

As the damper constraint λ in Eq. 2 is non-differentiable, gradient-based methods may struggle to escape that region once inside it, therefore the penalty is smoothed using the ReLU function:

$$\lambda = \lambda' \operatorname{ReLU}\left(0.85 - \max_i d_i\right), \tag{3}$$

where λ' is a penalty factor that enforces the damper constraint. Additionally, early stopping is applied to the Adam algorithm to terminate optimization when the objective fails to improve by a predefined threshold over consecutive iterations.

All hyperparameters were tuned through trial and error and are summarized in Table 1. The complete optimization procedure is outlined in Algorithm 1.

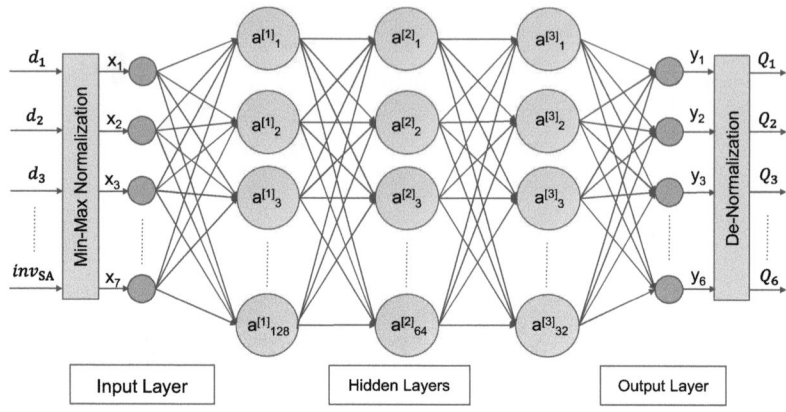

Fig. 4. Structure of the developed ANN surrogate model.

This hybrid scheme combines the global exploration strength of PSO with the efficiency of gradient-based refinement, enabling accurate and energy-efficient airflow balancing with runtimes suitable for real-time implementation.

Table 1. Hyper-parameters of the hybrid IPSO–Adam optimizer.

IPSO stage			Adam stage		
Parameter	Value	Comment	Parameter	Value	Comment
N_p	50	swarm size	learning-rate η	0.01	step size
N_{iter}^{max}	10	max. IPSO iterations	patience τ	20	early-stop window[a]
c_1	1.4	cognitive weight	improvement threshold δ	10%	early-stop criterion[a]
c_2	1.8	social weight	loss threshold	10^{-6}	stop if $L < 10^{-6}$
w_{max}	0.5	max. inertia weight	λ'	50	ReLU-penalty weight
w_{min}	0.1	min. inertia weight	w	0.0005	fan-energy weight in Adam loss
λ	500	penalty weight in IPSO cost			
w	0.0005	fan-energy weight in IPSO cost			

[a] Adam stops if the loss fails to improve by at least 10 % for 20 consecutive updates.

3 Case Study

3.1 Test Conditions

Simulation experiments were conducted to evaluate the performance of the proposed optimal air-balancing controller and the associated transfer learning scheme. The only exogenous disturbance provided to the controller is the six-zone occupancy schedule, shown in Fig. 5. Based on the instantaneous headcount $P_i(t)$ in each zone, the OA ventilation setpoint $Q_i^{set}(t)$ is computed using the ASHRAE Standard 62.1 rate method [2]:

Algorithm 1: Hybrid IPSO–Adam Algorithm.

Input: current time t, last control time t_{last}, control interval Δt, previous target flow $\mathbf{Q}_{\text{prev}}$
Data : Occupancy information $\Rightarrow$ zone set-points $\mathbf{Q}_{\text{set}}(t)$
$\mathbf{Q}_{\text{set}} \leftarrow \textsc{GetTargetFlow}(t)$
if $(t = t_0) \lor (t - t_{\text{last}} \geq \Delta t)$ **then**
    if $\mathbf{Q}_{\text{prev}} = \emptyset \lor \neg\textsc{AllClose}(\mathbf{Q}_{\text{set}}, \mathbf{Q}_{\text{prev}})$ **then**
        $\mathbf{Q}_{\text{set}}^{\text{sc}} \leftarrow \textsc{ScaleOut}(\mathbf{Q}_{\text{set}})$
        $(\mathbf{x}^{(0)}, f^{(0)}) \leftarrow \text{IPSO}(f, \mathbf{x}_{\min}, \mathbf{x}_{\max}, N_p, N_{\text{iter}}^{\max}, c_1, c_2, w_{\max}, w_{\min}, \lambda, w)$
        $\mathbf{x} \leftarrow \mathbf{x}^{(0)}$
        initialize Adam with learning-rate η
        $k \leftarrow 0$, $best\_loss \leftarrow \infty$, $c \leftarrow 0$
        while $k < \overline{K}_{\max}$ **do**
            $k \leftarrow k + 1$
            $\mathbf{x}_{\text{sc}} \leftarrow \textsc{ScaleIn}(\mathbf{x})$
            $\hat{\mathbf{Q}} \leftarrow F_\theta(\mathbf{x}_{\text{sc}})$
            $L \leftarrow \|\hat{\mathbf{Q}} - \mathbf{Q}_{\text{set}}^{\text{sc}}\|_2^2 + \lambda'\,\text{ReLU}(0.85 - \max(\mathbf{x}_{1:6})) + w\,x_7$
            $\textsc{BackProp}$; $\textsc{AdamStep}$
            $\mathbf{x} \leftarrow \textsc{Clip}(\mathbf{x}, 0.2, 1.0)$
            if $L < best\_loss\,(1-\delta)$ **then**
                | $best\_loss \leftarrow L$; $c \leftarrow 0$
            else
                $c \leftarrow c + 1$
            if $(c \geq \tau) \lor (L < 10^{-6})$ **then**
                break
    $\textsc{Deploy}\,\mathbf{x}$
    $\mathbf{Q}_{\text{prev}} \leftarrow \mathbf{Q}_{\text{set}}$;
    $t_{\text{last}} \leftarrow t$

$$Q_i^{\text{set}}(t) = R_z\,A_i + R_p\,P_i(t), \tag{4}$$

where $A_i = 76.8\text{m}^2$ is the zone floor area, $R_z = 0.30\text{Ls}^{-1}\text{m}^{-2}$ is the area-based ventilation rate, and $R_p = 2.5\text{Ls}^{-1}\text{person}^{-1}$ is the per-person rate.

3.2 Baseline Strategy

The proposed controller is benchmarked against the *trim-and-respond* (T&R) sequence recommended by ASHRAE Guideline 36 for high-performance VAV systems [8]. In this approach, each zone damper is controlled by an independent proportional-integral (PI) loop that regulates the measured airflow Q_i to match the setpoint Q_i^{set}. The supply fan is also governed by a PI controller, which maintains the static pressure p_{sp} downstream of the fan. This pressure setpoint is dynamically adjusted according to two rules:

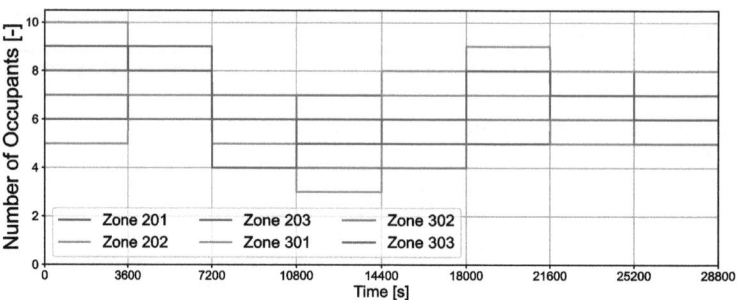

Fig. 5. Occupancy schedule used in the test case.

- **Trim.** When no zone issues a request (i.e., all dampers are < 85% open), the fan pressure setpoint p_{sp} is reduced by SP_{trim} every T seconds.
- **Respond.** When at least $I+1$ zones request more airflow (i.e., damper > 95% open), p_{sp} is increased by $SPres \times (I+1)$, capped at a maximum of SPres, max per interval.

The parameters used in this baseline control sequence are listed in Table 2, following ASHRAE Guideline 36 recommendations. All PI controllers (one for the fan and one per damper) were manually tuned via trial and error to ensure stable behavior and rapid recovery. The full T&R sequence is implemented in Python and interacts with the same FMU used by the proposed optimizer.

Table 2. Trim-and-respond control parameters

Symbol	Definition	Value
SP_0	Initial static-pressure set-point	10 Pa
I	Ignored-request threshold	0
SP_{trim}	Trim decrement	−3 Pa
SP_{res}	Response increment	+5 Pa
$SP_{res,max}$	Max. response per interval	20 Pa
T_{step}	Control interval	120 s

4 Results and Discussion

4.1 Operating Profiles of Fan and Dampers

Figure 6 compares the operational behavior of supply fan frequency and zone damper positions for the two control strategies. Under the T&R sequence, the fan set-point is continually trimmed or boosted to keep the most open damper within the recommended 85-95% range. However, there are prolonged periods where all dampers remain below 85%, resulting in increased system pressure losses and elevated fan energy consumption. Due to the reactive nature of T&R–responding only to discrete requests–the dampers exhibit pronounced hunting behavior even when zone airflow setpoints are unchanged. This issue is further exacerbated by actuator dynamics: the realized damper positions (output traces) lag behind the controller commands (input traces).

In contrast, the proposed ANN-based controller explicitly seeks control combinations that ensure at least one damper remains fully (or nearly fully) open at each optimization step. As a result, system resistance is minimized, and the fan operates at a lower static pressure. While actuator delays still cause short-term deviations between target and realized positions immediately following a schedule change, convergence is typically achieved within 100 s, leading to significantly more stable operation.

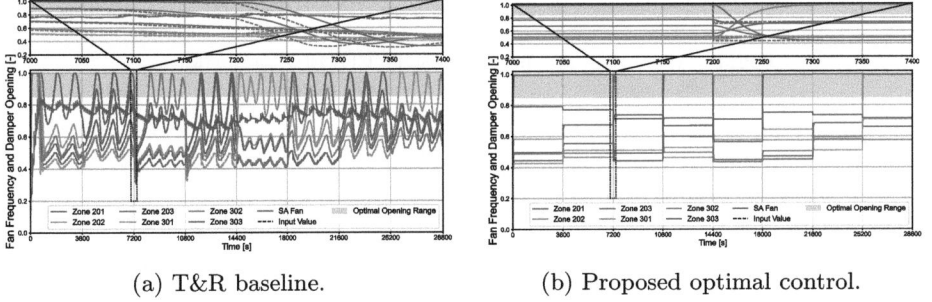

(a) T&R baseline.   (b) Proposed optimal control.

Fig. 6. Supply fan frequency and damper positions during operation.

4.2 Control Accuracy of Zone Airflow

Figures 7 and 8 present the delivered airflow rates and corresponding absolute percentage error (APE) for a representative zone:

$$\text{APE}_i(t) = \left| \frac{Q_i(t) - Q_i^{\text{set}}(t)}{Q_i^{\text{set}}(t)} \right| \times 100\%, \tag{5}$$

The T&R sequence generally maintains APE below 10%, but it can take several minutes to stabilize after occupancy changes. In contrast, the ANN controller consistently achieves convergence within approximately 120 s and maintains APE below 3% throughout the entire period.

4.3 Performance Summary

Table 3 summarizes the overall control performance. The overall balance accuracy across six zones is expressed as the mean absolute percentage error (MAPE):

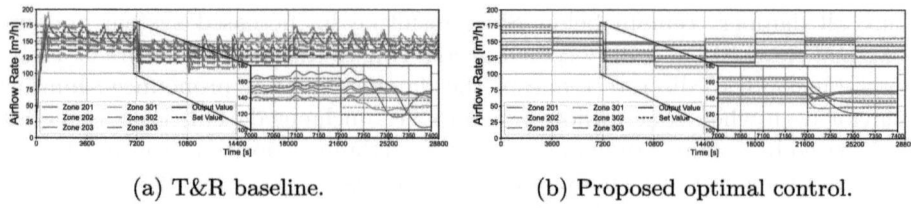

(a) T&R baseline. (b) Proposed optimal control.

Fig. 7. Zone supply airflow versus setpoint across six zones.

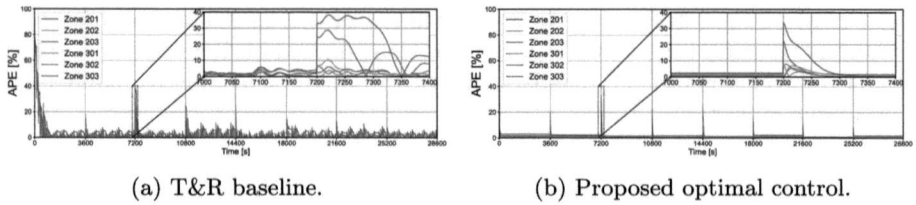

(a) T&R baseline. (b) Proposed optimal control.

Fig. 8. Absolute percentage error (APE) of zone airflows.

$$\text{MAPE} = \frac{1}{6T} \sum_{i=1}^{6} \sum_{t=1}^{T} \left| \frac{Q_i(t) - Q_i^{\text{set}}(t)}{Q_i^{\text{set}}(t)} \right| \times 100\% \tag{6}$$

with $T = 28{,}800$ seconds corresponds to the 8-hour simulation at a 1-second recording interval. The "Total SA deviation" column expresses the integrated difference between actual and target SA volumes (reference total $V_{\text{set}} = 8{,}103.97$ m^3). Fan energy use is obtained by time-integrating the FMU-reported electrical power.

Table 3. Comparison of control performance.

Strategy	MAPE [%]	Total SA deviation [%]	Fan energy [kWh]
T and R (Guideline 36)	2.48	−0.71	0.976
Proposed optimal control	1.00	−0.02	0.988 (+1.17%)

While the T&R strategy consumes approximately 1% less fan energy in this small-scale system due to consistent undersupply of air, it requires extensive manual tuning of seven PI loops and is highly sensitive to operating conditions. In contrast, the proposed surrogate-based optimizer offers three key advantages:

- **Improved control accuracy**: The optimizer ensures fast recovery to new setpoints (within two minutes) and maintains high balancing precision.
- **Energy-aware actuator coordination**: By keeping at least one damper fully open, duct pressure losses are minimized. The resulting fan-damper combination approaches global energy optimality. The energy benefit is expected

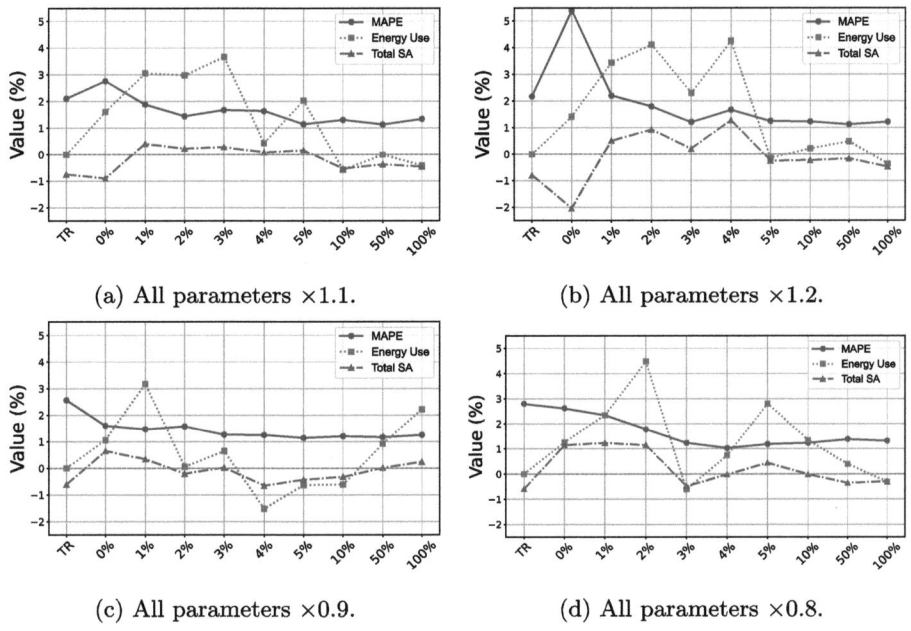

Fig. 9. Effect of uniform parameter scaling on control performance. MAPE is averaged over six zones; energy is expressed relative to the T&R baseline; total SA is shown relative to the setpoint.

to scale with system size, where damper losses represent a larger fraction of required fan head [3].
- **Reduced hardware and tuning requirements**: The method relies solely on airflow measurements for data collection. No static pressure sensor or PI-gain tuning is required, lowering commissioning costs.

4.4 Robustness to Model Mismatch and Transfer Learning Data Requirements

The previous results established that the proposed optimizer outperforms the T&R baseline under nominal conditions. This section examines the robustness of the controller to model-plant mismatch and evaluates the amount of operational data needed to restore performance through transfer learning.

Uniform Scaling. Four deterministic perturbations were applied uniformly to all fan, damper, and duct-loss parameters: $+10\%$ ($\times 1.1$), $+20\%$ ($\times 1.2$), -10% ($\times 0.9$), and -20% ($\times 0.8$). In each case, the design-stage surrogate model was fine-tuned with subsets of the new dataset, corresponding to $\rho \in [0, 1, 2, 3, 4, 5, 10, 50, 100]\%$ of the full training set ($N_{\text{full}} = 16{,}384$). Figure 9 summarizes the resulting MAPE, total SA deviation, and fan energy usage, expressed relative to the Guideline 36 baseline.

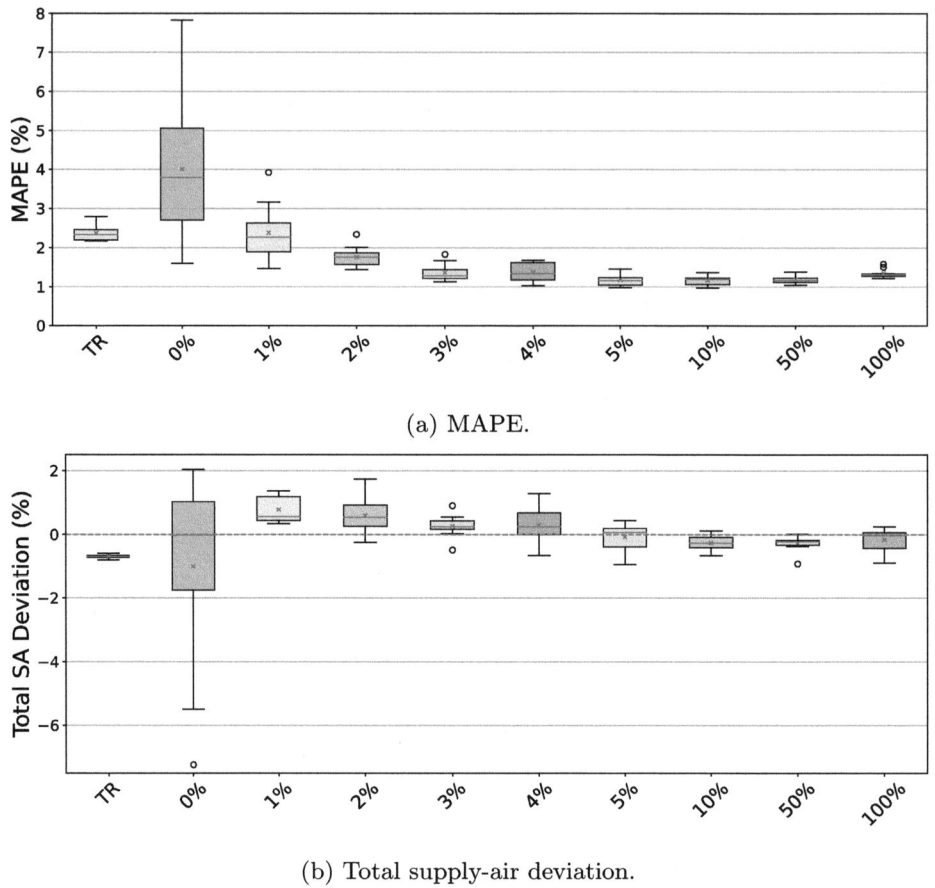

(a) MAPE.

(b) Total supply-air deviation.

Fig. 10. Performance under parameter-wise random scaling.

With as little as $\rho = 3\,\%$ (≈ 492 samples) the fine-tuned model matches the accuracy of a model retrained from scratch on the full dataset. When $\rho < 3\,\%$, larger parameter offsets translate into proportionally larger control errors, confirming that model mismatch degrades the optimization fidelity. In a few low-data cases the optimizer supplies less air yet consumes more fan energy, indicating that surrogate inaccuracy can result in inefficient fan-damper configurations.

Random Scaling. To emulate unstructured variation, six additional FMUs were generated by scaling each parameter independently by a factor drawn from the range of [0.8, 1.2]. Figure 10 shows the plot of the MAPE and total SA deviation for all ten FMUs (four uniform, six random). The observed trends mirror those in the deterministic cases: untuned or minimally tuned models ($\rho < 3\%$) exhibit significant control errors and may underperform T&R. Beyond this threshold, fine-tuned surrogates not only recover performance but often surpass models trained from scratch, highlighting the benefit of reusing pre-trained weights.

The design-stage surrogate captures the essential flow characteristics of the duct network. A few hundred post-installation samples are sufficient to compensate for substantial parameter drift. This data efficiency combined with rapid retraining makes the approach practical for real-world deployment and lifecycle adaptation of the control system.

5 Conclusion

This study proposed a data-driven, model-based air-balancing strategy that couples an ANN surrogate of the duct network with a hybrid IPSO–Adam optimizer. A high-fidelity Modelica testbed was used to benchmark the proposed strategy against the Guideline 36 T&R control sequence and to assess control performance and robustness to phase-change parameter drift. The main findings are as follows:

- The five-layer ANN reproduces the nonlinear mapping $[f_{\text{fan}}, d_1, \ldots, d_6] \mapsto [Q_1, \ldots, Q_6]$ with sufficient fidelity to support real-time optimization; each control step is solved in ≈ 0.76 s on an Intel i9-9980XE CPU @ 3.00 GHz.
- Relative to the high performance T&R control sequence, the proposed optimizer can (i) lower the MAPE to 1.00%, (ii) eliminate cumulative supply airflow bias, and (iii) keep at least one damper nearly full open with optimal fan frequency and damper opening combination, thereby reducing pressure losses and ensuring more energy-efficient operation.
- Uniform and random scalings of fan, damper and duct parameters were applied to emulate installation–operational stage mismatches. Fine-tuning the surrogate model with only $\sim 3\%$ (≈ 500 samples) of new data can restore or even surpass the performance of the model retrained from scratch on the full dataset. This demonstrates the data efficiency of the proposed approach and supports its early deployment following system commissioning.

Despite these promising results, the study has several limitations that need future investigation:

- Although synthetic data can be generated in abundance using the physical model, the number of required samples grows exponentially with the number of zones, limiting the scalability of the current approach. Future work will explore more compact and data-efficient surrogate architectures for large-scale multizone applications.
- Each scenario was executed only once in this study. Repeated trials with different random seeds are necessary to assess the variability in model training and optimization performance.
- While the Modelica-based testbed offers high fidelity, it assumes instantaneous airflow distribution and neglects communication delays between controllers, which may not accurately reflect real-world system dynamics. Incorporating transient models that account for these delays will be essential for more realistic evaluations.

Acknowledgements. This work was supported by JSPS KAKENHI Grant Number JP25KJ1173.

This study was conducted as part of the "Smart Building System Research Initiative." The authors would like to thank all individuals involved in this study.

References

1. FMPY. URL: httpps://github.com/CATIA-Systems/FMPy
2. ASHRAE Atlanta, G.: ANSI/ASHRAE standard 62.1-2010, ventilation and acceptable indoor air quality. American Society of Heating, Refrigerating, and Air-Conditioning Engineers, Inc (2010)
3. ASHRAE Atlanta, G.: ANSI/ASHRAE/IES standard 90.1-2010, energy standard for buildings except low-rise residential buildings. American Society of Heating, Refrigerating, and Air-Conditioning Engineers, Inc (2010)
4. Chenari, B., Carrilho, J.D., Da Silva, M.G.: Towards sustainable, energy-efficient and healthy ventilation strategies in buildings: a review. Renew. Sustain. Energy Rev. **59**, 1426–1447 (2016)
5. Cheng, F., Cui, C., Cai, W., Zhang, X., Ge, Y., Li, B.: A novel data-driven air balancing method with energy-saving constraint strategy to minimize the energy consumption of ventilation system. Energy **239**, 122146 (2022)
6. Cui, C., Zhang, X., Cai, W.: An energy-saving oriented air balancing method for demand controlled ventilation systems with branch and black-box model. Appl. Energy **264**, 114734 (2020)
7. Farooq, M.U., Ahmad, A., Hameed, A.: Opposition-based initialization and a modified pattern for inertia weight (IW) in PSO. In: 2017 IEEE International Conference on INnovations in Intelligent SysTems and Applications (INISTA), pp. 96–101. IEEE (2017)
8. Guideline, A.: Guideline 36-2024. high-performance sequences of operation for HVAC systems. American Society of Heating, Refrigerating, and Air-Conditioning Engineers, Inc (2024)
9. Haykin, S.: Neural Networks: A Comprehensive Foundation. Prentice Hall PTR (1994)
10. Jing, G., Cai, W., Chen, H., Zhai, D., Cui, C., Yin, X.: An air balancing method using support vector machine for a ventilation system. Build. Environ. **143**, 487–495 (2018)
11. Jing, G., Cai, W., Zhai, D., Liu, S., Cui, C.: A model-based air balancing method of a ventilation system. Energy Build. **174**, 506–512 (2018)
12. Jing, G., Cai, W., Zhang, X., Cui, C., Liu, H., Wang, C.: An energy-saving control strategy for multi-zone demand controlled ventilation system with data-driven model and air balancing control. Energy **199**, 117328 (2020)
13. Jing, G., Cai, W., Zhang, X., Cui, C., Yin, X., Xian, H.: An energy-saving oriented air balancing strategy for multi-zone demand-controlled ventilation system. Energy **172**, 1053–1065 (2019)
14. Jing, G., Cai, W., Zhang, X., Cui, C., Yin, X., Xian, H.: Modeling, air balancing and optimal pressure set-point selection for the ventilation system with minimized energy consumption. Appl. Energy **236**, 574–589 (2019)
15. Kennedy, J., Eberhart, R.: Particle swarm optimization. In: Proceedings of ICNN'95-International Conference on Neural Networks, vol. 4, pp. 1942–1948. IEEE (1995)

16. Kingma, D.P., Ba, J.: Adam: a method for stochastic optimization. arXiv preprint arXiv:1412.6980 (2014)
17. Li, B.: Advanced demand-controlled ventilation strategies for ACMV systems (2022)
18. Li, L., Bao, R., Cai, H., Zhang, X., Yin, Z.: A novel air balancing method based on an improved perceptron under multiple constraints for the energy conservation of ventilation system. Build. Environ. **248**, 111115 (2024)
19. Lu, X., Pang, Z., Fu, Y., O'Neill, Z.: The nexus of the indoor co2 concentration and ventilation demands underlying co2-based demand-controlled ventilation in commercial buildings: a critical review. Build. Environ. **218**, 109116 (2022)
20. Morawska, L., Allen, J., Bahnfleth, W., Bennett, B., Bluyssen, P.M., Boerstra, A., Buonanno, G., Cao, J., Dancer, S.J., Floto, A., et al.: Mandating indoor air quality for public buildings. Science **383**(6690), 1418–1420 (2024)
21. Nomura, A., Shi, S., Miyata, S., Akashi, Y., Momota, M., Sawachi, T.: Design-operation gap caused by parameter variance in HVAC system control sequences: a simulation-based study on energy efficiency and temperature controllability. J. Build. Eng. **87**, 109112 (2024)
22. Pinto, G., Wang, Z., Roy, A., Hong, T., Capozzoli, A.: Transfer learning for smart buildings: a critical review of algorithms, applications, and future perspectives. Adv. Appl. Energ. **5**, 100084 (2022)
23. Shi, S., Miyata, S., Akashi, Y.: Event-driven model-based optimal demand-controlled ventilation for multizone vav systems: enhancing energy efficiency and indoor environmental quality. Appl. Energy **377**, 124683 (2025)
24. Shi, S., Miyata, S., Akashi, Y., Momota, M., Sawachi, T., Gao, Y.: Model-based optimal control strategy for multizone vav air-conditioning systems for neutralizing room pressure and minimizing fan energy consumption. Build. Environ. **256**, 111464 (2024)
25. Wetter, M., Zuo, W., Nouidui, T.S., Pang, X.: Modelica buildings library. J. Build. Perform. Simul. **7**(4), 253–270 (2014)

Prosumer Optimization and Energy Storage in Local Energy Communities

Evaluating the Potential for Developing Local Energy Communities in Sweden: Case Studies at Jättesten and Chalmers Campus

Mohammadreza Mazidi[✉], Araavind Sridhar, David Steen, Elena Malakhatka, Sara Abouebeid, Felix Niklasson, Le Anh Tuan, and Holger Wallbaum

Chalmers University of Technology, 412 96 Gothenburg, Sweden
mazadi@chalmers.se

Abstract. As the Swedish electricity system transitions to cleaner and more sustainable energy sources, local energy communities (LECs), comprising groups of consumers and producers who share locally generated energy and energy-related infrastructure, are emerging as a promising solution to support the power grid. This paper aims to quantitatively evaluate the potential of LECs to improve the efficiency and sustainability of the Sweden's electricity system. To this end, two real-world demonstration sites in Sweden are analyzed: Jättesten, representing a residential load, and Chalmers Campus, representing a commercial load. The key performance indicators considered in these case studies include total annual operating cost, self-consumption (SC), self-sufficiency (SS), and peak shaving capability. The results show that combining residential and commercial loads within a single LEC significantly improves overall performance by leveraging demand diversity. Participation in LECs can reduce annual operating costs by up to 14 %, improve SC and SS by up to 4 %, and lower peak power demand by up to 20 %. Moreover, the analysis underscores the potential for further gains through the greater integration of photovoltaics (PVs) and battery energy storage system (BESS).

Keywords: Local energy community · energy management system · renewable energy integration · energy transition · real-world demonstration

1 Introduction

The transition to low-carbon energy systems has accelerated decentralization, flexibility, and active end-user participation. In Sweden, this shift is driven by ambitious climate goals, a high share of renewables, and rapid electrification of heating, transport, and industry [7]. While these trends enhance sustainability, they also stress existing power infrastructure—urban electrification is constrained by grid capacity, and the variability of wind and solar complicates real-time balancing [2]. In this context, Local Energy Communities (LECs) have emerged as viable solutions at the distribution level. By enabling local coordination among consumers and prosumers, LECs facilitate energy sharing and demand-side flexibility. Through the integration of local renewables, battery storage, and smart control, LECs offer a decentralized pathway to enhance grid resilience and accelerate the energy transition [1].

Although LECs present substantial opportunities to advance the energy transition, their implementation in Sweden remains hindered by various structural and regulatory challenges. The centralized electricity market, dominated by a few large utilities, limits prosumer engagement, and current policy frameworks do not sufficiently support community-led energy initiatives. Specific regulations for LECs are lacking, and the existing legal structure prohibits electricity sharing among neighbors without an internal grid—construction of which faces regulatory hurdles. In addition, the grid is not designed for reverse power flows, meaning that locally generated energy must be consumed immediately, restricting local participation. The lack of financial incentives, technical assistance, and administrative support further discourages the development of LEC. Finally, limited technical knowledge, bureaucratic complexities, and fragmented coordination among stakeholders weaken public motivation and engagement [2].

Despite systemic barriers, the development of LECs in Sweden is progressing, reflecting growing interest in their role in the national energy transition. The feasibility of a LEC in Sätra was demonstrated in [10], showing it is technically and economically viable, with benefits like increased local renewable generation, reduced dependence on centralized systems, and improved energy security. In another study about residential consumers living in 300 semi-detached houses in a mid-sized town in Sweden [4] found that economic incentives drive interest in LECs, though barriers such as complexity, limited social capital, lack of leadership, and trust concerns hinder formation. An analytical method to assess exergy retention in local systems was developed in [11], tested on 21 buildings in Uppsala. It showed that combining solar, heat pumps, EV charging, and battery storage can achieve nearly 40 % self-sufficiency, compared to 24 % with solar alone. In [5], a study on 48 dwellings in Ludvika found that future climate conditions may boost annual Photovoltaics (PVs) output by 10.7 %, with seasonal peaks, improving household self-sufficiency by 5.4–6.2 % depending on PV ownership, though oversizing PV systems was economically inefficient due to low grid sale returns.

In this paper, we investigate the potential for developing LECs within Sweden's electricity system, based on real-world demonstration sites. Drawing on two real-world demonstration sites—Jättesten (residential load) and Chalmers Campus (commercial load)—we evaluate the performance of LECs under varying load profiles, considering dynamic electricity pricing and existing grid tariffs. The study focuses on key performance indicators such as total annual operating cost, self-consumption, self-sufficiency, and peak shaving capability (Fig. 1).

The rest of the paper is organized as follows: Sect. 2 describes the demonstration sites. Section 3 presents the formulation and solution methodology. Section 4 discusses the results. Finally, Sect. 5 concludes the paper.

2 Description of Demonstration Sites

This study involves two demonstration sites:

- **Jättesten**: A residential area consisting of multiple apartment buildings located within the municipality of Gothenburg, Sweden.
- **Chalmers Campus**: A university campus that includes a mix of commercial buildings (e.g., lecture halls, laboratories, and offices) and student housing (residential buildings), also located within Gothenburg.

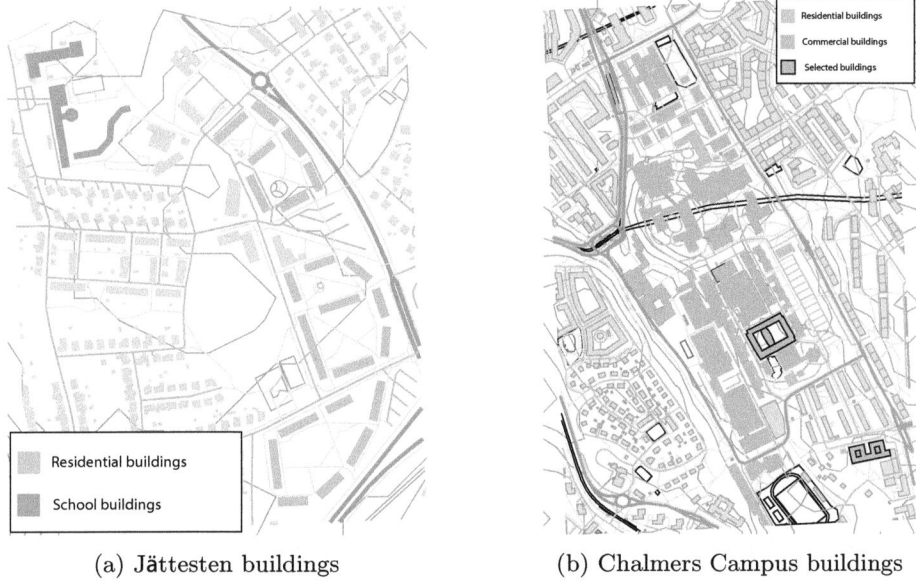

(a) Jättesten buildings (b) Chalmers Campus buildings

Fig. 1. Two demonstration sites

To evaluate the impact of LECs under varying compositions of residential and commercial buildings, different combinations of buildings from both demonstration sites are analyzed. Specifically, 24 buildings from the Jättesten site and two buildings from the Chalmers Campus are considered. The 24 buildings in Jättesten include primarily residential buildings as well as a school, reflecting a realistic mix of building types within an urban community. The selection of these two buildings from Chalmers is based on their comparable electricity load profiles to those of the residential buildings in Jättesten. A detailed description

Table 1. Buildings considered in Chalmers Campus

Building	Average Load (kWh)	Peak Load (kWh)	Total Energy Use (MWh)
Edit	151	344.4	1326
Gamla Matte	93	222.4	813
Both	244	568.8	2139

Table 2. Buildings considered in Jättesten

Buildings	Cluster	Average Load (kWh)	Peak Load (kWh)	Total Energy Use (MWh)
Baltzersgatan 1, Baltzersgatan 3–6, Baltzersgatan 12, Jättestensgatan 3, Jättestensgatan 5, Jättestensgatan 15, Sunnerviksgatan 19	J1	42.4	136.5	371.7
Jättestensgatan 11, Jättestensgatan 13, J1	J2	53.3	165.7	466.8
Baltzersgatan 7–8, Baltzersgatan 10, Baltzersgatan 14, Hakefjordsgatan 119, Jättestensgatan 1, Jättestensgatan 7, Jättestenskolan 119, Sunnerviksgatan 15, Sunnerviksgatan 17, Sunnerviksgatan 21	J3	113	435	994
All buildings	J4	209	737	1832

of the buildings and their associated load characteristics is provided in Tables 1 and 2.

From the description of loads in Jättesten and Chalmers Campus sites, it can be seen that Chalmers Campus has a higher average load and the total energy use in comparison to all buildings of Jättesten. But this order is reversed for the peak load. Overall the total energy use is roughly 300 MWh higher for Chalmers Campus over Jättesten site. In addition to this, there was one battery energy storage system (BESS) installed in Jättesten of capacity 295 kWh with a maximum charging and discharging power of 176 kW. In this study there has been no BESS considered within the Chalmers Campus buildings. In terms of PV production, there are roughly 1541 kW$_p$ installed in the buildings of Jättesten site and no PV production has been considered within Chalmers Campus site.

2.1 Scenario Formulation

To assess a variety of participation scenarios, different combinations of the Chalmers and Jättesten buildings are modeled. The scenarios span varying levels of residential and commercial load participation in the LEC. Table 3 summarizes the specific participation configurations analyzed.

Table 3. Participation scenarios considered in the LEC analysis

Participation Scenarios in LEC	S1	S2	S3	S4	S5	S6	S7	S8	S9	S10	S11	S12	S13	S14	S15	S16
Chalmers building	-	-	-	-	Both	Edit	Edit	Edit	Edit	Edit	Edit	Gamla Matte	Gamla Matte	Gamla Matte	Gamla Matte	Both
Jättesten Cluster	J4	J3	J2	J1	-	J4	J3	J2	J1	-	J4	J3	J2	J1	-	J4

From Fig. 2, it can be observed that the loads in Chalmers are very high during the day and during the nights, it reduces significantly. Similarly, the

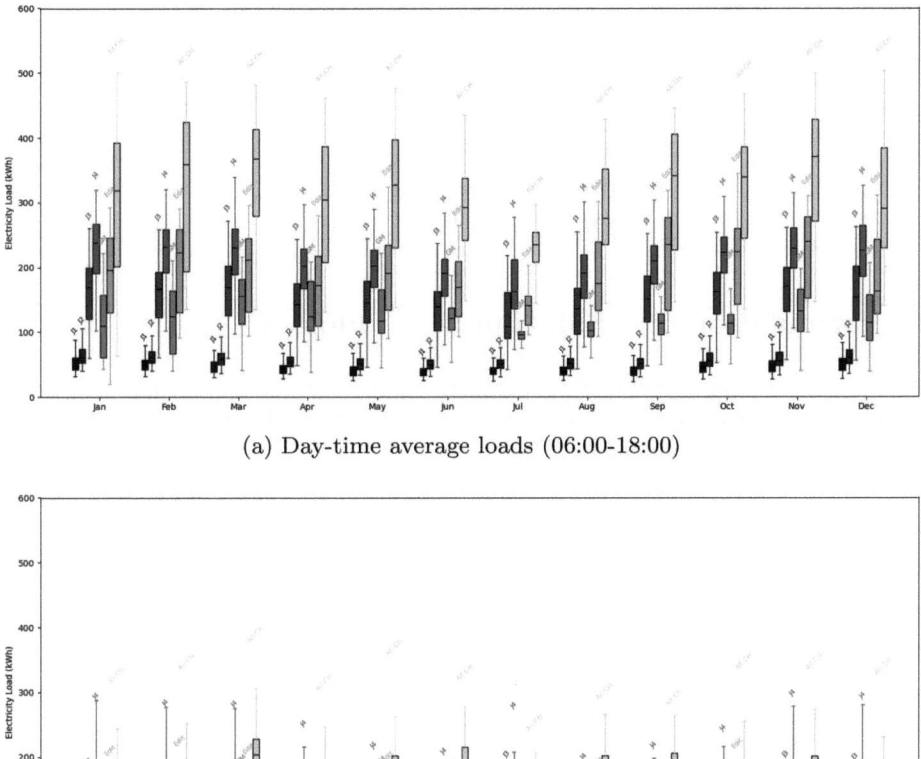

Fig. 2. Average loads in different month in both the demonstration sites

loads in Jättesten sites are also high during the day and lower during the nights, but this difference in consumption is not as drastic as that of Chalmers campus buildings.

2.2 Electricity Costs

The spot market prices for the study days are obtained from the Nord Pool market for the year 2023 [8]. The energy and power tariffs, as well as the tax fee, transmission fee, and incentive fee for electricity, are taken from the website of the Göteborg Energi and are presented in Table 4 [3].

Table 4. Network tariff structure used in the case study

Fee Type	Amount (SEK/kWh)
Transmission fee	0.204
Tax fee	0.428
Incentive fee	0.050
Peak fee	1.660

3 Formulation and Solution Methodology

In this section, the optimization problem of the energy management system, including the objective function and constraints, is formulated as a mixed integer linear programming model (MILP).

3.1 Objective Function

The aim of energy management system is to minimize the daily cost of the LEC given by:

$$f = \min \text{Cost}^{\text{LEC}} \tag{1}$$

$$\text{Cost}^{\text{LEC}} = C^{\text{Energy}} + C^{\text{Power}} + C^{\text{DEG}} \tag{2}$$

where the energy cost (C^{Energy}), power cost (C^{Power}), and degradation cost (C^{DEG}) can be calculated as follows:

$$C^{\text{Energy}} = \sum_{t=1}^{N_T} \left[\left(\pi^{\text{trans}} + \pi^{\text{tax}} + \pi_t^{\text{spot}} \right) \cdot P_t^{\text{market\_buy}} - \left(\pi^{\text{incen}} + \pi_t^{\text{spot}} \right) \cdot P_t^{\text{market\_sell}} \right] \tag{3}$$

$$C^{\text{Power}} = \pi^{\text{elec\_peak}} \cdot P^{\text{peak}} \tag{4}$$

$$C^{\text{DEG}} = \sum_{t=1}^{N_T} \left(\pi^{\text{deg}} \cdot (D_t^{\text{CAL}} + D_t^{\text{CYC}}) \right) \tag{5}$$

In Eqs. (3), (4), and (5), the set of agents is defined as $\mathcal{I} = \{1, 2, \ldots, N_I\}$, and the set of time intervals over the optimization horizon is given by $\mathcal{T} = \{1, 2, \ldots, N_T\}$. Likewise, π^{trans} represents the transmission fee, π^{tax} denotes the tax fee, and π_t^{spot} indicates the spot market price at time t, and π^{incen} is the incentive rate to sell electricity back to the grid. The electricity purchased from and sold to the power grid is represented by $P_t^{\text{market\_buy}}$ and $P_t^{\text{market\_sell}}$, respectively. The daily peak load of the LEC is denoted by P^{peak}, and the corresponding peak load fee is represented by $\pi^{\text{elec\_peak}}$. Finally, the cycle aging and the calendar aging of the BESS are indicated by D_t^{CAL} and D_t^{CYC}, respectively. The present value of BESS is given by π^{deg}.

3.2 Constraints

Load Balance Constraint: To ensure the stable operation of the LEC, the balance between energy exchanges of the LEC with the power grid and the energy exchanges with the agents must be maintained in each scheduling interval:

$$P_t^{\text{market\_buy}} - P_t^{\text{market\_sell}} = \sum_{i=1}^{N_I} P_{i,t}^{\text{LEC\_exp}} - \sum_{i=1}^{N_I} P_{i,t}^{\text{LEC\_imp}} \quad (6)$$

In Eq. (6), $P_{i,t}^{\text{LEC\_exp}}$ and $P_{i,t}^{\text{LEC\_imp}}$ represent the power exported and imported by agent i within the LEC to and from the internal network, respectively.

Grid Capacity Constraint: Due to the grid capacity limitation, the following constraints should be considered:

$$P_t^{\text{market\_buy}} \leq P^{\text{grid\_max}} \cdot u_t^{\text{market\_buy}} \quad (7)$$

$$P_t^{\text{market\_sell}} \leq P^{\text{grid\_max}} \cdot (1 - u_t^{\text{market\_buy}}) \quad (8)$$

In Eqs. (7) and (8), $P^{\text{grid\_max}}$ denotes the maximum grid exchange capacity. To prevent simultaneous buying and selling, a binary decision variable $u_t^{\text{market\_buy}}$ is introduced, where $u_t^{\text{market\_buy}} = 1$ indicates market purchase and 0 indicates market sale at time t.

Peak Power Constraint: In this study, peak demand costs were calculated on a daily basis for simplicity and to align with the short-term simulation horizon. The daily peak power is defined as the maximum power exchanged with the grid during the scheduling horizon and can be formulated as follows:

$$P^{\text{peak}} \geq P_t^{\text{market\_buy}} \quad (9)$$

Agent Constraint: Each component, or a combination of several identical or different components, within the LEC is modeled as an independent "agent" with its own operational characteristics, decision-making processes, and interaction capabilities. An agent may represent a single component, such as a PV system, or a group of related components, like a PV system combined with a BESS. These agents operate autonomously while communicating and coordinating with other agents in the LEC.

In the demonstration sites at Jättesten and Chalmers Campus, the agents are buildings equipped with PV system and BESS. For each building, the balance between energy exchanges with the LEC and the internal generation and consumption must be maintained in each scheduling interval, such that:

$$P_{i,t}^{\text{agent\_imp}} - P_{i,t}^{\text{agent\_exp}} = \sum_{j \in \text{BES}_i} P_{j,t}^{\text{cha}} + \sum_{j \in \text{EL}_i} P_{j,t}^{\text{load}} - \sum_{j \in \text{PV}_i} P_{j,t}^{\text{PV}} - \sum_{j \in \text{BES}_i} P_{j,t}^{\text{dis}} \quad (10)$$

In Eq. (10), the load demand and PV generation of agent i are indicated by $P_{j,t}^{\text{load}}$ and $P_{j,t}^{\text{PV}}$, respectively. Likewise, the charging and discharging power of the BESS are represented by $P_{j,t}^{\text{cha}}$ and $P_{j,t}^{\text{dis}}$, respectively. The power imported from and exported to the LEC internal network by agent i are indicated by $P_{i,t}^{\text{agent\_imp}}$ and $P_{i,t}^{\text{agent\_exp}}$, respectively. Due to the capacity limitation of internal network of LEC, the imported and exported power should be restricted as follows:

$$P_{i,t}^{\text{agent\_imp}} \leq P^{\text{agent\_max}} \cdot u_t^{\text{agent\_imp}} \tag{11}$$

$$P_{i,t}^{\text{agent\_exp}} \leq P^{\text{agent\_max}} \cdot (1 - u_t^{\text{agent\_imp}}) \tag{12}$$

where, $P^{\text{agent\_max}}$ is the maximum exchanged power between agent i and the LEC. To prevent simultaneous import and export, a binary decision variable $u_t^{\text{agent\_imp}}$ is introduced.

The BESS can be modeled using Eqs. (13)-(18). The discharging and charging power of BESS are limited to $P^{\text{BES\_max}}$ by Eq. (13) and Eq. (14), respectively. The SOC dynamic of BESS is given in Eq. (15). In this equation, η^{cha} and η^{dis} are charging and discharging efficiency, respectively. Likewise, the capacity of the BESS is denoted by E^{BES}. The initial SOC of BESS is defined in Eq. (16). Due to the technical limitations, the SOC of BESS is limited between a specified maximum and minimum values, i.e., SOC^{max} and SOC^{min}, as given in Eq. (17). Likewise, Eq. (18) ensures that concurrent charging and discharging of the BESS is prevented.

$$0 \leq P_{j,t}^{\text{BES\_dis}} \leq P^{\text{BES\_max}} u_{j,t}^{\text{BES\_dis}} \tag{13}$$

$$0 \leq P_{j,t}^{\text{BES\_cha}} \leq P^{\text{BES\_max}} u_{j,t}^{\text{BES\_cha}} \tag{14}$$

$$\text{SOC}_{j,t} = \text{SOC}_{j,t-1} + \frac{\eta^{\text{cha}} P_{j,t}^{\text{BES\_cha}} \Delta t}{E^{\text{BES}}} - \frac{P_{j,t}^{\text{BES\_dis}} \Delta t}{\eta^{\text{dis}} E^{\text{BES}}} \tag{15}$$

$$\text{SOC}_0 = \text{SOC}^{\text{ini}} \tag{16}$$

$$\text{SOC}^{\text{min}} \leq \text{SOC}_{j,t} \leq \text{SOC}^{\text{max}} \tag{17}$$

$$u_{j,t}^{\text{BES\_dis}} + u_{j,t}^{\text{BES\_cha}} \leq 1 \tag{18}$$

The the calendar and cycle aging models can be formulated as follows [9]:

$$D_{j,t}^{CAL} = \gamma_1 e^{\mu_1 (\tau_{j,t})^{-1}} \gamma_2 e^{\mu_2 \text{SOC}_{j,t}} T^{0.5} \tag{19}$$

$$D_{j,t}^{CYC} = \begin{cases} (\delta_1 D_{j,t}^2 + \delta_2 D_{j,t} + \delta_3) \cdot \mathcal{K} \cdot Ah_{j,t}^{0.87}, & \text{if } 0.10 \leq D_{j,t} \leq 0.50 \\ (\gamma_3 e^{\mu_3 D_{j,t}} + \gamma_4 e^{\mu_4 D_{j,t}}) \cdot \mathcal{K} \cdot Ah_{j,t}^{0.65}, & \text{otherwise} \end{cases} \tag{20}$$

where, μ_1, μ_2, δ_1, δ_2, δ_3, γ_1, γ_2, γ_3, and γ_4 are the coefficients of the extracted model, $\tau_{j,t}^{\text{BES}}$ represents the temperature of the battery cell during operation, T

represents the age, D is the depth of discharge, Ah is the Ah-throughput, and $\mathcal{K}$ is a complex balancing factor.

To keep MILP format of optimization problem, Eqs. (19) and (20) have been linearized using the method proposed by [6]. This study assumes unrestricted electricity transfer between buildings within the Local Energy Community, enabling optimal energy sharing. However, in real-world applications, such transfers are subject to technical and regulatory constraints, including grid capacity limits, transformer ratings, and local distribution rules. Ignoring these factors may overestimate the potential benefits of energy sharing, and future work should incorporate realistic transfer limitations to better reflect actual grid conditions.

3.3 Key Performance Indicators

This study evaluates LEC performance using three key indicators:

- **Total Operational Cost**: Electricity supply cost excluding capital expenditures for PV or BESS. Lower values indicate economic efficiency.
- **Self-Sufficiency (SS)**: Share of total electricity demand met by local generation (PV and BESS). Higher SS reflects reduced grid dependence.
- **Self-Consumption (SC)**: Share of local generation consumed within the community. Higher SC indicates better utilization of local resources and supports grid stability.

An optimal scenario features low operational costs alongside high self-sufficiency and self-consumption, reflecting a resilient and efficient LEC.

4 Results

The results for different scenarios have been performed for the year 2023 with the objective of minimizing costs and the results for this can be observed in

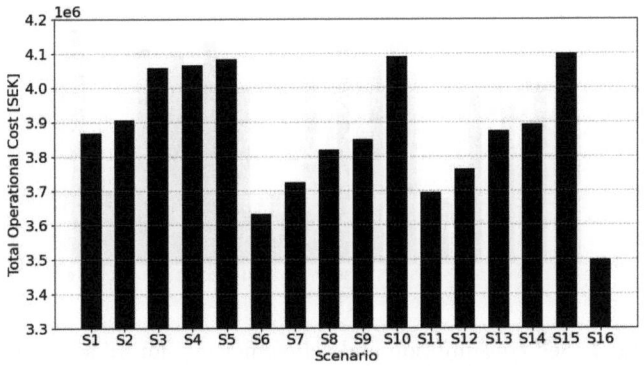

Fig. 3. Total operational cost for all scenarios

Fig. 3. From Fig. 3, it can be observed that as the share of buildings in Jättesten increases in LEC participation, the overall costs has been reducing this is visible when comparing scenarios S1 to S4, S6 to S9 and S11 to S14. Hence the addition of residential buildings to the LEC reduces the costs of the entire system. In terms of the buildings from Chalmers Campus, Edit building had a higher reduction in costs than in comparison to Gamla Matte building and this can be observed by comparing Scenarios S6 to S9 with S11 to S14. In addition to this, as more buildings are added to LEC from Chalmers, the overall costs reduces as well. The lowest costs can be seen for S16 in which all the buildings in both Chalmers Campus and Jättesten demonstration site has been considered to participate in LEC. This scenario results in up to a 14 % reduction in total annual operating costs. The results on other KPIs such as SS and SC can be observed in Fig. 4 where the bar graph with darker shade highlights the SS whereas the lighter shade bar graph highlights the SC. Similar results as to the operational costs is seen here with scenario S16 performing the best with the highest SC of 33 % and SS of 67 % which are up to 4 % higher than those in the other scenarios. The peak load values across all scenarios are illustrated in Fig. 5. The highest peak load, approximately 1000 kWh, is observed in S10, where only the Edit building from Chalmers Campus participates in the LEC while all other buildings remain excluded. In contrast, S16, which includes all buildings from both demonstration sites in the LEC, achieves the lowest peak load of 780 kWh—representing a reduction of up to 20 % compared to other scenarios. From the above results, it is evident that Scenario S16 is the best in terms of all KPIs and highlights the need for mixing multiple load profiles in LECs to maximize returns. But the above mentioned results is based on the current status-quo i.e., the existing PV and BESS installations in the demonstration sites. In order to analyze the effect of additional PV and BESS installations, the results might change. In order to analyze this, a sensitivity analysis is performed.

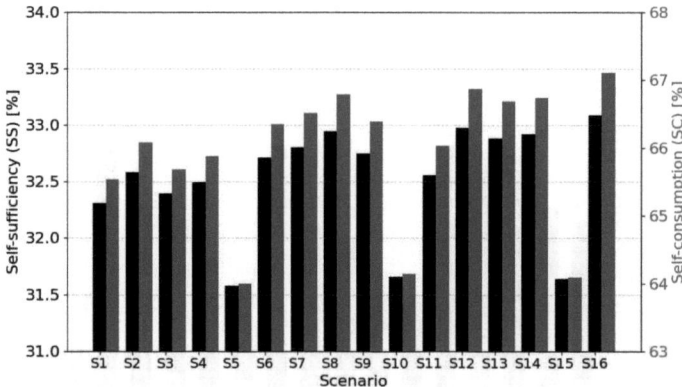

Fig. 4. Self consumption and self-sufficiency for all scenarios

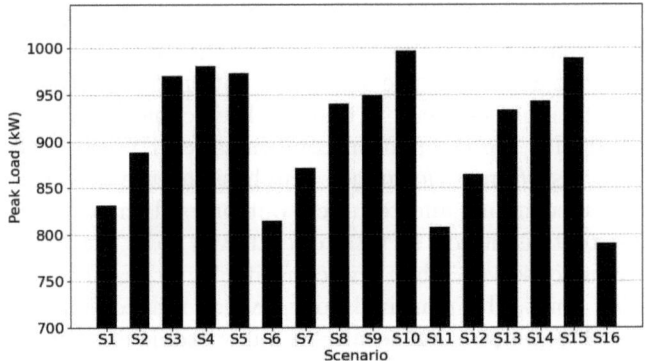

Fig. 5. Peak load for all scenarios

4.1 Sensitivity Analysis

A sensitivity analysis was conducted on scenario S16 by varying the levels of PV penetration and BESS capacity. The PV penetration was incremented by a factor of 0.25, ranging from 1 to 2 multiples of these base capacities, while the BESS capacity was increased in steps of 0.5, ranging from 1 to 3 multiples of these base capacities. Based on these changes, the updated results can be seen in Fig. 6.

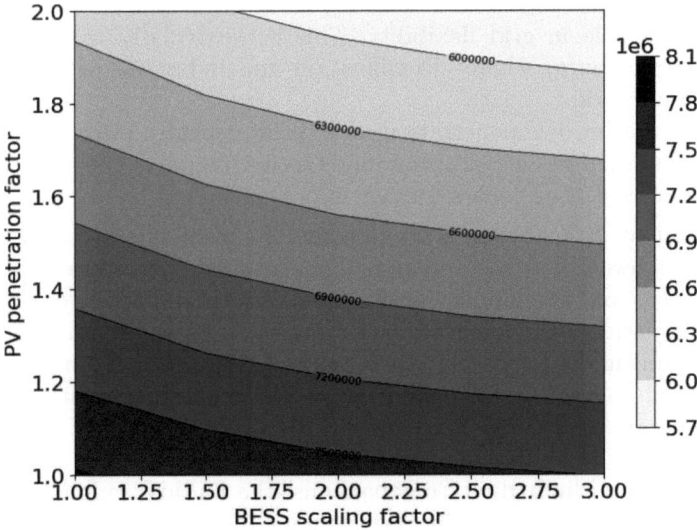

Fig. 6. Results on total operational costs for varying PV penetration and BESS installation capacity

As shown in Fig. 6, the capacities of PV and BESS are closely linked, as larger PV installations generate more surplus energy that requires sufficient storage to avoid curtailment and maximize self-consumption. Similarly, oversized BESS without enough PV input can lead to underutilized capacity and lower efficiency. Our results show that the calculation conditions for PV and BESS sizing significantly influence system performance, emphasizing the need for balanced co-design to optimize economic and technical outcomes. Increasing BESS capacity leads to a consistent reduction in total operational costs, with the most significant improvement observed when the capacity factor is increased from 1.0 to 1.5. Beyond this point, the marginal cost savings reduces but is still evident. Similarly, higher PV penetration results in a monotonic decrease in operational costs. In terms of other KPIs, the results of increasing PV penetration and BESS capacity increased the SC and SS of the LECs. These results highlight the potential for enhancing the performance of LECs through increased deployment of PV systems and BESS infrastructure beyond the current baseline configuration.

4.2 Key-Takeaway Points

Based on the above results there are three key-points from this study.

First, integrating diverse building types—particularly residential and commercial–within a LEC significantly improves performance across all KPIs. Increased demand diversity enhances self-consumption, self-sufficiency, and reduces operational costs, underscoring the limitations of single-sector LECs and the benefits of mixed participation.

Second, LEC participation enables up to 20 % reduction in peak demand, highlighting its role in grid flexibility. This is particularly relevant for urban areas like Gothenburg, where electrification and industrial activity stress the distribution network.

Third, increasing PV penetration and BESS capacity leads to lower operational costs and higher energy autonomy. Optimizing local generation and storage beyond current levels offers further improvements.

Comparison with Existing Knowledge: The results from this study extend findings from Swedish LECs research. For example, the Sätra case [10] validated technical and economic viability, and Åberg [11] reported up to 40 % self-sufficiency with DER integration. Huang et al. [5] projected 5.4–6.2 % self-sufficiency gains under future climate scenarios. In contrast, Scenario S16 in this study achieved up to 67 % self-sufficiency, a 20 % peak load reduction, and a 14 % drop in operational costs—highlighting the impact of combining real-world mixed-use profiles from Jättesten and Chalmers Campus. While methodological and site differences limit direct comparisons, the findings emphasize the value of heterogeneous participation in maximizing LEC benefits. This study's focus on quantifying these benefits using real-world data from mixed-use sites thus provides a novel perspective on optimizing LEC design for enhanced grid support and participant value in the Swedish context. While this study focuses on a specific set of DERs and a defined community size, the proposed framework is scalable and can be extended to larger energy communities or additional DER types such as heat pumps, electric boilers, or EV fleets. Incorporating these elements would enable a more comprehensive assessment of sector coupling and community-wide flexibility, further underlining the general applicability of the approach.

4.3 Limitations

While the results from this study provide valuable insights, certain limitations must be considered to accurately interpret the findings. First, the peak cost calculation within the MILP optimization model was performed on a daily basis, rather than over an entire month. This simplification was intended to minimize daily peak loads and reduce computational complexity, but in reality, the actual peak load costs should be based on the peak load over the full month. Second, the MILP model assumes unrestricted electricity transfer between buildings. In practice, however, transmission line constraints could limit the transfer of electricity, potentially affecting the results.

5 Conclusion

This study investigated the operational and economic benefits of LECs in the context of Sweden by incorporating mixed usage buildings and distributed energy resources specifically PV and BESS. A detailed MILP-based optimization framework was employed to assess key performance indicators including total operational cost, self-consumption, and self-sufficiency across various participation scenarios and building combinations while limiting battery aging. The results from this study clearly highlights the benefits of incorporating mixed usage of buildings within a LEC which outperforms the homogeneous mixture of buildings in LECs. Furthermore, the incorporation of commercial and residential buildings in LECs contributed to peak shaving which is essential in industry-intensive cities like Gothenburg while rapid electrification of transport and heating sector is to be expected in the following years. The sensitivity analysis of increasing PV penetration and BESS capacity increment improves the economic performance of LECs, though the marginal benefits decrease beyond certain thresholds. This indicates the importance of strategic sizing and deployment of distributed resources to maximize efficiency and cost-effectiveness. Overall, the findings support the adoption of mixed-use LECs and highlight the importance of flexible, data-driven planning in the transition toward decentralized and sustainable energy systems.

Acknowledgments. This paper is based on work conducted in the project Ecom4Future (Swedish energy agency project number: P2023-00948). The project has received funding in the framework of the joint programming initiative CETPartnership, the Clean Energy Transition Partnership under the 2022 joint call for research proposals, co-funded by the European Commission.

References

1. Bauwens, T., et al.: Conceptualizing community in energy systems: a systematic review of 183 definitions. Renew. Sustain. Energy Rev. **156**, 111999 (2022)
2. Bergek, A., Palm, J.: Energy communities in Sweden: challenging established ideas of aim, place and engagement. Energy Res. Soc. Sci. **115**, 103626 (2024)
3. Göteborg Energi: Elnätsavgiften (electricity network tariffs). https://www.goteborgenergi.se/foretag/vara-nat/elnat/elnatsavgiften (2025) [.Accessed 24 Apr 2025]
4. Hasselgren, P., Tawaha, M.: Energy Security for Sustainable Development: Exploring the Potential Contribution of Renewable Energy Communities in Sweden. Master's thesis, Malmö University (2023). https://www.diva-portal.org/smash/get/diva2:1777699/FULLTEXT01.pdf
5. Huang, P., Lovati, M., Shen, J., Chai, J., Zhang, X.: Investigation of the peer-to-peer energy trading performances in a local community under the future climate change scenario in Sweden. Energy Rep. **8**, 989–1001 (2022)
6. Mazidi, M., Khezri, R., Mohiti, M., Tuan, L.A., Steen, D.: Effects of calendar and cycle ageing on battery scheduling for optimal energy management: a case study of HSB living lab. In: 2023 IEEE International Conference on Energy Technologies for Future Grids (ETFG), pp. 1–5. IEEE (2023)
7. Millot, A., Krook-Riekkola, A., Maïzi, N.: Guiding the future energy transition to net-zero emissions: lessons from exploring the differences between France and Sweden. Energy Policy **139**, 111358 (2020)
8. Nord Pool: Nordic power market spot prices. https://www.nordpoolgroup.com (2025). [Accessed 24 Apr 2025]
9. Sarasketa-Zabala, E., Gandiaga, I., Martinez-Laserna, E., Rodriguez-Martinez, L., Villarreal, I.: Cycle ageing analysis of a lifepo4/graphite cell with dynamic model validations: towards realistic lifetime predictions. J. Power Sources **275**, 573–587 (2015)
10. Yamout, R., Krayem, A., Wallin, F.: Energy communities in Sweden: the case study of sätra, västerås. Energy Proc. **46** (2024)
11. Åberg, M.: Exergigemenskaper – för ett resurseffektivt energisystem. Tech. Rep. 2024-1064, Energiforsk (2024). https://energiforsk.se/media/34266/2024-1064-exergigemenskaper-fo-r-ett-resurseffektivt-energisystem.pdf

Data-Driven Correlated Uncertainty Sets for PV Generation and Electricity Demand

Debajyoti Biswas[1](✉), Cristian Aguayo[2], Anna Mutule[3], and Paula Carroll[1]

[1] College of Business, University College Dublin, Dublin, Ireland
{debajyoti.biswas,paula.carroll}@ucd.ie
[2] Département d'Informatique, Université libre de Bruxelles, Brussels, Belgium
cristian.aguayo.quintana@ulb.be
[3] Smart Grid Research Centre, Institute of Physical Energetics, Riga, Latvia
amutule@edi.lv

Abstract. Local energy communities (LECs) are viewed as key actors in the future clean energy system. However, uncertainty is inherent in renewable energy generation and electricity consumption. Renewable energy sources (RES) like solar and wind can exhibit considerable variation in power generation depending on weather and other factors. Optimisation techniques like Robust Optimisation (RO) aim to take uncertainty into account for decision making. It is important to consider uncertainty in both domains - power supply and electricity demand to facilitate the participation of LECs in the clean energy transition. In this paper, we examine empirical time-series data from the building energy management system (BEMS) of a public university in Ireland (University College Dublin) to characterise the temporal correlation between photovoltaic (PV) power generation and electricity consumption. We propose a data-driven approach to construct correlated uncertainty sets for supply and demand data by partitioning the day into specific time-windows. This data-driven approach can reduce the level of conservatism in RO models for LEC distribution network design and operational decision problems.

Keywords: energy community · renewable energy · correlated uncertainty · energy analytics · holistic optimisation

1 Introduction

The EU 2050 strategy to achieve climate neutrality and net-zero greenhouse gas emissions [6] envisages its citizens at the centre of the clean energy transition. Local energy communities (LECs) are citizen-led communities who actively participate in the decentralisation and decarbonisation of energy generation and distribution. Prioritising social and environmental benefits over financial profitability [15], LECs also aid in increasing consumer awareness about renewable energy [11], mitigating power losses by reducing the distance between generation and consumption points [7] and can help in building resilience for the grid during peak demand periods [8]. LECs serve their energy needs and may supply energy and services to the grid by leveraging renewable energy sources (RES) like wind and solar. Distributed Energy Resources (DERs) like photovoltaic (PV) panels and wind turbines, allow customers or groups of customers to become energy providers, known as "prosumers" [17].

Although LECs can offer clean energy solutions by adopting innovative low carbon technologies, they face several challenges when it comes to technology choice and decision support [3]. LECs need to make important long-term investment and short-term energy management decisions to achieve their goals. Recently, long-term investments in renewable energy sources—particularly PV —have become a subject of considerable debate due to emerging risks. These include policy uncertainty, as highlighted by the International Energy Agency (IEA) [10], where shifts such as the phase-out of feed-in tariffs and evolving market designs have increased investor exposure and revenue volatility. Technology risks are also significant, with rapid advancements making some PV assets obsolete.

LECs may wish to participate in energy markets after first serving their own energy needs, and may gain perspectives on multivariate Time-of-Use by jointly considering the correlation between supply and demand. Conventional stakeholders in the energy sector like Distribution System Operators (DSO) and Transmission System Operators (TSO) have access to historical empirical data and analytical tools for in-depth cost-benefit analysis of network-related decisions. LECs often lack access to sources of empirical data, and analytical tools to support their planning activities [1]. Energy analytics and informatics play a key role to aid data-driven decision-making and facilitate participation in the clean energy transition by LECs.

The PV industry is one of the fastest growing electricity generation industries. Solar power is slated to increase in generation from 2.2 TWh in 2019 to 34 TWh by 2050 [9]. Ground-mounted or rooftop PV panels intercept solar irradiance and convert it into electrical energy. PV is a popular form of RES harnessed by LECs to meet their energy needs but comes with its own set of challenges owing to the intermittent and variability of supply. Better PV prediction models are essential given the unpredictability in supply [2]. Although there are different kinds of uncertainty that LECs need to deal with, in this paper we restrict our focus to uncertainty in coincident PV supply and electricity demand.

It is important to factor in both the variation in RES supply and electricity demand, and their temporal relationship to make reliable data-driven decisions. Stochastic programming (SP) and robust optimisation (RO) are mathematical optimisation techniques that take uncertainty into account when computing decision recommendations. SP constructs a set of scenarios based on the distribution of uncertain parameters. In contrast, RO takes individual uncertain parameters into account by solving for their worst-case realisations possible. In practise, it is often difficult to obtain the true distribution of the uncertain parameters, hence RO may offer a more useful approach for decision-making under uncertainty.

Moreover, SP involves running many scenarios, increasing the computational burden for solving the problem [22]. On the flip-side, when the uncertain parameters are considered independently in RO, extremely unlikely outcomes of each individual parameter can lead to over-conservatism.

RO models capture uncertainty using "uncertainty sets" [5]. These are sets of values representing the expected variation of the uncertain parameters. Different mechanisms for defining the uncertainty sets can be used. Using a data-driven approach we construct correlated uncertainty sets directly from the distribution of empirical data. The sets bound the spread of the supply and demand points using an appropriate geometric shape (polydedral or ellipsoidal) that best captures the boundaries of the data and eliminates the void spaces in the bounding box. The most conservative estimate is the box uncertainty set where all uncertain parameters are considered to be independent and are characterised by the lower and upper bounds of the variation. Box uncertainty sets can be defined as:

$$\mathcal{U} = \{\tilde{P}_i = P_i + \zeta_i \hat{P}_i || \zeta_i| \leq \psi_i, \quad \forall i \in \mathcal{N}\}$$

where $\tilde{P}_i$ is the actual value of an uncertain parameter i, $i \in \mathcal{N}$, where $\mathcal{N}$ is the set of uncertain parameters, P_i is the nominal value, $\hat{P}_i$ is the maximum perturbation and ζ_i is an independent random variable such that $\zeta_i \in [-\psi_i, \psi_i]$ (ψ_i is a perturbation bound). This formulation of uncertainty sets accounts for several extreme realisations of the uncertain parameters which are highly unlikely, and can result in the RO optimal solution being overly conservative. When uncertain parameters are correlated, the uncertainty space can be restricted, thus reducing the conservatism level and accurately accounting for potential uncertainty in the concerned parameters. Based on the shape of the variation of the perturbation parameters in the uncertainty space, they can also be characterised as polyhedral or ellipsoidal. Further, decision makers can decide a budget for uncertainty [5] based on their risk preferences, by imposing a limit on the number of uncertain parameters that can simultaneously realise their worst value. This uncertainty is characterised as a polyhedral uncertainty set. After incorporating the uncertainty set of the uncertain parameters in the RO model, it is reformulated into a robust counterpart model, applying the concepts of strong duality [4]. The robust counterpart can be linear (polyhedral uncertainty set) or non-linear (ellipsoidal uncertainty set) based on the shape of the variation of the uncertain parameters, and is used for computing the optimal decisions feasible under all possible perturbations.

In this paper we investigate the correlation between PV supply and demand using data from the Building Energy Management System (BEMS) of a public university in Ireland, University College Dublin (UCD). We perform data analytics to examine how daily variations can be further granularised using time window sequences to characterise correlated uncertainty sets. We use the CRISP-DM (CRoss Industry Standard Process for Data Mining) framework to systematise our analysis, encompassing the steps of business understanding, data understanding and preparation, modeling, and evaluation before deployment [21].

Business Understanding: We begin by specifying the Business Understanding we seek for the correlated uncertainty problem, and formulate the following research questions to inform holistic energy decision support and optimisation:

1. How do time windows and empirical data influence the structure and properties of correlated uncertainty sets for PV supply and electricity demand?
2. How can data-driven methods be applied to characterise correlated uncertainty sets for PV supply and electricity demand?

Electricity consumption patterns and the correlation between photovoltaic supply and electricity demand depend on the type of building and load profile. We find much higher correlation between PV supply and demand in one of the academic buildings compared to the other. We partition the daily supply and demand data into homogeneous time window sequences during daylight hours and find that the maximum correlation across the time windows increases as the time window size decreases, whereas the average correlation may increase or decrease as the time window size increases. We also find that partitioning the day into time window sequences allows us to identify changes in both direction and strength of correlation between supply and demand leading to a more accurate characterisation of the relationship between PV supply and demand and more informative correlated uncertainty sets. These insights can be used by LECs and other actors in the energy space to design and operate their energy scheduling strategies.

The rest of the paper is structured as follows. In Sect. 2 we discuss related literature; in Sect. 3 we describe the dataset used and the methodology implemented; in Sect. 4 we present our analysis of correlated uncertainty sets and finally in Sect. 5 we summarise our findings and discuss future research directions.

2 Literature Review

In this section we briefly discuss related papers and position our work with respect to the modelling of correlated uncertainty for energy management.

Several papers have applied data-driven methods for creating correlated uncertainty sets using empirical distributions. In [19], a data-driven uncertainty set is created for correlation between demand and price uncertainty in a renewable energy microgrid dispatch problem. In [14], a data-driven polyhedral uncertainty set is implemented to characterise spatio-temporal dependencies between solar energy and loads for power management in an active distribution system. Convex hull-based uncertainty sets are proposed in [16] for time and spatial dependency of RES output where the degree of conservatism can be controlled by a scaling parameter. In [18] a historical-correlation-driven uncertainty set is proposed for an RO model for the microgrid dispatch problem. The authors apply a line-fitting approach for formulating the intervals that envelop data points of similar days, incorporating the spatio-temporal correlations to avoid unlikely scenarios. In [12], the authors construct a data-driven uncertainty set using autoregressive integrated moving average method (ARIMA) to solve the unit commitment problem considering spatio-temporal correlation between uncertain parameters, whereas in [13] a data-driven multi-ellipsoidal uncertainty set is formulated to capture temporal correlation of wind power to solve a two-stage robust optimisation model for managing a grid-connected microgrid.

Contrary to these papers, we propose the use of *time window sequences* for constructing data-driven correlated uncertainty sets. We model the correlation of the empirical distribution of the uncertain parameters (PV supply and electricity demand) and use time windows of various sizes to define the uncertainty sets. We show that this approach can reduce the conservatism level for RO models.

3 Materials and Methods

In this section, we describe the datasets' metadata, and CRISP-DM steps. The first CRISP-DM step is to specify Business Understanding questions. In this study we seek insights to our research questions. Our models aim to specify uncertainty sets for RO models in LEC operations and network design.

3.1 Data Understanding

We obtain solar PV generation and electricity consumption in kW units at a fifteen-minute resolution data from the UCD BEMS for the years 2022 to 2024. We select two different academic buildings on UCD's two Dublin campuses to allow diversity in building usage and load profiles for a more insightful analysis. In this study we present results and analysis of the UCD Engineering building in the Belfield campus, and Block D building in the Graduate Business School Blackrock campus. Both buildings have PV installations on their roofs. The capacity for the Engineering building PV system is 12.48 kW whereas for the Blackrock Block D it is 40.90 kW.

3.2 Data Preparation

We prepare and clean the data, removing anomalies to ensure reliable analysis. **Feature Engineering:** Based on the timestamp, we extract time-based features *day, month, year, hour*. The electricity demand data in the UCD BEMS is the net demand which is computed as the gross (actual) demand offset by the PV production that partially self-satisfies this demand. The gross demand is calculated per timestamp as the sum of the net demand and PV production. **Zero-truncation and Data Cleaning:** We apply zero truncation to remove non-daylight hours when no PV is produced, and hence PV correlation with demand cannot be defined. Daylight length is an important consideration at northerly latitudes where day length varies considerably by season. We filter the data to between sunrise and sunset times in Dublin from 2022 to 2024 [20]. In addition, we identify many near-zero values (0.0025 kW) in our dataset, which may correspond to low production at dawn and dusk. Some near-zero PV values

(0.0025 kW) were also identified which occur both during daylight (2.9%) and non-daylight hours (17.1%) for the Engineering building. A small percentage of zero values of PV production occurs during daylight hours for both buildings, possibly because of instrumentation errors or any other systemic glitches. We find that 25.9% and 43% of the PV production data from the Engineering and Block D buildings respectively have zero values during non-daylight hours, whereas 3.7% and 7.9% of the data has zero values for daylight hours. Some possible causes for near-zero PV values could be soiling and shading effects, dirt, dust, leaves, bird droppings, or even temporary disruptions in production due to inverter clipping and faults.

3.3 Modelling

In the CRISP-DM modeling step we use exploratory data analysis (EDA) to extract a deeper understanding of the underlying patterns in PV production and electricity consumption and potential relationships between the two. We use these insights to identify the most useful time window sequences to model and create correlated uncertainty sets.

Figures 1 and 2 show the distribution of PV supply and demand for both the buildings. We observe that PV supply exhibits a highly right-skewed pattern for both buildings, whereas for demand, we see a bimodal distribution for Engineering building and a slightly right-skewed distribution for Block D, indicating a difference in consumption patterns across the two buildings.

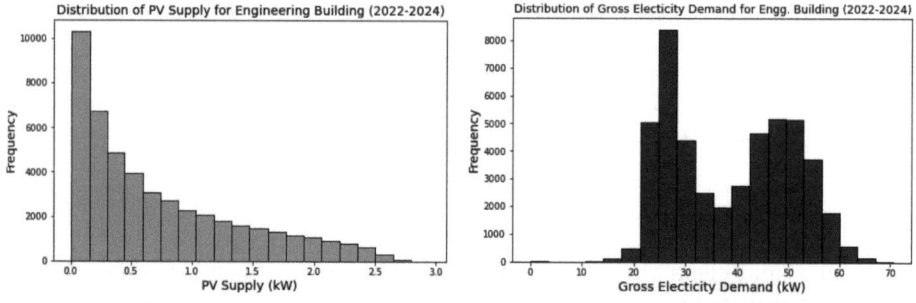

Fig. 1. PV Supply and Gross Electricity Demand distribution for Engineering building at 15 min intervals

Figure 3 shows the relationship between PV supply and demand in the form of a scatter plot of supply and demand pairs for each timestamp. For the Engineering building, we see two horizontal wedges signifying two demand clusters as noted in the demand distribution (Fig. 1 on right). For Block D, correlation (positive) between PV supply and electricity demand is more evident as compared to the Engineering building. Figure 4 shows the variation of average PV supply and electricity at an hourly level. We find that the supply and demand peaks

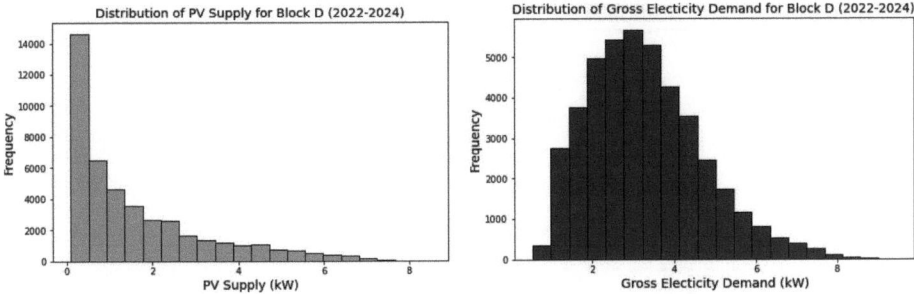

Fig. 2. PV Supply and Gross Electricity Demand distribution for Block D building at 15 min intervals

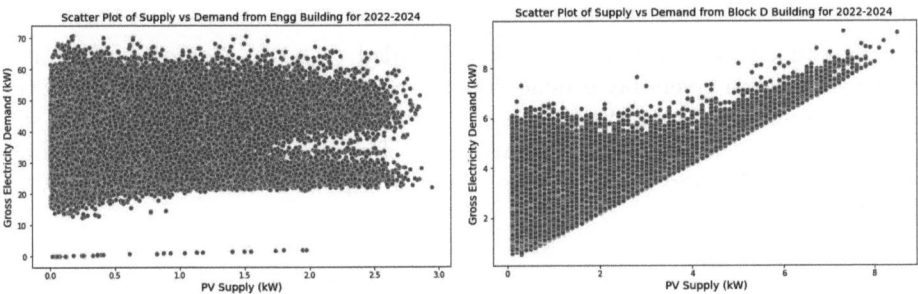

Fig. 3. Scatter plot for electricity demand and PV supply pairs at 15 min intervals for Engineering (left) and Block D buildings (right) respectively

are concurrent around mid-day for Block D, whereas the Engineering building, first demand peak between 10:00 to 15:00 h coincides with the supply peak.

After our EDA of the temporal correlation between PV supply and electricity demand, we next conceptualise how uncertainty sets can be created using time windows to capture the correlation. This allows us to examine the temporal relationship between PV supply and electricity at different granularity of time steps to define correlated uncertainty sets.

We first consider days broken into hourly time steps $t \in \mathcal{H} = \{0, \ldots, 23\}$, where daylight hours are a subset of those hours given by $\mathcal{D} = \{l, \ldots, u\}$ ($\mathcal{D} \subseteq \mathcal{H}$), and l and u are the sunrise and sunset times for a given day, respectively. Note that we disregard the correlation between PV supply and demand for non-daylight hours because of zero PV production. We denote the time window size or length as w. For a day length of $L = u - l$ hours, the number of time windows of size w is $\lfloor \frac{L}{w} \rfloor$. We index the time windows with $b \in \mathcal{T} = \{1, 2, \ldots, \lfloor \frac{L}{w} \rfloor\}$. A time window is defined as $\mathcal{W}_b = \{l + (b-1)w, \ldots, l + bw - 1\}$ comprising of the hours contained within the window. The daylight hours are partitioned into a sequence of time-windows $\{\{l, \ldots, l+w-1\}, \{l+w, \ldots, l+2w-1\} .. \{l + (\lfloor \frac{L}{w} \rfloor - 1)w, \ldots, u - 1\}\}$. Thus, the uncertainty corresponding to any hour t ($t \in \mathcal{D}$ for considering daylight hours) is represented by the uncertainty in the

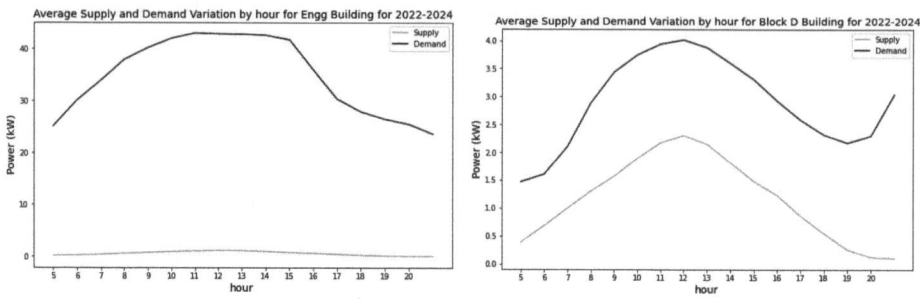

Fig. 4. Average hourly electricity demand and PV supply at 15 min intervals for Engineering (left) and Block D buildings (right) respectively

corresponding time window block $\mathcal{W}_b$, provided $t \in \mathcal{W}_b$. A sequence of time window sizes for a given day is denoted as $\mathcal{S} = \{|\mathcal{W}_1|, \ldots, |\mathcal{W}_{|\mathcal{T}|}|\}$ containing the set of time window sizes. When L is not perfectly divisible by the window size w we create sequences of $\lfloor \frac{L}{w} \rfloor$ time windows of size w followed by a single time window of size $L \mod w$. We define hour t to represent a 1 h interval between hours t and $t+1$.

For example, for a given day, with $l = 6, u = 18, L = 12$ and $\mathcal{D} = \{6, 7 \ldots, 18\}$ with time window size $w = 4$ and $\mathcal{T} = \{1, 2, 3\}$, we can define time windows as $\mathcal{W}_1 = \{6, 7, 8, 9\}$ (encompassing the hourly intervals 6–7, 7–8, 8–9, 9–10), $\mathcal{W}_2 = \{10, 11, 12, 13\}$ (encompassing the hourly intervals 10–11, 11–12, 12–13, 13–14) and $\mathcal{W}_3 = \{14, 15, 16, 17\}$ (encompassing the hourly intervals 14–15, 15–16, 16–17, 17–18). The time window sequence of time window sizes can be defined as $\mathcal{S} = \{4, 4, 4\}$. Hence, if the decision making is done at the hourly level, the uncertainty pertaining to a given hour, say uncertainty at $t = 11$ will correspond to the uncertainty related to the time window $\mathcal{W}_2$ ($\mathcal{W}_2 = \{10, 11, 12, 13\}$). For any parameter P_t under box-type uncertainty can be defined as $\tilde{P}_t = P_t + \zeta_b \hat{P}_t$ ($t \in \mathcal{W}_b$) where P_t is the nominal value, $\hat{P}_t$ is the maximum perturbation, and ζ_b is an independent random variable ($\zeta_b \in [-\psi_b, \psi_b]$) for time window b comprised of the hours in $\mathcal{W}_b$. By defining boundaries of the spread of the empirical data the total uncertainty space can be partitioned and refined to reduce void spaces. Hence we can eliminate void spaces corresponding to unlikely scenarios, by defining boundaries for the uncertainty sets such as polyhedral convex hulls, ellipsoids or other appropriate geometric shapes to enclose the observed supply/demand pairs, which can then directly feed into the RO model.

3.4 Evaluation

The scatter plot visualisations of the PV supply and electricity demand pairs give us a partial understanding of the direction and strength of their correlation. To better capture the correlation we partition the daylight hours into time window sequences with integer time window sizes w.

We consider contiguous time windows of equal size $w \in \{1, 2, 3, 4, L\}$ where L is the (variable) length of the daylight duration of the day. For constructing uncertainty sets, we consider the data based on these time window sequences for each day of the week (Monday to Sunday) for each month of the year and compute the correlation corresponding to them (discussed in the Analysis and Results later).

In order to visualise the distribution of correlations, we compute the average of the correlations ($\bar{r}$) and the maximum of the correlations (r_{max}) across time window sequences for different time window sizes, across all days in the dataset, considering daylight hours only. Referring to the previous example in Sect. 3.3, with $l = 6, u = 18, L = 12$ and $\mathcal{D} = \{6, 7 \ldots, 18\}$ with time window size $w = 4$, $\mathcal{T} = \{1, 2, 3\}$, and time window sequence $\mathcal{S} = \{4, 4, 4\}$, we can compute a corresponding set of correlations $\{r_1, r_2, r_3\}$ for the supply demand points contained in the corresponding time windows in the time window sequence. The average correlation $\bar{r}$ and the max correlation r_{max} for the time window sequence can be further computed. Note that we consider the absolute values of correlation ($|r| \in [0, 1]$) when computing the average and maximum correlations. However, later we relax this to compute correlations across different time window sequences for further numerical tests.

For brevity, we show the visualisation for one of the buildings (Block D) only (as it exhibits stronger correlation between PV supply and demand). Figures 5 and 6 show 3D histograms of the correlation frequency for different values of time window size w for Block D. In order to construct the histograms we consider the correlation between 15 min interval supply and demand pairs for each hour and plot their frequencies corresponding to the hour of the day.

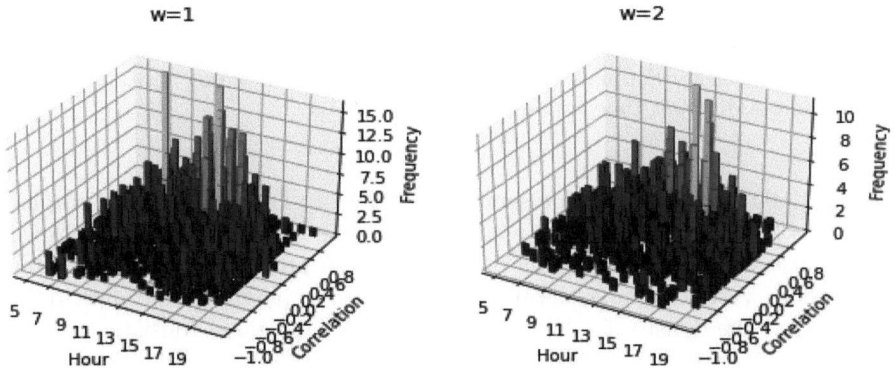

Fig. 5. Correlation frequency distribution between PV supply and electricity demand (at 15 min intervals) for Block D for time windows of 1 h and 2 h respectively, for daylight hours only.

We find that for Block D, the frequencies of higher correlation values dominate that of lower correlation values, with correlation peaks occurring between

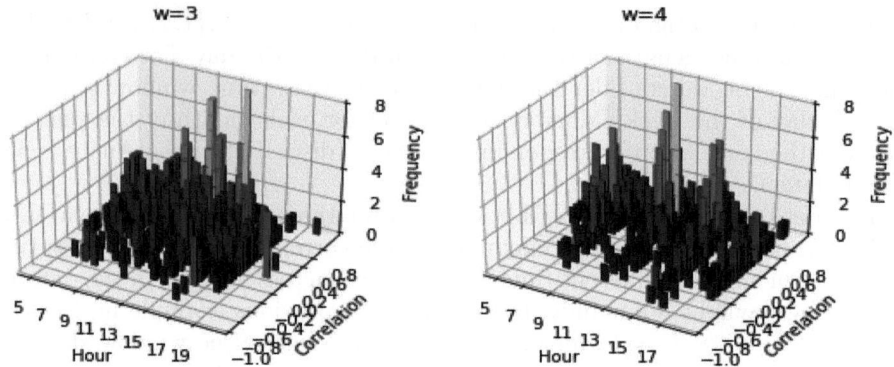

Fig. 6. Correlation frequency distribution between PV supply and electricity demand (at 15 min intervals) for Block D for time windows of 3 h and 4 h respectively, for daylight hours only.

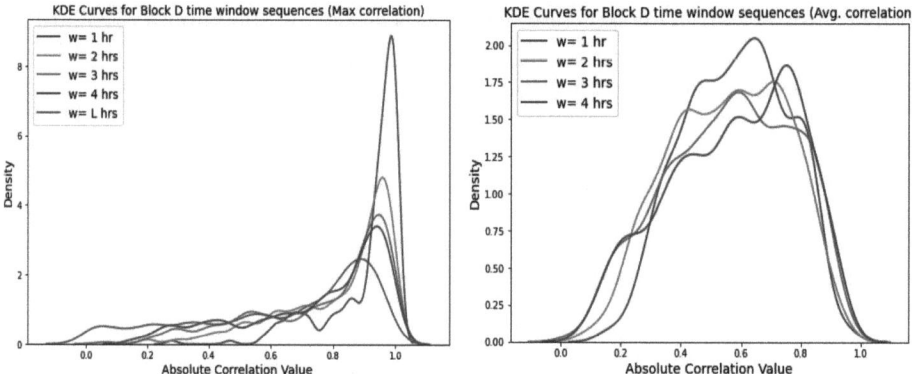

Fig. 7. Kernel Density Estimate (KDE) curves for Block D building for r_{max} (left) and $\bar{r}$ (right) across different time window sequences

11:00 to 13:00 h. In Fig. 7, we present Kernel Density Estimate (KDE) graphs of r_{max} and $\bar{r}$ for the different time window sequences for Block D. Kernel Density estimation is a non-parametric method to create a probability density estimate of a random variable and generate a smooth curve based on the data points. We find that the density for higher values of r_{max} increases consistently as the window size w decreases for the Block D building. However, we also observe that the density of lower values of $\bar{r}$ is higher for sequences with lower time window sizes (w). This highlights a trade-off in choosing the time window size w between the magnitude of r_{max} and $\bar{r}$. As w decreases, r_{max} increases, but $\bar{r}$ may decrease or increase. This has implications for the construction of correlated uncertainty sets. Smaller w results in multiple weakly correlated uncertainty sets. In contrast, for a bigger window size w, although r_{max} might be lower, the number of uncertainty sets are smaller with moderate to stronger correlations across them.

This could potentially reduce both the conservatism for the associated RO model and also the computational burden for solving the RO decision problem.

The final CRISP-DM Deployment step is addressed in Sect. 4 where we assess how the Correlated Uncertainty Sets perform.

4 Analysis and Results

In this section we answer the research questions posed in Sect. 1. We analyse the Correlated Uncertainty Sets and discuss the results of numerical experiments based on time windows for both the buildings' datasets. We then conceptualise the correlated uncertainty sets based on our findings.

4.1 Impact of Time Windows on Correlated Uncertainty Sets: Numerical Experiments

We focus on addressing our first research question 1: how time windows impact the structure and properties of correlated uncertainty sets.

Our empirical analysis in Sect. 3.4 shows the supply/demand correlation is more apparent when their daily variation is partitioned into time windows. Based on this finding, we look deeper into the correlation of supply and demand, by partitioning daily data into time windows and visualising the spread of the supply and demand points to understand how the correlation changes across time window sequences of different time window sizes. We characterise the spread of supply/demand points as the data-driven correlated uncertainty sets. For our tests, we aggregate data for each day of the week (Monday to Sunday, categorising them as 1 to 7 correspondingly) for each month of the year. Figures 8 and 9 show examples of these correlated uncertainty sets. The scatter plots of PV supply and demand are for the Block D building for day 5 (Fridays) for October, 2024, splitting the daylight hours between 7:00-18:00 h ($l = 7, u = 18, L = 11$) into time-windows with sizes of $w = 5$ h, and $w = 11$ h spanning the entire daylight duration for the day. Based on the observed relationship of PV supply and electricity demand for a given day and time window, we can define the range of uncertainty that can be expected for a similar day in the future for taking decisions that depend on both supply and demand.

We indicate the boundaries of the extremities of the spread with a box, which would be the most conservative estimate of the uncertainty assuming no correlation between PV supply and demand. Thus owing to the moderate to strong correlation across the different time window sequences, we can restrict the uncertainty space, doing away with the void spaces in the box.

In Fig. 8 interestingly, we find when we do not partition the day (length of 11 h) into time windows, the correlation obtained is 0.71, whereas in Fig. 9, for time-windows of size $w = 5$ (two windows of size 5 and one window of size 1), the correlation values are 0.74, 0.7 and 0.97, respectively. Thus, we conclude that higher granularity in the time-window design allows us to capture the relationship between the uncertain parameters more accurately. Hence, if an uncertainty set corresponding to a big time-window size (high w) is implemented to solve a RO model for delivering decisions at an hourly level (or a lower time step), it could lead to more conservative estimates of the correlated uncertainty increasing the computational burden for obtaining the optimal solution. On the other hand there can be situations where partitioning the day into time windows leads to very marginal change in the correlation values. We find that for one of the instances, without partitioning the day length (L) of 9 h, the correlation is 0.94 whereas with time windows of size $w = 5$ (1 window of size 5 and 1 window of size 4 hours), the correlations are 0.96 and 0.95 respectively.

Besides the strength of the correlation, it is also essential to account for the direction of correlation between two uncertain parameters. For example, in Figs. 10 and 11 we show the scatter plots for time windows for the Engineering building and observe that for a time window size of $w = 15$ h spanning the entire daylight duration ($L = 15$), the correlation observed is 0.2, whereas when partitioned into three time windows of size $w = 5$ h each, the correlations are $0.29, -0.41, 0.45$ respectively. Moreover, r_{max} and $\bar{r}$ of the absolute correlation values are both higher for the time window sequence $\mathcal{S} = \{5, 5, 5\}$ than the one corresponding to $\mathcal{S} = \{15\}$. Thus, without partitioning the day length into time windows, the change in direction of the correlation across the time intervals is lost. This has important consequences for LECs. A positive correlation between supply and demand would imply that LECs can self-supply and cater to the demand in the community, whereas for negative correlation, LECs may need to consider energy storage options (when supply increases and demand decreases), or LECs would have to draw energy from battery energy storage systems or import electricity from the grid (when supply decreases and demand increases) based on the shortfall of supply from demand.

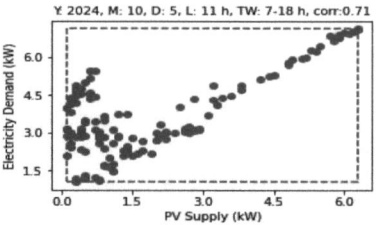

Fig. 8. Correlated Uncertainty Set of PV supply and demand for daylight hours for Block D for a single time window of size $w = L = 11$ h

These insights into the strength and direction of the correlation are important considerations for an LEC when considering how to match their supply and demand.

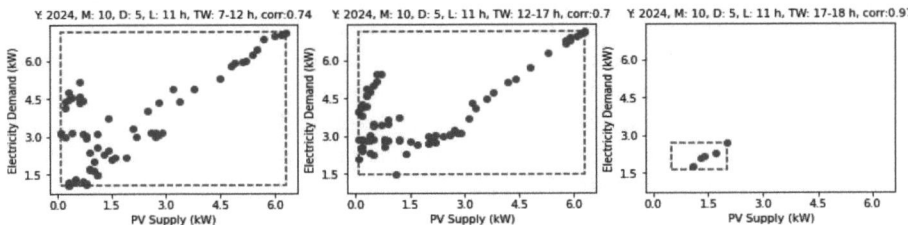

Fig. 9. Correlated Uncertainty Sets of PV supply and demand for daylight hours for Block D for time window size of $w = 5$ h for $L = 11$ h

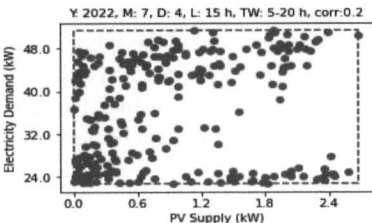

Fig. 10. Correlated Uncertainty Set of PV supply and demand for daylight hours for Engineering building for a single time window of size $w = L = 15$ h

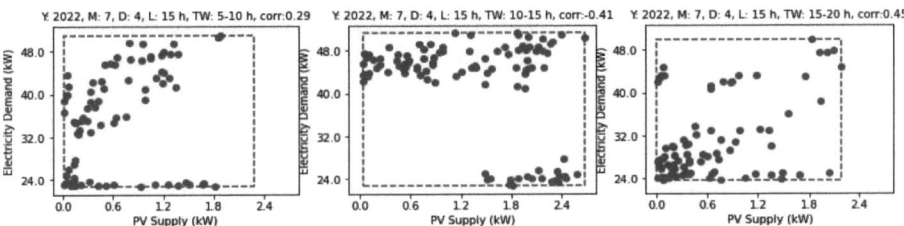

Fig. 11. Correlated Uncertainty Sets of PV supply and demand for daylight hours for Engineering building for time window size of $w = 5$ h and $L = 15$ h

4.2 Data-Driven Correlated Uncertainty Set Characterisation

Here, we characterise the uncertainty sets to answer our second research question. We define a general data-driven correlated uncertainty set for supply and demand as the following:

Let $\mathbf{X}_b$ be a vector of PV supply and electricity demand data for time window $b \in \mathcal{T}$ for a given day. Therefore, a generalised uncertainty set can be characterised as follows:

$$\mathcal{U}_b = \left\{ \mathbf{P}_b \in \mathbb{R}^2 \mid \mathbf{P}_b \in \mathcal{F}(\mathbf{X}_b) \right\} \qquad \forall b \in \mathcal{T}$$

where $\mathcal{F}(\mathbf{X}_b)$ is defined as a geometric envelope enclosing the supply and demand data points for time window b for a given day. The region could correspond to different shapes such as an ellipsoid or a polyhedron, based on the characteristics of the spread of the data points, and the level of conservatism and precision desired by the decision maker. Based on the time-step of the decision problem, the set $\mathcal{U}_b$ informs uncertainties for time-window b if it is solved corresponding to the time-window set $\mathcal{T}$ and if it is designed for a different granularity of time, then for such a time-step t, the uncertainty can be modeled based on the time-window it belongs to ($t \in \mathcal{W}_b$).

5 Conclusion

In this paper, we analyse PV supply and demand data from two buildings of a public university in two different geographic locations in Dublin, using the university BEMS and characterise correlated uncertainty sets for supply and demand. We consider only daylight hours data when correlation with demand can be defined. We partition the data according to time window sequences with time window sizes varying between 1 up to the length of the daylight hours for the day.

We find three key insights based on our analysis. Firstly, we observe that the correlation between supply and demand depends on the PV production and consumption patterns of the building and load profile, even if the building type and functional usage is similar.

Second, we find that the time window size and the length of the time window sequence has a bearing on the distribution of the strength of the correlation between PV supply and demand and thus impacts the correlated uncertainty set resulting from it. As the time window size decreases, the maximum value of correlation that can be obtained across the time windows of a sequence increases, however for the rest of the time windows in the sequence, the correlation may be weak, whereas for higher time window sizes and shorter sequences, the maximum correlation value might be smaller but there could be more number of moderate to strong correlation values across the time windows. Thus, an optimal design of time windows can strike a balance between the distribution of correlations obtained and the magnitude of correlations which based on the time step of the decision model (which can be aligned with the time window size) considering uncertainty can potentially reduce the conservatism level of the robust optimisation problem and the computational burden for solving it. Depending on the temporal variation of supply and demand and the temporal precision required, the decision-maker can optimise the granularity of the time windows for computing the correlation and constructing the correlated uncertainty sets, without ignoring major shifts in direction and strengths of correlation values. This is an important consideration for operational planning of an LEC.

Third, we show data-driven geometric contours or envelopes can be formulated (polyhedral convex hull or ellipse) to bound the 2-dimensional space enclosing the supply and demand points. These data-driven correlated uncertainty sets derived directly from the actual distribution of empirical data allow a decision-maker to decide the level of conservatism, and shape of the uncertainty set.

This paper is not devoid of limitations in the approach and analysis presented. Firstly, we base our analysis on the data of two university buildings, located in Ireland. For a more comprehensive analysis, different type of buildings (and more in number) across different geographies and weather characteristics can be explored to examine the relationship between PV supply and demand using our methodology to make the results more generalisable. Second, for our analysis on time windows, we assume simplistic time window sequences of the same time window size for an initial exploration. For a more intricate analysis, future research can explore heterogeneous time window sequences along with offsets in supply and demand time window sequences. An optimisation model can be designed to assign time window sequences to days, weeks or a user defined block of time based on the quality of the time window sequences captured by correlation metrics like max, average or a composite of the two. Given the variation of time window sizes, explicitly computing the correlation metric for a high number of sequence can be computationally challenging, necessitating advanced exact methods or metaheuristics. This can have interesting implications for Demand Response (DR) programs and time-of-use (ToU) pricing schemes which can greatly aid in peak-shifting and peak-shaving for LECs for achieving better energy efficiency. We restrict our analysis to temporal correlation between PV supply and demand specifically, in two dimensions and disregard spatial correlation or autocorrelation across supply and demand separately. Future research can analyse more complex spatio-temporal correlations in multiple dimensions for a more detailed analysis of correlated uncertainty. Finally, we do not discuss an RO model incorporating PV supply and electricity demand uncertainty, restricting our attention to characterisation of the uncertainty sets. There can be several interesting decision support models for LECs combining PV supply and electricity demand considering interactions with the DSOs, the grid, energy optimisation within the energy community etc., which would benefit from the conceptualisation of uncertainty sets we propose.

We believe that this paper offers interesting insights about the correlation between solar energy generated from PV panels and electricity demand in public university buildings. Partitioning the daily supply and demand data into time windows yields useful correlated uncertainty sets and contribute to improving RO decision models by reducing the conservatism level and improving the computational efficiency. These data-driven RO optimisation models can inform critical infrastructure and network expansion decisions for LECs and DSOs. Our study focuses on an application in two-dimensional space, $\in \mathbb{R}^2$. The framework we describe can be extended to n dimensions.

Acknowledgements. This work emanates from research supported by the ERA-NET Cofund grant under the CHIST-ERA IV Joint Call on Novel Computational Approaches for Environmental Sustainability (CES) project "Supporting Energy Communities-Operational Research and Energy Analytics" (SEC-OREA). The work of Cristian Aguayo was supported by the Fonds de la Recherche Scientifique-FNRS under Grant R801020F.

Disclosure of Interests. The authors have no competing interests.

References

1. Aguayo, C., Carroll, P., Kairiša, E.: Data, analytics and algorithms to support local energy communities. In: 2023 IEEE 64th International Scientific Conference on Power and Electrical Engineering of Riga Technical University (RTUCON), pp. 1–5. IEEE (2023)
2. Al-Shahri, O.A., et al.: Solar photovoltaic energy optimization methods, challenges and issues: a comprehensive review. J. Clean. Prod. **284**, 125465 (2021)
3. Araveti, S., et al.: Wind energy assessment for renewable energy communities. Wind **2**(2), 325–347 (2022)
4. Bertsimas, D., Sim, M.: The price of robustness. Oper. Res. **52**(1), 35–53 (2004)
5. Bertsimas, D., Thiele, A.: Robust and data-driven optimization: modern decision making under uncertainty. In: Models, methods, and applications for innovative decision making, pp. 95–122. INFORMS (2006)
6. European Commission: The European green deal striving to be the first climate-neutral continent (2021). https://commission.europa.eu/strategy-and-policy/priorities-2019-2024/european-green-deal. Accessed 16 April 2025
7. Fernández, J.M.R., Payán, M.B., Santos, J.M.R.: Profitability of household photovoltaic self-consumption in Spain. J. Clean. Prod. **279**, 123439 (2021)
8. Gui, E.M., MacGill, I.: Typology of future clean energy communities: an exploratory structure, opportunities, and challenges. Energy Res. Soc. Sci. **35**, 94–107 (2018)
9. Gupta, R., et al.: Spatial analysis of distribution grid capacity and costs to enable massive deployment of PV, electric mobility and electric heating. Appl. Energy **287**, 116504 (2021)
10. IEA: World energy investment 2023 (2023). https://iea.blob.core.windows.net/assets/8834d3af-af60-4df0-9643-72e2684f7221/WorldEnergyInvestment2023.pdf. Accessed 7 May 2025
11. Korõtko, T., et al.: Assessment of power system asset dispatch under different local energy community business models. Energies **16**(8), 3476 (2023). https://doi.org/10.3390/en16083476
12. Li, C., Zhao, J., Zheng, T., Litvinov, E.: Data-driven uncertainty sets: robust optimization with temporally and spatially correlated data. In: 2016 IEEE Power and Energy Society General Meeting (PESGM), pp. 1–5. IEEE (2016)
13. Li, X., Liu, Y., Guo, L., Li, X., Wang, C.: Data-driven based uncertainty set modeling method for microgrid robust optimization with correlated wind power. CSEE J. Power Energy Syst. **9**(2), 420–432 (2022)
14. Mancilla-David, F., Angulo, A., Street, A.: Power management in active distribution systems penetrated by photovoltaic inverters: a data-driven robust approach. IEEE Trans. Smart Grid **11**(3), 2271–2280 (2019)
15. Manso-Burgos, Á., Ribó-Pérez, D., Gómez-Navarro, T., Alcázar-Ortega, M.: Local energy communities modelling and optimisation considering storage, demand configuration and sharing strategies: a case study in Valencia (Spain). Energy Rep. **8**, 10395–10408 (2022)
16. Ono, T., Kawasaki, Y.: A scaled convex hull approach for robust voltage control with correlated uncertainties. In: 2024 IEEE Power & Energy Society General Meeting (PESGM), pp. 1–5. IEEE (2024)
17. Otamendi-Irizar, I., Grijalba, O., Arias, A., Pennese, C., Hernández, R.: How can local energy communities promote sustainable development in European cities? Energy Res. Soc. Sci. **84**, 102363 (2022)

18. Qiu, H., et al.: A historical-correlation-driven robust optimization approach for microgrid dispatch. IEEE Trans. Smart Grid **12**(2), 1135–1148 (2020)
19. Qiu, H., Liu, P., Gu, W., Zhang, R., Lu, S., Gooi, H.B.: Incorporating data-driven demand-price uncertainty correlations into microgrid optimal dispatch. IEEE Trans. Smart Grid **15**(3), 2804–2818 (2023)
20. Time&Date: Dublin, ireland — sunrise, sunset, and daylength, April 2025 (2021). https://www.timeanddate.com/sun/ireland/dublin. Accessed 16 Apr 2025
21. Wirth, R., Hipp, J.: CRISP-DM: towards a standard process model for data mining. In: Proceedings of the 4th International Conference on the Practical Applications of Knowledge Discovery and Data Mining, vol. 1, pp. 29–39. Manchester (2000)
22. Zhang, Y., Ai, X., Wen, J., Fang, J., He, H.: Data-adaptive robust optimization method for the economic dispatch of active distribution networks. IEEE Trans. Smart Grid **10**(4), 3791–3800 (2018)

Scheduling Heat Pumps for Balancing Thermal Storage and Grid Export

Aditya Somawanshi and Anupama Kowli

Indian Institute of Technology Bombay, Mumbai, India
{22d0522,anu.kowli}@iitb.ac.in

Abstract. This paper evaluates the operational performance of Smart Grid Ready (SG-ready) heat pumps integrated with rooftop photovoltaic (PV) systems for a single-family prosumer dwelling. A rule-based control logic is developed to dynamically determine the operating mode of the heat pump (Enhanced, Normal, or Off) as well as the room temperature setpoint based on the grid tariff, thermal requirements, and PV availability. In particular, the rule-based framework governs the routing of PV generation; deciding when to store excess as thermal energy and when to export to the grid. It also influences the amount of load drawn from the grid and at what time-of-day tariffs. Five different rules are considered spanning various combinations of SG-ready mode activation points and choice of room setpoints. Simulation of these five strategies over the winter period (December to February) for four cities – London, Oslo, Tokyo, and Berlin – is reported here. The dynamic use of SG-ready modes for the heat pump combined with setback temperature strategies and PV use reduces costs by nearly 13 to 50% in our simulations across the considered locations.

The maximum savings are observed in the strategy that uses SG-ready modes and uses higher setpoints at night and lower setpoints during the day to utilize solar heat gain. Results underscore the influence of local climate, electricity tariffs, and solar availability on system performance. This study demonstrates that integrating rule-based control with SG-ready capabilities significantly improves flexibility and operational efficiency in PV-enabled residential heating systems.

Keywords: Smart-Grid-Ready heat pumps · Rooftop solar · Prosumers · Electricity tariffs

1 Introduction

Space heating is a dominant energy end-use in buildings, accounting for approximately 50% of global building energy consumption. It also significantly contributes to peak electricity demand, especially during winter seasons [1]. This burden poses operational challenges for electricity grids, particularly as heating loads are increasingly being electrified while transitioning away from fossil fuels. However, there has been a notable rise in households equipped with rooftop photovoltaic (PV) systems. Such households act as *prosumers* – producers *and* consumers of electricity – and are expected to actively participate in the energy ecosystem by integrating local generation, storage, and intelligent controls [2]. Smart Grid-ready (SG-ready) heat pumps (HPs) – a demand-side intervention also gaining popularity – provide the prosumers with an additional degree of freedom in choosing SG-ready modes (on, off, enhanced) and affecting the load consumption. In this paper, we attempt to answer the following question: should excess PV production be stored in the thermal energy storage (TES) associated with the HP by exploiting the flexibility afforded by SG-ready modes or should it be exported to the grid.

Replacing natural gas boilers with heat pumps can reduce both energy costs and CO_2 emissions by a significant amount (41% and 73% respectively as computed in [3]). In particular, the study in [3] investigates various configurations – PV+TES, HP+TES, HP+PV and PV+HP+TES – and establishes how smart management of all three options can lead significant reductions in costs and emissions. Moreover, TES has proven benefits in optimizing energy costs and enabling demand shifting under optimal scheduling and model predictive (see examples in [4] and [5]). Therefore, TES can be deployed to address the mismatch between PV generation, which peaks around midday, and heating demand, which peaks in the morning and evening. Indeed, TES may be a better alternative than expensive battery-based energy storage options usually considered in literature (see recent example in [6] and the references there in) for addressing the supply-demand misalignment. The study in [7] uses real world data 357 houses to establish how optimal HP operation can have effects equivalent to the use of 2–4 kWh battery. Another study [8] emphasizes how HP integration reduces the optimal battery size by absorbing the midday PV surplus.

There is currently limited research that specifically explores the use of the HP water tank as a storage medium to absorb excess PV generation. Some existing works focus on control strategies that coordinate batteries and HPs/TES; see the predictive scheduling in [9]. Objectives such reduction in costs or CO_2 emissions may be considered, similar to the problem considered in [3]. Combined use of PV, HP and TES can reduce grid electricity demand by 50–80% and flatten the electricity load profile, as demonstrated in [10]. However, these research works do not directly employ SG-ready HP modes for accessing TES. In particular, the SG-ready enhanced mode can be used for charging the TES – allowing the water to be heated to a higher-than-normal temperature level. And with the HP turned off, the TES could be *discharged* to service the heating demand, allowing the water to return to usual operating temperature levels. References [11,12] demonstrate the demand-side flexibility that can be tapped into by leveraging these SG-ready modes in a similar manner for direct load control.

There is limited-to-no research discussing how SG-ready HP modes can be exploited to best use the available solar PV generation at an individual household level. Our paper addresses this research gap by proposing a simple, effective, rule-based control logic that determines which SG-ready HP modes should be activated to shift heating demand based on PV availability and tariff signals.

Unlike prior studies that rely on additional batteries, proposed approach uses the HP tank itself as a storage unit for excess solar energy, thereby providing a cost-effective and grid-supportive solution for prosumers.

SG-ready HPs are designed to respond dynamically to grid conditions, electricity tariffs, or renewable energy availability. However, the practical integration of these control capabilities within home energy management systems (HEMS) remains largely unexplored. The work we present here builds on our earlier work [13] which discusses HP integration in HEMS for electricity cost optimization. In the current paper, we examine how such integration can be used to align the heating demand with PV generation, thereby reducing grid dependency and improving energy efficiency. A simulation environment is created in Design Builder and a rule-based HP operating logic is devised. Inspired from the savings demonstrated in our prior work [13], the HP operating logic exploits the SG-ready modes as well as setback implementations [14]. Therefore, a holistic HP operating strategy is devised, which considers excess PV, grid tariffs and ambient temperature to determine both the SG-ready mode in HP is expected to operate and the room temperature setpoint.

To evaluate the robustness of the proposed strategy, we simulate its performance across four representative locations: London, Oslo, Tokyo, and Berlin. These cities reflect a diversity of climatic conditions, energy policies, and renewable integration levels. In London, the Boiler Upgrade Scheme [15] and widespread PV adoption [16] support residential electrification. Oslo, with abundant hydropower, leads globally in per-capita heat pump usage [1,17]. Tokyo promotes EcoCute heat pump water heaters under its Zero Emission Tokyo strategy [18], while Berlin advances flexible load integration via subsidies like BAFA [19] and initiatives like SolarPLUS [20]. Although the chosen locations reflect diverse climate and policy landscapes, energy costs are consistently reduced at all locations by deploying the proposed control logic. The studies outlined here thereby provide a comprehensive validation for potential adoption of such strategies by prosumers today.

The paper is structured as follows: Section 2 describes the system architecture, Section 3 outlines the time-of-day (TOD)-dependent control logic, Section 4 presents the simulation results and analysis, and Section 5 concludes the study with key insights and future work directions.

2 System Description

This section describes the simulation setup, covering aspects of building environment, thermal comfort considerations, HP configuration, solar PV system and electricity tariffs.

2.1 Building

The residential building under investigation is a $100\,\text{m}^2$ single-family prosumer dwelling. Modeled using DesignBuilder [21] and compliant with ASHRAE standards [22], the house features a total peak load of 10 kW, including heat pump

(6 kW) and other household loads, household loads make up the lighting load, catering load, and equipment loads, total of 4 kW with a base load of 500 W on the system. Furthermore, the property is equipped with a rooftop photovoltaic (PV) system for electricity generation during solar hours. To account for regional climatic differences across the four considered locations, the thermal insulation properties of the building envelope are modified accordingly. In colder climates such as Oslo, insulation levels are adapted to align with the Norwegian building code TEK17 [23], which enforces strict U-value and energy performance requirements for walls, roofs, and openings. As demonstrated in [24], improving insulation in residential buildings significantly reduces energy consumption for heating, especially under harsh winter conditions, thereby enhancing overall thermal performance and system efficiency.

2.2 Thermal Comfort

According to ASHRAE Standard 55 [25], the general recommended temperature range for maintaining thermal comfort is between 67° F (19.44 °C) and 82 °F (27.78 °C). However, this range can vary based on additional factors such as extreme outdoor temperatures and relative humidity. Specifically for winter, ASHRAE recommends maintaining indoor temperatures between 68 °F (20 °C) and 74 °F (23.33 °C) to ensure comfort. Taking this into consideration, the proposed model works with a 20 °C setpoint and a 18 °C setback temperature setpoint.

2.3 Heat Pump System

To determine the necessary heating capacity for maintaining a comfortable indoor temperature, the heating design calculations are conducted with EnergyPlus [26]. The steady-state heat loss (Q_{loss}), also known as zone sensible heating, is calculated as 4.76 kW. To ensure adequate performance under varying conditions, a design margin (M) of 1.25 is applied to this value, resulting in a design heating capacity $Q_{design} = Q_{loss} \times M = 5.95$ kW. Based on this requirement, a 6 kW air-source HP equipped with a hot water tank of 1000 l capacity is selected to efficiently meet the space heating demands of the house. The maximum temperature limit of the tank is 90 °C, the on and off cycle heat loss coefficients are 1 W/K and 2 W/K, respectively.

2.4 Solar Photovoltaic System

The solar photovoltaic (PV) system installed in the model is designed based on the available solar irradiance, typical system efficiencies, and load requirements. The PV system output is estimated using the following relation:

$$P_{\text{PV}}(t) = A_{\text{PV}} \times f_{\text{active}} \times \eta_{\text{PV}}(t) \times G_{\text{incident}}(t) \times \chi(t) \tag{1}$$

where $P_{\text{PV}}(t)$ is the electrical power output at time t, A_{PV} is the net surface area of the PV array, f_{active} is the fraction of active area, $\eta_{\text{PV}}(t)$ is the PV conversion efficiency, $G_{\text{incident}}(t)$ is the incident solar irradiance, and $\chi(t)$ is the system availability function. The equation (1) is derived from the PV model used in DesignBuilder [27] and the PV arrays are sized to meet the total peak house load of 10 kW provided that enough solar irradiance is available, the irradiation profile specific to the location (London / Oslo / Tokyo / Berlin) is considered. The PV panels are placed at an angle equal to the location's latitude, two such panels, each of $40\,\text{m}^2$. In addition, the PV system does not include a battery; the photovoltaic energy is stored in the hot water tank as heat energy through HP operation or exported to the grid.

2.5 Tariffs

Tariff data for London is available at Octopus Energy [28], providing a clear hourly structure for residential electricity costs. However, for Oslo, Tokyo, and Berlin, specific 24-hour import/export tariff data is not publicly available. Therefore, country-specific electricity price references from 2024 are used [29–31] alongside typical daily demand patterns to synthesize realistic tariff profiles. For Tokyo and Berlin, the study [32] showed that Japanese households are more open to dynamic pricing than German ones, especially when tariffs are predictable and tied to environmental benefits – guiding the use of greater variability in Tokyo and a more stable Time-of-use (TOU) structure in Berlin. For Norway, [33] demonstrated the effectiveness of sharp price signals in encouraging demand response, justifying steeper peak-to-off-peak differentials. This method ensured that the generated tariffs are realistic and aligned with regional consumption behavior.

The electricity tariff structures employed are simplified, omitting detailed components like grid tariffs, local taxes, and the typical lower remuneration for exported PV. While this may influence absolute cost savings, the study's conclusions on the relative effectiveness and trends of the control strategies remain robust.

To ensure a consistent basis for comparison across different regions, the country-specific electricity tariffs, originally in their local currencies, have been converted and are presented in pence per kilowatt-hour (pence/kWh) throughout this analysis. Table 1 shows the 24 h tariff rates for the respective locations.

3 HP and PV Operation Based on Time-of-Day (TOD)

The control algorithm for the SG-ready HP operates with a hierarchical decision-making process. Room temperature (T_R) always serves as the primary criterion for HP operation across all Time-of-Day (TOD) periods, ensuring occupant thermal comfort. Energy considerations, particularly regarding the hot water tank's stored energy (E_{tank}), then act as a secondary criterion, becoming more prominent as a focus for optimization depending on the current tariff period. The TOD at any given moment can be classified (based on the tariff during that period) into three categories, namely, High Peak Period (t_p), Mid/Shoulder

Table 1. Grouped Import and Export Tariffs (pence/kWh)

Hours	London		Oslo		Tokyo		Berlin	
	Import	Export	Import	Export	Import	Export	Import	Export
00–04	25.29	15.17	6.75	4.13	8.32	5.20	5.16	3.10
04–07	12.39	4.96	7.50	4.50	8.32–9.36	5.20–5.72	5.16–6.02	3.10–3.61
07–11	25.29	15.17	8.63	5.25	10.40	6.24	7.74	4.64
11–14	25.29	15.17	7.50	4.50	9.88	5.72	6.88	4.13
14–17	12.39	4.96	9.38	5.63	10.92	6.76	8.60	5.16
17–19	36.67	29.34	9.38	5.63	10.92	6.76	8.60	5.16
19–22	25.29	15.17	9.75	5.85	11.44	7.28	9.46	5.68
22–24	25.29	15.17	7.50	4.50	9.36	5.72	6.88	4.13

Peak Period (t_{mp}) and Low/Off Peak Period (t_{op}). Operating in a continuous, real-time control fashion, the algorithm identifies the TOD and PV output conditions to determine the control modes of the SG-ready HP during each period. The activation of SG-ready controls allow the HP to charge the hot water tank to different temperature levels, thus making it a variable heat (or energy) storage device. The hot water tank can be configured to respond to control signals by heating to a specified temperature. SG-ready control does not directly affect the room/zone temperature. The implementation considered in our simulations is shown in the Table 2. The operation logic for different time periods is explained in the following subsections.

Table 2. SG Ready signal description

Signal name	Resulting action
OFF mode	HP remains OFF
$Normal$ mode	HP charges the tank to 60 °C
$Enhanced$ mode	HP charges the tank to 70 °C

3.1 High Peak Period (t_p) Logic

The logic shown in Fig. 1 is executed to determine the state of HP and PV when $TOD \in t_p$. During t_p, the import tariff rate (C_{imp}) is high and it is beneficial to minimize power consumption. Therefore, HP operation is actively avoided, and power is only consumed when absolutely necessary to prevent thermal discomfort. So, logic checks whether the room temperature (T_r) is equal to setpoint temperature (T_s). If yes, then HP stays off and any excess PV power is exported to grid. However, if $T_r \neq T_s$, then heating is necessary to avoid thermal discomfort: depending on availability of PV power, HP chooses to draw power from grid or PV so that energy available inside the tank (E_{tank} is maintained at *tank threshold* (E_{thr})[1] - the energy inside tank below which T_r starts to drop below T_s leading to thermal discomfort.

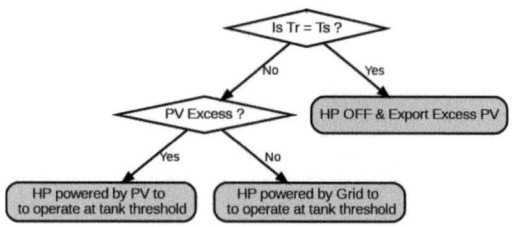

Fig. 1. High Peak Period Flowchart

As seen in Table 1, t_p corresponds to periods when C_{imp} is highest, that is, 36.67 pence/kWh for London, for Oslo $C_{imp} > 9$ pence/kWh, for Tokyo $C_{imp} > 10.5$ pence/kWh and for Berlin $C_{imp} > 8.5$ pence/kWh..

3.2 Mid/Shoulder Peak Period (t_{mp}) Logic

This logic is executed when $TOD \in t_{mp}$, wherein the C_{imp} is moderate. Given that the room temperature condition has been satisfied (i.e., thermal comfort is maintained), the algorithm then focuses on optimizing energy storage. As shown in Fig. 2, the energy available inside the tank E_{tank} is compared with E_{thr} to decide whether to turn off the HP or operate it at tank threshold level drawing power from PV or grid based on solar availability. For London t_{mp} corresponds to periods when C_{imp} is 25.29 pence/kWh, for Oslo $7 < C_{imp} < 9$ pence/kWh, for Tokyo $9.5 < C_{imp} < 10.5$ pence/kWh and for Berlin $6.5 < C_{imp} < 8.5$ pence/kWh.

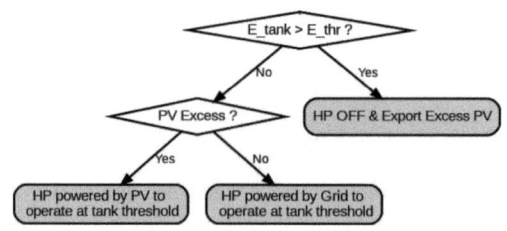

Fig. 2. Mid Peak Period Flowchart

---

[1] The computation of E_{thr} and E_{tank} is discussed in our working paper [34] and is not discussed here for brevity.

3.3 Low/Off Peak Period (t_{op}) Logic

The off-peak period logic shown in Fig. 3 is executed when $TOD \in t_{op}$. This period has the lowest C_{imp} values and it is beneficial for prosumers to maximize their HP operation during this time period. To further exploit more benefits, the algorithm aims at maximizing PV power usage rather than relying on grid import. In the absence of any excess PV power, the logic dictates HP to be operated in enhanced mode by drawing power from grid at low import prices. However, if excess PV is available then conditions related to E_{tank} are checked: that is, when E_{tank} is maximum ($T_{tank} \geq 70\,°C$) HP is turned off and excess PV is exported to grid. Else, we check if E_{tank} is greater than E_{thr}: if yes, then HP is powered by the available PV to reach the maximum tank capacity by operating in enhanced mode.

If $E_{tank} < E_{thr}$, then maintaining thermal comfort becomes a priority, and it dictates charging the tank to the threshold level. In this scenario, the import and export tariffs (C_{imp} and C_{exp}) are compared. In cases where $C_{imp} > C_{exp}$, exporting is not very beneficial and HP is used to charge the tank; operating in enhanced mode ensures that stored energy at lower prices ($TOD \in t_{op}$) can be used in upcoming t_{mp} or t_p periods. When $C_{exp} > C_{imp}$, it is beneficial to charge the tank to the threshold level while operating in normal mode and export the remaining PV power to the grid to ensure that we are taking advantage of the higher export prices.

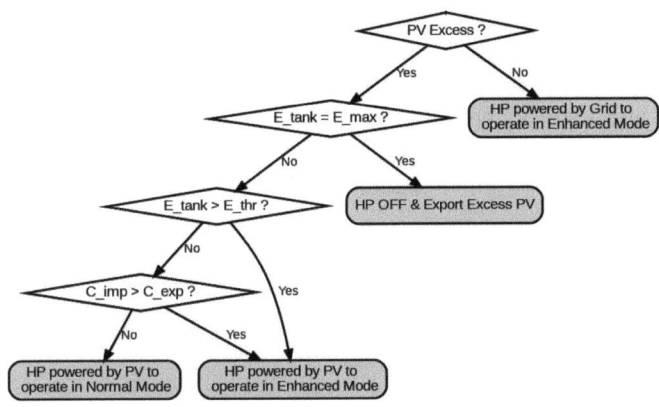

Fig. 3. Low Peak Period Flowchart

4 Results and Analysis

The developed simulation model is executed for the winter period, spanning from December 1st to February 28th, across the four chosen locations: London, Oslo, Tokyo, and Berlin. For each location, six operational scenarios are analyzed: the

Baseline case (fixed T_r, no SG-ready scheduling of HP), No-Setback case (fixed T_r with SG-ready signal scheduling), and Setback 1âĂŞ4 cases (dynamic T_r setpoint and SG-ready operation logics based on TOD and outside temperature (T_o) conditions).

Among all cases, the scenario achieving the maximum cost savings is identified individually for each location. This best-performing case is then analyzed further through comparative plots illustrating variations in power import, export, PV power used for storing heat in tank, and cumulative electricity costs. Furthermore, climate-specific (temperature variations, solar irradiance profiles) and tariff-specific (t_p, t_{mp}, t_{op} periods and pricing) characteristics are carefully discussed to highlight their impact on HP operation patterns, PV utilization effectiveness, and SG-ready mode switching behaviors. Key observations regarding the role of T_o and tariff structures in influencing HP performance and cost-effectiveness are detailed, establishing critical insights for the location-specific optimization of HP operation strategies.

4.1 Baseline Case Generation

This case serves as the reference, and comparisons are made against other cases to quantify net cost savings achieved over the simulation period, imported electricity from the grid, exported electricity back to the grid from surplus PV generation and PV energy stored as thermal energy in the hot water tank. As mentioned earlier, T_r is fixed at 20 °C and T_{tank} at 60 °C for this case, the setback temperature strategy and SG-ready HP scheduling based on TOD is not used. Figure 4 shows the system power flow, where, P_{imp} is the imported power, P_{exp} is the exported power, P_{pv} is the power generated by solar PV arrays and P_{load} is the total load of the system.

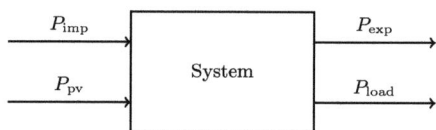

Fig. 4. System Power Flow

The power balance equation for the system is:

$$P_{imp} + P_{pv} = P_{exp} + P_{load} \tag{2}$$

The export rule for the baseline case is that when $P_{pv} > P_{load}$,

$$P_{exp} = P_{pv} - P_{load}$$
$$P_{imp} = 0$$

And the import rule, when $P_{load} > P_{pv}$,

$$P_{imp} = P_{load} - P_{pv}$$
$$P_{exp} = 0$$

4.2 Setback Temperature Cases

In this study, several operating strategies involving setpoint manipulation are explored to evaluate their impact on HP performance and energy costs. These strategies are designed to investigate the trade-offs between energy consumption and the level of thermal comfort provided, with all setpoints (18 °C and 20 °C) remaining within the acceptable range defined by ASHRAE 55 thermal comfort standards.

The No-Setback case implements SG Ready signals to control the HP but maintains a fixed T_r of 20 °C throughout the day, allowing the analysis of savings purely due to SG Ready HP mode switching without any temperature setbacks. The Setback 1 case introduces a dynamic setpoint where the T_r is reduced to 18 °C during daytime hours (7:00 to 19:00), assuming reduced occupancy, and then restored to the main setpoint of 20 °C during nighttime (20:00 to 7:00) to enhance comfort when occupants are presumed to return home.

On the other hand, the Setback 2 case reverses this logic, maintaining a setback temperature of 18 °C during nighttime and reverting to 20 °C during daytime, aligning indoor temperature closer to outdoor conditions and exploring its effects on thermal comfort and system efficiency. The Setback 3 case uses a dynamic outdoor-temperature-based approach, where if the instantaneous outdoor temperature (T_o) is less than or equal to the mean outdoor temperature (T_m) of the day, the room is maintained at the lower setback (18 °C); otherwise, it is set to the main temperature (20 °C). Conversely, the Setback 4 case swaps this logic: maintaining 20 °C when $T_o \leq T_m$, and reducing it to 18 °C during periods of higher solar gain, thereby leveraging passive heating to reduce energy consumption. All these cases are summarized in the Table 3.

Table 3. Summary of Setback Cases and Logic

Case	Description
No-Setback	Fixed 20 °C setpoint with SG Ready signal scheduling, no temperature setback.
Setback 1	18 °C from 7:00–19:00 (unoccupied), 20 °C during night (occupied).
Setback 2	20 °C during day, 18 °C at night; follows outdoor temperature trend.
Setback 3	18 °C if $T_o \leq T_m$, else 20 °C (dynamic with outdoor temperature).
Setback 4	20 °C if $T_o \leq T_m$, else 18 °C (benefits from passive solar heating).

In addition to the cost and energy savings achieved by applying SG Ready operational strategies and setpoint-based thermal demand management, in this study, the incorporation of a PV system into the household energy mix further improves savings. The local generation from PV panels not only offsets P_{imp} but also synergizes with thermal storage strategies, enhancing system efficiency and reducing reliance on the grid.

4.3 Winter Period Performance Analysis for London

The winter period analysis for London is conducted across six operational scenarios: Baseline, No-Setback, and Setback 1 to Setback 4. The Baseline case resulted in a total system load of 6036.71 kWh, with an imported energy of 5519.19 kWh and export energy of 524.98 kWh. Introducing SG Ready signals without any temperature setback (No-Setback case) increased the total system load to 6994.54 kWh, primarily due to dynamic heat pump operation; however, a reduction in net cost (£1093.38) is observed, assisted by PV integration and 200.98 kWh of thermal storage from solar energy.

Among the Setback cases, Setback-4 showed the most favorable results, achieving the lowest net cost (£915.24) with a reduced imported energy requirement (5620.03 kWh) while still utilizing 176.6 kWh of PV energy for thermal storage. Setback-1 and Setback-2 also provided significant improvements in net cost compared to the Baseline, driven by a more intelligent balance of occupancy-based setpoint management and solar energy utilization. Overall, the integration of SG Ready strategies, setback temperature operations, and PV energy storage significantly improved system efficiency and reduced operational costs compared to the Baseline. A summary of the key parameters for each case is presented in Table 4.

Table 4. Winter Period Analysis for London

Case	E_{imp} (kWh)	E_{exp} (kWh)	PV Stored (kWh)	Net Cost (£)	% Cost Savings
Baseline	5519.19	524.98	0	1231.82	0%
No-Setback	6402.85	450.81	200.98	1093.38	11.23%
Setback-1	5883.35	508.26	177.57	966.82	21.51%
Setback-2	5930.52	432.21	207.94	974.93	20.86%
Setback-3	6185.28	476.06	196.18	1030.28	16.36%
Setback-4	5620.03	484.29	176.60	915.24	25.69%

4.4 One-Day 24-Hour Analysis for Setback-4 Case Across Different Locations

As Setback-4 achieved the most favorable performance across all locations, 24-hour operation plots are presented for London, Oslo, Tokyo, and Berlin. These plots visualize T_o variations, HP load (P_{hp}), PV generation (P_{pv}), grid imports

(E_{imp}), exports (E_{exp}), T_r and T_{tank} evolution throughout a typical winter day (January 15th). The influence of climate conditions, tariff structures, and PV availability on the system behavior is discussed for each city.

London: T_o remained low (around $-1\,°C$ to $2\,°C$), requiring moderate HP operation primarily during early morning and evening hours. PV generation is limited, peaking around 5.3 kW mid-day, which marginally reduces grid imports. Energy exports are modest during solar hours but overall reliance on the grid remains high. T_{tank} is effectively managed to provide thermal storage before evening peak period. Refer to Fig. 5 for one-day plot of London city.

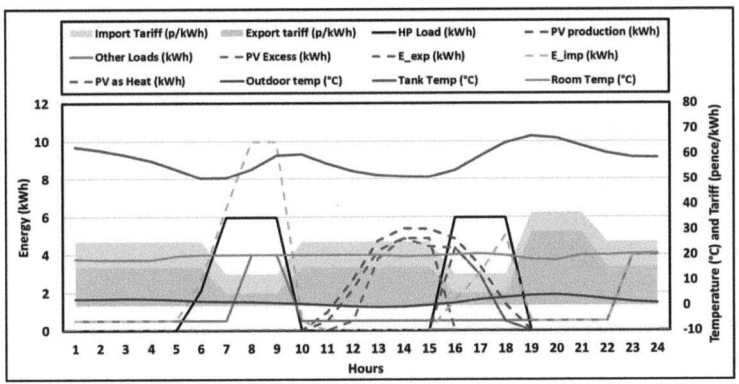

Fig. 5. January 15th energy and temperature variations for London

Observation: In London, modest PV generation coupled with cold temperatures enabled minor exports but heavy reliance on grid import persisted, especially during mornings and evenings.

Oslo: Outdoor temperatures are extremely cold (between $-12\,°C$ and $-9\,°C$), necessitating continuous HP operation throughout the day. Solar PV production is almost negligible, resulting in consistently high grid imports. Despite a relatively cheaper tariff structure, the system faces high operational costs due to heavy thermal demand. Refer to Fig. 6 for one-day plot of Oslo city.

Observation: In Oslo, due to severe winters and poor solar availability, the heat pump depends almost entirely on grid electricity, and PV contribution is negligible.

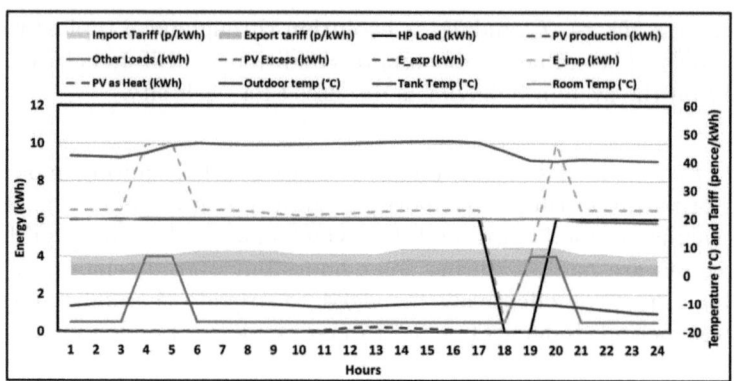

Fig. 6. January 15th energy and temperature variations for Oslo

Tokyo: Outdoor temperatures range from $-4\,°C$ to $1\,°C$, milder compared to Oslo. Significant PV generation is observed during mid-day (7.6 kW), substantially reducing grid imports and increasing energy exports. The heat pump operation is more flexible with strong solar support in the afternoon hours. Refer to Fig. 7 for one-day plot of Tokyo city.

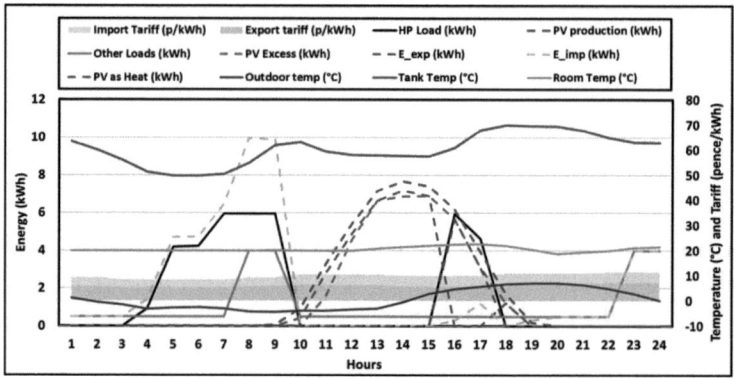

Fig. 7. January 15th energy and temperature variations for Tokyo

Observation : Tokyo showed the most efficient utilization of PV generation, significantly reducing mid-day imports and achieving large exports during sunny periods.

Berlin: Outdoor temperatures are milder ($2\,°C$ to $7\,°C$), resulting in lower HP loads compared to other locations. Moderate PV generation (3 kW peak) occurs during noon, allowing reduced imports and moderate exports. Thermal demand is comparatively low due to favorable weather conditions. Refer to Fig. 8 for one-day plot of Berlin city.

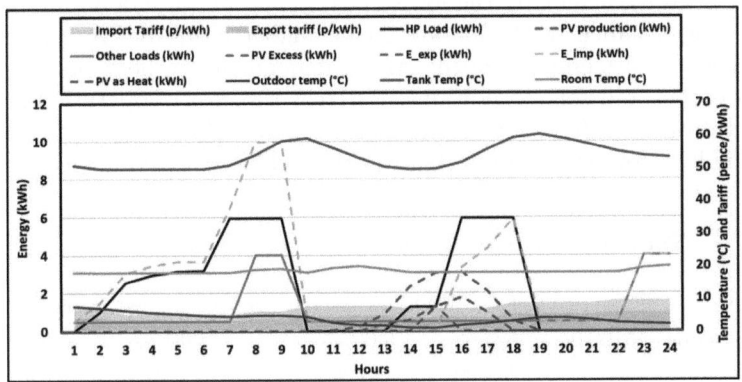

Fig. 8. January 15th energy and temperature variations for Berlin

Observation : Berlin presented a good balance between import reduction, PV thermal storage, and energy exports, owing to mild temperatures and moderate solar resource availability.

Comparative Summary: Table 5 summarizes the important findings across the four locations based on peak outdoor temperature, peak PV generation, major system behavior, and dominant energy source for a particular winter day (January 15th).

Table 5. January 15th performance comparison across locations

Location	Peak T_o (°C)	PV Peak (kW)	Major Behavior	Dominant Energy Source
London	−1 to 2	5.3	Grid import dominant	Grid + Small PV
Oslo	−12 to −9	∼0	Heavy HP load all day	Grid
Tokyo	−4 to 1	7.6	Large PV support mid-day	PV + Grid
Berlin	2 to 7	3	Balanced operation	PV + Grid

4.5 Winter Period Energy and Cost Summary

The winter period analysis highlights the influence of climate and solar availability on system performance across locations. Oslo had the highest energy import (9114.7 kWh) and minimal PV heat storage (32.85 kWh), resulting in higher reliance on the grid despite a relatively low net cost (£725.28), possibly due to favorable tariffs. Tokyo showed optimal performance with the lowest import (4259.9 kWh), highest export (2304.9 kWh), and maximum PV utilization (418.85 kWh), achieving the lowest cost (£266.71). London and Berlin had moderate performance, with London facing higher costs due to higher import tariffs. These results emphasize the strong dependence of heat pump efficiency on local weather and solar conditions. Whereas the cost of operation is majorly dependent on the tariff structure and also solar availability. Table 6 summarizes the specific location energy imports, exports and % cost savings.

Table 6. Summary of Winter Period for Different Cities

City	Case	E_{imp} (kWh)	E_{exp} (kWh)	PV Stored (kWh)	Net Cost (£)	% Cost Savings
London	Baseline	5519.19	524.98	0.00	1231.82	0.00
	Setback-4	5620.03	484.29	176.60	915.24	25.69
Oslo	Baseline	10358.26	101.83	0.00	833.89	0.00
	Setback-4	9114.69	156.09	32.85	725.28	13.03
Tokyo	Baseline	6294.36	2364.03	0.00	525.33	0.00
	Setback-4	4259.85	2304.92	418.85	266.71	49.23
Berlin	Baseline	8817.79	288.88	0.00	674.40	0.00
	Setback-4	7612.76	234.22	159.71	505.01	25.12

5 Conclusion

This paper presents a comprehensive assessment of Smart Grid Ready heat pumps integrated with photovoltaic systems for residential heating across four global cities. By implementing tariff-aware control strategies for HPs and dynamic room temperature setpoint manipulation, significant cost savings are achieved. Among all strategies, the one where the use of SG-ready modes along with higher nighttime and lower daytime room temperature setpoints consistently provided the lowest operational cost while maintaining thermal comfort across all the considered locations. Specifically, this strategy yielded cost savings of 25% for London, 13% for Oslo, 49% for Tokyo and 25% for Berlin, relative to their baselines. Location-specific simulations showed that the benefits of SG-ready operation are highly dependent on climatic conditions and local tariff structures. The integration of PV not only reduced reliance on grid-imported energy but also enabled effective thermal storage. Overall, this study demonstrates the effectiveness of SG-ready heat pump systems in reducing energy costs and enhancing grid flexibility, making them a viable solution for sustainable residential heating.

However, the study's primary limitation lies in its reliance on static occupancy assumptions and fixed time-based setbacks. In real-world scenarios, these may not reflect actual occupancy, potentially leading to discomfort, manual overrides, and negated energy savings due to the inherent rigidity of such approaches. Future work will prioritize developing real-time, user-centric control strategies. Exploring advanced methods like predictive control (MPC) can enable proactive optimization by leveraging forecasted data on occupancy, weather, and dynamic prices, ensuring more adaptive, energy-efficient, and comfort-aware operation.

References

1. International Energy Agency (IEA). The future of heat pumps. Technical report, IEA, Paris, 2022. Licence: CC BY 4.0, Accessed 7 Apr 2025
2. Oprea, S.-V., Bâra, A.: Generative literature analysis on the rise of prosumers and their influence on the sustainable energy transition. Utilities Policy **90**, 101799 (2024)
3. Facci, A.L., Krastev, V.K., Falcucci, G., Ubertini, S.: Smart integration of photovoltaic production, heat pump and thermal energy storage in residential applications. Solar Energy **192**, 133–143 (2019). Thermal Energy Storage for Solar Applications
4. Tarragona, J., Fernández, C., Gracia, Á.: Model predictive control applied to a heating system with PV panels and thermal energy storage. Energy **197**, 117229 (2020)
5. Weeratunge, H., Narsilio, G., de Hoog, J., Dunstall, S., Halgamuge, S.: Model predictive control for a solar assisted ground source heat pump system. Energy **152**, 974–984 (2018)
6. Raj, R.P., Kowli, A.: Handling forecast uncertainty and variability in solar generation to mitigate schedule deviation penalties. Solar Energy **271**, 112401 (2024)
7. Iwafune, Y., Kanamori, J., Sakakibara, H.: A comparison of the effects of energy management using heat pump water heaters and batteries in photovoltaic-installed houses. Energy Convers. Manage. **148**, 146–160 (2017)
8. Liu, X., Zhang, P., Pimm, A., Feng, D., Zheng, M.: Optimal design and operation of PV-battery systems considering the interdependency of heat pumps. J. Energy Storage **23**, 526–536 (2019)
9. Yousefi, M., Hajizadeh, A., Soltani, M.N., Hredzak, B.: Predictive home energy management system with photovoltaic array, heat pump, and plug-in electric vehicle. IEEE Trans. Ind. Inform. **17**(1), 430–440 (2020)
10. Li, Y., Rosengarten, G., Stanley, C., Mojiri, A.: Electrification of residential heating, cooling and hot water: load smoothing using onsite photovoltaics, heat pump and thermal batteries. J. Energy Storage **56**, 105873 (2022)
11. Fischer, D., Wolf, T., Triebel, M.-A.: Flexibility of heat pump pools: the use of SG-ready from an aggregator's perspective. In: 12th IEA Heat Pump Conference, pp. 1–12 (2017)
12. Fischer, D., Wolf, T., Wapler, J., Hollinger, R., Madani, H.: Model-based flexibility assessment of a residential heat pump pool. Energy **118**, 853–864 (2017)
13. Somawanshi, A.D., Dey, M.K., Kowli, A., Gugaliya, J., Choi, B., Nelakuditi, N.S.: Integration of smart grid ready heat pumps in home energy management systems. In *2024 IEEE PES Innovative Smart Grid Technologies - Asia (ISGT Asia)*, pp. 1–6, Bengaluru, India (2024)

14. Miara, M., Günther, D., Leitner, Z.L., Wapler, J.: Simulation of an air-to-water heat pump system to evaluate the impact of demand-side-management measures on efficiency and load-shifting potential. Energy technol. **2**(1), 90–99 (2014)
15. UK Government Grants Service. Boiler upgrade scheme. Accessed 5 Apr 2025
16. Statista. Solar energy share in the electricity mix in the united kingdom from 2010 to 2023. Accessed 5 Apr 2025
17. CINELDI Project. Annual report 2023. Technical report (2023). Accessed 7 Apr 2025
18. Tokyo Metropolitan Government. Outline of zero emission Tokyo strategy. Accessed 7 Apr 2025
19. Federal Office for Economic Affairs and Export Control (BAFA). Energy. Accessed 7 Apr 2025
20. IBB Business Team GmbH. Solarplus project. Accessed 7 Apr 2025
21. Goel, S., et al.: Enhancements to ashrae standard 90.1 prototype building models. Technical report, Pacific Northwest National Laboratory (2014)
22. Zhang, L.: Simulation analysis of built environment based on design builder software. Appl. Mech. Mater. **580**, 3134–3137 (2014)
23. Direktoratet for byggkvalitet (DiBK). Byggteknisk forskrift (tek17). Accessed 2 May 2025
24. Aditya, L., et al.: A review on insulation materials for energy conservation in buildings. Renew. Sustain. Energy Rev. **73**, 1352–1365 (2017)
25. De Dear, R.: Recent enhancements to the adaptive comfort standard in ashrae 55-2010. In: Proceedings of the 45th Annual Conference of the Architectural Science Association, pp. 16–19, Sydney, Australia (2011)
26. Alghoul, S.K.: A comparative study of energy consumption for residential HVAC systems using EnergyPlus. Am. J. Mech. Ind. Eng. **2**(2), 98–103 (2017)
27. DesignBuilder Software Ltd. Simple PV model. Accessed 5 Apr 2025
28. Jackson, G.: Octopus energy. Accessed 21 May 2024
29. Financial Times. Renewable energy developments in the UK. Accessed 8 Apr 2025
30. PV Magazine. Japan unveils 2024 feed-in tariff levels for residential, commercial PV. Accessed 8 Apr 2025
31. Bundesnetzagentur. German electricity market trends on SMARD. Accessed 8 Apr 2025
32. Nakai, M., Loessl, V., Wetzel, H.: Preferences for dynamic electricity tariffs: a comparison of households in Germany and Japan. Ecol. Econ. **223**, 108239 (2024)
33. Hofmann, M., Lindberg, K.B.: Evidence of households' demand flexibility in response to variable hourly electricity prices – results from a comprehensive field experiment in Norway. Energy Policy **184**, 113821 (2024)
34. Somawanshi, A., Kowli, A.: Integration of smart grid ready heat pumps in home energy management systems and their economic evaluation. Working Paper (2024)

Battery Energy Storage Integration with BIPV Systems: A Multi-scenario Economic Analysis and Optimization

Hashem Amini Toosi[✉]

Architecture, Built Environment, and Construction Engineering Department, Politecnico di Milano, Via Ponzio 31, 20133 Milan, Italy
`hashem.amini@polimi.it`

Abstract. The application of Building-Integrated Photovoltaics (BIPV) coupled with Battery Energy Storage Systems (BESS) in smart buildings is known as an effective solution to enhance the energy performance of buildings. However, the economic viability of these systems remains a complicated and challenging matter due to high upfront costs, variable market prices, and fluctuating energy and economic policy schemes such as Feed-in Tariffs (FiT) regimes. This study investigates the Life Cycle Cost (LCC) based optimum sizing of BESS for BIPV-equipped residential buildings under multiple scenarios of FiT schemes and BESS market prices in Italy. For this purpose, a residential building equipped with the aforementioned energy systems is parametrically modeled and evaluated with key LCC indicators, including Net Present Cost (NPC) and Saving to Investment Ratio (SIR), to elaborate on the economic performance of BESS adoption and accurate cost-effective size optimization. The results reveal a reverse relationship between FiT rates and BESS market price, with cost-effective BESS size due to high upfront costs imposed by higher BESS market prices and higher financial revenue for electricity export to the grid as a result of higher FiT rates, both discouraging BESS adoption and self-consumption. The results evaluate the impact of these economic factors, considering various BESS market prices under low, medium, and high FiTs scenarios. Moreover, the results highlight that the current high BESS market price is a major barrier to its adoption in the building sector under most FiT scenarios. Furthermore, this study identifies the economic viability thresholds of the BESS market price in various FiT scenarios and provides techno-economic and policy implications to further incentivize and promote BESS application in buildings equipped with BIPV.

Keywords: Photovoltaics · Energy storage · Battery systems · Optimization · Life cycle cost

1 Introduction

The rapid urbanization growth alongside the escalation of the global population has led to an increasing need to expand the building sector, which is identified as a major contributor to global energy consumption and environmental impacts [1–3]. The building sector accounts for a considerable share of final energy consumption and Greenhouse Gas (GHG) emissions worldwide. It is estimated that around 36% of final energy consumption, and 39% of CO_2 equivalent emission is attributed to the building sector, of which a significant portion is associated with the buildings' operational stage alone [4–6]. The situation in developed countries such as European Union (EU) member states is more critical, where a large share of existing buildings have been constructed decades ago, lacking the alignment with new energy performance criteria and directives, while around 85% of them are expected to remain in operation until 2050. These facts challenge the ambitious goals of the EU Green Deal to reduce GHG emissions by 55% by 2030 compared to 1990 levels and become carbon-neutral by 2050 [7, 8].To address this challenge, the building sector is recognized as a focal point in energy efficiency and decarbonization targets in EU member states. Integrating Renewable Energy Sources (RESs) with comparatively lower environmental footprint into the building sector as sustainable alternatives to fossil fuels [9] for supplying the energy needs of the building operational stage has emerged as a promising strategy and is being investigated and implemented progressively [10]. Nevertheless, resolving the complexity of the transition towards sustainable solutions and alternatives requires multi-disciplinary work, including methodological and technological advancement [11].

The expected growth of RESs capacity in the world [12] and the development and application of Building-Integrated Photovoltaic systems (BIPV) are examples of these advancements that offer multiple benefits including reducing the overall environmental footprint of the building sector [13] and lowering the dependency of the operational energy supply on the conventional electricity grid, particularly when coupled with energy storage systems. The economic feasibility of such integrated solutions (i.e., BIPV coupled with energy storage systems) could be analyzed and justified using Life Cycle Costing (LCC) methodologies [14] although it might be challenging when considering all upfront costs within different economic contexts and investment business models that require accurate and reliable cost-benefit analysis [15].

Energy storage systems including thermal storage and electrical batteries have been studied significantly in the literature and are known as effective technological solutions to increase renewable energy penetration, enhance self-consumption, and improve the economic and environmental performance of buildings [6, 16–18] and to enhance the grid resiliency [19]. A considerable share of the literature has explored the techno-economic aspects of integrating BIPV and Battery Energy Storage Systems (BESSs) to achieve Net Zero Energy Buildings (NZEBs) globally. Despite extensive evaluations, the economic viability of such systems remains a critical area of investigation. For instance, Sadat and Pearce [20] conducted an economic assessment in Canada (Ontario) with different financial metrics and concluded that under the baseline conditions, BESS integration fails to deliver economic viability unless significant cost reduction and policy reforms are implemented. Bird et al. [21] showed that although there are operational savings by integrating BIPV and BESSs in commercial buildings, the high upfront cost remains a major obstacle, making it necessary to either decrease the BESS market price or increase the electricity tariffs for economic justification of these solutions. The study performed by Chen et al. [22] revealed that electrical storage could be viable when the market price of BESSs drops to around 70 $/kWh. A similar study in Thailand also highlights the necessity of market price reduction of BESSs to make them financially viable, given their results indicating that the current price, ranging from 200–300 $/kWh, is too high to render the integrated BIPV-BESSs economically attractive [23]. Furthermore, Li et al. [24] and Wang et al. [25] have emphasized the impact of energy policies to make BESSs economically attractive by lowering feed-in tariffs, encouraging self-consumption and substantial subsidies for battery energy storage systems.

The present article aims to analyze the economic feasibility of BESSs coupled with BIPV in smart buildings under different economic scenarios. The main research question to be addressed is to find the LCC-based optimum size of BESSs under multiple scenarios of Feed-in Tariffs (FiT) and market price of BESSs. The cost-optimum size of BESSs in a multi-family residential building under each scenario is determined through parametric energy modeling. The results will provide a clear outcome to find the cost-optimum size of BESSs alongside the impact of their market price on the optimum size of storage systems. Furthermore, the results also elaborate on the impact of FiT rate variation on the cost-optimum BESSs sizing and the economic attractiveness of such integrated technological solutions. The results provide building designers and engineers with analytical results to understand the economic feasibility of their design alternatives under various economic situations and highlight the key points to be tackled by policymakers to encourage the building sector for wider adoption of BESSs.

2 Materials and Methods

To evaluate the impact of different FiT and market price scenarios on cost-optimum sizing of BESSs and the economic feasibility of energy storage systems coupled with BIPV systems, a parametric energy model of a multi-family residential building with 636 square meters net surface area in Italy is developed. The building is equipped with air-water efficient heat pump units to supply the heating, cooling, and domestic hot water needs of the building. The total annual electrical energy consumption of heat pump units is calculated equal to 22.51 kWh/m^2.year using the EnergyPlus simulation engine. The building is also equipped with BIPV installed on a slanted roof with a nominal power equal to 8.5 kWp and a control logic enabling the system to regulate the building-grid interaction. The control logic determines the quantity and time frame of activating electrical energy storage in BESSs based on hourly energy consumption and generation profile over a 24-h time frame. Therefore, in case of excess BIPV-electricity generation and the need for electricity import for the grid over the next 24 h, the needed electricity is stored in BESSs.

The energy model is enhanced with the smart control logic that simulates the profile of energy consumption, self-BIPV energy consumed, stored electrical energy, and imported/ exported energy from and to the grid on an hourly basis. These energy profiles are then used to calculate the total energy costs and revenues from imported and exported electricity from and to the grid. Table 1 presents the techno-economic input data to perform the economic performance evaluation of this case study.

Furthermore, three FiT scenarios are defined, including low, medium, and high FiTs in which FiT rates are set equal to 0.05, 0.1, and 0.15 €/kWh, respectively. Similarly, a range of various market prices of BESSs is included in this assessment, in which the

Table 1. Techno-economic data inputs for building energy and economic analysis

Techno-economic data	Input data
Annual electricity consumption	14316 kWh/year
PV size (Peak power)	8.5 kW$_p$
*BESS size (Li-ion)	0 to 10 kWh
*BESS market price	100 to 500/kWh
Study period	30 years
BESS technical life span	10 years
Electricity price (from the grid)	0.2 €/kWh
*Electricity FiTs	0.05 to 0.15 €/kWh
Electricity Price Inflation Rate	4%
Nominal discount rate	2%
Inflation rate for the goods' market price	2%

market price varies from 100 to 500 €/kWh of BESSs capacity. These input data and variables are then used to calculate the Net Present Cost (NPC) and Saving to Investment Ratio (SIR) as two reliable LCC indicators over a 30-year study period, to evaluate the economic viability of the studied BESS configuration. To calculate NPC and SIR, the imported electricity tariffs are chosen equal to 0.2 €/kWh, and the nominal discount rate and electricity price inflation rate are 2% and 4% respectively. Furthermore, while the battery performance degradation is not included in the energy model, the technical life span of BESSs is determined equal to 10 years, indicating two full replacements of BESSs during the chosen study period. Finally, the results will demonstrate the relationship between the different BESS capacities, BESS market price, and various FiT scenarios impacting NPC and SIR through a parametric energy modelling.

3 Results and Discussion

This section presents a detailed techno-economic analysis of coupling BESSs with BIPV in a residential building, focusing on finding the cost-optimum size of BESSs under different FiT and BESS market price scenarios. The investigation in this research aims to identify economically optimal BESS size concerning the NPC and SIR as LCC indicators for optimization objectives. The results are illustrated in Fig. 1 contains six subplots grouped into three scenarios for FiTs. The FiT scenarios cover low range (0.05 €/kWh), medium (0.10 €/kWh), and high (0.15 €/kWh) values.

Figure 1 illustrates the results of the techno-economic analysis to evaluate the impact of BESS market price and FiTs. In particular, the results represent the minimum NPC and the maximum achievable SIR that can be achieved by optimum BESS size under different pricing schemes. Subplot (a) presents the minimum NPC associated with the optimal BESS size for each combination of BESS market price and FiT scenarios. Likewise, subplot (b) displays the corresponding SIR attainable for the same parameter space.

These plots together clarify how economic parameters influence the cost-effectiveness of the BIPV-BESS configuration.

Subplot (a) in Fig. 1 reveals the strong dependence of the system's NPC on both BESS market price and FiT rates. As expected, NPC increases in scenarios with higher BESS market prices and lower FiTs, since the higher cost of BESS systems demands more initial investment, ultimately leading to a higher total cost of the system, while lower FiTs limit the compensation by exported electricity to the grid. The most favorable economic conditions are observed in the region with low BESS market price and higher FiTs that together reduce the required initial investment for BESS and allow for benefits from economic compensation achieved through electricity export to the grid. Although the results in Fig. 1(a) indicate that the combination of lower BESS market price with higher FiTs is the most favorable economic condition to minimize the total NPC of the whole system, it should be noted that such economic context (i.e. high FiT rate) might not necessarily encourage the application of BESS at all due to prioritizing the electricity export to the grid rather than storage in battery energy systems. These aspects are further addressed and discussed by the results illustrated in Fig. 2, where the relationship between optimum BESS size and economic parameters is elaborated.

Subplot (b) in Fig. 1, which evaluates the economic efficiency of the investment, presents a different image in which the SIR is the highest (i.e., better economic performance) in scenarios with low BESS market price and low FiTs. This image might seem contradictory to the NPC results at first glance, but it becomes clear when considering the role and effect of self-consumption. When FiT rates are low, exporting the excess BIPV-generated electricity to the grid is less economically attractive. In such a context, BESSs play a critical role in increasing the self-consumption rate by storing surplus electricity generated by BIPV for later use in the building.

As a result, the value of stored energy increases, leading to the improvement of the economic return on the investment and thus increasing the SIR. Conversely, at high FiT rates, electricity export becomes financially rewarding and the relative values of storage reduce (i.e., reflected in lower SIR) despite the existing potential to decrease NPC. Therefore, it is clear that the region with the highest SIR (bottom-left of the plot) in Fig. 1(b) does not coincide with the region of lowest NPC (bottom-right of the plot) in Fig. 1(a). This discrepancy highlights a critical trade-off in system design that indicates minimizing the total cost of the system does not necessarily mean maximizing investment efficiency. While lower NPC reflects economic viability from a total expenditure perspective, SIR emphasizes the relative economic gain over the investment, which is particularly important for stockholders focused on investment return rather than absolute cost.

The contradictory results displayed in Fig. 1 underline the importance of considering multiple economic performance indicators in the assessment and optimization of BIPV-BESS systems. If the objective is to minimize the total life cycle costs of the system (e.g., measured by NPC), then an economic context with high FiT rates and low BESS market price is ideal. However, if the goal is to maximize SIR corresponding with the highest return per investment, the ideal context is where the BESS market price is reduced and self-consumption is encouraged through lower FiT rates.

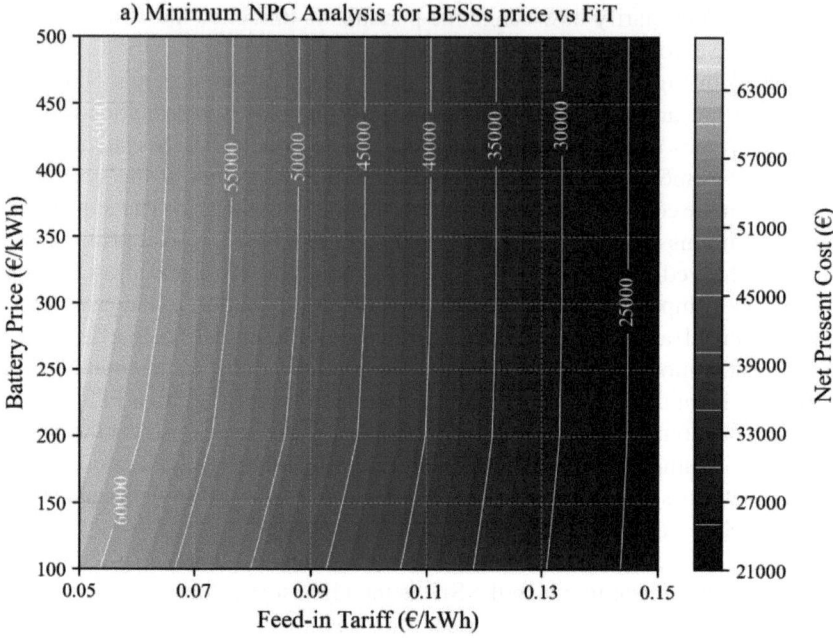

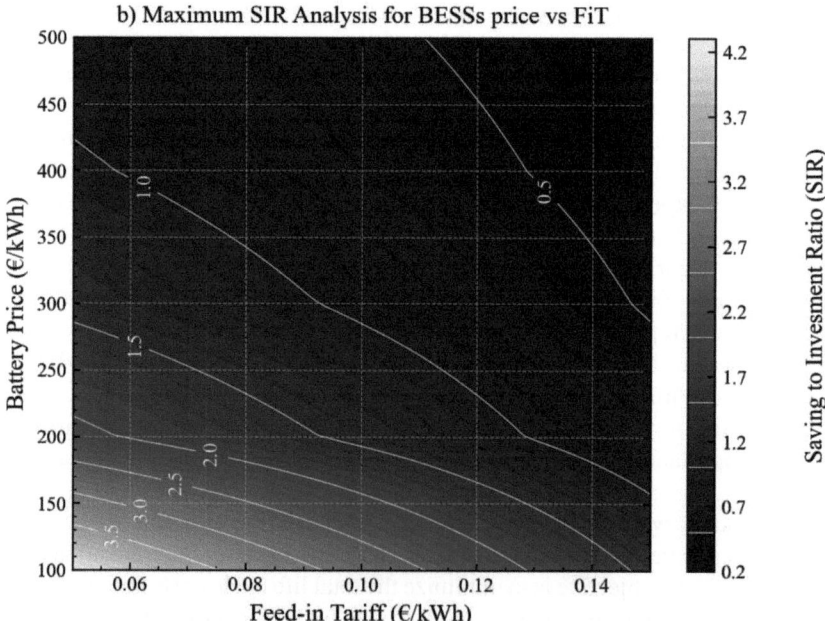

Fig. 1. The simulation results of the minimum NPC (a) and maximum SIR (b) achieveable for each combination of FiT scenarios and BESS market prices

The divergence between the results achieved by different economic indicators, including NPC and SIR, has noteworthy policy implications. Policymakers aiming to promote energy storage adoption alongside solar energy deployment should carefully balance FiT rates to ensure that energy storage strategies remain economically viable. This is because higher FiT rates normally encourage solar energy integration in the building sector, while the higher FiT rates can also diminish the attractiveness of energy storage strategies as they encourage feeding the excess generated electricity into the grid. Along with these findings, the results demonstrate that industrial efforts to reduce BESS market price are influential factors in promoting both solar energy penetration and energy storage system applications in the building sector, since they positively impact both economic performance indicators. From a design and optimization perspective, these findings highlight the need for multi-objective optimization frameworks aiming at balancing the total NPC and investment efficiency of energy storage systems, since an optimization based on a single economic indicator as the objective may lead to suboptimal design according to another indicator.

3.1 Low Feed-In Tariff (FiT) Scenario

As already discussed, the lower FiT encourages self-consumption over exporting excess BIPV generation to the grid, meaning prioritizing energy storage in BESSs. In Fig. 2(a-1), NPC shows an almost U-shaped relationship between BESS size and NPC, particularly at higher BESS market prices, and a declining trend as the market prices decrease. These trends indicate that for a low market price of BESSs, the larger BESS is more beneficial economically, although increasing the BESS market price limits the cost-optimum size of BESS, while BESS might still be beneficial at an optimum size. The optimization results based on NPC show that for a very high BESS price, the application of electrical storage is not economically viable due to the significant required initial investment. As the BESS market price decreases, the application of BESS becomes economically attractive by reducing the total NPC over the study period of the building. The cost optimum sizes of BESS obtained in this FiT scenario (low FiT = 0.05 €/ kWh) vary between 1–10 kWh when BESS market prices drop from 400 €/kWh to 100 €/kWh.

Subplot (a-2), in Fig. 2, demonstrates that in a low FiT scenario, BESS can yield highly favorable investment returns representing high SIR values, particularly for low BESS market price scenarios. The SIR reaches a peak higher than 4 for the scenarios with a market price equal to 100 €/kWh and higher than 2 when the market price is less than 200 €/kWh. However, SIR falls below the viability threshold (SIR < 1) for the scenario with a BESS market price higher than 420 €/kWh. This suggests that under a low FiT scenario, BESS can be economically viable only if the BESS market price remains under a critical threshold, and size optimization is essential to yield economic profits from energy storage and self-consumption strategies.

3.2 Medium Feed-In Tariff (FiT) Scenario

The results of the second scenario (low FiT), shown in subplots (b-1) and (b-2) in Fig. 2, represent a transitional policy landscape where both self-consumption through BESSs and grid export might provide competitive economic returns. NPC illustrated in these sub-plots still exhibits an almost U-shape trend for mid-range BESS market price, indicating that accurate cost-effective battery sizing is of essential importance to finding optimal BESS solutions for achieving higher economic benefits. The overall NPC in the medium-FiT scenario is reduced noticeably, even if the BESS is not optimal, which is directly attributed to higher financial returns from the exported electricity due to doubling the FiT rate in this scenario. In this scenario, NPC is less sensitive to the BESS sizing (compared to the low-FiT scenario), reflected in the milder slopes of lines in subplot (b-1), which can be explained by the fact that the higher FiT rates compensate for the penalty of inaccurate BESS size. However, the accurate BESS sizing, particularly concerning the BESS market price, can alter the total NPC of the building case study, which should be taken into account. The cost-optimum BESS size according to NPC in the medium FiT scenario is generally smaller than the values obtained for low-FiT scenarios.

Although the optimal size for the studied range of BESS market price varies between 10 kWh to 0 kWh by increasing the market price from 100 €/kWh to 500 €/kWh, the results show the BESS market price threshold for economic viability is lower (<290 €/kWh) in medium-FiT scenarios compared to the low-FiT scenario. The corresponding SIR results shown in subplot (b-2) in Fig. 2 further reaffirm the observed trends.

According to SIR, the economically profitable threshold for the BESS market price is lower than 290 €/kWh, meaning that any BESS size with a higher unit price is not economically attractive. Furthermore, the results demonstrate that the maximum SIR associated with the smallest BESS size is lower than the values found in the low-FiT scenario, indicating that increasing FiT leads to lower BESS size and lower investment returns. The results also indicate that while moderate battery storage remains beneficial, the economic margin is thinner, and battery implementation becomes increasingly sensitive to cost conditions.

3.3 High Feed-In Tariff (FiT) Scenario

The third scenario (high FiT), shown in subplots (c-1) and (c-2) in Fig. 2, represents a significant shift in the economic preferences toward exporting excess BIPV generation to the grids. As a result, prioritizing self-consumption by implementing BESSs becomes a less attractive investment strategy from an economic perspective. It is evident in subplot c-1 that in most scenarios of the BESS market price, the minimum NPC occurs at near-zero energy storage. However, at a very low market price (≤100 €/kWh), BESS is still economically profitable where 4 kWh capacity is found as the NPC-based optimum size. Nonetheless, in high-FiT scenarios, a smaller price threshold of economic viability is found compared with previous scenarios. In this scenario, BESS market price scenarios beyond 160 €/kWh are not economically attractive regardless of the BESS size. In high FiT scenarios, any increase in BESS market price (except for very low BESS market prices) leads to a steady rise in NPC. In this scenario, the total NPC is much lower than the values in the previous FiT scenarios due to higher potential revenue from high feed-in tariffs.

Subplot (c-2) also confirms the poor investment performance of BESS under high FiT conditions. The SIR always remains below 1.5 in high FiT scenarios across all BESS sizes and price conditions, which is considerably lower than the peak SIR values in previous

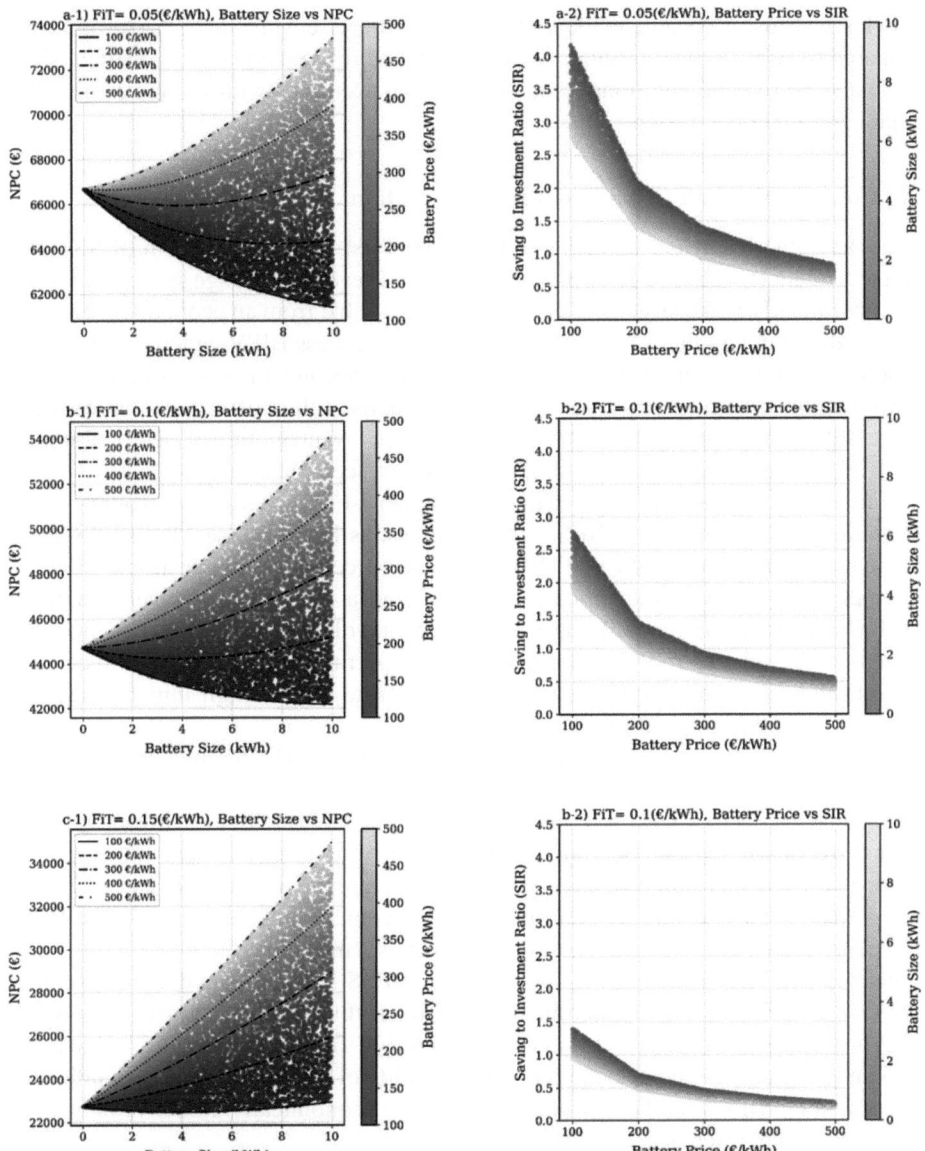

Fig. 2. The results of BESS size optimization under different market price scenarios and FiT regimes

FiT scenarios. According to the SIR indicator, most cases (except for an extremely low battery price of around 160 €/kWh) fall below the economic feasibility thresholds. These results indicate that at high feed-in tariffs, battery storage systems cannot be justified economically unless in the presence of an extreme reduction in battery system market price. Comparing the optimum BESS size based on NPC and SIR indicators across all FiT scenarios, it became evident that SIR is a more sensitive and stricter indicator compared to NPC to find optimum solutions with a threshold equal to 1, distinguishing viable and non-viable solutions, promoting design scenarios with the lowest possible initial investment per saving.

3.4 Comparative and Cross-Scenario Observation

Across all scenarios, two dominant trends emerge. First, the cost-optimum BESS size is inversely related to the feed-in tariff level. Lower FiT levels encourage self-consumption and consequently make larger BESS capacity more viable from an economic viewpoint. On the other hand, higher FiT levels favor exporting excess BIPV-generated electricity to the grid, leading to small electrical energy storage. Second, the economic viability of BESS is highly sensitive to its market price and depends on the existing economic setting. As the BESS market price falls at 100 €/kWh or lower, the integration of electrical storage into BIPV becomes significantly attractive in all FiT scenarios.

Furthermore, the results revealed that although low-FiT scenarios can promote BESS integration even at mid-range BESS market prices, as FiT increases, the BESS application in buildings equipped with BIPV cannot be economically justified unless in extremely low BESS market price scenarios. From a policy perspective, it suggests that BESS adoption in the building-integrated photovoltaic systems can be stimulated through either reduced FiT rates (to discourage export to the grid) or direct incentives and subsidies for battery systems to help compensate for the high initial investment required for purchasing and installing BESS.

Table 2, summarizes the influence of varying FiT rates and BESS market prices on the optimal size of BESSs coupled with BIPV based on NPC and SIR indicators, as shown in the table, at low (0.05 €/kWh) and medium (0.1 €/kWh) FiT rates, a wide range of optimal BESS size exists based on varying BESS market price however optimal BESS size decreases by increasing BESS market price. Nevertheless, as the FiT rate increases, the optimal BESS size shrinks even further and becomes viable only in case the BESS market price drops to 100 €/kWh or lower. Likewise, the economic viability threshold tightens as FiT rates increase. At low FiT rates, BESS is viable when its market price is below 430 €/kWh, while under medium FiT rates, this threshold drops to below 290 €/kWh, and at high FiT rates to lower than 160 €/kWh. These results highlight that under medium to high FiTs schemes, the economic viability of BESS application significantly depends on the BESS market price, and it could be economically attractive only when the BESS market price is extremely low.

For low FiT rates, the relationship between BESS size and NPC shows an almost U-shaped trend, indicating that a very large and small system could lead to higher NPC, while a moderate BESS size can minimize the total NPC. As the BESS market price decreases, NPC increases as well, making larger storage systems economically attractive. In contrast, for a medium FiT rate, this U shape is milder, meaning NPC is less sensitive to BESS size variation due to the better compensation from selling electricity to the grid. For a high FiT rate, the minimum NPC is found at near-zero BESS size, showing a steadily growing NPC as the BESS size increases. Furthermore, the cross-scenario observations highlight the difference in achievable peaks of SIR in different FiTs schemes. While SIR will reach 4 for low price ($\leq$ 100 €/kWh) battery

Table 2. The summary of cross-scenario observations and economic analysis

Key cross-scenario findings	Low FiT (0.05 €/kWh)	Medium FiT (0.1 €/kWh)	High FiT (0.15 €/kWh)
Optimal BESS size range- based on NPC	0–10 kWh (decreases as BESS market price rises)	0–10 kWh (smaller than in low FiT rates, decreases as BESS market prices rise)	Near-zero (4 kWh viable only at BESS market price ≤100 €/kWh)
Economic Viability Threshold based on SIR (BESS Market Price)	<430 €/kWh	<290 €/kWh	<160 €/kWh
Key NPC Trends	Almost U-shaped relationship with BESS size; larger BESS is beneficial at low prices. NPC declines as the BESS price decreases.	Milder U-shape; NPC is less sensitive to BESS size due to higher FiT compensation. Optimal size smaller than low-FiT.	Minimum NPC at near-zero storage. Steady NPC rises with BESS price except at <100 €/kWh.
Key SIR Trends	SIR peaks >4 (for appx 100 €/kWh), and >2 (for appx 200 €/kWh). Falls below viability (SIR <1) between 400–450 €/kWh.	Maximum SIR is lower than low-FiT. Viable only below appx 290 €/kWh; economic margins are thinner.	SIR <1.5 across all price scenarios. Viable only at <160 €/kWh.

energy storage systems, the application of BESS might become completely unattractive from an economic perspective under high FiT rates, except for BESS with an extremely low market price.

The summary of the cross-scenario observation demonstrates that under low FiT schemes, there is a greater economic motivation and opportunity to adopt a larger battery energy storage system. Conversely, under high FiT schemes, the economic profitability of storage scenarios is limited due to the higher potential of revenues from electricity export to the grid, where the adoption of BESS can be justified only if its market price is lowered significantly.

4 Conclusion

This study evaluates the economic feasibility and optimal sizing of Battery Energy Storage Systems (BESSs) integrated with Building-Integrated Photovoltaics (BIPV) under varying Feed-in Tariff (FiT) regimes and BESS market price through parametric energy modeling for a residential building complex in Italy. The findings reveal a complex interplay between the energy policy framework, technologies' market prices, and energy management strategies. The analysis proved that FiT policies have a significant impact on BESS adoption and cost-effective sizing. In low FiT scenarios, where there is a low compensation by exported electricity, self-consumption of BIPV-generated electricity becomes a promising strategy from an economic perspective. The finding in this paper highlights the critical interplay between energy and economic policies, such as FiT scenarios and the technology market price, in shaping optimal energy storage solutions and promoting the self-consumption of BIPV-generated electricity. It is expected that BESS adoption will be more viable with decreasing BESS global market price and regulatory energy economics on feed-in tariffs and further incentives for energy storage strategies. In such a scenario of low FiT schemes, BESS adoption leads to a cost-effective solution, particularly if the BESS market price is low. For instance, the application of BESS with a low market price around 100 €/kWh at a low FiT rate (0.05 €/kWh) can lead to SIR higher than 4, representing a significant economic return on investment.

Conversely, high FiT regimes (e.g., 0.15 €/kWh) create a different economic landscape. High compensation for exported electricity to the grid disincentivizes and discourages storage strategies, rendering BESS adoption economically unattractive except at extremely low BESS market prices (e.g., ≤ 100 €/kWh). In such FiT scenarios, the optimal BESS size tends to be near zero as the revenue from exported electricity to the grid outweighs the benefits of storage strategies. The finding in this section highlights a challenging paradox for policymakers, where the high FiT regimes, known as a promoting policy for solar energy penetration, inadvertently undermine the storage adoption. Nevertheless, to address this conflict, energy policies such as a dynamic tariff structure that penalizes peak-period exports or rewards stored energy during such periods could be adopted as a potential policy solution.

In the medium-FiT scenarios (i.e., 0.10 €/kWh), a transitional space is realized where partial storage remains economically viable but requires accurate sizing to balance the export revenues against the storage benefits. The optimum BESS sizes fall between the values obtained for the two previously described FiT schemes. Likewise, the economic return per investment is higher than high FiT scenarios and lower than low-FiT schemes. In such a scenario policy solution suggested in both previous scenarios, alongside the accurate BESS sizing, is of paramount importance to maximize the economic benefits of BESS adoption in the buildings.

Another finding of this study reveals the fact that high FiT rates minimize the NPC compared to the medium and low FiT rates due to compensation by the revenue from exported electricity and discourage the BESS adoption compared to the other FiT schemes, particularly from the building owner's perspective. While, from a policy viewpoint, aiming at grid resiliency, stability, and long-term sustainability, prioritizing low-FiT schemes that encourage BESS adoption is a favored option. Such divergence of interests therefore requires innovative financing mechanisms to balance the stakeholders' priorities, make the BESS adoption financially attractive, and continue promoting solar energy penetration and self-consumption in the building sector simultaneously.

Alongside the assessment of the influence of FiT schemes on the economic viability of BESS adoption in buildings, this study also evaluated the impact of BESS market price and the economic viability threshold of the market price of battery energy storage systems. The results indicated that although under ideal FiT scenarios for BESS adoption (i.e., low FiT), the application of BESS with a moderate market price might be economically viable, the current moderate-to-high BESS market price is a barrier to their adoption and application in buildings in most economic scenarios. Therefore, the results identify the need for incentivizing and reducing of BESS market price to the economic viability threshold as discussed in this research as a critical strategy for BESS adoption in the building sector.

To generalize the findings of this research, there are three types of limitations to be considered, including first the geographical context and the building typology, which can affect the energy need, solar radiation, and BIPV generation profile, ultimately impacting the need and possibility of storage. Moreover, the second and third limitations for generalizing the results are the fixed macro-economic parameters, including the nominal discount rate, electricity price, and inflation rate applied to the electricity purchasing rate, as well as the battery technology and its longevity, all impacting the life cycle cost analysis. Thus, further research is suggested to continue similar assessments under varying climatic conditions, focusing on other macroeconomic parameters and covering further storage technologies in the future.

References

1. Wang, D., Almojil, S.F., Ahmed, A.N., Chaturvedi, R., Almohana, A.I.: An intelligent design and environmental consideration of a green-building system utilizing biomass and solar having a bidirectional interaction with the grid to achieve a sustainable future. Sustain. Energy Technol. Assess. **57**, 103287 (2023). https://doi.org/10.1016/j.seta.2023.103287
2. Hafez, F.S., et al.: Energy efficiency in sustainable buildings: a systematic review with taxonomy, challenges, motivations, methodological aspects, recommendations, and pathways for future research. Energ. Strat. Rev. **45**, 101013 (2023). https://doi.org/10.1016/J.ESR.2022.101013
3. Amini Toosi, H., Lavagna, M., Leonforte, F., Del Pero, C., Aste, N.: Implementing life cycle sustainability assessment in building and energy retrofit design—an investigation into challenges and opportunities. In: Environmental Footprints and Eco-Design of Products and Processes, pp. 103–136 (2021). https://doi.org/10.1007/978-981-16-4562-4_6
4. Gupta, V., Deb, C.: Envelope design for low-energy buildings in the tropics: a review. Renew. Sustain. Energy Rev. **186**, 113650 (2023). https://doi.org/10.1016/J.RSER.2023.113650
5. McAllister, P., Nase, I.: Minimum energy efficiency standards in the commercial real estate sector: a critical review of policy regimes. J. Clean. Prod. **393**, 136342 (2023). https://doi.org/10.1016/J.JCLEPRO.2023.136342
6. Zhang, X., Xiao, F., Li, Y., Ran, Y., Gao, W.: Flexible coupling and grid-responsive scheduling assessments of distributed energy resources within existing zero energy houses. J. Build. Eng. **87**, 109047 (2024). https://doi.org/10.1016/j.jobe.2024.109047
7. European Commission: European Commission - The European Green Deal. European Commission – Press, p. 2, (2019), Accessed 06 Apr 2025. https://commission.europa.eu/strategy-and-policy/priorities-2019-2024/european-green-deal_en
8. Hernández, J.L., de Miguel, I., Vélez, F., Vasallo, A.: Challenges and opportunities in European smart buildings energy management: a critical review. Renew. Sustain. Energy Rev. **199**, 114472 (2024). https://doi.org/10.1016/J.RSER.2024.114472
9. Boulmrharj, S., Bakhouya, M., Khaidar, M.: Performance evaluation of grid-connected silicon-based PV systems integrated into institutional buildings: an experimental and simulation comparative study. Sustain. Energy Technol. Assess. **53**, 102632 (2022). https://doi.org/10.1016/j.seta.2022.102632

10. Ma, X., Ghosh, A., Cuce, E., Saboor, S.: Building integrated photovoltaic-thermal systems (BIPVT) and spectral splitting technology: a critical review. Next Sustainability **4**, 100056 (2024). https://doi.org/10.1016/J.NXSUST.2024.100056
11. Amini Toosi, H., Lavagna, M., Leonforte, F., Del Pero, C., Aste, N.: Towards sustainability assessment of the built environment: a classification of the existing challenges. Sustainability **15**(15), 12055 (2023). https://doi.org/10.3390/su151512055
12. Fan, P., Wang, D., Sun, Y., Wang, W.: A generalized flexibility potential quantification method of active thermal energy storage system for grid-interactive efficient buildings. J. Energy Storage **117**, 116120 (2025). https://doi.org/10.1016/j.est.2025.116120
13. Elkholy, A., Nafeh, A.E.S.A., Fahmy, F.H.: Impact of time resolution averaging analysis on integrated photovoltaic with office buildings and grid interaction metrics: case study. Energy Build. **257**, 111818 (2022). https://doi.org/10.1016/j.enbuild.2021.111818
14. Amini Toosi, H., Famiglietti, J., Motta, M.: Life cycle cost analysis of nearly-zero energy buildings: an introduction to the methodologies. Environ. Footprints Eco-Des. Prod. Process. **Part F1544**, 27–49 (2023). https://doi.org/10.1007/978-3-031-40993-6_2/TABLES/2
15. Amini Toosi, H.: Life cycle cost optimization of battery energy storage systems for BIPV-supported smart buildings: a techno-economic analysis. Sustainability **17**(13), 5820 (2025). https://doi.org/10.3390/SU17135820
16. Jia, S., Sheng, K., Huang, D., Hu, K., Xu, Y., Yan, C.: Design optimization of energy systems for zero energy buildings based on grid-friendly interaction with smart grid. Energy **284**, 129298 (2023). https://doi.org/10.1016/j.energy.2023.129298
17. Liu, J., Pan, Z., Huang, H., Wu, H.: Energy optimization of building-integrated photovoltaic for load shifting and grid robustness in high-rise buildings based on optimum planned grid output. Energy Convers. Manag. **324**, 119320 (2025). https://doi.org/10.1016/j.enconman.2024.119320
18. Amini Toosi, H., Lavagna, M., Leonforte, F., Del Pero, C., Aste, N.: Building decarbonization: assessing the potential of building-integrated photovoltaics and thermal energy storage systems. Energy Rep. **8**, 574–581 (2022). https://doi.org/10.1016/J.EGYR.2022.10.322
19. Pantoš, M., Lukas, L.: Enhancing power system reliability through demand flexibility of grid-interactive efficient buildings: a thermal model-based optimization approach. Appl. Energy **381**, 125045 (2025). https://doi.org/10.1016/j.apenergy.2024.125045
20. Sadat, S.A., Pearce, J.M.: Techno-economic evaluation of electricity pricing structures on photovoltaic and photovoltaic-battery hybrid systems in Canada. Renew. Energy **242**, 122456 (2025). https://doi.org/10.1016/J.RENENE.2025.122456
21. Bird, M., Andraos, R., Acha, S., Shah, N.: Lifetime financial analysis of a model predictive control retrofit for integrated PV-battery systems in commercial buildings. Energy Build. **332**, 115459 (2025). https://doi.org/10.1016/J.ENBUILD.2025.115459
22. Chen, Q., Kuang, Z., Liu, X., Zhang, T.: Optimal sizing and techno-economic analysis of the hybrid PV-battery-cooling storage system for commercial buildings in China. Appl. Energy **355**, 122231 (2024). https://doi.org/10.1016/J.APENERGY.2023.122231
23. Jivaganont, P., Limthongkul, P., Mongkoltanatas, J.: Design of photovoltaic and battery energy storage systems through load demand characterization: a case study in Thailand. Energy Rep. **12**, 4578–4593 (2024). https://doi.org/10.1016/J.EGYR.2024.10.025
24. Li, H., et al.: Can distributed photovoltaic-battery systems power buildings with favorable matching performance and techno-economic feasibility? Energy Convers Manag. **306**, 118260 (2024). https://doi.org/10.1016/J.ENCONMAN.2024.118260
25. Wang, Z., Luther, M., Horan, P., Matthews, J., Liu, C.: Technical and economic analyses of PV battery systems considering two different tariff policies. Sol. Energy **267**, 112189 (2024). https://doi.org/10.1016/J.SOLENER.2023.112189

Grid-Oriented AI, Simulation, and Resilience

A Data-Driven Analysis of Unscheduled Flows in the European Power System

Maurizio Titz[1,2](✉) and Dirk Witthaut[1,2]

[1] Institute of Climate and Energy Systems: Energy Systems Engineering (ICE-1),
Forschungszentrum Jülich, 52428 Jülich, Germany
`m.titz@fz-juelich.de`
[2] Institute for Theoretical Physics, University of Cologne, 50937 Köln, Germany

Abstract. Cross-border electricity trading is becoming increasingly important in the European power system. Unscheduled power flows induce additional costs and may lead to congestion and impair power grid operation. In this contribution we provide a data-centric analysis of unscheduled flows in the Central European power grid. Using methods from explainable machine learning, we identify the main driving factors for unscheduled flows and quantify their impact. Unscheduled flows in the meshed part of the grid can be attributed to transit or loop flows primarily and are well described by a linear model. The performance is substantially worse for unscheduled flows on bridges, with forecast errors being the most important drivers. This performance gap is probably due to data quality issues.

Keywords: Unscheduled Flows · Explainable AI · Transit Flows · Forecast Errors

1 Introduction

Unscheduled power flows - physical flows that deviate from commercially scheduled exchanges - are a persistent feature of the European electricity system [2]. These flows result from the mismatch between market-based scheduling and the physical laws governing the flow of alternating current. While they are an expected side-effect of zonal market design, their magnitude and impact can be significant, increasing costs [27] and complicating system operation [38].

Despite ongoing efforts to align market outcomes with physical constraints, such as the reconfiguration of bidding zones [8] and the introduction of flow-based market coupling [34], unscheduled flows remain a problem.

In this article, we provide a data-centric analysis of unscheduled flows in the Central European synchronous power grid based on publicly available data. We apply methods from explainable machine learning (ML) to identify the main driving factors for unscheduled flows and to quantify their dependencies. In the meshed part of the grid, unscheduled flows can be mainly attributed to transit flows and are well predicted from scheduled commercial exchanges. A linear model captures these relationships accurately and enables a causal interpretation. For bridges, the most important features are generally given by forecast errors. However, model performance on bridges is substantially lower.

Our contribution is organized as follows. We review the fundamentals of unscheduled flows and the recent literature in Sect. 2. The data sources and ML methods are described in Sects. 3 and 4, respectively. The results of our analysis are presented and discussed in Sect. 5 and summarized in Sect. 6. We remark that we focus on AC connections in this contribution, while DC interconnectors have been treated in [31].

2 Background

2.1 Cross-Border Electricity Trading in Europe

In liberalized electricity markets, the dispatch of power plants is mainly determined by electricity trading. Trading takes place on various time scales, from long-term contracts that are closed months in advance to intra-day contracts fixed minutes before delivery. Among these options, day-ahead spot markets are particularly relevant [18,41]. Day-ahead trading allows to adapt to the fluctuations of demand and renewable power generation via forecasts [16,36].

In Europe, day-ahead spot markets are auction-based with a trading interval of one hour. Generally, utility companies have to submit their bids and offers until 12:00 (noon) CET of the previous day. Market operators then set the market clearing price so that supply matches demand [9,29]. All offers below the clearing price and all bids above the clearing price are executed exactly at clearing price, this is commonly referred to as "pay-as-cleared".

The Central European synchronous power system is divided into bidding zones that reflect local market conditions [12]. Most countries correspond to one bidding zone, while some countries, such as Italy, are divided into several regional zones. Some smaller countries such as Luxembourg or Andorra, are integrated into the bidding zones of neighboring country. Each bidding zone constitutes a separate market with its own market clearing price.

The Single Day-Ahead Coupling (SDAC) mechanism allows electricity to be traded across bidding zones [11]. Market coupling aims to increase market efficiency by pooling demand and supply while respecting transmission constraints between bidding zones [28]. The SDAC employs the *EUPHEMIA* algorithm that aims to optimize the dispatch in all bidding zones to maximize the social welfare [3]. EUPHEMIA uses the order books from the 12:00 day-ahead auction and the network constraints and calculates the market price for all bidding zones as well as the commercial electricity exchange between interconnected bidding zones.

Before the introduction of flow-based market coupling (FBMC) [34], available transfer capacities were allocated before market clearing, typically through a bilateral agreement of the involved transmission system operators. In contrast, FBMC uses a grid model to quantify the grid load and allocates transfer capacities during market clearing. FBMC was first introduced for a few countries in

Central Western Europe in 2015 and extended to 13 other countries in June 2022 [30].

2.2 Unscheduled Flows

The physical power flow between two bidding zones does not necessarily match the commercial exchange scheduled on the day-ahead market. The difference between the physical flow and the scheduled commercial exchange is referred to as unscheduled flow. Transmission system operators aim to mitigate unscheduled flows as they can induce congestion or put the grid at risk [38]. Unscheduled flows can be caused by several different mechanisms (see Fig. 1 for a graphical overview):

- Transit flows: The power flows in an AC network are governed by Kirchhoff's and Ohm's laws and may therefore deviate from schedules. Consider for example a scheduled export of one Gigawatt from Germany to Austria. The physical power flow is not limited to the lines directly connecting Germany and Austria, but can also flow to Austria via Poland or the Czech Republic [35]. Transmission system operators try to reduce transit flows as they can induce congestion [19,38]. We note that the majority of academic articles focus on transit flows when analysing unscheduled flows. Sometimes the two terms are even used interchangeably.
- Forecast errors and intraday-trading: Day-ahead trading is based on forecasts, that are typically not perfect [39]. Forecasts are updated as the time of delivery approaches. A utility company may react via intra-day trading to correct for foreseen changes in demand and renewable power generation [6,42].
- Grid congestion and countertrading: The EUPHEMIA algorithm takes into account limited transmission capacities between bidding zones – but not within bidding zones. Hence, the day-ahead dispatch can induce congestion that must be resolved by the transmission system operators [40]. If congestion occurs close to a border, system operators can apply counter trading, buying electricity in one zone and selling it in another to mitigate congestion [25]. For example, a German grid operator can buy electricity in Germany and sell it in Denmark to reduce congestion-causing imports [40].
- Frequency control reserves: Some DC interconnectors are partly used for control reserves, where the power flow is adjusted in real time and thus deviates from the day-ahead schedule [31]. Consider for example the BritNed interconnector linking the British and the Continental European synchronous area. If power consumption exceeds power generation in the British synchronous area, the grid frequency drops. To prevent this, the operator can increase imports via the BritNed interconnector. As DC interconnectors have been analyzed in detail in [31], we will focus on AC connections in this article.

2.3 Literature on Unscheduled Flows

Potential negative effects and hazards of unscheduled flows have been reviewed in [19]: They can lead to congestion and induce transmission bottlenecks and thus

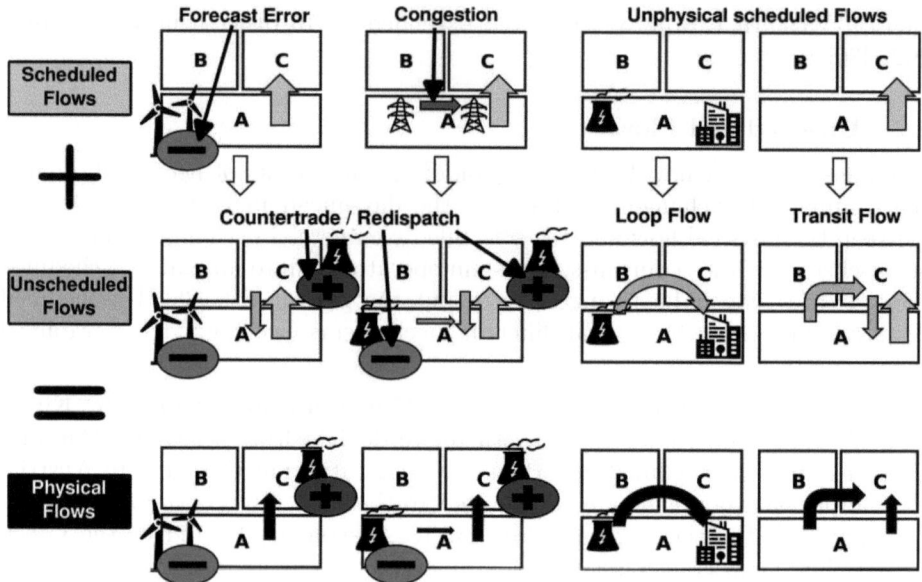

Fig. 1. Scheduled flows result from the dispatch determined by the EUPHEMIA algorithm, based on forecasts and market auction outcomes. Unscheduled flows quantify the deviation between scheduled and physical power flows. Forecast errors must be compensated through redispatch or countertrading. If this compensation occurs outside the bidding zone where the error originated, it induces unscheduled flows. Similarly, corrective actions taken by the grid operator to resolve congestion may lead to physical flows deviating from scheduled ones. Unscheduled flows can also occur when scheduled commercial exchanges conflict with the physical behavior of the grid. In the case of loop flows, flow scheduled between two locations within the same zone (e.g., A) may transit through external zones (e.g., B and C). In transit flows, electricity is scheduled from zone A to zone C but physically passes through an intermediate zone B. Since the direct flow between A and C is smaller than the scheduled exchange, this also results in unscheduled flows opposing the scheduled flow.

contribute to overloading of transmission lines which may eventually compromise grid reliability. Notably, unscheduled flows may have contributed to the 2003 North American blackout [7]. A particular example of an unscheduled power flow is the Lake Erie loop flow in the North American grid [5].

Several techniques to manage unscheduled transit flows are reviewed in [38]. Phase-shifting transformers (PSTs) enable the regulation of power flows in AC grids. Their optimized operation can therefore help manage unscheduled flows [21,24]. Other measures to manage unscheduled flows by topology modifications are discussed in [14]. The estimation of transit flows in power system operation from measurements has been discussed in [32,37].

Unscheduled flows in the European grid have been analyzed in various articles. An economic analysis focusing on the role of renewable energy and infrastructure policy has been presented in [1]. The impacts of market splitting and network extensions has been investigated using simulation models in [22] and via statistical analysis of the German-Austrian bidding zone split in [13]. Studies of the impact of wind power generation can be found in [26,43]. A detailed statistical analysis of unscheduled flows on DC interconnectors and the relation to load-frequency control has been provided in [31]. An early overview of the integration of European electricity markets and the fundamentals of cross-border trade can be found in [4].

The situation in Central and Eastern Europe has received particular attention. Singh et al. introduced the basic problem and analyzed the impact on the Polish transmission grid using numerical simulations in [35]. Further simulations focusing on the German borders have been presented in [33]. The impact of phase-shifting transformers at the borders of Germany, Poland and the Czech Republic is discussed in [20].

3 Data

We use publicly available data from the ENTSO-E Transparency Platform [10]. All data is open access and includes day-ahead generation forecasts and actual generation, day-ahead and actual load, day-ahead scheduled commercial exchanges and physical power flows. For the latter, data is reported for each direction individually. Load data is resampled to hourly resolution using the mean, to match the resolution of the flow data.

We define directional net flows between two zones i and j as

$$\hat{f}_{ij} = f_{ij} - f_{ji},$$

where f_{ij} is the physical flow from zone i to j, and f_{ji} the reverse. Net scheduled flows $\hat{s}_{ij}$ are computed analogously. From these we calculate the unscheduled flows as

$$\hat{u}_{ij} = \hat{s}_{ij} - \hat{f}_{ij}.$$

This approach thus captures directional net flow deviations but excludes internal loop flows between two zones.

For the load and the generation we compute the forecast errors as the difference between day-ahead forecasts and actual values

$$l_{i,err} = l_{i,\text{day-ahead}} - l_{i,\text{actual}}.$$

For instance, a load forecast error of +1GW means that the day-ahead prediction was 1GW larger than the actual load.

The data on the ENTSO-E Transparency Platform is not complete and requires pre-processing and filtering. For some bidding zones, individual features are not available and are thus discarded in the analysis. Many features miss individual data points, but for most this concerns less than 1% of data. We remove input features if more than 1.3% of the data is missing. We then remove all timestamps for which data is still missing for any input feature.

We excluded some outliers from the data, where flows are implausibly high. Furthermore for some connections we observe many occurrences of zero physical flows on AC links. We consider these values to be implausible under normal operating conditions and we assume this to result from reporting errors or outages. Therefore we excluded these data points from the analysis. While excluding these values has no significant impact on the results is raises questions about the overall data quality, which has been discussed in the past [17].

The European electricity system evolves slowly but continuously, through both physical developments and regulatory changes. Analyzing a long period – including major structural shifts – can obscure consistent patterns. For this reason, we focus on the period from the introduction of flow-based market coupling in June 2022 until the end of 2024.

4 Methods

4.1 Gradient Boosted Trees

We train gradient boosted decision trees (GBT) to model unscheduled flows. We selected Gradient Boosted Trees due to their strong performance on tabular, unstructured data [15] and because they offer efficient explainability with SHAP, as discussed below. They are also robust to multicollinearity and computationally efficient.

As input features we use scheduled flows, generation forecast errors, and load forecast errors for all European bidding zones, including those outside the Central European synchronous area. We train one separate model for each cross border connection.

We do not use a time-series split, since the model is used for explanation, not for forecasting. Instead we perform a group shuffle split with a block size of one week and a gap size of 24 h to avoid data leakage from auto-correlated samples. If two consecutive hours have correlated feature and target values, one in the training set and one in the test set, the GBT model can simply learn the correlated data points "by heart". This is prevented by leaving gaps between groups. Hyper-parameters are optimised using random search.

4.2 SHapley Additive ExPlanations

SHapley Additive exPlanations (SHAP) [23] is a widely used method for interpreting black-box models by attributing their outputs to individual input features. It uniquely satisfies the properties of local accuracy, missingness, and consistency–criteria that are essential for generating reliable and meaningful feature attributions.

For each prediction, SHAP quantifies the impact of each input feature on the model output. If the model predicts the value f from the feature values $x_1, \ldots, x_n$ we have

$$f(x_1, \ldots, x_n) = \phi_0(f) + \sum_{j=1}^{n} \phi_j(f; x_1, \ldots, x_n), \tag{1}$$

where $\phi_j(f;x_1,\ldots,x_n)$ denotes the SHAP values for the jth feature.

SHAP values thus give *local* explanations, i.e., explanations of individual predictions. To analyze these explanations across many samples, we use *dependency plots*, which show how the SHAP value of a specific feature $\phi_j(f;x_1,\ldots,x_n)$ varies as a function of the feature value x_j, see Fig. 3. If we want to gain a more *global* understanding of the model, and by extension the data it is trained on, we can use SHAP values to quantify the importance of individual features over the whole dataset. The feature importance of the jth feature is obtained by aggregating its SHAP values over all samples s

$$FI_j = \frac{1}{\mathcal{N}} \sum_s |\phi_j(f;x_1^{(s)},\ldots,x_n^{(s)})|. \tag{2}$$

The sum of all feature importances is often normalized to one.

When the number of input features is large, individual feature importances tend to diminish, as relevance is distributed across many potentially correlated variables. To retain interpretability, we aggregate importances for the three groups of features: (i) scheduled flows, (ii) generation forecast errors, and (iii) load forecast errors– and normalize them. This results in three group-level importance values that offer a high-level view of the mechanisms driving unscheduled flows.

4.3 Linear Model

We furthermore fit linear regression models to analyze transit flows in the meshed part of the Continental European synchronous area. Focusing on transit flows, we only use the scheduled flows on AC links within the Central European synchronous area as input features. Linear models are inherently transparent and facilitate a causal interpretation. Hence, they complement the previous analysis in terms of GBTs.

When giving the model all scheduled flows as input features, coefficients for lines with high distance can turn out to be high. These effects can only be interpreted as (spurious) correlations, not causal relationships. To restrict the model to more realistic local interactions, we thus constrain the inputs to lines within a topological distance of two from the target line. We fix the intercept to zero. This slightly decreases model performance but forces the model to attribute all unscheduled flows to scheduled flows. This makes the model more intuitive and easier to interpret. The model can be represented as

$$\boldsymbol{u} = \boldsymbol{As}, \tag{3}$$

where $\boldsymbol{u}$ and $\boldsymbol{s}$ are vectors that summarize the unscheduled flows $\hat{u}_{ij}$ and the scheduled commercial exchanges $\hat{s}_{ij}$ for all border (i,j). As described below, we fix $\boldsymbol{A}_{i,j} = 0$ if the shortest path distance from link i to j is larger than two. In the training and evaluation of the linear model we use a standard random train-test split.

5 Results

5.1 GBT Model

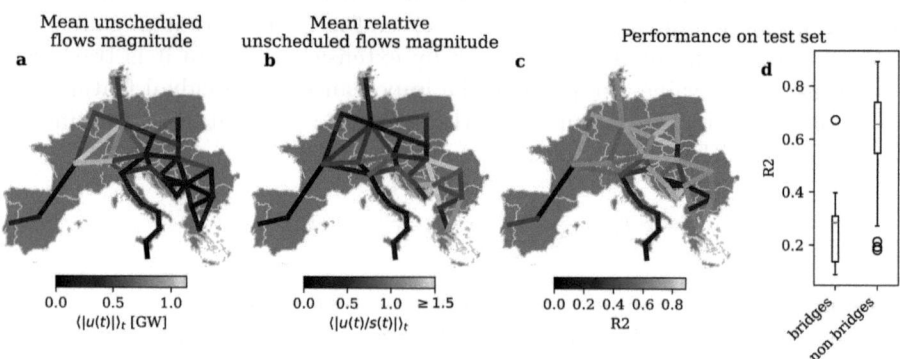

Fig. 2. Panel a (b) shows the mean (relative) magnitude of the unscheduled flows, where we divide the values shown in panel a by the mean magnitude of the scheduled flow to get the values in panel b. In panel b, we cropped the color scale at 1.5. The meshed part of western Europe shows the highest magnitudes of unscheduled flows, with DE-FR topping the list. However the relative values show, that this is in part due to the higher scheduled flows. Relatively speaking parts of the Balkan actually have the highest unscheduled flows, with multiple values larger than one. Panel c and d show the performance of the Gradient Boosted Tree (GBT) models. Apart from the DK1-DE link the performance on bridges is much worse than for non-bridges.

Unscheduled flows are largest in the meshed areas of central Europe, see Fig. 2. We compare the absolute value of the unscheduled flows $\langle |u_i(t)|\rangle_t$ and the relative unscheduled flows, i.e. $u_i^{rel} = \langle |u_i(t)|/|s_i(t)|\rangle_t$, where $\langle \cdot \rangle_t$ denotes the average over all timestamps t. We observe that relative unscheduled flows are no higher in central Europe than in the eastern Europe and the Balkan area. Indeed, for seven links in the south-east the relative magnitude is larger than one, while it is below 0.6 for DE-FR. On bridges, relative unscheduled flows are generally lower than on non-bridges.

The GBT models perform much better in the meshed region than on most bridge connections.

In the following, we discuss feature importances and dependencies for three representative connections in detail. The connection between Spain and Portugal (ES-PT) is a bridge, i.e. there is no indirect connection which can be subject to transit or loop flows. We find that forecast errors are the most important features in the GBT model. The generation forecast error is the most important factor and its SHAP values are approximately linear. The second most important feature, the load forecast errors in PT is much less important, since they are much smaller than generation forecast errors. The next important features relate to forecast errors or scheduled flows outside the Iberian peninsula. We hypothesize that these features capture only correlations, not causal effects.

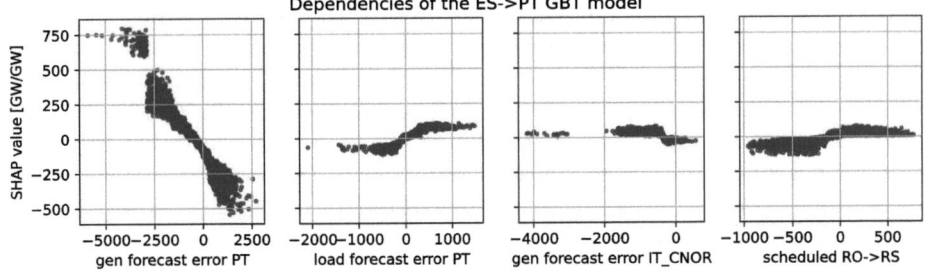

Fig. 3. Shap dependencies of the Gradient Boosted Trees model for the unscheduled flows on the line ES-PT, i.e. Spain to Portugal. By far the most important feature is the forecast error for renewable generation in Portugal. When there is a negative error, i.e. more generation than expected, the unscheduled flows are predicted to be higher, i.e. Portugal exports more or imports less than scheduled. Similarly, in the case of lower than expected generation, unscheduled flows to Spain are higher. The next most important feature, the generation forecast error in IT CSUD does already have a questionable relation to the cross border connection, which is most likely purely correlational.

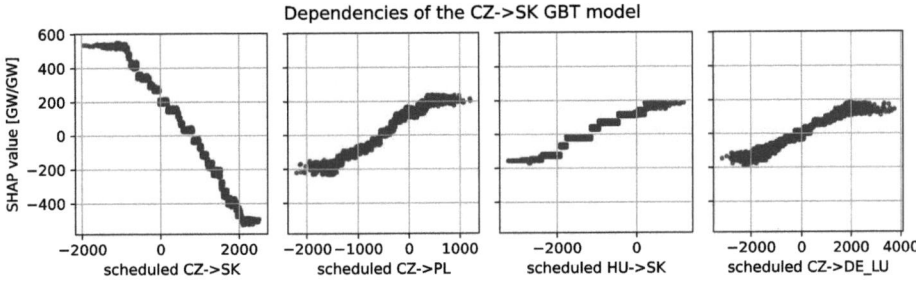

Fig. 4. The most important feature for the unscheduled flows on the CZ → SK connection is the corresponding scheduled flow. The relation is approximately linear except for extreme values, where the SHAP values saturate. The negative slope indicates that the unscheduled flows tend to oppose the scheduled flows. We also see that exports from CZ in other Zones, increase the unscheduled flows from CZ to SK.

The connection between the Czech Republic and Slovakia (CZ-SK) lies in the meshed part of the grid. Here, we find that the scheduled flow on the respective connection is the dominant factor. SHAP values show a near-linear response with saturation at the extremes for the scheduled flow on the line itself. The negative slope indicates that unscheduled flows oppose scheduled flows. On the other hand, scheduled flows from CZ to other zones show a positive slope. This can be explained by transit flows as in the case of CZ-PL. For HU-SK and CZ-DE LU the effect could be that these unscheduled flows are correlated because they are all driven by over-generation in CZ and under-generation in SK.

The bridge with the best performance is the DK-DE link. In contrast to other bridges, it is a bridge only when ignoring HVDC connections. The most important feature for the DK-DE connection is the corresponding scheduled flow. Here the model fits much stronger nonlinear effects than in other models. Surprisingly, the model does not strongly rely on forecast errors as would be expected for bridges. Instead, the next three most important features are all scheduled flows on HVDC lines. Unlike AC connections in the meshed grid, these do not have any direct physical effect on other power flows, since DC power transmission is fully controllable. Accordingly, unscheduled flows can only be affected through market effects but trying to explain these goes beyond the scope of this paper.

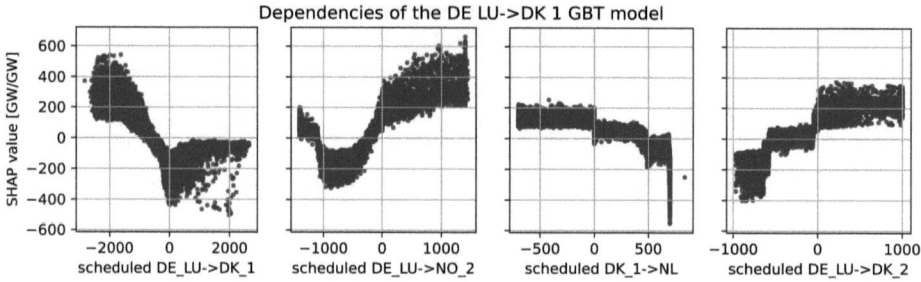

Fig. 5. The most important feature for the DE-DK unscheduled flows model is the corresponding scheduled flow. As with the CZ-SK model, we see the expected negative slope, though the dependencies show much stronger nonlinearities. Surprisingly, the next most important features are all scheduled flows on HVDC lines, instead of forecast errors.

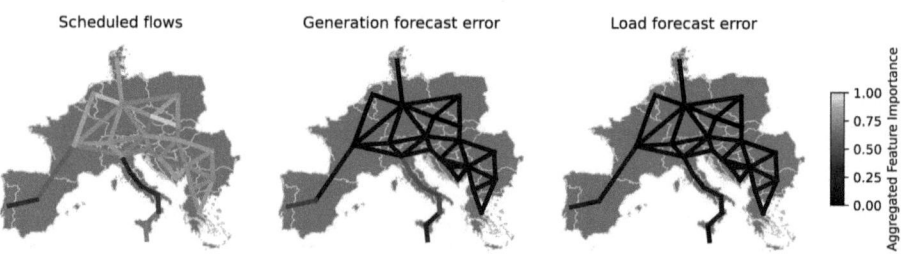

Fig. 6. Aggregated feature importances for the three types of input features. Each line corresponds to the GBT model for the unscheduled flows on that line. The feature importances for each model are normalized to sum to one. The importance of all features of each type are then summed to give the aggregated importance. Models for bridges stand out by utilizing forecast errors on a similar level as scheduled flows. For non bridges, they are barely used at all, and the predictions are heavily based on the scheduled flows instead. The DK1-DE LU link is a stark outlier. Load forecast errors are much less important than generation forecast errors.

To conclude, we collect cumulative feature importances results for all connections in the Central European synchronous area. Figure 6 highlights a clear separation between bridges and non-bridges. In meshed areas, predictions rely almost entirely on scheduled flows. On bridges, forecast errors become more important, though scheduled flows still dominate in some cases. The DK1âĂŞDE LU connection is an outlier in both importance and performance, as examined above.

Due to the simplicity of the relations for bridges and especially terminal links – unscheduled flows can only be caused from downstream forecast errors – one might expect the best performance here. This hints at problems with the data quality and availability. For instance, missing balancing actions in the generation data would make it impossible to capture these effects.

For all non-bridge and some bridge links the most important features are the scheduled flows. In many cases, the dependencies are close to linear, suggesting that linear models should be able to capture the relations similarly well.

5.2 Linear Model

For a detailed analysis of transit flows, we train a linear model to predict unscheduled flows using only scheduled flows as input. The intercept is fixed to zero, such that all unscheduled flows must be derived from scheduled flows. To avoid fitting spurious long-range correlations, we limit inputs to links within a topological distance of two from the target link, see Sect. 4.

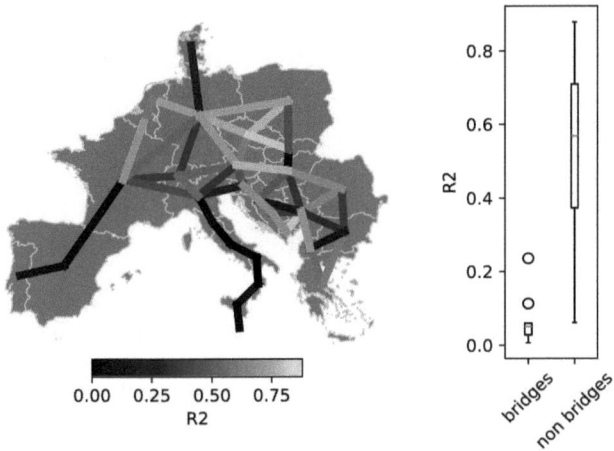

Fig. 7. Performance of the linear model. As expected, we see a big difference between bridges and non-bridges. The R2 score for bridges is below 0.1 for most bridges. For non-bridges, the R2 score is almost 0.6 on average. This matches with the GBT performances and feature importances.

The performance is in line with the GBT model (Fig. 7). R^2 scores are high for meshed connections and low for bridges. This supports the conclusion that in the meshed grid, unscheduled flows are largely driven by systematic mismatches between scheduled and physical flows (transit flows), while on bridges they reflect re-balancing effects driven by local forecast errors or other reasons.

We now analyze the effect of individual scheduled flows on the resulting unscheduled flows. This analysis is straightforward using the linear model (3) as the total unscheduled flows pattern decomposes into the sum of the effects from each individual line. These effects are captured in the columns of the learned coefficient matrix $\mathbf{A}$, where the lth column represents the impact of scheduled flow on line l across the entire system.

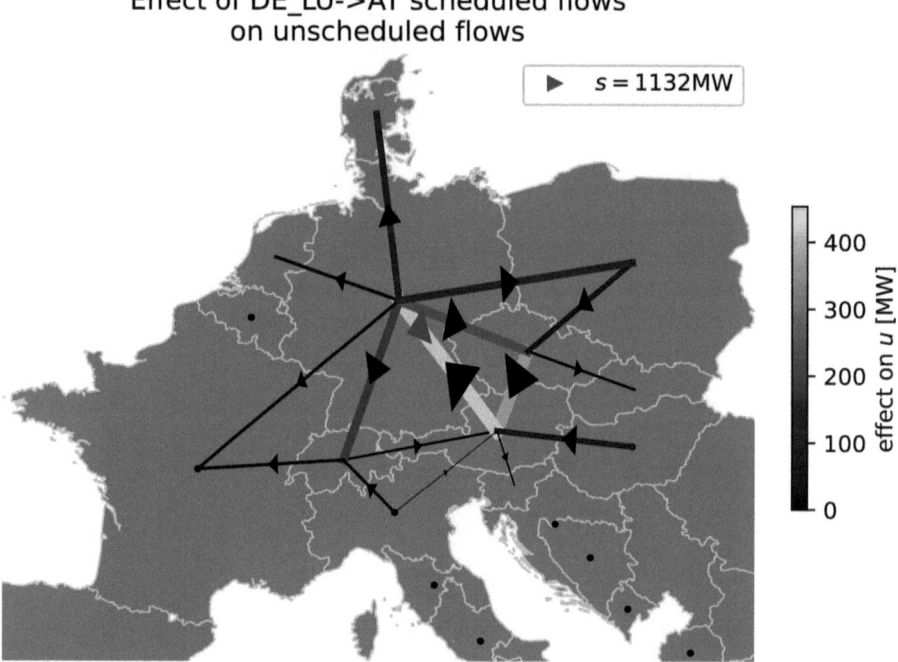

Fig. 8. Effect of scheduled flows from Germany to Austria on unscheduled flows as learned by the linear model. The scheduled flow of 1132 MW is the mean flow at times when Germany is exporting to Austria. The model learned that unscheduled flows of over 400 MW from AT to DE will result from the scheduled flows. In other words, more than one third of the scheduled exports will not take place or take another route. The latter can be seen as transit flows especially via Poland and the Czech Republic.

Figure 8 shows the case of scheduled exports from Germany to Austria. The model predicts that a significant portion of this flow –more than 400 MW– will not be directly realized, but instead be rerouted as unscheduled flows, primarily via neighboring countries such as Poland and the Czech Republic. This illustrates how scheduled flows can induce large-scale loop or transit flows even under simple linear assumptions.

Notably, the Czech Republic and Poland have repeatedly experienced congestion due to such transit flows [35]. As a consequence, TSOs have commissioned phase shifting transformers along the borders to Germany to regulate and constrain flows from Germany [20].

6 Discussion

To our knowledge, this is the first data-driven study to quantify the drivers of unscheduled flows across all cross-border links in Central Europe using explainable ML techniques. Our analysis demonstrates that unscheduled flows in the meshed part of the Central European power system can be explained to a large degree using only scheduled commercial exchanges. Gradient Boosted Tree (GBT) models perform well on meshed connections, while performance on bridges is consistently worse. SHAP analysis reveals that scheduled flows are by far the most important features across most models, and the relationship between scheduled and unscheduled flows is often close to linear. Forecast errors play a significant role only for some bridge connections in our models. Linear regression models using only scheduled flows as input confirm the dominant role of these features. They perform comparably well in meshed areas, but fail for bridge connections. These findings support the interpretation that unscheduled flows are still primarily caused by a mismatch between market-based scheduling and the physical realities of the power grid. In the meshed core of the grid, systematic transit flows and loop flows emerge due to the simplified network model used in market clearing, particularly in EUPHEMIA. For bridges, generation forecast errors are important drivers of unscheduled flows, while load forecast errors are generally smaller and thus less relevant. Surprisingly, however, even in terminal links, forecast errors do not allow reliable prediction of unscheduled flows at all. This is unexpected, as forecast errors should, in principle, hold all the information about net deviations from schedule. They should thus fully explain unscheduled flows on bridges. The low model performance therefore points to issues with data quality, such as misreported data, or missing balancing actions not reflected in the published data. Forecast errors are likely relevant in meshed areas as well. However, their effects are harder to capture, since the resulting imbalances can be compensated across multiple links. But once again, data quality might also be the problem.

The linear model provides further insight by making the relations indicated by the SHAP analysis explicit. By visualizing the coefficients, we can interpret the model as assigning each scheduled flow a contribution to unscheduled flows elsewhere in the network. In most cases, the resulting patterns correspond well to expected transit flows and confirm systematic deviations from schedules. These effects likely arise from the physical redistribution of power flows that is not fully captured by the simplified market model used in scheduling.

Our analysis is limited by the quality of publicly available data. Beyond missing values we found implausible zero flows. We might very well have been unable to identify further misreported data. Moreover, our models rely entirely on statistical relationships and do not incorporate physical constraints such as Kirchhoff's laws. All interpretations are based on correlation, not physical causation.

Future work could focus on integrating physical modeling or constraints with machine learning to improve interpretability and accuracy. However, the lack of public data on the transmission grid remains a major obstacle. Another direction is to analyze temporal changes in flow patterns in response to regulatory events such as bidding zone redefinitions, flow-based market coupling expansions, or grid extensions. Our preliminary investigations in this direction have shown little measurable effect.

A Appendix

Table 1. Performance (R^2 score) of the GBT model (first value) and linear model for unscheduled flows. Bridges link are marked by *. In some cases the linear model outperforms the GBT model, because of the different splits used, see method section.

CZ-SK	0.89 | 0.88	AT-CZ	0.67 | 0.62	ES-PT*	0.40 | 0.11		
ME-RS	0.83 | 0.82	CH-FR	0.67 | 0.37	IT NORD-SI	0.36 | 0.22		
CZ-PL	0.81 | 0.79	DE LU-DK 1*	0.67 | 0.24	HU-SK	0.31 | 0.06		
BA-ME	0.80 | 0.70	BG-GR	0.66 | 0.61	IT CSUD-IT SUD*	0.31 | 0.04		
AT-HU	0.78 | 0.79	GR-MK	0.63 | 0.57	IT CNOR-IT CSUD*	0.30 | 0.03		
BA-HR	0.77 | 0.69	BG-RO	0.62 | 0.36	IT CNOR-IT NORD*	0.28 | 0.05		
CZ-DE LU	0.76 | 0.77	CH-IT NORD	0.60 | 0.56	HR-RS	0.27 | 0.24		
AT-DE LU	0.75 | 0.72	DE LU-FR	0.59 | 0.56	BG-MK	0.21 | 0.15		
HR-SI	0.75 | 0.68	AT-CH	0.58 | 0.55	IT CALA-IT SUD*	0.20 | 0.01		
DE LU-NL	0.74 | 0.74	FR-IT NORD	0.56 | 0.45	BG-RS	0.19 | 0.33		
BE-FR	0.74 | 0.72	BE-NL	0.56 | 0.60	BA-RS	0.18 | 0.38		
DE LU-PL	0.73 | 0.74	HR-HU	0.55 | 0.51	IT CALA-IT SICI*	0.14 | 0.06		
HU-RO	0.73 | 0.67	CH-DE LU	0.55 | 0.36	IT SICI-MT*	0.12 | 0.02		
PL-SK	0.73 | 0.49	AT-IT NORD	0.47 | 0.34	ES-FR*	0.09 | 0.06		
RO-RS	0.70 | 0.66	AT-SI	0.46 | 0.48				
MK-RS	0.67 | 0.71	HU-RS	0.41 | 0.35				

References

1. Abrell, J., Rausch, S.: Cross-country electricity trade, renewable energy and European transmission infrastructure policy. J. Environ. Econ. Manag. **79**, 87–113 (2016)
2. ACER: Methodological paper: unscheduled flows (2018). https://www.acer.europa.eu/sites/default/files/documents/en/Electricity/Market%20monitoring/Documents_Public/ACER%20Methodological%20paper%20-%20Unscheduled%20flows.pdf

3. ALL NEMO COMMITTEE: Euphemia Public Describtion. https://www.nemo-committee.eu/assets/files/euphemia-public-description.pdf (2020)
4. Bower, J.: Seeking the single European electricity market: evidence from an empirical analysis of wholesale market prices (2002)
5. Coletta, T., Delabays, R., Adagideli, I., Jacquod, P.: Topologically protected loop flows in high voltage ac power grids. New J. Phys. **18**(10), 103042 (2016)
6. Cramer, E., Witthaut, D., Mitsos, A., Dahmen, M.: Multivariate probabilistic forecasting of intraday electricity prices using normalizing flows. Appl. Energy **346**, 121370 (2023)
7. Dozier, A.Q., Suryanarayanan, S., Liberatore, J.P., Veghte, M.C.: Unscheduled flow in deregulated electricity markets: Bridging the gap between the western electric power industry and academia. In: 2013 IEEE Green Technologies Conference (GreenTech), pp. 451–458. IEEE (2013)
8. European Federation of Energy Traders: Bidding zones delineation in Europe: Lessons from the past & recommendations for the future (2019). https://eepublicdownloads.entsoe.eu/clean-documents/Network%20codes%20documents/Implementation/stakeholder_committees/MESC/2019-09-17/5.2_EFET%20position%20paper_%20BZ%20review_16092019.pdf?Web=1
9. EPEX SPOT: Basics of the Power Market. https://www.epexspot.com/en/basicspowermarket. Accessed 07 Jan 2024
10. European Network of Transmission System Operators for Electricity: ENTSO-E Transparency Platform. https://transparency.entsoe.eu/ (2023)
11. European Network of Transmission System Operators for Electricity (ENTSO-E): Single Day-ahead Coupling (SDAC). https://www.entsoe.eu/network_codes/cacm/implementation/sdac/. Accessed 07 Jan 2024
12. European Union Agency for the Cooperation of Energy Regulators (ACER): Bidding Zone Review. https://www.acer.europa.eu/electricity/market-rules/capacity-allocation-and-congestion-management/bidding-zone-review. Accessed 07 Jan 2024
13. Graefe, T.: The effect of the Austrian-German bidding zone split on unplanned cross-border flows. arXiv preprint arXiv:2303.14182 (2023)
14. Granelli, G., Montagna, M., Zanellini, F., Bresesti, P., Vailati, R.: A genetic algorithm-based procedure to optimize system topology against parallel flows. IEEE Trans. Power Syst. **21**(1), 333–340 (2006)
15. Grinsztajn, L., Oyallon, E., Varoquaux, G.: Why do tree-based models still outperform deep learning on typical tabular data? Adv. Neural. Inf. Process. Syst. **35**, 507–520 (2022)
16. Han, C., et al.: Complexity and persistence of price time series of the European electricity spot market. PRX Energy **1**(1), 013002 (2022)
17. Hirth, L., Mühlenpfordt, J., Bulkeley, M.: The entso-e transparency platform – a review of Europe's most ambitious electricity data platform. Appl. Energy **225**, 1054–1067 (2018). https://doi.org/10.1016/j.apenergy.2018.04.048, https://www.sciencedirect.com/science/article/pii/S0306261918306068
18. Huisman, R., Huurman, C., Mahieu, R.: Hourly electricity prices in day-ahead markets. Energy Econ. **29**(2), 240–248 (2007)
19. Kavicky, J., Shahidehpour, S.: Parallel path aspects of transmission modeling. IEEE Trans. Power Syst. **11**(3), 1180–1190 (2002)
20. Korab, R., Owczarek, R.: Impact of phase shifting transformers on cross-border power flows in the central and eastern Europe region. Bulletin of the Polish Academy of Sciences. Tech. Sci. **64**(1), 127–133 (2016)

21. Korab, R., Połomski, M., Owczarek, R.: Application of particle swarm optimization for optimal setting of phase shifting transformers to minimize unscheduled active power flows. Appl. Soft Comput. **105**, 107243 (2021)
22. Kunz, F.: Quo vadis? (Un) scheduled electricity flows under market splitting and network extension in central Europe. Energy Policy **116**, 198–209 (2018)
23. Lundberg, S.M., Lee, S.I.: A unified approach to interpreting model predictions. In: Advances in Neural Information Processing Systems, vol. 30 (2017)
24. Marinakis, A., Glavic, M., Van Cutsem, T.: Minimal reduction of unscheduled flows for security restoration: application to phase shifter control. IEEE Trans. Power Syst. **25**(1), 506–515 (2009)
25. Meeus, L.: The evolution of electricity markets in Europe. Edward Elgar Publishing, Cheltenham (2020)
26. Mohanpurkar, M., Suryanarayanan, S.: A case study on the effects of predicted wind farm power outputs on unscheduled flows in transmission networks. In: 2013 IEEE Green Technologies Conference (GreenTech), pp. 277–284. IEEE (2013)
27. Newbery, D., Strbac, G., Viehoff, I.: The benefits of integrating European electricity markets. Energy Policy **94**, 253–263 (2016)
28. Nominated Electricity Market Operators Committee: Euphemia public description. https://www.nemo-committee.eu/assets/files/euphemia-public-description.pdf. Accessed 29 Jan 2024
29. Nord Pool: Day-ahead market. https://www.nordpoolgroup.com/en/the-power-market/Day-ahead-market/. Accessed 07 Jan 2024
30. Ovaere, M., Kenis, M., Bergh, K., Bruninx, K., Delarue, E.: The effect of flow-based market coupling on cross-border exchange volumes and price convergence in central western European electricity markets. Energy Econ. **118**, 106519 (2023)
31. Pütz, S., Schäfer, B., Witthaut, D., Kruse, J.: Revealing interactions between HVDC cross-area flows and frequency stability with explainable AI. Energy Inform. **5**(Suppl 4), 46 (2022)
32. Ronellenfitsch, H., Timme, M., Witthaut, D.: A dual method for computing power transfer distribution factors. IEEE Trans. Power Syst. **32**(2), 1007–1015 (2016)
33. Schneider, M., Barrios, H., Schnettler, A.: Evaluation of unscheduled power flows in the European transmission system. In: 2018 IEEE International Energy Conference (ENERGYCON), pp. 1–6. IEEE (2018)
34. Schönheit, D., Kenis, M., Lorenz, L., Möst, D., Delarue, E., Bruninx, K.: Toward a fundamental understanding of flow-based market coupling for cross-border electricity trading. Adv. Appl. Energy **2**, 100027 (2021)
35. Singh, A., Frei, T., Chokani, N., Abhari, R.S.: Impact of unplanned power flows in interconnected transmission systems-case study of central eastern European region. Energy Policy **91**, 287–303 (2016)
36. Staffell, I., Pfenninger, S.: The increasing impact of weather on electricity supply and demand. Energy **145**, 65–78 (2018)
37. Suryanarayanan, S., Farmer, R., Heydt, G., Chakka, S.: Estimation of unscheduled flows and contribution factors based on l/sub p/norms. IEEE Trans. Power Syst. **19**(2), 1245–1246 (2004)
38. Suryanarayanan, S.: Techniques for accommodating unscheduled flows in electricity networks and markets. In: 2008 IEEE Power and Energy Society General Meeting-Conversion and Delivery of Electrical Energy in the 21st Century, pp. 1–6. IEEE (2008)
39. Sweeney, C., Bessa, R.J., Browell, J., Pinson, P.: The future of forecasting for renewable energy. Wiley Interdisc. Rev. Energy Environ. **9**(2), e365 (2020)

40. Titz, M., Pütz, S., Witthaut, D.: Identifying drivers and mitigators for congestion and redispatch in the German electric power system with explainable AI. Appl. Energy **356**, 122351 (2024)
41. Wolff, G., Feuerriegel, S.: Short-term dynamics of day-ahead and intraday electricity prices. Int. J. Energy Sect. Manage. **11**, 557–573 (2017)
42. Ziel, F.: Modeling the impact of wind and solar power forecasting errors on intraday electricity prices. In: 2017 14th international conference on the European energy market (EEM), pp. 1–5. IEEE (2017)
43. Zugno, M., Pinson, P., Madsen, H.: Impact of wind power generation on European cross-border power flows. IEEE Trans. Power Syst. **28**(4), 3566–3575 (2013)

Green Hydrogen Under Uncertainty: Evaluating Power-to-X Strategies Using Agent-Based Simulation and Multi-criteria Decision Framework

Frederik Wagner Madsen[ID], Joy Dalmacio Billanes[ID], Bo Nørregaard Jørgensen[ID], and Zheng Ma[✉][ID]

SDU Center for Energy Informatics, The Faculty of Engineering, The Maersk Mc-Kinney Moller Institute, University of Southern Denmark, Odense, Denmark
{frm,joydbi,bnj,zma}@mmmi.sdu.dk

Abstract. The transition toward net-zero energy systems requires scalable and cost-effective deployment of Power-to-X technologies, particularly green hydrogen production. Despite increasing investments, a critical research gap remains in dynamically assessing how different operational strategies affect the feasibility of hydrogen production under real-world energy market conditions. Most existing studies rely on static, techno-economic models and overlook actor interactions, infrastructure limitations, and regulatory complexity. This paper presents a novel modeling framework that integrates agent-based simulation with multi-criteria decision-making to evaluate green hydrogen production strategies using co-located wind and solar generation. Three operational strategies—grid-only, on-site-only, and hybrid—are applied across three electrolyzer capacity levels (10 MW, 50 MW, and 100 MW) within a Danish case study. Real electricity tariffs, emissions factors, and market data are used to simulate technical, economic, and environmental performance indicators. The results show that hybrid strategies consistently outperform grid-only configurations in terms of cost and emissions while maintaining stable hydrogen output. Although on-site-only strategies minimize emissions and costs, they fail to meet fixed production demands. This framework offers novel scientific contributions by modeling dynamic actor interactions and integrating system performance evaluation into strategic planning. Practically, it provides actionable insights for energy planners and policymakers designing resilient and efficient Power-to-X systems in renewable-rich contexts.

Keywords: Green Hydrogen · Operational Strategy · Agent-Based Modeling · Multi-Criteria Decision Making · Renewable Energy Integration

1 Introduction

The global shift toward climate neutrality demands deep decarbonization of sectors heavily reliant on fossil fuels. In 2022, the energy sector alone was responsible for nearly half of global greenhouse gas emissions, necessitating urgent transformations in energy generation and consumption patterns[1]. While electrification and energy efficiency improvements are foundational to this transition, certain sectors—such as heavy industry, long-distance transport, and chemicals—are difficult to electrify directly. In this context, Power-to-X (PtX) technologies have emerged as a key enabler of sustainable energy systems, facilitating the conversion of renewable electricity into storable and versatile energy carriers like hydrogen, ammonia, and methanol [2, 3].

PtX offers critical benefits for integrating variable renewable energy (VRE) sources by enabling sector coupling and enhancing energy system flexibility [4, 5]. Among PtX pathways, green hydrogen production through electrolysis has gained significant attention due to its potential to decarbonize industrial processes and fuel markets. Denmark stands at the forefront of this transition with ambitious targets: a 70% reduction in emissions by 2030, 100% renewable electricity, and 4–6 GW of electrolyser capacity supported by strategic government funding [6, 7]. Flagship projects like Kassø and GreenLab Skive illustrate Denmark's leadership in integrating PtX into national energy infrastructure [8, 9].

Despite this momentum, major challenges hinder the effective deployment of PtX systems. These include high capital and operational costs, the need for advanced control strategies under renewable variability, and immature market mechanisms for hydrogen and e-fuels [14]. Additionally, PtX systems are technically complex, requiring seamless integration of distributed energy resources, electrolyzers, storage systems, and grid interaction. The economics of PtX projects are highly sensitive to electricity prices, tariffs, and operational strategies—factors that vary significantly depending on system design and policy frameworks [10].

Current literature primarily focuses on techno-economic assessments and energy system optimization of PtX configurations under static or idealized assumptions[7]. However, there is a lack of dynamic, agent-based modeling frameworks that simulate real-world PtX operation within evolving energy markets and tariff regimes, particularly at the scale of industrial on-site production. Moreover, limited research exists on how different operational strategies—such as grid reliance, hybrid sourcing, or exclusive on-site generation—impact the feasibility of hydrogen production across technical, economic, and environmental dimensions.

To address these gaps, this study presents an integrated simulation and decision-support framework that evaluates the feasibility of on-site green hydrogen production under varying operational strategies. The framework combines:

- Agent-based modeling (ABM) using AnyLogic to simulate the interactions among actors within a PtX ecosystem (e.g., PtX operators, electricity grid, renewable assets, transportation),
- Multi-Criteria Decision-Making (MCDM) methods (PROMETHEE, TOPSIS, VIKOR) to evaluate and rank the performance of different strategies based on key performance indicators (KPIs) such as production cost, emissions, grid usage, and storage needs.

A Danish case study simulates a renewable energy site comprising a 160-hectare PV installation and wind turbines, exploring three electrolyzer capacities (10, 50, and 100 MW) under three operational strategies: Full grid reliance (S1), Full on-site production (S2), and Hybrid approach (S3). Furthermore, the simulation results are assessed using MCDM tools to determine optimal configurations that balance cost, emissions, and infrastructure demands.

This work contributes to the literature by offering a novel dynamic modeling framework for PtX operational planning and decision-making, grounded in real-world tariff data and market mechanisms. It provides actionable insights for policymakers, planners, and investors navigating the complexity of large-scale hydrogen deployment in renewable-rich contexts.

2 Literature Review

2.1 Overview of Power-to-X Technologies and Their Role in Energy Transition

Power-to-X (PtX) technologies convert surplus renewable electricity into storable and transportable energy carriers such as hydrogen, methane, methanol, ammonia, and other synthetic fuels [11]. This conversion facilitates sector coupling across electricity, transport, gas, and heating domains, and is crucial for decarbonizing hard-to-electrify sectors such as heavy industry, shipping, and aviation [6].

Hydrogen production via electrolysis is a cornerstone of the PtX concept [4]. Hydrogen can be used directly or further synthesized into various e-fuels and e-chemicals (e.g., e-methanol, e-ammonia) [1]. These products support compatibility with existing energy infrastructures such as gas pipelines and storage tanks [3]. Moreover, emerging applications extend PtX's relevance to sectors like heat, desalination, and advanced materials (e.g., e-steel, e-carbon fibers) [11].

As Denmark transitions to 100% renewable electricity, PtX offers critical flexibility to integrate high shares of intermittent wind and solar power. PtX systems can act as virtual energy storage, helping mitigate curtailment and grid congestion issues [7]. Additionally, Denmark's policy and industrial context—strong offshore wind potential, progressive regulatory frameworks, and R&D investments—make it a particularly fertile ground for evaluating large-scale PtX integration [6].

Despite its potential, PtX faces several systemic challenges: high capital expenditures, fluctuating renewable supply, grid dependency, and technological immaturity (e.g., efficiency losses and degradation of electrolyzers under dynamic loads) [5]. These limitations underscore the need to explore and compare alternative operational strategies, such as full grid reliance, on-site-only generation, or hybrid sourcing, to identify viable business models under different boundary conditions.

2.2 Modeling and Decision Support Approaches for PtX Systems

To support strategic PtX planning, a variety of modeling and simulation tools have been developed. These include techno-economic simulation platforms (e.g., PyPSA, energyPRO), integrated energy system models, and process-level optimization tools that evaluate hydrogen and synthetic fuel production [12].

However, most of these tools assume deterministic conditions and lack the flexibility to capture the heterogeneous roles of system actors or evaluate real-time operational strategies across diverse market and tariff settings. Agent-Based Modeling (ABM), in contrast, enables simulation of complex ecosystems involving distributed actors—such as PtX plant operators, grid entities, and transportation services—and their interactions[13]. This is especially relevant for dynamic PtX configurations where infrastructure use, energy procurement, and hydrogen delivery are interdependent.

Complementing ABM, Multi-Criteria Decision Making (MCDM) methods have been extensively used to support infrastructure planning under uncertainty and conflicting objectives [14]. In the context of PtX systems, MCDM enables stakeholders to compare alternative operational strategies not just based on cost, but also environmental performance, storage requirements, infrastructure utilization, and grid impact.

Methods such as TOPSIS, PROMETHEE, and VIKOR are widely adopted due to their capacity to synthesize trade-offs among multiple quantitative and qualitative performance indicators [15]. These methods have been applied across the energy domain—from evaluating micro gas turbine performance to solar farm site selection and hydrogen storage options [16]. In this paper, MCDM tools are deployed to evaluate nine hydrogen production strategies (three capacities × three strategies) simulated through an ABM framework, aligning the decision process with real-world complexity.

2.3 Policy and Market Context for PtX in Denmark

Denmark's ambitious energy transition goals—such as achieving a 70% emissions reduction by 2030 and carbon neutrality by 2050—have positioned the country as a PtX policy and innovation leader [7]. Its national PtX strategy, introduced in 2021, promotes the deployment of 4–6 GW of electrolysis capacity by 2030, backed by a 1.25 billion DKK funding scheme [8].

Denmark's PtX ecosystem is supported by high renewable penetration (over 80% electricity from renewables), mature electricity markets, and favorable regulations that encourage behind-the-meter configurations and tariff exemptions for PtX operators co-located with renewable assets[7]. This legal environment enables flexible operational strategies, such as direct consumption of on-site electricity, that are modeled in this study.

Nevertheless, the economic viability of PtX remains precarious. Electrolysis is electricity-intensive, and grid tariffs can constitute a significant operational cost [6]. Participation in ancillary markets—such as FCR (fast activation time, low energy), aFRR (medium activation time, medium energy), and mFRR (slow activation time, high energy)—has shown potential to reduce Levelised Cost of Methanol (LCoM) and improve Net Present Value (NPV) of hydrogen projects [17]. However, commercial competitiveness is still hindered by the need for substantial price premiums for green fuels [9].

Given these market dynamics and infrastructure demands, assessing the trade-offs between full-grid, hybrid, and on-site-only PtX strategies becomes a critical task. This study simulates these strategies in a Danish context using real tariff data and evaluates them with MCDM tools to identify optimal pathways under realistic constraints.

3 Methodology

This study adopts a hybrid methodological approach combining agent-based modeling (ABM) and multi-criteria decision-making (MCDM) to evaluate the feasibility of Power-to-X (PtX) strategies under real-world conditions. Building on established business ecosystem modeling frameworks [18, 19], the ABM enables dynamic simulation of PtX operations by capturing how different sourcing strategies—grid-only, on-site-only, and hybrid—affect system performance over time in response to fluctuating tariffs, renewable availability, and actor interactions. Unlike static models, this approach reveals how operational choices impact hydrogen production reliability, cost-effectiveness, and emissions under variable market and infrastructure constraints.

3.1 Agent-Based Simulation Framework

The system under investigation is conceptualized as a business ecosystem comprising multiple interacting entities, each fulfilling distinct roles in hydrogen production, electricity procurement, and distribution logistics. These entities are modeled as software agents with dynamic behaviors and interactions.

The simulation is implemented using the AnyLogic™ multi-method modeling platform [20], which supports discrete-event, system dynamics, and agent-based modeling. Each agent represents a stakeholder in the PtX value chain. The key agents and their core responsibilities applied in the study are:

- PtX Company – Owns the electrolyzer facility; responsible for hydrogen production and financial flows.
- Operation Management System (OMS) – Oversees operational logic including dispatch strategy and storage utilization.
- Electrolyzer – Converts electricity (from grid or RE sources) into hydrogen; modeled with a non-linear efficiency curve.
- On-Site Storage – Buffers hydrogen output to align with transportation schedules and end-user delivery.
- Photovoltaic (PV) and Wind Turbine – Provide on-site electricity based on solar irradiation and wind profiles.
- Transportation Company – Manages hydrogen truck logistics to serve demand.
- Hydrogen Consumer – Purchases fixed daily volumes of hydrogen via bilateral agreements.
- Grid System – Provides electricity when RE is insufficient; includes interactions with:
    - o Distribution System Operator (DSO) – Applies capacity-based and time-varying tariffs.
    - o Transmission System Operator (TSO) – Manages day-ahead market pricing.
    - o DataHub – Supplies real-time price and tariff data to OMS.

The model simulates three electrolyzer capacity levels: 10 MW, 50 MW, and 100 MW, each with three operational strategies (grid-based, on-site only, and hybrid). For each experiment, the model tracks key performance indicators (KPIs), including hydrogen production, energy costs, CO_2 emissions, and infrastructure utilization (e.g., storage and trucks).

3.2 Operational Scenarios and Strategies

The model executes nine simulation experiments—three per capacity level—summarized as follows:

- Strategy 1 (S1) – Hydrogen is produced using electricity solely purchased from the grid; all on-site RE is sold to the market.
- Strategy 2 (S2) – Hydrogen is produced exclusively using on-site renewable energy (PV + wind); surplus is sold to the grid.
- Strategy 3 (S3) – A hybrid approach: RE is prioritized for hydrogen production; grid electricity is used only when RE is insufficient, and excess RE is sold.

All experiments consider a fixed daily hydrogen demand derived from electrolyzer sizing, assumed at 5,000 full load hours annually. Real 2024 market data on spot prices, CO_2 intensities, DSO/TSO tariffs, and efficiency profiles are integrated [21,22,23,24,25].

The simulation outputs a set of KPIs per experiment:

- Produced hydrogen (tonnes)
- Grid electricity consumption (MWh) and cost (DKK)
- Hydrogen production cost (DKK/kg)
- Electricity sold to grid and revenue
- CO_2 emissions (tonnes and kg CO_2/kg H_2)
- Electrolyzer utilization (hours)
- Storage and truck utilization rates

3.3 Multi-criteria Decision-Making (MCDM) Evaluation

To evaluate the relative performance of each strategy across competing dimensions, the simulation results are post-processed using three well-established MCDM methods [26, 27]:

- TOPSIS – Ranks alternatives based on closeness to an ideal solution.
- PROMETHEE II – Uses pairwise preference comparisons with outranking flows.
- VIKOR – Identifies compromise solutions based on regret and utility measures.

The decision matrix includes 13 KPIs (as criteria), standardized using min-max normalization. Each criterion is classified as either a benefit (e.g., hydrogen production) or a cost (e.g., grid electricity consumption, emissions).

To ensure fairness and robustness, criteria weights are derived using a hybrid method that averages:

- Equal weights – Emphasizing transparency.
- Entropy-based weights – Emphasizing information richness and data variability [15].

This integrated weighting approach balances subjective simplicity with data-driven objectivity.

3.4 Evaluation Workflow

The simulation and evaluation workflow consists of the following steps:

Model configuration with capacity and strategy inputs.
Agent-based simulation over a representative operational period.
Extraction and aggregation of performance metrics.
Construction and normalization of MCDM decision matrix.
Ranking of strategies using VIKOR, PROMETHEE, and TOPSIS.
Comparison and interpretation of method outputs to determine robust strategies.

This combined simulation-decision framework provides a scalable, actor-based method for PtX operational planning that is adaptable to evolving market conditions, regulatory changes, and infrastructure constraints.

4 Case Study and Scenario Design

4.1 Case Overview: Renewable Site and Hydrogen Production Concept

This study investigates the techno-economic feasibility and operational strategies of Power-to-X (PtX) systems for green hydrogen production in Denmark. The selected case simulates a PtX facility co-located with a high-capacity renewable energy site in a Danish context, reflecting the country's strategic investment in decentralized PtX production using wind and solar power.

The case comprises a 160-hectare photovoltaic (PV) installation and four 4.2 MW wind turbines, resulting in a total peak generation capacity of 272.8 MW. This hybrid RE configuration reflects realistic infrastructure scaling for future PtX hubs in Denmark, such as GreenLab Skive and the Kassø PtX cluster, and ensures a representative resource profile for evaluating hydrogen production scenarios.

The facility includes an electrolyzer system powered by both on-site renewables and the grid, with options for intermediate hydrogen storage and delivery by road transport. The operational model considers regulatory, market, and infrastructure constraints, including Danish grid tariffs, real-time electricity prices, and CO_2 emissions factors.

4.2 Electrolyzer Capacities and Design Assumptions

To assess scalability, the simulation models three electrolyzer capacity levels:

- 10 MW – representing pilot-scale PtX projects;
- 50 MW – medium-scale commercial plants;
- 100 MW – large-scale infrastructure aimed at export markets.

Each capacity scenario is evaluated using a fixed daily hydrogen demand based on 5,000 full-load hours of operation annually, in line with Danish hydrogen production forecasts. The key simulation parameters used across all scenarios, including tariff inputs, hydrogen density, and efficiency assumptions, are summarized in Table 1. Water use and waste heat recovery were excluded from this analysis to focus on electricity-driven process dynamics.

Table 1. Core parameters for electrolyzer case scenarios

Parameter	Values	Source
Electrolyzer capacity	10, 50, 100 MW	Assumed scale
Hydrogen demand (daily)	2,390; 11,952; 23,903 kg/day	Calculated
Electricity spot prices	2024 dataset	[21]
CO_2 emission factors	2024 dataset	[21]
Grid tariffs (TSO and DSO)	Dynamic for 2024	[22,23]
Electrolyzer efficiency	Dynamic efficiency curves	[24]
Hydrogen LHV	120 MJ/kg (33.33 kWh/kg)	[25]

4.3 Operational Strategies

Each electrolyzer capacity scenario is simulated using **three operational strategies**, designed to reflect varying levels of energy independence and market interaction.

- Strategy 1 (S1: Grid-Based). The PtX facility sells all on-site renewable energy (RE) to the grid and produces hydrogen using electricity purchased from the grid. This provides a baseline for evaluating grid dependency and associated costs/emissions.
- Strategy 2 (S2: On-Site Only). Hydrogen is produced exclusively using electricity from on-site PV and wind installations. Any surplus RE is sold to the grid. This strategy maximizes local energy utilization and avoids grid procurement costs.
- Strategy 3 (S3: Hybrid). On-site RE is prioritized for hydrogen production. When insufficient, grid electricity is procured to meet demand. Surplus RE is sold to the grid. This hybrid approach balances independence and reliability.

4.4 Simulation Parameters and Assumptions

The simulations are implemented in AnyLogic™ using an agent-based framework that models the interactions of key actors, including the PtX company, electrolyzer, storage tanks, grid operators, RE generation units, hydrogen consumers, and transport services.

All scenarios include real-world electricity market data (spot prices, CO_2 factors), dynamic efficiency curves for electrolyzers, and time-varying DSO/TSO tariffs for both consumption and production. Each experiment simulates one operational year, with hourly resolution.

The simulation tracks a consistent set of Key Performance Indicators (KPIs), including:

- Hydrogen production (tonnes);
- Grid electricity consumption and cost;
- Hydrogen production cost (DKK/kg);
- Electricity sales revenue;
- CO_2 emissions (total and per kg H_2);
- Storage and truck utilization rates;
- Electrolyzer full-load operating hours.

4.5 Summary of Simulation Experiments

A total of nine simulation experiments were conducted, representing all combinations of three electrolyzer capacities and three operational strategies. These are summarized in Table 2, which outlines the configuration of each experiment in terms of strategy, energy source, and daily hydrogen demand.

Table 2. Scenario–Strategy Matrix for Simulation Experiments

Experiment ID	Electrolyzer Capacity	Strategy	Electricity Source	Daily Hydrogen Demand
1.1	10 MW	S1	Grid only	2,390 kg
1.2	10 MW	S2	On-site RE only	2,390 kg
1.3	10 MW	S3	Hybrid (RE + Grid)	2,390 kg
2.1	50 MW	S1	Grid only	11,952 kg
2.2	50 MW	S2	On-site RE only	11,952 kg
2.3	50 MW	S3	Hybrid (RE + Grid)	11,952 kg
3.1	100 MW	S1	Grid only	23,903 kg
3.2	100 MW	S2	On-site RE only	23,903 kg
3.3	100 MW	S3	Hybrid (RE + Grid)	23,903 kg

5 Results

This section presents the outcomes of nine simulation experiments assessing the operational performance of three electrolyzer capacities (10 MW, 50 MW, and 100 MW) across three hydrogen production strategies (grid-only, on-site RE-only, and hybrid). Key performance indicators include hydrogen production, electricity consumption and costs, CO_2 emissions, and infrastructure utilization. Tables 3–5 present detailed results for each scenario, followed by an integrated MCDM-based ranking.

Scenario 1: 10 MW Electrolyzer. Table 3 summarizes the key performance indicators (KPIs) for the 10 MW electrolyzer configuration. Hydrogen production remains equal under Strategy 1 (grid-based) and Strategy 3 (hybrid), while Strategy 2 (on-site RE only) yields a 42% reduction in production due to intermittent resource availability. Grid electricity usage and emissions are highest under Strategy 1, while Strategy 2 achieves zero emissions and the lowest cost per kg of hydrogen. Strategy 3 offers a balance of full hydrogen delivery and reduced emissions and costs.

Table 3. Results for Scenario 1 – 10 MW Electrolyzer

Metrics	1.1 (S1: Grid-only)	1.2 (S2: On-site RE only)	1.3 (S3: Hybrid)
Produced hydrogen [ton]	868	502	868
Total grid electricity consumption [MWh]	49865	0	22267
Cost of grid electricity consumption [mDKK]	76	0	41
Hydrogen production cost [DKK/kg]	87	4	47
Total electricity sold to grid [MWh]	278536	248879	226102
Revenue from selling electricity [mDKK]	103	89	82
CO2 emissions [ton]	5170	0	2265
CO2 emissions [kgCO2/kgH2]	6	0	3
Electrolyzer usage [full load hours]	4987	2966	4987
On-site storage size [kgH2]	100	100	100
On-site storage utilization [%]	16	10	16
Number of trucks	2	2	2
Average hydrogen transportation truck utilization [%]	56	52	56

Scenario 2: 50 MW Electrolyzer. Table 4 presents the KPI results for the 50 MW electrolyzer case. Similar trends are observed: Strategy 1 and Strategy 3 meet full hydrogen demand, while Strategy 2 results in underproduction. Strategy 3 again achieves notable reductions in CO_2 emissions and electricity costs compared to full grid dependency. Infrastructure demands increase proportionally with electrolyzer capacity.

Table 4. Results for Scenario 2 – 50 MW Electrolyzer

Metrics	2.1 (S1: Grid-only)	2.2 (S2: On-site RE only)	2.3 (S3: Hybrid)
Produced hydrogen [ton]	4338	1735	4338
Total grid electricity consumption [MWh]	249317	0	156830
Cost of grid electricity consumption [mDKK]	378	0	262
Hydrogen production cost [DKK/kg]	87	4	60
Total electricity sold to grid [MWh]	278536	173287	109497
Revenue from selling electricity [mDKK]	103	59	36
CO_2 emissions [ton]	25848	0	16007
CO_2 emissions [$kgCO_2/kgH_2$]	6	0	4
Electrolyzer usage [full load hours]	4986	2105	4986
On-site storage size [kgH_2]	1000	1000	1000
On-site storage utilization [%]	36	21	36
Number of trucks	6	6	6
Hydrogen transportation truck utilization [%]	76	61	76

Scenario 3: 100 MW Electrolyzer. Table 5 provides the results for the 100 MW electrolyzer configuration. At this scale, Strategy 1 becomes prohibitively expensive and carbon-intensive. Strategy 2 maintains low cost and zero emissions but produces only 31% of the required hydrogen. Strategy 3 successfully combines production reliability with moderate emissions and cost savings. Again, the higher capacity electrolyzer increases the infrastructure need of both on-site storage and number of trucks, however the utilization rate of the infrastructure is better.

Table 5. Results for Scenario 3 – 100 MW Electrolyzer

Metrics	3.1 (S1: Grid-only)	3.2 (S2: On-site RE only)	3.3 (S3: Hybrid)
Produced hydrogen [ton]	8676	2732	8676
Total grid electricity consumption [MWh]	498633	0	359026
Cost of grid electricity consumption [mDKK]	757	0	589
Hydrogen production cost [DKK/kg]	87	4	68
Total electricity sold to grid [MWh]	278536	109497	32438
Revenue from selling electricity [mDKK]	103	35	9
CO_2 emissions [ton]	51695	0	36699
CO_2 emissions [$kgCO_2/kgH_2$]	6	0	4
Electrolyzer usage [full load hours]	4986	1690	4986
On-site storage size [kgH_2]	2000	2000	2000
On-site storage utilization [%]	41	25	41
Number of trucks	11	11	11
Hydrogen transportation truck utilization [%]	79	61	79

Multi-criteria Evaluation of Strategy-Scenario Combinations. Using VIKOR, PROMETHEE II, and TOPSIS methods, all nine configurations were evaluated based on 13 normalized KPIs. Figure 1 presents the ranking of the experiments using the three methods, while Table 6 summarizes the average scores. Figure 1 reveals consistency among the three MCDM methods regarding experiment rankings. Both PROMETHEE and the WPM rank Experiment 1.2 as the highest and Experiment 2.2 as the second highest. Conversely, TOPSIS ranks Experiment 2.2 first and Experiment 1.2 s. Examination of the KPIs in Tables 3 and 4 suggests that TOPSIS prioritizes hydrogen production and the utilization of storage and trucks, whereas PROMETHEE and WPM place greater emphasis on cost-related KPIs. Nevertheless, all three methods identify Experiment 3.1 as the least favorable.

From Table 6 it is seen that Strategy 2 consistently outperforms the two other strategies across all electrolyzer size scenarios, whereas Strategy 1 exhibits the lowest performance. Overall, Experiment 1.2 achieves the highest average ranking score of 8.67, closely followed by Experiment 2.2 with a score of 8.33.

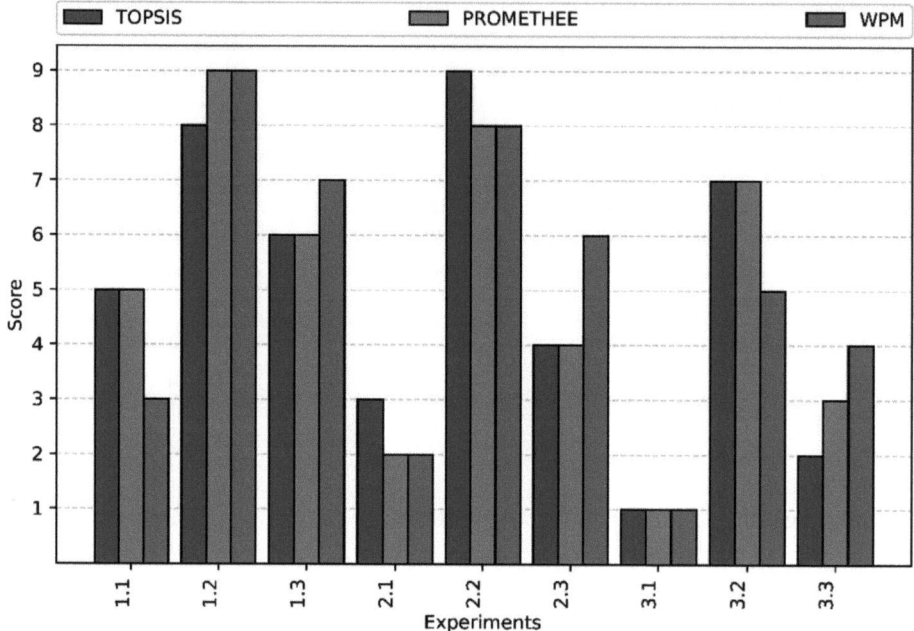

Fig. 1. Rankings of strategies under VIKOR, TOPSIS, and PROMETHEE methods

Table 6. MCDM-based ranking of experiments (average of 3 methods)

Experiment ID	Strategy	Electrolyzer Capacity	Average Score
1.2	S2	10 MW	8.67
2.2	S2	50 MW	8.33
1.3	S3	10 MW	6.33
3.2	S2	100 MW	6.33
2.3	S3	50 MW	4.67
1.1	S1	10 MW	4.33
2.1	S1	50 MW	2.33
3.3	S3	100 MW	3.00
3.1	S1	100 MW	1.00

6 Discussion

This section interprets the results in the context of existing literature, drawing conclusions regarding the scalability, emissions performance, and economic viability of Power-to-X (PtX) systems in Denmark and similar energy systems.

Scalability and Production Security. The consistent underperformance of Strategy 2 (on-site RE only) across all capacity levels demonstrates the practical limitations of relying solely on local renewables for firm hydrogen output. This aligns with [3], that PtX operations must accommodate variability in renewable generation through flexible system design and supplemental power sources. Strategy 3 emerges as the most robust approach, maintaining high hydrogen production levels while reducing dependency on grid electricity. This supports findings by [28] and [14] that emphasized the importance of hybridization and grid-assisted designs in achieving stable PtX operations.

Emissions and Environmental Implications. Consistent with [4] and [1], the study demonstrates that grid-based strategies incur significant emissions due to the carbon intensity of electricity, even in relatively clean systems like Denmark's. Strategy 2 eliminates emissions but sacrifices production quantity. Strategy 3 significantly reduces emissions without compromising output, which is critical in scenarios requiring consistent fuel supply to decarbonize hard-to-electrify sectors [5, 29]. This suggests that hybrid PtX systems are essential for meeting environmental goals while preserving system resilience, especially in transition periods before full renewable grid penetration is achieved.

Economic Viability and Tariff Sensitivity. Hydrogen production costs under Strategy 1 far exceed those reported in techno-economic benchmarks (e.g., [10]), primarily due to grid electricity prices and DSO/TSO tariffs. In contrast, Strategy 3 offers a feasible cost-performance compromise, aligning with analysis by [6], who reported significant cost advantages in hybrid configurations with dynamic market participation. The advantage of Strategy 3 also aligns with findings by Søgaard-Deakin and Xydis [8], who noted that optimal site location and tariff configurations can significantly enhance PtX economics. By using behind-the-meter RE and selectively accessing grid supply, Strategy 3 leverages regulatory provisions while securing supply.

Infrastructure Optimization. The simulation results confirm that larger electrolyzer systems dramatically increase storage and transportation requirements. This finding supports [3] and [11], which stressed the importance of logistics integration in PtX scale-up. The higher utilization rates of infrastructure under Strategy 2 indicate its efficiency in asset use, but this comes at the cost of reduced hydrogen output. Strategy 3 again balances infrastructure use and energy yield.

Strategic and Policy Implications. The superiority of hybrid approaches has clear implications for PtX policy design. As shown in this study and in the Danish context outlined by [7] and [22], policies that incentivize on-site generation with partial grid support—such as tariff exemptions or dynamic pricing—can enhance both the cost-efficiency and environmental performance of PtX facilities. From a system planning perspective, this study supports the EU Green Deal's call for regional hydrogen networks by illustrating how localized hybrid plants can anchor flexible PtX clusters, as discussed by [9].

7 Conclusion

This study proposed and evaluated an integrated simulation and decision-support framework for assessing Power-to-X (PtX) system operations under varying production strategies and scale levels. By applying agent-based modeling (ABM) and Multi-Criteria Decision-Making (MCDM) methods, the paper explored how different operational configurations—full-grid reliance, exclusive on-site renewables, and hybrid sourcing—impact the techno-economic feasibility, environmental performance, and infrastructure requirements of green hydrogen production in Denmark.

The results demonstrate that while on-site renewable-only strategies offer the lowest emissions and production costs, they consistently fail to meet fixed hydrogen demand across all electrolyzer capacity levels. Grid-based strategies, by contrast, meet production targets but suffer from significantly higher emissions and electricity costs due to their dependence on market-based electricity prices and tariffs. Hybrid strategies emerge as a robust middle ground, achieving full production volumes while considerably reducing emissions and costs compared to grid-only approaches. This strategic balance is further supported by the MCDM results, where hybrid strategies consistently ranked high across multiple performance indicators and decision criteria.

Scientifically, this study contributes a novel combination of ABM and MCDM techniques for dynamic, actor-based PtX system analysis—addressing a critical gap in existing literature, which often relies on static or deterministic techno-economic models. The proposed methodology not only allows for a granular simulation of stakeholder interactions and market constraints but also enhances decision quality by incorporating environmental, operational, and infrastructural trade-offs into an integrated evaluation framework.

Practically, the findings offer concrete insights for PtX developers, policymakers, and system planners. The hybrid model presented here aligns with Denmark's PtX strategy and demonstrates how partial reliance on the grid, combined with behind-the-meter renewable production, can improve cost efficiency while mitigating carbon emissions. This supports ongoing policy efforts related to tariff exemptions, ancillary service market participation, and infrastructure planning for decentralized PtX deployment.

Nonetheless, the study presents several limitations. First, the simulation assumes constant electrolyzer efficiency and does not account for degradation effects, which could influence long-term viability. Second, the scope of KPIs, while comprehensive, excludes considerations such as heat integration and water use, which are critical for full system life-cycle assessment. Third, while MCDM methods capture decision complexity, the weighting approach—though hybridized—may still introduce subjective bias depending on the use case.

To address these limitations, future work should extend the model to include component degradation, water consumption, and thermal energy recovery. Integration with carbon capture and e-fuel synthesis pathways would also enhance relevance for sector coupling scenarios. Furthermore, additional MCDM sensitivity analysis or stakeholder-informed weighting schemes could improve robustness and applicability in participatory planning contexts. A regional-scale extension of the simulation framework—such as linking multiple PtX hubs or evaluating national PtX deployment strategies—would offer further value for system-level optimization and investment planning.

In summary, this paper advances both methodological and applied understanding of PtX operations in renewable-rich energy systems. The proposed framework provides a scalable foundation for evaluating real-world PtX strategies under dynamic and uncertain market conditions, and supports the responsible, data-driven deployment of green hydrogen infrastructure across Denmark and beyond.

Acknowledgments. This paper is part of the project "INNOMISSION II: MissionGreenFuel-Digitalization and test for dynamic and flexible operation of PtX components and systems (DYNFLEX)" funded by Innovation Fund Denmark; Part of the project titled "Danish Participation in IEA IETS Task XXI - Decarbonizing industrial systems in a circular economy framework", funded by EUDP (project number: 134233-511205); Part of the project titled "Danish participation in IEA IETS Task XXII - Climate Resilience and Energy Adaptation in Industry under Uncertainty", funded by EUDP (project number: 95–41006-2410288).

Disclosure of Interests. The authors have no competing interests to declare that are relevant to the content of this article.

References

1. Majanne, Y., et al.: Integration of Power to X Economy in existing energy system – case Finland. IFAC-PapersOnLine **58**(13), 739–744 (2024)
2. Mohammed, R.K., Farzaneh, H.: Power-to-X in Southern Iraq: techno-economic assessment of solar-powered hydrogen electrolysis combined with carbon capture and storage for sustainable energy solutions. Energy Conv. Manag. X **26**, 100918 (2025)
3. Bram, M.V., et al.: Challenges in Power-to-X: a perspective of the configuration and control process for E-methanol production. Int. J. Hydrogen Energy **76**, 315–325 (2024)
4. Skov, I.R., et al.: Power-to-X in Denmark: an analysis of strengths, weaknesses, opportunities and threats. Energies **14**(4), 913 (2021)
5. Battaglia, V., Vanoli, L.: Optimizing renewable energy integration in new districts: power-to-X strategies for improved efficiency and sustainability. Energy **305**, 132312 (2024)
6. Andreae, E., et al.: Cost minimization of a hybrid PV-to-methanol plant through participation in reserve markets: a Danish case study. Int. J. Hydrogen Energy **68**, 190–201 (2024)
7. Nielsen, F.D., Skov, I.R., Sorknæs, P.: Feasibility of integrating excess heat from power-to-methanol: case study of a Danish district heating network. Appl. Energy **386**, 125590 (2025)
8. Søgaard-Deakin, J., Xydis, G.: Prefeasibility study on optimal site location for Power-to-X: an experiment for the Danish energy system. Energy Rep. **12**, 1859–1875 (2024)
9. Kountouris, I., et al.: Power-to-X in energy hubs: a Danish case study of renewable fuel production. Energy Policy **175**, 113439 (2023)
10. Zhu, M., et al.: Techno-economic analysis of green hydrogen production using a 100 MW photovoltaic power generation system for five cities in North and Northwest China. Sol. Energy **269**, 112312 (2024)

11. Khalili, S., Lopez, G., Breyer, C.: Role and trends of flexibility options in 100% renewable energy system analyses towards the power-to-X economy. Renew. Sustain. Energy Rev. **212**, 115383 (2025)
12. Taslimi, M.S., et al.: Optimization and analysis of methanol production from CO2 and solar-driven hydrogen production: a Danish case study. Int. J. Hydrogen Energy **69**, 466–476 (2024)
13. Abdullah, A.G., et al.: Multi-criteria decision-making for wind power project feasibility: trends, techniques, and future directions. Cleaner Eng. Technol. **27**, 100987 (2025)
14. Wu, L., et al.: Site selection for underground bio-methanation of hydrogen and carbon dioxide using an integrated multi-criteria decision-making (MCDM) approach. Energy **306**, 132437 (2024)
15. Espie, P., Ault, G.W., McDonald, J.R.: Multiple criteria decision making in distribution utility investment planning. in DRPT2000. In: International Conference on Electric Utility Deregulation and Restructuring and Power Technologies. Proceedings (Cat. No.00EX382) (2000)
16. Yifan, J., et al.: Assessment of the photovoltaic potential at urban level based on parameterization and multi criteria decision-making (MCDM): a case study and new methodological approach. Energy Sustain. Dev. **83**, 101585 (2024)
17. Zheng, Y., et al.: Economic evaluation of a power-to-hydrogen system providing frequency regulation reserves: a case study of Denmark. Int. J. Hydrogen Energy **48**(67), 26046–26057 (2023)
18. Ma, Z.: Business ecosystem modeling- the hybrid of system modeling and ecological modeling: an application of the smart grid. Energy Info. **2**(1), 35 (2019)
19. Værbak, M., et al.: A generic agent-based framework for modeling business ecosystems: a case study of electric vehicle home charging. Energy Informatics **4**(2), 28 (2021)
20. AnyLogic. [.Accessed 15 May 2025]. Available from: https://www.anylogic.com/
21. Service, E.D. [.Accessed 05 May 2025]. Available from: https://www.energidataservice.dk/
22. Energinet. [.Accessed 15 April 2025]. Available from: https://energinet.dk/
23. Elnetselskabet N1. [.Accessed 16 April 2025]. Available from: https://n1.dk/
24. Liponi, A., et al., Techno-economic analysis of hydrogen production from PV plants. E3S Web Conf. **334** (2022)
25. Danish Energy Agency. *Technology Data for Renewable Fuels*. [cited 2025 03–04]; Available from: https://ens.dk/en/analyses-and-statistics/technology-data-renewable-fuels
26. Hosouli, S., Hassani, R.A.: Application of multi-criteria decision making (MCDM) model for solar plant location selection. Results Eng. **24**, 103162 (2024)
27. Hosouli, S., et al.: Optimizing photovoltaic thermal (PVT) collector selection: a multi-criteria decision-making (MCDM) approach for renewable energy systems. Heliyon **10**(6), e27605 (2024)
28. Kim, J., et al.: Revealing the impact of renewable uncertainty on grid-assisted power-to-X: A data-driven reliability-based design optimization approach. Appl. Energy **339**, 121015 (2023)
29. Samitha Weerakoon, A.H., Assadi, M.: Techno economic analysis and performance based ranking of 3–200 kW fuel flexible micro gas turbines running on 100% hydrogen, hydrogen fuel blends, and natural gas. J. Clean. Prod. **477**, 143819 (2024)

Synthesizing Fault Localization Datasets

Zhonghe Chen[1](✉), Adi Botea[2], Paula Carroll[3], and Deepak Ajwani[1]

[1] School of Computer Science, University College Dublin, Dublin, Ireland
zhonghe.chen@ucdconnect.ie, deepak.ajwani@ucd.ie
[2] Centre for Intelligent Power, Eaton Intelligent Power Ltd., Dublin, Ireland
AdiBotea@eaton.com
[3] School of Business, Quinn, University College Dublin, Dublin, Ireland
paula.carroll@ucd.ie

Abstract. The reliability of power distribution networks is critical to maintaining the continuous delivery of electricity to all consumers and sectors of the economy. Fault localization plays a key role in minimizing downtime and repair costs. In recent years, a growing number of studies have leveraged machine learning techniques to enhance the precision and the speed of fault detection and localization. However, a major challenge remains: the scarcity of comprehensive datasets that capture the complexities of power system faults. This study addresses this limitation by developing an enriched dataset and proposing methods to mitigate overfitting, a phenomenon in which a model captures noise or patterns specific to the training data, impairing its performance on unseen data. By augmenting existing data with simulated fault scenarios, our framework improves robustness and generalizability, and reduces the risk of overfitting of machine learning models.

Keywords: Power System · Distribution System · Dataset · Machine Learning · Graph Neural Network · Fault Localization

1 Introduction

Modern electrical power systems are critically vulnerable to cascading faults, underscoring the urgent need for rapid fault detection and localization to ensure grid stability and prevent catastrophic failures [2,9,23]. A multitude of factors, including lightning strikes, high winds, animal interference, physical and cyber-attacks, electromagnetic pulses, and other environmental events, can disrupt power delivery to end-users. However, accurately identifying the precise cause and location of a fault's origin can be a protracted process. For example, the "ground zero" of the extensive blackout that impacted the Iberian Peninsula in April 2025 was only discovered on May 15th, 2025, and the definitive cause was still under investigation past that date.[1]

---

[1] https://www.euronews.com/my-europe/2025/05/15/spain-identifies-power-failure-ground-zero-as-search-for-iberian-blackout-cause-continues.

While traditional fault detection and localization methods provide a foundational framework, their high accuracy often relies on specific assumptions, such as linearity and consistent impedance [15]. Conventional techniques, including traveling wave and impedance-based methods, were primarily developed for transmission lines and encounter substantial limitations when applied to distribution systems. In contrast to transmission lines, which typically exhibit simpler, linear topologies and consistent line characteristics, distribution networks are characterized by greater complexity, featuring numerous branches, varied configurations, and fluctuating load conditions [1]. Consequently, the underlying assumptions of traditional methods frequently do not hold true in distribution grids, thereby limiting their reliability for accurate fault localization [27].

In recent years, machine learning (ML) techniques have achieved widespread adoption across diverse domains, ranging from natural language processing (NLP) and image recognition to healthcare diagnostics and autonomous vehicles. These advancements highlight ML's versatility and its potential to address intricate problems through data-driven insights. Within the context of power systems, ML techniques have also been increasingly applied to tasks such as demand forecasting, predictive maintenance, and fault detection [4,20,22].

Building upon these advancements, current research is exploring the application of ML techniques, particularly convolutional neural networks (CNNs) [19, 24] and graph neural networks (GNNs) [12], for fault localization in distribution networks. These models are particularly well-suited for this task due to their inherent capability to learn the complex topological features characteristic of these grids, with GNNs offering a distinct advantage in modeling spatial dependencies across nodes in networked systems [25]. By effectively leveraging data from distributed sensors, CNNs and GNNs can analyze temporal sequences and spatial correlations, enabling more precise identification of fault locations.

It is crucial to differentiate between fault detection, which involves identifying the occurrence of a fault, and fault localization, which aims to pinpoint the specific location or component of the fault's origin. While detection often presents a simpler classification problem, localization poses a significantly greater challenge, especially in distribution systems marked by diverse topologies and limited sensor coverage.

Despite the promise of CNNs and GNNs, significant challenges persist in their effective application for fault localization. A major limitation is the scarcity of large-scale, diverse datasets that accurately reflect a broad spectrum of network configurations and fault scenarios. Power system operators are often reluctant to share real-world operational data due to concerns over revealing sensitive infrastructure information, compromising system security, breaching confidentiality agreements, or disclosing commercially sensitive details.

The lack of comprehensive datasets significantly limits the effectiveness of machine learning models for fault localization. When models are highly complex and contain a large number of parameters, limited training data can lead to overfitting. In such cases, the models may learn noise and spurious correlations in the training data, resulting in strong performance on the training set but poor generalization to unseen network topologies. Overfitting occurs when a model captures patterns that are overly specific to the training data, including artifacts or noise, instead of learning generalizable patterns. Here, generalization refers to a model's ability to maintain high performance when applied to new or previously unseen system configurations, rather than merely memorizing training patterns. As a result, models that overfit perform poorly in real-world settings, where power grid configurations can vary significantly. Conversely, reducing the number of parameters to prevent overfitting can result in models that are overly simplistic, impairing their ability to localize faults accurately.

The fact that the learning models either overfit or become overly simplistic and the failure to find a hyperparameter setting that learns a generalizable model in between the two extremes indicates that the training data is not sufficient for learning such a model. It underscores the need for large, diverse datasets to train machine learning models capable of effective fault localization. Given the unlikelihood of obtaining large-scale real-world datasets in the near future – due to data sensitivity, national security, and privacy concerns – it is imperative to generate extensive synthetic datasets that realistically simulate fault behavior.

In this paper, we present a novel framework for generating large-scale synthetic datasets derived from publicly available IEEE and DISCO bus systems. Our datasets are developed using the widely adopted OpenDSS simulator and include a rich set of feature values for all network nodes. We intend to release these synthetic datasets publicly. This contribution not only improves the generalizability of learning-based fault localization models but also provides a valuable resource for future research in power system analysis. For instance, we demonstrate that the GGNN model proposed by Freitas et al. [8], when trained on our large synthetic dataset, exhibits significantly improved generalizability across different bus system topologies.

Contribution. Our key contributions in this manuscript are three-fold:

- We identify and analyze a critical limitation in prior work on machine learning-based fault localization in power distribution systems – namely, the tendency of models to either overfit or become overly simplistic due to the limited size and diversity of available training datasets.
- We develop a large-scale synthetic dataset by conducting extensive fault simulations using the widely adopted OpenDSS simulation tool. The dataset is derived from a variety of IEEE and DISCO bus systems, encompassing approximately 33,000 distinct fault scenarios and providing rich feature representations for all network nodes.[2]
- We demonstrate that the Gated Graph Neural Network (GGNN) model, when trained on our synthetic dataset, achieves high accuracy in fault localization, and more importantly, the learned model generalizes effectively across different network topologies.

Outline. In Sect. 2, we describe the work most closely related to ours. Section 3 presents our methodology for generating the synthetic dataset. Section 4 demonstrates that models trained on our synthetic dataset can generalize effectively

---

[2] https://github.com/Zhonghe-Chen/Gnn-Fault-Localisation.

to unseen topologies from the same distribution. Finally, in Sect. 5, we present conclusions, limitations and future work ideas.

2 Related Work

In the domain of power system fault analysis, ML techniques have been predominantly employed for fault detection and classification. For example, Support Vector Machines (SVMs), one of the most well-established supervised learning models, have been successfully used to diagnose faults using both historical and real-time data [12]. Bouchiba et al. [3] proposed a hybrid approach combining SVMs with deep learning, achieving improved accuracy in fault detection tasks across various power system configurations. Mrabet et al. [7] proposed a Random Forest regressor identifying both fault location and duration. However, their generalizability across different network topologies remains uncertain.

In recent years, advancements in deep learning have further improved the scalability and performance of ML methods, particularly for high-dimensional datasets inherent in power systems. Zhao et al. [26] introduced a deep Convolutional Neural Networks (CNNs) architecture for real-time fault localization in distribution grids under wildfire conditions, demonstrating the model's ability to handle dynamic fault scenarios effectively. Jana et al. [11] proposed a CNN-based transformer model for fault detection that combines convolutional layers with transformer blocks to capture both local and global patterns in power system data. Ren et al. [18] utilized CNNs for power system event classification and localization, effectively addressing complex fault scenarios by leveraging spatial correlations in sensor data. Zain et al. [16] developed a multi-output deep learning framework for fault classification and localization in photovoltaic systems, addressing challenges that are unique to that setting. To achieve high accuracy, their machine learning models are trained on an extensive dataset that includes 6,912,000 samples collected through automated simulation of a PV array modeled using PSCAD/EMTDC. In contrast, our goal is to generate a large synthetic dataset for faults in distribution lines.

Despite their success, neural network models that do not explicitly encode the topology of power distribution networks often lack robustness and struggle to adapt to variations in network topology and configurations. To address this limitation, recent studies have explored the use of Graph Neural Networks (GNNs) for fault localization, capitalizing on their inherent ability to model network structures explicitly [5,8,14]. For example, Chen et al. [5] applied deep Graph Convolutional Networks (GCNs) to fault localization in power distribution systems, leveraging the network's topological structure and electrical features to improve fault detection and scalability. Liang et al. [14] developed a fault localization method based on Multi-head Graph Attention Networks (GATs), which dynamically weigh the relevance of neighboring nodes and edges using attention mechanisms. In addition, Freitas and Coelho [8] utilized Gated Graph Neural Networks (GGNNs) that employs gated message passing to model directional current flow and fault propagation in radial networks.

GNN-based methods have proved particularly effective in adapting to the unique structural and operational challenges of distribution systems, offering robust fault localization even in dynamic network settings. Building on this line of research, our study evaluates the approach proposed by Freitas and Coelho [8]. Although their model is designed to generalize across different network configurations, our analysis reveals that when trained on the small dataset provided with their publicly available code, the learned model either overfits to the small training set or is overly simplistic struggling to meet the accuracy requirement. In both scenarios, the learned model is ineffective when applied to feeder topologies that differ from those encountered during training. A detailed discussion of these limitations is provided in Sect. 4. This motivates our goal of generating a large synthetic datasets for effective training of machine learning techniques for fault localization in distribution lines.

3 Methodology

This study primarily focuses on generating a comprehensive dataset designed to mitigate the overfitting and oversimplification issues encountered in previous research on power system fault localization. The methodology involves systematically simulating faults, constructing a detailed dataset, and verifying the dataset's quality and effectiveness through a Gated Graph Neural Network (GGNN).

3.1 Fault Simulation and Dataset Generation

We perform fault simulations using OpenDSS [6], a widely adopted tool for power flow analysis, focusing on line-to-ground (LG) faults due to their high occurrence rate [10]. Simulations are conducted on six bus systems–IEEE 30, IEEE 34, IEEE 123, IEEE LV, DISCO p1uhs21, and DISCO p1uhs23 [17,21]–selected for their diverse topologies and realistic representation of distribution networks.

We simulate faults at all valid combinations of buses and phases to ensure comprehensive coverage of possible fault conditions in the network, resulting in approximately 33,000 unique fault scenarios. For each simulation, we record four key electrical parameters at every node, both before and after the fault: current magnitude, current phase angle, voltage magnitude, and voltage phase angle, forming the first eight features. The ninth feature encodes the node type, indicating whether it hosts special devices such as transformers or reclosers, which significantly affect current and voltage behavior.

Reliable fault insertion across nodes and phases required careful handling of OpenDSS Fault objects and validation of phase connectivity. Before inserting a fault at a given bus, we checked its available phases using OpenDSS bus data— for instance, if a bus was connected only to phases A and B, faults were applied only to those phases, avoiding invalid configurations involving phase C. To introduce variability and prevent duplicate results, load multipliers were randomized by scaling each load's power consumption using a uniform factor in the range [0.9, 1.1].

In contrast to the original work of Freitas and Coelho [8], we make our network topologies undirected by replacing each directed edge with a bidirectional edge. Instead, we introduce voltage and current phase angles as node features to implicitly capture the direction of power flow.

Each simulated fault scenario is represented as a feature matrix of size $n \times 9$, where n is the number of nodes in the graph and each row contains the corresponding node's feature values. To rigorously evaluate the model's generalization and reduce overfitting, the dataset is split into training and testing sets using an 80:20 ratio.

The dataset used in this study, comprising all fault simulation results and extracted features, is available at our GitHub repository.[3]

3.2 GGNN Model for Dataset Verification

To evaluate the dataset's ability to prevent overfitting and oversimplification, we adopt a Gated Graph Neural Network (GGNN) [13]. The model takes a node feature matrix $n \times 9$ and an edge index representing the network structure.

There are several layers in GGNN. The first one is a Rectified Linear Unit (ReLU) activation layer, introducing non-linear transformations. Then the embeddings will be passed to a Gated Recurrent Unit (GRU). This GRU updates each node's hidden state by computing two learnable gating functions: an update gate that controls how much of the new information should be incorporated, and a reset gate that controls how much of the previous state should be forgotten. This mechanism enables each node to integrate information from its neighbors over multiple steps while maintaining stability during training. After message passing, dropout is applied to the node embeddings to prevent overfitting, and each node's final hidden state is passed through a linear layer that outputs a single score representing the likelihood of that node being the fault location. These scores are then passed through a softmax function to compute a node-level probability distribution.

Training is performed using the negative log-likelihood (NLL) loss function, which is well-suited for multi-class node classification tasks where only one node is labeled as faulty in each graph.

4 Results and Analysis

This section presents an evaluation of our synthetic dataset. Through a series of carefully structured experimental setups, we assess the effectiveness of our generated dataset and the trained Gated Graph Neural Network (GGNN) model under various experimental settings designed to test generalization, overfitting, and robustness.

---

[3] https://github.com/Zhonghe-Chen/Gnn-Fault-Localisation.

4.1 Motivation for a New Dataset

To highlight the need for a large and diverse dataset, we consider the GGNN model from Freitas et al. [8]. We ran it on the dataset reported in their paper and the provided train/test split. We observed substantial divergence between the training and test loss (see Fig. 1a). The training loss decreased rapidly converging to a low value (approximately 1.5 to 3), while the test loss showed minimal improvement even after 60 epochs (approximately 5.5) – clearly indicating overfitting (poor generalization performance). This overfitting stemmed mainly from limited training dataset size (around 600 samples) relative to the number of parameters (around 40,000 parameters), as well as insufficient variability and information content in the training dataset. This imbalance led the model to fit closely to the limited training data, failing to generalize effectively to the test set.

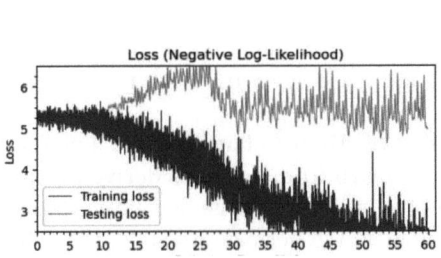

(a) Overfitting in GGNN caused by limited training dataset size relative to the large number of parameters in the machine learning model.

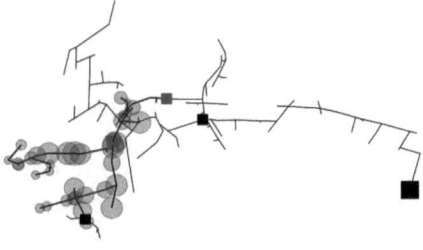

(b) With the reduced number of parameters, the learned model predicted equal likelihood for all nodes in the downstream of an open recloser (shown in red rectangle) to be a fault location.

Fig. 1. Experiment result using GGNN on a dataset from Freitas et al. [8]

To prevent overfitting, we gradually reduced the size of the neural network by reducing the number of neurons from 64 to 32 in each layer of GRU (that updates the embedding of a node based on its neighbor), reducing the number of hidden layers in GRU and reducing the number of neurons in the initial layer before the attribute matrix is passed to GRU. Overall, this reduces the number of learned parameters from approximately 40,000 to 10,000. However, this results in learning models that are overly simplistic. Figure 1b shows a typical fault probability prediction output of this reduced parameter model. In this figure, the circles around the nodes indicate the predicted probability of a node to be a fault location (the bigger the circle, the higher the probability). The red cross indicates the target fault location. We observe that the resulting model often assigns roughly equal fault probabilities to all nodes downstream of an open recloser. In other words, the model fails to differentiate between nodes located beyond the recloser on the feeder line, instead predicting that all such nodes had the same likelihood of being the fault location. While this behavior aligns with domain knowledge in power systems and suggests that the model has learned a basic functional relationship based on limited features, it does not go beyond this domain intuition and lacks the precision needed for accurate fault localization.

4.2 Experimental Setup and Objectives

To systematically evaluate the quality and usefulness of our generated dataset, we conducted experiments across multiple training and testing setups. Specifically, we designed three distinct experimental settings:

1. **Train and test on the same single topology:** In this setting, the model is trained and evaluated on the same network topology. This is to determine whether the model can learn the mapping between input features and fault locations when the topology is fixed. A high performance in this setting confirms that the input features are informative and the model architecture is functioning correctly. This setting is used to ascertain if our larger synthetic datasets enable the learning model to avoid overfitting and oversimplification and if the learned models can achieve good accuracy with both training and test loss reducing fast.
2. **Train and test on the same collection of diverse topologies:** The main advantage of GNN models is to be able to learn from datasets derived from a diverse range of network topologies. In this setting, a large synthetic dataset is generated from a mix of network topologies. We perform an 80:20 train-test split of the nodes in the collection of diverse topologies. A good performance in this setting will indicate that the learned model has not simply memorized the structure of a particular topology, but is capable of learning from faults in a collection of different network topologies.
3. **Train on multiple topologies and test on an unseen topology:** In this setting, we evaluate the generalization capabilities across network topologies. We evaluate whether training on diverse topologies helps the learned model to also be effective on different network topologies. If the learned model performs well, it shows potential for adaptation and robustness, suggesting that sufficient variety in training data can overcome the domain shift problem.

4.3 Accuracy and Generalization with the Synthetic Dataset

We empirically evaluate the accuracy and generalization capabilities of the GGNN model in the different settings described above. To ensure fairness, the same GGNN architecture (with around 10,000 parameters) is used and trained on the different datasets. Hyperparameters are fine-tuned for each dataset individually, as different network topologies exhibit varying structural properties. For example, graph diameter – the longest shortest-path distance between any pair of nodes – differs significantly across topologies. This property is generally correlated with the number of propagation steps required by the GGNN to achieve optimal performance.

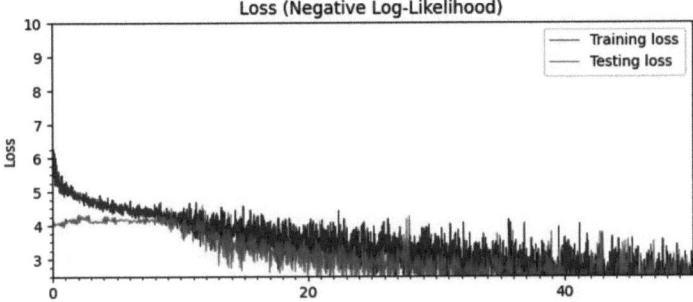

Fig. 2. GGNN training and testing loss on the synthetic dataset generated from IEEE 34.

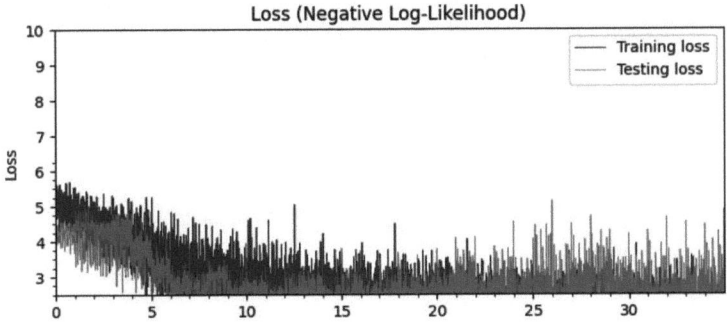

Fig. 3. GGNN training on our dataset synthesized from IEEE 123, IEEE 34, IEEE 30 and DISCO pluhs23, and testing on DISCO pluhs21.

We first consider the divergence between the training and testing loss in experimental setting 1 and 3. For setting 1, we consider the synthetic dataset generated using network topology of IEEE 34 bus system. Figure 2 shows that on this dataset, both the training and testing loss of the GGNN model (with around 10,000 parameters) reduce quite fast and in sync. This is in contrast to Fig. 1a where the loss on the test data didn't reduce and diverged from the loss on the training data. This indicates that our synthetic dataset using the IEEE34 bus is large enough to alleviate the overfitting issues on a 10,000-parameter GGNN model and the learning model trained on this dataset is likely to generalize well to unseen data from similar topologies.

For setting 3, we trained on a dataset synthesized from IEEE 123, IEEE 34, IEEE 30 and DISCO pluhs23 and tested on a dataset derived from a different network topology of DISCO pluhs21. Even in this difficult setting which tests the generalization ability across network topologies, we observe from Fig. 3 that the training and test loss reduce quite fast and they both converge to a small value. The results indicate that our synthetic dataset is large and diverse enough that the learned GGNN model is able to generalize across network topologies.

Table 1 presents the experimental results for these experimental settings. In this table, we refer to the dataset used in Freitas and Coelho [8] as "Baseline". The table includes results based on the Top-k evaluation metrics. Top-k (for k=1,3,5) accuracy measures whether the actual fault location is among the top k most probable fault nodes predicted by the model. Higher Top-k accuracy values indicate better performance.

Table 1. Fault localization Top-k accuracy under different experimental settings

Row No.	Training Topologies	Test Topologies	Top-1 Accuracy (%)	Top-3 Accuracy (%)	Top-5 Accuracy (%)
1	Baseline	Baseline	5.04	17.38	29.47
2	DISCO pluhs23	DISCO pluhs23	29.14	47.43	55.54
3	IEEE 34	IEEE 34	37.00	64.67	74.33
4	IEEE 123, DISCO pluhs21, DISCO pluhs23	IEEE 123, DISCO pluhs21, DISCO pluhs23	46.97	59.63	64.50
5	IEEE 123, IEEE 34, IEEE 30, DISCO pluhs23	DISCO pluhs21	45.67	66.27	71.27

Experimental Setting 1 We first observe that with the 80:20 train-test split on the "Baseline" dataset, the GGNN model of Freitas and Coelho [8] had a Top-1 accuracy of only 5.04% and a Top-5 accuracy of only 29.47%. In contrast, when our synthetic dataset based on DISCO pluhs21 and IEEE 34 bus topology was used (with a similar 80:20 split), the GGNN model (with the same architecture) achieved a Top-1 accuracy of 29.14% and 37.00%, respectively and a Top-5 accuracy of 55.54% and 74.33%, respectively. This clearly indicates that by training on these larger datasets, the GGNN model is able to avoid the oversimplification of the learned model and learns a more nuanced mapping between the node features and the prediction probability.

Setting 2 Row 4 corresponds to the second setting, where the model is trained and tested on multiple topologies, including IEEE 123, DISCO pluhs21 and pluhs23, again using an 80:20 train-test node split. The observed Top-1 accuracy of 46.97% is substantially higher than that in rows 2 and 3, where the model was trained and tested on single topologies, further confirming the effectiveness and general applicability of our dataset for training fault localization models.

Setting 3 Row 5 corresponds to the final experimental setting, in which the model is trained on four different topologies—IEEE 123, IEEE 34, DISCO pluhs23, and IEEE 30—and tested on a previously unseen topology, DISCO pluhs21. The high Top-k accuracy results in this setting suggest that the model is capable of learning some transferrable features from our dataset. It provides evidence that the GGNN model learned using our synthetic dataset generalizes across network topologies by avoiding the extremes of overfitting and oversimplification.

Table 2. Fault localization macro precision, recall and F1-score under different experimental settings

Row No.	Training Topologies	Test Topologies	Precision (%)	Recall (%)	F1-score (%)
1	Baseline	Baseline	2.62	5.09	2.86
2	DISCO pluhs23	DISCO pluhs23	28.61	20.78	23.29
3	IEEE 34	IEEE 34	26.47	14.56	16.88
4	IEEE 123, DISCO pluhs21, DISCO pluhs23	IEEE 123, DISCO pluhs21, DISCO pluhs23	45.79	29.71	34.31
5	IEEE 123, IEEE 34, IEEE 30, DISCO pluhs23	DISCO pluhs21	60.40	50.84	51.32

Table 2 presents additional evaluation metrics, including the macro-averaged precision, recall, and F1-score. These metrics evaluate the model's classification performance by treating each node in the network as a distinct class. Macro precision reflects the average accuracy of positive predictions across all nodes, while macro recall indicates the average ability to correctly identify actual faults. The macro F1-score, calculated as the harmonic mean of precision and recall, provides an overall measure of classification balance. Together, these metrics complement the Top-k accuracy by offering a more holistic view of model performance.

Across all experimental settings, the GGNN model trained on our synthetic dataset achieves significantly higher precision, recall, and F1-scores compared to the model trained on the "Baseline" dataset. The "Baseline" dataset yields macro precision, recall, and F1-score values of only 2.62, 5.09, and 2.86, respectively, indicating poor generalization and limited fault identification capability. In contrast, our models trained on our synthetic dataset consistently outperform this benchmark. The highest scores are observed in the setting combining IEEE 123, IEEE 34, IEEE 30, and DISCO pluhs23 (with DISCO pluhs21 as test set), achieving a macro F1-score of 51.32. This demonstrates not only improved accuracy but also strong generalization across multiple unseen networks. Even when trained and tested on individual systems, such as IEEE 34 or DISCO pluhs23, the model maintains substantial improvements over the Baseline, with macro F1-scores of 16.88 and 23.29, respectively. These results suggest that using a more diverse and extensive dataset enhances the model's ability to generalize fault localization across different network topologies.

5 Conclusion

In this work, we presented a methodology for generating a large-scale synthetic dataset tailored to the fault localization task in power systems. The dataset integrates simulated fault scenarios across a range of topologies and fault locations, enabling robust model evaluation.

Our results show that increasing the scale and diversity of the dataset, in conjunction with reducing model complexity, significantly enhances the generalization performance of learning models. This contribution addresses a critical gap in existing resources and supports the scalable deployment of machine-learning techniques for smart grid fault management.

Nonetheless, this study has several limitations. First, we evaluate only one type of neural network architecture. While our findings suggest promising generalization from Gated Graph Neural Network (GGNN) models, it remains unclear how well other architectures, such as attention-based or hybrid models, might perform under the same dataset conditions. Second, the current dataset omits edge-level features that may be critical in real-world fault analysis. Attributes such as line impedance, physical distance between nodes, switch status, and conductor type can all affect current flow patterns during a fault. Incorporating these features could improve model interpretability and performance.

Future extensions of this work can focus on incorporating edge-level features into both the dataset and the model architecture. Additionally, a wider range of fault types can be simulated to improve the dataset's coverage.

Acknowledgements. This publication has emanated from research supported in part by a grant from Science Foundation Ireland (Grant number 18/CRT/6183) and Centre for Intelligent Power, Eaton Intelligent Power Ltd. For the purpose of Open Access, the authors have applied a CC BY public copyright licence to any author-accepted manuscript version arising from this submission.

References

1. IEEE guide for determining fault location on ac transmission and distribution lines. IEEE Std C37.114-2014 (Revision of IEEE Std C37.114-2004), pp. 1–76 (2015)
2. Abedi, A., Gaudard, L., Romerio, F.: Review of major approaches to analyze vulnerability in power system. Reliab. Eng. Syst. Saf. **183**, 153–172 (2019)
3. Bouchiba, N., Kaddouri, A., Ounissi, A.: Power system faults detection based on deep learning and support vector machine supervised machine learning techniques. In: 2022 8th International Conference on Control, Decision and Information Technologies (CoDIT), vol. 1, pp. 1190–1195 (2022)
4. Carvalho, T.P., Soares, F.A.A.M.N., Vita, R., da P. Francisco, R., Basto, J.P., Alcalá, S.G.S.: A systematic literature review of machine learning methods applied to predictive maintenance. Comput. Ind. Eng. **137**, 106024 (2019)
5. Chen, K., Hu, J., Zhang, Y., Yu, Z., He, J.: Fault location in power distribution systems via deep graph convolutional networks. IEEE J. Sel. Areas Commun. **38**(1), 119–131 (2020)

6. Dugan, R.C., McDermott, T.E.: An open source platform for collaborating on smart grid research. In: 2011 IEEE Power and Energy Society General Meeting, pp. 1–7 (2011)
7. El Mrabet, Z., Sugunaraj, N., Ranganathan, P., Abhyankar, S.: Random forest regressor-based approach for detecting fault location and duration in power systems. Sensors **22**(2) (2022)
8. Freitas, J.T., Coelho, F.G.F.: Fault localization method for power distribution systems based on gated graph neural networks. Electr. Eng. **103**(5), 2259–2266 (2021). https://doi.org/10.1007/s00202-021-01223-7
9. Gjorgiev, B., Sansavini, G.: Identifying and assessing power system vulnerabilities to transmission asset outages via cascading failure analysis. Reliab. Eng. Syst. Saf. **217**, 108085 (2022)
10. Glover, J.D., Sarma, M.S., Overbye, T.J.: Power System Analysis and Design. Cengage Learning, 6 edn. (2012), see p. 430 for specific discussion
11. Jana, D., Patil, J., Herkal, S., Nagarajaiah, S., Duenas-Osorio, L.: CNN and convolutional autoencoder (CAE) based real-time sensor fault detection, localization, and correction. Mech. Syst. Signal Process. **169**, 108723 (2022)
12. Lal, M.D., Varadarajan, R.: A review of machine learning approaches in synchrophasor technology. IEEE Access **11**, 33520–33541 (2023)
13. Li, Y., Tarlow, D., Brockschmidt, M., Zemel, R.: Gated graph sequence neural networks. arXiv preprint arXiv:1511.05493 (2015)
14. Liang, L., Zhang, H., Cao, S., Zhao, X., Li, H., Chen, Z.: Fault location method for distribution networks based on multi-head graph attention networks. Front. Energy Res. **12** (2024)
15. Mamishev, A., Russell, B., Benner, C.: Analysis of high impedance faults using fractal techniques. IEEE Trans. Power Syst. **11**(1), 435–440 (1996)
16. Mustafa, Z., Awad, A.S., Azzouz, M., Azab, A.: Fault identification for photovoltaic systems using a multi-output deep learning approach. Expert Syst. Appl. **211**, 118551 (2023)
17. Palmintier, B., et al.: SMART-DS synthetic electrical network data OpenDSS models for SFO, GSO, and AUS. Open Energy Data Initiative (OEDI) (2020). Accessed 18 May 2025
18. Ren, H., Hou, Z.J., Vyakaranam, B., Wang, H., Etingov, P.: Power system event classification and localization using a convolutional neural network. Front. Energy Res. **8** (2020)
19. Rezapour, H., Jamali, S., Bahmanyar, A.: Review on artificial intelligence-based fault location methods in power distribution networks. Energies **16**(12) (2023)
20. Román-Portabales, A., López-Nores, M., Pazos-Arias, J.J.: Systematic review of electricity demand forecast using ANN-based machine learning algorithms. Sensors **21**(13) (2021)
21. Schneider, K.P., et al.: Analytic considerations and design basis for the IEEE distribution test feeders. IEEE Trans. Power Syst. **33**(3), 3181–3188 (2018)
22. Shakiba, F.M., Azizi, S.M., Zhou, M., Abusorrah, A.: Application of machine learning methods in fault detection and classification of power transmission lines: a survey. Artif. Intell. Rev. **56**(7), 5799–5836 (2023)
23. Stott, B.: Review of load-flow calculation methods. Proc. IEEE **62**(7), 916–929 (1974)
24. Vaish, R., Dwivedi, U., Tewari, S., Tripathi, S.: Machine learning applications in power system fault diagnosis: research advancements and perspectives. Eng. Appl. Artif. Intell. **106**, 104504 (2021)

25. Zhang, J., Tal, I.: A systematic review of contemporary applications of privacy-aware graph neural networks in smart cities. In: Proceedings of the 19th International Conference on Availability, Reliability and Security (2024). https://doi.org/10.1145/3664476.3669980
26. Zhao, M., Barati, M.: A real-time fault localization in power distribution grid for wildfire detection through deep convolutional neural networks. IEEE Trans. Ind. Appl. **57**(4), 4316–4326 (2021)
27. Zhou, M., Kazemi, N., Musilek, P.: Distribution grid fault classification and localization using convolutional neural networks. Smart Grids Sustain. Energy **9**(1), 1–17 (2024)

Machine Learning-Based Cyberattack Detection in Power Data

Robert A. Becker[✉], Nikolai Kamenev, Celina Koelsch, Aashay Kulkarni, and Thomas Bleistein

August-Wilhelm Scheer Institut für digitale Produkte und Prozesse gGmbH, 66123 Saarbrücken, Germany
robert.becker@aws-institut.de

Abstract. The broader context of this study lies in the growing importance of securing power systems against increasingly sophisticated cyberattacks. As power grids and other critical infrastructures become more digitized, the potential attack surfaces expand, making robust anomaly detection systems crucial. Smart homes, which increasingly rely on IoT-based devices, are particularly vulnerable to cyberattacks. These attacks can have grave consequences, such as breaches of privacy, property damage, and even physical harm. The growing use of these devices by consumers highlights the importance of protecting them as a key sociotechnical issue. This work is based on the findings of a previous study, where attacks on ten smart home devices were simulated, identified visually in their power consumption data, and grouped based on similarities in their time series data. The primary objective of the present study is to develop and evaluate various classical machine learning models for the automated detection of cyberattacks using power consumption data. Given that many of the IoT devices in this study are consumer-focused, the practical relevance of these solutions for real-world smart home environments is emphasized. The initial time series data is used to create new features which are well suited for real-time monitoring. The performances of various Machine Learning models are examined, and the best models in terms of time and performance are presented. The results indicate that Extreme Gradient Boosting is particularly well-suited for real-time anomaly detection in power consumption monitoring systems, offering both high accuracy and efficiency across different device types.

Keywords: Smart home security · cyberattacks · anomaly detection · IoT devices · consumer IoT · power consumption patterns · machine learning

1 Introduction

Smart homes and the integration of Internet-of-things (IoT) sensors transform our daily lives due to increasing digitalization and connectivity of everyday objects. They provide individuals with a convenient and efficient way of controlling and automating their homes and everyday devices. However, the spread of these internet-connected devices and the data which is stored have made smart homes vulnerable to a wide range of cyberthreats and attacks. Attacks on smart homes can have severe consequences, such as compromised privacy, property damage, and worst-case physical harm. Thus, the need for systems that can detect cyberattacks on smart homes is apparent, especially those that can seamlessly integrate into the everyday lives of users and enhance trust in connected home technologies. Those systems can automatically warn users about an on-going attack and can identify the associated problems.

Our previous research conference paper explored the potential of analyzing power consumption data generated by various smart home devices to detect cyberattacks (Title: power consumption analysis as a detection indicator for cyberattacks on smart home devices [1]). The work demonstrated the feasibility of using power consumption data for detecting hacking attacks and will be shortly summarized at the beginning of this paper. The research determined limitations and further research possibilities.

This present extensional paper aims to build on the previous findings by further exploring the potential of using power consumption data for detecting cyberattacks on smart home devices. The motivation is to develop a method for detecting cyberattacks in device power consumption automatically, with the assistance of Machine Learning (ML) models, thus providing an accessible, user-friendly solution that enhances household security for a broad range of consumers. The primary objective is to develop and evaluate different classical ML models for detecting cyberattacks, considering the insights gained from the initial study. The accuracy and possibilities of the various models are examined, and the best models are presented. The research question is whether automated detection of cyberattacks in power consumption is possible using ML-supported systems, and how accurately different models can predict them on different devices. Hence, the present study introduces a benchmark for ML models for power consumption analysis and the influence of cyberattacks on different power consumption patterns from various devices.

2 Summarization of the Initial Study

The initial study was part of the BMBF-funded research project KIASH (funding code: 16KIS1614, acronym for German project name "KI-gestützte Anomalieerkennung für Smart Homes") and aimed to investigate the feasibility of detecting cyberattacks on smart home devices through the analysis of power consumption data. For this purpose, a hardware testbed was built up in cooperation with Hochschule Worms. This testbed included ten smart home devices typically used by consumers in household environments. These devices were connected to an intelligent measuring device to simulate cyberattacks and record the resulting power consumption data. [1]

Several IoT-based cyberattacks, i.e., Distributed Denial of Service (DDoS) with different parameters, were simulated. Specifically, Internet Control Message Protocol (ICMP) flooding was conducted.

After analyzing the power consumption of the devices statistically, graphical representations were used to visualize the attacks. This initial study identified visible changes in power consumption data during cyberattacks for all devices. Power consumption increased during the attacks and decreased again after the end of the attacks. Depending on the device, different patterns in power consumption were observed during the standby phase and during the attack phase. Thus, the devices were grouped into four distinct categories, which are further explained below.

Group 1 (G1). Devices exhibiting a clear upward change in power consumption during the attacks, followed by a return to the previous stand-by power consumption. This group includes Apple Homepod, Amazon Alexa, Bosch Smart Home Controller, and Philips Hue.

Group 2 (G2). Devices showing small, intermittent spikes in power consumption during the attacks, both upwards and downwards. The group consists of Netatmo Weather Station, Netatmo Thermostat, Netatmo Alarm System, Homematic IP Access Point, and Google Nest Mini.

Group 3 (G3). Devices with occasional upward spikes in power consumption during the attacks, such as the Canon Printer.

Group 4 (G4). A subset of Group 2 devices that experienced a significant increase in power consumption for several hours following the attack, specifically the Netatmo Thermostat and Netatmo Weather Station.

In this extensional study, anomaly detection algorithms were developed, for minimizing false alarms and adapting to different smart home devices, as well as to detach detection from optical and manual detection for automatizing the attack detection. The previous findings suggest that monitoring and analyzing power data could provide a promising method for real-time detection of cyberattacks in household devices. Considering the device groups, different expectations are placed on the effectiveness of the ML methods for detection anomalies. We expect that the models trained on Group 2 data should perform less good as they only experience small intermittent spikes during the attack which should be difficult to detect. Group 3 devices should be easier to detect than Group 2 as there are occasionally prominent upward spikes. Since Group 4 devices have had a significant increase in power consumption for a long time after attacks, the detection via ML models is expected to be more accurate with Group 4 data than with Group 2 and 3 data. Group 1 devices have clear upward change during the attack and hence the detection is expected to perform best for the data from those devices.

3 Related Work

Several works have utilized network data to detect attacks on IoT devices. The studies mentioned in this section can be considered as a foundational paradigm for detecting cyberattacks on IoT devices. We will give a quick overview of these works and then move towards the approaches that utilize power data for the same task, i.e., anomaly detection from power consumption data.

The research of Krishnan et al. [2] achieved high accuracy in network attack detection using SVC, RF, and XGB on the IoTID20 dataset [3]. The models were able to detect attacks with remarkably high accuracy. However, they utilized only one month's data and for only for two IoT devices, which gives limited insights when dealing with different kind of consumers and long-term running devices. In addition, they did not use power consumption data since the used dataset is based on network traffic.

The work of Anwer et al. [4] was based on the NSL KDD dataset [5] which is suited for cyberattack detection. They trained three models on this dataset namely, RF, SVM and Gradient Boosted Decision Tree. Here, RF performed best with 85.34% accuracy, while SVM had the lowest accuracy with 32.38%. However, the system was trained on network traffic instead of power consumption data.

Abbas et al. used the CIC-IoT Dataset 2023 [6] for creating a detection model with 47 network-based features [7]. Deep learning models based on Deep Neural Network (DNN), Convolution Neural Network (CNN) and Recurrent Neural Network (RNN) architectures were trained. The model based on the RNN architecture achieved a remarkably high accuracy of around 96.5%.

The importance of data availability for detection model training is crucial as discussed in the works above. This is further supported by the findings of Haque et al. [8], who identified ten datasets suitable for the use in ML applications for anomaly detection.

Shi et al. [9] noted that using power consumption data for anomaly detection offers greater robustness as it is independent of the attack itself. Hence, changes in power consumption can still be observed even if the kernel of an operating system is compromised. This is not always true for network traffic data.

The following paragraphs discuss some of the important works that use power consumption data in different steps of model creation. In addition, we will evaluate the limitations of the usage of power consumption data as training data.

3.1 Data Gathering

In the works of Shi et al., Li et al. and Hernandes Jimenez et al. [9–11], data was gathered instead of using public datasets. Hernandes Jimenez et al. [11] collected both network traffic and power data from voltage rails in a testbed with Dell OptiPlex 755 computers, using Wireshark and energy meters, respectively. In the work of Shi et al. [9], energy meters were also used, by recording data over a few hours from four devices, including both malicious and non-malicious. In the work of Li et al. [10], 12 Raspberry Pi were used to simulate IoT nodes and their power consumption.

3.2 Data Processing and Feature Generation

In [11], the features were created from 30 min time series intervals in which either normal or malware-based software were executed. Seven power-based features and eighteen network based features were created which would prove useful for malware detection. In the work of Shi et al. [9] applied filtering and noise reduction, generated multiple features, and used PCA to reduce dimensionality to ten features. In [10], the data was pre-processed and interpolated to maintain the waveform and the sampling frequency of energy meters. Edge-preserving filtering was used to reduce the negative effects of noise. The data was finally normalized before passing it to the model.

3.3 Machine Learning

In the study [11], ten ML algorithms were evaluated, finding that combining network and power data is best suited for anomaly detection. If only one dataset is used, using solely power features performed better than network features. In the work of Shi et al. [9]

developed models for short- and long-term prediction. Li et al. [10] used a more complex approach involving two deep learning models and statistical analysis of prediction error to detect anomalies. The power consumption data obtained after preprocessing was sent to a modified seq2point model that was used as a model to disaggregate power consumption into three components namely, CPU, TX, and disk performance. These three components were then sent into an aggregation-based model to predict power consumption. The difference between predicted and actual power consumption was used to detect anomalies.

3.4 Limitations and the Presented Approach

Although there are several public network traffic data sets available to create models for anomaly detection, the same does not apply to power consumption data requiring researchers to collect their own. If they want to create models for anomaly detection based on power consumption. In general, all the approaches discussed above worked well, however the approaches which used power consumption data had the limitation that the data required prominent levels of data processing and complicated models to achieve satisfactory performance. The aim of the present work is to develop an approach for cyberattack detection using power consumption data with simpler data processing and classical ML models, minimizing the number and complexity of features while maintaining good performance across different devices.

4 Methodology

This section outlines the complete workflow involved in the implementation phase of this research. The **'Data Collection and Preparation'** section describes the process of obtaining data from the testbed and the creation of features from this data. Subsequently, the **'Data Splitting'** and **'Data Augmentation'** sections outline how the data was divided into distinct training and testing datasets, and how dataset imbalance was addressed. Then, the **'Model Training'** section provides a detailed explanation of the selected models, hyperparameter tuning techniques, and the cross-validation setup. Finally, the **'Evaluation Metrics'** and **'Time Metrics'** sections present the metrics used for model evaluation, along with a custom parameter designed to measure computational efficiency. In Fig. 1, a scheme of the methodology process is pictured.

4.1 Data Collection and Preparation

The power consumption data was collected from a network consisting of ten consumer devices. Cyberattacks in the form of DDoS were deliberately conducted on the network to generate anomalies that resemble real-world conditions. These anomalies are the basis for both training our anomaly detection models and evaluating their robustness. To be able to use the time series data with classical ML models, the power data was transformed by segmenting it into 2-min intervals. Then, for each interval, the following statistical features were computed: mean, median, and variance. To capture temporal dependencies, the same features were computed for the preceding 2-min interval. Therefore, for each device, we had the following features:

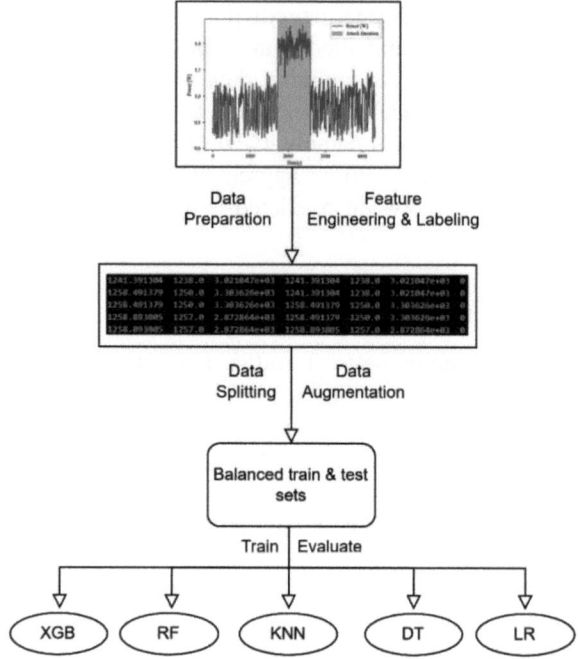

Fig. 1. The process from time series data to balanced & labeled datasets to the trained models.

Power_SMX_mean
Power_SMX_median
Power_SMX_var
Power_SMX_mean_before
Power_SMX_median_before
Power_SMX_var_before

where X represents the smart meter number of the smart meter to which a device was attached. Features labeled with the suffix "before" representing the power consumption features during the previous 2-min interval. The features from the previous interval were included based on the assumption that during an attack, at least one feature would exhibit meaningful change and that the difference between two intervals might play a crucial role for detection. Finally, each interval was labeled with a binary class if a cyberattack happened during that time or not.

4.2 Data Splitting

The dataset was split into training and testing sets using an 80:20 ratio. This split was done to ensure that the models were trained on a substantial portion of the data while preserving a separate set for evaluation.

4.3 Data Augmentation

Given the imbalance in the dataset, with fewer intervals labeled as "attacks", we used a random under sampling technique without replacement to reduce the number of non-attack data points. This technique balanced the occurrence frequency of attack and non-attack records, and thereby reducing the bias of the majority.

4.4 Model Training

We utilized the following ML models from scikit-learn to detect anomalies:

Random Forest (RF)
K-Nearest Neighbors (KNN)
Extreme Gradient Boosting (XGB)
Decision Tree (DT)
Logistic Regression (LR)

These ML models have several hyperparameters which can affect performance. Thus, the "RandomizedSearchCV" function from the sklearn package was used for hyperparameter tuning. Therefore, the parameters which lead to the best performance regarding the F1 score of each model for each device were determined.

Each model was trained using KFold cross-validation on the training set and subsequently evaluated on the test set. KFold cross-validation was employed to reduce overfitting and provide a clearer understanding of the performance of the models.

4.5 Evaluation Metrics

The performance of each model was evaluated using standard classification metrics such as accuracy, precision, recall, and F1 score. These metrics provided a comprehensive overview of the performance of each model.

4.6 Time Metrics

To measure the computational efficiency of the models, we tracked the time required for training each individual model and the time each model needed for 100 predictions. This efficiency measurement is particularly relevant for deployment in consumer IoT devices, where real-time performance is critical, especially when the software must be executable on weaker edge devices.

The measured times were normalized with their respective maximum values across all models and devices. These normalized training and prediction times are added up to form a new time metric called Relative Efficiency Score (RES). The RES is computed in Eq. (1) as follows:

$$RES_{i,j} = \frac{t_{i,j}}{max([t_{1,j}, \ldots, t_{11,j}])} + \frac{\tau_{i,j}}{max([\tau_{1,j}, \ldots, \tau_{11,j}])} \quad (1)$$

where i is a specific device out of the 10 devices, j is one of the following ML algorithms [KNN, DT, RF, XGB, LR], $RES_{i,j}$ is the Relative Efficiency Score of the ML algorithm

j for a specific device i, $t_{i,j}$ denotes the time for training the ML model j on the training data of device i and $\tau_{i,j}$ is the time for 100 predictions of the trained model j with the test data of device i.

4.7 Summary

This methodology outlines the process of data collection, feature extraction, data augmentation, model training, and evaluation used to detect anomalies in power consumption data under simulated attack conditions.

5 Results

We evaluated the performance of five ML models—KNN, DT, RF, LR and XGB—on their ability to detect anomalies in power consumption data across different devices in a network. Each point in our analysis represents a distinct device, providing an overview of model performance across diverse power consumption patterns.

Figures 2 and 3 illustrate the relationship between model accuracy and F1 Score with the RES. Relationships are crucial for the understanding of the trade-off between performance and efficiency in real-time anomaly detection systems. In the next paragraphs, we will highlight the general observations and insights of each model after evaluation.

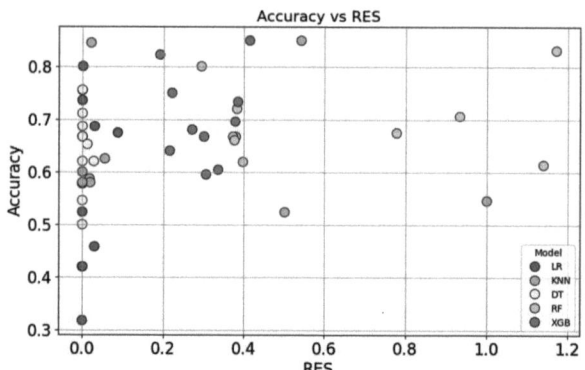

Fig. 2. Accuracy vs. RES.

As shown in Figs. 2 and 3, LR and DT models are clustered towards lower RES, indicating a fast training and prediction time in relation to other models. This is also reflected in the second lowest average prediction time as shown in Table 2. However, the accuracy and F1 scores of LR and DT vary significantly, ranging from ~0.30 to ~0.80. This means the performance of these models is highly dependent on the underlying data. Thus, LR and DT are computationally efficient, but they do not generalize well for different kinds of devices. Generally, DT models perform better with data from devices of groups G1 and G4 as shown in Fig. 4. This observation fits our initial assumption.

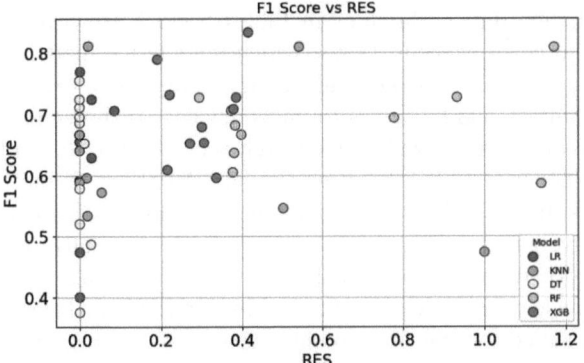

Fig. 3. F1 Score vs. RES.

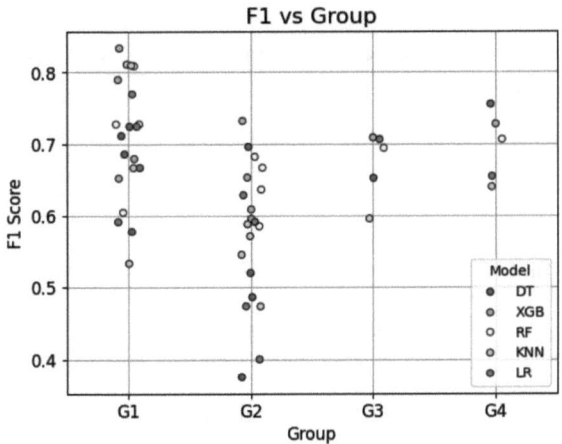

Fig. 4. F1 Scores in distinct groups.

Seven KNN models show a low RES, like the LR and DT models. However, three of the devices show a high RES in relation to the other models. Those three models were trained by using slow "brute" algorithm to find the nearest neighbors. Thus, the prediction time is in some cases remarkably high, which leads to a RES of over 0.4. As mentioned, the brute algorithm was chosen by RandomizedSearchCV to find the best parameters for the models. The accuracy and F1 of KNN models vary between values of ~0.50 and >0.80. However, the majority is clustered around a moderate performance (accuracy ~0.60, F1 ~ 0.60). KNN models perform worse for the groups G2-G4 and better for the group G1 as shown in Fig. 4.

RF models exhibit a moderate range of RES and accuracy and F1 scores. Four models have a high accuracy (> 0.7) and high F1 score (>0.7). No trained model shows a performance of less than 0.6 in accuracy and only one is slightly lower than 0.6 in terms of F1 score. The trade-off for RF appears to be higher computational time compared to simpler models like LR, KNN or DT as indicated by the high RES and the high training and prediction time highlighted in Tables 1 and 2. However, it was found that the prediction time never exceeds 31 ms, which renders RF models still decent for a real-time anomaly detection tool. Despite the high training time, RF models are robust, providing high accuracy and F1 scores for most devices, as shown in Fig. 4.

XGB models are characterized by their high accuracy (~0.8) and F1 scores (~0.7) with a moderate consistent RES between 0.2 and 0.4 (Figs. 2 and 3). As shown in Table 2, XGB has the second lowest maximum prediction time among all models and the third lowest average prediction time next to LR. Additionally, as shown in Fig. 4, XGB models perform reliably good over all kinds of training data of all four groups. Their superior performance over all device types and low and reliable training and prediction times make them suited for real-time anomaly detection on edge devices, where a high generalization is crucial because of heterogenous devices types in the environment.

Table 1. Overview of elapsed time during training

	DT	KNN	LR	RF	XGB
t_m [ms]	2.28	1.12	4.37	306.26	163.10
t_{min} [ms]	<0.01	<0.01	<0.01	164.89	95.69
t_{max} [ms]	15.95	10.11	17.11	572.65	230.29

Table 2. Overview of elapsed time for 100 predictions

	DT	KNN	LR	RF	XGB
τ_m [ms]	<0.01	39.17	1.32	16.12	3.22
τ_{min} [ms]	<0.01	<0.01	<0.01	<0.01	<0.01
τ_{max} [ms]	<0.01	183.29	13.16	31.26	10.09

Now, recall vs. RES and precision vs. RES will be discussed. Figures 5 and 6 show the relationship between recall and precision and RES, respectively.

LR models exhibit a broad range of precision and recall scores. For instance, one LR model for a specific device achieves a recall score close to 1.00, while another model for a different device attains a precision score of approximately 0.32. This variation indicates that LR models do not perform consistently well across different devices.

KNN models also display a wide range of recall scores, with precision consistently falling between 0.50 and 0.60.

DT models demonstrate recall scores between 0.60 and 0.70 across multiple devices, though there are outliers, with two models scoring below 0.45 and two others exceeding 0.90. In contrast, precision scores for DT models are more stable, with most models scoring between 0.55 and 0.65.

RF models consistently show high recall scores across all devices, ranging from 0.60 to 0.90. Precision scores for RF models fall between 0.55 and 0.65, with only two models scoring above 0.65.

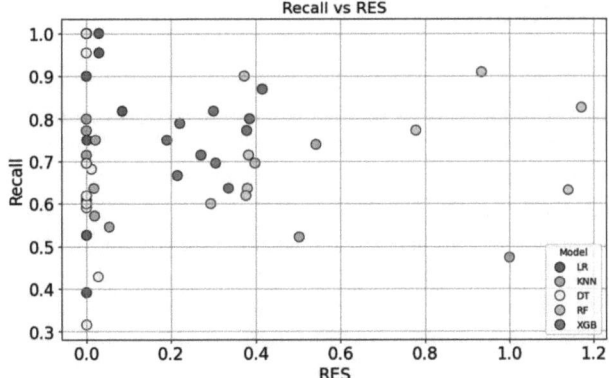

Fig. 5. Recall vs. RES.

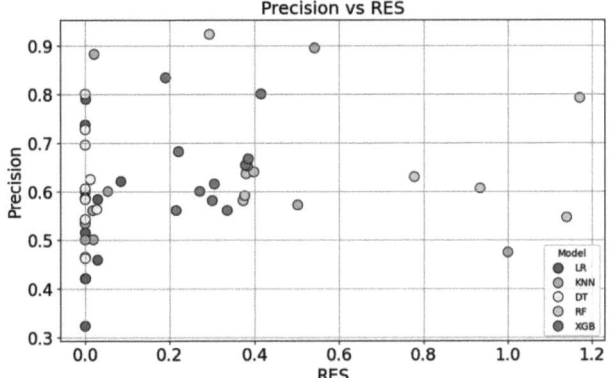

Fig. 6. Precision vs. RES.

XGB models achieve high recall scores, with all models scoring above 0.65. In terms of precision, all XGB models score above 0.55. Overall, XGB models exhibit the most reliable performance in both precision and recall across all devices. In general, these findings are very similar to the findings in accuracy and F1-Scores.

Overall, Fig. 4 shows the performance of models with respect to their F1 Scores across distinct groups of devices. Most models of Group 1 have F1 scores of 0.65 or higher. In this Group, there are models reaching highest F1 scores seen across all the groups (around 0.80). Group 2 models have the highest range of values, indicating no reliability in prediction. Here, models with F1 Scores as low as 0.35 are observed. Group 3 models performed well with majority values around 0.70 but not as good as Group 4 models where a lot of models can be seen to have values around and above 0.7. These observations are in line with our initial assumptions of the group's behaviors.

6 Summary of Results

The results indicated that LR and DT models do not perform consistently across different devices. However, DT models are by far the fastest models during training and prediction. KNN models perform well, but they are not efficient in terms of computational time. RF models perform very well in general, but they have high computational time. XGB models perform decently across all metrics and have low RES. The data on XGB models indicates that they are consistent in performance and in computational time, which makes them robust against different consumers and suitable for edge devices at the same time. These findings suggest that XGB is well-suited for real-time anomaly detection in power consumption monitoring systems, providing both accuracy, efficiency, and reliability. The observation of F1 score in the different device groups helped to uncover patterns. Models on Group 1 devices performed best followed by Group 4 and Group 3 while Group 2 models showed a high range of values models having the lowest values of F1 Scores across all devices. Here, XGB is among the highest scoring models in those groups.

7 Discussion

This study evaluated the effectiveness of anomaly detection models by identifying cyberattacks based on power consumption variations across different device groups. Our findings align with our initial hypotheses, revealing important nuances regarding anomaly detection in power consumption monitoring.

The varying performance across device groups shows the complexity introduced by diverse power consumption behaviors during attacks. As anticipated, models struggled most with Group 2 devices, where subtle, intermittent spikes in power consumption created a weak anomaly signal, which makes it difficult to distinguish between normal fluctuations and attack-induced variations. Suggesting that traditional anomaly detection models may require enhancements or supplementary techniques, like incorporating temporal context or leveraging more sophisticated pattern recognition methods, to improve detection in scenarios where anomalies are less pronounced.

Performance was better in Groups 1, 3, and 4 where clearer, more consistent attack patterns were present. Group 1 devices with their pronounced upward shifts during attacks, were the easiest anomalies to track. Highlighting that distinct signal patterns significantly influence model effectiveness. This finding is consistent with broader research in anomaly detection, which often finds that the more distinct the anomaly signal, the higher the model's detection accuracy.

These results have significant implications for real-time anomaly detection in smart homes. The high performance on devices with clear attack signatures suggests that traditional anomaly detection methods can be robust enough in such cases, essential for building trust and ensuring security. However, our environments are dominated by devices out of Group 2, our findings indicate that relying solely on traditional models may result in a higher risk of undetected attacks, potentially leading to severe consequences.

We anticipated all the models to face challenges with Group 2 devices, due to the subtle and intermittent spikes in power consumption during cyberattacks. In contrast, we expected that attacks on Group 3 devices would be easier to detect because of the occasional upward spikes in power consumption during attacks, providing a more distinct signal, albeit still limited. For Group 4 devices, we predicted a moderate level of detection, given the significant and prolonged increase in power consumption following an attack, which offers a clearer signal. Lastly, we hypothesized that Group 1 devices, with their pronounced upward changes in power consumption during attacks, would be the most straightforward for the anomaly detection models to identify.

ML models like XGB are good candidates for real-time anomaly detection systems, particularly for Group 1 devices, further work is needed to enhance performance, especially for groups with subtle anomalies. However, it is known that XGB's tree-based structure is well suited to resource-constrained (edge) devices because inference involves only simple conditional branches and additions. A trained model can be exported to a lightweight runtime such as xgboost4micro and compiled directly onto common HEMS controllers (Raspberry Pi, ESP32). With modest hyper-parameters ($\leq$ 200 trees, depth $\leq$ 6) the memory footprint remains below 1 MB and latency is typically <5 ms, satisfying real-time requirements. Integrating the XGB module as a plug-in to existing HEMS middleware (e.g., Home Assistant) therefore offers an immediately deployable path to decent-accuracy, low-latency anomaly detection—especially for Group 1 devices.

A key takeaway from this study is the necessity of tailored approaches to anomaly detection models and its devices. Instead of a one-size-fits-all model, which might perform well in some cases but poorly in others, a hybrid approach could be more effective. For example, combining ML models with rule-based systems or integrating domain-specific knowledge could enhance detection capabilities, particularly for devices with subtle anomaly signals.

8 Conclusion

The growing adoption of smart home devices has introduced a range of cyber threats that pose significant risks to privacy, property, and physical safety. This study extends previous research on cyberattack detection through power consumption analysis by developing and testing classical ML models for real-time anomaly detection. Our findings demonstrate that XGB is particularly effective for detecting cyberattacks in power consumption monitoring systems, offering a balance of accuracy and efficiency across various devices.

In evaluating different ML models, including RF, KNN, DT, LR, and XGB, we found that XGB consistently outperformed the other models in terms of accuracy, F1 score, and RES for training and prediction. These results corroborate our initial hypotheses regarding the performance of anomaly detection models, particularly the effectiveness of XGB on devices exhibiting distinct increases in power consumption during attacks.

The study's outcomes have important implications for enhancing smart home security. The use of power consumption data as a basis for anomaly detection presents a promising approach for identifying cyberattacks, providing early warnings to users and contributing to a safer smart home environment. Future research should aim to further improve the performance of these models and assess the applicability of this approach to a broader range of devices and attack scenarios.

9 Limitations and Future Works

The broader context of this study lies in the growing importance of securing power systems against increasingly sophisticated cyberattacks. As power grids and other critical infrastructures become more digitized, the potential attack surfaces expand, making robust anomaly detection systems crucial. Our findings contribute by demonstrating that while current techniques effectively monitor some devices, others pose significant challenges requiring further attention.

Although this research yielded successful results in terms of the objectives the researchers had in consideration, the following limitations were identified:

1. The process of obtaining attack data was difficult and only helps in creating systems resistant to similar kinds of attacks.
2. The research was only based on a two-minute time interval.
3. DDoS attacks were the only type of attacks considered for research.
4. Although multiple devices were considered, they do not represent the full spectrum of consumer IoT devices commonly found in smart homes, and they were all evaluated in standby mode. A more comprehensive study would require considering devices under various usage scenarios.

Future work should focus on:

1. Creating approaches such as autoencoders based attack detection that can capture the general trends of use and detect any deviant behavior.
2. Trying out different time intervals. It would be insightful to see how robustness of models varies based on different time intervals.
3. Checking the robustness of the approach in response to other types of attacks.
4. How well the models perform when data is logged in actual consumer environments, considering more categories of devices available in smart homes. Future work should also aim to simulate real-world usage patterns to better understand the practical applications of anomaly detection systems.

The main goal of future works should be to create a system that can experiment and deploy best-suited models for individual devices, which, when paired with Home Energy Management Systems (HEMS), will make smart homes much more secure.

Acknowledgements. This research was conducted as part of the KIASH project funded by Federal Ministry of Education and Research of Germany under the "KMU-innovativ" initiative. We are grateful for the invaluable support provided by "Hochschule Worms, University of Applied Sciences" during the initial study for creating the testbed and simulating the cyberattacks.

Data Availability. The datasets generated and analyzed during the current study are available from the corresponding author upon reasonable request.

References

1. Schorr, V., Kamenev, N., Bleistein, T., Werth, D., Wendzel, S., Weigold, T.: Power consumption analysis as a detection indicator for cyberattacks on smart home devices. In: Jørgensen, B.N., da Silva, L.C.P., Ma, Z. (eds.) Energy Informatics. EI.A 2023. LNCS, vol. 14468. Springer, Cham (2023). https://doi.org/10.1007/978-3-031-48652-4_15
2. Krishnan, S., Neyaz, A., Liu, Q.: IoT network attack detection using supervised machine learning **10**, 18–32 (2021)
3. Ullah, Mahmoud, Q.: A scheme for generating a dataset for anomalous activity detection in IoT networks, pp. 508–520 (2020)
4. Anwer, M., Khan, S.M., Farooq, M.U., Waseemullah, N.: Attack detection in IoT using machine learning. Eng. Technol. Appl. Sci. Res **11**(3), 7273–7278 (2021)
5. Tavallaee, M., Bagheri, E., Lu, W., Ghorbani, A.A.: A detailed analysis of the KDD CUP 99 data set. In: 2009 IEEE Symposium on Computational Intelligence for Security and Defense Applications, pp. 1–6 (2009)
6. Neto, E.C.P., Dadkhah, S., Ferreira, R., Zohourian, A., Lu, R., Ghorbani, A.A.: CICIoT2023: a real-time dataset and benchmark for large-scale attacks in IoT environment. Sensors **23** (2023)
7. Abbas, S., et al.: Evaluating deep learning variants for cyber-attacks detection and multi-class classification in IoT networks. PeerJ Comput. Sci. **10**, e1793 (2024). https://doi.org/10.7717/peerj-cs.1793
8. Haque, S., El-Moussa, F., Komninos, N., Muttukrishnan, R.: A systematic review of data-driven attack detection trends in IoT. Sensors **23**(16), 7191 (2023). https://doi.org/10.3390/s23167191
9. Shi, Y., Li, F., Song, W., Li, X.-Y., Ye, J.: Energy audition based cyber-physical attack detection system in IoT. In: Proceedings of the ACM Turing Celebration Conference - China (ACM TURC '19). Association for Computing Machinery, New York, NY, USA, Article 27, 1–5. https://doi.org/10.1145/3321408.3321588, 2019
10. Li, F., Shi, Y., Shinde, A., Ye, J., Song, W.: Enhanced cyber-physical security in internet of things through energy auditing **6**, 5224–5231 (2019). https://doi.org/10.1109/JIOT.2019.2899492
11. Hernandes Jimenez, J., Goseva-Popstojanova, K.: Malware detection using power consumption and network traffic data (2019). https://doi.org/10.1109/ICDIS.2019.00016

Optimization of Second-Life Battery Energy Storage System in Buildings with Photovoltaic Panels: A Norwegian Case Study

Italo Aldo Campodonico-Avendano[1](✉), Amin Moazami[1,2], Aileen Yang[2], and Hicham Johra[2]

[1] Department of Ocean Operations and Civil Engineering, Faculty of Engineering, NTNU, Larsgårdsvegen 2, 6009 Ålesund, Norway
  `italo.a.c.avendano@ntnu.no`
[2] SINTEF Community, Børrestuveien 3, 0373 Oslo, Norway

Abstract. This study investigates the techno-economic feasibility of deploying a second-life battery energy storage system (BESS), using a school in Oslo, Norway, as a pilot case. A mixed-integer linear programming (MILP) model is developed to evaluate the performance of one to six second-life battery modules (40 kWh/20 kW each), integrated with on-site photovoltaic (PV) generation. Two operational strategies are assessed: a baseline case involving self-consumption and dynamic price optimization, and a local flexibility market (LFM) case that enables the system to provide capacity reserves. The model used 2024 load and generation measured data to simulate energy flows and economic performance. Under the baseline scenario, a system with six second-life battery modules had a simple payback period of approximately 11.4 years. Participation in the LFM significantly improved economic outcomes, reducing the payback period by 1.4 years, given the current market activation rates. The findings indicate that second-life BESS can be economically viable in non-residential buildings, especially when integrated into LFM. Additionally, targeted subsidies and improved on-site solar self-consumption can enhance the attractiveness of these investments by offsetting capital costs and increasing the value derived from energy. These results highlight the potential of second-life batteries as a cost-effective solution for storage and flexibility, as well as for supporting broader energy transition goals by extending battery lifespans and promoting circular energy practices.

Keywords: Battery Energy Storage Systems (BESS) · Second-life · PV generation · Dynamic Prices · Local Flexibility Market

1 Introduction

In 2020, the steps toward a clean energy transition were established by the European Union (EU) through the European Green Deal [1]. Alongside the expansion of renewable energy generation, the electrification of the demand side is identified as a central measure to support this transition. In this context, Norway is presented as a leading example. The

© The Author(s), under exclusive license to Springer Nature Switzerland AG 2026
I. Martinac et al. (Eds.): EIA Nordic 2025, LNCS 16096, pp. 300–317, 2026.
https://doi.org/10.1007/978-3-032-03098-6_20

electrification rate in the building sector reaches 81% (2020), mainly driven by a national total ban on oil- and gas-based heating technologies [2]. In parallel, Norway stands out as a global leader in the adoption of electric vehicles (EVs) [3].

From the early 1990s, the Norwegian government introduced several fiscal incentives to accelerate EV adoption. As a result, by 2024, 34.9% of the vehicle stock consists of electric or plug-in hybrid vehicles, and 88.9% of newly registered vehicles are fully electric [4]. These developments create new opportunities but also introduce challenges. In 2022, Norway experienced the highest electricity prices on record [5], while in areas such as Oslo, there is a lack of capacity for new customers (2024) [6].

Environmental concerns are raised regarding the end-of-life (EoL) stage of EV batteries. Typically, EV batteries reach an EoL at a state-of-health (SoH) of approximately 75–80% [7]. At this point, they are no longer suitable for use in vehicles. However, they can be repurposed as second-life battery energy storage systems (BESS) for stationary applications. However, when integrated into building systems, second-life BESS contributes to circularity while offering technical and economic benefits. These systems increase self-consumption of photovoltaic (PV) generation, reduce electricity costs through load shifting and peak shaving, and provide flexibility services to relieve grid congestion and support energy balancing [8].

This study provides a comprehensive design and techno-economic analysis of a second-life BESS installed at Voldsløkka School in Oslo, Norway. The analysis evaluates a range of system sizes and includes integration with on-site PV generation. The BESS's operational control is modeled and optimized using a mixed-integer linear programming (MILP) model, incorporating real-world electricity consumption data, dynamic spot market prices, and participation in a local flexibility market currently active in the Oslo region.

The structure of this work is as follows: Sect. 2 offers a comprehensive review of the current literature on second-life BESS and identifies the research gaps that this study addresses. Section 3 presents the case study examined in this work, detailing the building pilot, the BESS, and the electric market conditions. Section 4 outlines the methodology used to optimize the BESS using a MILP model and explains the procedures for conducting Monte Carlo simulations of LFM flexibility activation. Section 5 discusses the results of this study, and Sect. 6 concludes with a summary of the findings and suggestions for future research.

2 Literature Review

Interest in BESS for buildings has grown in recent years [9]. However, research on the viability of second-life battery systems in the Nordic context primarily focuses on life-cycle assessment (LCA) analyses or relies on simulated data and hypothetical scenarios [10, 11]. Modeling BESS with PV integration using MILP is a well-established field [8, 12]. Recently, this area expanded to include the modeling of grid services and dynamic spot pricing [13]. In the Nordic region, most economic assessments of BESS focus on residential applications, utilizing both simulated [14] and real data [15]. Similarly, the literature in non-residential buildings is also limited, with a single study [16] considering solely PV data (not demand). Notably, none of the existing studies explicitly consider second-life BESS within the modeling framework (only one non-building-related study was found [17]), despite the growing availability of retired electric vehicle batteries [18], distributed PV [19] and their potential for cost-effective stationary storage.

Despite advancements in the field, several key gaps remain unaddressed: the lack of simulation studies based on real building demand data in Norwegian non-residential settings; the absence of second-life batteries in techno-economic optimization frameworks; and limited consideration of LFMs in the design of building-scale energy systems. By addressing these issues, this work contributes to filling the empirical and methodological gaps in the literature, providing new insights into the economic viability and operational value of second-life BESS under real-world market and consumption conditions.

3 Case Study

3.1 Building Pilot

The building case of the current study is the Voldsløkka School, located in Oslo, Norway [20]. This school comprises two main buildings: a newly constructed classroom-building (9,267 m^2, accommodating 810 students) and a renovated cultural center (2,332 m^2). Heating and domestic hot water are provided by a hybrid energy system that combines a ground-source heat pump (GSHP) and a connection to the local district heating network. The classroom-building complies with the FutureBuilt Plus-Energy definition [21], being Oslo's first plus-energy school. Its 1,217-module PV system (337 kWp), installed on roofs and façades, is designed to have a yearly production that is 2 kWh/m^2 above the energy demand of the buildings. However, in 2024, the school used 655.5 MWh of electricity (monthly average: 54.6 ± 7.6 MWh), while PV generation totaled 215.0 MWh (ranging from 40.1 MWh in May to 1.5 MWh in December (see Fig. 1). 2024 had typical solar conditions, with a global horizontal irradiance that is only 3% below the 2019–2024 average. The production of the PV system fits its design performance. The school uses more energy than the expected design projections; nevertheless, it is significantly more energy efficient than other schools in Oslo [20].

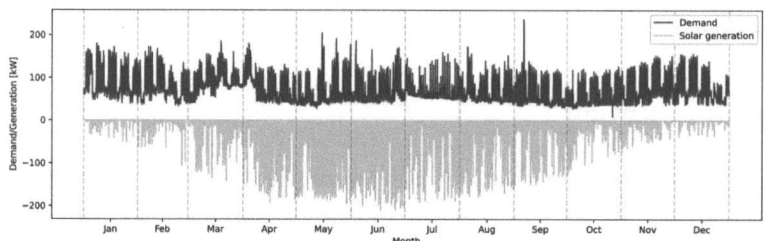

Fig. 1. Demand and PV generation for the year 2024.

3.2 BESS Module

The case study examines the installation of second-life battery systems recycled from EVs. It focuses on commercially available battery packs from the Renault ZOE, which has a first-life capacity of 22 kWh, and the third-generation Nissan Leaf, which has a first-life capacity of 28 kWh. These batteries are mounted in ready-to-install cabinet modules, with a measured second-life capacity of 40 kWh (utilizing two battery packs) and inverters capable of delivering 20 kW. Additional specifications, including costs and dimensions given by the technology provider ECO-STOR, are provided in Table 1.

Table 1. Battery modules and system characteristics.

Value	Unit	Description
W:800x D:1200x H:1800	*mm*	Module dimensions
160 000	*NOK/module*	Cost per module
4 000	*NOK/kWh*	Cost per effective capacity
40	*kWh*	Second life capacity
20	*kW*	Charge/discharge power
90.0	%	Maximum state of charge SOC_{max} [22]
20.0	%	Minimum state of charge SOC_{min} [22]
82.6	%	Round-trip AC2AC efficiency η_{RTE} [23]
90.9	%	Charging efficiency η_c
90.9	%	Discharging efficiency η_d
60.0 (first life) – 75.0 (second life)	%	EoL– Minimum SOC limit [7]

3.3 Tariff Scheme

The building is located in the southeastern Norway bidding area N01, and the distribution is managed by the distribution system operator (DSO) Elvia. In this study, the BESS is optimized by monitoring the grid's hourly dynamic electricity prices from N01 (for 2024 prices [24], see Fig. 2). This optimization also considers grid costs and incentives associated with a prosumer status, as described in Table 2.

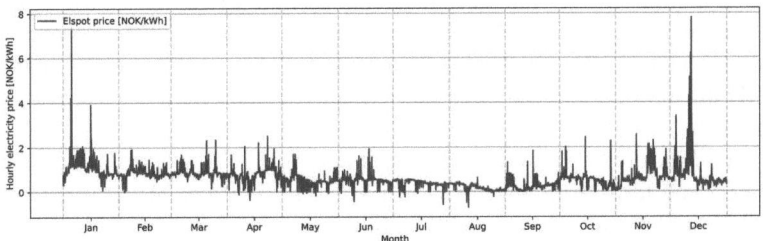

Fig. 2. Hourly electricity prices [NOK/kWh] during the year 2024.

Table 2. Electricity and grid prices gathered from ELVIA (January 2024) [24].

Value	Unit	Description
0.608 ± 0.479	NOK/kWh	Yearly average electricity price (hourly - 2024)
1.148	NOK/kWh	Maximum monthly average price (Jan – 2024)
0.162	NOK/kWh	Minimum monthly average price (Agu – 2024)
0.05	NOK/kWh	Fixed energy tax on imports e_{buy}
0.0302	NOK/kWh	Flat incentive paid for every kWh exported e_{sell}
44 in summer, 104 in winter	NOK/kW	Monthly demand charge per kW $Cost_{peak}$
25	%	VAT

3.4 Local Flexibility Market

The battery energy storage system is configured not only for dynamic pricing optimization but also to participate in the LFM operated by Elvia under the EuroFlex scheme with NODES. This market offers two products: ShortFlex, a pay-as-bid contract similar to stock market auctions, and LongFlex, a capacity reservation contract that allows the distribution system operator to secure flexibility weeks or months in advance, thereby relieving grid congestion [25]. In this study, only LongFlex is analyzed. For the 2025 to 2026 season the market requires in building's area turn up capacity reserves from January through March and October through December on Tuesdays through Saturdays between 07:00 and 10:00 and between 15:00 and 18:00. Reserved capacity is remunerated at NOK 0.12 per kWh per hour while full activation yields NOK 4.00 per kWh per hour, about 6.5 times the 2024 NO1 zone average energy price, and no payment or penalty applies if activation does not occur. Current market information presents activation rates of 5% in the Oslo zone [26].

4 Methods

This section includes three main components. First, the MILP model used to schedule BESS operation is presented, minimizing costs under dynamic tariffs. Second, a battery degradation model accounts for capacity fading and ageing, enabling multi-year lifecycle analysis. Third, a Monte Carlo simulation estimates payback periods under varying LFM activation rates.

Two scenarios are compared. In the baseline, the BESS is optimized only for self-consumption and tariff arbitrage. In the LFM case, the same MILP is extended with additional variables and revenues for flexibility reservations. This isolates the impact of LFM participation. Both scenarios are evaluated over a 20-year horizon with annual degradation effects.

4.1 System Optimization

The decision variables and the parameters considered in the MILP model are presented in Tables 3 and 4, respectively.

Table 3. Decision variables of the MILP model.

Decision variable	Unit	Description
$G_{imp}[t] \in \mathbb{R}$	kW	Grid import power flow
$G_{exp}[t] \in \mathbb{R}$	kW	Grid export power flow
$P_{ch}[t] \in \mathbb{R}$	kW	Battery charging power. Always negative
$P_{dis}[t] \in \mathbb{R}$	kW	Battery discharging power. Always positive
$SOC[t] \in \mathbb{R}$	%	State-of-Charge of the battery
$\sigma[t] \in \{0,1\}$	-	Binary variable ensuring mutually exclusive battery modes
$P_{max}[t] \in \mathbb{R}$	kW	Monthly import power peak
$P_{dem}[t] \in \mathbb{R}$	kW	Battery discharge that feeds the on-site load
$P_{grd}[t] \in \mathbb{R}$	kW	Battery discharge sent to the grid

Table 4. Defined parameters of the MILP model.

Parameter	Unit	Description
Time/Load		
t	h	Time step
T	–	Total number of time steps
M_t	kWh	Net load (demand – solar)
Market		
p_t	NOK/kWh	Dynamic electricity spot price at time t
e_{buy}	NOK/kWh	Fixed energy tax on imports
e_{sell}	NOK/kWh	Flat incentive paid for every kWh exported
$Cost_{peak}$	NOK/kW	Monthly demand charge per kW
$\rho_{act}[t]$	NOK kWh/h	Capacity activation cost
$\rho_{res}[t]$	NOK kWh/h	Capacity reserve cost
Battery		
P_{ch}^{max}	kW	Maximum charging rate
P_{dis}^{max}	kW	Maximum discharge rate
C	kWh	Battery capacity
η_c	%	Charging efficiency

(*continued*)

Parameter	Unit	Description
η_d	%	Discharging efficiency
SOC_{min}	%	Minimum allowed state-of-charge
SOC_{max}	%	Maximum allowed state-of-charge
SOC_0	%	Initial allowed state-of-charge
$P_{act}[t]$	kWh	Reserved/activated capacity for LFM
$\gamma_{act}[t]$	–	Binary flag that indicates activation when the value equals 1
$\gamma_{res}[t]$	–	Binary flag that indicates activation when the value equals 1

Optimization Problem

The objective function reflects a streamlined billing model that accounts for variable tariff components, non-reactive power charges, and revenues from both reserve and capacity services. It therefore consists of four primary components:

1. **Energy import term**: The imported energy from the grid is charged at the hourly market price p_t (including 25% VAT) and a fixed-rate energy tax e_{buy}.

$$(P_t + e_{buy})G_{imp}(t) \qquad (1)$$

2. **Energy export term**: A flat incentive for exporting energy, aiming for grid decongestion, is subtracted from the costs.

$$E_{sell}G_{exp}(t) \qquad (2)$$

3. **Peak charge**: The maximum monthly peak is penalized in the MILP problem. In the post calculations, the maximum absolute peak is replaced by the average of the three maximum monthly power peaks $\overline{P}_{max}$.

$$Cost_{peak}P_{max} \qquad (3)$$

4. **Capacity Allocations**: This objective term accounts for revenues from holding reserve capacity (when $\gamma_{res}(t) = 1$) and delivering power during activations (when $\gamma_{act}(t) = 1$).

$$\rho_{res}\gamma_{res}(t)P_{act}(t) + \rho_{act}\gamma_{act}(t)P_{act}(t) \qquad (4)$$

The final objective function is defined as follows:

$$\min \sum_{t=0}^{T-1}\left[(p_t + e_{buy})G_{imp}(t) - e_{sell}G_{exp(t)} - (\rho_{res}\gamma_{res}(t)P_{act}(t) + \rho_{act}\gamma_{act}(t)P_{act}(t))\right]$$
$$+ Cost_{peak}P_{max} \qquad (5)$$

Constraints

Eight constraint terms are defined in the MILP model.

1. **Power Balance**: Ensure energy balance at the building level at each hour. All power sources (grid import, battery discharge) and sinks (grid export, battery charging) must match the **net site demand** (load minus solar).

$$G_{imp}(t) - G_{exp}(t) + P_{dem}(t) + P_{ch}(t) = M_t \tag{6}$$

2. **SoC Dynamics**: Battery modelling capacity C at each hour. Charging increases the energy, and it is adjusted by the charging efficiency η_c. Similarly, the discharging process is adjusted with efficiency η_d.

$$SOC(t) = SOC(t-1) + \eta_c \frac{-P_{ch}(t)}{C} - \frac{P_{dist}(t)}{\eta_d C} \tag{7}$$

3. **SoC Bounds**: Boundaries of the SoC.

$$SOC_{min} \leq SOC(t) \leq SOC_{max} \tag{8}$$

4. **Charge/Discharge Linking**: Binary variable σ that indicates if the battery is idle (σ = 0) or if it is charging or discharging (σ = 1).

$$-P_{ch}(t) - \sigma(t)P_{ch}^{max} \leq 0, \; P_{dis}(t) - (1-\sigma(t))P_{dis}^{max} \leq 0 \tag{9}$$

5. **Peak Import Constraint**: The maximum monthly import power peak constrains the import of energy (P_{max}).

$$G_{imp}(t) \leq P_{max} \tag{10}$$

6. **Battery Internal Coupling Constraint**: The split of the power flows in the battery forbids the system from feeding the load while charging.

$$P_{dis}(t) = P_{dem}(t) + P_{grd}(t) \tag{11}$$

7. **Reserve/activation delivery**: The binary flag $\gamma_{act}(t)$ indicates the activation (and reserve) obligation at time t. The delivery is constrained based on the activation size $P_{act}(t)$ contracted.

$$P_{dis}(t) \geq P_{act}(t)\gamma_{act}(t), \; G_{exp}(t) \geq P_{act}(t)\gamma_{act}(t) \tag{12}$$

8. **Capacity allocation**: During hours reserved for capacity reserves, the battery must be fully available to discharge if activated, and it cannot be charged.

$$P_{ch}(t) = 0 \text{ if } \gamma_{res} = 1 \tag{13}$$

4.2 Battery Degradation Model

After each annual simulation, the remaining capacity of the battery energy storage system is updated using the semi-empirical degradation model developed by Xu et al. [27]. This approach captures both calendar ageing and cycling effects to project capacity fade over multiple years.

$$C_y = 1 - (1 - C_{y-1})e^{-f_{d,y}} \tag{14}$$

where "y" is the capacity at the end of the previous year and $f_{d,y}$ is the linearized annual degradation rate.

The degradation rate $f_{d,y}$ itself decomposes into three multiplicative stress factors: calendar ageing $S_t(y)$, cycling $S_{SOC}(SOC)$, and temperature-related stress $S_T(T)$, such that

$$F_{d,y} = S_t(y) \cdot S_{SOC}(SOC) \cdot S_T(T) = e^{k_t} \cdot e^{k_{SOC}(\overline{SOC} - SOC_{ref})} \cdot e^{\frac{k_T(T - T_{ref})T_{ref}}{T}} \quad (15)$$

In this formulation, $S_t(y)$ represents capacity loss from calendar ageing, $S_{SOC}(SOC)$ captures cycle-induced degradation, and $S_T(T)$ quantifies thermal-stress effects. All constants and variable definitions are provided in Table 5.

Table 5. Variables utilized in the battery degradation model.

Variable	Unit	Value	Description
SOC_{ref}	%	50	Reference state-of-charge
T_{ref}	K	295.15	Reference temperature
k_t	–	1.31e–02	Calendar constant
k_{SOC}	–	1.04	SOC constant
k_T	–	6.93e–02	Temperature constant
$\overline{SOC}$	%	0.60	Yearly average SOC
T	K	298.15	Module temperature

4.3 Monte Carlo Simulation for LFM Case

This study employs a Monte Carlo simulation framework to evaluate the long-term economic performance of BESSs that provide capacity for LFM in buildings, despite uncertainty in activation. While reserve capacity is allocated deterministically based on fixed contractual requirements, the DSO's actual dispatch of these reserves is subject to uncertainty. Each Monte Carlo trial generates 50 randomized activation signals to model this stochastic behavior using a Bernoulli process with predefined activation rates. This rate represents the probability that a reserved hour will be activated. Importantly, this randomized activation is not confined to a single year; instead, it is independently redrawn for each year throughout a 20-year simulation horizon, allowing for the capture of interannual variability in system utilization. Additionally, based on the historical price data for zone NO1, an annual growth rate of 6.38% is used for future year simulations in the hourly electricity price, activation costs, and other related energy charges and benefits, aiming to increase the variance in costs. Moreover, capacity-related costs, such as the monthly demand charge and capacity allocation costs, are dependent on the level of investment in the grid. Therefore, annual variations are based on the historical variation of the Consumer Price Index (CPI) in Norway, which is 3.23%.

In the results and discussion section, the overall findings, ranging from no activation to complete activation, are presented. However, the current market activation rate of 5% is highlighted, along with higher rates of 25% and 50%, since the authors believe that as the maturity of the LFM increases and buildings become active demand-side flexibility providers, activation rates are expected to grow in the future.

5 Key Performance Indicators

Four key performance indicators (KPIs) are used to evaluate the economic and operational performance of the BESS. The first is the return on investment (ROI), defined as the number of years required for the initial capital expenditure (CAPEX) to be recovered through the net operational savings relative to the baseline case (which considers only demand and solar generation). Each battery module (including inverter) carries a price of approximately 160,000 NOK (equivalent to 4,000 NOK per usable kWh), based on ECO-STOR estimates. The payback period PB is calculated without accounting for interest as:

$$PB = \frac{CAPEX_{tot}}{OPEX_{baseline} - OPEX_{bess}} \tag{16}$$

The second KPI is self-consumption (SC), which quantifies the fraction of photovoltaic generation that is consumed on-site rather than exported to the grid. It is expressed as:

$$SC = \frac{\sum_t solar_t - \sum_t G_{exp}(t)}{\sum_t solar_t} \tag{17}$$

and ranges from 0 (no on-site use) to 1 (all generation consumed locally).

The third KPI is self-sufficiency (SS), which measures the fraction of the total building load met without importing energy from the grid. It is defined as

$$SS = \frac{\sum_t load_t - \sum_t G_{imp}(t)}{\sum_t load_t} \tag{18}$$

Similarly to SC, SS ranges from 0 to 1. During the discussion and presentation of results, SC and SS are reported only for the baseline case, while PB is evaluated for both the baseline and the LFM case.

Finally, the willingness-to-pay (t_{WTP}) is defined as the maximum payback period that commercial building owners consider financially viable. Empirical evidence from solar PV adopters indicates that payback periods of five years or less are required for adoption [28]. Due to the similar motivations for the end use of both technologies, a five-year t_{WTP} threshold is used as a practical reference point for BESS. This timeframe is backed by studies indicating that such payback periods can be achieved under favorable conditions, such as demand response strategies [29] or with the help of subsidies [30]. Under this assumption, the subsidy required to achieve a five-year payback is given by:

$$S = CAPEX_{tot} - \sum_{t=0}^{t_{WTP}} \left(OPEX_{baseline,t} - OPEX_{BESS,t}\right) \tag{19}$$

To facilitate comparison across projects, S is normalized by effective storage capacity and reported in [NOK/kWh] and percentage compared to the CAPEX.

6 Results and Discussion

This section presents the results and discussion on the second-life BESS modeling and simulation. The section covers the first analysis of yearly energy usage, imports, exports, and generation, as well as the self-consumption and self-sufficiency of the pilot, comparing the current state with the installation of 1 to 6 battery modules in the initial year. Next, an analysis of utilizing the building for participating in demand-side flexibility schemes, such as LFMs, is presented and discussed. Due to the baseline independence of BESS systems, the pilot has the potential to participate in capacity markets; thus, this case analyzes this market under current conditions (prices and activation rates of 5%). Moreover, as the LFM matures and the participation of grid-interactive buildings is expected to increase, larger activation rates are also presented and discussed. Finally, possible subsidies for making second-life BESS attractive for new stakeholders are discussed.

This work, even when presenting long-term analyses, still has limitations that need to be addressed. These include projecting future loads, as current data do not provide enough evidence for establishing typical long-term load patterns. Additionally, the LFM is still in the early stages, which means that participation and activation costs for flexibility may change in the future. The rates for activated flexibility and the periods during which activation occurs are also subject to variation. Nonetheless, incorporating trends in dynamic prices, along with changes in costs and benefits based on CPI, aims to reduce uncertainties related to this issue.

Figure 3 illustrates the monthly grid import and export profiles for varying battery capacities. From January to March and from November to December, grid exchange remains relatively stable, consisting entirely of imports. This stability reflects consistent demand and limited photovoltaic generation during the heating season. In contrast, pronounced export peaks are observed from April to July, with June representing the peak in solar production, followed by May and then July (see Fig. 1). While export levels in these months remain relatively similar, imports are at their lowest in May and June, before rising in July. This pattern reflects the influence of baseline demand, which is higher in July. Hence, it suggests that the existing battery sizes are bounding the absorption of all available PV surplus when demand rises, thereby limiting the potential for further reducing exports. Next, introducing a single battery module tends to increase both imports and exports during these months, as limited storage cannot fully accommodate the generation surplus. As additional modules are added, these peaks are progressively smoothed out, demonstrating that larger storage capacity captures the surplus solar energy and reduces dependence on the distribution grid.

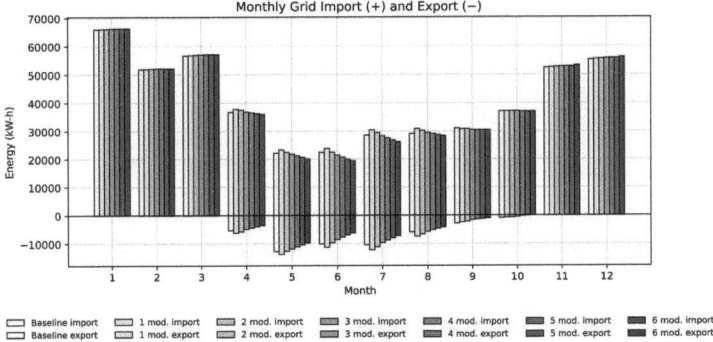

Fig. 3. Monthly energy imports and exports in [kWh/month] for the initial year calendar. The simulation includes 1 to 6 battery modules.

For the baseline case, the monthly self-consumption is presented in Fig. 4. Considering no installed BESS (baseline), 77.4% of the yearly PV output is consumed on-site. When a single battery module is added, on-site consumption decreases slightly to 74.8%, prioritizing cost optimization over self-consumption. With six modules in place, SC rises to 85.2%, reflecting the system's improved ability to shift solar energy into periods of local demand during the summer months, which can differ up to 10.2% compared to the baseline in June and July. Changes over the winter remain minimal because low irradiance limits both generation and storage opportunities.

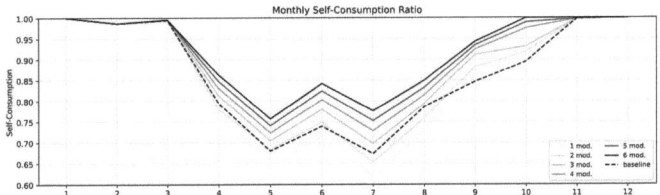

Fig. 4. Self-consumption ratio for the different BESS modules.

Figure 5 depicts the monthly self-sufficiency results. The baseline SS is estimated to be 25.4%, with significant peaks during the summer months, reaching approximately 55.0%. The implementation of BESS is shown to enhance SS during the summer period. However, the opposite effect is observed during the winter months. This behavior can be attributed to seasonal variations in generation availability. These variations can lead to greater grid independence when combined with increased storage capacity and optimal control strategies. During the summer, a maximum percentage increase of 6% in SS is observed in June when compared to the baseline scenario.

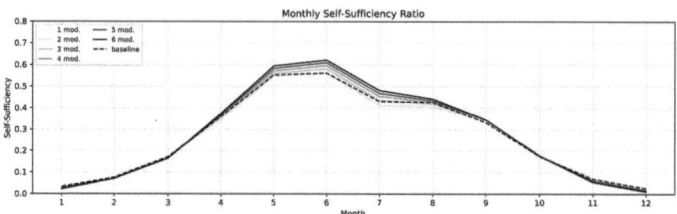

Fig. 5. Self-sufficiency ratio for the different BESS modules.

The ROI is assessed using a cumulative cash-flow chart (see Fig. 6) for battery configurations ranging from one to six modules, with each module costing 160,000 NOK. Under baseline conditions and focusing solely on the variable billing components for building demand and solar generation, the total cost amounts to 551,585 NOK in the initial year. The payback period is 7.0 years for a single module and extends to 11.4 years for a total of six modules. Next, the EoL second-life battery packs are reached after 19 years, defined at 60 percent remaining state of charge, which is 7.5 years beyond the payback of the six-module case.

When considering LFM revenues, three activation rates are illustrated in Fig. 6: 5%, 25%, and 50%. This calculation is based on 786 h of activation, which generates 799.83 NOK per module for capacity reservation, and a maximum of 26,661.12 NOK per module for activation settlements when activation reaches 100% in year 0. For a single module, the PB period varies depending on the activation rate: it decreases to 6.7 years at a 5% activation rate, 6.1 years at a 25% activation rate, and a minimum of 5.3 years at a 50% activation rate. Compared to the baseline case, this represents a reduction of 0.3 years with the current activation rate of 5% and to 1.7 years for a single module and a 50% activation rate. Similar patterns are observed for additional modules. For six modules, the payback periods are 10.0 years at a 5% activation rate, 8.1 years at a 25% activation rate, and 6.8 years at a 50% activation rate of reserves. This shows the most significant difference from the baseline case, with reductions ranging from 1.4 to 4.7 years in the sample activation rates. By considering the limits of the activation range, first by reserving the load only, the payback period is reduced by 0.8 years. Next, with full activation, the payback period can be further decreased to 6.5 years, based on the 6-module system.

In both scenarios, steeper cumulative cash-flow trajectories indicate that once capital costs are recovered, larger installations generate higher annual savings compared to smaller ones. However, revenues can vary from one to six modules at the EoL between 0.30 and 0.9 million NOK with a 5% activation rate, and between 4.7 and 2.1 million NOK with 50% activation, while baseline cases do not exceed 0.64 million NOK.

Optimization of Second-Life Battery Energy Storage System in Buildings 313

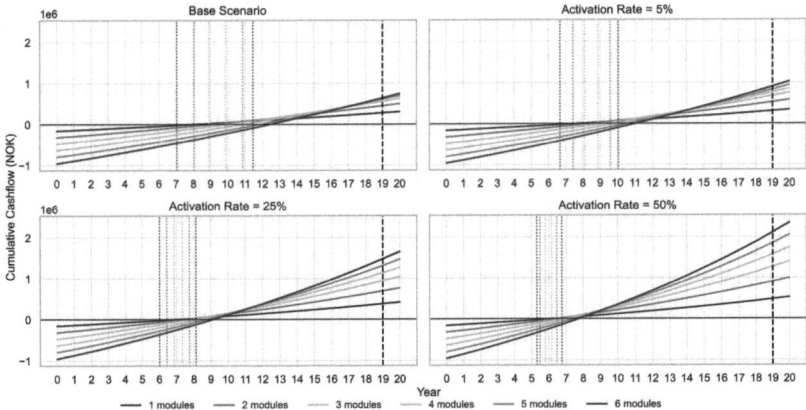

Fig. 6. Average cumulative cash flow for the different BESS sizes, considering the baseline and LFM cases with 5%, 25%, and 50% activation rates.

In Fig. 7, the PB periods are contrasted with the activation rate, which ranges from no activation (0%) to full activation (100%). As shown, all modules exhibit exponential decay in their curves as activation rates increase. Furthermore, when there are fewer modules, the behavior of the curves tends to be more linear. Notably, with activation rates above 65% for one module and 95% for six modules, the 5-year willing-to-pay PB period is exceeded.

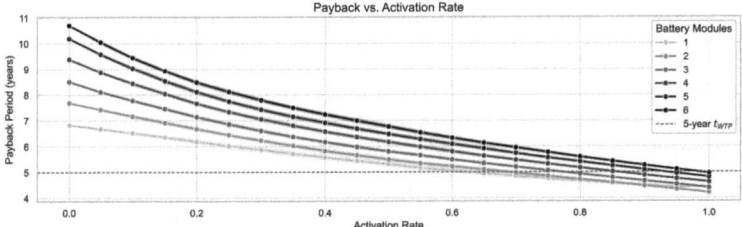

Fig. 7. Payback periods for the different activation rates for the Monte Carlo simulation of the LFM (the results are presented as the average of these simulations).

Figure 8 illustrates the subsidy required to achieve a five-year payback period for both the baseline and LFM (with different activation rates) cases across installations ranging from one to six battery modules. In the baseline scenario, the required subsidy is 1,641.2 [NOK/kWh] for a single module, which steadily increases to 2,573.2 [NOK/kWh] for six modules. This represents a 23.3% total increase, reflecting the higher relative capital expenditure on larger systems.

In contrast, under the LFM scenario, the subsidy requirements vary significantly depending on the activation rates. For instance, at an activation rate of 5%, the average subsidy decreases by 990.5 [NOK/kWh] for a one-module installation and by approximately 2001.8 [NOK/kWh] for a six-module installation. Similarly, for 25% and 50% activation rates, the required subsidies range from 684.8 [NOK/kWh] to 1042.8

[NOK/kWh], respectively. These reductions align with the shorter payback periods and greater operating cost savings observed in the LFM case.

When expressed as a percentage of total CAPEX, the subsidy in the LFM with six battery modules ranges from 53.1% when no activation is performed to no subsidy with full activation of the reserves. At a 50% activation rate and six battery modules, an average of 26.1% of the initial investment is required to achieve a PB period of five years. This highlights how LFM strategies enhance cost-effectiveness. These results demonstrate that while the absolute subsidies increase with system size and activation rates, the proportional capital support required is lower in the LFM case, emphasizing the advantages of participating in LFM in reducing the need for fiscal incentives.

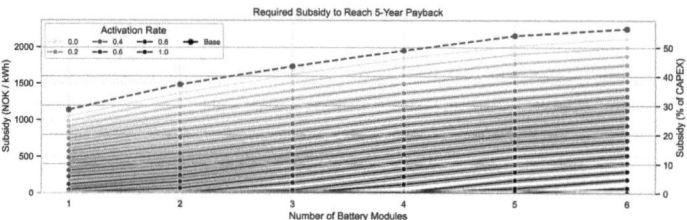

Fig. 8. The subsidy amount required to achieve a 5-year payback in the baseline and LFM cases. The results are shown normalized per NOK/kWh and in a fraction of the initial CAPEX.

7 Conclusions

This study modeled a BESS for Voldsløkka Skole using a MILP approach. It utilized load and generation data from 2024 to evaluate the performance of one to six second-life battery modules (40 kWh/20 kW each), installed in a 13.5 m2 technical room. The assessment was conducted under two operational frameworks: a simple self-consumption "baseline" scenario and an active LFM scenario leveraging capacity contracts.

In the baseline scenario, the BESS increased self-consumption by up to 10% and self-sufficiency by up to 6% when six modules were installed, while also reducing grid imports. However, due to relatively high upfront capital costs, the undiscounted payback periods remained lengthy, with approximately seven years with a single module, extending to eleven years with six modules. In contrast, when the school participated in the EuroFlex LFM and optimized its ability to provide capacity reserves, the payback periods decreased substantially. Under the current activation rates of the LFM (5%), the system with six modules can reduce the payback period by 1.4 years on average and is expected to experience an even further decrease of 4.7 years (50% activation rate) as the LFM matures. This improvement was achieved through additional revenues and operational savings from capacity reserve activations. When considering a five-year willingness-to-pay payback period, the baseline case required a subsidy covering 64.3% of capital costs with six modules. Participation in the LFM reduced this requirement to 50.0% at a 5% activation rate and to 26.1% at a 50% activation rate.

Overall, integrating BESS with on-site PV at Voldsløkka Skole demonstrated the potential to modulate peak demand, reduce energy costs, and enhance self-consumption and self-sufficiency. However, substantial capital costs and extended payback horizons constrained the system's economic viability. Participation in the LFM significantly alleviated these challenges, reducing payback periods and minimizing required subsidies. This offers a promising pathway for the broader adoption of second-life battery storage in non-residential buildings.

7.1 Suggestions for Future Work

While this study provides a long-term analysis, several aspects warrant further investigation. A key limitation lies in the projection of future load profiles, as it remains uncertain whether the current data adequately captures the building's typical long-term consumption behavior. Future research should focus on improving load forecasting by leveraging extended datasets and identifying underlying patterns of occupancy and usage. Furthermore, LFMs are still in the early stages of development. As these markets mature, the associated costs of participation and activation, remuneration schemes, and regulatory frameworks are likely to evolve. It will be essential to consider a variety of future market scenarios, including potential changes in tariffs, incentives, and activation periods. To enhance the generalizability of the findings, comparative studies across different contexts should be undertaken. This involves analyzing buildings of various types and uses, testing different battery technologies and manufacturers, and accounting for a range of weather conditions and regional market structures. Such comparisons would offer valuable insight into the scalability and robustness of the proposed approach. Finally, although this work incorporates trends in dynamic pricing and cost adjustments based on the CPI, future efforts could explore alternative economic modeling techniques and perform sensitivity analyses to better address long-term financial uncertainties.

Acknowledgment. The authors gratefully acknowledge the support from the Horizon 2020 European Union-funded project ARV-Climate Positive Circular Communities (grant agreement ID: 101036723).

This work has been written with the LifeLine-2050 project, funded by the Faculty of Engineering (IV) at the Norwegian University of Science and Technology (NTNU). The LifeLine-2050 project is a flagship project with the NTNU's Centre for Green Shift in the Built Environment (Green2050). The authors gratefully acknowledge the support of Green2050's partners and the encouragement of the innovation committee of IV faculty at NTNU.

References

1. Directorate-General for Research and Innovation (European Commission): European Green Deal: research & innovation call. Publications Office of the European Union (2021)
2. IEA: Norway 2022: Energy Policy Review. International Energy Agency (IEA) (2022)
3. Korpås, M., et al.: Learning from the norwegian electric vehicle success: an overview. IEEE Power Energ. Mag. **21**, 18–27 (2023). https://doi.org/10.1109/MPE.2023.3308246
4. Norsk Elbilforening: Statistikk Elbil. https://elbil.no/om-elbil/elbilstatistikk/. Accessed 14 May 2025
5. Holstad, M.: SSB: Record high electricity price in 2022 – curbed by Electricity support for households. https://www.ssb.no/en/energi-og-industri/energi/statistikk/elektrisitetspriser/article-for-electricity-prices/record-high-electricity-price-in-2022--curbed-by-electricity-support-for-households. Accessed 18 May 2025

6. Gonzalez, S.I.A.: Fullt strømnett på Østlandet til 2035: – Må snu hver sten. https://www.nettavisen.no/5-95-1385671. Accessed 18 May 2025
7. Salek, F., Resalati, S., Babaie, M., Henshall, P., Morrey, D., Yao, L.: A review of the technical challenges and solutions in maximising the potential use of second life batteries from electric vehicles. Batteries. **10**, 79 (2024). https://doi.org/10.3390/batteries10030079
8. Tang, H., Wang, S.: Life-cycle economic analysis of thermal energy storage, new and second-life batteries in buildings for providing multiple flexibility services in electricity markets. Energy **264**, 126270 (2023). https://doi.org/10.1016/j.energy.2022.126270
9. Pantelatos, L., Boks, C., Verhulst, E.: Repurposing lithium-ion batteries for the household context: an industry investigation in Norway. In: Fukushige, S., Nonaka, T., Kobayashi, H., Tokoro, C., Yamasue, E. (eds.) EcoDesign for Circular Value Creation: Volume II. pp. 133–147. Springer Nature, Singapore (2025). https://doi.org/10.1007/978-981-97-9076-0_9
10. Ahmed, S., Verhulst, E., Boks, C.: Second life of electric vehicle lithium-ion batteries from a sustainable business model perspective. In: Fukushige, S., Nonaka, T., Kobayashi, H., Tokoro, C., Yamasue, E. (eds.) EcoDesign for Circular Value Creation: Volume I. pp. 229–243. Springer Nature, Singapore (2025). https://doi.org/10.1007/978-981-97-9068-5_15
11. Wrålsen, B., O'Born, R.: Use of life cycle assessment to evaluate circular economy business models in the case of Li-ion battery remanufacturing. Int. J. Life Cycle Assess. **28**, 554–565 (2023). https://doi.org/10.1007/s11367-023-02154-0
12. Mohamed, A.A.R., Best, R.J., Liu, X., Morrow, D.J.: A Comprehensive robust techno-economic analysis and sizing tool for the small-scale PV and BESS. IEEE Trans. Energy Convers. **37**, 560–572 (2022). https://doi.org/10.1109/TEC.2021.3107103
13. Mirzaei Alavijeh, N., Khezri, R., Mazidi, M., Steen, D., Le, A.T.: Profit benchmarking and degradation analysis for revenue stacking of batteries in Sweden's day-ahead electricity and frequency containment reserve markets. Appl. Energy **381**, 125151 (2025). https://doi.org/10.1016/j.apenergy.2024.125151
14. Bjarghov, S., Korpås, M., Zaferanlouei, S.: Value comparison of EV and house batteries at end-user level under different grid tariffs. In: 2018 IEEE International Energy Conference (ENERGYCON), pp. 1–6 (2018). https://doi.org/10.1109/ENERGYCON.2018.8398742
15. Nygård, H.S., Ottesen, S.Ø., Skonnord, O.H.: Profitability analyses for residential battery investments: a norwegian case study. Energies **17**, 4048 (2024)
16. Agathokleous, C., Tuan, L.A., Steen, D.: Stochastic operation scheduling model for a swedish prosumer with PV and BESS in nordic day-ahead electricity market. In: 2019 IEEE Milan PowerTech, pp. 1–6 (2019). https://doi.org/10.1109/PTC.2019.8810651
17. Lieskoski, S., Tuuf, J., Björklund-Sänkiaho, M.: Techno-economic analysis of the business potential of second-life batteries in Ostrobothnia Finland. Batter. **10**, 36 (2024). https://doi.org/10.3390/batteries10010036
18. Yu, X., et al.: Current challenges in efficient lithium-ion batteries' recycling: a perspective. Global Chall. **6**, 2200099 (2022). https://doi.org/10.1002/gch2.202200099
19. Gholami, H.: Technical potential of solar energy in buildings across Norway: capacity and demand. Sol. Energy **278**, 112758 (2024). https://doi.org/10.1016/j.solener.2024.112758
20. Sørensen, Å.L., Johra, H., Lolli, N., Høiaas, I.E., Andresen, I.: Influence of PV system orientation and design on energy self-consumption and cost savings: a Norwegian case study. In: Journal of Physics: Conference Series. Proceedings of the CISBAT Conference (2025)
21. Andresen, I., Thyholt, M., Dokka, T.: Kriterier for Futurebuilt Plusshus. SINTEF Byggforsk. (2014)
22. Thomas, C.E.: Fuel cell and battery electric vehicles compared. Int. J. Hydrogen Energy **34**, 6005–6020 (2009). https://doi.org/10.1016/j.ijhydene.2009.06.003
23. Viswanathan, V., Mongird, K., Franks, R., Li, X., Sprenkle, V., Baxter, R.: 2022 grid energy storage technology cost and performance assessment. Energy **2022**, 1–151 (2022)

24. ELVIA: Dagens og historiske priser innenfor elvias nettområd. https://www.elvia.no/nettleie/alt-om-nettleie/dagens-og-historiske-priser-innenfor-elvias-nettomrade/. Accessed 1 May 2025
25. Stølsbotn, D., Staude, A.: White Paper: Trading in NorFlex 2020–23 (2023)
26. NODESmarket: NODES platform. https://portal.nodesmarket.com/onboarding/dashboard. Accessed 15 May 2025
27. Xu, B., Oudalov, A., Ulbig, A., Andersson, G., Kirschen, D.S.: Modeling of lithium-ion battery degradation for cell life assessment. IEEE Trans. Smart Grid **9**, 1131–1140 (2018). https://doi.org/10.1109/TSG.2016.2578950
28. Dong, C., Sigrin, B.: Using willingness to pay to forecast the adoption of solar photovoltaics: a "parameterization + calibration" approach. Energy Policy **129**, 100–110 (2019). https://doi.org/10.1016/j.enpol.2019.02.017
29. Elio, J., Milcarek, R.J.: Assessment of optimal energy storage dispatch control strategies for cost savings in 606 commercial and industrial facilities leveraging utility demand response programs. Appl. Energy **384**, 125513 (2025). https://doi.org/10.1016/j.apenergy.2025.125513
30. Al-Wreikat, Y., Attfield, E.K., Sodré, J.R.: Model for payback time of using retired electric vehicle batteries in residential energy storage systems. Energy **259**, 124975 (2022). https://doi.org/10.1016/j.energy.2022.124975

Non-Intrusive Load Monitoring and Data Competitions

ADRENALIN: Energy Data Preparation and Validation for HVAC Load Disaggregation in Commercial Buildings

Balázs András Tolnai[1](✉), Zheng Grace Ma[1], Igor Sartori[2], Surya Venkatesh Pandiyan[3], Matt Amos[4], Gustaf Bengtsson[5], Synne Krekling Lien[2], Harald Taxt Walnum[2,6], Akram Hameed[4], Jayaprakash Rajasekharan[3], Rafeal Gomez Garcia[5], and Bo Nørregaard Jørgensen[1]

[1] SDU Center for Energy Informatics, The Faculty of Engineering, Maersk Mc-Kinney Moeller Institute, University of Southern Denmark, 5230 Odense, Denmark
bnj@mmmi.sdu.dk
[2] Department of Architectural Engineering, SINTEF Community, Oslo, Norway
[3] Department for Electric Energy, Norwegian University of Science and Technology (NTNU), NO-7491, Trondheim, Norway
[4] CSIRO Energy, Commonwealth Scientific and Industrial Research Organisation (CSIRO), Newcastle, Australia
[5] Department of Built Environment, RISE Research Institutes of Sweden, Borås, Sweden
[6] Department of Engineering Cybernetics, NTNU, Trondheim, Norway

Abstract. Accurately monitoring and managing energy consumption in buildings is critical for improving efficiency and reducing environmental impact. Non-Intrusive Load Monitoring (NILM) enables energy disaggregation from aggregate meter data, but disaggregating heating and cooling loads presents unique challenges due to their continuously variable nature and dependence on external weather conditions. This paper presents a structured methodology for preparing a dataset specifically designed for temperature-dependent load disaggregation in commercial and public buildings. The dataset includes energy consumption from multiple buildings across diverse climate zones, integrating sub-metered heating and cooling loads with weather data. A rigorous data cleaning and preprocessing pipeline was implemented to ensure consistency, including unit normalization, outlier detection, cross-meter validation, and alignment with meteorological data. The resulting dataset provides researchers with high-quality energy and weather time series, enabling the development and validation of NILM algorithms for HVAC disaggregation. By documenting the dataset preparation process, this work establishes best practices for handling real-world energy data, ensuring reliability and reproducibility. This paper serves as a reference for future dataset curation efforts in NILM and temperature-dependent load analysis.

Keywords: Non-Intrusive Load Monitoring (NILM) · Load Disaggregation · Temperature-Dependent Energy Use · HVAC Disaggregation · Smart Buildings · Energy Data Preprocessing · Weather Data Integration · Public Building Energy Dataset

1 Introduction

Buildings represent a major share of global energy consumption, making efficiency improvements critical for climate goals [1]. A key strategy for optimizing energy use is gaining detailed insight into how energy is consumed within buildings. Non-intrusive load monitoring (NILM) enables the disaggregation of energy consumption from aggregate meter data [2], helping to identify end-use patterns without additional hardware. Initially introduced by Hart in the 1990s [3], NILM has been extensively researched, particularly in residential settings. However, its application in commercial buildings has been less explored due to data availability constraints [4], and it remains largely undeployed in real-world scenarios [5].

Space heating and cooling systems account for a substantial portion of building energy use, often up to 50% [6]. Separately monitoring their consumption offers practical benefits, including smart HVAC control, demand-side response, and energy optimization. Real-time HVAC monitoring enables adaptive management, optimizing energy use while maintaining occupant comfort. Additionally, distinguishing HVAC demand allows for better participation in demand-side flexibility programs, reducing peak loads and improving grid stability [7].

HVAC load disaggregation differs from typical NILM applications. The strong dependency of HVAC systems on weather conditions introduces opportunities for improving disaggregation accuracy. Correlations with temperature, humidity, and solar radiation provide additional contextual information that can be leveraged to enhance NILM models, particularly for low-frequency data [8].

Preparing a dataset for temperature-dependent disaggregation requires careful preprocessing to standardize units, remove outliers, and align energy data with weather conditions. Missing readings, inconsistencies in units, and sampling rate mismatches between energy meters must be addressed to prevent errors in NILM models. This paper presents a structured dataset designed for temperature-dependent load disaggregation in commercial and public buildings, integrating sub-metered heating and cooling data with weather data.

The dataset initially included 18 buildings from various sources but was refined to 9 buildings to ensure quality and suitability for disaggregation. It spans multiple climates and building types, including offices, schools, and public institutions, with metered heating and cooling loads providing reliable ground-truth data. A rigorous preprocessing pipeline was implemented, including unit normalization, missing data handling, and outlier detection using a Mean Absolute Deviation (MAD)-based approach. Suspicious readings, such as negative consumption values, were addressed.

To support temperature-dependent energy analysis, meteorological parameters such as outdoor temperature, solar radiation, wind speed, and humidity were integrated. Extensive validation checks—including multi-year consistency analysis and temperature-load regression tests—were conducted to confirm the reliability of HVAC sub-metering. Additionally, power and energy meter readings were cross-validated, consistency over different frequencies was ensured, and virtual meters were created to represent total energy use where needed.

The remainder of the paper is structured as follows: Sect. 2 reviews related work on NILM and existing energy datasets. Section 3 describes data sources and building selection criteria. Section 4 details data cleaning and preprocessing, while Sect. 5 discusses weather data integration. Section 6 presents validation and sanity checks. Section 7 explains dataset structuring and formatting. Section 8 summarizes lessons learned and best practices, and Sect. 9 concludes the paper with suggestions for future work. Section 10 provides dataset availability details.

2 Related Work

2.1 NILM and Temperature-Dependent Disaggregation

Non-intrusive load monitoring (NILM) has evolved significantly since Hart's seminal work [3], with research spanning traditional signal processing to modern deep learning-based techniques [9]. While much NILM research focuses on residential settings, HVAC disaggregation in commercial buildings has received less attention [10].

A key NILM challenge is load disaggregation on low-frequency smart meter data, which lacks the transient electrical signatures required for precise appliance detection [11, 12]. While high-frequency NILM approaches excel in capturing appliance switching events, they are impractical for many real-world deployments that rely on 15-min or hourly smart meter readings.

Recent studies have incorporated weather data into NILM frameworks to improve HVAC disaggregation [13, 14]. Given HVAC consumption's strong correlation with temperature, humidity, and solar radiation, these external factors provide critical context for distinguishing heating and cooling loads [15]. Machine learning methods, regression-based models, and hybrid physical-statistical approaches have demonstrated improved accuracy by integrating weather information into NILM models [16, 17].

HVAC disaggregation remains an open challenge in NILM, requiring advanced modeling techniques that accommodate complex consumption patterns and environmental influences. The dataset presented in this paper contributes to this area by providing detailed HVAC sub-metering combined with weather data to facilitate accurate load disaggregation.

2.2 Smart Building Energy Datasets and Preprocessing

Public NILM datasets have significantly contributed to the field. The REDD dataset (2011) [18] was among the first, providing high-frequency voltage and current readings along with 1 Hz appliance-level data for several U.S. homes. UK-DALE [19] offered appliance-level power measurements at 10-s intervals, while REFIT [20] provided 8-s resolution data for 20 UK households. The ECO dataset [21] collected 1 Hz data from 6 Swiss homes, uniquely incorporating ground-truth occupancy information. AMPds [22] contained 1-min data for a Canadian household, covering electrical, water, and natural gas usage. The Pecan Street project [23] expanded on these efforts by collecting 15-min data from thousands of homes. The Plug-Level Appliance Identification Datasets [24, 25] feature data from 11 appliance types at 30kHz frequency across 56 households in PLAID 1 and 9 households in PLAID 2.

Most existing NILM datasets focus on residential settings and often lack explicit HVAC sub-metering. While some datasets targeting commercial buildings exist, such as the office building dataset by Alesanco et al. [26], they remain scarce. In contrast, our dataset is specifically designed for commercial and public buildings, where HVAC systems represent a major energy load. These buildings utilize diverse heating and cooling technologies, including district heating and heat pumps, which are rarely covered in traditional NILM datasets.

Data preprocessing is critical in NILM research but is often underreported. Standard tasks include resampling irregular time-series, filtering erroneous readings, and normalizing units. NILMTK [27] was developed to standardize these tasks across datasets, offering tools for converting REDD, UK-DALE, ECO, and others into a common format. Even with such tools, manual cleaning remains necessary. As Klemenjak et al. [28] observed, model performance varies significantly between raw and preprocessed aggregate signals, emphasizing the need for structured preprocessing.

Our work builds on prior NILM research by focusing on temperature-driven load disaggregation in commercial buildings, integrating high-quality HVAC sub-metering with weather data. By documenting the data preparation process in detail, we contribute to transparency in NILM dataset development, supporting advancements in energy disaggregation methodologies.

3 Data Collection and Sources

The dataset was constructed by aggregating data from multiple sources, focusing on buildings with measurable heating or cooling loads alongside main electricity consumption. The initial dataset consisted of eighteen buildings collected from five different data providers. These included CSIRO in Australia, ReMoni in Denmark, Synavision in Germany, and Kiona and SINTEF in Norway. CSIRO data was retrieved from the Data Clearing House (DCH) smart building and energy flexibility platform [29], while SINTEF data was retrieved via the Energinet energy management platform. The buildings in the dataset represent a diverse mix of climate conditions, building types, and energy systems.

While the initial dataset consists of 18 buildings, after the cleaning and validation processes presented in this paper, nine buildings were retained after it was determined they met all selection criteria.

3.1 Building Selection Criteria

The primary objective of this dataset was to include non-residential buildings with relatively standard usage profiles, such as offices, schools, and public institutions, where heating and cooling energy use is significant and varies predictably with weather. Although some of the buildings were removed during the cleaning process, the dataset still encompasses a healthy variety of building types.

The most common issues leading to exclusion were incomplete or unreliable main meter readings, missing temperature-dependent sub-metering, and excessive missing data or irregular energy patterns that could not be reliably interpolated. In some cases, buildings were excluded due to suspected data leakage, as identified through energy per square meter analysis—such as a grocery store where refrigeration loads were substantial, and the overall consumption was likely influenced by the larger building it was part of. The nine retained buildings were those that provided high-quality, structured data that would best support temperature-dependent energy analysis. The filtering process and quality control measures applied during data selection are discussed further in Sect. 4.

The final dataset represents buildings with a variety of heating and cooling systems, including district heating, electric heating, heat pumps with electric boilers, and air handling units. The diversity of energy systems within the dataset ensures robust testing of temperature-dependent disaggregation methodologies and supports a comprehensive understanding of different heating and cooling load behaviors.

3.2 Data Sources

The dataset includes buildings from multiple regions, each contributing unique characteristics to the study. The Norwegian buildings sourced via Drammen Municipality's profile at Energinet include public buildings such as schools, offices, a kindergarten, and a nursing home. The energy data for these buildings spans multiple years and includes multiple metering points per building, covering main electricity consumption, district heating, ventilation, and hot water systems. District heating meters provided critical heating energy measurements separate from the total electricity consumption, making these buildings particularly valuable for heating disaggregation analysis.

Norwegian data was also collected from Kiona, which provided records for shopping centers, grocery stores, and mixed-use offices. The Danish dataset, sourced from ReMoni, included a municipal office building with electric heating as part of its primary energy consumption. Synavision contributed data from public schools and office buildings. These buildings featured both electric heating and district heating systems, allowing for a diverse dataset representative of different heating infrastructures.

Australian buildings were sourced from CSIRO's existing smart building and flexibility platform, the Data Clearing House (DCH), which uses the Brick schema [30], an open standard for building metadata, to identify energy and HVAC resources. These buildings had sub-metered energy monitoring, including photovoltaic systems, battery energy storage, and heating and cooling managed through air handling units. Unlike the Norwegian and Danish buildings that rely on external heating networks such as district heating, the Australian buildings in the dataset are entirely electric and feature on-site energy generation.

3.3 Building Metadata and Dataset Structure

In addition to the energy time series, each building in the dataset was characterized by detailed metadata, including location, building type, gross floor area, the presence of on-site photovoltaic generation or battery storage, and the type of heating and cooling system used. An example of this is shown in Table 1. Metadata was obtained directly from building owners, public records, and energy management platforms.

Table 1. Metadata of Building L03_B02

Building	L03_B02
Country	Denmark
Provider	ReMoni
Building Type	Office
Floor Area	8685 m^2
PV	NO
Battery	NO
Heating System	District Heating

For the SINTEF buildings, Drammen Municipality provided documentation detailing building areas and energy systems, while CSIRO supplied structured metadata extrapolated from its building management system. Among the buildings retained in the final dataset, two have solar photovoltaic systems, one in Norway and one in Australia. Additionally, one of the Australian buildings includes battery storage. These features were carefully accounted for to ensure that net-metered energy usage did not misrepresent actual consumption patterns.

The dataset spans multiple years, with varying coverage depending on the building and data provider. The SINTEF buildings have records starting from January 2018, with data extending to mid-2022 for most sites. The CSIRO buildings in Australia contain records from 2021 to 2022. Buildings from Kiona, Synavision, and ReMoni exhibit more diverse coverage periods.

Each building has a dedicated file containing time-series data for main electricity consumption, heating energy usage, photovoltaic generation, and battery storage (if applicable), as well as weather variables such as outdoor temperature, solar radiation, and wind speed. The dataset was resampled to multiple time resolutions, with hourly data serving as the default resolution and finer-granularity data available at 30-min, 15-min, and 5-min intervals for selected buildings.

4 Data Cleaning and Preprocessing

Raw sensor data often contains errors or irregularities that must be addressed prior to analysis. This section describes the cleaning steps applied to each building's time-series. This process was essential to ensure data reliability and usability for temperature-dependent load disaggregation.

Our goal was to standardize all readings to comparable units and sampling intervals and to remove data that was unreliable while preserving as much valid information as possible. The data cleaning and preprocessing steps were as follows.

4.1 Unit Normalization

Different meters recorded energy consumption in varying units and formats. Energy meters provided data as energy (kWh) over a time interval, while power meters recorded instantaneous power (kW) at a timestamp; sometimes both measures were available. To ensure consistency across all buildings, all energy measurements were converted to kilowatt-hour per hour (kWh/h), which represents the average power consumption during each hourly interval.

4.2 Handling Invalid and Missing Data

At the start and end of some datasets, extended periods of missing or zero values were detected, typically due to the initialization of metering equipment or system failures. If an entire segment contained no valid measurements across all meters, it was removed. For example, in one building, the first two weeks of data showed only zeros across all energy streams, indicating that metering had not yet begun. These periods were excluded to focus on valid data. Additionally in the SINTEF buildings, if a meter had more than 23 consecutive readings, the entire day was marked as unreliable and excluded from analysis.

No synthetic interpolation was applied, ensuring transparency regarding data availability. If necessary, users may apply their own interpolation methods, but the dataset explicitly marks large gaps rather than filling them artificially.

4.3 Meter Quality Assurance and Virtual Aggregation

Some meters exhibited persistent issues such as frequent dropouts, unrealistic fluctuations, or mislabeling. To address this, each meter's data integrity was evaluated across the full measurement period. Meters with pervasive errors, such as erratic spikes or long-term unreliability, were excluded from further analysis.

For buildings with multiple submeters, potential discrepancies were examined. If multiple meters collectively represented a single logical energy load, their readings were aggregated into a virtual meter. Additionally, in buildings using district heating, total energy use was derived by summing electricity and district heat into a virtual meter. These adjustments ensured consistency across buildings and provided a more comprehensive representation of energy consumption.

To maintain accuracy, all aggregations were performed at the highest available time resolution (e.g., 15-min data for buildings where this resolution was available), ensuring that energy totals remained consistent across different datasets.

4.4 Outlier Detection and Removal

Outliers were identified using a robust statistical method based on the Mean Absolute Deviation (MAD). Instead of relying on arbitrary thresholds, we computed the mean value m and MAD for each energy stream and removed readings that deviated by more than $10 \times$ MAD. These were replaced with NaN to prevent distortion of the dataset.

4.5 Correction of Negative Values

Negative values in energy data are usually anomalies, as energy consumption cannot be negative under normal circumstances. However, in buildings with solar PV, net electricity export can result in negative main meter values. These cases were preserved, as they reflect real building behavior. Negative electricity readings arise from the net export of excess PV generation or drawing grid power to charge batteries. The PV and main meter values always account for total load, storage, and export. Conversely, negative heating values were deemed physically implausible and were corrected to NaN.

5 Weather Data Integration

To support temperature-dependent load disaggregation, each building's energy data was paired with hourly weather information retrieved using the Open-Meteo API [31]. This service provides access to high-resolution reanalysis data from the ERA5 [32] and CERRA [33] datasets, maintained by the Copernicus Climate Data Store. These datasets offer spatially and temporally consistent climate records that are well-suited for retrospective analysis and modeling. While a wide range of meteorological variables is available from these sources, only those considered relevant for disaggregating temperature-dependent loads were included.

In cases where multiple buildings were located in the same area but had different submetering periods, weather data was initially collected over a broad time range to ensure full coverage for all buildings. However, for the version of the dataset used in the competition, this data was trimmed individually for each building to match the specific period of its associated energy data. This trimming also served to conceal the test period and prevent participants from inferring evaluation windows during training. In practice, only one shared-location group remained, and those buildings had identical time spans, making the process straightforward.

The dataset includes six weather variables selected for their relevance to HVAC energy behavior. These are: air temperature (°C, abbreviation: T) and relative humidity (%, Rh), both measured at 2 m height; wind speed (km/h, Ws) and wind direction (degrees, Wd), measured at 10 m; and two solar radiation variables, direct solar radiation (Rd) and diffuse solar radiation (Rr), both measured in W/m2 at surface level. All features are provided in hourly resolution.

6 Validation and Sanity Checks

After assembling the cleaned energy data and integrating weather information, a series of validation and sanity checks were performed to ensure the dataset's integrity and confirm that sub-metered heating and cooling data were consistent with expectations. These checks were essential in verifying that the dataset was reliable for training and evaluating disaggregation models. Additionally, as part of the overall data preparation, buildings that exhibited major inconsistencies or unresolvable data issues were excluded, which resulted in the reduction of the initial 18 buildings to the final nine.

6.1 Multi-year Consistency

For buildings with data spanning multiple years, energy consumption trends were examined to determine whether they remained stable over time when normalized for Heating Degree Days (HDD). In a well-functioning building with no significant occupancy changes or retrofits, total energy use should generally follow expected variations based on weather conditions.

To verify this, total annual energy consumption was calculated for each building and compared against annual HDD data. A strong correlation between colder years and higher heating demand indicated that the dataset reflected realistic building behavior. In most cases, expected patterns were observed, where energy use remained within a reasonable variance from year to year.

However, certain anomalies were detected, particularly in public buildings affected by the COVID-19 pandemic in 2020 and 2021. These buildings, including schools and offices, experienced significantly reduced occupancy, which led to lower overall energy consumption during those periods.

6.2 Energy Use Per Area

To support validation of the overall energy data quality, annual energy consumption was normalized by building floor area and expressed in kWh/m2/year. These area-based energy use values were compared against typical benchmarks for each building type to identify outliers. Buildings with significantly higher or lower energy use per square meter were flagged for further review, as such deviations can indicate issues like partial submetering, non-HVAC energy loads, or data logging errors.

This check contributed to the decision to discard one building—a grocery store located within a larger commercial complex—where energy use per area appeared unreasonably high. The result supported existing suspicions of data leakage from the surrounding building.

6.3 HVAC Load Capture Verification

An essential validation step involved verifying that the meters designated for heating and cooling loads truly captured the majority of temperature-driven energy consumption. If significant portions of heating consumption were instead hidden within general electricity usage, such as plug-in space heaters drawing power from the main electrical meter, it would complicate disaggregation efforts.

To test this, a temperature-load regression analysis was conducted to examine the relationship between residual electricity consumption (total consumption minus heating) and outdoor temperature. Ideally, residual consumption should be largely independent of temperature, indicating that most temperature-sensitive loads are correctly assigned to the heating meter.

A linear regression model was applied on all frequencies, where residual energy use was compared against outdoor temperature. If the heating sub-meter successfully captured all heating-related consumption, the temperature dependency in the residual load would be negligible. In most cases, the heating sub-meter accounted for over 90%

of temperature-sensitive consumption, confirming that HVAC loads were appropriately captured. However, in some buildings, a small temperature-dependent residual load was detected, likely due to additional electric heating sources that were not included in the heating meter. All included buildings had above 75% of their temperature-sensitive consumption explained by the submetering. This issue was noted in the dataset description of the competition.

Buildings, where heating sub-metering failed to capture a significant fraction of total heating consumption, were ultimately removed during data cleaning to prevent inaccurate load disaggregation results.

6.4 Cross-Meter Consistency

To ensure consistency, sub-metered energy use was compared to the main electricity meter's total reading to confirm that the sum of individual meters did not exceed the main meter values. In cases where sub-meters were installed for HVAC, lighting, and other building loads, their combined energy consumption should never surpass the total electricity consumption recorded by the main meter.

Before data cleaning, several inconsistencies were detected. In some instances, heating meters recorded higher values than the total electricity meter, suggesting possible misalignment or erroneous readings. Other cases exhibited abrupt discontinuities or unexplained jumps in energy consumption, which were likely caused by metering failures or data logging errors. Through careful data synchronization and outlier removal, these discrepancies were addressed. Any buildings where cross-meter consistency could not be reliably validated were excluded from the final dataset.

6.5 Negative Residual Analysis

As discussed in Sect. 4, we verified instances where the main meter recorded negative values, which typically indicated net energy export in buildings with PV. To ensure data consistency, we checked whether PV generation was sufficient to explain these negative readings. If the main meter showed a negative value while heating consumption was zero, it confirmed that PV was exporting enough power to account for the difference. These cases, which mostly occurred during sunny periods with low building consumption, were retained as valid data points. For disaggregation purposes, PV can be treated as a separate known input, or users can assume that negative main meter values correspond to PV export.

6.6 Energy Balance and Resampling

Because the dataset was structured at multiple time resolutions (5-min, 15-min, 30-min, and hourly intervals), it was necessary to ensure that total energy values remained consistent across different aggregation levels.

To verify this, total daily and annual energy values were summed across all resolutions to confirm that they matched. Resampling from higher-frequency data to lower resolutions was carefully checked to ensure that no artificial changes in energy totals occurred. Additionally, missing data handling was reviewed to confirm that no erroneous energy values were introduced during time aggregation.

The final structured dataset maintained total energy consistency within 0.5% across all resolutions, confirming that down sampling and aggregation procedures were executed correctly.

6.7 Summary of Validation and Checks

The validation process confirmed that energy consumption patterns remained stable across multiple years, with expected variations due to weather and operational factors. HVAC sub-metering successfully captured heating and cooling loads with minimal leakage into residual energy use. Cross-meter consistency was verified, ensuring that total energy use did not exceed main meter readings. Where both power and energy readings were available, they were aligned to prevent discrepancies. Negative residual loads were either resolved or documented, with PV-related exports properly accounted for. Lastly, total energy consistency was preserved across different time resolutions, ensuring a reliable dataset.

Buildings that failed any of these validation steps were removed during the data cleaning process, ensuring that the final dataset consists of high-quality, validated energy data suitable for temperature-dependent load disaggregation research.

7 Dataset Structuring and Formatting

To ensure the dataset is convenient for various analyses and research applications, we structured and formatted it in a consistent and flexible way. The dataset underwent careful reformatting, standardization of time resolutions, and the creation of virtual meters where necessary. In this section, we describe the steps taken to produce the final structured dataset and how it was organized to ensure usability.

7.1 Standardized Time Resolutions

The raw data originated from different sources, each having distinct sampling intervals. Norwegian and Danish buildings provided data in hourly resolution, while Australian data included 5-min and 15-min readings. To support a wide range of research applications and disaggregation challenges, we resampled the dataset to the following standardized time intervals: hourly (60 min), 30 min, 15 min, and 5 min.

For buildings that originally provided higher-frequency data, down sampling was performed by aggregating smaller time intervals into larger ones. For example, when converting 5-min data to an hourly format, values were summed to represent total energy consumption per hour. If the data was instantaneous power readings, an average over the hour was used instead.

For buildings that did not have higher resolution data, no up-sampling was done, so these buildings were only provided in the highest resolution that was available.

In all cases, missing data was preserved and not interpolated unless necessary for summation. If an entire hour was missing, the corresponding 15-min intervals remain blank rather than being filled with estimated values. This ensures that the dataset maintains integrity for researchers who may wish to apply their own missing data handling techniques.

7.2 Virtual Meter Creation

Some buildings lacked a single main energy meter that covered all energy use. In such cases, virtual meters were created by summing individual energy streams. This approach was particularly important for buildings that used multiple energy sources, such as district heating in addition to electricity.

For buildings using district heating, the total energy consumption was computed by summing the district heat meter and the main electricity meter, shown in Fig. 1. The choice of resolution for virtual meters was determined based on the source data's native resolution. For instance, if one meter provided hourly readings while another provided 15-min readings, the combined virtual meter was created at the coarser resolution (hourly). This prevented artificial high-frequency variations from being introduced through interpolation.

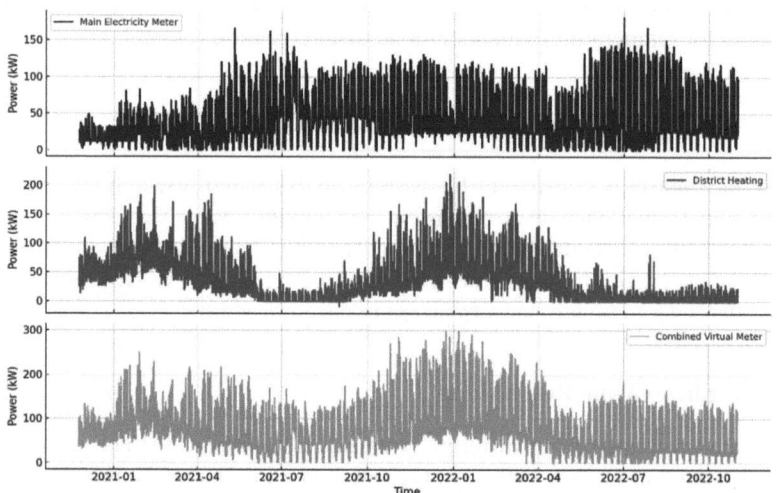

Fig. 1. Virtual meter creation for building L03.B02

In cases where multiple submeters existed, such as in the Australian building, a virtual main meter was created by aggregating all electrical sub-circuits. Since this building had separate meters for HVAC loads, we structured the dataset to include both the aggregated main load (including HVAC) and the separately metered HVAC consumption. This design ensures that researchers can either work with a "blind" disaggregation challenge (using the main meter alone) or validate models using the explicit HVAC metering.

7.3 File Format and Structure

The dataset follows a standardized format to ensure ease of use and consistency across all buildings. Each building's data is stored in comma-separated values (CSV) files at multiple time resolutions, including hourly, 30-min, 15-min, and 5-min intervals. The highest available resolution is used as the base file, with lower-resolution versions created through resampling. Figure 2 shows the final dataset's structure.

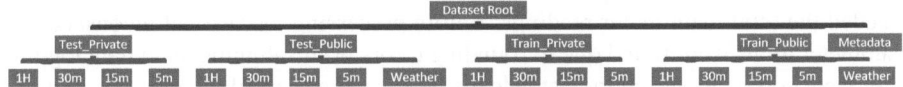

Fig. 2. Folder structure of the final dataset.

Building metadata is included in the dataset separately, containing information about the building's name (anonymized), location, type, floor area, presence of photovoltaic generation or battery storage, and heating and cooling system characteristics. This information was shared as a table during the competition. The header row specifies column names and units. The timestamps are recorded in ISO 8601 format (e.g., 2020-01-01T00:00:00Z) in Coordinated Universal Time (UTC) to avoid inconsistencies related to daylight-saving time.

The dataset includes time-series data for total electrical energy consumption, heating energy consumption, and solar PV generation (if applicable), all measured in kilowatts (kW), shown in Table 2. Table 3 shows the weather variables included, such as air temperature at 2 m (°C), relative humidity at 2 m (%), wind speed at 10 m (km/h), wind direction at 10 m(degrees), direct solar radiation (W/m^2), and diffuse solar radiation (W/m^2) are also included. All energy-related fields are standardized to kilowatts to ensure consistency across different buildings. Missing data is represented as blank fields or NaN, allowing users to apply their own interpolation techniques if needed. By structuring the dataset in this way, it remains both flexible for various research applications and aligned with best practices for energy data analysis.

Table 2. The header of a building energy characteristics file

timestamp	main_energy_consumption (kW)	heating_energy_consumption (kW)	PV_and_Battery_System (kW)

Table 3. The header of a weather information file

air_temperature_at_2m (°C)	relative_humidity_at_2m (%)	direct_solar_radiation (W/m²)	diffuse_solar_radiation (W/m²)	wind_speed_at_10m (km/h)	wind_direction_at_10m (°)	air_temperature_at_2m (°C)

7.4 Data Integrity Checks in Structured Files

After structuring and formatting the dataset, validation checks were performed to ensure internal consistency. The total annual energy consumption in different resolutions was compared to verify that resampling did not introduce significant discrepancies. Summing hourly data over a year, for example, was checked against summing 15-min data over the same period, ensuring that the total energy remained within an acceptable margin of error (typically $< 0.5\%$).

A cross-check was also performed to confirm that the sum of submeters never exceeded the total main meter readings. Before processing, occasional inconsistencies in submeter totals were found due to rounding errors or misalignments in data logging. These were corrected during the data cleaning process, as described in earlier sections.

7.5 Summary of Dataset Structure

The final structured dataset provides a well-documented, standardized collection of building energy data across different time resolutions. Virtual meters ensure completeness in buildings with multiple energy sources, and time resampling enables flexible usage in various research scenarios. By maintaining transparency in data processing and ensuring consistency across files, this dataset is designed to support robust load disaggregation analysis while minimizing preprocessing efforts for users.

8 Lessons Learned and Best Practices

The process of compiling, cleaning, and structuring this dataset provided key insights into real-world energy data complexities. A rigorous validation and cleaning workflow proved essential. The initial dataset contained 18 buildings, but issues such as missing main meters, unreliable HVAC sub-metering, and dominant non-HVAC loads reduced it to 9 buildings, ensuring suitability for temperature-dependent load disaggregation.

Variability in data quality underscored the importance of early collaboration with data providers. The dataset, sourced from CSIRO (Australia), ReMoni (Denmark), Synavision (Germany), Kiona (Norway), and SINTEF (Norway via Energinet), included both well-documented data and datasets requiring extensive preprocessing. Early clarification of metering setups and data structures was crucial to resolving inconsistencies and ensuring accurate representation of building energy use.

Defining clear building selection criteria was another key takeaway. While the dataset initially covered diverse buildings, including shopping centers, grocery stores, educational institutions, a nursing home and mixed-use office-production spaces, some were excluded due to unreliable meters, missing HVAC sub-metering, or irregular patterns that couldn't be resolved through preprocessing. Requiring buildings to have independent heating/cooling meters, minimal missing data, and distinct temperature-driven load variations was vital in refining the dataset.

Weather data integration was equally critical. Weather series were trimmed to match each building's energy data, ensuring alignment for temperature-load correlation.

Transparent documentation and reproducibility were essential. Maintaining metadata to track cleaning decisions, dataset changes, and time series adjustments enhanced usability and ensured future researchers could replicate preprocessing steps with consistency.

These lessons highlight the need for rigorous validation, careful selection criteria, and proactive engagement with data providers to build high-quality datasets for energy disaggregation research.

9 Conclusion and Future Work

This work presents a methodology for preparing a multi-building energy dataset for temperature-dependent load disaggregation. The dataset was initially compiled from 18 buildings, sourced from energy management platforms, including CSIRO (Australia), ReMoni (Denmark), Synavision (Germany), Kiona (Norway), and SINTEF (Norway via Energinet). Following a rigorous validation process, 9 buildings were retained to ensure reliability, completeness, and suitability for heating and cooling disaggregation.

The dataset underwent preprocessing steps, including time alignment, missing data handling, and cross-meter consistency checks. Buildings with unreliable metering, excessive missing data, or non-temperature-dependent loads (e.g., refrigeration) were excluded.

Challenges in dataset preparation highlighted key best practices: early engagement with data providers, thorough documentation of metering setups, and structured preprocessing. Matching weather and energy data periods, validating temperature-load relationships, and robust quality control checks were essential for refining the dataset.

Future work can expand the dataset by incorporating buildings from diverse climates, increasing data resolution, and integrating advanced metering sources, such as smart thermostats and occupancy sensors. Further validation efforts—such as benchmarking disaggregation methods—could help refine dataset structuring and establish best practices for building energy analytics.

10 Dataset Availability

The dataset used in the load disaggregation competition is publicly available through the competition's CodaLab platform, including preprocessed energy time-series and weather data for the selected buildings. This version of the dataset was prepared specifically for the challenge and includes necessary formatting and cleaning to support algorithm development.

In addition, the full dataset—including all 18 buildings, extended time coverage, and metadata—will be made available via the Zenodo research data repository. This will ensure long-term access, versioning, and citation support. All building identifiers are anonymized, and no personally identifiable information is included. Researchers using the dataset are requested to cite this paper in any publications or derived works.

Acknowledgement. This paper is part of the ADRENALIN (Data-driven smart buildings: data sandbox and competition) project. Funded by the Energy Technology Development and Demonstration Programme (EUDP) In Denmark. (Case no.64021-6025).

References

1. Programme, U.E.: 2021 Global Status Report for Buildings and Construction. UNEP—United Nations Environment Programme Nairobi, Kenya (2021)
2. Massidda, L., Marrocu, M.: A bayesian approach to unsupervised, non-intrusive load disaggregation. Sensors (Basel) **22**(12) (2022)
3. Hart, G.W.: Nonintrusive appliance load monitoring. Proc. IEEE **80**(12), 1870–1891 (1992)
4. Henriet, S., et al.: A generative model for non-Intrusive load monitoring in commercial buildings. Energy Build. **177**, 268–278 (2018)
5. Gawin, B., Malkowski, R., Rink, R.: Will NILM technology replace multi-meter telemetry systems for monitoring electricity consumption? Energies **16**(5) (2023)
6. Rousselot, M., Pinto Da Rocha, F.: Energy efficiency trends in buildings in the EU. ODYSSEE-MURE Policy Brief (2021)
7. Massidda, L., Marrocu, M.: Total and thermal load forecasting in residential communities through probabilistic methods and causal machine learning. Appl. Energy **351**, 121783 (2023)
8. Gong, H., et al.: Forecast of community total electric load and HVAC component disaggregation through a new LSTM-based method. Energies **15**(9), 2974 (2022)
9. Lien, S.K., Najafi, B., Rajasekharan, J.: Advances in machine-learning based disaggregation of building heating loads: a review. In: Energy Informatics Academy Conference. Springer (2023)
10. Tolnai, B.A., Ma, Z., Jørgensen, B.N.: A scoping review of energy load disaggregation. in progress in artificial intelligence. Springer Nature Switzerland, Cham (2023)
11. Kaselimi, M., et al.: Towards trustworthy energy disaggregation: a review of challenges, methods, and perspectives for non-intrusive load monitoring. Sensors **22**(15), 5872 (2022)
12. Brudermueller, T., Breer, F., Staake, T.: Disaggregation of heat pump load profiles from low-resolution smart meter data. In: Proceedings of the 10th ACM International Conference on Systems for Energy-Efficient Buildings, Cities, and Transportation (2023)
13. Eiraudo, S., et al.: Non-intrusive load disaggregation of industrial cooling demand with LSTM neural network. In: 2022 IEEE International Conference on Environment and Electrical Engineering and 2022 IEEE Industrial and Commercial Power Systems Europe (EEEIC/I&CPS Europe) (2022)
14. Kaneko, N., et al.: Non-intrusive thermal load disaggregation and forecasting for effective HVAC systems. Appl. Energy **367**, 123379 (2024)
15. Hossain, M., et al.: Unsupervised non-intrusive energy disaggregation for commercial buildings (2017)
16. Kazuki, O., et al.: Evaluation of deep learning-based non-intrusive thermal load monitoring. Energies **17**(9) (2024)
17. Mingzhe, Z., et al.: Heating and lighting load disaggregation using frequency components and convolutional bidirectional long short-term memory method. Energies **14**(16) (2021)
18. Kolter, J.Z., Johnson, M.J.: REDD: a public data set for energy disaggregation research. In: Workshop on data mining applications in sustainability (SIGKDD), San Diego, CA. Citeseer (2011)
19. Kelly, J., Knottenbelt, W.: The UK-DALE dataset, domestic appliance-level electricity demand and whole-house demand from five UK homes. Sci. Data **2**(1), 150007 (2015)
20. Murray, D., Stankovic, L., Stankovic, V.: An electrical load measurements dataset of United Kingdom households from a two-year longitudinal study. Sci. Data **4**(1), 160122 (2017)
21. Beckel, C., et al.: The ECO data set and the performance of non-intrusive load monitoring algorithms. In: Proceedings of the 1st ACM Conference on Embedded Systems for Energy-Efficient Buildings (2014)

22. Makonin, S.: AMPds2: the almanac of minutely power dataset (Version 2). Harvard Dataverse (2016)
23. Parson, O., et al.: Dataport and NILMTK: a building data set designed for non-intrusive load monitoring. In: 2015 IEEE Global Conference on Signal and Information Processing (GlobalSIP) (2015)
24. Gao, J., et al.: PLAID: a public dataset of high-resoultion electrical appliance measurements for load identification research: demo abstract. In: Proceedings of the 1st ACM Conference on Embedded Systems for Energy-Efficient Buildings, pp. 198–199. Association for Computing Machinery: Memphis, Tennessee (2014)
25. Baets, L.D., et al.: Handling imbalance in an extended PLAID. In: 2017 Sustainable Internet and ICT for Sustainability (SustainIT) (2017)
26. Bazenkov, N.I., et al.: An office building power consumption dataset for energy grid analysis and control algorithms. IFAC-PapersOnLine **55**(9), 111–116 (2022)
27. Batra, N., et al.: NILMTK: an open source toolkit for non-intrusive load monitoring. In: Proceedings of the 5th International Conference on Future Energy System, pp. 265–276. Association for Computing Machinery: Cambridge, United Kingdom (2014)
28. Klemenjak, C., Makonin, S., Elmenreich, W.: Investigating the performance gap between testing on real and denoised aggregates in non-intrusive load monitoring. Energy Inform. **4**, 3 (2021)
29. Hugo, D., et al.: A smart building semantic platform to enable data re-use in energy analytics applications: the Data Clearing House. In: Climate Smart Engineering. Engineers Australia, Melbourne, Australia (2023)
30. Balaji, B., et al.: Brick: towards a unified metadata schema for buildings. In Proceedings of the 3rd ACM International Conference on Systems for Energy-Efficient Built Environments, pp. 41–50, Association for Computing Machinery: Palo Alto, CA, USA (2016)
31. Zippenfenig, P.: Open-Meteo.com Weather API. Zenodo (2023)
32. Hersbach, H., et al.: ERA5 hourly data on single levels from 1940 to present. Copernicus Climate Change Service (C3S) Climate Data Store (CDS) (2023)
33. Schimanke, S., et al.: CERRA sub-daily regional reanalysis data for Europe on single levels from 1984 to present. Copernicus Climate Change Service (C3S) Climate Data Store (CDS) (2021)

Advancing Non-intrusive Load Monitoring: Insights from the Winning Algorithms in the ADRENALIN 2024 Load Disaggregation Competition

Balázs András Tolnai[1(✉)], Rafael Sudbrack Zimmermann[2], Yangxinyu Xie[2], Ngoc Tran[3], Cihat Emre Çeliker[4], Zheng Grace Ma[1], Igor Sartori[4], Matt Amos[5], Gustaf Bengtsson[6], Synne Krekling Lien[4], Clayton Miller[7], Akram Hameed[5], and Bo Nørregaard Jørgensen[1]

[1] SDU Center for Energy Informatics, The Faculty of Engineering, Maersk Mc-Kinney Moeller Institute, University of Southern Denmark, 5230 Odense, Denmark
bnj@mmmi.sdu.dk
[2] Department of Statistics and Data Science, The Wharton School, University of Pennsylvania, Philadelphia, PA, USA
[3] Institute for Foundations of Machine Learning, The University of Texas at Austin, Austin, TX, USA
[4] Department of Architectural Engineering, SINTEF Community, Oslo, Norway
[5] CSIRO Energy, Commonwealth Scientific and Industrial Research Organisation (CSIRO), Newcastle, Australia
[6] Department of Built Environment, RISE Research Institutes of Sweden, Borås, Sweden
[7] Department of the Built Environment, College of Design and Engineering, National University of Singapore, Singapore 119077, Singapore

Abstract. The ADRENALIN 2024 Load Disaggregation Challenge: Energy Use in Buildings aimed to advance non-intrusive load monitoring (NILM) by developing unsupervised machine learning models capable of separating temperature-dependent heating, ventilation, and air conditioning (HVAC) loads from total building energy consumption. Unlike traditional NILM approaches that rely on labeled training data, this competition required participants to design scalable and generalizable methods without access to appliance-level ground truth data. The top three solutions demonstrated three distinct methodologies: an adjusted Seasonal-Trend decomposition using LOESS (STL) model leveraging reference weeks for seasonal adjustments, a Gaussian Mixture Model (GMM) clustering-based approach, and a base load decomposition technique distinguishing operational and HVAC-related loads. The highest-performing model achieved an average Normalized Mean Absolute Error ($\overline{NMAE}$) of 0.235, successfully capturing seasonal HVAC trends while maintaining scalability and robustness. The competition results highlighted key challenges in automating HVAC disaggregation, improving model generalization across diverse building types, and integrating additional contextual data sources. Future research should focus on self-supervised learning, multi-modal NILM techniques, federated learning for privacy-preserving disaggregation, and computational efficiency for real-time NILM applications.

These advancements will be instrumental in enabling energy-efficient building management, demand response strategies, and smart grid integration.

Keywords: Load Disaggregation · NILM · HVAC · Unsupervised Learning · Building Energy Management

1 Introduction

Buildings account for approximately a third of global final energy consumption [1], and around 40% in the European Union [2]. In contrast, buildings in Australia account for only 19% of total energy use [3]. This amounts to approximately 24% of the country's electricity consumption for each of the residential [4] and commercial building sectors [5]. This makes energy efficiency a critical factor in reducing CO_2 emissions and balancing power grids. As the demand for energy-efficient solutions grows, understanding and optimizing building-level energy consumption has become increasingly important [6]. One of the key technologies enabling this optimization is Non-Intrusive Load Monitoring (NILM), which disaggregates total energy usage into individual appliance-level consumption without requiring physical submetering [7].

NILM techniques offer several advantages, such as providing detailed insights into energy usage patterns, enabling personalized energy-saving recommendations [8], monitoring of individuals [9], and facilitating fault detection in ventilation, and air conditioning (HVAC) systems [10], and accommodating more accurate demand-side management [11]. However, accurate NILM remains a significant challenge, particularly for heating, and cooling systems. Unlike conventional appliances with distinct on/off states, HVAC systems often operate in a continuously variable manner, making their disaggregation more complex [12]. While most NILM applications focus on pattern recognition in high-resolution data, there are few demonstrations of disaggregation of HVAC load decomposition on low resolution (e.g. 1 h) [13–15].

To advance the state of the art in HVAC load disaggregation, the ADRENALIN 2024 Load Disaggregation Competition was launched. This competition aimed to develop unsupervised machine learning approaches capable of distinguishing temperature-dependent HVAC loads from total energy consumption. While many NILM approaches rely on supervised learning or appliance-specific models [16], unsupervised methods have also been explored in prior work, including clustering-based and probabilistic modeling approaches [17–20]. The ADRENALIN 2024 Load Disaggregation Competition required participants to develop scalable and generalizable unsupervised machine learning methods, distinguishing temperature-dependent loads from total energy consumption without access to labeled training data.

Participants worked with a diverse dataset collected from nine buildings across Norway, Denmark, and Australia, representing various climatic zones and building types such as offices, schools, shopping centers, and nursing homes. The dataset included energy meter readings at multiple time resolutions (5, 15, 30 and 60 min), along with weather-related features such as temperature, solar radiation, and wind speed. The competition was structured into two phases: an initial development phase, where participants fine-tuned their models on a training dataset, and a final evaluation phase, where they submitted results on the test dataset.

The competition attracted 47 teams in the first phase and 13 teams in the final phase, leading to the development of multiple innovative NILM algorithms. The winning solutions utilized distinct approaches, including seasonal-trend decomposition (STL) [21], Gaussian Mixture Models (GMM) [22], and base load decomposition techniques, demonstrating the feasibility of unsupervised NILM methods for temperature-dependent load disaggregation.

The remainder of the paper is structured as follows: Sect. 2 describes the competition methodology, detailing the dataset, evaluation metrics, and competition structure. Section 3 introduces the three winning algorithms, explaining their respective approaches. Section 4 presents the results of the competition and an in-depth analysis of algorithmic performance. Section 5 discusses the key findings and limitations. Section 6 provides a summary, concluding remarks and future directions for NILM research.

2 Competition Methodology

The ADRENALIN 2024 Load Disaggregation Challenge was designed to advance research in unsupervised NILM by encouraging participants to develop scalable and generalizable algorithms for disaggregating temperature-dependent HVAC loads from overall energy consumption. Unlike NILM tasks that often rely on supervised learning or detailed appliance-level labels, this competition required contestants to disaggregate temperature-dependent energy usage without access to ground truth data during model development, ensuring that solutions were adaptable across various building types and climates.

The competition was hosted on the Codalab platform [23], where participants accessed the ADRENALIN dataset and submitted their predictions for evaluation. The dataset consisted of energy consumption measurements collected from nine buildings across Norway, Denmark, and Australia, covering offices, schools, shopping centers, nursing homes, and kindergartens. As detailed in Table 1. Each building had different HVAC configurations, with some having only heating systems while others included both heating and cooling. The dataset was provided at multiple sampling resolutions (hourly, 30-min, 15-min, and 5-min intervals), allowing teams to test the robustness of their models at different time granularities. Additionally, meteorological data, including outdoor temperature, relative humidity, solar radiation, wind speed, and wind direction, was included to support temperature-dependent load analysis. For buildings with photovoltaic (PV) systems, energy generation and battery storage data were also provided. To ensure data consistency, the dataset was preprocessed and resampled, with missing values handled before distribution.

To create a competitive yet realistic testing environment, aligning with common practice [24], the challenge was structured into two distinct phases. In Phase I (development phase), participants received a training dataset containing raw energy consumption data but without ground truth labels for temperature-dependent loads. They were allowed to develop and refine their models based on the observed correlations between energy consumption and temperature variations. To improve performance, competitors could submit their predictions and receive immediate feedback on a public leaderboard. This phase provided an opportunity for teams to experiment with different methodologies and optimize their approaches before entering the final stage.

Table 1. The dataset available for the training phase

Name	Country	Building type	Floor Area [m²]	PV/Battery system	Time resolution in minutes				HVAC type	data for Phase I - Devel-opment	data for Phase II - Evaluation
					60	30	15	5		From – To	From – To
L03_B02	Denmark	Office	8 685		x				Heat	01.12.20 – 15.11.21	16.11.21 – 31.10.22
L06_B01	Norway	Shopping centre	2 200	x	x				Heat	01.04.21 – 15.02.22	16.02.22 – 31.12.22
L09_B01	Australia	Office	8700	x	x	x	x	x	Heat & Cool	01.01.21 – 31.12.21	01.01.22 – 31.12.22
L10_B01	Norway	Office	18 000		x	x	x		Heat & Cool	01.01.20 – 31.07.21	01.08.21 – 31.12.22
L14_B01	Norway	School	6 084		x				Heat	01.01.18 – 31.12.18	01.01.19 – 31.12.19
L14_B02		Nursing home	2 700		x						
L14_B03		School	6 546		x						
L14_B04		Office	11 502		x						
L14_B05		Kindergarten	988		x						

In Phase II (final evaluation phase), a new, unseen dataset was released, and participants had a strict limit of five submissions. This restriction was implemented to prevent overfitting to the test set, ensuring that only the most generalizable and robust models performed well.

The evaluation metric used for ranking submissions was Normalized Mean Absolute Error (NMAE), a widely used error measure for NILM tasks. The NMAE for each building was calculated individually using Eq. 1, where y_i represents the actual measured temperature-dependent consumption, $\hat{y}_i$ represents the model's predicted values, and $\bar{y}$ is the mean ground truth value. The final competition score was then determined by averaging the NMAE scores across all buildings using Eq. 2. The NMAE metric was chosen because it provides scale-invariant error measurement, allowing fair comparison across buildings with different energy consumption levels.

$$NMAE_j = \frac{\sum_{i=1}^{n}|y_i - \hat{y}_i|}{n \cdot \bar{y}} \tag{1}$$

$$\overline{NMAE} = \frac{1}{m}\sum\nolimits_{j=1}^{m} NMAE_j \tag{2}$$

The competition attracted a diverse group of participants, with 47 teams submitting entries during Phase I. However, only 13 teams advanced to Phase II, highlighting the challenge of generalizing unsupervised NILM models. To qualify as a high-performing solution, participants were required to achieve an $\overline{NMAE}$ below 0.5. Among the teams that progressed to Phase II, nine successfully met this criterion, demonstrating strong performance in temperature-dependent load disaggregation. The final winners were selected based on their ranking on the Phase II leaderboard and their compliance with documentation requirements, ensuring transparency and reproducibility of their methods.

The ADRENALIN 2024 competition successfully demonstrated the potential of unsupervised NILM approaches for temperature-dependent load disaggregation and provided valuable insights into the scalability of different machine-learning models.

3 Winning Solutions

The ADRENALIN 2024 Load Disaggregation Competition resulted in three distinct winning approaches, each offering unique methodologies for unsupervised temperature-dependent load disaggregation. These solutions demonstrated how different machine learning and statistical techniques could be leveraged to separate temperature-dependent loads from total building energy consumption without access to labeled training data. The top three teams employed three different approaches: 1) STL, 2) clustering-based GMM, and 3) a base load decomposition framework, showcasing diverse strategies for tackling the problem. The following sub-chapters describe these strategies in more detail.

3.1 Team Rafaelzimmermann's Algorithm

The first-place solution, developed by Team Rafaelzimmermann, introduced an Adjusted STL decomposition algorithm designed to isolate HVAC loads by leveraging stable reference weeks and seasonal adjustment techniques. STL (Seasonal-Trend decomposition using LOcally Estimated Scatterplot Smoothing LOESS [21]) is a well-established time-series decomposition method that separates a signal into trend, seasonal, and residual components. In this approach, the key innovation was the identification of reference weeks, which are periods where temperature-dependent loads are minimal or absent. These weeks served as a baseline for refining the seasonal component of the STL decomposition, ensuring more accurate disaggregation. The model adjusted seasonal estimates using multiplicative scaling factors derived from the reference periods, improving robustness against seasonal fluctuations and noise. Unlike traditional STL decomposition, which assumes fixed seasonality, the adjusted version adapts to varying seasonal trends, making it particularly effective in buildings with irregular heating and cooling patterns. The preprocessing stage included timestamp synchronization, missing value imputation, and outlier detection using statistical smoothing methods. This model was particularly strong in buildings with clear heating-dominated consumption patterns but required manual reference week selection, limiting full automation, which in turn limits scalability for large datasets.

3.2 Team HashBrown's Algorithm

The second-place solution, developed by Team HashBrown, employed a clustering-based approach using GMM combined with a time-as-predictor model. This method classified energy consumption into three demand categories: no demand, low demand, and high demand-based on temperature values. The GMM component was used to cluster energy readings into distributions representing different states of HVAC activity, assuming that energy demand patterns could be modeled as a mixture of Gaussian distributions. The time-as-predictor model estimated the base load by analyzing historical consumption trends during periods of minimal HVAC activity, enabling the separation of temperature-independent loads. A key advantage of this method was its automatic adaptability across different building types, as it required minimal customization and relied on data-driven clustering rather than predefined thresholds. The preprocessing pipeline included PV energy adjustments, outlier filtering, and missing data handling using forward-fill interpolation. While the model performed well in buildings with predictable HVAC schedules, its accuracy suffered in cases where HVAC operation was highly variable or influenced by external non-temperature factors such as occupancy changes or equipment malfunctions. An additional innovation was the incorporation of unsupervised holiday detection, which improved the accuracy of disaggregation in schools and office buildings by automatically identifying periods of reduced energy use.

3.3 Team Cteceliker's Algorithm

The third-place solution, developed by Team Cteceliker, implemented a base load decomposition framework that separated temperature-dependent consumption by subtracting estimated base and operational loads from total energy use. This method did not rely on explicit temperature correlations but instead modeled operational energy patterns using clustering techniques. The base load was determined by extracting the minimum observed power usage per hour, under the assumption that this represents non-temperature-dependent energy consumption, such as lighting and essential building operations. The operational load was then identified using a K-Means clustering approach, grouping power usage patterns into different operational states. The final temperature-dependent load was computed as the residual energy consumption after subtracting the base and operational loads. The algorithm further applied buffer corrections and clipping thresholds to account for fluctuations in heating and cooling energy. For buildings with cooling systems, seasonal scaling factors were introduced to correct underestimated cooling loads, particularly in commercial settings where temperature-dependent usage varies with business activity. While this approach was highly scalable and did not require temperature data, its performance was sensitive to base load estimation inaccuracies and struggled in buildings with highly irregular consumption patterns.

3.4 Summary

A comprehensive comparison of these methodologies is provided in Table 2. The table encapsulates the differences of each approach—from the underlying techniques

Table 2. Comparison of the Top Three Winning Solutions

Feature	Team Rafaelzimmermann (1st)	Team HashBrown (2nd)	Team Cte-celiker (3rd)
Approach	Adjusted STL decomposition	Time-based predictor + GMM	Base/operational load removal + K-Means
Main Technique	STL with seasonal adjustment via ref. weeks	GMM clustering + statistical time predictor	Residual calc. after subtracting base/operational
Uses Temp. Data?	No (uses seasonal trends)	Yes (temp thresholds for clustering)	No (infers HVAC via patterns)
Base Load Est	From low-HVAC ref. weeks	Time-of-day/week patterns	Hourly minima
HVAC Load ID	Seasonal signal after STL adjustment	3-state clustering: no/low/high demand	Residual after subtracting other loads
Preprocessing	Sync, imputation, outlier removal	PV adj., interpolation, holiday detection	PV handling, buffer correction, clustering
Generalizability	High (default works, tuning improves)	Fully auto., needs consistent HVAC	Scalable, struggles with non-HVAC variance
Strengths	Accurate seasonal split; low customization	No temp data needed; auto. clustering	Handles noise; good for irregular occupancy
Limitations	Needs tuning; weak w/ irregular HVAC	Base load errors hurt accuracy	Hard to separate non-HVAC ops
Best Buildings	Seasonal HVAC patterns	Predictable HVAC demand	Clear operational/non-operational loads
Weakest Buildings	Year-round HVAC use	Occupant-driven fluctuations	Complex or variable op. loads

and use of temperature data to preprocessing requirements, generalizability, strengths, limitations, and performance across different building types.

Each of these three approaches demonstrated unique advantages and limitations, reflecting the diverse methodologies applicable to NILM-based HVAC load disaggregation. The Adjusted STL method was highly accurate but its best results required manual reference week selection, making automation more challenging. The clustering-based GMM model was interpretable and required minimal customization, but its performance was dependent on consistent HVAC operation schedules. The base load decomposition method was scalable across different buildings but faced difficulties in distinguishing temperature-dependent loads from other operational loads. Together, these solutions highlighted the potential of unsupervised NILM techniques, offering valuable insights

4 Competition Results

4.1 Overall Results

The first phase of the competition had 47 entrants, while the second phase had fewer, 13 submitters. Out of these 13 submissions, nine performed better than 0.5 $\overline{\text{NMAE}}$. The number of submissions from individual teams varied. The team topping the test phase leaderboard made 151 submissions but elected not to participate in the final phase. The winning team made the most submissions during the test phase, a total of 342 submissions, second place made 88 while the third-place finisher made 218 submissions.

The top three contestants achieved a score of 0.235, 0.265, and 0.274 combined $\overline{\text{NMAE}}$. The previously set threshold that the contestant's score had to be above to be eligible to be a winner was 0.5 $\overline{\text{NMAE}}$, which was reached by 9 of the 13 participants. This is shown on Table 3, the final leaderboard. This table shows the 13 participants or teams that made submissions during the test stage of the competition, their final placement, and their best achieved $\overline{\text{NMAE}}$ score. Figure 1 shows the distribution of the contestants' scores for each building while Fig. 2 shows the same for all contestants. These two figures show that the performance of the algorithms varies from building to building, and the best and worst-performing buildings can vary between solutions. The multiple sampling rates included for buildings L09.B01 and L10.B01 had similar results, which meant that the performance on these buildings largely impacted the final scoring. L06.B01 was also a critical building, as it was the weak point of many algorithms, while L14.B05 proved to be the building that could be disaggregated the most accurately.

Table 3. The final leaderboard

placement	User	NMAE
1	rafaelzimmermann	0.235
2	Xieyangxinyu (Team HashBrown)	0.265
3	cteceliker	0.274
4	mattuw	0.276
5	Antelope3440	0.285
6	rasyidridha	0.352
7	aqib16	0.468
8	amtsh	0.468
9	matifj23	0.468
10	madi12	0.524
11	dr_molu	0.556

(*continued*)

Table 3. (*continued*)

placement	User	$\overline{\text{NMAE}}$
12	BasuHela	0.639
13	wij	0.798

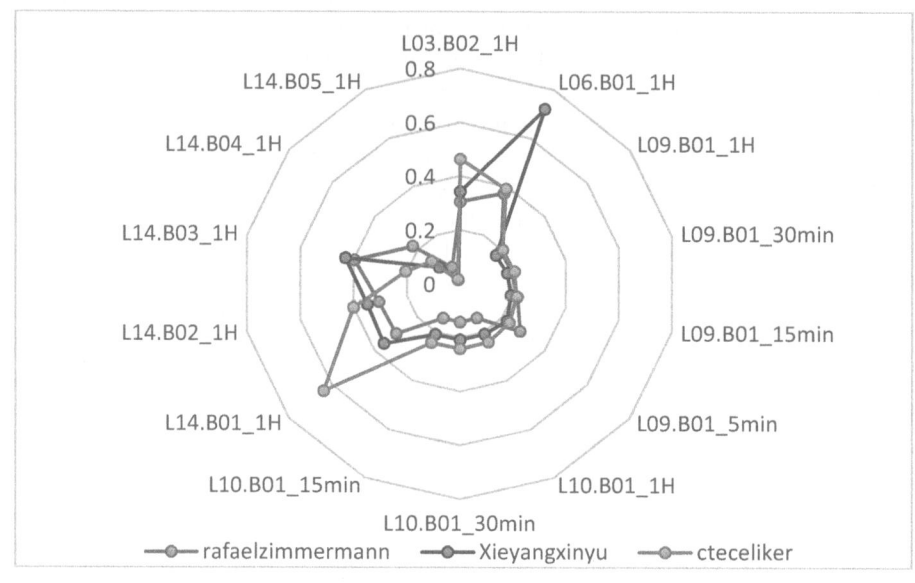

Fig. 1. Scores of the top three contestants on each building.

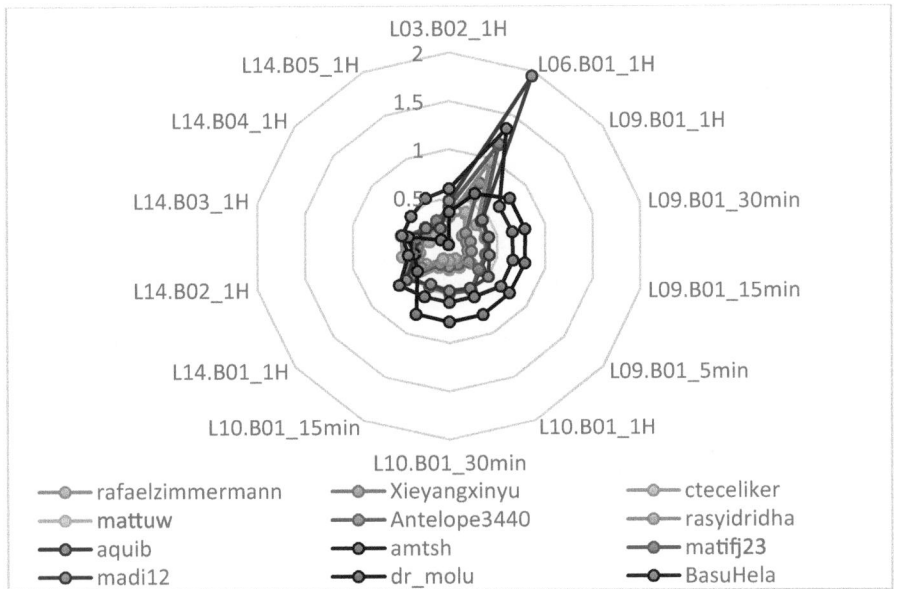

Fig. 2. Scores of all contestants on each building.

4.2 Team Rafaelzimmermann's Algorithm

The adjusted STL algorithm achieved the best overall result during the final evaluation phase, with 0.235 $\overline{\text{NMAE}}$. For individual buildings, the method performed best on L10.B0, L14.B01, L14.B02, L03.B02, and L06.B01. The method fell behind the other top solutions on buildings L14.B04, L14.B05, and also on L09.B01 with a 5-min frequency. Detailed results in Fig. 3, show that the algorithm provided very stable results, as even the buildings with the least accurate disaggregation had an NMAE below 0.4. During the development phase of the competition, the same algorithm provided results with an $\overline{\text{NMAE}}$ of 0.255, placing it in second place on Phase I leaderboard.

The team experimented with other methods, mainly based on the STL decomposition and classical decomposition. Classical decomposition demonstrated promising results in buildings where heating was the primary factor, achieving an $\overline{\text{NMAE}}$ of 0.320 in the competition's phase I submissions. However, its performance declined in cases requiring both heating and cooling analyses. Standard STL decomposition produced suboptimal results, leading to an $\overline{\text{NMAE}}$ exceeding 0.4.

A hybrid approach combining adjusted STL and classical decomposition was tested on select buildings, yielding an $\overline{\text{NMAE}}$ of 0.243. This suggests a potential for further refinement in integrating both methods where improvements were observed. Additionally, a filtering mechanism adjusting predictions based on temperature data further improved results, reducing the $\overline{\text{NMAE}}$ to 0.240. However, its increased complexity and data demands limit its practicality.

Other techniques, including regression models, deep learning, and unsupervised NILM approaches, were explored but ultimately dismissed due to excessive complexity and inferior performance compared to adjusted STL.

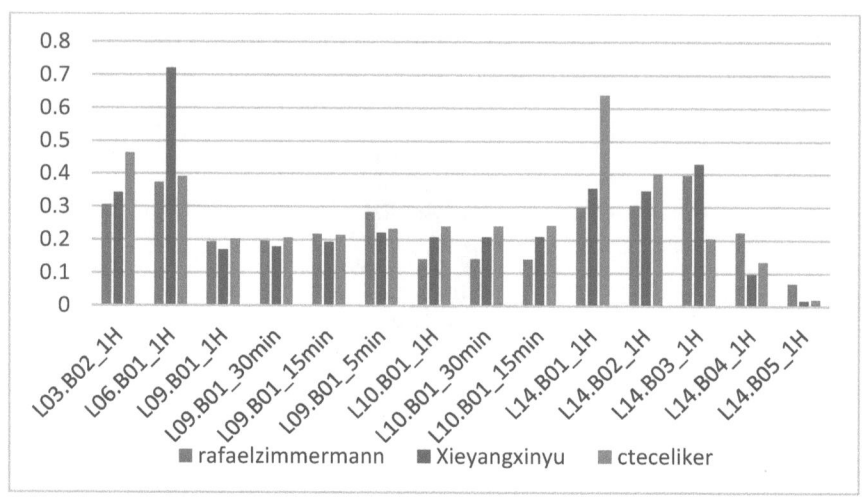

Fig. 3. Results of the top 3 algorithms for all buildings (NMAE)

4.3 Team HashBrown's Algorithm

The second-best disaggregation approach also provided strong results across all buildings, as seen in Fig. 3. The algorithm's notable weak point is building L06.B01, where it was significantly outperformed by the other winning algorithms. The rest of the buildings showed results similar to the other algorithms, with only one other building having an NMAE above 0.4. The strongest buildings for this approach were L14.B04, L14.B05, and all frequencies of L09.B01, where it provided the best result of the three winning algorithms.

During the final evaluation phase, it achieved an $\overline{\text{NMAE}}$ of 0.285, while in the development phase, the best-recorded $\overline{\text{NMAE}}$ was 0.298. The model effectively captured daily and seasonal energy consumption patterns, with HVAC energy use strongly correlating with temperature variations in buildings requiring both heating and cooling.

Performance varied among different building categories. For heating-only buildings, the model provided stable and accurate predictions, particularly in settings where temperature thresholds clearly delineated HVAC usage. In buildings with both heating and cooling, the model effectively adjusted for seasonal variations, producing HVAC estimates that aligned well with observed consumption patterns. The approach performed best when demand patterns exhibited consistent weekday and weekend variations, with correlation values exceeding 90% between predicted and actual temperature-dependent consumption across most buildings.

In specific cases, refinements improved prediction accuracy. The introduction of an unsupervised holiday detection method enhanced HVAC demand estimation for schools and office buildings, correctly identifying low-energy periods during breaks. Additionally, targeted adjustments to Australian office buildings corrected inconsistencies in predicted consumption levels, leading to more reliable results.

4.4 Team Cteceliker's Algorithm

The third approach also provided good results, less than 0.01 $\overline{\text{NMAE}}$ behind the second solution, with consistent values across most buildings, as seen in Fig. 3, with only two buildings above 0.4 NMAE. Compared to the other algorithms, the solution provided the best results on building L14.B03 where it had the best performance by a margin of 0.2 NMAE. The building least fitting for this algorithm was L14.B01, where it produced the highest NMAE and was outperformed by the other algorithms.

The model achieved a leaderboard score below 0.3 during the development phase, indicating strong predictive capability. Results showed that HVAC consumption patterns aligned with seasonal and daily variations in energy use, with higher consumption during peak heating or cooling periods. The model successfully captured expected energy trends, performing particularly well in buildings with predictable operational schedules.

For buildings with regular usage patterns, the model provided accurate estimates of HVAC energy consumption, demonstrating a strong correlation with external temperature fluctuations. The results confirmed that heating and cooling loads were well-disaggregated, particularly in buildings with clear distinctions between operational and non-operational hours. In contrast, buildings with irregular energy consumption presented greater challenges, leading to increased uncertainty in disaggregation results.

The model also demonstrated improvements in estimating HVAC consumption in buildings with cooling systems. Refinements such as buffer adjustments helped reduce underestimation, while upper clipping prevented overestimation of HVAC loads. These refinements resulted in more stable and reliable HVAC energy usage estimates, particularly in commercial buildings with fluctuating energy demands.

5 Discussion

The results of the ADRENALIN 2024 Load Disaggregation Competition demonstrated the feasibility of unsupervised machine learning techniques for accurately identifying HVAC loads in building energy data. The competition successfully showcased how different methodologies - adjusted seasonal-trend decomposition (STL), clustering-based Gaussian Mixture Models (GMM), and base load decomposition techniques can be leveraged to separate temperature-dependent HVAC loads from total energy consumption without labeled training data. Each of the winning solutions had distinct strengths and weaknesses, highlighting key areas where NILM approaches perform well and where challenges remain.

All three top-performing models were lightweight and implemented using standard Python libraries. The fastest models produced results within 2 to 20 s per building, while the others relied on efficient statistical or clustering-based operations that require no specialized hardware. This confirms the practical deployability of unsupervised NILM methods even at scale.

A significant finding of the competition was the effectiveness of unsupervised learning for NILM, particularly in real-world applications where appliance-level labels are unavailable. The results reinforced that purely data-driven methods can effectively infer HVAC consumption using statistical decomposition, clustering, and pattern recognition techniques. This finding is critical for scalable NILM implementations, as it eliminates the need for extensive manual data labeling, making these methods more practical for deployment across diverse building types and climatic conditions. Nevertheless, while the top-performing models functioned without building-specific tuning, participants often performed manual adjustments to boost leaderboard performance. This highlights a tension between benchmark optimization and real-world scalability, where the absence of ground truth complicates fine-tuning and limits the practicality of such adjustments. Model generalization remains a challenge, as performance varies significantly depending on building type, HVAC configuration, and energy consumption patterns.

The comparison of Normalized Mean Absolute Error (NMAE) across buildings with district heating and electric heating reveals clear differences in NILM model performance. L14.B05, a district heating building, stands out with the lowest NMAE, indicating that it was the easiest to disaggregate. In contrast, L06.B01, an electric heating building, has a significantly higher NMAE, making it one of the most difficult to model accurately. This suggests that electric heating introduces more variability or complexity that the models struggle to capture. Other buildings show a more mixed pattern. L09.B01 and L10.B01, despite having different heating types (electric and district, respectively), exhibit NMAE values that are relatively close, indicating that heating type alone does not always determine difficulty.

Average model performance varied by building type as shown in Table 4. Kindergartens showed the lowest normalized mean absolute errors across all models, suggesting simpler HVAC load patterns that facilitated disaggregation. Shopping centers presented the greatest challenge, particularly for the model by team HashBrown, indicating greater variability or complexity in energy use. Offices, schools, and nursing homes demonstrated intermediate accuracy levels. These trends highlight the influence of building function on NILM model effectiveness and underscore the need for tailored approaches to accommodate diverse building usage profiles.

Table 4. Average results per building type

Building type	rafaelzimmermann	team hashbrown	cteceliker
office	0.2053	0.203433	0.2422
shopping center	0.3728	0.7205	0.3903
school	0.34795	0.39385	0.4222
nursing home	0.3053	0.3485	0.4002
kindergarten	0.0687	0.0167	0.0195

The adjusted STL approach, which ranked first, performed well by using automatically identified stable reference weeks to refine seasonal decomposition and isolate HVAC loads. However, while the default setting provided solid performance, achieving the best results required manual tuning of the reference weeks, highlighting a limitation in terms of full automation. The second-place solution, based on Gaussian Mixture Models and time-as-predictor models, proved to be highly adaptable and required minimal manual tuning. However, it struggled with irregular occupancy-driven fluctuations, particularly in buildings with unpredictable HVAC operation schedules. The third-place solution, which employed a base and operational load decomposition approach, was highly scalable and effective in commercial buildings, where clear operational schedules helped in estimating base loads. However, it faced difficulties in distinguishing non-HVAC operational loads, leading to potential inaccuracies in buildings with fluctuating energy consumption patterns.

Another key takeaway was the importance of incorporating diverse data sources into NILM methods. While the competition primarily focused on energy meter readings, many real-world NILM applications benefit from additional contextual data, such as weather information, occupancy patterns, and indoor climate conditions. The findings suggest that future NILM solutions could benefit from integrating external environmental data to improve accuracy in disaggregating temperature-dependent loads.

Beyond the methodological findings, the competition highlighted the importance of evaluation constraints in NILM research. Since the competition followed an unsupervised evaluation protocol, participants did not have access to ground truth HVAC labels during model development. While this ensured that models were tested on their ability to generalize, it also introduced challenges in hyperparameter tuning, as competitors had to rely on leaderboard feedback rather than direct validation on labeled data. These insights emphasize the need for NILM research to explore new evaluation methodologies that balance generalization with real-time performance optimization.

The competition reinforced that unsupervised NILM techniques can be highly effective in separating temperature-dependent and independent loads while also revealing areas where improvement is needed. The variability in model performance across buildings, the challenges of automating model adaptation, and the need for multi-source data integration are all factors that must be addressed in future NILM developments. By refining these approaches, NILM can play an even more significant role in optimizing energy management, supporting demand response strategies, and enabling more energy-efficient buildings.

6 Conclusion and Future Work

The ADRENALIN 2024 Load Disaggregation Competition has provided valuable insights into the potential and limitations of unsupervised NILM techniques for HVAC load disaggregation in buildings. By challenging participants to develop models that could separate temperature-dependent loads from total energy consumption without labeled training data, the competition successfully demonstrated the viability of scalable NILM implementations. The winning solutions, which employed adjusted STL decomposition, Gaussian Mixture Models, and base load decomposition techniques each exhibited unique strengths and weaknesses, underscoring the need for adaptive and hybrid NILM approaches.

The results confirmed that no single NILM approach is universally optimal across all buildings. The adjusted STL method excelled in buildings with seasonal HVAC usage and while default settings could extract reference weeks, the best results required manual tuning. The clustering-based approach was automated and adaptable but was sensitive to occupancy-driven fluctuations. The base load decomposition method was highly scalable but faced challenges in accurately distinguishing non-HVAC operational loads. These findings highlight the importance of hybrid models that can combine statistical decomposition, clustering, and machine learning-based feature extraction to improve NILM accuracy and generalizability.

Looking ahead, several research directions could enhance NILM methodologies and improve real-world deployment. Automating reference week selection in STL-based approaches could significantly reduce manual intervention, making them more practical for large-scale deployment. Self-supervised learning techniques could improve clustering-based NILM models, enabling them to adapt to dynamic HVAC behavior in real-time. Multi-modal NILM methods that incorporate temperature, humidity, CO_2 levels, and motion sensor data could further improve load disaggregation accuracy by integrating contextual building information. Additionally, federated learning-based NILM models could enable privacy-preserving energy analytics, allowing buildings to optimize energy usage without sharing raw energy data.

The competition dataset included a diverse range of building types, including offices, schools, and retail spaces, and spanned multiple climate zones and HVAC configurations. However, the total number of buildings was limited to nine, which constrains the statistical strength of any generalization. Future competitions should consider expanding the number of buildings while maintaining realistic, high-quality, and diverse data to better support robust cross-building evaluation.

In addition to methodological improvements, computational efficiency and deployment scalability remain key considerations for NILM adoption. While the competition did not impose strict computational constraints, real-world applications require NILM models that can operate on edge devices or cloud-based platforms with minimal latency. Future work should focus on developing lightweight NILM models optimized for IoT-based energy monitoring systems, ensuring that energy disaggregation can be performed in real-time without excessive computational overhead.

Beyond HVAC disaggregation, NILM techniques can support a wide range of energy management applications. Expanding NILM models to include appliance fault detection, real-time demand response, and smart grid energy management could significantly improve building energy efficiency and grid stability. Future competitions could further advance NILM research by incorporating real-time disaggregation challenges, grid-level NILM tasks, and dynamic demand-side management scenarios.

The ADRENALIN 2024 competition has demonstrated the practical viability and scalability of unsupervised NILM techniques for HVAC load disaggregation. While the competition results showcased several promising methodologies, they also revealed key challenges in model generalization, automation, and handling irregular energy patterns. Future advancements in self-supervised learning, multi-modal data integration, federated NILM, and edge computing optimization will be critical for developing next-generation NILM solutions. These advancements will play an essential role in enabling energy-efficient buildings integrated into the future grid.

Acknowledgement. This paper is part of the ADRENALIN (Data-driven smart buildings: data sandbox and competition) project. Funded by the Energy Technology Development and Demonstration Programme (EUDP) In Denmark. (Case no.64021-6025).

References

1. International Energy, A., A. International Renewable Energy, and U.N.C.C.H.-L. Champions, Breakthrough Agenda Report 2023. IEA, Paris (2023)
2. European, U., Directive (EU) 2024/1275 of the European Parliament and of the Council of 24 April 2024 on the energy performance of buildings, in Official Journal of the European Union. Publications Office of the European Union, p. 1–87 (2024)
3. Department of Climate Change, E.t.E. and Water. Buildings Overview. https://www.dcceew.gov.au/energy/energy-efficiency/buildings
4. Department of Climate Change, E.t.E. and Water. Residential Buildings. https://www.dcceew.gov.au/energy/energy-efficiency/buildings/residential-buildings
5. Department of Climate Change, E.t.E. and Water, Commercial Building Baseline Study 2022. Commonwealth of Australia: Canberra, Australia (2022)
6. Min, J., et al.: The effect of carbon dioxide emissions on the building energy efficiency. Fuel **326**, 124842 (2022)
7. Taghvaei, F., Safa, R.: Efficient energy consumption in smart buildings using personalized NILM-based recommender system. Big Data Comput. Vis. **1**(3), 161–169 (2021)
8. Ehrhardt-Martinez, K., Donnelly, K.A., Laitner, S.: Advanced metering initiatives and residential feedback programs: a meta-review for household electricity-saving opportunities. American Council for an Energy-Efficient Economy Washington, DC (2010)
9. Dai, S., Wang, Q., Meng, F.: A telehealth framework for dementia care: an ADLs patterns recognition model for patients based on NILM. In: 2021 International Joint Conference on Neural Networks (IJCNN) (2021)
10. Rafati, A., Shaker, H.R., Ghahghahzadeh, S.: Fault detection and efficiency assessment for HVAC systems using non-intrusive load monitoring: a review. Energies **15** (2022). https://doi.org/10.3390/en15010341
11. Lu, N.: An evaluation of the HVAC load potential for providing load balancing service. IEEE Trans. Smart Grid **3**(3), 1263–1270 (2012)
12. Zoha, A., et al.: Non-intrusive load monitoring approaches for disaggregated energy sensing: a survey. Sensors **12**, 16838–16866 (2012). https://doi.org/10.3390/s121216838
13. Lien, S.K., Najafi, B., Rajasekharan, J.: Advances in machine-learning based disaggregation of building heating loads: a review. in energy informatics. Springer Nature Switzerland, Cham (2024)
14. De Baets, L., et al.: On the Bayesian optimization and robustness of event detection methods in NILM. Energy Build. **145**, 57–66 (2017)
15. Li, J., et al.: Air conditioning load monitoring in NILM using low frequency power data. In: 2024 3rd Asian Conference on Frontiers of Power and Energy (ACFPE) (2024)
16. Tolnai, B.A., Ma, Z., Jørgensen, B.N.: A scoping review of energy load disaggregation. In: Moniz, N., Vale, Z., Cascalho, J., Silva, C., Sebastião, R. (eds.) Progress in Artificial Intelligence. EPIA 2023. LNCS, vol. 14116. Springer, Cham (2023). https://doi.org/10.1007/978-3-031-49011-8_17
17. Gonçalves, H., et al.: Unsupervised disaggregation of appliances using aggregated consumption data. In: The 1st KDD Workshop on Data Mining Applications in Sustainability (SustKDD). ACM San Diego, CA, USA (2011)
18. Wang, L., Luo, X., Zhang, W.: Unsupervised energy disaggregation with factorial hidden Markov models based on generalized backfitting algorithm. In: 2013 IEEE International Conference of IEEE Region 10 (TENCON 2013). IEEE (2013)
19. Zaeri, N., Gunay, H.B., Ashouri, A.: Unsupervised energy disaggregation using time series decomposition for commercial buildings. In: Proceedings of the 9th ACM International Conference on Systems for Energy-Efficient Buildings, Cities, and Transportation (2022)

20. Egarter, D., Bhuvana, V.P., Elmenreich, W.: PALDi: online load disaggregation via particle filtering. IEEE Trans. Instrum. Meas. **64**(2), 467–477 (2014)
21. Cleveland, R.B., et al.: STL: a seasonal-trend decomposition. J. off. Stat **6**(1), 3–73 (1990)
22. Reynolds, D.A.: Gaussian mixture models. In: Encyclopedia of Biometrics (2018)
23. Adrien, P., et al.: CodaLab competitions: an open source platform to organize scientific challenges. J. Mach. Learn. Res. **24**(198), 1–6 (2023)
24. Tolnai, B.A., Ma, Z., Jørgensen, B.N.: Standard energy data competition procedure: a comprehensive review with a case study of the ADRENALIN load disaggregation competition. In: Jørgensen, B.N., da Silva, L.C.P., Ma, Z. (eds.) Energy Informatics. EI.A 2023. LNCS, vol. 14467. Springer, Cham (2024). https://doi.org/10.1007/978-3-031-48649-4_4

Comparison of Three Algorithms for Low-Frequency Temperature-Dependent Load Disaggregation in Buildings Without Submetering

Balázs András Tolnai(✉), Zheng Ma, and Bo Nørregaard Jørgensen

SDU Center for Energy Informatics, The Faculty of Engineering, Maersk Mc-Kinney Moeller Institute, University of Southern Denmark, 5230 Odense, Denmark
bnj@mmmi.sdu.dk

Abstract. Heating, Ventilation, and Air Conditioning (HVAC) systems account for a significant portion of global energy consumption, making their efficient operation critical for energy savings and demand-side management. Non-Intrusive Load Monitoring (NILM) techniques provide a promising approach for disaggregating HVAC loads from aggregate energy consumption using smart meter data. However, most NILM research focuses on high-frequency data, which is often impractical for large-scale deployment due to hardware and infrastructure constraints. This study addresses the challenge of temperature-dependent NILM using low-frequency data by evaluating three algorithms: Bayesian Disaggregation, Time-Frequency Mask Estimation, and BI-LSTM. The Bayesian approach models energy consumption as a probabilistic distribution to estimate HVAC loads, the Time-Frequency Mask method applies spectral transformations for enhanced signal separation, and BI-LSTM leverages deep learning to capture long-term energy dependencies. Using the ADRENALIN and AMPds2 datasets, we compare these models based on accuracy, computational efficiency, and applicability across residential and commercial buildings. The results indicate that the Time-Frequency Mask Estimation model provides the most consistent accuracy, while Bayesian Disaggregation performs well in environments with clear seasonal variations. The BI-LSTM model demonstrates stable performance but struggles with dataset inconsistencies. This study contributes to the field by providing a comparative analysis of NILM algorithms for low-frequency HVAC load disaggregation and offering insights into model selection for real-world applications. Future research should explore hybrid approaches that integrate spectral transformations with advanced deep-learning architectures to enhance NILM accuracy and generalizability.

Keywords: Non-Intrusive Load Monitoring · HVAC Disaggregation · Bayesian Estimation · Time-Frequency Mask · BI-LSTM · Low-Frequency Energy Data · Smart Meter Analytics

1 Introduction

Buildings account for approximately 40% of European [1] and 30% of global [2] energy consumption, with heating, ventilation, and air conditioning (HVAC) systems representing a significant portion of this demand. Optimizing HVAC energy use is essential for improving energy efficiency and implementing demand-side management strategies [3]. Energy load disaggregation, or non-intrusive load monitoring (NILM), is a technique used to break down total energy consumption into individual components, allowing for a more detailed understanding of energy usage patterns [4]. NILM has widespread applications, including improving demand-side management, enabling energy-saving behaviors, identifying inefficient or faulty appliances faults, and tracking user behaviors [5–7].

Most NILM research has focused on high-frequency data (typically above 1 Hz), as it allows for detailed feature extraction based on transient patterns [8]. However, in practical applications where only low-frequency, aggregated data is available, disaggregating energy consumption becomes significantly more complex, especially for temperature-dependent loads like HVAC systems[9–11]. Unlike fixed-load appliances such as lighting and refrigeration, HVAC energy use fluctuates based on environmental conditions and occupancy patterns, making it more difficult to isolate from aggregate consumption data [12, 13]. While heating and cooling loads are strongly correlated with outdoor temperature, other seasonal variations, such as shifts in occupancy behavior and lighting usage, introduce further complexities in distinguishing HVAC consumption. Accurately disaggregating heating and cooling loads is particularly valuable, as they are considered shiftable [14] and can support grid-responsive demand-side management. Moreover, disaggregating these loads enables benchmarking of building energy performance and helps identify candidates for HVAC or envelope retrofits, which are important strategies for reducing overall energy consumption.

Given the increasing need for scalable and cost-effective NILM solutions, this study investigates methods for disaggregating HVAC energy consumption from low-frequency smart meter data, incorporating external environmental variables to improve accuracy. To address the lack of comparative evaluations for temperature-dependent load disaggregation at low resolutions, we benchmark three previously proposed algorithms selected from a recent literature review [15]. These methods were chosen based on their ability to operate without appliance-level sub-metering and their compatibility with low-frequency building data.

The Bayesian Disaggregation approach [16] applies an unsupervised probabilistic approach that models total energy consumption as the sum of a temperature-dependent thermal load and a base load, which is estimated using mild-temperature periods. The model iteratively refines its HVAC consumption estimates using Bayesian inference to update prior assumptions based on observed energy data.

Time-Frequency Mask Estimation [17] utilizes a deep neural network (DNN)-based approach to generate adaptive masks in the time-frequency domain, effectively separating target energy signatures from aggregated signals. By leveraging spectral decomposition and mask learning, the method dynamically adjusts the proportion of disaggregated loads based on temperature dependency and operational patterns, enhancing load separation accuracy.

The Bi-LSTM model is designed to enhance HVAC load disaggregation by incorporating frequency-domain transformations alongside deep learning [18]. Rather than operating on raw time-series data, the model processes frequency components extracted via Fourier series decomposition, allowing it to learn long-term dependencies in energy consumption patterns more effectively. The Bi-LSTM architecture consists of bidirectional recurrent layers, which capture both past and future sequences, improving disaggregation accuracy.

By comparing these approaches across residential and commercial buildings using two real-world datasets, ADRENALIN and AMPds2 [19], this study evaluates their effectiveness in accurately identifying heating and cooling loads.

The primary contributions of this work include a comprehensive analysis of three distinct NILM algorithms for low-frequency temperature-dependent disaggregation and a comparative assessment of their accuracy. This research provides valuable guidance for future efforts in developing scalable NILM solutions that do not rely on high-frequency or appliance-level data. To address these challenges, the next section provides a detailed review of related work in NILM and highlights prior approaches to heating and cooling load separation.

The remainder of the paper is organized as follows. Section 2 provides a review of related work in NILM and discusses prior approaches to HVAC load separation. Section 3 describes the datasets used in this study and the evaluation metrics applied for performance comparison. Section 4 outlines the methodology, including the preprocessing steps and implementation details of the Bayesian Disaggregation, Time-Frequency Mask Estimation, and BI-LSTM models. Section 5 presents the results and analysis of model performance across different datasets and building types. Section 6 discusses the findings, highlighting the strengths and limitations of each approach. Finally, Sect. 7 concludes the paper with key takeaways and directions for future research.

2 Literature Review and Model Selection

Energy load disaggregation has been extensively studied in the past decade, with a predominant focus on high frequency data based methods [20]. Approaches such as Hidden Markov Models (HMMs), Convolutional Neural Networks (CNNs), and Long Short-Term Memory (LSTM) networks have been widely used in NILM [15]. However, these models often rely on data sampled at rates higher than 1 Hz, which is not always available in real-world scenarios where smart meters operate at hourly or half-hourly intervals.

While there have been several advances in NILM methodologies, the study of temperature-dependent NILM using low-frequency data remains limited. Some studies have attempted to use probabilistic models to estimate HVAC consumption by identifying baseline energy usage during non-operational periods, while others have explored frequency-domain transformations to separate HVAC signals from background consumption.

Given the limitations of previous approaches, this study applies three models that have been previously developed for NILM and evaluates their performance in HVAC load disaggregation using low-frequency data: Bayesian Disaggregation, Time-Frequency

Mask Estimation, and BI-LSTM. These models were chosen because they align directly with the objective of disaggregating heating and cooling loads from aggregate energy consumption without requiring high-resolution data. Bayesian Disaggregation provides a probabilistic approach that estimates HVAC consumption based on historical patterns of base load variations. The Time-Frequency Mask Estimation model applies spectral transformations to extract HVAC signals, addressing the issue of overlapping loads in aggregate consumption data. BI-LSTM, a hybrid deep learning model combining convolutional and recurrent layers, learns sequential patterns in energy usage and captures long-term dependencies within low-frequency datasets.

The selection of these models was guided by a systematic literature review that identified studies relevant to low-frequency NILM and HVAC load disaggregation. From an initial pool of 72 articles [15], a subset of 10 papers specifically addressing low-frequency data was examined, with four studies focusing directly on heating and cooling load separation. These papers highlighted key challenges in low-frequency NILM, including the difficulty of state identification and load overlap, and provided insights into effective algorithmic strategies.

By implementing and comparing Bayesian Disaggregation, Time-Frequency Mask Estimation, and BI-LSTM, this study aims to evaluate their effectiveness in disaggregating HVAC loads across different building types. The results will provide insights into the trade-offs between model accuracy, computational efficiency, and generalizability, ultimately contributing to the development of scalable NILM solutions for real-world energy management applications.

3 Datasets and Evaluation Metrics

To evaluate the performance of the selected NILM models, two datasets were chosen: ADRENALIN and AMPds2. These datasets provide a diverse representation of energy consumption patterns in commercial and residential buildings, respectively, ensuring that the models can generalize in different environments. ADRENALIN consists of data collected from commercial and public buildings across different geographical locations, offering hourly-resolution readings. AMPds2, on the other hand, is a widely used residential dataset that originally contains minute-level energy readings, which were resampled to hourly intervals to align with the ADRENALIN dataset. Table 1 provides a summary of the key characteristics of these datasets.

3.1 Evaluation Metrics

To comprehensively evaluate the performance of the tested NILM models, five different metrics were selected. These metrics were chosen to provide a balance between absolute error measurement, scale-invariant evaluation, and the ability to assess predictive accuracy across different datasets. Each metric serves a distinct purpose in assessing how well the models disaggregate HVAC loads from aggregate energy consumption.

The Mean Absolute Error (MAE) [21] and Root Mean Square Error (RMSE) [21] are standard error measures in regression problems. In NILM, MAE is particularly useful for evaluating overall accuracy, while RMSE helps identify large misestimations, which are common in HVAC load disaggregation due to seasonal variations. The MAE is given in Eq. 1 where X_i and Y_i are the actual and predicted HVAC consumption values, respectively.

$$MAE = \sum_{i=1}^{n} \frac{|X_i - Y_i|}{n} \tag{1}$$

RMSE, shown in Eq. 2 gives higher weight to larger errors. This characteristic ensures that large disaggregation errors, which can disproportionately affect energy management decisions, are more prominently reflected in the final evaluation.

$$RMSE = \sqrt{\sum_{i=1}^{n} \frac{(X_i - Y_i)^2}{n}} \tag{2}$$

The Normalized Mean Absolute Error (NAME) provides a scale-independent error measure that allows comparison across different buildings. Unlike MAE, which is influenced by total energy consumption, NAME accounts for variations in baseline consumption, making it a more reliable metric for NILM evaluation. The NAME is given by Eq. 3.

$$nMAE = \frac{\sum_{i=1}^{n} |y_i - \hat{y}_i|}{n \cdot \bar{y}} \tag{3}$$

Table 1. Dataset Characteristics

Dataset	Resolution	Building Type	Number of Buildings	HVAC Loads Available
ADRENALIN	Hourly	Commercial/Public	9	Yes
AMPds2	1 min (Resampled to Hourly)	Residential	1	Yes

By normalizing the error relative to total energy consumption, this metric avoids biases introduced by datasets with large differences in total consumption.

The Coefficient of Determination (R^2 Score) [22] measures how well the predicted energy consumption explains the variance in actual HVAC consumption. The R^2 score is calculated as shown in Eq. 4, where $\overline{X}$ is the mean of the actual HVAC consumption values. However, in NILM, R^2 can sometimes be misleading if small over- and underpredictions cancel each other out, resulting in a lower R^2 score even when the overall disaggregation is accurate. Therefore, it should be interpreted alongside other metrics such as MAE and RMSE to provide a more holistic evaluation.

$$R^2 = 1 - \frac{\sum_{i=1}^{n} (X_i - Y_i)^2}{\sum_{i=1}^{n} (X_i - \overline{X})^2} \tag{4}$$

These evaluation metrics collectively provide a robust framework for assessing NILM performance. By incorporating absolute error measurements, scale-independent comparisons, and variance-based accuracy indicators, this study ensures a comprehensive and unbiased assessment of HVAC load disaggregation methods.

4 Methodology

This section details the methodology used to implement and evaluate the selected NILM models: Bayesian Disaggregation, Time-Frequency Mask Estimation, and BI-LSTM. These models were chosen based on their suitability for low-frequency NILM and their ability to disaggregate HVAC loads from aggregate energy consumption. The methodology includes data preprocessing steps, model architectures, training procedures, and validation strategies to ensure reliable performance assessment.

4.1 Data Preprocessing

The data preprocessing pipeline was designed to enhance the quality and usability of the ADRENALIN and AMPds2 datasets. The first step involved resampling the AMPds2 dataset from minute-level readings to hourly resolution to match the ADRENALIN dataset. Following this, missing values were interpolated using a linear interpolation method to maintain data continuity. Additionally, outlier detection techniques were applied. The final step involved normalizing the energy consumption values using min-max scaling, ensuring consistency across the datasets.

4.2 Model Descriptions

The three selected models were implemented using a structured approach to ensure consistency in their evaluation. Each model is introduced with a brief explanation, followed by its theoretical foundation and implementation details.

Bayesian Disaggregation. Bayesian Disaggregation is an unsupervised probabilistic model that estimates HVAC energy consumption by separating total load into a base load and a temperature-dependent thermal load. The base load is inferred from mild-temperature periods when heating and cooling are inactive, while the thermal load is estimated using Bayesian inference. The model updates its HVAC consumption estimates using Bayes' theorem, refining prior knowledge based on observed total energy consumption. The Approximate Bayesian Computation (ABC) method is used to determine the best-fit prior distribution by minimizing divergence between simulated and observed data. Since this is an unsupervised approach, the solutions were generated for each building individually.

Time-Frequency Mask Estimation. The Time-Frequency Mask Estimation (TFM) method operates in three stages: pre-clustering, mask estimation, and load decomposition. First, a pre-clustering step groups energy data based on environmental factors such as temperature dependency and day type (workday vs. non-workday) to enhance the accuracy of load separation. The model then transforms aggregate energy consumption into the time-frequency (T-F) domain using Short-Time Fourier Transform (STFT). T The T-F masks were calculated from the ground truth and served as the learning objective for the DNN. The deep neural network (DNN) estimates this T-F mask, the Adaptive Optimal Ratio Mask (AORM), which dynamically adjusts the weight of HVAC consumption based on the correlation between target and residual loads. The extracted HVAC signal is reconstructed in the time domain for evaluation. The AORM is defined by Eq. (5). In this equation $T_{t,f}$ represents the spectral values of the target load, $S_{t,f}$ denotes the residual load, $C_{t,f}$ is the correlation measure, and $R(T_{t,f}S^{*}_{t,f})$ is the real value of the product between the target and residual load's conjugate.

$$AORM_{t,f} = \frac{|T_{t,f}|^2 C_{t,f} + R(T_{t,f}S^{*}_{t,f})\sqrt{C_{t,f}(1-C_{t,f})}}{|T_{t,f}|^2 C_{t,f} + |S_{t,f}|^2(1-C_{t,f}) + 2R(T_{t,f}S^{*}_{t,f})\sqrt{C_{t,f}(1-C_{t,f})}} \quad (5)$$

BI-LSTM Model. The Bi-LSTM model is a deep learning architecture specifically designed to capture long-term dependencies in HVAC energy consumption patterns. Unlike standard LSTMs, Bi-LSTM processes sequential data in both forward and backward directions, allowing it to learn relationships across different time scales more effectively. The architecture consists of two bidirectional LSTM layers followed by a fully connected dense output layer. Unlike traditional NILM approaches that rely on high-frequency data, Bi-LSTM is optimized to work with low-frequency aggregate energy data by leveraging its ability to model long-range dependencies. The model's hyperparameters, including the number of LSTM units, learning rate, and dropout rate, were optimized using Bayesian Optimization to minimize disaggregation error. The training was conducted using the Adam optimizer rather than RMSprop, as it was found to improve convergence stability. The loss function used was Mean Squared Error (MSE), which penalizes large deviations from the actual consumption values while ensuring robustness against minor fluctuations in energy demand.

4.3 Training and Validation

Each model was trained and validated using a systematic approach to ensure reliable performance evaluation. The dataset was split into training and test sets using a leave-one-building-out cross-validation approach for the Time-Frequency Mask Estimation and BI-LSTM models, while the Bayesian model statistically created the results from the building's consumption patterns. Hyperparameter tuning was performed using Bayesian optimization, which iteratively adjusts parameters to minimize disaggregation errors. This method improves efficiency compared to traditional grid search by adaptively selecting parameter configurations rather than exhaustively testing all combinations.

4.4 Implementation Details

The models were implemented using Python with TensorFlow framework for deep learning-based models. Bayesian Disaggregation was implemented using NumPy and SciPy, leveraging probabilistic inference libraries for posterior estimation. The Time-Frequency Mask Estimation model was implemented using TensorFlow and trained with an RMSprop optimizer.

With the methodology established, the next section presents the results of the NILM models, comparing their accuracy and effectiveness in HVAC load disaggregation.

5 Results

This section presents the performance evaluation of the three selected NILM models, Bayesian Disaggregation, Time-Frequency Mask Estimation, and BI-LSTM, on the ADRENALIN and AMPds2 datasets. The models were assessed using multiple performance metrics, including normalized Mean Absolute Error (NAME), Mean Absolute Error per hour (MAE), Root Mean Square Error (RMSE), and R^2. The differences in performance across buildings and datasets highlight the strengths and weaknesses of each approach, revealing insights into their effectiveness for HVAC load disaggregation in low-frequency settings.

5.1 Performance of the Bayesian Approach

The Bayesian approach was tested in two different configurations: with and without distinguishing between weekends and weekdays. These results are visible in Tables 2 and 3. This shows that this separation usually did not yield positive results. This is most likely due to the reduced number of samples available for the statistical model.

Table 2. Results of the Bayesian method, without separating the weekends.

House	NAME	MAE	RMSE	r^2
Building 1	0.54	19.05	28.17	0.35
Building 2	1.66	10.91	15.60	−0.90
Building 3	3.91	41.12	44.76	−3.86
Building 4	2.61	76.24	79.75	−1.24
Building 5	0.71	31.41	38.93	−1.04
Building 6	0.29	4.44	6.48	0.76
Building 7	0.37	10.53	19.63	0.70
Building 8	0.24	25.91	35.84	0.90
Building 9	0.50	49.64	70.31	0.62

The Bayesian model performed best in Building 6 (NAME: 0.29), where HVAC consumption exhibited strong seasonal correlation with temperature, making it easier for the model to estimate temperature-dependent loads. However, it struggled in Building 3 (NAME: 3.91), where HVAC usage was present year-round, violating the model's assumption that the lowest energy consumption at mild temperatures represents the baseload. This incorrect assumption led to severe underestimation of HVAC loads, as seen in Figs. 1 and 2.

Table 3. Results of the Bayesian method, treating weekends and weekdays separately.

Building	NAME	MAE	RMSE	r^2
Building 1	0.59	16.40	22.90	0.57
Building 2	1.66	10.59	15.15	−0.80
Building 3	3.36	39.58	42.76	−3.35
Building 4	3.46	81.71	86.18	−1.61
Building 5	0.58	31.03	39.07	−1.07
Building 6	0.29	4.47	6.51	0.75
Building 7	0.39	10.92	19.65	0.70
Building 8	0.16	15.76	23.33	0.96
Building 9	0.44	46.64	65.07	0.67

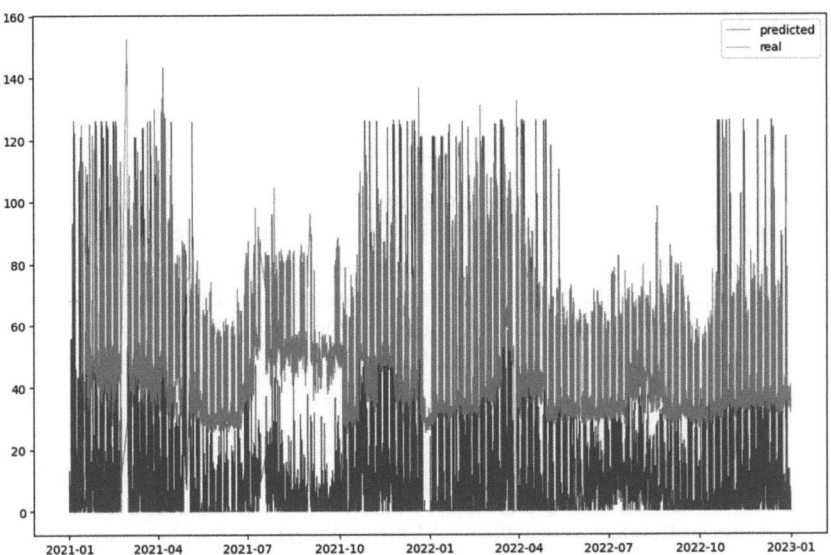

Fig. 1. Bayesian algorithm disaggregation results on Building 3

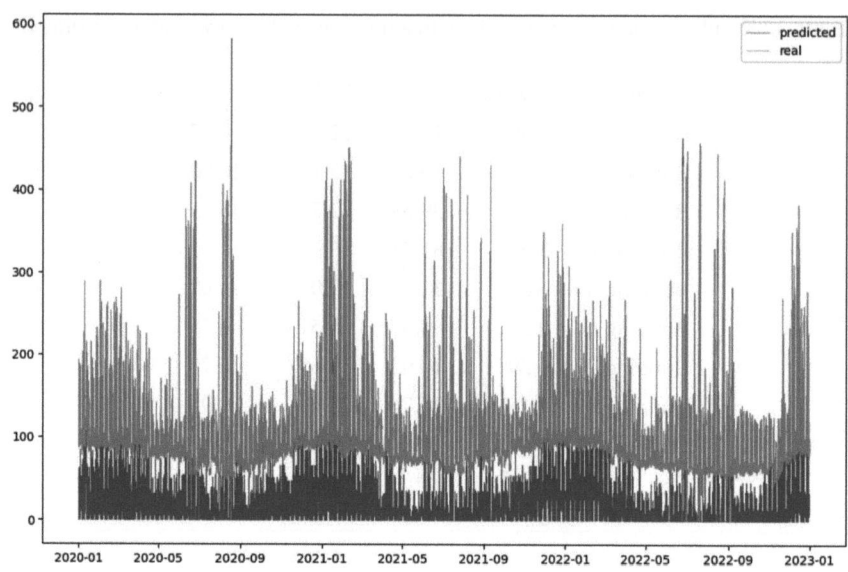

Fig. 2. Bayesian algorithm disaggregation results on Building 4

5.2 Performance of the Time-Frequency Mask Estimation Model

The Time-Frequency Mask estimation model outperformed the other approaches, achieving the lowest NAME in most buildings. Its superior performance is attributed to the transformation of the time-series data into time frequency masks, where overlapping consumption patterns can be more effectively separated. This transformation allows the model to better isolate temperature-dependent HVAC loads. As shown in Table 4, the model achieved the lowest NAME of 0.241 in Building 4.

Table 4. Performance of the Mask based algorithm

Building	NAME	MAE	RMSE	r^2
Building 1	0.396	17.276	24.864	0.480
Building 2	0.706	31.448	40.011	−3.776
Building 3	0.605	34.803	40.540	−2.908
Building 4	0.241	33.167	47.609	0.249
Building 5	0.403	15.453	22.077	0.515
Building 6	0.450	11.616	12.749	0.337
Building 7	0.305	11.463	17.218	0.836
Building 8	0.480	87.340	97.195	0.122
Building 9	0.419	29.005	42.561	0.831

A key advantage of this model was its ability to generalize across different buildings. The model leveraged cross-learning from multiple buildings to good effect. This resulted in improved performance in commercial buildings, as seen in Fig. 3. However, it struggled in Building 2 (NAME: 0.706), where disaggregated values were significantly larger than real HVAC consumption, except for a single peak, as illustrated in Fig. 4.

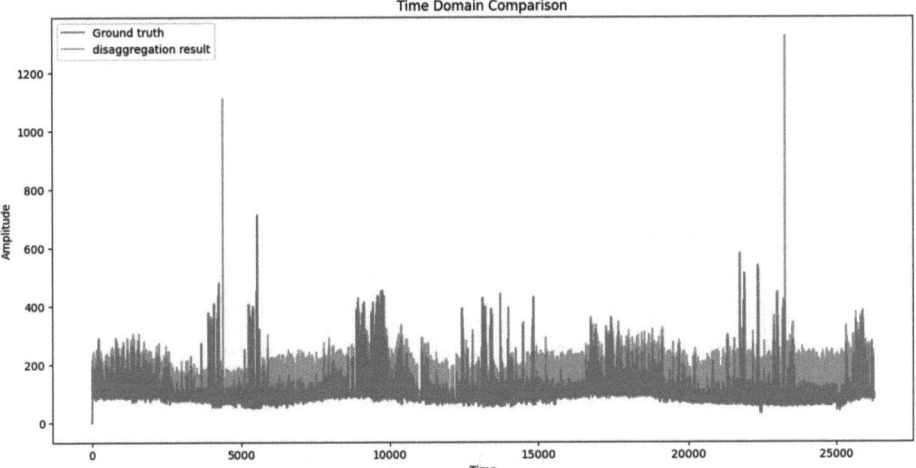

Fig. 3. Result of the Mask based algorithm on building 4

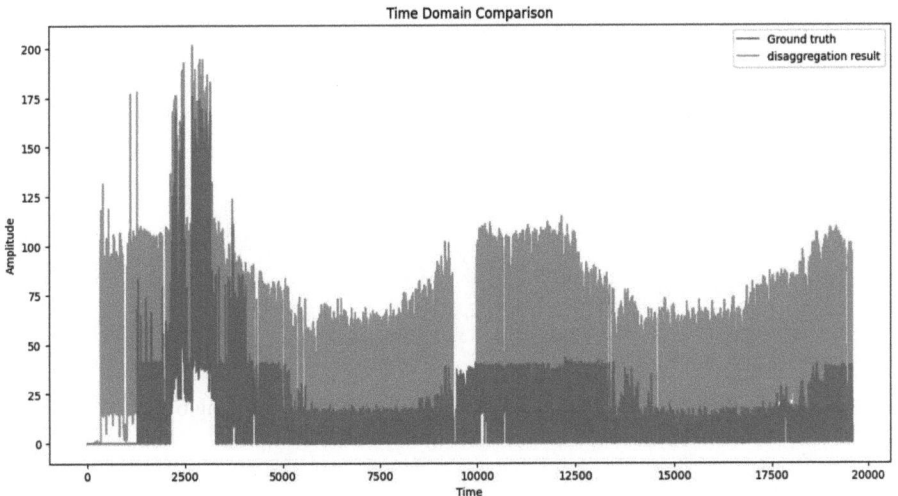

Fig. 4. Result of the Mask based algorithm on building 2

5.3 Performance of the BI-LSTM Model

The BI-LSTM model demonstrated stable performance across different buildings, benefiting from its ability to capture temporal dependencies in HVAC energy consumption, as shown in Table 5. BI-LSTM effectively modeled consumption patterns over extended periods, however, while its stability was an advantage, its overall accuracy remained slightly lower than the Time-Frequency Mask model.

Table 5. Performance of the BI-LSTM Model

Building	NAME	MAE	RMSE	r^2
Building 1	0.56	17.23	23.51	0.4
Building 2	0.67	9.58	14.03	−0.25
Building 3	0.68	34.22	40.31	−0.29
Building 4	0.47	49.84	69.76	−0.82
Building 5	0.53	12.99	19.99	0.6
Building 6	0.44	6.43	9.15	0.61
Building 7	0.51	20.9	30.26	0.27
Building 8	0.61	57.95	66.44	−0.14
Building 9	0.65	62.32	92.53	−5.6

The best performance for the BI-LSTM model was recorded in Building 6, with an NAME of 0.44, aligning with the Bayesian approach's strongest result on the same building, as illustrated in Fig. 5. Conversely, the worst performance occurred in Building 3, where the model failed to capture the complex HVAC load characteristics (Fig. 6).

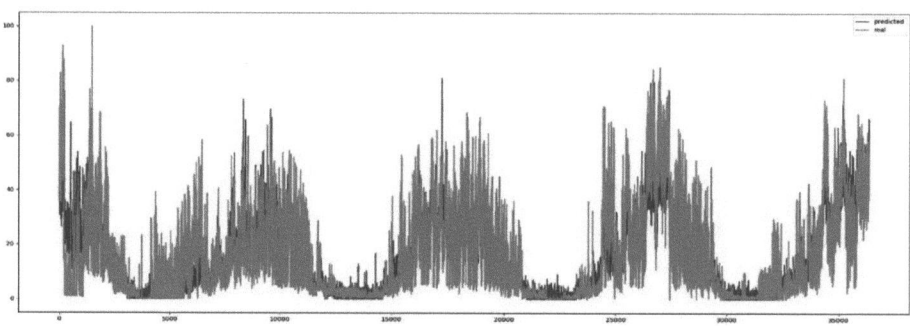

Fig. 5. Result of the Mask based algorithm on building 6

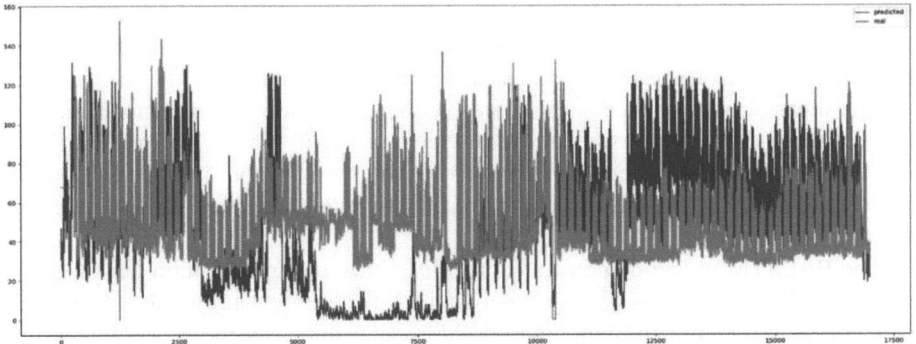

Fig. 6. Result of the Mask based algorithm on building 3

5.4 Comparison of Algorithm Performance

Table 6 summarizes the best and worst performance of each algorithm. The Time-Frequency Mask model demonstrated the most consistent accuracy, while the Bayesian method struggled with irregular seasonal loads. The BI-LSTM method provided stable results but was outperformed by the Time-Frequency Mask estimation model in most cases.

Table 6. Comparison of results on the three methods

Algorithm	Best-Performing Building (Lowest NAME)	Worst-Performing Building (Highest NAME)
Bayesian	Building 6 (NAME: 0.29)	Building 3 (NAME: 3.91)
Time-Frequency Mask	Building 4 (NAME: 0.241)	Building 2 (NAME: 0.706)
BI-LSTM	Building 6 (NAME: 0.44)	Building 3 (NAME: 0.68)

These findings highlight the strengths and weaknesses of each model. The Bayesian approach performed well on buildings with clear heating and cooling trends but struggled with irregular loads. The Time-Frequency Mask estimation model was the most effective method overall, likely due to the mask-based approach. The BI-LSTM method provided a stable alternative but did not outperform the Time-Frequency Mask model in most cases.

6 Discussion

The results of this study highlight the challenges and opportunities in low-frequency, temperature-dependent energy load disaggregation. The comparison of three different approaches revealed that different models excel in different conditions, suggesting that no single approach is universally optimal.

One of the key takeaways is the importance of adapting models to the characteristics of the dataset. The Bayesian model, while offering a simple and interpretable method, assumes that the base load remains stable across seasons, which is often not the case. Seasonal variations in lighting, appliance usage, and occupancy patterns introduce fluctuations that the Bayesian approach cannot fully account for.

The superior performance of the Time-Frequency Mask estimation model suggests that frequency-domain transformations provide a powerful tool for energy disaggregation, particularly for low-frequency datasets. By moving beyond time-series modeling and leveraging spectral analysis, this approach can better separate overlapping energy consumption patterns.

The BI-LSTM model demonstrated stability in capturing long-term dependencies, but its overall accuracy was slightly lower than the Time-Frequency Mask model. While it integrated Fourier transformation-based additional features, the model was trained only on data in the time domain. Deep learning models can capture complex relationships in energy data, their reliance on large training datasets and computational resources may limit their applicability in real-time energy monitoring systems. Future work could focus on incorporating attention mechanisms or hybrid architectures to better leverage frequency-domain information and improve model efficiency.

The findings highlight the trade-offs between model interpretability, accuracy, and computational efficiency in NILM applications. While probabilistic methods like Bayesian Disaggregation offer greater transparency and adaptability, deep learning approaches such as BI-LSTM and Time-Frequency Mask Estimation leverage more sophisticated techniques for load separation. The selection of an appropriate NILM model depends on the specific requirements of a given energy monitoring application, including data availability, real-time constraints, and generalization needs.

7 Conclusion

This study investigated the performance of three NILM models, Bayesian Disaggregation, Time-Frequency Mask Estimation, and BI-LSTM, on low-frequency HVAC load disaggregation using the ADRENALIN and AMPds2 datasets. The results demonstrated that different approaches excel in different conditions, with the Time-Frequency Mask model achieving the best overall accuracy across buildings. The Bayesian model demonstrated strong performance in temperature-dependent HVAC disaggregation, particularly in environments where HVAC loads dominate seasonal energy variations. However, its reliance on mild-temperature periods for base load estimation led to inaccuracies in buildings with year-round HVAC usage or significant seasonal variations in non-HVAC loads. Future improvements could involve integrating additional contextual features, such as occupancy schedules or lighting patterns, to enhance model robustness. The BI-LSTM model offers stable but slightly less accurate predictions. These findings highlight the trade-offs between model interpretability, generalization ability, and computational complexity in NILM applications.

The study contributes to the field of energy disaggregation by demonstrating the effectiveness of frequency-domain transformations for low-frequency HVAC load separation. Additionally, it provides insights into the challenges of low-frequency NILM, particularly in handling diverse building types and seasonal variations. The findings suggest that energy management systems in commercial and residential buildings could benefit from integrating frequency-domain-based disaggregation models, while policymakers and energy providers could leverage these insights to develop demand response strategies that optimize HVAC energy consumption without compromising occupant comfort.

Despite its contributions, this study has limitations. The evaluation was conducted on two datasets, ADRENALIN and AMPds2, which, while providing valuable insights into commercial and residential building energy use, may not fully capture the wide variability of HVAC consumption patterns present across different building types, climates, and usage scenarios. Notably, industrial and mixed-use buildings are not represented in these datasets. This limitation constrains the generalizability of the findings and underscores the need for future work to validate and extend these models across a broader range of building types and environmental conditions.

Future research should investigate hybrid models that integrate spectral analysis with advanced deep learning techniques, such as attention mechanisms and graph neural networks. Additionally, validating these models on industrial and mixed-use buildings would provide further insight into their applicability beyond residential and commercial settings. By refining model architectures and exploring hybrid approaches, future studies can enhance the effectiveness of low-frequency energy load disaggregation, making it more accessible for real-world deployment.

As energy efficiency becomes increasingly critical in the transition toward sustainable power systems, advances in NILM techniques, such as those explored in this study, will play a crucial role in optimizing building energy management and grid stability. Continued research and development in this field will contribute to more intelligent, adaptive, and scalable solutions for energy monitoring and conservation.

Acknowledgement. This paper is part of the ADRENALIN (Data-driven smart buildings: data sandbox and competition) project. Funded by the Energy Technology Development and Demonstration Programme (EUDP) In Denmark. (Case no.64021-6025).

References

1. Commission, E., Energy performance of buildings directive (2018)
2. International Energy, A., A. International Renewable Energy, and U.N.C.C.H.-L. Champions, Breakthrough Agenda Report 2023. IEA, Paris (2023)
3. Salani, M., et al.: Non intrusive load monitoring for demand side management. Energy Inform. **3**, 1–12 (2020)
4. Hart, G.W.: Nonintrusive appliance load monitoring. Proc. IEEE **80**(12), 1870–1891 (1992)
5. Dash, S., Sodhi, R., Sodhi, B.: An appliance load disaggregation scheme using automatic state detection enabled enhanced integer programming. IEEE Trans. Industr. Inf. **17**(2), 1176–1185 (2021)
6. Wang, W., et al.: Bats: an appliance safety hazards factors detection algorithm with an improved nonintrusive load disaggregation method. Energies **14**(12) (2021)
7. Chalmers, C., et al.: Detecting activities of daily living and routine behaviours in dementia patients living alone using smart meter load disaggregation. IEEE Trans. Emerg. Top. Comput. **10**(1), 157–169 (2022)

8. Rehman, A.U., et al.: Comparative evaluation of machine learning models and input feature space for non-intrusive load monitoring. J. Mod. Power Syst. Clean Energy **9**(5), 1161–1171 (2021)
9. Lien, S.K., Najafi, B., Rajasekharan, J.: Advances in machine-learning based disaggregation of building heating loads: a review. In: Jørgensen, B.N., da Silva, L.C.P., Ma, Z. (eds.) Energy Informatics. EI.A 2023. LNCS, vol. 14467. Springer, Cham (2024). https://doi.org/10.1007/978-3-031-48649-4_1
10. Huber, P., et al.: Review on deep neural networks applied to low-frequency NILM. Energies **14** (2021), https://doi.org/10.3390/en14092390
11. Brudermueller, T., Breer, F., Staake, T.: Disaggregation of heat pump load profiles from low-resolution smart meter data. In: Proceedings of the 10th ACM International Conference on Systems for Energy-Efficient Buildings, Cities, and Transportation (2023)
12. Luan, W., et al.: A training-free non-intrusive air conditioning load monitoring method based on fuzzy comprehensive evaluation. Appl. Energy **376**, 124058 (2024)
13. Li, J., et al.: Air conditioning load monitoring in nilm using low frequency power data. In: 2024 3rd Asian Conference on Frontiers of Power and Energy (ACFPE) (2024)
14. Wang, D., et al.: Quantifying the potential of load flexibility for building HVAC system using model predictive control strategy. Energy Build. **323**, 114819 (2024)
15. Tolnai, B.A., Ma, Z., Jørgensen, B.N.: A scoping review of energy load disaggregation. In: Moniz, N., Vale, Z., Cascalho, J., Silva, C., Sebastião, R. (eds.) Progress in Artificial Intelligence. EPIA 2023. LNCS, vol. 14116. Springer, Cham (2023). https://doi.org/10.1007/978-3-031-49011-8_17
16. Massidda, L., Marrocu, M.: A bayesian approach to unsupervised, non-intrusive load disaggregation. Sensors **22**(12) (2022)
17. Song, J., Lee, Y., Hwang, E.: Time-frequency mask estimation based on deep neural network for flexible load disaggregation in buildings. IEEE Trans. Smart Grid **12**(4), 3242–3251 (2021)
18. Zou, M.Z., et al.: Heating and lighting load disaggregation using frequency components and convolutional bidirectional long short-term memory method. Energies **14**(16) (2021)
19. Makonin, S.: AMPds2: the almanac of minutely power dataset (Version 2). Harvard Dataverse (2016)
20. Tolnai, B.A., Ma, Z., Jørgensen, B.N.: A scoping review of energy load disaggregation. In: EPIA 2023. 2023. Springer, Cham
21. Chai, T., Draxler, R.R.: Root mean square error (RMSE) or mean absolute error (MAE)? – arguments against avoiding RMSE in the literature. Geosci. Model Develop. **7**(3), 1247–1250 (2014)
22. Chicco, D., Warrens, M.J., Jurman, G.: The coefficient of determination R-squared is more informative than SMAPE, MAE, MAPE, MSE and RMSE in regression analysis evaluation. PeerJ Comput. Sci. **7**, e623 (2021)

Lessons Learned from the ADRENALIN Load Disaggregation Challenge

Balázs András Tolnai[1](✉), Zheng Ma[1], Igor Sartori[2], Clayton Miller[3], Stephen White[4], Matt Amos[4], Gustaf Bengtsson[5], Akram Hameed[4], and Bo Nørregaard Jørgensen[1]

[1] SDU Center for Energy Informatics, The Faculty of Engineering, Maersk Mc-Kinney Moeller Institute, University of Southern Denmark, 5230 Odense, Denmark
bnj@mmmi.sdu.dk
[2] Department of Architectural Engineering, SINTEF Community, Oslo, Norway
[3] Department of the Built Environment, College of Design and Engineering, National University of Singapore, Singapore 119077, Singapore
[4] CSIRO Energy, Commonwealth Scientific and Industrial Research Organisation (CSIRO), Newcastle, Australia
[5] Department of Built Environment, RISE Research Institutes of Sweden, Borås, Sweden

Abstract. Crowdsourced data science competitions have emerged as a powerful mechanism for advancing research in energy informatics, offering scalable pathways for developing machine learning solutions that enhance energy efficiency and smart building operations. The ADRENALIN Load Disaggregation Challenge addressed a central problem in energy analytics—non-intrusive load monitoring (NILM) of heating and cooling loads in commercial buildings—while emphasizing the importance of model generalization across different buildings. This paper presents a comprehensive reflection on the lessons learned from organizing and executing the ADRENALIN competition, including technical insights, organizational challenges, and recommendations for future energy data challenges. In addition to the ADRENALIN case, a comparative analysis is conducted with recent energy informatics competitions, including ASHRAE Great Energy Predictor III, BigDEAL 2022, CityLearn 2022, the Global AI Challenge, AIcrowd's Brick by Brick competition, and the NYSERDA RTEM Hackathon. This analysis identifies common challenges and effective strategies, such as the importance of dataset quality and preprocessing, the impact of evaluation metric selection, and trade-offs between large-scale open platforms (e.g., Kaggle) and research-oriented platforms (e.g., CodaLab, AIcrowd). Based on these insights, the paper outlines a set of best practices for designing energy data competitions, including multi-phase evaluation structures, clearly defined scoring frameworks, enhanced participant engagement strategies, and pathways for post-competition implementation to maximize real-world impact.

Keywords: Energy Data Competitions · Crowdsourced Data Challenges · Non-Intrusive Load Monitoring (NILM) · Energy Load Disaggregation

© The Author(s), under exclusive license to Springer Nature Switzerland AG 2026
I. Martinac et al. (Eds.): EIA Nordic 2025, LNCS 16096, pp. 371–387, 2026.
https://doi.org/10.1007/978-3-032-03098-6_24

1 Introduction

Load disaggregation - often framed as non-intrusive load monitoring (NILM) - is an important problem in energy informatics with significant practical implications [1]. By separating an aggregated energy signal (e.g., a building's total electricity usage) into its constituent loads, one can gain detailed insights into individual appliance or sub-system consumption. This has been shown to aid in balancing power grids through enhanced demand-side management [2] and to promote electricity-saving behavior by increasing consumer awareness of usage patterns [3, 4]. Traditional approaches require intrusive sub-metering of each device (Intrusive Load Monitoring), but NILM techniques use only aggregate device meter data to infer individual loads, offering a more cost-effective and deployable solution [5].

Despite considerable research in this area, the field has lacked comprehensive overviews of its scope and methods. A recent scoping review [6] assessed dozens of studies and found that residential electricity consumption is the most researched domain in load disaggregation, whereas other contexts (e.g., commercial or industrial buildings) are relatively under-explored [4, 5, 7]. It also noted that the majority of studies use mid-range frequency data (sampling intervals on the order of seconds to minutes) and a wide variety of computational methods - with artificial neural networks (ANNs) being the most common [8], followed by optimization strategies, Hidden Markov Models, and other techniques [6]. These findings highlight both the progress and the gaps in current research. In particular, the scarcity of work on non-residential buildings and the challenges of applying models across different buildings point to an opportunity for new advances.

Crowdsourced data science competitions have emerged as a powerful mechanism to drive innovation in domains like energy. Over the past decade, competitive platforms (e.g., Kaggle and others) have become immensely popular for tackling complex data problems by harnessing the collective intelligence of global participants [9, 10]. Such competitions are a cost-effective alternative to traditional in-house R&D [11], often yielding creative solutions from diverse teams around the world. They also provide valuable learning opportunities for participants to sharpen skills and contribute to open challenges. In a typical competition, participants are provided with a curated dataset and a clearly defined problem statement [9]. During the development phase, teams build models or algorithmic solutions that are evaluated against a standardized performance metric. A public leaderboard offers real-time feedback based on a designated validation dataset, fostering a competitive and iterative environment. Final rankings are then determined using a withheld test set—unseen by participants—to prevent overfitting and ensure robustness of the submitted solutions. In the energy sector, data competitions have been used to address problems ranging from energy efficiency optimization to renewable integration and grid stability. However, detailed documentation of the process and best practices of running these competitions remains limited [9].

The ADRENALIN Load Disaggregation Challenge was conceived against this backdrop to accelerate research and solutions in building energy disaggregation. This competition was organized as part of the ADRENALIN research project—a strategic initiative focused on data-driven smart building solutions—with the goal of crowdsourcing innovative algorithms for disaggregating building energy loads. The ADRENALIN project collected data from real buildings across multiple countries and continents to create a "data sandbox" and hosted competitions to source novel approaches to specific challenges [12]. In particular, the load disaggregation challenge sought to leverage the community's expertise to address the identified gaps (e.g., disaggregating in commercial/public buildings using low-frequency data [13]) and to test the transferability of models to different buildings, and building types. The competition was expected not only to yield high-performing models but also to foster engagement and learning in the energy informatics community.

While this paper primarily reflects on the lessons learned from designing and running the ADRENALIN Load Disaggregation Challenge, it is important to place these findings in a broader context. In recent years, several energy-related data competitions have been conducted across different domains, including load forecasting (ASHRAE Great Energy Predictor III [14], BigDEAL 2022 [15]), and grid-interactive optimization of neighborhood energy consumption (CityLearn 2022 [16]). Additional examples include the Global AI Challenge [17], which focused on sustainability-oriented data science solutions; AIcrowd's Brick by Brick 2024 [18], a classification-based competition exploring energy data in new formats; and the NYSERDA RTEM Hackathon [19], a competition focused on applying real-time energy data in building analytics. These competitions have faced similar challenges in dataset curation, participant engagement, competition design, and ensuring real-world impact.

A key contribution of this paper is to document the lessons from ADRENALIN as well as compare them with insights from other recent competitions. By examining similarities and differences across these events, we can extract best practices for organizing energy data challenges, and identifying strategies that have proven effective across multiple domains. This comparative perspective strengthens the findings of this paper and provides actionable recommendations for future competitions.

The remainder of the paper is organized as follows: Sect. 2 provides an overview of the competition's design, dataset, and participation. Section 3 discusses the key lessons learned, from technical hurdles to community engagement, now integrating comparisons with lessons from other energy data competitions and highlighting shared challenges and unique solutions. Section 4 offers recommendations for future data competitions, incorporating cross-competition insights to suggest improvements in competition design, dataset preparation, and evaluation criteria. Section 5 concludes with final reflections and directions for future work in this area. By embedding ADRENALIN's lessons within the broader field of energy data competitions, this paper aims to contribute to the ongoing refinement of best practices in running effective data challenges in energy informatics.

2 Overview of the ADRENALIN Load Disaggregation Challenge

2.1 Competition Design and Objectives

The ADRENALIN 2024 Load Disaggregation Challenge was an integral part of the ADRENALIN project's efforts to advance smart building analytics. The overall theme was non-intrusive load disaggregation in buildings, with a particular focus on heating and cooling loads. The task for participants was to develop machine learning or statistical models that could disaggregate a building's aggregate energy signal into its constituent temperature-dependent loads (primarily HVAC-related loads). By doing so, one can, for example, identify how much of the energy consumption is due to heating or cooling systems, which in turn helps detect buildings with sub-optimal insulation or aging HVAC equipment and identifies shiftable loads for demand response While several prior works have explored disaggregation of heating loads, most rely on high-resolution data and lack adaptation to the physical characteristics of heating systems or low-frequency smart meter data [20].

A core objective of the challenge was to create flexible models that generalize well, allowing application in real buildings without dedicated sub-metering. The design of the competition explicitly encouraged unsupervised approaches, as traditional NILM techniques often struggle with model adaptability when deployed in new buildings [21]. To ensure models were evaluated under realistic conditions, the competition dataset included only whole-building meter readings and weather data, while the hidden ground truth sub-metered HVAC loads were used solely for evaluation.

2.2 Benchmarking Against Other Energy Competitions

This focus on model generalization and unsupervised learning is not common in most energy data competitions. For example, the Great Energy Predictor III (GEPIII) competition, hosted on Kaggle by ASHRAE, worked on predicting hourly building energy consumption from weather and operational data. In GEPIII, participants had access to extensive training labels (historical metered data for thousands of buildings), meaning the task was purely supervised learning. By contrast, ADRENALIN specifically tested how well models could generalize between buildings without access to ground truth, making it a more challenging problem in terms of real-world deployment.

Similarly, the CityLearn Challenge (2022), which focused on reinforcement learning for energy management, used a simulation-based dataset rather than real-world collected data. This allowed precise control over the training environment but also meant that results were dependent on the fidelity of the simulator rather than real building characteristics. In contrast, ADRENALIN used real-world building data, ensuring that the winning models were developed and tested in an actual operational context. A brief comparison of the competitions is presented in Table 1.

By emphasizing real-world data constraints and model transferability, ADRENALIN filled an important gap in existing energy competitions, addressing the practical limitations of NILM deployment in commercial buildings.

Table 1. Compared competitions

Competition	Domain	Platform	Teams	Metric
GEPIII (2019)	Residential forecasting	Kaggle	4000+	RMSLE
BigDEAL (2022)	Industrial peak prediction	Academic site	78	Top-3 Accuracy
CityLearn (2022)	Neighborhood control (RL)	AIcrowd	100+	Cost–Carbon–Ramp score

(continued)

Table 1. (*continued*)

Competition	Domain	Platform	Teams	Metric
ADRENALIN (2024)	HVAC disaggregation	CodaLab	200+	NMAE

2.3 Dataset Characteristics

A unique aspect of this competition was its dataset, which was collected by the ADRENALIN project consortium to provide a rich, real-world testbed. The dataset assembled for the challenge comprised data from multiple buildings in different countries, contributed by various project partners. The dataset was derived from commercial and public facilities (e.g., office buildings, kindergartens), rather than residential sources. Prior to inclusion in the competition, the data was stripped of any personally identifiable information (PII) to ensure privacy compliance. For each building, the dataset included the main meter measurements (overall electricity or heating consumption) as well as sub-metered readings for the key temperature-dependent loads (such as heating/cooling systems), which served as the ground truth for disaggregation. The dataset is available on the competition's Codalab page [22].

Data was recorded at the available sampling frequency within each unique building, leading to inconsistencies in sampling frequency across the dataset as a whole. To ensure consistency and alignment across all supplied building data, resampling was applied at 5-min, 15-min, 30-min, and hourly intervals, reflecting typical smart meter and building management system capabilities. In addition to power readings, the dataset provided contextual features: basic building attributes (e.g., floor area, building type) and local weather data (e.g., outdoor temperature) synchronized with the consumption data. These additional features were included to help participants' models account for external factors (for instance, linking heating load to outdoor temperature).

2.4 Comparing Dataset Scope Across Competitions

Dataset quality and scope are critical factors in energy informatics competitions, as they directly impact the realism and applicability of the resulting models. ADRENALIN's dataset strategy was unique in several ways:

- Unlike ASHRAE GEPIII, which provided historical hourly energy data for 1,448 buildings but no sub-metering, ADRENALIN included both whole-building meter readings and sub-metered HVAC loads for ground truth validation.
- BigDEAL 2022, a peak demand forecasting competition, provided a multi-year dataset with granular electricity load curves for various grid zones but focused on aggregate consumption trends rather than individual building-level disaggregation.
- CityLearn 2022 used a fully synthetic dataset modeled after a neighborhood of homes, which allowed controlled experiments but did not reflect real-world noise or sensor variability. ADRENALIN, by contrast, worked with real metered data from diverse building types, increasing deployment relevance.

This underscores a key strength of the ADRENALIN dataset: it blended real-world complexity with carefully structured evaluation splits to assess how models generalize across different buildings, an aspect often overlooked in other competitions that focus purely on historical forecasting.

2.5 Competition Format and Participant Engagement

The challenge was conducted in multiple phases to guide participant engagement. Following best practices identified in other data competitions, the organizers adopted a three-stage structure, as shown in Table 2.

Table 2. Competition phases

Phase	Dates	Key Characteristics
Training Phase	July 8 – September 15, 2024	Participants developed models using whole-building meter and weather data, with feedback provided via a public leaderboard
Test Phase	September 23 – September 30, 2024	Final model submissions were evaluated on a previously hidden dataset with a strict submission limit of 5. Documentation was required along with the submissions
Knowledge Transfer	October 2024 – January 2025	No direct submissions took place, but the focus shifted towards industry adoption of top-performing models. Post-competition collaboration ensured real-world application

The ADRENALIN Load Disaggregation Challenge attracted a mix of participants from academia and industry, all interested in energy analytics and machine learning. Over the course of the competition, a high level of engagement was observed: many teams made regular submissions to improve their models, and the discussion forum featured exchanges about data interpretation. By the end of the development phase, over 200 teams were registered. Although no formal survey was conducted, interactions with top-performing teams revealed a mix of academic researchers and independent data scientists, many of whom regularly participate in machine learning competitions.

While large-scale competitions like ASHRAE GEPIII or Kaggle forecasting challenges typically see much higher engagement, ADRENALIN's participation levels were more in line with specialized research competitions, such as CityLearn, where only a few dozen dedicated teams compete but produce highly impactful solutions.

Training Phase (July 8 – September 15, 2024): During this phase, participants registered for the competition and developed their models using the provided training dataset. They had access to the data and could experiment with different approaches to improve their disaggregation models. A public leaderboard was available, allowing participants to evaluate their models on the training data and receive feedback. Engagement occurred in cycles with bursts of intense submissions followed by drops. A significant surge in submissions occurred in the final three days as teams finalized their models before submission restrictions began.

Test Phase (September 23 – September 30, 2024): In this final phase, participants submitted their trained models for evaluation on a hidden test dataset, which included data from the same buildings but covering different time periods. Limited feedback was provided during this stage, but to prevent overfitting, participants were restricted to a maximum of five submissions. This ensured that final rankings reflected true model generalization. Submission patterns became more deliberate and strategic, with performance improvements plateauing in the later stage. Limited leaderboard feedback encouraged the careful selection of final models.

Knowledge Transfer (October 2024 – January 2025): This phase allowed industry partners to understand and integrate the competition's top-performing models into real-world applications, ensuring that the innovations generated during the competition had practical impact. No direct submissions took place, but the focus shifted to industry adoption and real-world implementation of top-performing models. Post-competition collaboration ensured real-world application. Future competitions could provide follow-up grants for further model testing.

3 Lessons Learned from Running the Competition

The experience of organizing and executing the ADRENALIN Load Disaggregation Challenge yielded numerous insights. These *lessons learned* span technical challenges related to data and modeling, as well as organizational and logistical aspects of managing a data competition. We also observed the impact such a competition can have on community engagement and knowledge generation. In this section, we reflect on these lessons, comparing them with findings from other recent energy-related data competitions to identify common trends, challenges, and best practices.

3.1 Technical Challenges and Insights

Data Quality and Preparation. One of the foremost challenges in running the ADRENALIN competition was ensuring the dataset's quality. As the dataset was compiled from multiple real buildings via different project partners, harmonizing it required extensive preprocessing. Issues such as inconsistent formats, missing values, validating meter hierarchies within supplied buildings, and varying sensor accuracies surfaced throughout the data curation process. The competition organizers followed a structured data collection protocol, iteratively cleaning and validating the dataset to minimize noise and inconsistencies [12].

This lesson is not unique to ADRENALIN. The ASHRAE Great Energy Predictor III (GEPIII) competition on Kaggle faced similar challenges due to the massive dataset provided years of hourly metering data from 1,448 buildings. The competition's top-performing teams noted that extensive feature engineering and careful preprocessing were key differentiators in model performance. Likewise, BigDEAL 2022 encountered dataset sparsity and missing values, forcing participants to develop innovative imputation techniques. These findings highlight that dataset curation is often as important as model development, reinforcing the need for competition organizers to prioritize data quality before launching a challenge.

A key differentiator of ADRENALIN was its explicit focus on promoting model generalization across buildings. The competition returned a single aggregated score that combined results across all buildings. This design choice was to prevent participants from overfitting to individual buildings and encouraged the development of models capable of performing well across diverse conditions. Similarly, CityLearn 2022, a reinforcement learning competition for building energy control, found that many reinforcement learning (RL) models struggled to generalize beyond the specific training scenarios provided in the competition. This suggests that designing competitions that explicitly test generalization (as ADRENALIN and CityLearn did) is an effective way to push the development of deployable, rather than overfitted, machine learning models.

Defining Evaluation Metrics. Selecting the appropriate evaluation metric was another major consideration in ADRENALIN. After reviewing common NILM performance measures, the organizers selected Normalized Mean Absolute Error (NMAE) as the primary ranking metric, ensuring that errors were fairly compared across buildings of different sizes [9].

Other competitions have taken similar approaches. BigDEAL 2022, for example, used multiple leaderboards, each tracking different error components (peak timing, peak magnitude, overall load profile accuracy), to ensure models performed well across multiple criteria. In contrast, ASHRAE GEPIII used a single primary metric: Root Mean Squared Logarithmic Error (RMSLE), which was chosen to accommodate buildings with widely varying energy usage levels. However, post-competition discussions revealed that this metric sometimes disproportionately penalized under-predictions compared to over-predictions, leading some teams to optimize for the metric rather than real-world forecasting needs.

The takeaway from these competitions is that metric choice profoundly influences how participants develop their models. Unlike competitions that employed multiple evaluation metrics, ADRENALIN exclusively used Normalized Mean Absolute Error (NMAE) as its single ranking criterion. This decision provided a straightforward and consistent evaluation approach, avoiding potential conflicts between competing objectives. While multi-objective evaluation frameworks can be beneficial in some contexts, ADRENALIN's approach emphasized clarity and comparability across buildings. Future competitions should carefully consider whether a single well-chosen metric or a multi-metric framework is more suitable for their specific problem domain.

Modeling Approaches and Comparisons. The ADRENALIN competition saw a diverse range of unsupervised modeling approaches. Participants experimented with statistical methods, including probabilistic modeling, as well as clustering-based approaches that identified consumption patterns across different time periods. A detailed technical analysis of the three top-performing algorithms is provided in a companion paper [23], which describes their methodology, strengths, and performance characteristics in depth.

This diversity of approaches mirrors findings from other competitions. CityLearn 2022 reported that some teams preferred simple, rule-based controllers, while others developed deep reinforcement learning (DRL) algorithms, often with similar final performance. Likewise, BigDEAL 2022 found that while complex neural networks outperformed simpler models on peak forecasting tasks, the computational cost and instability of deep learning models made some teams favor gradient-boosted trees or hybrid solutions. These insights suggest that in competitions involving dynamic energy environments, simpler, interpretable models often perform comparably to complex architectures, particularly when generalization is a concern.

ADRENALIN showed that competitions should welcome diverse solutions while aligning evaluation with real-world feasibility. To counter overfitting, future contests could promote unsupervised methods, enforce interpretability, or require model justification.

3.2 Organizational and Logistical Lessons

Platform Selection and Constraints. One of the earliest decisions in organizing ADRENALIN was the choice of competition platform. Due to budget constraints, the organizers selected CodaLab, an open-source competition hosting platform. While CodaLab offered flexibility in designing the evaluation pipeline, it lacked some of the engagement features of commercial platforms like Kaggle, which have built-in forums, code-sharing, and large participant bases [9].

This decision significantly influenced participation numbers. ASHRAE GEPIII, which was hosted on Kaggle, attracted over 4,000 participants, whereas BigDEAL 2022 and CityLearn 2022, hosted on more specialized platforms, had only a few dozen teams. The trade-off here is scale vs. research focus: Kaggle competitions tend to attract thousands of participants, but many of them may be casual entrants with limited domain expertise. By contrast, niche competitions on academic platforms (like CodaLab, AIcrowd, or EvalAI) often attract fewer but highly skilled participants.

ADRENALIN's experience suggests that platform selection should align with competition goals. If the objective is to engage the largest possible number of participants and promote visibility, Kaggle or DrivenData may be preferred. However, if the goal is to attract focused, domain-specific teams, academic platforms like CodaLab remain a strong alternative.

Participant Engagement and Communication. Keeping participants engaged throughout a competition is critical for maintaining momentum. ADRENALIN organizers found that regular updates, clear documentation, and prompt responses to questions helped sustain participation over the competition's multi-month duration. Unlike a steady decline or continuous engagement, participation followed a dynamic pattern with bursts of submission activity followed by periods of offline refinement. This suggests that teams worked in cycles—experimenting, analyzing results, and refining their models before resubmitting. A last-minute surge before the deadline indicated that many participants delayed final submissions while refining their best models offline. The submission pattern of the competition is shown in Fig. 1.

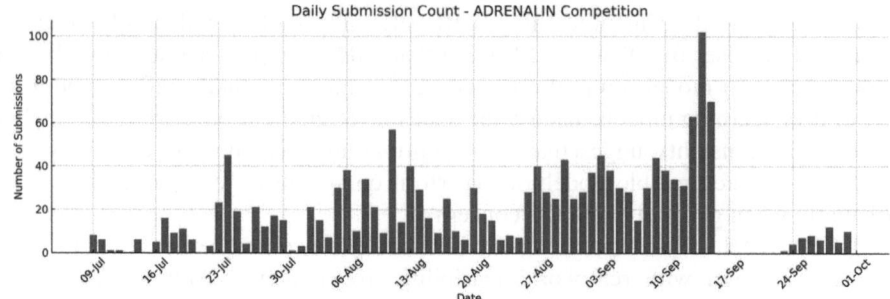

Fig. 1. Participation pattern in the ADRENALIN competition

This aligns with experiences from CityLearn 2022, which saw mid-competition engagement drops and suggested that structured milestone challenges (e.g., periodic mini-leaderboards or webinars) could help sustain interest. Similarly, BigDEAL 2022 found that rolling deadlines encouraged teams to stay active, rather than submitting everything at the last minute. In ADRENALIN, while final deadlines were a strong motivator, participation trends showed that many teams iterated early but held back final submissions until just before restrictions took effect.

A best practice emerging from these insights is to actively manage community engagement throughout a competition. Organizers should send periodic updates, highlight interesting findings, and foster participant interactions, which can be done through forums, webinars, or even informal Q&A sessions. Additionally, incorporating structured milestone deadlines or staged challenges could help maintain steady participation while still allowing for the natural iterative process of model development.

4 Recommendations for Future Data Competitions

Based on our experiences with the ADRENALIN challenge, and drawing upon best practices highlighted in recent energy data competitions such as ASHRAE GEPIII, BigDEAL 2022, and CityLearn 2022, we propose the following recommendations for organizing future data competitions, particularly in the field of energy informatics. These recommendations cover competition design, dataset preparation, participant engagement, and real-world impact, ensuring that competitions are both technically rigorous and practically valuable.

4.1 Competition Design and Dataset Preparation

Define a Clear Scope and Objective. A well-defined problem scope is the foundation of a successful competition. Organizers should invest substantial time upfront in narrowing the competition's focus to a specific, meaningful challenge. ADRENALIN's focus on unsupervised load disaggregation made it unique, as most NILM research relies on labeled datasets, but this choice also introduced significant complexity. Similarly, BigDEAL 2022's focus on peak demand forecasting forced teams to address not just energy prediction but also peak timing, which had seen little prior work.

A best practice observed across ASHRAE GEPIII, BigDEAL, and CityLearn is that clarity in problem framing directly impacts solution quality. BigDEAL organizers explicitly separated their competition into three tracks (magnitude, peak timing, overall shape) to guide participants toward building well-rounded models. CityLearn organizers noted that without separate tracks, some teams gravitated toward overly simple approaches. Future competitions should consider multi-track evaluations to encourage both basic and advanced solutions, ensuring accessibility for newcomers while pushing the boundaries of state-of-the-art methods.

Follow a Robust Data Collection Protocol. Dataset quality is arguably the single most important factor in determining competition outcomes. Poorly curated datasets lead to models that exploit artifacts rather than solving the actual problem. The ADRENALIN dataset was carefully curated from real-world building measurements, with sub-metered HVAC loads serving as ground truth. However, integrating data from multiple partners introduced format inconsistencies, missing values, and sensor calibration issues, requiring significant preprocessing.

This experience aligns with challenges faced in ASHRAE GEPIII, where missing values and extreme variations in building sizes made dataset preprocessing critical. Similarly, BigDEAL 2022 participants found that imputing missing demand data was as important as model selection. Competitions must ensure rigorous data validation and documentation before launch. A best practice, as seen in ASHRAE GEPIII and BigDEAL, is to release a "data quality report" along with the dataset, detailing known issues, anomalies, and recommended preprocessing steps to avoid confusion.

Additionally, simulated datasets, like those in CityLearn, offer unique advantages in control optimization but come with drawbacks, participants in CityLearn found that some reinforcement learning models performed well in simulation but failed in real-world settings. Future competitions should weigh the trade-offs of real-world vs. synthetic data, and if using simulated environments, should conduct validation tests against real data to ensure model transferability.

Ensure a Fair Evaluation Process. Evaluation criteria must align with real-world objectives, as they dictate what participants optimize for. ADRENALIN's use of Normalized Mean Absolute Error (NMAE) as its sole evaluation metric, ensured that models were assessed based on a single, consistent measure across all test buildings. Unlike competitions that use multi-track evaluation systems, ADRENALIN's single-metric approach streamlined the evaluation process and reinforced the importance of generalization across buildings.

This approach contrasts with BigDEAL 2022, where organizers introduced three separate evaluation tracks to ensure that teams optimized for multiple aspects of the forecast rather than focusing on a single measure. Conversely, ASHRAE GEPIII relied solely on RMSLE, but post-competition analysis revealed that it disproportionately penalized under-predictions, leading some teams to favor models that slightly overestimated energy use. ADRENALIN followed a different path by intentionally using only NMAE as its sole evaluation criterion, prioritizing a clear and consistent ranking methodology. While multi-metric evaluation frameworks can offer additional insights, ADRENALIN's approach highlights the benefits of using a single, well-defined metric to enforce fairness and simplicity in competition design.

Another strategy observed in CityLearn 2022 was using reward functions combining multiple objectives (e.g., energy cost, emissions, comfort). Future competitions could explore custom scoring mechanisms, such as weighting interpretability, robustness, or computational efficiency alongside raw predictive accuracy.

4.2 Participant Engagement and Experience

Choose the Right Hosting Platform. The choice of competition platform significantly influences participation. ASHRAE GEPIII, hosted on Kaggle, saw over 4,00 participants, whereas BigDEAL 2022, CityLearn 2022 and AIcrowd's Brick by Brick competition, hosted on smaller academic platforms, attracted fewer but highly specialized teams. Simmilarly, ADRENALIN, hosted on CodaLab, attracted a targeted, domain-specific audience rather than thousands of casual entrants.

Competitions aimed at wider public engagement (e.g., industry and data science professionals) should leverage platforms like Kaggle or DrivenData, which have built-in community features, large user bases, and robust submission infrastructures. By contrast, competitions aimed at academic research advancements may benefit from open-source platforms like CodaLab, AIcrowd, or EvalAI, which offer more flexibility but require active management by organizers.

Maintain Active Communication and Support. Keeping participants engaged throughout a competition is critical for maintaining momentum. ADRENALIN's organizers found that regular updates, clear documentation, and timely responses to questions helped sustain participation across its multi-month duration.

This aligns with experiences from CityLearn 2022, where organizers noted that interest dipped mid-competition, leading them to recommend structured engagement milestones, such as midway check-ins, mini-leaderboards, or live Q&A sessions. While in BigDEAL 2022 the rolling deadlines encouraged participants to stay active rather than submitting everything at the last minute.

ADRENALIN's participation patterns suggest that many teams refined their models early and strategically selected submission timings. A key recommendation is to actively manage community engagement, whether through email updates, competition forums, webinars, or interactive leaderboards.

Encourage Code and Knowledge Sharing. One of the most valuable outcomes of competitions is the dissemination of knowledge. Kaggle competitions like ASHRAE GEPIII encourage participants to share notebooks and insights, fostering a strong learning community. ADRENALIN organizers required winners to open-source their code after the competition, ensuring transparency and knowledge transfer.

Future competitions could consider requiring open-source solutions from top teams (with appropriate licensing) and hosting post-competition workshops where winners explain their methods. This approach, already adopted in ASHRAE GEPIII, helps ensure that competition findings extend beyond the event itself and contribute to broader advancements in energy informatics.

4.3 Maximizing Real-World Impact

Align Competition Goals with Practical Needs. To ensure that competition outcomes are valuable beyond academic interest, organizers should align tasks with real-world deployment challenges. ADRENALIN did this by promoting unsupervised approaches, with strong generalization. The tasks introduced in BigDEAL 2022 are relevant to grid operators, increasing the likelihood of real-world adoption of winning models.

A recommendation for future competitions is to collaborate with industry stakeholders early in the design phase. This ensures that competition objectives are directly tied to practical applications, increasing the likelihood that winning solutions will transition from competition settings to real-world implementation.

Support Post-Competition Integration of Winning Solutions. A major shortcoming of many data competitions is that the results are often limited to leaderboard rankings without clear pathways to deployment. ADRENALIN mitigated this by requiring a post-competition collaboration period for winning teams, ensuring that top solutions were properly documented and tested for industry use.

Future competitions should consider offering follow-up grants or research funding for the top solutions, encouraging continued development and real-world piloting. Competitions that produce open datasets, like ASHRAE GEPIII and BigDEAL, also provide long-term value to the research community, allowing future benchmarking efforts. By maintaining public access to high-quality, well-documented data, such competitions ensure that researchers can revisit the problem over time using emerging tools and techniques, potentially unlocking new solutions even years after the competition has ended.

5 Conclusion and Future Work

The ADRENALIN Load Disaggregation Challenge provided a rich learning experience for both participants and organizers. Through this competition, we addressed a pressing energy informatics problem, disaggregating building-level energy usage into heating and cooling loads using only whole-building metering data, while also testing model generalization across unseen buildings. By structuring the competition around real-world data constraints and generalization challenges, ADRENALIN made important contributions to advancing practical NILM techniques.

However, ADRENALIN's lessons extend beyond this single competition. A comparative analysis with other recent energy data competitions: ASHRAE GEPIII, BigDEAL 2022 and CityLearn 2022, reveals that many of the challenges, solutions, and best practices identified in ADRENALIN are common across different types of energy informatics competitions. These comparisons highlight key areas where ADRENALIN aligned with or diverged from other competitions, strengthening our understanding of what makes an energy data competition successful and impactful.

5.1 Key Takeaways from ADRENALIN and Other Competitions

Dataset Quality is Critical. Across ADRENALIN, ASHRAE GEPIII, and BigDEAL, data curation was identified as one of the most important yet challenging aspects. Inconsistent formats, missing values, and the need for domain-specific preprocessing all proved to be major hurdles. Future competitions should invest in extensive data validation before launch, ensuring participants work with a dataset that is both realistic and reliable.

Evaluation Metrics Shape Competition Outcomes. Evaluation strategies varied across competitions. ADRENALIN's use of a single metric (NMAE) simplified evaluation and emphasized generalization, while BigDEAL and CityLearn explored multi-objective scoring.

Generalization is a Key Challenge Across Domains. One of ADRENALIN's primary objectives was to test model generalization across buildings, a problem that is often overlooked in machine learning-based energy forecasting. CityLearn 2022 faced a similar challenge, where reinforcement learning models struggled to adapt beyond their training environments. ADRENALIN's results confirmed that ensuring cross-building generalization is difficult but necessary for practical NILM applications. Future competitions should explicitly design evaluation procedures that test real-world adaptability, rather than allowing participants to fine-tune models exclusively for a fixed dataset.

Competition Structure and Platform Choice Affect Engagement. ADRENALIN, BigDEAL, and CityLearn all relied on specialized academic platforms (CodaLab, AIcrowd, EvalAI), which helped attract domain-specific experts but limited the overall number of participants. In contrast, ASHRAE GEPIII leveraged Kaggle, reaching over 4,000 participants but at the cost of less direct engagement with energy professionals. The takeaway is that competitions must balance visibility with participant expertise. Large-scale competitions benefit from open platforms like Kaggle, while targeted research competitions thrive on domain-specific platforms that allow for more controlled evaluation and participant interaction.

Ensuring Real-World Impact Requires Post-Competition Follow-Up. Many energy competitions struggle to translate winning solutions into real-world deployment. ADRENALIN aimed to bridge this gap by requiring a post-competition collaboration period for winners, ensuring that their models were tested for practical applicability. This approach aligns with ASHRAE GEPIII, which encouraged open-source solutions, which required competitors to submit detailed documentation for industry use. Future competitions should consider offering funding, implementation grants, or direct industry collaboration to ensure that top solutions extend beyond the leaderboard.

5.2 Future Work and Next Steps

The lessons from ADRENALIN, coupled with insights from other competitions, point toward several areas for improvement in future energy informatics challenges:

Expanding Competition Scope. While ADRENALIN focused on disaggregating HVAC loads in commercial buildings, future competitions could explore other under-researched NILM problems, such as industrial load disaggregation, multi-appliance classification, or real-time streaming disaggregation. BigDEAL 2022's focus on peak timing forecasting suggests that competitions tackling previously unexplored subproblems can significantly advance the state of the art.

Hybrid Evaluation Frameworks. A key takeaway from BigDEAL and CityLearn is that multi-track evaluation can lead to better-rounded models. ADRENALIN, by contrast, successfully demonstrated the effectiveness of a single, well-defined metric (NMAE) to drive generalization. Future competitions should incorporate hybrid evaluation frameworks that balance accuracy, interpretability, computational efficiency, and generalizability.

Open Science and Community Collaboration. Many competitions, including ASHRAE GEPIII and ADRENALIN, highlighted the importance of open-source sharing of data, models, and insights. Future competitions should incentivize participants to document and share their findings, potentially through post-competition workshops, public dataset releases, or follow-up research collaborations.

Longitudinal Competitions. Rather than one-off events, future competitions could adopt longitudinal formats, where models are tested over time on new, unseen datasets. This would encourage participants to develop robust, deployable solutions rather than simply optimizing for a fixed dataset.

Interdisciplinary Collaboration. As energy data competitions continue to evolve, there is potential for greater interdisciplinary collaboration; for example, combining machine learning, physics-based modeling, and behavioral analytics. CityLearn demonstrated the value of reinforcement learning, while BigDEAL incorporated time-series forecasting expertise. Future competitions could encourage interdisciplinary teams to tackle energy informatics problems from multiple perspectives.

5.3 Final Remarks

The ADRENALIN Load Disaggregation Challenge was one of the first competitions to explicitly test unsupervised NILM models generalization across buildings, making it a valuable contribution to the energy informatics community. However, its findings are not isolated, the lessons learned align with broader trends observed in forecasting (BigDEAL), grid-interactive neighborhood energy optimization (CityLearn), sustainability-focused predictive modeling (Global AI Challenge), and energy efficiency modeling (ASHRAE GEPIII).

By synthesizing insights from multiple competitions, this paper not only documents ADRENALIN's specific outcomes but also provides a framework for designing better energy informatics competitions in the future. As the field evolves, future competitions should build upon these lessons, refining their structure, evaluation metrics, and engagement strategies to maximize both research impact and real-world deployment of energy analytics solutions.

The future of energy data science is collaborative, interdisciplinary, iterative, and well-designed competitions will continue to play a crucial role in accelerating innovation in this space.

Acknowledgement. This paper is part of the ADRENALIN (Data-driven smart buildings: data sandbox and competition) project. Funded by the Energy Technology Development and Demonstration Programme (EUDP) In Denmark (Case no. 64021-6025).

References

1. Angelis, G.-F., et al.: NILM applications: literature review of learning approaches, recent developments and challenges. Energy Build. **261**, 111951 (2022)
2. Salani, M., et al.: Non intrusive load monitoring for demand side management. Energy Inform. **3**, 1–12 (2020)
3. Ehrhardt-Martinez, K., Donnelly, K.A., Laitner, S.: Advanced metering initiatives and residential feedback programs: a meta-review for household electricity-saving opportunities. American Council for an Energy-Efficient Economy Washington, DC (2010)
4. Tolnai, B.A., Ma, Z., Jørgensen, B.N.: A scoping review of energy load disaggregation. In: EPIA 2023. Springer, Cham (2023)
5. Hart, G.W.: Nonintrusive appliance load monitoring. Proc. IEEE **80**(12), 1870–1891 (1992)
6. Tolnai, B.A., Ma, Z., Jørgensen, B.N.: A scoping review of energy load disaggregation. In: Moniz, N., Vale, Z., Cascalho, J., Silva, C., Sebastião, R. (eds.) Progress in Artificial Intelligence. EPIA 2023. LNCS, vol 14116. Springer, Cham (2023). https://doi.org/10.1007/978-3-031-49011-8_17
7. Nalmpantis, C., Vrakas, D.: Machine learning approaches for non-intrusive load monitoring: from qualitative to quantitative comparison. Artif. Intell. Rev. **52**(2), 217–243 (2019)
8. Huber, P., et al.: Review on deep neural networks applied to low-frequency NILM. Energies **14**(9), 2390 (2021)
9. Tolnai, B.A., Ma, Z., Jørgensen, B.N.: Standard energy data competition procedure: a comprehensive review with a case study of the ADRENALIN load disaggregation competition. In: Energy Informatics. Springer Nature Switzerland, Cham (2024)
10. Mozafari, B., et al.: Scaling up crowd-sourcing to very large datasets: a case for active learning. Proc. VLDB Endow. **8**(2), 125–136 (2014)
11. Yan, W., et al.: Crowdsourcing data science for innovation. In: 2017 IEEE International Conference on Data Mining Workshops (ICDMW) (2017)
12. Tolnai, B.A., Ma, Z., Jørgensen, B.N.: Energy Data Collection Protocol: A Case Study on the ADRENALIN Project. In: Energy Informatics. Springer Nature Switzerland, Cham (2025)
13. Henriet, S., et al.: A generative model for non-intrusive load monitoring in commercial buildings. Energy Build. **177**, 268–278 (2018)
14. Miller, C., et al.: The ASHRAE Great Energy Predictor III competition: overview and results. Sci. Technol. Built Environ. **26**(10), 1427–1447 (2020)
15. Shukla, S., Hong, T.: BigDEAL challenge 2022: forecasting peak timing of electricity demand. IET Smart Grid **7**(4), 442–459 (2024)
16. Nweye, K., et al.: The CityLearn Challenge 2022: overview, results, and lessons learned. in Proc. NeurIPS 2022 Competitions Track (2022)
17. Global AI Challenge 2021. 2021 2025. https://2021.globalaichallenge.com/en/home
18. AIcrowd | Brick by Brick 2024 (2024) [cited 2025]. https://www.aicrowd.com/challenges/brick-by-brick-2024

19. NYSERDA RTEM Hackathon (Building Energy Exchange) (2023) 2025. https://be-exchange.org/nyserda-rtem-hackathon-demo-day/
20. Lien, S.K., Najafi, B., Rajasekharan, J.: Advances in machine-learning based disaggregation of building heating loads: a review. In: Energy Informatics. Springer Nature Switzerland, Cham (2024)
21. Pujić, D., Tomašević, N., Batić, M.: A semi-supervised approach for improving generalization in non-intrusive load monitoring. Sensors (Basel) **23**(3) (2023)
22. ADRENALIN Load Disaggregation Challenge Dataset: Energy Use in Buildings. (2024) [cited 2025]. https://codalab.lisn.upsaclay.fr/competitions/19659
23. Tolnai, B.A., et al.: Advancing non-intrusive load monitoring: insights from the winning algorithms in the ADRENALIN 2024 load disaggregation competition. In: Nordic Energy Informatics Academy Conference 2025. Springer, Stockholm, Sweden (2025)

Business Model Innovation in Data Competitions: Insights from the 2024 ADRENALIN Load Disaggregation Challenge

Zheng Grace Ma(✉) [id], Balázs András Tolnai [id], and Bo Nørregaard Jørgensen [id]

SDU Center for Energy Informatics, The Faculty of Engineering, The Maersk Mc-Kinney Moller Institute, University of Southern Denmark, Odense, Denmark
zma@mmmi.sdu.dk

Abstract. Data competitions have become an essential mechanism for fostering open innovation in domains such as computer vision, natural language processing, and energy informatics. Despite their growing prominence, the underpinning business models that sustain these competitions remain underexplored, leading to uncertain long-term adoption and limited value capture. This paper addresses these gaps by examining the 2024 ADRENALIN Load Disaggregation Competition as a case study of both technical and business model innovation within energy informatics. The research adopts an embedded single-case design, supported by multiple data sources and a comparative analysis with the digital gaming industry. Findings indicate that integrating multi-sided platform principles—derived from gaming ecosystems—can catalyze scalable Non-Intrusive Load Monitoring (NILM) solutions, enhance stakeholder engagement, and establish viable revenue pathways. Empirical results show that unsupervised NILM algorithms developed under zero ground truth constraints achieved NMAE values below 0.30, demonstrating high performance across diverse building types and climates. The study concludes that a hybrid revenue approach, combining sponsorships, IP licensing, and post-competition collaborations, enables sustainable operations beyond the typical prize-based model. These insights contribute to both academic literature and practical guidelines, illustrating how data competitions can evolve into robust, multi-stakeholder ecosystems with enduring economic and societal benefits.

Keywords: Business Model Innovation · Data Competitions · Load Disaggregation · Multi-Sided Platforms · Non-Intrusive Load Monitoring

1 Introduction

Data-driven competitions have emerged as an increasingly influential approach to advancing research and innovation, particularly in complex domains such as energy informatics and artificial intelligence. By mobilizing a diverse pool of global participants, these competitions harness collective intelligence to generate inventive solutions, often at substantially lower cost and reduced development timelines compared to traditional R&D initiatives. Prominent competition platforms, including Kaggle, AIcrowd, and Codalab, have demonstrated the potential of open calls to address a spectrum of technical challenges, spanning computer vision, natural language processing, and energy optimization. Despite this success, the business models underpinning data competitions remain insufficiently examined in existing scholarship.

Within energy informatics, non-intrusive load monitoring (NILM) has benefitted from multiple data competitions that push methodological frontiers [1]. NILM researchers seek to disaggregate whole-building power consumption into end-use profiles, e.g., heating, ventilation, and air conditioning (HVAC), to enable targeted energy efficiency interventions. However, while competitions have proved effective in stimulating algorithmic innovation, two key challenges persist. First, most NILM competitions rely on supervised data with labeled sub-metered appliances, an assumption that does not always hold in real-world building settings. Second, little is known about the economic frameworks or post-competition pathways that can sustain such initiatives and secure long-term industry adoption.

This study addresses these research gaps by examining the 2024 ADRENALIN Load Disaggregation Competition as a focal case of both technical and business model innovation (BMI). ADRENALIN challenged participants to develop unsupervised NILM algorithms for HVAC disaggregation across diverse commercial buildings and climatic regions. In addition to technical goals, the competition organizers explicitly designed a multi-sided business model, drawing inspiration from digital gaming platforms that profit from multi-stakeholder interactions [2, 3]. Such parallels between online gaming and data competitions offer a novel theoretical lens to assess how competitions can create, deliver, and capture value in a sustainable manner.

A critical limitation in the literature is that while data competitions increasingly generate meaningful technical results, they often lack robust monetization mechanisms, structured industry engagement strategies, or formalized procedures for implementing winning solutions. By contrast, digital games utilize multi-faceted revenue streams—such as microtransactions, subscriptions, and in-game advertising—to support ongoing platform viability. Extending these insights to data competitions could help address fundamental challenges: the reliance on short-term sponsorships, the uncertain post-competition uptake of solutions, and the absence of sustainable ecosystems around competition platforms.

In this context, the primary objectives of this paper are threefold. First, it proposes an analytical framework that adopts concepts from business model innovation and platform economics to dissect the value proposition, platform structure, revenue logic, and stakeholder engagement of data competitions. Second, it applies this framework to the ADRENALIN case to illustrate how unsupervised HVAC disaggregation challenges can be simultaneously pursued with novel business model elements, including indirect monetization and stakeholder co-creation. Third, it presents empirically grounded recommendations for data competition organizers, policymakers, and industry partners, with an emphasis on achieving long-term impacts in energy informatics and beyond.

To achieve these objectives, this study employs a qualitative, embedded single-case design [4]. Multiple data sources—including competition reports, official documentation, and post-competition evaluations—were analyzed to reveal the interplay between competition design, stakeholder incentives, and the resulting business model innovations [5]. A comparative perspective with the digital gaming industry further highlights both commonalities (multi-sided interactions, network effects) and differences (non-commercial, research-oriented goals).

The paper is organized as follows. Section 2 reviews literature on data competitions, business model innovation, and multi-sided platforms in computer gaming. Section 3 describes the case study methodology and analytical framework. Section 4 analyzes the ADRENALIN competition, focusing on objectives, participants, and revenue structures. Section 5 discusses findings in relation to existing theories, noting similarities and differences from gaming models. Section 6 concludes with key insights, limitations, and suggestions for future research.

2 Literature Review

There are three key areas relevant to the study: (1) data competitions as a crowdsourcing mechanism in scientific and engineering domains, (2) business model innovation within digital platform ecosystems, and (3) the application of multi-sided business models in the computer game industry.

2.1 Data Competitions

Data competitions have gained significant traction in fields such as computer vision, natural language processing, and energy informatics, largely driven by platforms like Kaggle, AIcrowd, and Codalab. These platforms leverage a global pool of experts who compete to develop novel algorithms under standardized evaluation criteria, effectively democratizing innovation and reducing the time-to-market for cutting-edge solutions. Prior research highlights how these open contests can accelerate progress in specialized areas—ranging from medical image analysis to energy load forecasting—by tapping into a diverse talent base [6].

In the energy domain, NILM has particularly benefited from data competitions that encourage methodological diversity and robust benchmarking. Traditional NILM studies often rely on labeled datasets that may not generalize beyond specific building contexts [7]. To address this gap, recent competitions, including the ADRENALIN initiative, have introduced unsupervised or semi-supervised frameworks in which participants must learn building-specific load signatures without direct access to labeled training data. While these competitions have substantially advanced the technical front, the underlying business models are typically ad hoc, funded through grants or industry sponsorships without a clear plan for post-competition revenue or sustained stakeholder engagement. This deficiency underscores the need for a deeper understanding of the economic and strategic dimensions of data competitions.

2.2 Business Model Innovation in Digital Platform Ecosystems

BMI is broadly understood as the reconfiguration of existing business logic, value creation, delivery, and capture, to exploit emerging opportunities or counter disruptive threats [8]. Traditional frameworks of BMI emphasize the importance of multi-sided platforms, wherein different stakeholder groups (e.g., producers, consumers, partners) co-create value through a shared digital infrastructure [9]. These platforms often rely on network effects, where each additional participant enhances the ecosystem's value, facilitating rapid growth and collective innovation [10].

While BMI theory has been extensively applied to industries such as e-commerce and software services, its applicability to data competitions remains underexplored. Recent work suggests that data-driven contests can function as specialized multi-sided platforms linking participants (data scientists), organizers, domain experts, and industry sponsors [11]. However, unlike consumer-facing digital platforms that can monetize through subscriptions or advertising, many data competitions lack a robust, long-term revenue model. Organizers typically rely on one-off sponsorships and grants, raising questions about sustainability and repeatability over time [12].

Therefore, there is the need for competition platforms to move beyond simple prize-based incentives by integrating more sophisticated forms of value capture such as intellectual property rights, licensing agreements, or spin-off services. A few studies underscore that data competitions can emulate platform tactics from other digital industries by building communities around shared data resources, engaging participants in extended problem-solving phases, and creating mechanisms for long-tail monetization (e.g., commercializing winning solutions) [13, 14]. Nonetheless, empirical analyses that map these ideas onto real-world data competitions, especially in fields like energy informatics, remain sparse.

2.3 Computer Game Industry

The computer game industry provides a rich context for examining multi-sided business models, as evidenced by a substantial body of research. These studies reveal how game developers leverage platform-based ecosystems, monetize user engagement, and orchestrate community-driven innovation—all strategies that could inform the design of sustainable data competitions.

Multi-sided Business Models and Creative Ecosystems. Multi-sided platform theory holds that digital gaming ecosystems often involve multiple stakeholders: game developers, players, advertisers, and content creators, [15, 16]. By fostering openness—allowing user-generated content or "modding"—some game studios orchestrate highly creative ecosystems that encourage user participation and loyalty. Data competitions can analogously benefit from participant-led innovation, open-source contributions, and a sense of shared community ownership [14].

Microtransactions and Revenue Diversification. One hallmark of modern gaming business models is the transition from single-purchase box sales to ongoing revenue streams via microtransactions, subscriptions, and downloadable content [17, 18]. This approach alleviates reliance on one-time sales, ensuring continuous engagement and a more stable financial outlook. For data competitions, a parallel could involve licensing winning algorithms or offering premium consulting services post-competition, thereby diversifying beyond a single prize pool [19, 20].

Community Engagement and Actor Participation. Several studies highlight how actor engagement—from active players to community influencers—reshapes the value proposition, creation, and capture within gaming ecosystems [21]. Building a robust participant community can also yield network effects, as seen in large-scale multiplayer platforms. In the context of data competitions, fostering long-term relationships among participants, industry sponsors, and academia may similarly amplify impact and extend the lifecycle of competition outputs [22, 23].

Ethical and Sustainability Considerations. Recent debates in gaming also address ethical aspects of monetization and user engagement, examining how design choices impact trust and long-term ecosystem viability [22]. While data competitions do not typically face the same ethical controversies as pay-to-win gaming models, the principle of transparent and fair value distribution remains pertinent. Ensuring that competition outputs—such as winning algorithms—are accessible to stakeholders without exploitation reinforces trust and can enhance the competition brand's reputation [1].

Table 1 synthesizes select studies on data competitions and computer game business models, highlighting key themes relevant to understanding how data competition organizers can innovate their business models.

As shown in Table 1, both data competitions and computer games face the dual challenge of (1) crafting compelling value propositions that attract and retain participants, and (2) sustaining engagement through business model mechanisms. The ADRENALIN competition's design focusing on NILM and unsupervised methods addresses a critical research gap but also highlights the need for advanced monetization and stakeholder engagement strategies reminiscent of successful gaming platforms. Building on these insights, Table 2 offers a focused comparison of core business model elements in data competitions versus computer gaming, illustrating how principles from the latter might inform the former.

From a strategic management perspective, lessons from the gaming industry suggest that data competitions might benefit from hybrid revenue models, persistent community engagement channels, and pre-defined pathways for real-world implementation. While a purely "freemium" approach may not translate directly into scientific competitions, the underlying principles—recurring value propositions, network effects, community cocreation—can significantly enhance the sustainability and impact of data competitions in domains like energy informatics.

Despite parallels to well-established multi-sided ecosystems in the gaming sector, the scholarly discourse on data competitions has largely focused on technical outcomes rather than on holistic business model considerations. Key open questions include how to structure competitions for repeatable revenue, how to engage a stable community of solvers and sponsors over time, and how to integrate winning algorithms into industry practice. Existing research seldom addresses post-competition adoption pathways or formalized value-capture mechanisms. Consequently, a clear gap exists in understanding how data competitions can evolve from short-lived innovation "sprints" into sustainable platforms that generate enduring economic and societal benefits.

Positioning the ADRENALIN Load Disaggregation Competition at the nexus of these issues, this study aims to build on the rich findings from digital platform ecosystems—particularly from computer gaming—and adapt them to the context of large-scale data challenges in energy informatics. The subsequent sections elucidate how

Table 1. Key Studies Comparing Data Competitions and Computer Game Models

Context/Industry	Key Findings	Relevance to ADRENALIN Case	Ref.
NILM Data Competitions	Demonstrates the technical value of crowdsourced energy disaggregation solutions	Highlights the need for scaling solutions beyond a single challenge	[1]
Digital Platforms	Multi-sided platforms can create sustained value through network effects and strategic openness	Suggests how data competitions could adopt platform-based growth strategies	[2]
Online Gaming	Analyzes freemium/microtransaction models that drive recurring revenue	Inspires potential recurring revenue models for data competition organizers	[3]
Video Game Ecosystems	Managing openness is key to harness user creativity and innovation	Applies to open-source and collaborative aspects of ADRENALIN	[24]
Video Game Platforms	Compares platform economics and revenue models; underscores importance of multi-sided interactions	Informs strategic design choices for data competition monetization	[25]
Computer Game Industry	Discuss multi-sided business models, creative ecosystems, monetization strategies, and user engagement	Provides a suite of potential best practices for sustainable data competitions	[15–23, 26, 27]

ADRENALIN's business model elements align with or diverge from established practices in the gaming industry, providing empirical insights that inform future competition design and academic discourse.

3 Methodology

This study uses a case study approach to investigate business model innovations in data competitions, focusing on the 2024 ADRENALIN Load Disaggregation Competition. This method is well-suited to exploring complex, real-world phenomena such as stakeholder dynamics and strategic implications [1]. An embedded single-case design is applied, with the competition as the main unit of analysis and key elements—like

Table 2. Core Business Model Elements in Data Competitions vs. Computer Games

Element	Data Competitions	Computer Games
Value Proposition	Crowdsourced R&D, problem-solving for complex domains (e.g., energy, healthcare)	Immersive entertainment experiences, often extended with user-generated content
Platform Structure	Multi-sided: participants, organizers, industry sponsors, domain experts	Multi-sided: players, developers, advertisers, content creators
Revenue Model	Primarily external grants/sponsorship, limited IP licensing post-competition	Freemium, subscriptions, in-game purchases, downloadable content (DLC), advertising
Community Engagement	Forum-based collaboration, open-source sharing of code, limited post-competition follow-up	Extended community building via online forums, tournaments, social media integration
Long-Term Impact	Ad hoc integration of winning solutions, variable industry uptake	Continual revenue from updates, expansions, microtransactions, strong brand loyalty

participant engagement, platform dynamics, and post-competition implementation—as sub-units. This enables in-depth analysis while linking findings to broader digital business model theories.

A multi-source data collection strategy was employed to ensure robustness and triangulation. The primary sources of data include:

1. Official reports documenting the competition's design, objectives, dataset characteristics, evaluation metrics, and post-competition insights were analyzed [12]. These reports provide structured reflections on the competition's execution and the performance of submitted models.
2. Documentation related to the competition's platform architecture, dataset structure, evaluation framework, and benchmark models was reviewed to understand the technical constraints and opportunities that shaped participant engagement and model development [28].
3. The application form and strategic documents associated with the EUDP (Energy Technology Development and Demonstration Program) were examined to contextualize the competition within broader research and industry initiatives. These documents offer insights into the intended value capture mechanisms and long-term implementation plans.

An analytical framework was adapted from business model innovation literature, particularly research on multi-sided platforms in digital industries such as computer games and online service ecosystems [29, 30]. The framework examines four key dimensions as shown in Table 3. This framework provides a structured lens for systematically extracting key business model insights from the ADRENALIN competition, allowing for meaningful comparisons with established digital business ecosystems.

To position the ADRENALIN competition within broader business model innovation trends, this study conducts a comparative analysis with business models observed in the video game industry and other multi-sided digital platforms. The rationale for this comparison is twofold:

1. Similar Business Model Mechanics: Like video game platforms, data competitions operate within a multi-sided market, where different user groups (e.g., participants, competition organizers, industry sponsors) interact through a shared digital infrastructure. Both industries rely on engagement-driven value creation, whether through gameplay mechanics in video games or algorithmic development in data competitions [31].
2. Divergent Value Capture Mechanisms: While video game platforms have well-defined monetization strategies—such as in-game purchases, advertisements, and subscription models—data competitions typically rely on external funding sources and industry partnerships. The study explores how lessons from gaming business models might inform more sustainable monetization approaches for future data competitions.

Table 3. Analytical Framework for ADRENALIN's Business Model

Dimension	Aim	Considerations
Value Proposition	Understanding how the competition created and delivered value to different stakeholders, including participants (data scientists and AI researchers), industry sponsors, and competition organizers	What were the primary incentives for participant engagement? How was knowledge generated, shared, and leveraged post-competition? How did the competition balance innovation and practical applicability?
Platform Dynamics	Analyzing the multi-sided nature of the ADRENALIN competition platform and its role in facilitating value exchange among different actors	The structure of the competition platform and its alignment with established multi-sided platform models. The degree of openness in competition participation and model dissemination. Mechanisms employed to foster collaboration and interaction between participants and stakeholders

(*continued*)

Table 3. (*continued*)

Dimension	Aim	Considerations
Revenue and Cost Structures	Investigating how the business model of the competition aligns with value capture mechanisms seen in other digital industries	The role of external funding (e.g., grants, industry sponsorship) in sustaining competition costs Direct vs. indirect monetization strategies, such as intellectual property agreements, post-competition commercialization of winning models, and industry partnerships Comparisons with freemium and microtransaction models commonly used in online gaming platforms
Stakeholder Engagement and Knowledge Transfer	Examining how the competition engaged participants before, during, and after the event to maximize impact	Participant onboarding processes, including dataset access, technical guidelines, and community engagement forums Incentive structures, such as prize allocation, recognition, and potential commercialization pathways Post-competition dissemination of results, including publication strategies, open-source contributions, and industry partnerships

The comparative analysis follows a pattern-matching approach, where observed business model characteristics in ADRENALIN are mapped against known patterns from video game ecosystems. Table 4 provides a preliminary comparison of key business model elements. This comparative analysis highlights both shared and distinct business model dynamics, offering insights into how data competitions can optimize engagement strategies, value creation, and revenue generation models.

To ensure rigor and reliability, the study applies data triangulation, where findings from different sources (reports, documents, literature) are cross-verified. Additionally, the comparative component provides external validation by situating the ADRENALIN competition within a broader theoretical and industrial context.

Table 4. Preliminary Business Model Comparison: ADRENALIN vs. Video Game Industry

Business Model Element	ADRENALIN Competition	Video Game Industry
Value Proposition	Crowdsourced algorithm development for energy applications	Immersive entertainment experience
Platform Structure	Multi-sided platform connecting data scientists, building operators, and competition organizers	Multi-sided ecosystem linking players, developers, advertisers, and content creators
Revenue Model	Primarily external funding, industry sponsorships, and grant support	Freemium, in-game purchases, subscription-based services
Participant Engagement	Open-source community, knowledge sharing, and academic dissemination	Social features, in-game events, and community-driven content
Post-Competition Monetization	Potential commercial deployment of winning solutions	Long-tail revenue from continuous player engagement

4 Case Analysis of the 2024 ADRENALIN Load Disaggregation Competition

The ADRENALIN 2024 Load Disaggregation Competition was organized by the SDU Center for Energy Informatics, with coordination led by SINTEF and significant contributions from RISE, CSIRO, and other consortium partners. The competition's central goal was to advance machine learning approaches for HVAC load disaggregation in commercial buildings. Unlike traditional contests primarily focused on short-term algorithmic improvements, ADRENALIN integrated strategic considerations such as crowdsourced R&D, multi-sided platform dynamics, and post-competition revenue pathways, thereby offering unique insights into the feasibility of long-term value capture.

4.1 Data and Problem Formulation

The core challenge of the ADRENALIN competition was to identify HVAC energy consumption within aggregate building power measurements using purely unsupervised or semi-supervised techniques. The competition dataset spanned nine commercial buildings located in Norway, Denmark, and Australia, representing a diverse range of energy usage patterns and HVAC system configurations. Each building's dataset included total power consumption readings, sub-metered HVAC ground truth data for ex-post model evaluation, and localized weather information (temperature, humidity, wind speed, solar radiation).

All data were recorded at multiple temporal resolutions, including 5-min, 15-min, 30-min, and hourly intervals. To encourage generalizable and robust solutions, the competition prohibited the use of labeled training data. Participants were instead required to devise algorithms capable of inferring HVAC load signatures directly from aggregated consumption time series. This zero ground truth requirement posed significant modeling challenges but also aligned with the real-world constraints often faced by building operators who lack dedicated sub-metering for all appliances.

4.2 Competition Design and Workflow

The ADRENALIN competition was structured into three consecutive phases, each designed to balance flexibility in model development with rigorous evaluation criteria. The development phase allowed participants to access partial data and utilize a public leaderboard for iterative feedback. The subsequent final evaluation phase restricted submissions to a hidden test set and imposed submission limits to mitigate overfitting tendencies. The final implementation phase evaluated the real-world viability of top-performing models, as organizers and industry partners collaborated to test solutions in live building energy management settings.

Figure 1 illustrates the phased workflow. During the development phase, partial feedback scores were computed on a subset of building data. Once participants finalized their models and moved into the final evaluation phase, they submitted up to five entries, each of which was scored against an unseen test partition. The evaluation metric was the normalized mean absolute error (NMAE), chosen for its capacity to compare results across buildings with varying load levels.

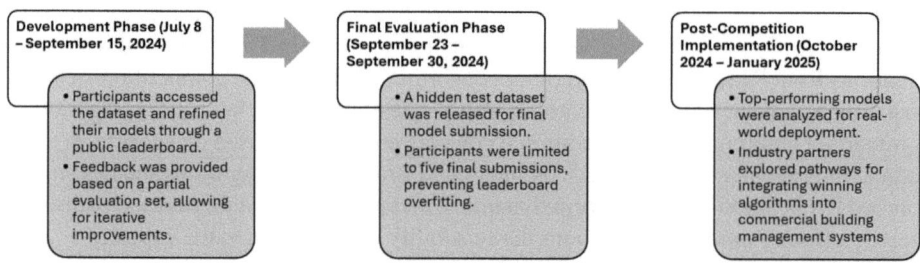

Fig. 1. Phased workflow of the 2024 ADRENALIN Load Disaggregation Competition [32]

Participants came from diverse professional and academic backgrounds, reflecting the competition's multi-sided platform nature. While researchers and data scientists benefited from exposure to a real-world dataset and potential academic recognition, industry partners gained early access to potentially transformative NILM algorithms. Table 5 summarizes the key stakeholders, their roles, and their incentives for participating in the ADRENALIN ecosystem, emphasizing the competition's alignment with multi-sided platform principles discussed in digital industries.

Table 5. Stakeholders, Roles, and Incentives in the ADRENALIN Ecosystem

Stakeholder	Role	Incentive
Data Scientists	Developed unsupervised NILM models for leaderboard rankings	Access to unique dataset, potential prize, academic recognition
Building Operators	Provided real-world building data and verified data integrity	Early insights into advanced HVAC disaggregation solutions
Industry Partners	Co-funded competition expenses, explored winning model adoption	Potential licensing agreements, improved energy management products
Research Institutions	Curated the dataset, ensured methodological rigor, disseminated results	Enhanced visibility of NILM research, alignment with grants and long-term academic collaboration

4.3 Business Model Considerations

One of the central innovations of the ADRENALIN competition was its attention to business model design, in parallel with the technical demands of the challenge. Organizers positioned ADRENALIN as a multi-sided platform, drawing inspiration from approaches in the video game industry where developers, players, and other stakeholders co-create value [14]. This structure facilitated direct collaboration between data scientists, building operators, and industry sponsors, each of whom had distinct motivations and value propositions.

A key aspect of ADRENALIN's business model was the exploration of indirect monetization strategies. Although industry sponsorships and grant funding underwrote the initial operational costs, organizers introduced mechanisms to ensure long-term viability and follow-up. Once proven effective, top-performing algorithms could be licensed to industry partners for integration into commercial building management systems. Competition participants were also invited to explore pilot projects, mirroring the "freemium to premium" transitions observed in modern gaming ecosystems. This revenue diversification approach sought to address a common shortfall in data competitions, where value often evaporates once the final leaderboard is published [33].

4.4 Competition Outcomes and Performance

The winning solutions from ADRENALIN exemplified the competition's focus on real-world applicability. Table 6 presents the top three teams, their methodological approaches, and their respective NMAE scores, all of which fell below 0.30. These results validated the feasibility of zero ground truth modeling techniques, demonstrating that unsupervised learning could, in many cases, approximate or even rival traditional supervised methods.

Table 6. Top-Performing ADRENALIN 2024 Solutions and Their Accuracy

Rank	Team	Methodology	NMAE
1st	Rafaelzimmermann	Adjusted STL Decomposition	0.235
2nd	Team HashBrown	Gaussian Mixture Models (GMM)	0.265
3rd	Cteceliker	Base Load Decomposition + Clustering	0.274

These methodologies varied in terms of algorithmic complexity and assumptions about underlying consumption patterns. The top team employed an adjusted seasonal-trend decomposition (STL) approach, while second- and third-place teams relied on probabilistic clustering methods. All three demonstrated strong generalization to unseen building data, which was essential given the international scope of the dataset and the practical objective of scaling solutions across diverse energy contexts. Paper [34] includes a more detailed breakdown of the results, while further algorithmic insights can be found in [35].

Post-Competition Implementation

A distinguishing feature of ADRENALIN was the explicit focus on commercializing top-performing solutions. Industry partners commenced pilot tests to integrate leading algorithms into building energy management systems, aiming to validate the performance under operational conditions. Early field trials indicated promising results, particularly for real-time HVAC load monitoring in office and educational buildings. This transition from competition to deployment underscores how thoughtfully designed data challenges can bridge the gap between open innovation and marketable technology, reflecting a fundamental objective in multi-sided platforms.

Organizers also facilitated follow-up engagements for continued knowledge transfer. Several top-ranking teams collaborated on joint publications with research institutions and entered licensing discussions with sponsors who saw a direct path to monetizing advanced NILM technologies. Such activities illustrated the extended lifecycle of a competition that, rather than concluding upon leaderboard publication, evolved into a sustained R&D and commercialization ecosystem.

4.5 Lessons Learned and Implications

The ADRENALIN experience revealed several insights that have broader implications for future data competitions. First, the multi-phase structure was deemed vital for encouraging incremental improvements and preventing leaderboard overfitting. Second, restricting participants to zero ground truth training stimulated novel solution strategies grounded in domain understanding, potentially accelerating methodological advances. Third, forging early relationships with industry partners ensured that promising algorithms did not remain purely academic exercises but found pathways toward widespread adoption.

From a business model standpoint, ADRENALIN demonstrated the viability of hybrid monetization through sponsorships, licensing, and post-competition collaborations, which parallels the evolution of multi-sided gaming ecosystems that profit from continuous user engagement and revenue streams. These outcomes suggest that competition organizers can benefit from pre-arranged industry alliances, clearly defined intellectual property agreements, and structured post-competition engagement plans that extend the value of winning solutions.

Despite common goals, stakeholders may have diverging incentives that hinder adoption. Academics often focus on publishing novel methods, while industry seeks deployable, market-ready solutions. Building operators may face procurement barriers, legacy systems, or resistance to external tools. IP uncertainties and unclear post-competition support can further slow uptake. Early alignment through clear IP terms, joint pilot planning, and operator involvement can improve commercialization outcomes.

5 Discussion

One of the central insights from the ADRENALIN case study is how a multi-sided business model architecture—mirroring gaming ecosystems—can catalyze value creation in data competitions. By uniting data scientists, building operators, and industry partners via a shared digital platform, the ADRENALIN competition harnessed network effects, as the participation of additional data scientists enriched the algorithmic solution pool and the involvement of more building operators diversified the dataset.

This design aligns with the value creation perspective [2], which underscores the importance of stakeholder engagement and platform openness for sustained competitive advantages. Publicly available building energy data and evaluation protocols nurtured collective learning among participants, mirroring the culture of user-generated content in gaming platforms [3]. The improved generalization and lower NMAE scores highlight the benefits of openly sharing data across different building contexts.

The ADRENALIN results also confirm findings in prior work on data competitions, which demonstrate that open R&D challenges can effectively solve specialized tasks such as NILM at reduced cost and in shorter timeframes than traditional approaches [1]. The competition's multi-phase structure, featuring a development phase followed by a final evaluation, aligns with recognized methods of mitigating leaderboard overfitting while driving iterative model enhancement [33].

In contrast to typical data competitions relying on prize money or short-term grants, ADRENALIN introduced multiple indirect monetization pathways similar to those employed in gaming environments [31]. These included licensing winning solutions for immediate deployment in commercial building management systems and paid pilot projects with top-performing teams. While microtransactions and subscription-based approaches are common in digital games [3], they have been less common in scientific contests, making ADRENALIN's model a salient example of how data competitions can sustain themselves through continuous revenue streams and strategic industry partnerships.

While the ADRENALIN challenge focused on NILM, similar competition-based frameworks could be adapted to address data science problems in other energy subdomains, including demand response, forecasting, or grid analytics. Although such competitions are not policy instruments, their design and outcomes may indirectly inform future initiatives in smart building standardisation and applied decarbonisation strategies.

A key contribution of this study is illustrating how multi-sided, open innovation events can be aligned with financially viable business models. Although earlier research focuses predominantly on the technical dimension of data competitions or on revenue mechanics in gaming, the ADRENALIN competition demonstrates that these dimensions can be integrated effectively. Early engagement with industry sponsors played a critical role in ensuring immediate real-world application for winning solutions, thereby mitigating the tendency for competition outputs to remain unused after final leaderboard announcements.

Another notable outcome is the establishment of a hybrid revenue approach. Table 7 compares ADRENALIN's financial strategies with conventional data competition funding methods, showing how reliance on sponsorships, IP licensing, and ongoing service engagements can collectively generate recurring revenue. As Table 7 indicates, this paradigm allows data competitions to be less dependent on lump-sum grants and to cultivate more robust stakeholder relationships. The flexibility observed in gaming's "freemium" and "microtransaction" models thus finds a parallel in ADRENALIN, reinforcing that data competitions have the potential to transition from short-lived novelty events into enduring platforms that deliver both commercial and societal benefits.

While freemium, microtransaction, and subscription models in gaming generate strong revenue, their direct application to energy efficiency services faces challenges. Procurement rules, public-sector risk aversion, and strict data privacy policies can hinder recurring payments. Additionally, energy users prioritize cost savings over discretionary spending. Thus, while gaming models offer useful inspiration, they must be adapted to sector-specific constraints. Hybrid approaches—like licensing, service contracts, and public-private partnerships—are more viable, as reflected in ADRENALIN's focus on post-competition collaborations and pilot deployments.

Table 7. ADRENALIN's Hybrid Revenue Model vs. Conventional Data Competitions

Aspect	Conventional Data Competitions	ADRENALIN Hybrid Model
Funding Source	Single source (e.g., prize funds)	Multiple sources (sponsorships, grants, licensing)
Post-Competition Monetization	Limited or none	Licensing agreements, paid pilot projects
Industry Integration	Uncertain adoption	Early involvement, direct deployment pathways
Sustainability	Dependent on recurring external support	Potentially self-sustaining via recurring revenue

The research bridges two key areas of scholarship: the literature on data competitions, which typically underscores algorithmic success or organizational aspects, and the literature on business model innovation, predominantly centered on entertainment or software platforms. By adapting proven monetization and engagement strategies from gaming ecosystems—such as platform openness, revenue diversification, and collaborative value creation—ADRENALIN provides a grounded framework for advancing data competitions in other specialized domains.

Finally, the ADRENALIN experience suggests that multi-phase structures and zero ground truth configurations can enhance both algorithmic originality and practical relevance, especially in contexts like NILM where building conditions vary widely. The multi-phase structure fostered incremental improvements, while the zero ground truth approach encouraged participants to devise generalizable methods. These competition design features, coupled with an early articulation of IP rights and revenue-sharing mechanisms, established trust among participants, policymakers, and industry sponsors. This multi-stakeholder collaboration ultimately facilitated swift technology deployment in commercial buildings, illustrating how a well-structured competition can bridge the gap between experimental prototypes and scalable solutions.

6 Conclusion

This paper analyzed the 2024 ADRENALIN Load Disaggregation Competition as a case study of integrating unsupervised NILM research with a multi-sided, revenue-driven platform model. The findings show that unsupervised NILM algorithms operating under zero ground truth constraints can achieve high accuracy (NMAE < 0.30) across diverse building contexts, validating the technical feasibility of data competition–based innovation in energy informatics. Beyond the technical dimension, the study highlights how early collaborations with industry, flexible licensing agreements, and strategically phased competition workflows enable data competitions to extend beyond single-sponsor events, adopting business model elements reminiscent of multi-sided gaming ecosystems.

The study enhances the literature on data competitions by demonstrating that entrepreneurial revenue strategies—from IP licensing to pilot project collaborations—can be seamlessly incorporated into open innovation events. This approach helps overcome the "value evaporates" problem often encountered when competition outputs remain unused after their initial development. By detailing how early sponsorship and well-articulated IP rights foster stakeholder buy-in, the ADRENALIN model offers an actionable blueprint for achieving both technical breakthrough and financial viability.

Despite these promising insights, three primary limitations remain. The study was confined to a single case within the energy informatics domain, raising concerns about the generalizability of the findings to other sectors such as healthcare, finance, or autonomous systems. The analysis was primarily retrospective, relying on post-competition documentation rather than real-time participant feedback, and no interview data from participants or sponsors was collected, which limits direct triangulation of perspectives. Additionally, participant-level analytics, such as team composition or geographic spread, were not recorded systematically, which limits the depth of platform usage insights. Ethical considerations concerning privacy, data ownership, and monetization of open-source contributions were not exhaustively explored, though they are critical for the long-term sustainability of competition-driven innovation ecosystems.

Future research can address these limitations by replicating the ADRENALIN approach in diverse application areas, enabling cross-domain comparisons of competition design and business models. Longitudinal methods could more fully capture the evolution of algorithm deployment from prototype to mainstream adoption, while surveys and interviews would provide deeper insights into participant motivations, perceived barriers, and ethical concerns. Comparative analyses of differing monetization frameworks, ranging from subscription-based licensing to microtransaction-like features, would help pinpoint which models are most effective in various organizational and domain-specific contexts. Such inquiries will refine data competition practices to ensure that they remain both scientifically productive and economically robust, further solidifying open innovation challenges as a significant driver of progress in fields like energy informatics and beyond.

Acknowledgement. This paper is part of the ADRENALIN (Data-driven smart buildings: data sandbox and competition) project. Funded by the Energy Technology Development and Demonstration Programme (EUDP) In Denmark. (Case no.64021-6025).

References

1. Tolnai, B.A., Ma, Z., Jørgensen, B.N.: Standard energy data competition procedure: a comprehensive review with a case study of the ADRENALIN load disaggregation competition. In: Energy Informatics Academy Conference. Springer (2023)
2. Amit, R., Zott, C.: Creating value through business model innovation. MIT Sloan management review (2012)
3. Coutinho, T.: The Microtransaction Business Model: A Study on Modern Videogame Monetization and the Economic Sustainability of Microtransactions. ISCTE-Instituto Universitario de Lisboa (Portugal) (2021)
4. Yin, R.K.: Case study research and applications: design and methods. Sage publications (2017)
5. Hatzitaskos, K., Card, D., Howell, V.: Guidelines on quantitative techniques for competition analysis. The Regional Competition (2012)
6. Luitse, D., Blanke, T., Poell, T.: AI competitions as infrastructures of power in medical imaging. Information, Communication & Society, p. 1–22
7. Renaux, D.P.B., et al.: A dataset for non-intrusive load monitoring: design and implementation. Energies **13**(20), 5371 (2020)
8. Fallahi, S.: A process view of business model innovation. Chalmers Tekniska Hogskola (Sweden) (2017)
9. Hoch, N.B., Brad, S.: Managing business model innovation: an innovative approach towards designing a digital ecosystem and multi-sided platform. Bus. Process. Manag. J. **27**(2), 415–438 (2021)
10. Abdelkafi, N., et al., Multi-sided platforms, pp. 553–559. Springer (2019)
11. Haucap, J.: Competition and competition policy in a data-driven economy. Intereconomics **54**(4), 201–208 (2019)
12. Anderson-Cook, C.M., et al.: How to host an effective data competition: statistical advice for competition design and analysis. Statist. Anal. Data Min.: ASA Data Sci. J. **12**(4), 271–289 (2019)
13. Yamamoto, K., Hayashi, T.: Understanding user interactions and community formation on data competition platform, pp. 6690–6696 (2024)

14. Exploring Participants' collaboration behaviors of open data competitions in digital humanities: a value co-creation perspective. information studies: theory and application, vol. 45, pp. 112–119 (2022)
15. Gandia, R., Parmentier, G.: The role of multi-sided business models in managing creative ecosystems: the case of the online video game industry. In: Business Model Innovation in Creative and Cultural Industries, pp. 89–109. Routledge (2025)
16. Parmentier, G., Gandia, R.: Managing openness within a multi-sided business model: the case of online video game. Revue Francaise de Gestion **254**, 107–128 (2016)
17. Kovsca, V., Lackovic, Z., Antun, V.T.: The impact of microtransactions on the development of computer game business models. EMC Rev. Econ. Mark. Commun. Rev. **13**(2), 462–474 (2023)
18. Lantano, F., Petruzzelli, A.M., Panniello, U.: Business model innovation in video-game consoles to face the threats of mobile gaming: Evidence from the case of Sony PlayStation. Technological Forecasting and Social Change, vol. 174 (2022)
19. Sebastian Morillas, A., Nunez Cansado, M., Munoz Sastre, D.: New business models for advertisers: the video games sector in Spain. Advergaming Vs Ingame Advertising. Revista Icono 14-Revista Cientifica de Comunicacion y Tecnologias **14**(2), 256–279 (2016)
20. Goumagias, N., et al.: Literature review: business model components in the computer and video games industry
21. A phylogenetic classification of the video-game industry's business model ecosystem. In: IFIP Advances in Information and Communication Technology, pp. 285–294 (2014)
22. Kleer, N., Kunz, R.E.: The impact of actor engagement on the business models of video game developers. JMM Int. J. Media Manage. **23**, 204–237 (2021)
23. Roy, N.: Applying kant's ethics to video game business models: which ones pass muster? Bus. Prof. Ethics J. **40**, 109–127 (2021)
24. Waldner, F., et al.: Cross-industry innovation: the transfer of a service-based business model from the video game industry to the music industry. In: 2011 International Conference on Emerging Intelligent Data and Web Technologies (2011)
25. Parmentier, G., Gandia, R.: Managing openness within a multi-sided business model. The case of online video game. Revue Française de Gestion **42**(254), 107–128 (2016)
26. Kim, J.: The platform business model and business ecosystem: quality management and revenue structures. Eur. Plan. Stud. **24**(12), 2113–2132 (2016)
27. Vanhala, E., Kasurinen, J.: The role of business model and its elements in computer game start-ups. In: 5th International Conference on Software Business (ICSOB). Paphos, CYPRUS: Springer-Verlag Berlin (2014)
28. Waldner, F., Zsifkovits, M., Heidenberger, K.: Are service-based business models of the video game industry blueprints for the music industry? Int. J. Serv. Econ. Manage. **5**, 5–20 (2013)
29. Attanasio, G., et al.: DSLE: a smart platform for designing data science competitions. In: 2020 IEEE 44th Annual Computers, Software, and Applications Conference (COMPSAC). IEEE (2020)
30. Ardolino, M., et al.: A business model framework to characterize digital multisided platforms. J. Open Innov.: Technol. Mark. Complex. **6**(1), 10 (2020)
31. Daxhammer, K., et al.: Development of a strategic business model framework for multi-sided platforms to ensure sustainable innovation in small and medium-sized enterprises. Procedia Manufac. **39**, 1354–1362 (2019)
32. Majander, V.: Revenue models for video games (2019)
33. Tolnai, B.A., Ma, Z., Jørgensen, B.N.: Energy data collection protocol: a case study on the ADRENALIN project. Springer Nature Switzerland, Cham (2025)

34. Lu, L., Anderson-Cook, C.M.: Incorporating uncertainty for enhanced leaderboard scoring and ranking in data competitions. Qual. Eng. **33**, 189–207 (2021)
35. Tolnai, B.A., et al.: Advancing non-intrusive load monitoring: insights from the winning algorithms in the ADRENALIN 2024 load disaggregation competition. In: Nordic Energy Informatics Academy Conference 2025. Springer, Stockholm, Sweden (2025)

Author Index

A
Abouebeid, Sara II-173
Aguayo, Cristian II-187
Ahammer, Florian II-95
Aiswarya, T. S. II-78
Ajwani, Deepak II-271
Akashi, Yasunori II-114, II-144, II-154
Alaliyat, Saleh Abdel-Afou I-3
Alex, A. II-78
Al-Habaibeh, Amin I-198
Amideo, Annunziata Esposito I-255
Amini Toosi, Hashem II-221
Amos, Matt II-321, II-338, II-371
Ayyathurai, Vignesh Pechiappan I-95

B
Bansal, Ramesh C. I-309
Becker, Robert A. II-285
Beigaitė, Rita II-35
Bengtsson, Gustaf II-321, II-338, II-371
Billanes, Joy Dalmacio I-79, I-215, II-254
Biswas, Debajyoti II-187
Blaabjerg, Frede I-60
Bleistein, Thomas II-285
Bolaños-Zuñiga, Johanna II-67
Bordin, Chiara I-60
Botea, Adi II-271

C
Caetano, Luis II-130
Campodonico-Avendano, Italo Aldo II-300
Carroll, Paula I-255, I-267, II-187, II-271
Çeliker, Cihat Emre II-338
Chen, Zhonghe II-271
Christensen, Kristoffer I-371
Clauß, John II-130
Cong, Lu I-237

D
Daniel, Lius II-35
Davidsson, Henrik I-131

Derbas, Abd Alelah I-60

E
Engström, Jesper I-131

F
Faisal, Mohammed Farhan I-15
Fellerer, Jonathan II-3
Fernengel, Natascha I-323
Ford, Ryan II-35
Förderer, Kevin I-323

G
Garcia, Rafeal Gomez II-321
German, Reinhard II-3
Gölles, Markus II-95
Guðjónsdóttir, Maria Sigríður II-23
Gudmundsson, Steinn I-341

H
Hagenmeyer, Veit I-323
Hajsok, Lucija I-283
Hameed, Akram II-321, II-338, II-371
Harini, N. II-78
Hasan, Agus I-3
He, Yue II-144
Hehemann, Michael I-323
Helbrecht, Jana II-3
Holly, Stefanie I-354
Holtwerth, Alexander I-323
Hoppe, Eugen I-323
Huang, Haoyu I-323
Huang, Pei I-299

J
Johansson, Dennis I-131
Johra, Hicham II-300
Jørgensen, Bo Nørregaard I-215, I-237, I-371, II-254, II-321, II-338, II-355, II-371, II-388

Author Index

K
Kamenev, Nikolai II-285
Kandemir, Ege I-3
Kayo, Genku I-110
Khajoei, Najmeh I-341
Kind, Reidar II-130
Koelsch, Celina II-285
Kowli, Anupama II-204
Kulkarni, Aashay II-285

L
L., Alberto J. Lamadrid II-67
Lassen, Thomas Elvrum II-130
Liberado, Eduardo I-185
Lichtenegger, Klaus II-95
Lien, Synne Krekling II-321, II-338
Lin, Jeremy I-309
Lygnerud, Kristina I-79

M
Ma, Zheng Grace I-215, I-237, I-371, II-321, II-338, II-388
Ma, Zheng I-79, II-254, II-355, II-371
Madsen, Frederik Wagner II-254
Malakhatka, Elena II-173
Marumoto, Shoya II-114
Mazidi, Mohammadreza II-173
Medjdoub, Benachir I-198
Mehmood, Khawaja Khalid I-32
Miller, Clayton II-338, II-371
Mishra, Sambeet I-60
Miyata, Shohei II-114, II-144, II-154
Moazami, Amin II-300
Mori, Taro I-149, I-164, I-173
Moura, Ranier Alexsander Arruda I-32
Müller, Dirk I-323
Muschick, Daniel II-95
Mutule, Anna II-187

N
Najmadin, Abdelmomen I-95
Nguyen, Phuong Hong I-32
Niklasson, Felix II-173
Nixon, Nimisha I-15
Nordanger, Knut II-130

O
Osawa, Hisato I-149, I-164, I-173
Otani, Kazuma I-164, I-173

P
Pandiyan, Surya Venkatesh II-321
Parvaz, Md I-131
Plompen, Hendrik I-32
Pradeep, Jayarama II-78
Þorvaldsson, Einar Örn I-131

R
Radtke, Malin I-354
Rajasekharan, Jayaprakash II-321
Ravindra, Nikhil I-198
Richter, Christiaan I-230

S
Safavi, Aysan I-230
Santana, Emerson I-185
Sartori, Igor II-321, II-338, II-371
Schopper, Fabian II-95
Seema, II-51
Serrao, Nikith Jude II-78
Sharma, Desh Deepak I-309
Shé, Clíodhna Ní I-267
Shi, Shanrui II-144, II-154
Sirjani, Reza II-51
Slimani, Mohamed El-Amine II-23
Somawanshi, Aditya II-204
Sridhar, Araavind II-173
Stark, Sanja I-354
Steen, David II-173
Suzuki, Konatsu I-149, I-164, I-173

T
Taniguchi, Keiichiro II-114
Theocharis, Andreas II-51
Titz, Maurizio II-237
Tolnai, Balázs András II-321, II-338, II-355, II-371, II-388
Tran, Ngoc II-338
Tuan, Le Anh II-173

U
Unnthorsson, Runar I-230, I-341

Author Index

V
van der Molen, Anne I-32
van der Wielen, Peter I-32
Varma, Pamba Raja I-15

W
Waczowicz, Simon I-323
Walker, Sara I-119
Wallbaum, Holger II-173
Walnum, Harald Taxt II-321
White, Stephen II-371
Witthaut, Dirk II-237

X
Xhonneux, André I-323
Xiang, Jingyu I-255
Xie, Yangxinyu II-338

Y
Yan, Hui I-119
Yang, Aileen II-300

Z
Zafar, Rehman I-299
Žakula, Tea I-283
Zimmermann, Rafael Sudbrack II-338

MIX
Papier aus verantwortungsvollen Quellen
Paper from responsible sources
FSC® C105338

If you have any concerns about our products,
you can contact us on
ProductSafety@springernature.com

In case Publisher is established outside the EU,
the EU authorized representative is:
Springer Nature Customer Service Center GmbH
Europaplatz 3, 69115 Heidelberg, Germany

Printed by Libri Plureos GmbH
in Hamburg, Germany